Weiss Ratings' Guide to Life and Annuity Insurers

Weiss Ratings'
Guide to
Life and Annuity Insurers

A Quarterly Compilation of Insurance
Company Ratings and Analyses

Spring 2019

GREY HOUSE PUBLISHING

Weiss Ratings
4400 Northcorp Parkway
Palm Beach Gardens, FL 33410
561-627-3300

Independent. Unbiased. Accurate. Trusted.

Published by Grey House Publishing, Inc., located at 4919 Route 22, Amenia, NY 12501; telephone 518-789-8700. Grey House Publishing neither guarantees the accuracy of the data contained herein nor assumes any responsibility for errors, omissions or discrepancies. Grey House Publishing accepts no payment for listing; inclusion in the publication of any organization, agency, institution, publication, service or individual does not imply endorsement of the publisher.

Grey House
Publishing
4919 Route 22
PO Box 56
Amenia, NY 12501-0056

Edition No. 115, Spring 2019

ISBN: 978-1-64265-184-3
ISSN: 2158-527X

Contents

Terms and Conditions

This document is prepared strictly for the confidential use of our customer(s). It has been provided to you at your specific request. It is not directed to, or intended for distribution to or use by, any person or entity who is a citizen or resident of or located in any locality, state, country or other jurisdiction where such distribution, publication, availability or use would be contrary to law or regulation or which would subject Weiss Ratings or its affiliates to any registration or licensing requirement within such jurisdiction.

No part of the analysts' compensation was, is, or will be, directly or indirectly, related to the specific recommendations or views expressed in this research report.

This document is not intended for the direct or indirect solicitation of business. Weiss Ratings, LLC., and its affiliates disclaims any and all liability to any person or entity for any loss or damage caused, in whole or in part, by any error (negligent or otherwise) or other circumstances involved in, resulting from or relating to the procurement, compilation, analysis, interpretation, editing, transcribing, publishing and/or dissemination or transmittal of any information contained herein.

Weiss Ratings has not taken any steps to ensure that the securities or investment vehicle referred to in this report are suitable for any particular investor. The investment or services contained or referred to in this report may not be suitable for you and it is recommended that you consult an independent investment advisor if you are in doubt about such investments or investment services. Nothing in this report constitutes investment, legal, accounting or tax advice or a representation that any investment or strategy is suitable or appropriate to your individual circumstances or otherwise constitutes a personal recommendation to you.

The ratings and other opinions contained in this document must be construed solely as statements of opinion from Weiss Ratings, LLC., and not statements of fact. Each rating or opinion must be weighed solely as a factor in your choice of an institution and should not be construed as a recommendation to buy, sell or otherwise act with respect to the particular product or company involved.

Past performance should not be taken as an indication or guarantee of future performance, and no representation or warranty, expressed or implied, is made regarding future performance. Information, opinions and estimates contained in this report reflect a judgment at its original date of publication and are subject to change without notice. Weiss Ratings offers a notification service for rating changes on companies you specify. For more information visit WeissRatings.com or call 1-877-934-7778. The price, value and income from any of the securities or financial instruments mentioned in this report can fall as well as rise.

This document and the information contained herein is copyrighted by Weiss Ratings, LLC. Any copying, displaying, selling, distributing or otherwise reproducing or delivering this information or any part of this document to any other person or entity is prohibited without the express written consent of Weiss Ratings, LLC, with the exception of a reviewer or editor who may quote brief passages in connection with a review or a news story.

Message To Insurers

All survey data received on or before January 16, 2019 has been considered or incorporated into this edition of the Directory. If there are particular circumstances which you believe could affect your rating, please use the online survey **(http://weissratings.com/survey/)** or e-mail Weiss Ratings, LLC **(insurancesurvey@weissinc.com)** with documentation to support your request. If warranted, we will make every effort to incorporate the changes in our next edition.

Welcome to Weiss Ratings'
Guide to Life and Annuity Insurers

Most people automatically assume their insurance company will survive, year after year. However, prudent consumers and professionals realize that in this world of shifting risks, the solvency of insurance companies can't be taken for granted.

If you are looking for accurate, unbiased ratings and data to help you choose life and annuity insurance for yourself, your family, your company or your clients, *Weiss Ratings' Guide to Life and Annuity Insurers* gives you precisely what you need.

In fact, it's the only source that currently provides ratings and analyses on over 650 life and annuity insurers.

Weiss Ratings' Mission Statement

Weiss Ratings' mission is to empower consumers, professionals, and institutions with high quality advisory information for selecting or monitoring a financial services company or financial investment.

In doing so, Weiss Ratings will adhere to the highest ethical standards by maintaining our independent, unbiased outlook and approach to advising our customers.

Why rely on Weiss Ratings?

Weiss Ratings provides fair, objective ratings to help professionals and consumers alike make educated purchasing decisions.

At Weiss Ratings, integrity is number one. Weiss Ratings never takes a penny from insurance companies for its ratings. And, we publish Weiss Safety Ratings without regard for insurers' preferences. However, other rating agencies like A.M. Best, Fitch, Moody's and Standard & Poor's are paid by insurance companies for their ratings and may even suppress unfavorable ratings at an insurer's request.

Our ratings are more frequently reviewed and updated than any other ratings. You can be sure that the information you receive is accurate and current – providing you with advance warning of financial vulnerability early enough to do something about it.

Other rating agencies focus primarily on a company's current claims paying ability and consider only mild economic adversity. Weiss Ratings also considers these issues, but in addition, our analysis covers a company's ability to deal with severe economic adversity and a sharp increase in claims.

Our use of more rigorous standards stems from the viewpoint that an insurance company's obligations to its policyholders should not depend on favorable business conditions. An insurer must be able to honor its policy commitments in bad times as well as good.

Our rating scale, from A to F, is easy to understand. Only a few outstanding companies receive an A (Excellent) rating, although there are many to choose from within the B (Good) category. An even larger group falls into the broad average range which receives C (Fair) ratings. Companies that demonstrate marked vulnerabilities receive either D (Weak) or E (Very Weak) ratings.

How to Use This Guide

The purpose of the *Guide to Life and Annuity Insurers* is to provide policyholders and prospective policy purchasers with a reliable source of insurance company ratings and analyses on a timely basis. We realize that the financial strength of an insurer is an important factor to consider when making the decision to purchase a policy or change companies. The ratings and analyses in this Guide can make that evaluation easier when you are considering:

- Life insurance

- Annuities

- Health insurance

- Guaranteed Investment Contracts (GICs) and other pension products

This Guide also includes ratings for some Blue Cross Blue Shield plans.

The rating for a particular company indicates our opinion regarding that company's ability to meet its commitments to the policyholder – not only under current economic conditions, but also during a declining economy or in an environment of increased liquidity demands.

To use this Guide most effectively, we recommend you follow the steps outlined below:

Step 1   To ensure you evaluate the correct company, verify the company's exact name and state of domicile as it was given to you or appears on your policy. Many companies have similar names but are not related to one another, so you want to make sure the company you look up is really the one you are interested in evaluating.

Step 2   Turn to Section I, the Index of Companies, and locate the company you are evaluating. This section contains all companies analyzed by Weiss Ratings including those that did not receive a Safety Rating. It is sorted alphabetically by the name of the company and shows the state of domicile following the name for additional verification. Once you have located your specific company, the first column after the state of domicile shows its Weiss Safety Rating. Turn to *About Weiss Safety Ratings* for information about what this rating means. If the rating has changed since the last issue of this Guide, a downgrade will be indicated with a down triangle ▼ to the left of the company name; an upgrade will be indicated with an up triangle ▲.

Step 3   Following Weiss Safety Rating are some of the various indexes that our analysts used in rating the company. Refer to the Critical Ranges in our Indexes table for an interpretation of which index values are considered strong, good, fair or weak. You can also turn to the introduction of Section I to see what each of these factors measures. In most cases, lower rated companies will have a low index value in one or more of the factors shown. Bear in mind, however, that a Weiss Safety Rating is the result of a complex propriatory quantitative and qualitative analysis which cannot be reproduced using only the data provided here.

Step 4   The quality of a company's investment portfolio – bonds, mortgages and other investments – is an integral part of our analysis. So, the right hand page of Section I shows you where the company has invested its premiums. Again, refer to the introduction of Section I for a description of each investment category.

Step 5   Some insurers have a bullet ● preceding the company name on the right hand page of Section I. If the company you are evaluating is identified with a bullet, turn to Section II, the Analysis of Largest Companies, and locate it there (otherwise skip to step 8). Section II contains the largest insurers rated by Weiss Ratings, regardless of rating. It too is sorted alphabetically by the name of the company.

Step 6   Once you have identified your company in Section II, you will find its Safety Rating and a description of the rating immediately to the right of the company name. Then, below the company name is a description of the various rating factors that were considered in assigning the company's rating. These factors and the information below them are designed to give you a better feel for the company and its strengths and weaknesses. See the Section II introduction, to get a better understanding of what each of these factors means.

Step 7   To the right, you will find a five-year summary of the company's Safety Rating, capitalization and income. Look for positive or negative trends in this data. Below the five-year summary, we have included a graphic illustration of the most critical factor or factors impacting the company's rating. Again, the Section II introduction provides an overview of the content of each graph or table.

Step 8   If the company you are evaluating is not highly rated and you want to find an insurer with a higher rating, turn to the page in Section IV that has your state's name at the top. This section contains those Recommended Companies (rating of A+, A, A- or B+) that are licensed to underwrite insurance in your state, sorted by rating. From here you can select a company and then refer back to Sections I and II to analyze it.

Step 9   If you decide that you would like to contact one of Weiss Recommended Companies about obtaining a policy or for additional information, refer to Section III. Following each company's name is its address and phone number to assist you in making contact.

Step 10   In order to use Weiss Safety Ratings most effectively, we strongly recommend you consult the Important Warnings and Cautions listed. These are more than just "standard disclaimers"; they are very important factors you should be aware of before using this Guide. If you have any questions regarding the precise meaning of specific terms used in the Guide, refer to the Glossary.

Step 11   The Appendix contains information about State Guaranty Associations and the types of coverage they provide to policyholders when an insurance company fails. Keep in mind that while guaranty funds have now been established in all states, many do not cover all types of insurance. Furthermore, all of these funds have limits on their amount of coverage. Use the table to determine whether the level of coverage is applicable to your policy and the limits are adequate for your needs. You should pay particular attention to the notes regarding whether the coverage is for residents of the state or companies domiciled in the state.

Step 12   If you want more information on your state's guaranty fund, call the State Commissioner's Office directly.

Step 13   Keep in mind that good coverage from a state guaranty association is no substitute for dealing with a financially strong company. Weiss Ratings only recommends those companies which we feel are most able to stand on their own, even in a recession or downturn in the economy.

Step 14 Make sure you stay up to date with the latest information available since the publication of this Guide. For information on how to set up a rating change notification service, acquire follow-up reports or receive a more in-depth analysis of an individual company, call 1-877-934-7778 or visit www.weissratings.com.

Data Sources: Annual and quarterly statutory statements filed with state insurance commissioners and data provided by the insurance companies being rated. The National Association of Insurance Commissioners has provided some of the raw data. Any analyses or conclusions are not provided or endorsed by the NAIC.

Date of data analyzed: September 30, 2018 unless otherwise noted.

About Weiss Safety Ratings

The Weiss Ratings of insurers are based upon the annual and quarterly financial statements filed with state insurance commissioners. This data may be supplemented by information that we request from the insurance companies themselves. However, if a company chooses not to provide supplemental data, we reserve the right to rate the company based exclusively on publicly available data.

The Weiss Ratings are based on a complex analysis of hundreds of factors that are synthesized into a series of indexes: capitalization, investment safety (life, health and annuity companies only), reserve adequacy (property and casualty companies only), profitability, liquidity, and stability. These indexes are then used to arrive at a letter grade rating. A weak score on any one index can result in a low rating, as financial problems can be caused by any one of a number of factors, such as inadequate capital, unpredictable claims experience, poor liquidity, speculative investments, inadequate reserving, or consistent operating losses.

Our **Capital Index** gauges capital adequacy in terms of each insurer's ability to handle a variety of business and economic scenarios as they may impact investment performance, claims experience, persistency, and market position. The index combines two Risk-Adjusted Capital ratios as well as a leverage test that examines pricing risk.

Our **Investment Safety Index** measures the exposure of the company's investment portfolio to loss of principal and/or income due to default and market risks. Each investment area is rated by a factor that takes into consideration both quality and liquidity. (This factor is measured as a separate index only for life, health, and annuity insurers.)

Our **Profitability Index** measures the soundness of the company's operations and the contribution of profits to the company's financial strength. The profitability index is a composite of five sub-factors: 1) gain or loss on operations; 2) consistency of operating results; 3) impact of operating results on surplus; 4) adequacy of investment income as compared to the needs of policy reserves (life, health and annuity companies only); and 5) expenses in relation to industry norms for the types of policies that the company offers.

Our **Liquidity Index** evaluates a company's ability to raise the necessary cash to settle claims and honor cash withdrawal obligations. We model various cash flow scenarios, applying liquidity tests to determine how the company might fare in the event of an unexpected spike in claims and/or a run on policy surrenders.

Our **Stability Index** integrates a number of sub-factors that affect consistency (or lack thereof) in maintaining financial strength over time. These sub-factors will vary depending on the type of insurance company being evaluated but may include such things as 1) risk diversification in terms of company size, group size, number of policies in force, types of policies written, and use of reinsurance; 2) deterioration of operations as reported in critical asset, liability, income and expense items, such as surrender rates and premium volume; 3) years in operation; 4) former problem areas where, despite recent improvement, the company has yet to establish a record of stable performance over a suitable period of time; 5) a substantial shift in the company's operations; 6) potential instabilities such as reinsurance quality, asset/liability matching, and sources of capital; and 7) relationships with holding companies and affiliates.

In order to help guarantee our objectivity, we reserve the right to publish ratings expressing our opinion of a company's financial stability based exclusively on publicly available data and our own proprietary standards for safety.

Each of these indexes is measured according to the following range of values.

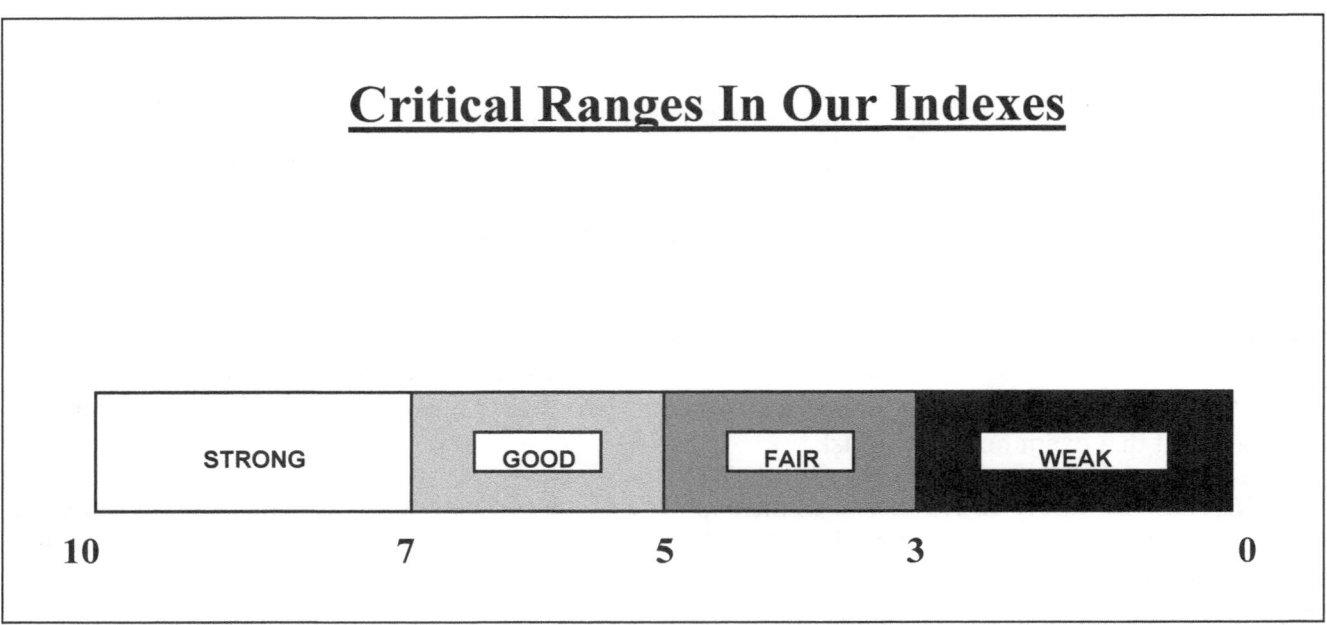

What Our Ratings Mean

A   **Excellent.** The company offers excellent financial security. It has maintained a conservative stance in its investment strategies, business operations and underwriting commitments. While the financial position of any company is subject to change, we believe that this company has the resources necessary to deal with severe economic conditions.

B   **Good.** The company offers good financial security and has the resources to deal with a variety of adverse economic conditions. It comfortably exceeds the minimum levels for all of our rating criteria, and is likely to remain healthy for the near future. However, in the event of a severe recession or major financial crisis, we feel that this assessment should be reviewed to make sure that the firm is still maintaining adequate financial strength.

C   **Fair.** The company offers fair financial security and is currently stable. But during an economic downturn or other financial pressures, we feel it may encounter difficulties in maintaining its financial stability.

D   **Weak.** The company currently demonstrates what, in our opinion, we consider to be significant weaknesses which could negatively impact policyholders. In an unfavorable economic environment, these weaknesses could be magnified.

E   **Very Weak.** The company currently demonstrates what we consider to be significant weaknesses and has also failed some of the basic tests that we use to identify fiscal stability. Therefore, even in a favorable economic environment, it is our opinion that policyholders could incur significant risks.

F   **Failed.** The company is deemed failed if it is either 1) under supervision of an insurance regulatory authority; 2) in the process of rehabilitation; 3) in the process of liquidation; or 4) voluntarily dissolved after disciplinary or other regulatory action by an insurance regulatory authority.

+   The **plus sign** is an indication that the company is in the upper third of the letter grade.

-   The **minus sign** is an indication that the company is in the lower third of the letter grade.

U   **Unrated.** The company is unrated for one or more of the following reasons: (1) total assets are less than $1 million; (2) premium income for the current year was less than $100,000; (3) the company functions almost exclusively as a holding company rather than as an underwriter; (4) in our opinion, we do not have enough information to reliably issue a rating.

How Our Ratings Differ From Those of Other Services

Weiss Safety Ratings are conservative and consumer-oriented. We use tougher standards than other rating agencies because our system is specifically designed to inform risk-averse consumers about the financial strength of life and annuity insurers.

Our rating scale (A to F) is easy to understand by the general public. Users can intuitively understand that an A+ rating is at the top of the scale rather than in the middle like some of the other rating agencies.

Other rating agencies give top ratings more generously so that most companies receive excellent ratings.

More importantly, other rating agencies focus primarily on a company's *current* claims paying ability or consider only relatively mild economic adversity. We also consider these scenarios but extend our analysis to cover a company's ability to deal with severe economic adversity and potential liquidity problems. This stems from the viewpoint that an insurance company's obligations to its policyholders should not be contingent upon a healthy economy. The company must be capable of honoring its policy commitments in bad times as well.

Looking at the insurance industry as a whole, we note that several major rating firms have poor historical track records in identifying troubled companies. The 1980s saw a persistent decline in capital ratios, increased holdings of risky investments in the life and health industry as well as recurring long-term claims liabilities in the property and casualty industry. The insurance industry experienced similar issues before and during the Great Recession of 2007-2009. Despite these clear signs that insolvency risk was rising, other rating firms failed to downgrade at-risk insurance companies. Instead, they often rated companies by shades of excellence, understating the gravity of potential problems.

Other ratings agencies have not issued clear warnings that the ordinary consumer can understand. Few, if any, companies receive "weak" or "poor" ratings. Surely, weak companies do exist. However, the other rating agencies apparently do not view themselves as consumer advocates with the responsibility of warning the public about the risks involved in doing business with such companies.

Additionally, these firms will at times agree *not* to issue a rating if a company denies them permission to do so. In short, too often insurance rating agencies work hand-in-glove with the companies they rate.

At Weiss Ratings, although we seek to maintain good relationships with the firms, we owe our primary obligation to the consumer, not the industry. We reserve the right to rate companies based on publicly available data and make the necessary conservative assumptions when companies choose not to provide additional data we might request.

Comparison of Insurance Company Rating Agency Scales

Weiss Ratings [a]	Best [a]	S&P	Moody's	Fitch
A+, A, A-	A++, A+	AAA	Aaa	AAA
B+, B, B-	A, A-	AA+, AA AA-	Aa1, Aa2, Aa3	AA+, AA, AA-
C+, C, C-	B++, B+,	A+, A, A-, BBB+, BBB, BBB-	A1, A2, A3, Baa1, Baa2, Baa3	A+, A, A-, BBB+, BBB, BBB-
D+, D, D-	B, B- C++, C+, C, C-	BB+, BB, BB-, B+, B, B-	Ba1, Ba2, Ba3, B1, B2, B3	BB+, BB, BB-, B+, B, B-
E+, E, E- F	D E, F	CCC R	Caa, Ca, C	CCC+, CCC, CCC- DD

[a] Weiss Ratings and Best use additional symbols to designate that they recognize an insurer's existence but do not provide a rating. These symbols are not included in this table.

Rate of Insurance Company Failures

Weiss Ratings provides quarterly Safety Ratings for thousands of insurance companies each year. Weiss Ratings strives for fairness and objectivity in its ratings and analyses, ensuring that each company receives the rating that most accurately depicts its current financial status, and more importantly, its ability to deal with severe economic adversity and a sharp increase in claims. Weiss Ratings has every confidence that its Safety Ratings provide an accurate representation of a company's stability.

In order for these ratings to be of any true value, it is important that they prove accurate over time. One way to determine the accuracy of a rating is to examine those insurance companies that have failed, and their respective Weiss Safety Ratings. A high percentage of failed companies with "A" ratings would indicate that Weiss Ratings is not being conservative enough with its "secure" ratings, while conversely, a low percentage of failures with "vulnerable" ratings would show that Weiss Ratings is overly conservative.

Over the past 29 years (1989–2017) Weiss Ratings has rated 637 insurance companies, for all industries, that subsequently failed. The chart below shows the number of failed companies in each rating category, the average number of companies rated in each category per year, and the percentage of annual failures for each letter grade.

	Safety Rating	Number of Failed Companies	Average Number of Companies Rated per year	Percentage of Failed Companies per year (by ratings category)*
Secure	A	1	153	0.02%
	B	6	1,111	0.02%
	C	70	1,610	0.15%
Vulnerable	D	278	744	1.29%
	E	282	217	4.48%

A=Excellent, B=Good, C=Fair, D=Weak, E=Very Weak

On average, only 0.09% of the companies Weiss Ratings rates as "secure" fail each year. On the other hand, an average of 2.01% of the companies Weiss Ratings rates as "vulnerable" fail annually. That means that a company rated by Weiss Ratings as "Vulnerable" is 21.7 times more likely to fail than a company rated as "Secure".

When considering a Weiss Safety Rating, one can be sure that they are getting the most fair, objective, and accurate financial rating available anywhere.

*Percentage of Failed Companies per year = (Number of Failed Companies) / [(Average Number of Companies Rated per year) x (years in study)]

Data as of December 2017 for Life & Annuity Insurers, Property & Casualty Insurers and Health Insurers.

What Does Average Mean?

At Weiss Ratings, we consider the words average and fair to mean just that – average and fair. So when we assign our ratings to insurers, a large percentage of companies receive an average C rating. That way, you can be sure that a company receiving Weiss B or A rating is truly above average. Likewise, you can feel confident that companies with D or E ratings are truly below average. In recent years, life and health insurers have experienced consistent, solid performance resulting in a shift in the rating distribution so that more insurers than ever are rated B or better.

Current Weiss Ratings Distribution for Life and Annuity Insurers

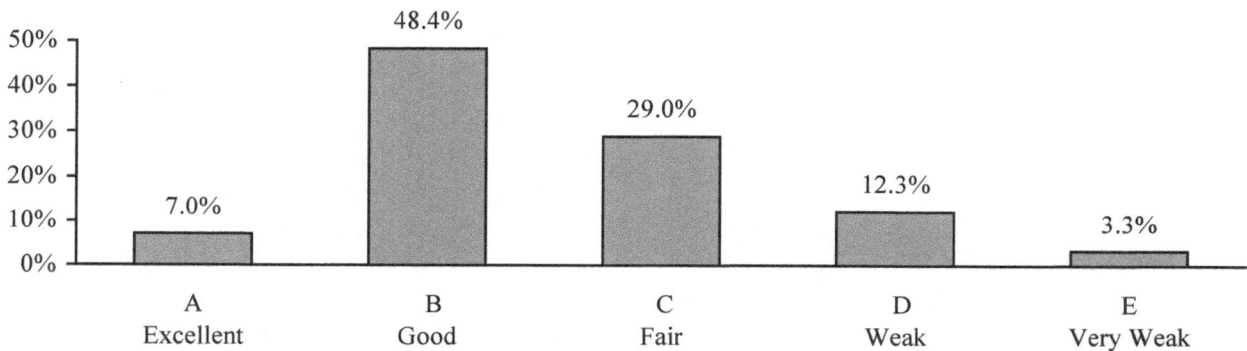

Important Warnings and Cautions

1. A rating alone cannot tell the whole story. Please read the explanatory information contained in this publication. It is provided in order to give you an understanding of our rating philosophy, as well as paint a more complete picture of how we arrive at our opinion of a company's strengths and weaknesses.

2. Weiss Safety Ratings represent our opinion of a company's insolvency risk. As such, a high rating means we feel that the company has less chance of running into financial difficulties. A high rating is not a guarantee of solvency nor is a low rating a prediction of insolvency. Weiss Safety Ratings are not deemed to be a recommendation concerning the purchase or sale of the securities of any insurance company that is publicly owned.

3. Company performance is only one factor in determining a rating. Conditions in the marketplace and overall economic conditions are additional factors that may affect the company's financial strength. Therefore, a rating upgrade or downgrade does not necessarily reflect changes in the company's profits, capital or other financial measures, but may be due to external factors. Likewise, changes in Weiss indexes may reflect changes in our risk assessment of business or economic conditions as well as changes in company performance.

4. All firms that have the same Safety Rating should be considered to be essentially equal in strength. This is true regardless of any differences in the underlying numbers which might appear to indicate greater strengths. Weiss Safety Rating already takes into account a number of lesser factors which, due to space limitations, cannot be included in this publication.

5. A good rating requires consistency. If a company is excellent on four indicators and fair on one, the company may receive a fair rating. This requirement is necessary due to the fact that fiscal problems can arise from any *one* of several causes including speculative investments, inadequate capital resources or operating losses.

6. We are an independent rating agency and do not depend on the cooperation of the companies we rate. Our data are derived from annual and quarterly financial statements that we obtain from federal regulators and filings with state insurance commissioners. The latter may be supplemented by information insurance companies voluntarily provide upon request. Although we seek to maintain an open line of communication with the companies, we do not grant them the right to stop or influence publication of the ratings. This policy stems from the fact that this publication is designed for the protection of the consumer.

7. Affiliated companies do not automatically receive the same rating. We recognize that a troubled company may expect financial support from its parent or affiliates. Weiss Safety Ratings reflect our opinion of the measure of support that may become available to a subsidiary, if the subsidiary were to experience serious financial difficulties. In the case of a strong parent and a weaker subsidiary, the affiliate relationship will generally result in a higher rating for the subsidiary than it would have on a stand-alone basis. Seldom, however, would the rating be brought up to the level of the parent. This treatment is appropriate because we do not assume the parent would have either the resources or the will to "bail out" a troubled subsidiary during a severe economic crisis. Even when there is a binding legal obligation for a parent corporation to honor the policy obligations of its subsidiaries, the possibility exists that the subsidiary could be sold and lose its parental support. Therefore, it is quite common for one affiliate to have a higher rating than another. This is another reason why it is especially important that you have the precise name of the company you are evaluating.

Section I

Index of Companies

An analysis of all rated and unrated

U.S. Life and Annuity Insurers.

Companies are listed in alphabetical order.

Section I Contents

This section contains the key rating factors and investment portfolio analysis for all rated and unrated insurers analyzed by Weiss Ratings. An explanation of each of the footnotes and stability factors appears at the end of this section.

Left Pages

1. Insurance Company Name

The legally registered name, which can sometimes differ from the name that the company uses for advertising. If you cannot find the company you are interested in, or if you have any doubts regarding the precise name, verify the information with the company before looking the name up in this Guide. Also, determine the domicile state for confirmation. (See column 2.)

2. Domicile State

The state which has primary regulatory responsibility for the company. It may differ from the location of the company's corporate headquarters. You do not have to be living in the domicile state to purchase insurance from this firm, provided it is licensed to do business in your state.

Also use this column to confirm that you have located the correct company. It is possible for two unrelated companies to have the same name if they are domiciled in different states.

3. Safety Rating

Our rating is measured on a scale from A to F and considers a wide range of factors. Please see What Our Ratings Mean for specific descriptions of each letter grade. Also, refer to how our ratings differ from those of other rating agencies. Most important, when using this rating, please be sure to consider the warnings regarding the ratings' limitations and the underlying assumptions. Notes in this column refer to the date of the data included in the rating evaluation and are explained.

4. Total Assets

All assets admitted by state insurance regulators in millions of dollars. This includes investments, current business assets, and separate accounts. The year-end figure is used to correspond with the figures on the right-hand pages, some of which are only available on an annual basis.

The overall size is an important factor which affects the ability of a company to manage risk. Mortality, morbidity (sickness) and investment risks can be more effectively diversified by large companies. Because the insurance business is based on probability, the number of policies must be large enough so that actuarial statistics are valid. Life insurance policies, for example, are based on mortality tables containing the expected number of deaths per thousand at various ages.

The larger the number of policyholders, the more reliable the actuarial projections will be. A large company with a correspondingly large policy base can spread its risk and minimize the effects of claims experience that exceeds actuarial expectations.

5. Capital and Surplus

The company's statutory net worth in millions of dollars. Consumers may wish to limit the size of any policy so that the policyholder's maximum benefits do not exceed approximately 1% of the company's capital and surplus. For example, when buying a policy from a company with capital and surplus of $10,000,000, the 1% limit would be $100,000. (When performing this calculation, do not forget that figures in this column are expressed in millions of dollars.)

Critical Ranges In Our Indexes and Ratios

Indicators	Strong	Good	Fair	Weak
Risk-Adjusted Capital Ratio #1	—	1.0 or more	0.75 - 0.99	0.74 or less
Risk-Adjusted Capital Ratio #2	1.0 or more	0.75 - 0.99	0.5 - 0.74	0.49 or less
Capitalization Index	6.9 – 10	4.9 - 6.8	2.9 - 4.8	Less than 2.9
5 Year Profitability Index	6.9 – 10	4.9 - 6.8	2.9 - 4.8	Less than 2.9
Liquidity Index	6.9 – 10	4.9 - 6.8	2.9 - 4.8	Less than 2.9
Investment Safety Index	6.9 – 10	4.9 - 6.8	2.9 - 4.8	Less than 2.9
Stability Index	6.9 – 10	4.9 - 6.8	2.9 - 4.8	Less than 2.9

6. Risk-Adjusted Capital Ratio #1

This ratio examines the adequacy of the company's capital base and whether the company has sufficient capital resources to cover potential losses which might occur in an average recession or other moderate loss scenario. Specifically, the figure cited in the table answers the question: For every dollar of capital that we feel would be needed, how many dollars in capital resources does the company actually have? (See the table above for the levels which we believe are critical.) You may find that some companies have unusually high levels of capital. This often reflects special circumstances related to the small size or unusual operations of the company.

7. Risk-Adjusted Capital Ratio #2

This is similar to item 6. But in this case, the question relates to whether the company has enough capital cushion to withstand a *severe* recession or other severe loss scenario.

8. Capitalization Index

An index that measures the adequacy of the company's capital resources to deal with a variety of business and economic scenarios. It combines Risk-Adjusted Capital Ratios #1 and #2 as well as a leverage test that examines pricing risk. (See the table above for the levels which we believe are critical.)

9. Investment Safety Index

An index that measures the exposure of the company's investment portfolio to a loss of principal and/or income due to default and market risks. It is the composite of a series of elements, some of which are shown on the right pages. Each investment area is rated by a factor that takes into consideration both quality and liquidity. (See the table on the next page for the levels which we believe are critical.)

10. 5-Year Profitability Index

An index that measures the soundness of the company's operations and the contribution of profits to the company's fiscal strength. The Profitability Index is a composite of five factors: (1) gain or loss on operations; (2) consistency of operating results; (3) impact of operating results on surplus; (4) adequacy of investment income as compared to the needs of policy reserves; and (5) expenses in relation to industry averages for the types of policies that the company offers.

This factor is especially important among health insurers including Blue Cross Blue Shield companies that rely more heavily on current earnings than do life and annuity writers. After factoring out the normal cycle, companies with stable earnings and capital growth are viewed more favorably than those whose results are erratic from year to year. (See the table for the levels which we believe are critical.)

11. Liquidity Index

An index which measures the company's ability to raise the necessary cash to meet policyholder obligations. This index includes a stress test which considers the consequences of a spike in claims or a run on policy surrenders. Sometimes a company may appear to have the necessary resources, but may be unable to sell its investments at the prices at which they are valued in the company's financial statements. (See the table for the levels which we believe are critical.)

12. Stability Index

An index which integrates a number of factors such as: (1) risk diversification in terms of company size, number of policies in force, use of reinsurance and other items related to spread of risk; (2) deterioration of operations as reported in critical asset, liability, income or expense items such as surrender rates and premium volume; (3) former problem areas where, despite recent improvement, the company has yet to establish a record of stable performance over a suitable period of time; (4) a substantial shift in the company's operations; (5) potential instabilities such as reinsurance quality, asset/liability matching and sources of capital; plus (6) relationships to holding companies and affiliates. (See the table for the levels which we believe are critical.)

13. Stability Factors   Indicates those specific areas that have negatively impacted the company's Stability Index.

Right Pages

1. Net Premiums   The amount of insurance premiums received from policyholders less any premiums that have been transferred to other companies through reinsurance agreements. This figure is updated through the most recent quarterly report available. Generally speaking, companies with large net premium volume generally have more predictable claims experience.

2. Invested Assets   The value of the firm's total investment portfolio, measured in millions of dollars. The year-end figure is used to correspond with the following figures, some of which are only available on an annual basis. Use the figure in this column to determine the actual dollar amounts invested in each asset category shown in columns 3 through 11 on the right-side pages. For example, if the firm has $500 million in invested assets and column 3 shows that 10% of its portfolio is in cash, the company has $50 million in cash.

     Looking at the right-side pages, columns 3 through 11 will, unless otherwise noted, add up to approximately 100%. Column 12 (investments in affiliates) is already included in other columns (usually 4, 5 or 6) depending upon the specific investment vehicle.

3. Cash   Cash on hand and demand deposits at year-end. A negative cash position implies checks outstanding exceed cash balances, a situation not unusual for insurance companies.

4. CMOs (Collateralized Mortgage Obligations) and Other Structured Securities   Mortgage-backed bonds at year-end that split the payments from mortgage pools into different classes, called tranches. The split may be based on maturity dates or a variety of other factors. For example, the owner of one type of CMO, called a PAC, receives principal and interest payments made by the mortgage holders between specific dates. The large majority of CMOs held by insurance companies are those issued by government agencies and carry very little risk of default. Virtually all of the CMOs included here are investment grade. However, they all carry some measure of risk based on the payment speed of the underlying mortgages.

5. Other Investment Grade Bonds

All year-end investment grade bonds other than the CMOs included in column 4. Specifically, this includes: (1) issues guaranteed by U.S. and foreign governments which are rated as "highest quality" (Class 1) by state insurance commissioners; (2) nonguaranteed obligations of governments, such as Fannie Maes, which do not carry full faith and credit guarantees; (3) obligations of governments rated as "high quality" (Class 2) by state insurance commissioners; (4) state and municipal bonds; plus (5) investment-grade corporate bonds as defined by the state insurance commissioners. The data shown in this column are based exclusively on the definition used by state insurance commissioners. However, on the companies for which a more detailed breakdown of bond ratings is available, the actual bond ratings - and not the data shown in this column - are used in our rating process to calculate the Investment Safety Index.

6. Noninvestment Grade Bonds

Low-rated issues at year-end– commonly known as "junk bonds" – which carry a high risk as defined by the state insurance commissioners. In an unfavorable economic environment, we generally assume that these will be far more subject to default than other categories of corporate bonds.

7. Common and Preferred Stock

Year-end common and preferred equities. Although a certain amount is acceptable for the sake of diversification, excessive investment in this area is viewed as a factor that can increase the company's overall vulnerability to market declines.

8. Mortgages In Good Standing

Year-end mortgages which are current in their payments. Mortgage-backed securities are excluded.

9. Non-performing Mortgages

Mortgages which are (a) 90 days or more past due; or (b) in process of foreclosure. These are year-end figures. If the mortgages have already been foreclosed, the asset is transferred to the next category - real estate. Clearly, a high level of nonperforming mortgages is a negative, reflecting on the quality of the entire mortgage portfolio.

10. Real Estate

Year-end direct real estate investments including (a) property occupied by the company; and (b) properties acquired through foreclosure. A certain amount of real estate investment is considered acceptable for portfolio diversification. However, excessive amounts may subject the company to losses during a recessionary period.

11. Other Investments

Items such as premium notes, collateral loans, short-term investments, policy loans and a long list of miscellaneous items at year-end.

12. Investments in Affiliates

Year-end bonds, preferred and common stocks, as well as other vehicles which many insurance companies use to invest in - and establish a corporate link with - affiliated companies. Since these can often be non-income-producing paper assets, they are considered less desirable than the equivalent securities of publicly traded companies. Investments in affiliates are also included in other columns (usually 4, 5 or 6). Therefore, the percentage shown here represents a duplication of some of the amounts shown in the other columns.

Footnotes:

(1) Data items shown are from the company's 2017 annual statutory statement except for Risk-Adjusted Capital Indexes 1 and 2, Profitability Index, Investment Safety Index, Liquidity Index and Stability Index which have been updated using the company's June 2018 quarterly statutory statement. Other more recent data may have been factored into the rating when available.

(2) Data items shown are from the company's 2017 annual statutory statement except for Risk-Adjusted Capital Indexes 1 and 2, Profitability Index, Investment Safety Index, Liquidity Index and Stability Index which have been updated using the company's March 2018 quarterly statutory statement. Other more recent data may have been factored into the rating when available.

(3) Data items shown are from the company's 2017 annual statutory statement. Other more recent data may have been factored into the rating when available.

(4) Data items shown are from the company's 2016 annual statutory statement except for Risk-Adjusted Capital Indexes 1 and 2, Profitability Index, Investment Safety Index, Liquidity Index and Stability Index which have been updated using the company's September 2017 quarterly statutory statement. Other more recent data may have been factored into the rating when available.

(5) These companies have data items that are older than June 30, 2017. They will be unrated (U) if they are not failed companies (F).

(*) Breakdown of the company's investment portfolio, shown in percentages in columns 3-11 on the right hand page, does not total to 100% due to the inclusion of non–admitted assets in the bond or mortgage figures, or due to other accounting adjustments.

Stability Factors

(A)   Stability Index was negatively impacted by the financial problems or weaknesses of a parent or **affiliate** company.

(C)   Stability Index was negatively impacted by past results on our Risk-Adjusted **Capital** tests. In general, the Stability Index of any company can be affected by past results even if current results show improvement. While such improvement is a plus, the improved results must be maintained for a period of time to assure that the improvement is not a temporary fluctuation. During a five-year period, the impact of poor past results on the Stability Index gradually diminishes.

(D)   Stability Index was negatively impacted by limited **diversification** of general business, policy, and/or investment risk. This factor especially affects smaller companies that do not issue as many policies as larger firms. It can also affect firms that specialize in only one line of business.

(E)   Stability Index was negatively impacted due to a lack of operating **experience**. The company has been in operation for less than five years. Consequently, it has not been able to establish the kind of stable track record that we believe is needed to demonstrate financial permanence and strength.

(F)   Stability Index was negatively impacted by negative cash **flow**. In other words, the company paid out more in claims and expenses than it received in premiums and investment income.

(G)   Stability Index was negatively impacted by fast asset or premium **growth**. Fast growth can pose a serious problem for insurers. It is generally achieved by offering policies with premiums that are too low, benefits that are too costly, or agents commissions that are too high. Due to the highly competitive nature of the insurance marketplace, rapid growth has been a factor in many insurance insolvencies.

(I)   Stability Index was negatively impacted by past results on our **Investment** Safety Index. This can pose a problem for insurers even after risky investments have been sold off. To illustrate, consider those companies that have sold off their junk bonds and now carry much smaller junk bond risk. For a period of time the company that had the junk bonds incorporated the expectation of higher yields into its policy design and marketing strategy. Only time will tell how the company's investment income margins and future sales will be affected by the junk bond sell off. So, while the Investment Safety Index would improve right away, the Stability Index would improve only gradually over a period of three years, if the transition to lower yielding investments is handled smoothly.

(L)   Stability Index was negatively impacted by past results on our **liquidity** tests. In general, the Stability Index of any company can be affected by past results even if current results show improvement. While such improvement is a plus, the improved results must be maintained for a period of time to assure that the improvement is not a temporary fluctuation. During a five-year period, the impact of poor past results on the Stability Index gradually diminishes.

(O)   Stability Index was negatively impacted by significant changes in the company's business **operations**. These changes can include shifts in the kinds of insurance offered by the company, a temporary or permanent freeze on the sale of new policies, or recent release from conservatorship. In these circumstances, past performance cannot be a reliable indicator of future financial strength.

(R)   Stability Index was negatively impacted by concerns about the financial strength of its **reinsurers**.

(T)   Stability Index was negatively impacted by significant **trends** in critical asset, liability, income or expense items. Examples include increasing surrender rates, increasing mortgage defaults, and shrinking premium volume.

(Z)   This company is unrated due to data, as received by Weiss Ratings, that are either incomplete in substantial ways or contain items that, in the opinion of Weiss Ratings analysts, may not be reliable.

INSURANCE COMPANY NAME	DOM. STATE	RATING	TOTAL ASSETS ($MIL)	CAPITAL & SURPLUS ($MIL)	RISK ADJUSTED CAPITAL RATIO 1	RISK ADJUSTED CAPITAL RATIO 2	CAPITAL-IZATION INDEX (PTS)	INVEST. SAFETY INDEX (PTS)	PROFIT-ABILITY INDEX (PTS)	LIQUIDITY INDEX (PTS)	STAB. INDEX (PTS)	STABILITY FACTOR
4 EVER LIFE INS CO	IL	B	190.1	84.8	6.56	4.32	10.0	6.6	5.0	6.8	5.0	A
AAA LIFE INS CO	MI	B	677.0	170.5	3.30	1.88	8.3	6.4	6.7	6.5	6.1	I
AAA LIFE INS CO OF NY	NY	B	7.7	5.2	2.52	2.27	8.9	6.8	1.9	6.8	4.8	ADI
ABILITY INS CO	NE	D	1320.8	17.9	0.39	0.22	0.0	0.8	1.4	8.7	0.3	CFIT
ACADEME INC	WA	U (3)	--	--	--	--	--	--	--	--	--	Z
ACCORDIA LIFE & ANNUITY CO	IA	C	9246.6	702.8	1.16	0.79	5.3	5.1	3.4	6.0	4.4	
ACE LIFE INS CO	CT	B-	45.9	7.6	1.19	1.07	7.1	8.5	1.5	3.8	4.4	AFGLT
ADVANCE INS CO OF KANSAS	KS	B+	61.6	50.9	3.90	2.54	9.3	4.4	8.4	7.0	6.8	AI
AETNA HEALTH & LIFE INS CO	CT	C	175.2	106.0	9.72	5.45	4.0	4.6	5.8	0.0	2.9	FLT
AETNA LIFE INS CO	CT	B	21702.3	4062.4	1.48	1.12	5.2	6.2	6.7	6.2	5.4	AIT
AGC LIFE INS CO	MO	U (3)	--	--	--	--	--	--	--	--	--	Z
▲ ALABAMA LIFE REINS CO INC	AL	D	24.3	9.2	2.42	2.17	8.8	6.7	2.0	9.2	1.5	DFT
ALFA LIFE INS CORP	AL	B-	1479.5	272.2	2.72	1.53	7.8	5.0	4.3	6.4	5.2	I
ALL SAVERS INS CO	IN	C	703.8	557.0	8.56	6.29	10.0	8.1	2.8	7.4	2.4	T
ALL SAVERS LIFE INS CO OF CA	CA	U (3)	--	--	--	--	--	--	--	--	--	Z
ALLIANZ LIFE INS CO OF NORTH AMERICA	MN	C	147319.7	6683.6	2.20	1.23	7.3	6.0	2.7	5.2	4.3	
ALLIANZ LIFE INS CO OF NY	NY	B+	3461.1	186.8	5.00	2.89	9.8	7.6	5.5	9.3	5.3	A
ALLIED FINANCIAL INS CO	TX	U (5)	--	--	--	--	--	--	--	--	--	Z
ALLSTATE ASR CO	IL	C+	699.2	160.9	4.26	2.25	8.9	6.5	1.8	5.8	3.3	DGT
ALLSTATE LIFE INS CO	IL	B	30993.3	3680.8	2.17	1.27	7.4	4.5	4.0	6.7	4.8	FIT
ALLSTATE LIFE INS CO OF NEW YORK	NY	B-	6223.9	685.3	2.74	1.45	7.7	5.6	3.6	6.5	5.0	
AMALGAMATED LIFE & HEALTH INS CO	IL	C	5.0	3.9	2.37	2.13	8.7	8.7	6.2	7.7	4.2	DT
AMALGAMATED LIFE INS CO	NY	A	140.3	65.3	4.42	3.38	10.0	8.2	8.1	6.3	7.1	
AMERICAN BANKERS LIFE ASR CO OF FL	FL	C+	334.1	56.1	5.45	3.05	10.0	6.5	7.4	7.4	3.6	AGT
AMERICAN BENEFIT LIFE INS CO	OK	C	158.3	23.4	2.46	1.54	7.8	5.0	8.7	6.3	3.5	AD
AMERICAN CENTURY LIFE INS CO	OK	D+	84.3	6.5	0.91	0.81	5.5	0.8	4.1	3.6	2.5	DFILT
AMERICAN CENTURY LIFE INS CO TX	TX	C-	7.4	0.6	0.65	0.59	3.7	2.3	8.3	8.4	3.0	CDGIT
AMERICAN COMMUNITY MUT INS CO	MI	F (5)	--	--	--	--	--	--	--	--	--	Z
AMERICAN CONTINENTAL INS CO	TN	C+	268.1	109.9	1.74	1.31	5.9	7.7	2.9	5.7	4.6	D
AMERICAN CREDITORS LIFE INS CO	DE	U (3)	--	--	--	--	--	--	--	--	--	Z
AMERICAN EQUITY INVEST LIFE INS CO	IA	B-	54487.2	3244.8	2.40	1.26	7.4	5.4	8.6	4.7	5.3	ILT
AMERICAN EQUITY INVESTMENT LIFE NY	NY	B	201.4	36.7	3.82	2.35	9.0	6.7	6.4	5.6	5.3	ADF
AMERICAN FAMILY LIFE ASR CO OF NY	NY	A-	1000.3	295.8	5.40	3.59	10.0	8.0	9.0	7.9	7.2	AD
AMERICAN FAMILY LIFE INS CO	WI	A+	5269.9	644.4	3.27	1.78	8.2	5.9	6.5	6.3	6.3	AIT
AMERICAN FARM LIFE INS CO	TX	B	4.5	2.0	1.54	1.38	7.6	8.3	8.1	7.0	4.1	AD
AMERICAN FARMERS & RANCHERS LIFE INS	OK	C	30.2	2.3	0.53	0.48	2.8	7.2	3.5	1.6	2.8	ACDL
AMERICAN FEDERATED LIFE INS CO	MS	B	31.6	15.0	3.21	2.88	9.8	8.5	6.6	7.8	5.2	A
AMERICAN FIDELITY ASR CO	OK	B+	6090.1	471.9	1.90	1.11	7.2	6.0	8.5	6.2	6.8	I
AMERICAN FIDELITY LIFE INS CO	FL	B	402.5	66.2	1.74	1.25	7.4	5.8	5.8	6.0	5.8	DI
AMERICAN FINANCIAL SECURITY L I C	MO	D	14.3	6.8	2.49	1.93	8.4	8.4	7.2	7.3	2.4	DG
AMERICAN GENERAL LIFE INS CO	TX	B	179039.2	6273.9	2.48	1.16	7.2	3.9	6.2	5.9	4.0	AGIT
AMERICAN HEALTH & LIFE INS CO	TX	A-	1018.0	155.6	2.74	1.74	8.1	6.3	6.3	8.9	5.8	AGIT
AMERICAN HERITAGE LIFE INS CO	FL	B	2026.5	367.1	1.25	0.95	6.6	5.4	5.4	6.4	5.9	AI
AMERICAN HOME LIFE INS CO	KS	C-	263.0	22.2	2.19	1.20	7.3	6.0	3.0	4.3	3.2	DL
AMERICAN HOME LIFE INS CO	AR	E	22.6	0.5	0.20	0.18	0.0	0.2	1.7	0.2	0.0	CIL
AMERICAN INCOME LIFE INS CO	IN	B-	4094.0	307.6	1.49	0.87	6.0	4.6	5.1	2.2	4.2	IL
AMERICAN INTEGRITY LIFE INS CO	AR	C- (1)	1.4	1.0	1.98	1.78	8.2	7.8	5.7	8.5	3.0	D
AMERICAN LABOR LIFE INS CO	AZ	D	10.4	8.0	3.42	3.07	10.0	7.0	9.0	10.0	1.5	D
AMERICAN LIFE & ACC INS CO OF KY	KY	C	252.6	138.6	2.62	1.59	7.9	2.3	5.9	6.9	3.5	DFIT
AMERICAN LIFE & ANNUITY CO	AR	D+	53.4	3.5	0.55	0.49	2.9	3.9	4.7	2.6	2.4	CDIL
▼ AMERICAN LIFE & SECURITY CORP	NE	E-	21.1	1.6	0.37	0.33	1.0	0.8	0.3	2.2	0.8	CDILT
AMERICAN LIFE INS CO	DE	C	10706.5	5037.1	0.94	0.91	6.3	3.0	6.4	9.2	3.4	I

See Page 27 for explanation of footnotes and Page 28 for explanation of stability factors.
Arrows denote recent upgrades ▲ or downgrades▼ (see Section VI for explanations)

30

www.weissratings.com

NET PREMIUM ($MIL)	IN-VESTED ASSETS ($MIL)	CASH	CMO & STRUCT. SECS.	OTH.INV. GRADE BONDS	NON-INV. GRADE BONDS	CMMON & PREF. STOCK	MORT IN GOOD STAND.	NON-PERF. MORT.	REAL ESTATE	OTHER INVEST-MENTS	INVEST. IN AFFIL	INSURANCE COMPANY NAME
53.4	174.0 (*)	11.3	23.6	46.1	4.3	6.0	0.0	0.0	0.0	5.3	0.0	● 4 EVER LIFE INS CO
90.3	573.9 (*)	1.3	18.0	67.0	8.9	2.4	0.0	0.0	0.0	1.2	1.1	● AAA LIFE INS CO
3.1	7.3	7.9	0.0	86.3	5.2	0.0	0.0	0.0	0.0	0.1	0.0	● AAA LIFE INS CO OF NY
103.1	1,164.2 (*)	4.9	25.0	30.1	3.1	4.3	9.0	0.6	0.1	19.7	0.0	ABILITY INS CO
--	--	--	--	--	--	--	--	--	--	--	--	ACADEME INC
224.6	8,293.8 (*)	1.7	23.3	45.9	1.9	5.9	10.4	0.0	0.0	7.7	6.8	● ACCORDIA LIFE & ANNUITY CO
2.1	31.6 (*)	0.2	0.0	38.2	0.0	0.0	0.0	0.0	0.0	0.0	0.0	● ACE LIFE INS CO
8.2	59.1 (*)	0.3	32.2	31.6	0.0	32.3	0.0	0.0	0.0	0.0	2.4	● ADVANCE INS CO OF KANSAS
270.6	353.9 (*)	0.0	14.2	23.1	3.7	0.4	0.0	0.0	0.0	60.9	28.2	● AETNA HEALTH & LIFE INS CO
14,973.9	10,621.9 (*)	0.0	10.9	56.9	7.9	1.2	13.0	0.0	2.4	10.9	5.9	● AETNA LIFE INS CO
--	--	--	--	--	--	--	--	--	--	--	--	AGC LIFE INS CO
0.3	24.5	47.9	0.0	40.5	0.0	11.2	0.0	0.0	0.0	0.4	0.0	ALABAMA LIFE REINS CO INC
116.5	1,407.9 (*)	0.5	4.7	61.4	5.9	8.0	0.0	0.0	0.0	14.1	0.0	● ALFA LIFE INS CORP
353.7	1,096.9 (*)	0.9	28.1	61.3	0.0	0.0	0.0	0.0	0.0	2.8	0.0	● ALL SAVERS INS CO
--	--	--	--	--	--	--	--	--	--	--	--	ALL SAVERS LIFE INS CO OF CA
8,547.1	109,328.0 (*)	0.0	13.7	68.5	1.6	1.3	10.8	0.0	0.1	1.0	1.2	● ALLIANZ LIFE INS CO OF NORTH AMERICA
218.3	630.2	0.0	24.4	70.4	0.9	0.0	0.0	0.0	0.0	3.3	0.0	● ALLIANZ LIFE INS CO OF NY
--	--	--	--	--	--	--	--	--	--	--	--	ALLIED FINANCIAL INS CO
115.6	663.5	-0.1	6.0	63.5	6.8	0.0	17.1	0.0	0.0	6.2	0.0	● ALLSTATE ASR CO
703.8	27,564.4	0.1	5.4	50.3	10.6	6.9	11.6	0.0	0.4	14.3	3.4	● ALLSTATE LIFE INS CO
142.8	5,723.2	0.0	3.3	69.9	5.2	3.6	10.7	0.0	0.0	7.3	0.1	● ALLSTATE LIFE INS CO OF NEW YORK
1.9	5.7 (*)	9.3	22.5	52.8	0.0	0.0	0.0	0.0	0.0	11.6	0.0	AMALGAMATED LIFE & HEALTH INS CO
72.9	111.9	0.0	26.9	61.2	0.0	0.0	0.0	0.0	0.0	11.9	0.0	● AMALGAMATED LIFE INS CO
68.5	291.6 (*)	9.3	9.4	55.7	1.3	0.8	4.2	0.0	14.2	1.3	0.0	● AMERICAN BANKERS LIFE ASR CO OF FL
21.5	130.6	2.1	3.4	64.5	1.8	2.6	20.6	1.0	0.9	3.0	2.1	AMERICAN BENEFIT LIFE INS CO
7.5	81.6	1.9	0.0	82.8	12.1	2.6	0.0	0.0	0.5	0.1	0.0	AMERICAN CENTURY LIFE INS CO
4.8	2.8	20.0	1.5	18.2	1.8	12.6	31.7	0.0	14.3	0.0	0.0	AMERICAN CENTURY LIFE INS CO TX
--	--	--	--	--	--	--	--	--	--	--	--	AMERICAN COMMUNITY MUT INS CO
377.1	254.6 (*)	0.0	29.6	74.5	1.0	0.0	2.3	0.0	0.0	0.6	0.0	● AMERICAN CONTINENTAL INS CO
--	--	--	--	--	--	--	--	--	--	--	--	AMERICAN CREDITORS LIFE INS CO
2,600.0	51,117.9 (*)	0.0	21.5	64.5	2.8	1.1	6.2	0.0	0.0	1.6	0.4	● AMERICAN EQUITY INVEST LIFE INS CO
0.1	206.2 (*)	0.3	17.7	75.3	3.7	0.0	0.0	0.0	0.0	1.6	0.0	● AMERICAN EQUITY INVESTMENT LIFE NY
251.2	858.6	0.0	0.6	90.6	2.0	0.0	0.0	0.0	0.0	6.8	0.0	● AMERICAN FAMILY LIFE ASR CO OF NY
276.3	5,263.5 (*)	0.3	18.7	56.1	2.8	3.3	12.1	0.0	0.0	3.7	0.0	● AMERICAN FAMILY LIFE INS CO
0.3	4.0 (*)	4.5	0.3	84.6	2.5	0.0	0.0	0.0	0.0	3.1	0.0	AMERICAN FARM LIFE INS CO
1.7	28.5 (*)	0.6	5.6	91.9	0.0	0.0	0.0	0.0	0.0	0.3	0.0	AMERICAN FARMERS & RANCHERS LIFE INS
12.8	28.5	2.7	2.5	94.8	0.0	0.0	0.0	0.0	0.0	0.0	0.0	AMERICAN FEDERATED LIFE INS CO
757.4	4,892.8	4.9	18.0	63.1	1.6	0.6	9.8	0.0	0.4	1.6	0.3	● AMERICAN FIDELITY ASR CO
7.7	403.8	2.5	0.0	70.6	0.5	9.1	8.2	0.0	6.6	2.6	14.4	● AMERICAN FIDELITY LIFE INS CO
12.5	6.8	11.9	0.0	79.3	0.0	0.9	0.0	0.0	8.0	0.0	0.0	AMERICAN FINANCIAL SECURITY L I C
-14,405.8	121,303.0 (*)	0.0	26.4	46.5	5.0	0.3	13.1	0.0	0.2	6.1	5.4	● AMERICAN GENERAL LIFE INS CO
272.1	800.4 (*)	0.9	20.4	73.8	3.1	0.6	0.0	0.0	0.0	0.1	0.0	● AMERICAN HEALTH & LIFE INS CO
722.2	1,706.0 (*)	0.0	4.7	47.7	6.7	13.0	9.0	0.0	2.2	17.8	7.8	● AMERICAN HERITAGE LIFE INS CO
19.1	251.0 (*)	0.3	24.6	60.8	1.9	2.4	1.0	0.0	0.4	5.8	0.0	AMERICAN HOME LIFE INS CO
2.2	21.2 (*)	1.0	0.0	66.1	3.9	11.3	5.4	0.0	5.9	0.8	0.0	AMERICAN HOME LIFE INS CO
635.7	3,601.9	0.6	0.9	82.3	4.8	2.2	0.0	0.0	0.0	8.9	2.6	● AMERICAN INCOME LIFE INS CO
0.2	1.2	12.8	2.1	79.4	0.0	5.4	0.0	0.0	0.0	0.0	0.0	AMERICAN INTEGRITY LIFE INS CO
2.1	9.7	65.8	0.0	17.1	0.0	13.4	3.1	0.0	0.0	0.6	3.1	AMERICAN LABOR LIFE INS CO
47.5	249.8	1.6	1.9	17.0	0.0	72.2	0.0	0.0	7.2	0.1	0.0	● AMERICAN LIFE & ACC INS CO OF KY
3.5	51.5 (*)	0.3	57.5	28.5	2.1	5.1	0.0	0.0	0.3	0.2	0.0	AMERICAN LIFE & ANNUITY CO
2.2	23.4	3.9	5.8	83.9	2.4	0.0	0.0	0.0	2.2	1.7	0.0	AMERICAN LIFE & SECURITY CORP
1,188.3	9,548.5	6.8	5.8	18.0	13.4	53.7	0.0	0.0	0.1	2.2	55.2	● AMERICAN LIFE INS CO

INSURANCE COMPANY NAME	DOM. STATE	RATING	TOTAL ASSETS ($MIL)	CAPITAL & SURPLUS ($MIL)	RISK ADJUSTED CAPITAL RATIO 1	RISK ADJUSTED CAPITAL RATIO 2	CAPITAL-IZATION INDEX (PTS)	INVEST. SAFETY INDEX (PTS)	PROFIT-ABILITY INDEX (PTS)	LIQUIDITY INDEX (PTS)	STAB. INDEX (PTS)	STABILITY FACTORS
▼ AMERICAN MATURITY LIFE INS CO	CT	B-	63.1	48.6	6.69	6.02	10.0	9.5	4.2	7.0	4.9	G
AMERICAN MEMORIAL LIFE INS CO	SD	B-	3314.8	149.1	1.50	0.77	5.8	3.9	7.1	5.6	4.9	CI
AMERICAN MODERN LIFE INS CO	OH	B	38.3	32.9	2.57	2.48	9.2	8.0	9.0	6.9	4.1	FGT
AMERICAN NATIONAL INS CO	TX	B	20831.3	3294.7	1.16	0.95	6.6	5.3	4.2	6.6	6.1	I
AMERICAN NATIONAL LIFE INS CO OF TX	TX	B-	127.2	34.2	3.85	2.81	9.7	7.1	2.3	6.4	5.0	F
AMERICAN PROGRESSIVE L&H I C OF NY	NY	C	259.4	121.4	1.12	0.91	5.5	7.4	3.5	0.8	2.8	DFL
AMERICAN PUBLIC LIFE INS CO	OK	B	99.1	33.3	2.15	1.63	7.9	7.9	8.3	6.9	5.9	T
AMERICAN REPUBLIC CORP INS CO	IA	C	21.7	7.7	2.02	1.81	8.0	8.6	5.0	7.4	3.8	A
AMERICAN REPUBLIC INS CO	IA	B-	1016.1	473.9	3.55	2.53	9.3	5.8	6.8	6.9	4.8	AG
AMERICAN RETIREMENT LIFE INS CO	OH	C+	120.7	64.2	1.23	0.95	5.3	7.6	1.4	0.7	3.3	CDFGI
AMERICAN SAVINGS LIFE INS CO	AZ	C	62.0	15.9	1.11	0.73	5.2	1.8	7.9	5.2	3.6	DI
AMERICAN SERVICE LIFE INS CO	AR	B	1.3	1.3	2.63	2.37	9.1	9.1	9.2	9.2	4.6	ADT
AMERICAN UNITED LIFE INS CO	IN	B+	29575.8	1029.1	2.30	1.14	7.2	5.4	6.9	7.5	6.6	I
AMERICAN-AMICABLE LIFE INS CO OF TX	TX	C	303.0	39.5	0.68	0.59	3.7	6.4	2.7	5.2	3.7	CD
AMERICO FINANCIAL LIFE & ANNUITY INS	TX	B-	4642.1	534.2	1.89	1.10	7.2	4.6	8.1	6.1	5.3	AI
AMERITAS LIFE INS CORP	NE	B	21881.9	1584.6	2.23	1.32	7.5	4.9	4.9	6.1	4.4	IT
AMERITAS LIFE INS CORP OF NY	NY	B-	1316.4	108.7	2.34	1.23	7.3	6.0	4.0	5.0	4.9	I
AMICA LIFE INS CO	RI	B+	1302.6	330.3	5.28	3.05	10.0	7.0	5.7	6.5	6.5	A
ANNUITY INVESTORS LIFE INS CO	OH	A-	3232.6	315.1	3.21	1.62	7.9	6.4	8.6	5.2	6.9	AIL
ANTHEM LIFE & DISABILITY INS CO	NY	B	24.6	18.6	4.31	3.17	10.0	8.6	2.9	6.8	5.2	FT
ANTHEM LIFE INS CO	IN	B	720.0	131.9	2.31	1.59	7.9	7.5	7.6	6.0	4.7	T
ARKANSAS BANKERS LIFE INS CO	AR	D	2.6	1.5	1.67	1.50	7.8	9.8	2.2	9.5	2.1	FT
ASSURITY LIFE INS CO	NE	B+	2729.5	334.7	2.54	1.47	7.7	5.5	5.9	5.4	6.6	IL
ASSURITY LIFE INS CO OF NY	NY	B	8.3	7.5	3.75	3.37	10.0	9.1	3.6	7.6	5.1	DEG
ATHENE ANNUITY & LIFE ASR CO	DE	C	20718.3	1551.1	0.96	0.70	4.7	3.6	4.7	6.4	3.7	ACFGI
ATHENE ANNUITY & LIFE ASR CO OF NY	NY	C	3174.7	293.8	1.97	1.10	7.2	4.1	8.5	9.1	4.0	ACGIT
ATHENE ANNUITY & LIFE CO	IA	C	57378.9	1231.5	0.99	0.52	4.9	2.4	7.5	6.4	3.7	CIT
ATHENE LIFE INS CO	DE	U (3)	--	--	--	--	--	--	--	--	--	Z
ATHENE LIFE INS CO OF NEW YORK	NY	C	970.0	83.9	2.58	1.25	7.4	5.6	6.5	9.0	2.7	AGIT
ATLANTA LIFE INS CO	GA	D+	22.7	9.0	1.15	0.74	5.2	2.9	2.6	5.8	2.4	DFIT
ATLANTIC COAST LIFE INS CO	SC	B-	542.2	27.4	1.45	0.69	5.7	3.4	2.7	10.0	3.5	ACDG
AURORA NATIONAL LIFE ASR CO	CA	B	3097.8	145.4	1.69	0.88	6.0	5.6	5.5	6.8	5.5	ACFI
AUTO CLUB LIFE INS CO	MI	C+	814.0	78.7	0.99	0.70	4.9	5.6	2.6	5.0	4.4	C
AUTO-OWNERS LIFE INS CO	MI	B	3995.6	488.4	3.12	1.66	8.0	6.0	5.0	6.4	4.4	GIT
AUTOMOBILE CLUB OF SOUTHERN CA INS	CA	B-	1285.6	63.7	1.04	0.58	5.1	3.2	1.9	3.6	5.1	CIL
AXA CORPORATE SOLUTIONS LIFE REINS	DE	B	258.4	160.3	1.43	1.36	7.5	4.9	3.4	9.1	4.9	FIT
▲ AXA EQUITABLE LIFE & ANNUITY CO	CO	B	474.4	19.7	0.91	0.47	4.3	6.8	1.5	0.0	4.7	CLT
AXA EQUITABLE LIFE INS CO	NY	B+ (2)	191807.0	7320.1	3.79	1.95	8.4	7.1	6.7	6.2	6.6	
BALTIMORE LIFE INS CO	MD	B	1286.6	83.3	1.62	0.85	5.9	4.8	5.7	3.1	5.1	CIL
BANKERS CONSECO LIFE INS CO	NY	D	494.3	60.2	3.34	1.66	8.0	4.4	2.2	6.8	1.8	DI
BANKERS FIDELITY ASR CO	GA	C+	11.2	9.3	3.67	3.30	8.0	8.3	3.1	7.0	4.3	AI
BANKERS FIDELITY LIFE INS CO	GA	C	146.1	30.8	1.06	0.82	5.6	4.8	2.1	4.5	3.8	DFIL
BANKERS LIFE & CAS CO	IL	D+	15550.0	1233.0	2.02	1.08	7.1	4.3	4.8	5.6	2.7	AI
BANKERS LIFE INS CO	FL	C-	385.7	36.8	3.35	1.53	4.0	3.5	2.0	5.9	2.8	CFGIT
BANKERS LIFE INS CO OF AMERICA	TX	D+	6.1	1.1	0.71	0.64	4.1	4.0	2.8	5.9	2.5	CDI
BANKERS LIFE OF LOUISIANA	LA	C	18.3	6.7	2.06	1.86	8.3	8.5	5.3	7.6	4.1	A
BANNER LIFE INS CO	MD	B-	4020.8	496.0	2.61	1.76	8.1	6.3	5.3	9.0	4.8	GT
BENEFICIAL LIFE INS CO	UT	B	2157.1	193.2	2.09	1.16	7.2	5.5	5.7	5.6	5.4	FIT
BENEVOLENT LIFE INS CO INC	LA	D (3)	2.1	0.4	0.61	0.55	3.4	8.8	2.0	9.6	1.6	CDF
BERKLEY LIFE & HEALTH INS CO	IA	A	325.8	157.3	4.50	3.33	10.0	7.8	8.7	6.8	7.8	AD
BERKSHIRE HATHAWAY LIFE INS CO OF NE	NE	C+	18380.3	5447.6	1.51	1.20	7.3	3.7	3.0	10.0	3.2	GIT
BERKSHIRE LIFE INS CO OF AMERICA	MA	B	3893.2	205.4	2.53	1.20	7.3	4.1	5.5	7.9	6.1	I

See Page 27 for explanation of footnotes and Page 28 for explanation of stability factors. 32 www.weissratings.com

Arrows denote recent upgrades ▲ or downgrades ▼ (see Section VI for explanations)

NET PREMIUM ($MIL)	IN-VESTED ASSETS ($MIL)	CASH	CMO & STRUCT. SECS.	OTH.INV. GRADE BONDS	NON-INV. GRADE BONDS	CMMON & PREF. STOCK	MORT IN GOOD STAND.	NON-PERF. MORT.	REAL ESTATE	OTHER INVEST-MENTS	INVEST. IN AFFIL	INSURANCE COMPANY NAME
0.1	49.0	0.1	0.0	99.9	0.0	0.0	0.0	0.0	0.0	0.0	0.0	● AMERICAN MATURITY LIFE INS CO
429.1	3,060.2	0.0	11.5	69.4	4.8	0.7	9.4	0.0	0.0	4.4	0.0	● AMERICAN MEMORIAL LIFE INS CO
0.4	39.2	0.1	4.4	62.0	0.0	32.7	0.0	0.0	0.0	0.1	32.7	● AMERICAN MODERN LIFE INS CO
1,559.5	18,762.5 (*)	0.0	1.2	47.4	2.3	14.3	24.2	0.0	1.7	7.6	21.6	● AMERICAN NATIONAL INS CO
28.9	118.3	0.0	0.2	92.7	2.5	0.0	0.0	0.0	0.0	4.6	0.0	● AMERICAN NATIONAL LIFE INS CO OF TX
456.0	168.3 (*)	1.9	7.7	85.1	0.0	2.5	0.0	0.0	0.0	0.0	0.0	● AMERICAN PROGRESSIVE L&H I C OF NY
73.8	94.6	5.1	24.1	60.0	0.0	1.1	7.9	0.0	0.9	0.9	0.0	● AMERICAN PUBLIC LIFE INS CO
0.0	11.3 (*)	20.6	22.4	55.6	0.0	0.0	0.0	0.0	0.0	0.0	0.0	AMERICAN REPUBLIC CORP INS CO
510.7	810.7 (*)	0.6	19.2	54.8	3.3	4.4	10.9	0.0	4.0	1.6	3.8	● AMERICAN REPUBLIC INS CO
298.1	108.9	-14.4	0.0	114.4	0.0	0.0	0.0	0.0	0.0	0.0	0.0	● AMERICAN RETIREMENT LIFE INS CO
1.5	60.5	9.7	2.9	4.9	0.9	6.3	58.9	8.0	7.1	1.2	0.5	AMERICAN SAVINGS LIFE INS CO
0.3	1.0 (*)	20.3	0.0	47.4	0.0	5.8	0.0	0.0	0.0	0.0	5.8	AMERICAN SERVICE LIFE INS CO
2,836.4	13,649.3 (*)	0.6	21.5	53.7	2.0	1.0	14.4	0.0	0.7	3.7	0.0	● AMERICAN UNITED LIFE INS CO
59.8	276.8	0.0	0.6	68.8	0.0	17.8	5.0	0.0	1.5	6.3	17.4	● AMERICAN-AMICABLE LIFE INS CO OF TX
399.7	4,049.9 (*)	0.4	33.0	35.8	3.5	13.6	7.8	0.0	0.0	3.5	2.9	● AMERICO FINANCIAL LIFE & ANNUITY INS
2,094.8	12,156.3 (*)	0.1	13.9	53.4	3.5	4.8	14.8	0.0	0.5	7.1	1.3	● AMERITAS LIFE INS CORP
96.2	1,129.9	0.0	13.4	63.5	3.1	0.1	15.4	0.0	0.0	4.4	0.0	● AMERITAS LIFE INS CORP OF NY
53.4	1,204.8	0.6	29.6	53.7	2.0	4.6	3.8	0.0	0.0	4.8	0.0	● AMICA LIFE INS CO
148.7	2,519.9	0.0	23.0	68.5	1.5	0.2	0.0	0.0	0.0	6.0	0.0	● ANNUITY INVESTORS LIFE INS CO
6.0	23.5 (*)	2.9	0.0	21.9	0.0	0.0	0.0	0.0	0.0	0.0	0.0	ANTHEM LIFE & DISABILITY INS CO
324.4	634.0 (*)	0.0	33.6	59.7	0.5	1.5	0.0	0.0	0.0	3.1	0.0	● ANTHEM LIFE INS CO
0.4	2.7	89.6	0.0	9.4	0.0	0.0	0.0	0.0	0.0	0.0	0.0	ARKANSAS BANKERS LIFE INS CO
146.8	2,551.7	0.0	12.0	55.9	1.9	4.9	16.4	0.0	2.1	6.7	1.2	● ASSURITY LIFE INS CO
0.2	7.6 (*)	0.3	0.0	97.8	0.0	0.0	0.0	0.0	0.0	0.0	0.0	ASSURITY LIFE INS CO OF NY
4,162.9	9,928.7	1.9	31.3	26.0	7.4	12.9	10.3	0.1	0.0	9.4	23.1	● ATHENE ANNUITY & LIFE ASR CO
15.6	3,119.8	0.5	33.7	50.0	7.2	2.3	3.8	0.0	0.0	2.5	1.9	● ATHENE ANNUITY & LIFE ASR CO OF NY
714.3	50,121.4	0.8	28.2	50.8	4.4	1.0	9.6	0.0	0.0	4.2	2.9	● ATHENE ANNUITY & LIFE CO
--	--	--	--	--	--	--	--	--	--	--	--	ATHENE LIFE INS CO
1.1	940.8	2.9	3.6	81.2	3.6	0.4	8.1	0.0	0.0	0.2	0.0	● ATHENE LIFE INS CO OF NEW YORK
4.8	14.9 (*)	0.2	0.0	13.9	1.4	37.0	0.0	0.0	0.0	0.6	0.0	ATLANTA LIFE INS CO
-38.6	441.3 (*)	1.6	18.6	57.9	3.8	1.3	5.5	0.0	0.7	5.0	0.0	● ATLANTIC COAST LIFE INS CO
0.4	3,028.1	0.2	7.8	68.9	2.0	0.8	14.2	0.0	0.0	5.5	0.0	● AURORA NATIONAL LIFE ASR CO
135.0	709.1	0.0	20.7	62.6	8.2	6.1	0.0	0.0	0.0	1.8	5.9	● AUTO CLUB LIFE INS CO
-89.5	3,429.2	0.4	15.7	67.1	1.8	3.4	3.1	0.0	4.2	4.6	0.0	● AUTO-OWNERS LIFE INS CO
225.8	1,105.4	0.0	22.7	67.6	8.1	0.2	0.0	0.0	0.0	0.7	0.0	● AUTOMOBILE CLUB OF SOUTHERN CA INS
2.0	243.7 (*)	4.5	0.9	44.1	0.1	48.6	0.0	0.0	0.0	0.0	48.6	● AXA CORPORATE SOLUTIONS LIFE REINS
-0.4	469.8 (*)	0.1	1.3	27.1	0.0	0.0	0.0	0.0	0.0	64.1	0.0	● AXA EQUITABLE LIFE & ANNUITY CO
2,422.7	53,451.8 (*)	0.5	1.2	61.2	2.0	1.0	20.4	0.0	0.0	11.4	4.5	● AXA EQUITABLE LIFE INS CO
91.1	1,227.0	0.5	4.1	76.7	3.6	1.4	2.0	0.0	0.7	10.1	0.1	● BALTIMORE LIFE INS CO
46.9	460.8	6.0	25.7	60.3	3.5	1.5	0.0	1.5	0.0	1.7	0.1	● BANKERS CONSECO LIFE INS CO
0.0	10.8 (*)	11.3	3.4	80.0	2.3	0.0	0.0	0.0	0.0	0.0	0.0	BANKERS FIDELITY ASR CO
89.2	134.9 (*)	2.4	5.5	67.1	7.9	11.5	0.0	0.0	0.0	3.8	7.0	● BANKERS FIDELITY LIFE INS CO
1,874.6	17,695.9	1.4	25.7	56.2	4.2	2.1	6.1	0.0	0.0	3.5	1.3	● BANKERS LIFE & CAS CO
218.3	219.3 (*)	6.6	20.2	60.7	3.6	0.2	0.0	0.0	0.0	2.3	2.3	● BANKERS LIFE INS CO
0.8	5.7	2.1	0.0	60.3	1.6	1.4	0.0	0.0	26.1	8.5	0.0	BANKERS LIFE INS CO OF AMERICA
8.8	16.3 (*)	1.0	1.2	86.1	0.0	2.8	0.0	0.0	0.0	0.0	0.0	BANKERS LIFE OF LOUISIANA
598.6	2,869.0 (*)	0.0	9.1	64.3	3.8	4.1	10.5	0.0	0.0	0.7	4.1	● BANNER LIFE INS CO
21.7	2,186.1 (*)	0.8	10.6	74.5	1.9	5.2	0.0	0.0	0.0	5.4	0.0	● BENEFICIAL LIFE INS CO
0.2	2.1 (*)	45.5	4.9	18.6	0.0	1.6	0.0	0.0	1.2	0.0	0.0	BENEVOLENT LIFE INS CO INC
202.5	260.6 (*)	0.0	44.9	56.4	0.4	0.0	0.0	0.0	0.0	0.0	0.0	● BERKLEY LIFE & HEALTH INS CO
1,901.6	18,760.9	5.4	2.5	47.1	0.3	20.5	0.0	0.0	0.0	23.8	25.3	● BERKSHIRE HATHAWAY LIFE INS CO OF NE
98.3	3,600.2	0.1	0.6	91.5	4.1	0.0	0.3	0.0	0.5	3.0	0.5	● BERKSHIRE LIFE INS CO OF AMERICA

● Bullets denote a more detailed analysis is available in Section II.
(*) Asset category percentages do not add up to 100%

INSURANCE COMPANY NAME	DOM. STATE	RATING	TOTAL ASSETS ($MIL)	CAPITAL & SURPLUS ($MIL)	RISK ADJUSTED CAPITAL RATIO 1	RISK ADJUSTED CAPITAL RATIO 2	CAPITAL-IZATION INDEX (PTS)	INVEST. SAFETY INDEX (PTS)	PROFIT-ABILITY INDEX (PTS)	LIQUIDITY INDEX (PTS)	STAB. INDEX (PTS)	STABILITY FACTORS
BEST LIFE & HEALTH INS CO	TX	B+	22.7	17.6	1.82	1.47	7.7	8.0	8.4	6.9	6.0	
BEST MERIDIAN INS CO	FL	B-	348.6	59.6	1.79	1.16	7.2	6.3	5.2	6.7	4.3	DT
BLUE CROSS BLUE SHIELD OF KANSAS INC	KS	B	1791.6	874.2	2.01	1.50	7.8	4.5	5.8	6.5	5.4	I
BLUE SHIELD OF CALIFORNIA L&H INS CO	CA	B	303.9	189.5	5.05	3.74	10.0	8.1	5.8	7.0	4.9	T
BLUE SPIRIT INS CO	VT	U	--	--	--	--	--	--	--	--	--	Z
BLUEBONNET LIFE INS CO	MS	B+	64.3	59.8	8.28	7.45	10.0	8.1	9.4	10.0	6.4	D
BOSTON MUTUAL LIFE INS CO	MA	B+	1461.7	221.7	2.20	1.42	7.6	6.2	7.2	6.0	6.4	I
BRIGHTHOUSE LIFE INS CO OF NY	NY	C+	8005.3	274.0	2.33	1.20	7.3	6.5	2.0	6.3	4.4	GT
BRIGHTHOUSE LIFE INSURANCE CO	DE	B	172096.6	5033.3	2.65	1.38	7.6	6.2	5.4	7.4	4.5	AIT
BROOKE LIFE INS CO	MI	B-	4657.8	4322.2	1.26	1.12	7.2	1.2	6.8	9.5	4.1	GIT
CALPERS LONG-TERM CARE PROGRAM		U	--	--	--	--	--	--	--	--	--	Z
CANADA LIFE ASSURANCE CO-US BRANCH	MI	C	4624.3	185.9	1.37	0.73	5.6	5.9	4.0	4.9	3.7	CFLT
CANYON STATE LIFE INS CO	AZ	U (5)	--	--	--	--	--	--	--	--	--	Z
CAPITOL LIFE INS CO	TX	C	299.9	28.0	2.88	1.44	7.7	4.4	5.5	5.4	3.6	ADGIT
CAPITOL SECURITY LIFE INS CO	TX	D-	4.3	1.5	1.07	0.97	6.8	9.4	2.5	6.5	1.1	ADF
CAREAMERICA LIFE INS CO	CA	U (3)	--	--	--	--	--	--	--	--	--	Z
CARIBBEAN AMERICAN LIFE ASR CO	PR	B	39.7	13.0	2.25	1.92	8.4	8.6	7.0	8.4	5.5	AF
CASS COUNTY LIFE INSURANCE CO	TX	U (3)	--	--	--	--	--	--	--	--	--	Z
CATERPILLAR LIFE INS CO	MO	U (3)	--	--	--	--	--	--	--	--	--	Z
CENTRAL SECURITY LIFE INS CO	TX	D+	87.2	5.5	0.62	0.56	3.5	4.7	4.7	0.7	2.7	CFIL
CENTRAL STATES H & L CO OF OMAHA	NE	B	389.7	131.9	3.94	2.87	9.8	5.8	6.2	7.3	4.7	FGIT
CENTRE LIFE INS CO	MA	B-	1703.5	93.7	4.03	2.56	9.3	6.7	2.8	9.0	4.7	FT
CENTURION LIFE INS CO	IA	C	1047.7	819.9	37.09	16.05	10.0	6.9	6.6	6.7	3.3	FT
▲ CHESAPEAKE LIFE INS CO	OK	B+	195.4	120.9	2.95	2.34	9.0	8.8	7.4	7.5	6.5	D
CHESTERFIELD REINS CO	MO	C	330.3	90.1	1.57	1.10	7.2	6.8	2.3	0.0	2.9	DEL
CHRISTIAN FIDELITY LIFE INS CO	TX	B+	64.2	32.9	3.78	2.77	9.7	7.9	7.3	7.3	6.5	ADT
CHURCH LIFE INS CORP	NY	B	303.4	68.7	4.83	2.64	9.5	6.4	7.7	6.5	6.2	DFI
CICA LIFE INS CO OF AMERICA	CO	D	169.5	58.3	1.22	0.97	6.8	4.8	4.1	4.0	2.0	CILT
CIGNA ARBOR LIFE INS CO	CT	U (3)	--	--	--	--	--	--	--	--	--	Z
CIGNA HEALTH & LIFE INS CO	CT	B	10572.2	4929.1	2.23	1.69	7.1	3.7	9.9	4.2	5.6	AIL
CIGNA LIFE INS CO OF NEW YORK	NY	A-	407.5	102.4	2.50	1.63	7.9	6.3	7.4	7.0	7.0	ADI
CIGNA NATIONAL HEALTH INS CO	OH	B-	14.6	13.7	1.68	1.56	7.8	4.5	6.3	9.8	5.2	DIT
▲ CIGNA WORLDWIDE INS CO	DE	B-	63.0	10.9	1.57	1.42	4.0	8.3	3.8	10.0	4.3	IT
▼ CINCINNATI EQUITABLE LIFE INS CO	OH	D	154.8	9.5	1.15	0.73	5.2	3.6	2.0	1.8	2.2	CDIL
CINCINNATI LIFE INS CO	OH	B-	4517.0	204.7	1.35	0.73	5.5	3.6	3.6	4.6	5.0	CIL
CITIZENS FIDELITY INS CO	AR	C+	70.3	12.9	1.92	1.28	7.4	3.4	7.3	6.6	4.5	DI
CITIZENS NATIONAL LIFE INS CO	TX	C	11.9	1.9	3.02	2.72	9.6	7.8	1.1	6.7	3.0	ADFT
CITIZENS SECURITY LIFE INS CO	KY	C	29.5	16.0	0.81	0.72	4.8	2.9	8.7	6.9	4.1	CI
CLEAR SPRING LIFE INS CO	TX	U (3)	--	--	--	--	--	--	--	--	--	Z
CM LIFE INS CO	CT	B	8471.3	1546.5	2.85	1.81	8.2	5.3	8.4	6.6	4.7	IT
CMFG LIFE INS CO	IA	B-	18854.8	2180.1	1.63	1.25	7.4	4.8	8.0	6.9	5.0	I
COLONIAL LIFE & ACCIDENT INS CO	SC	C+	3368.4	526.9	2.23	1.40	7.6	5.9	7.1	6.9	4.4	A
COLONIAL LIFE INS CO OF TX	TX	C-	20.1	14.7	4.49	2.94	9.9	4.6	3.9	7.3	3.3	DF
COLONIAL PENN LIFE INS CO	PA	D+	871.8	97.1	1.23	0.71	5.3	4.0	1.9	2.5	2.7	ACIL
COLONIAL SECURITY LIFE INS CO	TX	D+	2.7	1.9	2.14	1.93	8.4	7.3	7.3	7.0	2.6	D
COLORADO BANKERS LIFE INS CO	NC	C	2618.4	155.6	2.27	1.08	7.1	5.5	3.0	9.1	2.1	GT
COLUMBIAN LIFE INS CO	IL	C	342.1	34.3	2.57	1.42	7.6	7.4	2.5	3.5	4.2	LRT
COLUMBIAN MUTUAL LIFE INS CO	NY	B	1454.3	105.2	1.60	1.02	7.0	6.4	5.0	3.6	5.4	IL
COLUMBUS LIFE INS CO	OH	C+	4144.8	257.5	1.80	0.93	6.4	4.8	1.9	5.4	4.4	I
COMBINED INS CO OF AMERICA	IL	B-	1561.1	237.7	1.72	1.23	7.3	5.5	4.7	6.3	5.3	ACI
COMBINED LIFE INS CO OF NEW YORK	NY	C+	464.1	50.4	1.35	0.96	6.7	7.3	2.9	7.1	4.5	C
COMM TRAVELERS LIFE INS CO	NY	B-	27.1	14.1	3.15	2.84	9.8	8.1	2.8	8.8	4.2	CGT

See Page 27 for explanation of footnotes and Page 28 for explanation of stability factors.
Arrows denote recent upgrades ▲ or downgrades▼ (see Section VI for explanations)

34

www.weissratings.com

NET PREMIUM ($MIL)	IN-VESTED ASSETS ($MIL)	CASH	CMO & STRUCT. SECS.	OTH. INV. GRADE BONDS	NON-INV. GRADE BONDS	CMMON & PREF. STOCK	MORT IN GOOD STAND.	NON-PERF. MORT.	REAL ESTATE	OTHER INVEST-MENTS	INVEST. IN AFFIL	INSURANCE COMPANY NAME
					% OF INVESTED ASSETS IN:							
32.8	19.7 (*)	26.4	0.2	37.2	0.8	27.8	0.0	0.0	0.0	0.1	0.0	BEST LIFE & HEALTH INS CO
87.2	278.8 (*)	14.7	14.8	40.6	0.7	1.4	13.8	0.0	10.7	2.1	1.4 ●	BEST MERIDIAN INS CO
1,691.4	1,540.7	0.0	19.2	30.8	1.6	27.5	0.0	0.0	2.1	18.8	5.9 ●	BLUE CROSS BLUE SHIELD OF KANSAS INC
182.0	296.6	-0.2	41.9	56.5	0.0	0.0	0.0	0.0	0.0	1.8	0.0 ●	BLUE SHIELD OF CALIFORNIA L&H INS CO
--	--	--	--	--	--	--	--	--	--	--	--	BLUE SPIRIT INS CO
3.4	60.3	1.0	28.8	57.1	0.7	0.8	0.0	0.0	0.0	11.5	0.0 ●	BLUEBONNET LIFE INS CO
152.1	1,301.6	2.2	5.9	56.2	1.6	5.6	14.8	0.0	0.8	12.8	2.5 ●	BOSTON MUTUAL LIFE INS CO
325.9	2,417.9	0.6	18.8	58.4	5.4	0.0	16.4	0.0	0.0	0.3	0.0 ●	BRIGHTHOUSE LIFE INS CO OF NY
4,420.0	61,425.6 (*)	0.4	17.6	51.9	4.2	0.9	14.8	0.0	0.0	6.5	1.1 ●	BRIGHTHOUSE LIFE INSURANCE CO
24.8	4,288.7	0.0	1.5	7.3	0.3	90.6	0.0	0.0	0.0	0.4	90.6 ●	BROOKE LIFE INS CO
--	--	--	--	--	--	--	--	--	--	--	--	CALPERS LONG-TERM CARE PROGRAM
91.7	3,249.9 (*)	0.3	11.0	66.1	0.6	0.0	11.2	0.0	0.0	8.6	0.0 ●	CANADA LIFE ASSURANCE CO-US BRANCH
--	--	--	--	--	--	--	--	--	--	--	--	CANYON STATE LIFE INS CO
14.1	245.9	0.0	2.7	72.4	3.0	0.4	20.8	0.0	0.4	0.6	0.0 ●	CAPITOL LIFE INS CO
0.4	4.1	2.5	0.0	97.5	0.0	0.0	0.0	0.0	0.0	0.0	0.0	CAPITOL SECURITY LIFE INS CO
--	--	--	--	--	--	--	--	--	--	--	--	CAREAMERICA LIFE INS CO
7.4	36.8 (*)	12.2	6.2	65.0	0.0	11.7	0.0	0.0	0.0	0.0	11.7	CARIBBEAN AMERICAN LIFE ASR CO
--	--	--	--	--	--	--	--	--	--	--	--	CASS COUNTY LIFE INSURANCE CO
--	--	--	--	--	--	--	--	--	--	--	--	CATERPILLAR LIFE INS CO
1.6	87.3	0.2	53.3	37.0	0.8	2.6	0.3	0.0	0.0	5.0	2.5	CENTRAL SECURITY LIFE INS CO
84.7	395.6	0.0	23.8	41.9	1.2	12.5	4.9	0.0	1.2	13.5	6.5 ●	CENTRAL STATES H & L CO OF OMAHA
1.0	1,765.4	-0.2	18.2	81.6	0.0	0.0	0.0	0.0	0.0	0.1	0.0 ●	CENTRE LIFE INS CO
1.9	1,239.2 (*)	2.2	27.7	43.3	3.0	0.0	0.0	0.0	0.0	0.9	0.0 ●	CENTURION LIFE INS CO
159.0	138.9 (*)	1.4	8.0	67.0	0.0	0.0	0.0	0.0	0.0	0.6	0.0 ●	CHESAPEAKE LIFE INS CO
155.5	76.9 (*)	0.6	17.3	80.9	0.0	0.0	0.0	0.0	0.0	0.0	0.0 ●	CHESTERFIELD REINS CO
20.5	56.6	6.2	4.1	84.3	0.5	0.0	4.1	0.0	0.0	0.8	0.0 ●	CHRISTIAN FIDELITY LIFE INS CO
34.2	290.9	0.0	26.2	61.2	3.9	5.5	0.0	0.0	0.0	3.2	0.0 ●	CHURCH LIFE INS CORP
-723.9	962.9	1.1	1.6	84.5	2.6	3.0	0.0	0.0	0.2	7.1	3.0 ●	CICA LIFE INS CO OF AMERICA
--	--	--	--	--	--	--	--	--	--	--	--	CIGNA ARBOR LIFE INS CO
12,381.2	5,856.9 (*)	0.0	1.8	50.2	19.7	6.7	7.8	0.0	0.0	15.1	12.6 ●	CIGNA HEALTH & LIFE INS CO
151.7	379.1	0.0	3.2	88.0	9.2	0.0	0.0	0.0	0.0	0.0	0.0 ●	CIGNA LIFE INS CO OF NEW YORK
2.1	12.8	1.0	0.0	45.8	0.0	53.2	0.0	0.0	0.0	0.0	53.2	CIGNA NATIONAL HEALTH INS CO
0.0	47.7	42.3	0.0	57.7	0.0	0.0	0.0	0.0	0.0	0.0	34.3	CIGNA WORLDWIDE INS CO
29.1	133.7	0.3	12.8	72.7	4.0	9.1	0.0	0.0	0.0	0.3	2.3	CINCINNATI EQUITABLE LIFE INS CO
216.0	3,427.9	1.0	6.3	82.9	6.2	0.2	0.0	0.0	0.0	3.4	0.9 ●	CINCINNATI LIFE INS CO
2.3	69.6 (*)	2.3	0.1	69.0	6.1	10.0	0.1	0.0	5.1	0.8	0.0	CITIZENS FIDELITY INS CO
0.7	11.6	6.2	1.5	86.2	0.0	5.0	0.0	0.0	0.0	1.2	0.0	CITIZENS NATIONAL LIFE INS CO
55.6	20.2	22.8	0.0	12.4	2.3	36.3	0.0	0.0	26.3	0.4	0.0	CITIZENS SECURITY LIFE INS CO
--	--	--	--	--	--	--	--	--	--	--	--	CLEAR SPRING LIFE INS CO
242.9	6,657.2 (*)	0.2	10.0	46.8	9.5	5.2	14.1	0.0	0.0	8.3	9.8 ●	CM LIFE INS CO
2,493.4	12,319.7 (*)	0.5	13.1	49.3	3.5	8.9	14.2	0.0	0.6	7.5	15.2 ●	CMFG LIFE INS CO
1,190.0	2,923.4	0.0	2.8	76.5	3.4	0.8	12.8	0.0	1.7	2.7	0.0 ●	COLONIAL LIFE & ACCIDENT INS CO
0.6	19.2 (*)	0.3	14.9	42.9	6.9	28.7	0.0	0.0	0.0	1.3	0.0	COLONIAL LIFE INS CO OF TX
294.5	789.7	1.9	16.8	70.2	4.1	1.2	0.7	0.0	1.0	4.1	0.0 ●	COLONIAL PENN LIFE INS CO
0.4	2.6	1.6	0.1	88.1	0.0	1.0	0.0	0.0	0.0	9.1	0.0	COLONIAL SECURITY LIFE INS CO
1,206.5	1,251.0 (*)	11.4	10.9	56.6	1.6	0.0	0.0	0.0	0.0	1.1	4.3 ●	COLORADO BANKERS LIFE INS CO
44.6	307.5 (*)	1.6	21.7	62.6	0.0	0.0	5.5	0.0	0.0	7.3	0.0	COLUMBIAN LIFE INS CO
136.7	1,364.3	0.0	14.1	64.4	0.4	2.5	12.6	0.0	0.3	5.8	2.0 ●	COLUMBIAN MUTUAL LIFE INS CO
244.4	3,904.2 (*)	0.2	16.0	60.7	5.2	3.1	5.8	0.0	0.0	6.5	2.5 ●	COLUMBUS LIFE INS CO
383.7	1,295.5 (*)	0.7	19.4	56.6	10.4	3.4	0.0	0.0	0.0	2.7	3.4 ●	COMBINED INS CO OF AMERICA
125.4	424.2	0.0	48.6	47.3	0.3	0.1	0.0	0.0	0.0	3.8	0.0 ●	COMBINED LIFE INS CO OF NEW YORK
3.5	24.7 (*)	25.8	35.6	33.2	0.0	1.5	0.0	0.0	1.1	0.0	0.3	COMM TRAVELERS LIFE INS CO

● Bullets denote a more detailed analysis is available in Section II.
(*) Asset category percentages do not add up to 100%

INSURANCE COMPANY NAME	DOM. STATE	RATING	TOTAL ASSETS ($MIL)	CAPITAL & SURPLUS ($MIL)	RISK ADJUSTED CAPITAL RATIO 1	RISK ADJUSTED CAPITAL RATIO 2	CAPITAL-IZATION INDEX (PTS)	INVEST. SAFETY INDEX (PTS)	PROFIT-ABILITY INDEX (PTS)	LIQUIDITY INDEX (PTS)	STAB. INDEX (PTS)	STABILIT FACTOR
COMMENCEMENT BAY RISK MGMT INS	WA	U (3)	--	--	--	--	--	--	--	--	--	Z
COMMONWEALTH ANNUITY & LIFE INS CO	MA	B-	19628.2	2465.7	0.87	0.74	4.9	4.7	7.8	7.6	3.7	CFGIT
COMMONWEALTH DEALERS LIFE INS CO	VA	U (5)	--	--	--	--	--	--	--	--	--	Z
COMPANION LIFE INS CO	NY	B-	1170.0	55.0	1.54	0.81	5.8	4.1	2.0	4.0	4.9	IL
COMPANION LIFE INS CO	SC	B+	401.6	226.4	2.77	2.12	8.7	4.4	8.6	6.9	6.6	AI
COMPANION LIFE INS CO OF CA	CA	B	24.4	11.5	3.37	3.03	10.0	9.5	3.0	10.0	4.9	GT
CONCERT HEALTH PLAN INS CO	IL	F (5)	--	--	--	--	--	--	--	--	--	Z
CONNECTICUT GENERAL LIFE INS CO	CT	B-	19355.3	5637.9	1.48	1.31	7.5	4.4	8.1	7.3	5.2	AIT
CONSECO LIFE INS CO OF TX	TX	U (3)	--	--	--	--	--	--	--	--	--	Z
CONSTITUTION LIFE INS CO	TX	D	393.5	35.0	2.37	1.30	7.5	4.3	2.2	7.0	2.3	AFT
CONSUMERS LIFE INS CO	OH	B	44.4	30.5	2.06	1.59	7.9	9.2	6.8	7.1	4.9	GT
CONTINENTAL AMERICAN INS CO	SC	B	804.5	159.2	1.68	1.24	7.4	7.6	4.5	7.1	5.7	
CONTINENTAL GENERAL INS CO	OH	C+ (1)	1407.1	68.4	1.05	0.63	5.1	2.8	5.9	6.7	4.7	CIT
▲ CONTINENTAL LIFE INS CO	PA	C-	27.7	3.0	0.74	0.67	4.4	3.5	4.6	4.8	3.0	ACDIL
CONTINENTAL LIFE INS CO OF BRENTWOOD	TN	C+	376.4	214.9	1.19	1.07	7.1	5.4	2.2	6.4	4.6	D
COOPERATIVA DE SEGUROS DE VIDA DE PR	PR	C- (4)	511.4	23.0	1.15	0.53	5.2	2.2	5.6	4.3	2.9	CIL
COOPERATIVE LIFE INS CO	AR	D	6.9	2.7	1.60	1.44	7.7	4.5	4.0	7.1	1.4	DI
CORVESTA LIFE INS CO	AZ	U (3)	--	--	--	--	--	--	--	--	--	Z
COTTON STATES LIFE INS CO	GA	A-	339.7	74.7	4.78	2.62	9.4	6.6	7.3	6.2	7.3	ADFI
COUNTRY INVESTORS LIFE ASR CO	IL	A-	303.5	196.6	14.64	7.13	8.0	8.2	7.6	7.4	7.1	
COUNTRY LIFE INS CO	IL	A+	9673.9	1223.6	2.11	1.39	7.6	5.8	6.9	5.8	7.6	IT
CROWN GLOBAL INS CO OF AMERICA	DE	E	661.2	1.9	0.11	0.10	0.0	8.0	3.0	10.0	0.0	CFIT
CSI LIFE INS CO	NE	B-	24.6	17.7	4.52	4.06	10.0	9.4	3.5	6.5	4.9	DGT
DAKOTA CAPITAL LIFE INS CO	ND	D	7.2	1.6	0.91	0.82	5.6	4.8	2.4	6.5	1.4	AGIT
DEARBORN NATIONAL LIFE INS CO	IL	B+	1737.6	488.0	3.47	2.14	8.7	6.1	6.0	6.3	6.5	AFIT
DEARBORN NATIONAL LIFE INS CO OF NY	NY	B+	23.6	12.7	3.15	2.83	9.7	8.3	4.0	7.0	4.9	AFT
DELAWARE AMERICAN LIFE INS CO	DE	B+	122.9	68.7	3.79	2.83	9.7	7.6	6.3	6.8	6.1	ADT
DELAWARE LIFE INS CO	DE	C	37022.2	1481.5	1.13	0.70	5.2	4.7	2.6	8.1	4.1	IT
DELAWARE LIFE INS CO OF NEW YORK	NY	B-	2382.2	378.7	9.41	4.50	10.0	6.4	5.7	6.9	4.6	AT
DELTA LIFE INS CO	GA	E+	65.0	6.5	0.43	0.26	0.2	1.0	1.9	3.9	0.2	CIL
DESERET MUTUAL INS CO	UT	B	42.8	17.0	3.53	2.39	9.1	6.6	6.9	7.7	5.6	AD
DESTINY HEALTH INS CO	IL	U (5)	--	--	--	--	--	--	--	--	--	Z
DIRECT GENERAL LIFE INS CO	SC	C	32.4	21.7	4.43	3.98	10.0	8.4	9.7	9.0	4.0	ADT
▲ DIRECTORS LIFE ASR CO	OK	E+	36.4	2.3	0.37	0.34	1.1	0.8	5.1	0.7	0.6	CIL
DL REINSURANCE CO	DE	U (3)	--	--	--	--	--	--	--	--	--	Z
EAGLE LIFE INS CO	IA	B+	1070.1	180.5	3.89	1.81	8.2	6.5	7.7	7.8	6.8	ADGI
EDUCATORS LIFE INS CO OF AMERICA	IL	U (3)	--	--	--	--	--	--	--	--	--	Z
ELAN INSURANCE USVI INC	VI	E+ (2)	2.6	1.6	1.80	1.54	7.8	8.6	1.4	7.2	0.7	DEFG
ELCO MUTUAL LIFE & ANNUITY	IL	C+	821.4	63.0	2.10	1.00	7.0	3.7	5.1	4.4	4.7	DIL
EMC NATIONAL LIFE CO	IA	B	963.0	118.6	2.88	1.62	7.9	6.7	7.4	5.2	6.0	FL
EMPIRE FIDELITY INVESTMENTS L I C	NY	B+	3035.0	88.5	2.62	2.10	8.7	8.1	5.5	7.0	6.7	
EMPLOYERS REASSURANCE CORP	KS	D	13630.6	794.5	1.08	0.81	5.5	5.6	1.8	6.6	1.9	AGT
▲ ENTERPRISE LIFE INS CO	TX	B+	73.7	49.3	1.29	1.15	7.2	5.7	9.2	7.5	6.4	ACDG
EPIC LIFE INSURANCE CO	WI	C	33.2	17.7	2.04	1.43	7.6	4.9	3.8	6.7	3.8	IT
EQUITABLE LIFE & CASUALTY INS CO	UT	C+	371.9	42.4	0.84	0.66	4.3	6.3	3.2	7.2	4.3	CDG
EQUITABLE NATIONAL LIFE INS CO	CT	U (3)	--	--	--	--	--	--	--	--	--	Z
EQUITRUST LIFE INS CO	IL	B-	18410.4	951.1	1.39	0.68	5.6	3.7	6.6	7.5	5.0	CI
ERIE FAMILY LIFE INS CO	PA	A-	2512.1	311.9	2.99	1.63	7.9	5.9	6.3	6.1	7.1	AI
EVERENCE INS CO	IN	U (3)	--	--	--	--	--	--	--	--	--	Z
EVERGREEN LIFE INS CO	TX	U (3)	--	--	--	--	--	--	--	--	--	Z
FAMILY BENEFIT LIFE INS CO	MO	C	159.1	8.2	0.95	0.67	4.6	3.3	2.9	2.4	3.2	ACDIL
FAMILY HERITAGE LIFE INS CO OF AMER	OH	B+	1444.8	106.0	1.66	1.02	7.0	5.9	5.3	7.6	6.5	AI

See Page 27 for explanation of footnotes and Page 28 for explanation of stability factors.

Arrows denote recent upgrades ▲ or downgrades▼ (see Section VI for explanations)

36

www.weissratings.com

NET PREMIUM ($MIL)	INVESTED ASSETS ($MIL)	CASH	CMO & STRUCT. SECS.	OTH.INV. GRADE BONDS	NON-INV. GRADE BONDS	CMMON & PREF. STOCK	MORT IN GOOD STAND.	NON-PERF. MORT.	REAL ESTATE	OTHER INVEST-MENTS	INVEST. IN AFFIL	INSURANCE COMPANY NAME
--	--	--	--	--	--	--	--	--	--	--	--	COMMENCEMENT BAY RISK MGMT INS
1,326.0	8,554.4 (*)	1.8	26.5	33.9	1.1	26.2	2.0	0.0	0.0	4.3	30.4 ●	COMMONWEALTH ANNUITY & LIFE INS CO
--	--	--	--	--	--	--	--	--	--	--	--	COMMONWEALTH DEALERS LIFE INS CO
69.6	1,001.0	0.0	21.6	65.0	0.6	0.5	9.0	0.0	0.0	3.4	0.0 ●	COMPANION LIFE INS CO
208.2	284.2	3.6	11.5	46.8	0.3	37.2	0.0	0.0	0.0	0.0	9.3 ●	COMPANION LIFE INS CO
3.5	19.8	37.5	2.6	60.0	0.0	0.0	0.0	0.0	0.0	0.0	0.0	COMPANION LIFE INS CO OF CA
--	--	--	--	--	--	--	--	--	--	--	--	CONCERT HEALTH PLAN INS CO
268.5	9,601.5	0.1	2.0	34.4	3.0	38.5	2.8	0.0	1.9	17.5	40.4 ●	CONNECTICUT GENERAL LIFE INS CO
--	--	--	--	--	--	--	--	--	--	--	--	CONSECO LIFE INS CO OF TX
32.9	344.8	1.6	26.3	68.0	2.5	0.0	0.0	0.0	0.0	1.4	0.7 ●	CONSTITUTION LIFE INS CO
20.9	39.9	41.8	0.0	57.6	0.0	0.0	0.0	0.0	0.0	0.0	0.0 ●	CONSUMERS LIFE INS CO
449.7	502.2	0.0	0.0	90.5	1.8	0.0	0.0	0.0	0.0	7.7	0.0 ●	CONTINENTAL AMERICAN INS CO
41.1	1,359.4 (*)	0.2	20.0	60.4	7.1	5.5	3.8	0.0	0.0	1.5	2.1 ●	CONTINENTAL GENERAL INS CO
3.6	24.6	0.4	4.0	71.3	0.3	0.0	16.2	0.0	1.8	6.0	0.0	CONTINENTAL LIFE INS CO
377.2	339.5 (*)	0.0	25.5	41.7	0.7	33.9	2.6	0.0	0.0	0.4	33.9 ●	CONTINENTAL LIFE INS CO OF BRENTWOOD
53.9	375.7	2.5	0.0	64.0	19.8	1.5	0.3	1.1	9.7	1.0	0.0	COOPERATIVA DE SEGUROS DE VIDA DE PR
0.3	6.8	9.1	1.7	59.8	9.0	19.9	0.0	0.0	0.3	0.3	0.0	COOPERATIVE LIFE INS CO
--	--	--	--	--	--	--	--	--	--	--	--	CORVESTA LIFE INS CO
15.9	324.9	0.0	21.9	60.3	2.8	4.4	0.0	0.0	0.0	10.5	0.0 ●	COTTON STATES LIFE INS CO
0.0	222.8	0.0	24.9	64.3	2.0	0.0	0.0	0.0	0.0	8.8	0.0 ●	COUNTRY INVESTORS LIFE ASR CO
458.6	9,207.2 (*)	0.0	18.4	58.5	4.2	7.2	3.2	0.0	0.4	6.3	3.8 ●	COUNTRY LIFE INS CO
36.1	2.4 (*)	1.8	47.2	39.3	0.0	0.0	0.0	0.0	0.0	0.0	0.0	CROWN GLOBAL INS CO OF AMERICA
1.5	17.7 (*)	5.8	0.0	67.9	0.0	0.0	0.0	0.0	0.0	0.1	48.1	CSI LIFE INS CO
1.3	4.8 (*)	5.1	0.0	72.5	10.2	11.0	0.0	0.0	0.0	0.1	0.0	DAKOTA CAPITAL LIFE INS CO
340.7	1,706.6	0.0	18.6	61.5	9.5	0.8	6.3	0.0	0.0	2.9	0.8 ●	DEARBORN NATIONAL LIFE INS CO
0.4	24.7 (*)	3.1	18.0	70.9	0.8	0.0	0.0	0.0	0.0	0.1	0.0	DEARBORN NATIONAL LIFE INS CO OF NY
72.5	91.8	4.9	24.2	66.3	0.0	0.0	0.0	0.0	0.0	4.6	4.6 ●	DELAWARE AMERICAN LIFE INS CO
-10,894.6	12,113.0 (*)	-0.1	17.4	46.3	3.1	6.0	4.1	0.0	0.0	16.9	7.5 ●	DELAWARE LIFE INS CO
10.9	1,158.8 (*)	0.5	21.9	62.2	0.8	2.8	3.1	0.0	0.0	0.5	0.0 ●	DELAWARE LIFE INS CO OF NEW YORK
11.0	65.4	4.6	0.0	23.0	4.4	37.6	0.0	0.0	22.3	8.2	17.5	DELTA LIFE INS CO
11.5	40.1	13.0	0.0	74.1	0.0	12.9	0.0	0.0	0.0	0.0	0.0	DESERET MUTUAL INS CO
--	--	--	--	--	--	--	--	--	--	--	--	DESTINY HEALTH INS CO
8.1	23.9	16.4	30.6	53.0	0.0	0.0	0.0	0.0	0.0	0.0	0.0 ●	DIRECT GENERAL LIFE INS CO
4.5	33.8	0.2	0.4	93.1	5.0	0.0	0.0	0.0	0.0	1.3	0.0	DIRECTORS LIFE ASR CO
--	--	--	--	--	--	--	--	--	--	--	--	DL REINSURANCE CO
253.3	803.0 (*)	0.7	39.3	44.3	1.8	0.0	5.5	0.0	0.0	0.2	0.0 ●	EAGLE LIFE INS CO
--	--	--	--	--	--	--	--	--	--	--	--	EDUCATORS LIFE INS CO OF AMERICA
1.3	2.4	100.0	0.0	0.0	0.0	0.0	0.0	0.0	0.0	0.0	0.0	ELAN INSURANCE USVI INC
162.5	718.6 (*)	6.1	0.0	78.7	5.3	0.4	0.3	0.0	0.4	0.0	0.0 ●	ELCO MUTUAL LIFE & ANNUITY
41.1	906.4 (*)	0.0	6.6	79.9	1.3	3.8	3.4	0.0	0.1	2.2	0.0 ●	EMC NATIONAL LIFE CO
93.3	209.4	0.0	1.2	96.1	0.4	0.0	0.0	0.0	0.0	2.3	0.0 ●	EMPIRE FIDELITY INVESTMENTS L I C
262.9	10,970.2 (*)	0.1	15.8	68.1	2.0	5.2	5.7	0.0	0.0	1.8	6.1 ●	EMPLOYERS REASSURANCE CORP
105.8	46.2 (*)	26.1	3.9	14.9	0.6	47.0	0.0	0.0	0.0	0.0	47.0 ●	ENTERPRISE LIFE INS CO
20.9	30.7	0.0	11.4	60.5	0.0	25.2	0.0	0.0	0.0	2.8	0.0	EPIC LIFE INSURANCE CO
69.3	308.5	0.0	9.5	66.8	1.6	7.9	5.4	0.0	0.0	8.9	7.8 ●	EQUITABLE LIFE & CASUALTY INS CO
--	--	--	--	--	--	--	--	--	--	--	--	EQUITABLE NATIONAL LIFE INS CO
1,107.4	16,370.3 (*)	0.3	19.5	45.8	4.4	1.6	6.2	0.0	0.0	15.2	3.1 ●	EQUITRUST LIFE INS CO
132.0	2,328.0 (*)	1.0	3.2	83.8	1.6	2.0	0.0	0.0	0.0	2.3	0.0 ●	ERIE FAMILY LIFE INS CO
--	--	--	--	--	--	--	--	--	--	--	--	EVERENCE INS CO
--	--	--	--	--	--	--	--	--	--	--	--	EVERGREEN LIFE INS CO
17.0	145.9	3.2	0.1	51.6	1.4	0.1	40.6	0.8	0.2	1.5	0.0	FAMILY BENEFIT LIFE INS CO
229.2	1,101.6	0.0	2.7	92.8	1.4	0.0	0.3	0.0	0.0	2.8	0.0 ●	FAMILY HERITAGE LIFE INS CO OF AMER

● Bullets denote a more detailed analysis is available in Section II.
(*) Asset category percentages do not add up to 100%

INSURANCE COMPANY NAME	DOM. STATE	RATING	TOTAL ASSETS ($MIL)	CAPITAL & SURPLUS ($MIL)	RISK ADJUSTED CAPITAL RATIO 1	RISK ADJUSTED CAPITAL RATIO 2	CAPITAL-IZATION INDEX (PTS)	INVEST. SAFETY INDEX (PTS)	PROFIT-ABILITY INDEX (PTS)	LIQUIDITY INDEX (PTS)	STAB. INDEX (PTS)	STABILIT FACTOR
FAMILY LIBERTY LIFE INS CO	TX	D	34.9	9.5	2.05	1.28	7.4	4.4	2.7	6.1	2.2	DI
FAMILY LIFE INS CO	TX	C	146.4	29.4	3.16	2.57	9.4	8.2	3.0	5.8	4.2	DF
FAMILY SECURITY LIFE INS CO INC	MS	C	6.8	1.7	0.93	0.83	5.6	5.6	3.5	6.5	3.4	CD
FAMILY SERVICE LIFE INS CO	TX	U (3)	--	--	--	--	--	--	--	--	--	Z
FARM BUREAU LIFE INS CO	IA	B+	9267.1	634.1	2.17	1.13	7.2	5.5	8.0	4.0	6.0	IL
FARM BUREAU LIFE INS CO OF MICHIGAN	MI	A-	2502.3	458.6	3.70	2.06	8.6	6.1	7.1	5.7	6.9	I
FARM BUREAU LIFE INS CO OF MISSOURI	MO	A-	604.4	71.1	1.68	1.11	7.2	5.2	5.3	5.7	6.9	I
FARM FAMILY LIFE INS CO	NY	B (2)	2259.2	253.2	2.61	1.44	7.7	5.0	6.0	5.6	6.0	GI
FARMERS NEW WORLD LIFE INS CO	WA	B-	5159.1	480.9	2.14	1.18	4.0	5.4	3.0	4.3	4.7	FILT
FEDERAL LIFE INS CO	IL	C-	241.1	13.2	1.74	0.96	6.7	3.7	1.9	4.0	2.8	DIL
FEDERATED LIFE INS CO	MN	A	1969.7	411.9	4.96	2.68	9.5	6.7	8.8	6.4	7.4	AI
FIDELITY & GUARANTY LIFE INS CO	IA	C+	24281.8	946.4	1.09	0.58	5.1	2.6	5.8	6.0	4.6	CI
FIDELITY & GUARANTY LIFE INS CO NY	NY	B-	539.9	94.4	4.62	2.36	9.0	5.2	7.1	6.1	4.8	AFIT
FIDELITY INVESTMENTS LIFE INS CO	UT	A-	30960.8	934.0	3.39	2.03	8.5	6.6	9.2	7.0	7.0	I
FIDELITY LIFE ASSN A LEGAL RESERVE	IL	C+	404.2	118.0	5.99	3.20	10.0	6.3	3.7	6.7	4.8	D
FIDELITY MUTUAL LIFE INS CO	PA	F (5)	--	--	--	--	--	--	--	--	--	Z
FIDELITY SECURITY LIFE INS CO	MO	B	931.6	234.7	4.44	2.70	9.6	6.7	7.6	6.6	5.5	FT
FIDELITY SECURITY LIFE INS CO OF NY	NY	B	44.4	11.6	2.30	2.02	8.5	5.5	7.1	6.8	6.2	AI
FIDELITY STANDARD LIFE INS CO	AR	E+	3.4	0.6	0.57	0.51	3.1	3.0	5.0	5.8	0.8	ACI
FINANCIAL AMERICAN LIFE INS CO	KS	D-	3.5	2.0	1.46	1.31	4.0	9.1	0.9	6.7	1.3	ADFT
FINANCIAL ASSURANCE LIFE INS CO	TX	U (3)	--	--	--	--	--	--	--	--	--	Z
FIRST ALLMERICA FINANCIAL LIFE INS	MA	B	3333.8	236.8	5.16	2.45	9.2	6.6	6.0	5.9	5.8	AFT
FIRST ASR LIFE OF AMERICA	LA	B	41.6	36.9	3.35	3.12	10.0	8.4	8.3	8.4	5.9	AT
FIRST BERKSHIRE HATHAWAY LIFE INS CO	NY	C+	215.8	119.0	12.05	6.26	10.0	3.7	2.8	10.0	4.4	GIT
FIRST COMMAND LIFE INS CO	TX	B-	41.3	11.4	2.07	1.86	8.3	7.5	6.9	6.6	4.3	D
FIRST CONTINENTAL LIFE & ACC INS CO	TX	D-	3.0	1.6	1.25	0.82	5.6	4.6	0.9	0.6	1.1	FLT
FIRST DIMENSION LIFE INS CO INC	OK	U (3)	--	--	--	--	--	--	--	--	--	Z
FIRST GUARANTY INS CO	LA	D	54.2	5.6	0.88	0.79	5.3	3.1	6.5	2.2	2.3	ACILT
FIRST HEALTH LIFE & HEALTH INS CO	TX	C+	420.1	166.9	1.61	1.33	7.5	5.4	3.9	1.8	3.2	DFLT
FIRST LANDMARK LIFE INS CO	NE	U (3)	--	--	--	--	--	--	--	--	--	Z
FIRST NATIONAL LIFE INS CO	NE	C	6.9	2.6	1.08	0.70	5.1	2.6	3.9	6.6	3.6	CFIT
FIRST PENN-PACIFIC LIFE INS CO	IN	B	1418.1	163.5	2.53	1.37	7.6	6.0	4.4	4.0	5.1	AFIL
▼ FIRST RELIANCE STANDARD LIFE INS CO	NY	A-	208.0	59.6	4.77	3.16	10.0	6.6	3.6	7.0	5.7	AI
FIRST SECURITY BENEFIT LIFE & ANN	NY	B	599.1	31.4	1.66	0.79	6.0	2.8	6.0	3.6	4.0	CDFIL
FIRST SYMETRA NATL LIFE INS CO OF NY	NY	B+	2070.2	115.3	1.80	0.91	6.3	4.6	7.8	5.1	6.3	ACIL
FIRST UNUM LIFE INS CO	NY	C+	3656.0	234.1	2.02	1.04	7.1	3.6	5.5	7.6	4.8	AI
FIVE STAR LIFE INS CO	NE	C	294.2	27.4	1.79	1.12	7.2	6.7	1.4	5.0	3.9	F
FLORIDA COMBINED LIFE INS CO INC	FL	C	70.5	43.6	6.73	3.36	8.0	4.8	2.8	7.8	4.3	I
FORESTERS LIFE INS & ANNUITY CO	NY	C+	2619.6	72.1	1.78	0.95	6.6	6.1	3.0	6.0	4.5	I
FORETHOUGHT LIFE INS CO	IN	B	30391.4	1693.7	2.20	1.05	4.0	4.7	7.1	7.3	4.4	IT
FORETHOUGHT NATIONAL LIFE INS CO	TX	U (3)	--	--	--	--	--	--	--	--	--	Z
FOUNDATION LIFE INS CO OF AR	AR	D	5.5	1.4	1.16	1.04	7.1	4.5	2.1	8.4	2.0	
FRANDISCO LIFE INS CO	GA	A	93.8	79.8	9.51	8.56	10.0	8.9	9.7	9.1	6.9	AD
FREEDOM LIFE INS CO OF AMERICA	TX	B+	213.2	127.9	1.47	1.22	7.3	6.7	8.4	7.1	6.5	CGI
FREMONT LIFE INS CO	CA	F (5)	--	--	--	--	--	--	--	--	--	Z
FRINGE BENEFIT LIFE INS CO	TX	C-	27.2	20.4	4.70	3.09	4.0	4.6	5.4	9.0	2.8	DFIT
FUNERAL DIRECTORS LIFE INS CO	TX	B-	1386.8	126.9	2.42	1.30	7.5	6.3	7.9	2.7	4.7	L
GARDEN STATE LIFE INS CO	TX	A	135.5	79.3	8.68	7.81	10.0	6.7	8.8	6.9	7.8	ADI
▲ GENERAL FIDELITY LIFE INS CO	SC	C	22.1	15.6	4.13	3.72	10.0	9.7	2.7	10.0	3.5	DFT
▼ GENERAL RE LIFE CORP	CT	C	4272.2	931.7	0.41	0.32	0.8	4.1	2.9	7.9	3.0	CFIT
GENWORTH INSURANCE CO	NC	U (3)	--	--	--	--	--	--	--	--	--	Z
GENWORTH LIFE & ANNUITY INS CO	VA	C-	22016.7	1315.4	1.82	1.05	7.1	6.0	2.5	6.0	2.0	AT

See Page 27 for explanation of footnotes and Page 28 for explanation of stability factors.
Arrows denote recent upgrades ▲ or downgrades▼ (see Section VI for explanations)

38 · www.weissratings.com

NET PREMIUM ($MIL)	IN-VESTED ASSETS ($MIL)	% OF INVESTED ASSETS IN:										INSURANCE COMPANY NAME
		CASH	CMO & STRUCT. SECS.	OTH. INV. GRADE BONDS	NON-INV. GRADE BONDS	CMMON & PREF. STOCK	MORT IN GOOD STAND.	NON-PERF. MORT.	REAL ESTATE	OTHER INVEST-MENTS	INVEST. IN AFFIL	
1.4	34.2 (*)	1.9	0.0	73.8	1.9	19.4	0.0	0.0	0.1	0.0	0.0	FAMILY LIBERTY LIFE INS CO
19.5	136.3 (*)	0.8	2.9	71.9	0.0	1.1	2.5	0.0	0.0	9.7	0.0 ●	FAMILY LIFE INS CO
0.6	6.8 (*)	0.4	6.5	63.1	1.5	1.6	0.0	0.0	3.5	0.0	0.0	FAMILY SECURITY LIFE INS CO INC
--	--	--	--	--	--	--	--	--	--	--	--	FAMILY SERVICE LIFE INS CO
471.4	8,167.9	0.0	25.2	53.3	2.9	1.9	11.9	0.0	0.0	4.5	0.1 ●	FARM BUREAU LIFE INS CO
80.6	2,358.8	0.0	1.4	69.1	1.1	6.9	17.5	0.0	0.4	3.5	0.4 ●	FARM BUREAU LIFE INS CO OF MICHIGAN
32.2	571.3	0.3	13.5	66.1	0.2	14.7	0.0	0.0	0.0	5.2	3.1 ●	FARM BUREAU LIFE INS CO OF MISSOURI
73.2	1,342.8	0.0	1.1	71.2	4.2	9.7	9.2	0.3	0.4	3.9	0.0 ●	FARM FAMILY LIFE INS CO
398.5	4,054.6 (*)	0.5	13.3	54.5	2.9	0.1	14.3	0.0	3.5	9.6	3.4 ●	FARMERS NEW WORLD LIFE INS CO
15.6	205.8	0.0	23.5	60.5	4.2	3.3	0.0	0.0	1.0	7.4	1.3	FEDERAL LIFE INS CO
138.7	1,830.6 (*)	0.0	14.1	75.9	3.8	1.5	0.0	0.0	0.0	1.9	0.0 ●	FEDERATED LIFE INS CO
2,201.5	21,359.2	1.8	23.8	56.6	5.8	5.1	2.6	0.0	0.0	3.6	1.7 ●	FIDELITY & GUARANTY LIFE INS CO
8.5	508.7	0.0	16.3	64.5	3.7	5.6	0.0	0.0	0.0	9.1	0.0 ●	FIDELITY & GUARANTY LIFE INS CO NY
1,094.1	1,050.6	0.0	1.4	75.0	6.8	7.9	0.0	0.0	0.0	8.9	7.9 ●	FIDELITY INVESTMENTS LIFE INS CO
45.6	384.0	2.7	25.7	48.4	7.7	2.0	11.2	0.0	0.0	2.4	0.0 ●	FIDELITY LIFE ASSN A LEGAL RESERVE
--	--	--	--	--	--	--	--	--	--	--	--	FIDELITY MUTUAL LIFE INS CO
91.5	904.7 (*)	2.7	36.3	50.9	0.6	2.8	0.3	0.0	0.0	2.3	1.6 ●	FIDELITY SECURITY LIFE INS CO
2.0	39.0 (*)	1.6	20.6	75.2	0.0	0.8	0.0	0.0	0.0	0.0	0.0	FIDELITY SECURITY LIFE INS CO OF NY
0.1	3.3	8.3	0.0	39.2	12.3	30.2	4.1	0.0	0.0	6.0	0.0	FIDELITY STANDARD LIFE INS CO
-0.1	3.3	6.0	0.0	93.9	0.0	0.0	0.0	0.0	0.0	0.1	0.0	FINANCIAL AMERICAN LIFE INS CO
--	--	--	--	--	--	--	--	--	--	--	--	FINANCIAL ASSURANCE LIFE INS CO
21.4	2,574.8 (*)	2.5	18.5	71.5	0.8	0.0	0.6	0.0	0.0	2.1	0.5 ●	FIRST ALLMERICA FINANCIAL LIFE INS
1.4	40.3 (*)	0.8	0.0	66.8	1.2	25.0	0.0	0.0	0.0	0.0	25.0 ●	FIRST ASR LIFE OF AMERICA
4.0	221.0 (*)	17.2	11.0	50.9	17.6	4.8	0.0	0.0	0.0	0.0	3.6 ●	FIRST BERKSHIRE HATHAWAY LIFE INS CO
1.7	38.9 (*)	0.2	18.7	75.0	2.6	0.0	0.0	0.0	0.0	0.4	0.0	FIRST COMMAND LIFE INS CO
1.4	2.5	17.5	0.0	48.4	0.0	23.7	0.0	0.0	10.4	0.0	23.7	FIRST CONTINENTAL LIFE & ACC INS CO
--	--	--	--	--	--	--	--	--	--	--	--	FIRST DIMENSION LIFE INS CO INC
1.1	54.2 (*)	0.4	3.9	67.2	5.2	1.4	14.7	0.0	0.9	0.4	0.0	FIRST GUARANTY INS CO
427.1	140.3 (*)	33.6	15.0	38.4	10.6	0.0	0.0	0.0	0.0	0.0	0.0 ●	FIRST HEALTH LIFE & HEALTH INS CO
--	--	--	--	--	--	--	--	--	--	--	--	FIRST LANDMARK LIFE INS CO
1.8	5.7	4.1	30.9	16.1	0.0	49.8	0.0	0.0	-1.2	0.4	0.0	FIRST NATIONAL LIFE INS CO
96.0	1,323.1	-0.5	10.5	76.5	4.2	0.2	6.0	0.0	0.0	3.0	1.4 ●	FIRST PENN-PACIFIC LIFE INS CO
54.9	187.2	0.0	16.8	73.5	6.9	0.0	0.0	0.0	0.0	2.9	0.0 ●	FIRST RELIANCE STANDARD LIFE INS CO
12.0	527.6	0.0	45.0	43.9	4.5	0.1	0.0	0.0	0.0	6.5	0.5 ●	FIRST SECURITY BENEFIT LIFE & ANN
352.3	1,782.5	0.1	8.2	77.7	1.2	0.0	12.8	0.0	0.0	0.0	0.0 ●	FIRST SYMETRA NATL LIFE INS CO OF NY
340.3	3,370.1	0.0	5.2	79.9	8.8	0.0	5.2	0.0	0.0	1.0	0.0 ●	FIRST UNUM LIFE INS CO
98.6	237.1 (*)	2.7	18.8	70.5	3.3	0.3	0.0	0.0	0.0	3.2	0.1 ●	FIVE STAR LIFE INS CO
0.0	49.4	5.5	2.4	16.1	0.1	0.0	0.0	0.0	0.0	75.4	75.4 ●	FLORIDA COMBINED LIFE INS CO INC
211.0	948.1	0.8	0.2	83.7	4.5	0.0	0.0	0.0	0.0	10.8	0.0 ●	FORESTERS LIFE INS & ANNUITY CO
3,349.0	26,981.6 (*)	0.4	52.1	29.7	1.3	0.5	13.5	0.1	0.0	0.9	0.2 ●	FORETHOUGHT LIFE INS CO
--	--	--	--	--	--	--	--	--	--	--	--	FORETHOUGHT NATIONAL LIFE INS CO
1.2	4.9	33.9	0.0	40.3	7.4	16.2	0.0	0.0	0.0	2.2	0.0	FOUNDATION LIFE INS CO OF AR
13.3	85.0 (*)	0.2	0.0	97.6	0.0	0.0	0.0	0.0	0.0	0.0	0.0 ●	FRANDISCO LIFE INS CO
306.2	126.4 (*)	14.3	13.2	43.8	0.2	23.6	0.0	0.0	0.0	0.0	23.6	FREEDOM LIFE INS CO OF AMERICA
--	--	--	--	--	--	--	--	--	--	--	--	FREMONT LIFE INS CO
0.0	30.1 (*)	8.7	3.4	39.8	1.7	16.6	12.5	0.0	0.0	21.7	0.0	FRINGE BENEFIT LIFE INS CO
174.0	1,288.6	0.1	2.8	84.6	2.4	0.4	7.9	0.0	1.3	0.4	0.9 ●	FUNERAL DIRECTORS LIFE INS CO
16.5	118.1	0.0	0.9	94.1	1.7	0.0	0.0	0.0	0.0	3.4	0.0 ●	GARDEN STATE LIFE INS CO
0.1	23.2 (*)	44.0	0.0	49.2	0.0	0.0	0.0	0.0	0.0	0.0	0.0	GENERAL FIDELITY LIFE INS CO
995.3	3,342.9 (*)	0.3	0.1	67.0	2.0	11.7	0.0	0.0	0.0	15.0	15.4 ●	GENERAL RE LIFE CORP
--	--	--	--	--	--	--	--	--	--	--	--	GENWORTH INSURANCE CO
261.6	14,431.2	0.0	18.9	55.8	3.5	1.8	12.3	0.0	0.1	6.7	1.4 ●	GENWORTH LIFE & ANNUITY INS CO

● Bullets denote a more detailed analysis is available in Section II.
(*) Asset category percentages do not add up to 100%

INSURANCE COMPANY NAME	DOM. STATE	RATING	TOTAL ASSETS ($MIL)	CAPITAL & SURPLUS ($MIL)	RISK ADJUSTED CAPITAL RATIO 1	RISK ADJUSTED CAPITAL RATIO 2	CAPITAL-IZATION INDEX (PTS)	INVEST. SAFETY INDEX (PTS)	PROFIT-ABILITY INDEX (PTS)	LIQUIDITY INDEX (PTS)	STAB. INDEX (PTS)	STABILITY FACTORS
GENWORTH LIFE INS CO	DE	C+	39956.4	2514.7	1.12	0.79	5.3	4.8	2.5	7.0	4.7	AIT
GENWORTH LIFE INS CO OF NEW YORK	NY	C	7736.8	311.4	1.53	0.78	5.8	4.0	1.5	6.0	3.7	AFIT
GERBER LIFE INS CO	NY	B+	3909.7	297.1	1.79	1.05	7.1	6.0	4.8	4.8	6.4	IL
GERMANIA LIFE INS CO	TX	C+	94.3	9.5	1.19	1.04	7.1	5.0	3.0	4.7	4.4	AIL
GERTRUDE GEDDES WILLIS LIFE INS CO	LA	F (5)	--	--	--	--	--	--	--	--	--	Z
GLOBE LIFE & ACCIDENT INS CO	NE	C+	4652.8	318.2	1.11	0.70	5.2	4.1	5.2	1.8	3.8	CIL
GLOBE LIFE INSURANCE CO OF NY	NY	B	248.9	28.4	1.73	1.07	7.1	4.5	6.1	4.2	6.0	AIL
GMHP HEALTH INS LMTD	GU	U (3)	--	--	--	--	--	--	--	--	--	Z
GOLDEN RULE INS CO	IN	B	534.7	283.1	1.67	1.31	5.1	8.0	6.8	6.2	5.4	ACT
GOVERNMENT PERSONNEL MUTUAL L I C	TX	B	821.2	114.8	2.58	1.65	8.0	6.6	5.9	5.6	5.8	D
GPM HEALTH & LIFE INS CO	WA	B	143.3	14.2	1.60	1.44	7.7	3.7	5.1	4.3	5.4	ADFGIL
GRANGE LIFE INS CO	OH	C	390.8	41.1	2.65	1.59	7.9	6.5	1.8	5.9	2.9	FGT
GREAT AMERICAN LIFE INS CO	OH	B-	35805.2	2333.2	1.75	0.97	6.8	5.2	8.8	5.5	5.3	AI
GREAT CENTRAL LIFE INS CO	LA	C+ (3)	24.9	9.0	1.51	0.99	6.9	3.3	6.8	8.2	4.2	DI
GREAT REPUBLIC LIFE INS CO	WA	F (5)	--	--	--	--	--	--	--	--	--	Z
GREAT SOUTHERN LIFE INS CO	TX	B	212.0	53.1	5.75	3.17	10.0	6.5	9.3	7.0	6.3	AT
GREAT WEST LIFE ASR CO	MI	C+	73.3	25.9	3.33	2.83	9.7	7.5	3.0	6.6	4.8	F
GREAT WESTERN INS CO	UT	C-	1402.4	27.5	0.54	0.28	1.3	0.5	0.9	5.4	1.5	CIT
GREAT WESTERN LIFE INS CO	MT	U (3)	--	--	--	--	--	--	--	--	--	Z
GREAT-WEST LIFE & ANNUITY INS CO	CO	B-	57765.4	1270.0	1.32	0.71	5.5	5.5	6.2	5.7	4.2	CGIT
GREAT-WEST LIFE & ANNUITY INS OF NY	NY	B	2258.1	89.0	2.14	1.13	7.2	5.9	4.4	4.4	5.9	AIL
GREATER GEORGIA LIFE INS CO	GA	B	61.0	21.8	1.24	0.92	6.4	8.2	4.2	6.4	5.6	C
GREENFIELDS LIFE INS CO	CO	B	16.1	8.8	3.10	2.79	4.0	8.7	2.2	7.8	4.9	AFT
GRIFFIN LEGGETT BURIAL INS CO	AR	U (3)	--	--	--	--	--	--	--	--	--	Z
GUARANTEE TRUST LIFE INS CO	IL	B	637.7	94.9	2.07	1.35	7.5	6.5	7.8	7.2	5.4	T
▲ GUARANTY INCOME LIFE INS CO	LA	B	812.7	66.5	3.31	1.48	7.7	4.5	8.9	5.5	5.4	DGI
GUARDIAN INS & ANNUITY CO INC	DE	B	15824.8	342.0	1.89	0.96	6.7	5.4	3.5	9.0	4.7	CGIT
GUARDIAN LIFE INS CO OF AMERICA	NY	A	57852.7	7110.3	2.89	1.84	8.3	6.6	7.2	6.1	7.5	I
GUGGENHEIM LIFE & ANNUITY CO	DE	B- (2)	13884.9	606.4	1.57	0.79	5.9	4.1	6.9	6.2	4.2	CIT
GULF GUARANTY LIFE INS CO	MS	C+	18.6	10.1	1.48	1.12	7.2	3.6	6.7	8.1	3.6	DGI
GULF STATES LIFE INS CO INC	LA	U (5)	--	--	--	--	--	--	--	--	--	Z
HALLMARK LIFE INS CO	AZ	C (4)	4.8	4.0	1.22	1.09	7.1	9.8	5.8	2.2	2.6	ADFLT
HANNOVER LIFE REASSURANCE CO OF AMER	FL	B+	16338.8	442.5	1.75	0.96	6.7	6.8	7.6	6.7	6.5	CGI
HARLEYSVILLE LIFE INS CO	OH	B	401.8	50.1	3.20	1.71	8.1	6.4	5.6	5.2	5.4	ADFIL
HARTFORD LIFE & ACCIDENT INS CO	CT	C	12962.6	2267.8	4.01	2.53	9.3	7.0	2.0	6.3	3.9	AFGT
HAWKEYE LIFE INS GROUP INC	IA	C	12.5	10.0	3.69	3.32	10.0	8.7	8.3	8.4	3.3	D
HAWTHORN LIFE INS CO	TX	D	10.1	1.9	0.21	0.21	0.0	3.0	5.5	3.9	0.5	ACDIL
HAYMARKET INS CO	NE	D	1016.4	41.3	1.24	0.71	5.4	3.8	3.0	0.0	2.0	CDEGII
HCC LIFE INS CO	IN	B	1086.9	516.9	3.37	2.66	9.5	8.4	6.8	6.6	5.7	AD
HEALTH NET LIFE INS CO	CA	C	748.8	391.3	3.22	2.56	9.3	8.5	1.9	6.8	3.9	AT
HEARTLAND NATIONAL LIFE INS CO	IN	B-	13.0	5.0	1.84	1.66	8.0	8.9	6.3	7.0	4.7	T
HERITAGE LIFE INS CO	AZ	C+	3923.4	937.5	3.76	1.73	8.1	3.7	6.7	8.0	4.2	FIT
HIGGINBOTHAM BURIAL INS CO	AR	F (5)	--	--	--	--	--	--	--	--	--	Z
HM LIFE INS CO	PA	B	721.2	396.5	3.91	2.63	9.4	4.8	6.8	6.2	5.4	ADIT
HM LIFE INS CO OF NEW YORK	NY	B	67.2	44.4	5.54	4.28	10.0	8.8	6.4	6.9	5.4	ADT
HOMESTEADERS LIFE CO	IA	B	3035.3	202.0	2.26	1.20	7.3	6.1	5.5	7.1	5.5	I
HORACE MANN LIFE INS CO	IL	B	9548.2	479.7	1.76	0.91	6.3	5.3	8.1	4.3	5.4	ACIL
HUMANA INS CO OF KENTUCKY	KY	B	209.8	180.8	6.80	5.00	10.0	7.3	6.9	7.3	4.5	DT
▼ HUMANA INS CO OF PUERTO RICO INC	PR	C+	77.8	46.1	2.12	1.70	8.1	8.3	2.5	6.6	4.8	
IA AMERICAN LIFE INS CO	TX	C+	140.8	40.0	0.81	0.73	4.8	4.5	3.5	6.5	4.8	ACIT
IBC LIFE INS CO	TX	U (5)	--	--	--	--	--	--	--	--	--	Z
IDEALIFE INS CO	CT	B-	21.5	15.2	4.26	3.83	10.0	9.5	2.4	9.8	5.0	DF

See Page 27 for explanation of footnotes and Page 28 for explanation of stability factors.

40

www.weissratings.com

Arrows denote recent upgrades ▲ or downgrades▼ (see Section VI for explanations)

NET PREMIUM ($MIL)	IN-VESTED ASSETS ($MIL)	CASH	CMO & STRUCT. SECS.	OTH.INV. GRADE BONDS	NON-INV. GRADE BONDS	CMMON & PREF. STOCK	MORT IN GOOD STAND.	NON-PERF. MORT.	REAL ESTATE	OTHER INVEST-MENTS	INVEST. IN AFFIL	INSURANCE COMPANY NAME
					% OF INVESTED ASSETS IN:							
1,712.7	38,936.8 (*)	0.0	13.2	61.1	4.3	4.4	10.1	0.0	0.0	5.7	4.4 ●	GENWORTH LIFE INS CO
185.6	7,239.9	0.0	22.6	59.8	2.7	0.7	8.9	0.0	0.0	4.8	0.0 ●	GENWORTH LIFE INS CO OF NEW YORK
565.9	3,426.1	0.1	22.7	67.6	4.1	0.3	0.0	0.0	0.0	4.7	0.0 ●	GERBER LIFE INS CO
5.2	84.7	0.0	20.7	68.2	5.4	2.4	0.0	0.0	0.0	3.2	0.0	GERMANIA LIFE INS CO
--	--	--	--	--	--	--	--	--	--	--	--	GERTRUDE GEDDES WILLIS LIFE INS CO
555.8	4,139.1	0.7	1.6	85.4	5.1	2.4	0.2	0.0	0.0	4.5	5.0 ●	GLOBE LIFE & ACCIDENT INS CO
53.2	218.5 (*)	1.6	4.8	78.8	5.6	0.0	0.0	0.0	0.0	4.6	0.0 ●	GLOBE LIFE INSURANCE CO OF NY
--	--	--	--	--	--	--	--	--	--	--	--	GMHP HEALTH INS LMTD
935.2	421.3	0.7	18.7	76.2	0.0	0.0	0.0	0.0	0.6	3.2	0.0 ●	GOLDEN RULE INS CO
34.8	798.3 (*)	2.7	0.0	62.7	2.6	2.8	15.6	0.0	1.7	8.5	2.4 ●	GOVERNMENT PERSONNEL MUTUAL L I C
4.7	137.8 (*)	2.0	1.3	76.6	5.3	0.9	0.0	0.0	0.0	9.6	0.0	GPM HEALTH & LIFE INS CO
40.0	351.5	4.7	28.0	57.8	6.1	0.0	0.0	0.0	0.0	3.4	0.0 ●	GRANGE LIFE INS CO
3,780.9	31,571.7 (*)	0.1	27.9	56.7	2.0	3.3	3.1	0.0	0.3	3.1	1.0 ●	GREAT AMERICAN LIFE INS CO
2.3	24.9	14.7	0.0	15.7	0.0	38.1	20.3	0.0	10.7	0.0	10.0	GREAT CENTRAL LIFE INS CO
--	--	--	--	--	--	--	--	--	--	--	--	GREAT REPUBLIC LIFE INS CO
0.1	208.1	0.0	50.4	38.1	1.9	5.9	0.1	0.0	0.0	4.0	0.0 ●	GREAT SOUTHERN LIFE INS CO
1.9	68.8 (*)	1.0	22.0	70.1	0.0	0.0	0.0	0.0	1.8	1.6	0.0 ●	GREAT WEST LIFE ASR CO
-8.8	1,282.0	0.1	10.9	72.5	1.2	0.9	12.5	0.0	0.3	0.7	0.4 ●	GREAT WESTERN INS CO
--	--	--	--	--	--	--	--	--	--	--	--	GREAT WESTERN LIFE INS CO
10,500.9	28,848.9	0.0	17.8	50.4	1.0	0.4	13.4	0.0	0.1	15.9	1.0 ●	GREAT-WEST LIFE & ANNUITY INS CO
187.1	1,403.7 (*)	0.1	16.1	72.0	1.3	0.0	6.5	0.0	0.0	2.2	0.0 ●	GREAT-WEST LIFE & ANNUITY INS OF NY
26.8	53.7 (*)	2.4	18.0	66.3	0.5	0.0	0.0	0.0	0.0	0.0	0.0	GREATER GEORGIA LIFE INS CO
2.2	13.3	7.5	55.1	34.8	0.0	0.0	0.0	0.0	0.0	2.0	0.0	GREENFIELDS LIFE INS CO
--	--	--	--	--	--	--	--	--	--	--	--	GRIFFIN LEGGETT BURIAL INS CO
177.6	569.8 (*)	0.6	31.5	50.6	2.7	1.3	9.4	0.0	0.2	2.0	1.4 ●	GUARANTEE TRUST LIFE INS CO
159.8	654.4	0.4	37.5	53.4	2.4	2.5	0.4	0.0	1.9	0.6	0.0 ●	GUARANTY INCOME LIFE INS CO
1,233.9	3,632.4	-0.7	3.3	77.7	3.2	0.8	11.2	0.0	0.0	4.6	0.9 ●	GUARDIAN INS & ANNUITY CO INC
6,222.0	50,454.9	0.0	8.4	64.8	3.5	3.0	7.9	0.0	0.7	11.7	3.7 ●	GUARDIAN LIFE INS CO OF AMERICA
137.2	9,481.0 (*)	1.0	22.6	50.7	2.2	1.6	3.2	0.0	0.0	15.8	5.6 ●	GUGGENHEIM LIFE & ANNUITY CO
8.1	18.1 (*)	16.8	0.0	13.4	0.0	40.4	7.7	0.0	11.2	1.7	21.7	GULF GUARANTY LIFE INS CO
--	--	--	--	--	--	--	--	--	--	--	--	GULF STATES LIFE INS CO INC
0.0	0.1	21.1	0.0	78.9	0.0	0.0	0.0	0.0	0.0	0.0	0.0	HALLMARK LIFE INS CO
289.0	2,787.6	0.0	6.4	86.3	2.7	0.1	0.3	0.0	0.0	4.3	0.1 ●	HANNOVER LIFE REASSURANCE CO OF AMER
11.1	390.7 (*)	0.2	9.4	84.7	0.5	0.0	0.0	0.0	0.0	1.5	0.0 ●	HARLEYSVILLE LIFE INS CO
3,406.3	12,134.0 (*)	0.1	14.9	68.5	2.7	0.9	7.1	0.0	0.0	3.6	0.3 ●	HARTFORD LIFE & ACCIDENT INS CO
1.5	11.3	1.2	18.5	80.3	0.0	0.0	0.0	0.0	0.0	0.0	4.2	HAWKEYE LIFE INS GROUP INC
0.3	9.5	2.7	21.3	0.0	0.0	76.0	0.0	0.0	0.0	0.0	75.7	HAWTHORN LIFE INS CO
67.9	186.6 (*)	10.1	50.5	26.1	0.0	0.0	6.2	0.4	0.0	2.7	0.0	HAYMARKET INS CO
1,021.5	916.2	0.0	38.4	61.1	0.0	0.2	0.0	0.0	0.0	0.3	0.2 ●	HCC LIFE INS CO
591.7	560.9 (*)	29.8	13.0	37.2	0.1	0.0	0.0	0.0	0.0	0.3	0.0 ●	HEALTH NET LIFE INS CO
3.6	10.2 (*)	1.4	1.1	77.2	0.0	0.0	0.0	0.0	0.0	0.0	0.0	HEARTLAND NATIONAL LIFE INS CO
30.3	4,065.8 (*)	0.3	23.6	41.8	12.1	2.1	0.0	0.0	0.0	18.8	1.8 ●	HERITAGE LIFE INS CO
--	--	--	--	--	--	--	--	--	--	--	--	HIGGINBOTHAM BURIAL INS CO
325.4	614.3 (*)	-0.7	13.2	40.6	11.4	10.9	0.0	0.0	0.0	0.1	0.0 ●	HM LIFE INS CO
27.2	65.2 (*)	2.5	20.1	42.9	0.4	0.0	0.0	0.0	0.0	0.0	0.0 ●	HM LIFE INS CO OF NEW YORK
376.9	2,855.0	0.6	18.6	75.2	2.6	0.0	1.3	0.0	0.4	0.4	0.0 ●	HOMESTEADERS LIFE CO
407.7	6,981.5	0.0	30.7	59.5	1.7	1.6	0.2	0.0	0.0	5.7	0.1 ●	HORACE MANN LIFE INS CO
102.3	179.4	0.1	26.4	69.0	4.2	0.0	0.0	0.0	0.0	0.0	0.0 ●	HUMANA INS CO OF KENTUCKY
98.5	69.3	0.0	31.7	51.6	2.6	0.0	0.0	0.0	0.0	14.1	0.0 ●	HUMANA INS CO OF PUERTO RICO INC
19.5	142.1	2.0	0.3	52.4	0.0	38.6	1.1	0.0	0.0	5.1	47.4 ●	IA AMERICAN LIFE INS CO
--	--	--	--	--	--	--	--	--	--	--	--	IBC LIFE INS CO
0.8	18.9 (*)	4.9	0.0	64.0	0.0	0.0	0.0	0.0	0.0	11.5	0.0	IDEALIFE INS CO

● Bullets denote a more detailed analysis is available in Section II.
(*) Asset category percentages do not add up to 100%

INSURANCE COMPANY NAME	DOM. STATE	RATING	TOTAL ASSETS ($MIL)	CAPITAL & SURPLUS ($MIL)	RISK ADJUSTED CAPITAL RATIO 1	RISK ADJUSTED CAPITAL RATIO 2	CAPITAL-IZATION INDEX (PTS)	INVEST. SAFETY INDEX (PTS)	PROFIT-ABILITY INDEX (PTS)	LIQUIDITY INDEX (PTS)	STAB. INDEX (PTS)	STABILIT FACTOR
ILLINOIS MUTUAL LIFE INS CO	IL	B	1447.8	240.3	3.82	2.14	8.7	6.5	5.9	6.5	6.2	
INDEPENDENCE INS INC	DE	U (5)	--	--	--	--	--	--	--	--	--	Z
INDEPENDENCE LIFE & ANNUITY CO	DE	D	3172.7	164.5	4.55	3.51	4.0	7.9	6.5	6.9	2.1	A
INDIVIDUAL ASR CO LIFE HEALTH & ACC	OK	D	26.6	12.4	2.10	1.40	7.6	4.2	2.4	7.1	1.6	GIT
INDUSTRIAL ALLIANCE INS & FIN SERV	TX	C	272.5	65.7	5.69	3.33	10.0	5.8	2.9	5.7	4.0	DI
INTEGRITY LIFE INS CO	OH	B-	9713.5	1147.9	1.82	1.19	7.3	5.0	2.9	7.5	5.0	I
INTERNATIONAL AMERICAN LIFE INS CO	TX	U (3)	--	--	--	--	--	--	--	--	--	Z
INTRAMERICA LIFE INS CO	NY	B	34.8	10.3	2.05	1.85	8.3	8.8	7.6	10.0	5.3	AT
INVESTORS HERITAGE LIFE INS CO	KY	C+	466.9	39.3	1.56	1.01	7.0	4.9	4.2	3.2	4.6	CDILR
INVESTORS LIFE INS CO NORTH AMERICA	TX	B	597.6	58.8	2.99	1.62	4.0	5.2	7.4	5.9	6.1	AFI
INVESTORS PREFERRED LIFE INS CO	SD	E	478.0	2.1	0.13	0.12	0.0	9.8	2.8	10.0	0.0	CDFG
▲ JACKSON GRIFFIN INS CO	AR	D-	12.8	1.2	0.51	0.46	2.5	2.2	2.1	5.6	1.3	CFI
JACKSON NATIONAL LIFE INS CO	MI	B	237904.4	4262.1	1.64	0.91	6.3	5.7	6.1	7.7	6.0	CI
JACKSON NATIONAL LIFE INS CO OF NY	NY	B	13730.6	580.6	4.73	2.97	10.0	5.4	8.4	7.0	6.0	AFI
JAMESTOWN LIFE INS CO	VA	B-	127.3	57.7	6.26	5.64	10.0	7.3	7.0	8.2	5.1	ADT
JEFF DAVIS MORTUARY BENEFIT ASSOC	LA	D	7.9	1.6	0.86	0.77	5.2	6.3	2.6	6.7	2.1	DT
JEFFERSON LIFE INS CO	TX	D	2.2	1.5	1.96	1.77	8.2	9.8	2.1	9.4	1.7	DFT
JEFFERSON NATIONAL LIFE INS CO	TX	C	6534.9	42.4	0.96	0.57	4.7	6.1	4.6	7.0	4.2	CFGI
JEFFERSON NATIONAL LIFE INS CO OF NY	NY	B-	110.2	6.6	0.77	0.70	4.6	8.5	2.7	7.0	4.4	ACDE
JOHN ALDEN LIFE INS CO	WI	B-	208.0	17.7	4.38	3.78	4.0	7.7	2.4	6.4	3.5	AFT
JOHN HANCOCK LIFE & HEALTH INS CO	MA	B	13974.9	929.6	3.54	1.91	8.4	5.2	8.9	9.1	4.0	GIT
JOHN HANCOCK LIFE INS CO (USA)	MI	B	240600.9	9115.0	1.76	1.08	7.1	4.4	6.1	7.2	6.1	CIT
JOHN HANCOCK LIFE INS CO OF NY	NY	B	17266.2	1474.5	4.03	2.07	8.6	5.9	3.0	6.6	4.3	IT
JORDAN FUNERAL & INS CO INC	AL	F (5)	--	--	--	--	--	--	--	--	--	Z
JRD LIFE INS CO	AZ	U	--	--	--	--	--	--	--	--	--	Z
K-TENN INSURANCE CO	TN	D-	2.2	2.1	3.29	2.96	9.9	9.3	1.9	9.1	1.2	DEFG
KANSAS CITY LIFE INS CO	MO	B	3401.6	289.8	1.80	1.04	7.1	4.5	5.6	5.7	5.9	I
KENTUCKY FUNERAL DIRECTORS LIFE INS	KY	B-	22.8	5.9	1.62	1.46	7.7	7.6	8.3	6.1	4.8	AD
KENTUCKY HOME LIFE INS CO	KY	C-	5.2	3.4	2.96	2.67	9.5	7.5	3.1	6.9	3.0	AF
KILPATRICK LIFE INS CO	LA	E+	193.2	7.5	0.66	0.38	2.3	0.4	3.0	1.1	0.5	CDIL
LAFAYETTE LIFE INS CO	OH	B	5572.4	318.2	1.75	0.87	6.1	4.6	6.1	5.4	5.6	ACIL
LANDCAR LIFE INS CO	UT	U (3)	--	--	--	--	--	--	--	--	--	Z
LANDMARK LIFE INS CO	TX	C	46.2	5.0	0.85	0.77	5.2	4.0	5.7	2.4	4.1	CFIL
LANGHORNE REINSURANCE AZ LTD	AZ	C	8.6	7.3	2.75	2.48	9.2	5.7	6.3	9.2	2.7	T
LASSO HEALTHCARE INSURANCE CO	TX	U (3)	--	--	--	--	--	--	--	--	--	Z
LEADERS LIFE INS CO	OK	B	6.2	2.7	1.57	1.42	7.6	3.7	2.0	4.2	5.7	AFIL
LEGACY LIFE INS CO OF MO	MO	U (3)	--	--	--	--	--	--	--	--	--	Z
LEWER LIFE INS CO	MO	C	32.9	12.7	2.78	1.79	8.2	5.5	5.9	6.8	3.4	D
LIBERTY BANKERS LIFE INS CO	OK	D+	1974.6	203.8	1.08	0.73	5.1	3.7	6.6	6.3	2.8	I
LIBERTY LIFE ASR CO OF BOSTON	NH	B-	4034.0	526.3	1.80	1.07	7.1	3.1	5.2	6.1	4.7	IT
LIBERTY NATIONAL LIFE INS CO	NE	B	7484.1	477.6	1.75	0.92	6.4	4.2	6.0	4.4	5.7	ACIL
LIFE ASR CO OF AMERICA	IL	U (3)	--	--	--	--	--	--	--	--	--	Z
LIFE ASSURANCE CO INC	OK	C-	4.1	2.2	1.59	1.43	7.6	9.7	2.8	9.8	3.0	DT
LIFE INS CO OF ALABAMA	AL	B	124.2	42.3	3.50	2.32	9.0	4.2	6.7	6.4	5.7	I
LIFE INS CO OF BOSTON & NEW YORK	NY	A-	157.5	32.2	3.56	2.26	8.9	6.8	6.1	6.6	7.0	AI
LIFE INS CO OF LOUISIANA	LA	D (3)	10.4	4.5	2.10	1.51	7.8	3.3	2.5	7.0	2.1	DI
LIFE INS CO OF NORTH AMERICA	PA	B	8743.9	1846.5	2.66	1.71	8.1	5.4	8.0	6.7	5.8	AI
LIFE INS CO OF THE SOUTHWEST	TX	B	19754.5	1346.7	2.50	1.21	7.3	5.1	8.3	4.4	5.5	AGILT
LIFE OF AMERICA INS CO	TX	C	12.0	2.4	0.77	0.59	3.7	6.6	2.3	0.9	2.9	CDFL
LIFE OF THE SOUTH INS CO	GA	C	106.6	20.8	0.73	0.56	3.5	3.4	5.9	7.5	3.5	CI
LIFECARE ASSURANCE CO	AZ	C	2516.7	60.6	1.13	0.58	5.2	1.8	1.8	8.9	3.2	I
LIFEMAP ASR CO	OR	B-	100.7	49.5	1.99	1.45	7.7	5.0	3.4	6.8	5.0	I

See Page 27 for explanation of footnotes and Page 28 for explanation of stability factors.
Arrows denote recent upgrades ▲ or downgrades▼ (see Section VI for explanations)

42

www.weissratings.com

NET PREMIUM ($MIL)	INVESTED ASSETS ($MIL)	CASH	CMO & STRUCT. SECS.	OTH.INV. GRADE BONDS	NON-INV. GRADE BONDS	CMMON & PREF. STOCK	MORT IN GOOD STAND.	NON-PERF. MORT.	REAL ESTATE	OTHER INVEST-MENTS	INVEST. IN AFFIL	INSURANCE COMPANY NAME
77.2	1,318.5	0.5	24.2	61.5	3.2	4.3	3.3	0.0	0.2	2.3	0.2 ●	ILLINOIS MUTUAL LIFE INS CO
--	--	--	--	--	--	--	--	--	--	--	--	INDEPENDENCE INS INC
-0.3	185.3 (*)	0.3	40.4	48.0	0.5	0.0	0.0	0.0	0.0	6.8	0.0 ●	INDEPENDENCE LIFE & ANNUITY CO
6.2	15.3 (*)	14.6	0.0	20.3	0.0	1.4	28.4	0.0	19.1	13.9	0.0	INDIVIDUAL ASR CO LIFE HEALTH & ACC
54.6	214.8	0.8	0.3	90.9	0.0	0.0	-0.4	2.4	3.8	1.7	0.0 ●	INDUSTRIAL ALLIANCE INS & FIN SERV
481.5	6,653.4 (*)	0.2	28.7	43.1	5.7	8.8	6.9	0.0	0.0	4.8	6.2 ●	INTEGRITY LIFE INS CO
--	--	--	--	--	--	--	--	--	--	--	--	INTERNATIONAL AMERICAN LIFE INS CO
0.0	14.1	2.7	0.0	97.3	0.0	0.0	0.0	0.0	0.0	0.0	0.0	INTRAMERICA LIFE INS CO
33.2	426.4	0.6	14.9	68.2	2.2	2.7	9.4	0.0	0.1	1.5	2.5 ●	INVESTORS HERITAGE LIFE INS CO
0.0	394.5	0.0	34.9	48.1	4.1	7.3	0.0	0.0	0.0	5.5	1.3 ●	INVESTORS LIFE INS CO NORTH AMERICA
7.3	1.0	100.0	0.0	0.0	0.0	0.0	0.0	0.0	0.0	0.0	0.0	INVESTORS PREFERRED LIFE INS CO
0.8	12.4	6.0	0.0	70.3	5.4	18.3	0.0	0.0	0.0	0.0	0.0	JACKSON GRIFFIN INS CO
13,799.6	61,904.0 (*)	0.0	11.7	56.9	2.3	1.1	13.6	0.0	0.4	10.4	1.6 ●	JACKSON NATIONAL LIFE INS CO
105.7	1,225.1	0.0	25.0	62.3	3.5	0.0	0.0	0.0	0.0	8.7	0.0 ●	JACKSON NATIONAL LIFE INS CO OF NY
0.8	127.5 (*)	10.5	25.7	45.6	1.3	0.0	0.0	0.0	0.0	2.4	0.0 ●	JAMESTOWN LIFE INS CO
1.8	6.7	9.2	0.0	88.4	0.0	2.1	0.0	0.0	0.0	0.0	0.0	JEFF DAVIS MORTUARY BENEFIT ASSOC
0.3	2.2 (*)	69.6	0.0	16.1	0.0	0.0	0.0	0.0	0.0	0.3	0.0	JEFFERSON LIFE INS CO
900.0	494.3 (*)	2.2	32.6	52.7	2.8	3.8	2.9	0.0	0.0	1.8	1.4 ●	JEFFERSON NATIONAL LIFE INS CO
22.4	6.9 (*)	1.2	4.0	88.5	0.0	0.0	0.0	0.0	0.0	0.0	0.0	JEFFERSON NATIONAL LIFE INS CO OF NY
0.1	200.3 (*)	1.0	12.5	72.6	1.2	1.7	0.0	0.0	0.0	8.0	0.0	JOHN ALDEN LIFE INS CO
515.4	4,879.1 (*)	0.1	4.8	56.9	0.9	2.7	6.7	0.0	3.4	16.4	1.0 ●	JOHN HANCOCK LIFE & HEALTH INS CO
7,405.7	95,296.0 (*)	-0.3	6.7	46.0	2.3	4.1	12.5	0.0	6.0	12.6	5.4 ●	JOHN HANCOCK LIFE INS CO (USA)
810.7	7,961.7 (*)	0.1	5.4	56.6	1.9	2.1	9.6	0.0	2.9	12.7	0.0 ●	JOHN HANCOCK LIFE INS CO OF NY
--	--	--	--	--	--	--	--	--	--	--	--	JORDAN FUNERAL & INS CO INC
--	--	--	--	--	--	--	--	--	--	--	--	JRD LIFE INS CO
0.2	1.7	42.1	0.0	57.9	0.0	0.0	0.0	0.0	0.0	0.0	0.0	K-TENN INSURANCE CO
214.0	2,907.5	0.1	3.7	63.2	1.6	2.8	19.0	0.2	5.4	3.4	1.7 ●	KANSAS CITY LIFE INS CO
2.2	21.4	1.0	0.0	94.3	3.6	0.7	0.0	0.0	0.0	0.0	0.0	KENTUCKY FUNERAL DIRECTORS LIFE INS
1.1	5.2	3.1	3.5	83.4	0.0	10.0	0.0	0.0	0.0	0.0	0.0	KENTUCKY HOME LIFE INS CO
11.0	186.0	0.4	21.8	54.3	4.1	1.9	5.4	0.0	3.4	8.4	6.8	KILPATRICK LIFE INS CO
421.7	5,306.4 (*)	0.3	16.8	49.4	5.1	2.2	8.6	0.0	0.0	15.0	1.2 ●	LAFAYETTE LIFE INS CO
--	--	--	--	--	--	--	--	--	--	--	--	LANDCAR LIFE INS CO
6.0	42.7	2.8	16.8	63.6	1.3	0.1	5.8	0.0	6.5	3.1	0.0	LANDMARK LIFE INS CO
0.0	12.1 (*)	1.0	0.1	81.1	0.0	15.3	0.0	0.0	0.0	1.1	0.0	LANGHORNE REINSURANCE AZ LTD
--	--	--	--	--	--	--	--	--	--	--	--	LASSO HEALTHCARE INSURANCE CO
3.2	4.0	8.7	0.0	57.5	22.6	8.6	0.0	0.0	0.0	2.0	0.0	LEADERS LIFE INS CO
--	--	--	--	--	--	--	--	--	--	--	--	LEGACY LIFE INS CO OF MO
7.3	30.7 (*)	0.4	12.2	66.3	0.1	15.4	0.0	0.0	0.0	1.0	0.0	LEWER LIFE INS CO
207.2	1,656.5	3.0	4.4	52.4	2.2	9.7	21.4	0.3	4.2	2.4	7.2 ●	LIBERTY BANKERS LIFE INS CO
-14,185.6	18,564.9 (*)	0.0	8.0	77.0	2.8	0.1	6.0	0.0	0.0	3.7	0.1 ●	LIBERTY LIFE ASR CO OF BOSTON
661.7	7,069.4	0.1	1.3	76.3	6.3	4.0	0.4	0.0	0.0	11.3	7.7 ●	LIBERTY NATIONAL LIFE INS CO
--	--	--	--	--	--	--	--	--	--	--	--	LIFE ASR CO OF AMERICA
0.7	4.1	75.7	2.6	21.8	0.0	0.0	0.0	0.0	0.0	0.0	0.0	LIFE ASSURANCE CO INC
27.9	116.1 (*)	0.5	0.0	78.8	9.0	5.6	0.0	0.0	0.6	3.6	0.0 ●	LIFE INS CO OF ALABAMA
16.5	140.8	2.2	8.5	63.4	1.7	2.6	0.0	0.0	0.0	20.8	0.0 ●	LIFE INS CO OF BOSTON & NEW YORK
0.2	9.4 (*)	4.7	0.0	30.6	0.0	37.3	6.9	0.0	0.0	18.0	24.2	LIFE INS CO OF LOUISIANA
2,798.4	7,674.4	0.0	2.0	72.7	8.3	0.4	11.1	0.0	0.0	6.3	7.0 ●	LIFE INS CO OF NORTH AMERICA
1,558.4	18,340.1 (*)	0.0	16.8	52.4	3.8	0.5	15.5	0.0	0.0	6.0	0.0 ●	LIFE INS CO OF THE SOUTHWEST
7.2	3.0 (*)	32.8	0.0	49.8	6.8	1.1	0.0	0.0	0.0	0.2	0.0	LIFE OF AMERICA INS CO
46.9	88.6 (*)	2.3	16.1	34.3	0.0	16.9	0.0	0.0	11.6	17.6	11.6	LIFE OF THE SOUTH INS CO
127.9	2,370.3	0.1	31.5	62.8	2.9	0.0	0.0	0.0	0.0	2.4	0.0 ●	LIFECARE ASSURANCE CO
59.9	88.4 (*)	5.5	38.7	31.3	0.3	22.1	0.0	0.0	0.0	0.0	2.0 ●	LIFEMAP ASR CO

● Bullets denote a more detailed analysis is available in Section II.
(*) Asset category percentages do not add up to 100%

INSURANCE COMPANY NAME	DOM. STATE	RATING	TOTAL ASSETS ($MIL)	CAPITAL & SURPLUS ($MIL)	RISK ADJUSTED CAPITAL RATIO 1	RISK ADJUSTED CAPITAL RATIO 2	CAPITAL- IZATION INDEX (PTS)	INVEST. SAFETY INDEX (PTS)	PROFIT- ABILITY INDEX (PTS)	LIQUIDITY INDEX (PTS)	STAB. INDEX (PTS)	STABILITY FACTORS
LIFESECURE INS CO	MI	D	404.4	47.7	2.55	1.66	8.0	7.3	1.9	9.0	1.9	DI
LIFESHIELD NATIONAL INS CO	OK	B-	86.1	28.8	1.97	1.35	7.5	3.9	7.9	6.7	5.0	GI
LIFEWISE ASR CO	WA	A	193.1	148.0	7.52	5.54	10.0	8.0	9.3	7.1	7.1	AD
LILY LIFE INS CO	TX	E+	2.0	0.3	0.39	0.35	1.2	4.8	1.0	5.6	0.4	CDT
LINCOLN BENEFIT LIFE CO	NE	C+	10952.9	446.1	1.39	0.70	5.6	3.9	6.0	5.4	4.8	CFI
LINCOLN HERITAGE LIFE INS CO	IL	B-	1018.0	97.2	2.42	1.31	7.5	6.5	2.7	6.1	5.1	D
LINCOLN LIFE & ANNUITY CO OF NY	NY	B	15062.1	1191.5	4.46	2.26	8.9	5.9	6.5	6.5	4.1	AIT
LINCOLN NATIONAL LIFE INS CO	IN	B	249329.3	7941.7	1.31	0.91	6.3	6.2	7.6	6.1	5.8	ACGI
LOCOMOTIVE ENGRS&COND MUT PROT ASSN	MI	B+	73.6	62.7	8.21	4.83	10.0	5.2	7.4	7.0	6.0	DI
LOMBARD INTL LIFE ASR CO	PA	E	7065.7	24.1	0.34	0.19	0.0	8.1	1.9	7.0	0.0	CFG
LOMBARD INTL LIFE ASR CO OF NY	NY	U (3)	--	--	--	--	--	--	--	--	--	Z
LONDON LIFE INS CO	MI	B-	21.1	14.0	2.43	1.59	7.9	8.3	3.0	9.2	4.8	FT
LONDON LIFE REINSURANCE CO	PA	C+	200.0	60.4	6.42	4.27	10.0	7.7	5.6	7.2	4.0	T
LONE STAR LIFE INS CO	TX	F (5)	--	--	--	--	--	--	--	--	--	Z
LONGEVITY INS CO	TX	B	7.8	7.7	3.79	3.41	8.0	9.6	2.7	10.0	5.6	AF
LOYAL AMERICAN LIFE INS CO	OH	B-	334.0	117.7	1.10	0.94	6.5	6.1	6.2	6.6	4.9	D
LUMICO LIFE INSURANCE CO	MO	C	58.4	44.5	6.50	5.85	10.0	7.9	2.5	8.2	4.0	DT
M LIFE INS CO	CO	B+	307.3	129.0	7.89	5.22	10.0	7.8	7.2	6.7	5.3	D
MADISON NATIONAL LIFE INS CO INC	WI	B	339.1	202.0	1.62	1.51	7.8	5.9	8.1	7.0	6.3	IT
MAGNOLIA GUARANTY LIFE INS CO	MS	C	10.7	1.9	0.81	0.73	4.8	6.3	1.1	8.4	3.3	ACD
MAJESTIC LIFE INS CO	LA	D (3)	12.8	3.3	1.00	0.60	3.0	1.5	1.9	7.0	1.6	DFIT
MANHATTAN LIFE INS CO	NY	B	623.8	58.0	1.37	0.98	6.8	6.1	5.1	5.5	5.4	AIT
MANHATTAN NATIONAL LIFE INS CO	OH	B-	152.0	9.9	1.20	1.08	7.1	3.6	2.0	6.4	3.9	DFGIT
MANHATTANLIFE ASSR CO OF AM	AR	C	675.1	107.8	0.59	0.52	3.2	5.2	5.3	5.8	3.2	CG
MAPFRE LIFE INS CO	DE	C	40.7	39.9	10.53	9.48	10.0	9.2	3.1	9.6	4.1	FGT
MAPFRE LIFE INS CO OF PR	PR	C- (4)	58.5	23.0	1.19	0.96	5.3	8.7	1.8	4.1	3.0	CLT
MARQUETTE INDEMNITY & LIFE INS CO	AZ	D+	5.6	1.9	1.17	1.05	7.1	3.7	2.1	7.6	2.5	FIT
MASSACHUSETTS MUTUAL LIFE INS CO	MA	A-	245872.2	14722.1	1.30	0.97	6.8	6.1	6.3	6.7	6.6	CI
MCS LIFE INS CO	PR	D-	92.7	45.0	0.96	0.79	4.8	9.4	5.3	4.6	1.0	ACDG
MEDAMERICA INS CO	PA	C	973.5	23.6	0.76	0.42	3.1	0.6	1.7	8.2	3.3	CI
▲ MEDAMERICA INS CO OF FL	FL	B	44.5	5.5	0.97	0.87	6.0	5.0	3.1	9.8	4.2	ACDI
MEDAMERICA INS CO OF NEW YORK	NY	C	808.5	11.7	0.79	0.47	3.3	3.2	1.0	8.1	3.3	CI
MEDICAL BENEFITS MUTUAL LIFE INS CO	OH	D	14.9	10.7	2.50	1.81	8.2	3.3	1.9	7.5	1.7	DFIT
MEDICO CORP LIFE INS CO	NE	B-	70.6	26.1	3.53	3.17	8.0	8.3	7.0	7.0	4.8	A
MEDICO INS CO	NE	B-	84.6	40.3	4.95	4.46	10.0	7.7	6.3	6.8	4.8	A
MEDICO LIFE & HEALTH INS CO	IA	C	15.6	14.0	4.82	4.33	8.0	8.0	5.2	10.0	4.1	AT
MELANCON LIFE INS CO	LA	D	10.8	1.3	0.71	0.46	2.7	1.8	2.0	7.0	1.9	DIT
MELLON LIFE INS CO	DE	U (3)	--	--	--	--	--	--	--	--	--	Z
MEMBERS LIFE INS CO	IA	C	151.4	17.7	1.92	1.73	8.0	9.3	3.6	7.0	3.4	G
MEMORIAL INS CO OF AMERICA	AR	D	1.1	1.1	2.23	2.01	8.5	7.7	3.8	10.0	2.3	AF
MEMORIAL LIFE INS CO	LA	C (3)	3.6	1.4	1.32	1.03	7.0	2.6	3.6	9.2	3.1	DIT
MERIT LIFE INS CO	IN	B	386.6	111.9	8.66	4.45	10.0	6.7	5.1	7.9	4.1	FT
METLIFE INSURANCE LTD	GU	U (5)	--	--	--	--	--	--	--	--	--	Z
METROPOLITAN LIFE INS CO	NY	B-	389582.7	10506.8	1.08	0.71	5.1	4.1	6.3	7.0	3.8	CGIT
METROPOLITAN TOWER LIFE INS CO	NE	B- (2)	5013.0	733.8	3.30	1.47	7.7	3.3	6.1	6.3	4.6	GIT
▲ MID-WEST NATIONAL LIFE INS CO OF TN	TX	C+	62.6	28.2	3.89	3.50	10.0	8.0	5.8	8.0	3.4	FT
MIDLAND NATIONAL LIFE INS CO	IA	B+	58240.4	3510.9	2.00	1.01	7.0	4.6	9.1	5.9	6.5	IL
MIDWESTERN UNITED LIFE INS CO	IN	B	234.5	127.3	12.87	11.31	10.0	7.8	4.0	6.9	5.8	DF
MILILANI LIFE INS CO	HI	U (3)	--	--	--	--	--	--	--	--	--	Z
MINNESOTA LIFE INS CO	MN	B+	49271.3	3054.8	2.25	1.40	7.6	5.6	6.7	6.6	6.5	I
MML BAY STATE LIFE INS CO	CT	B	5026.5	310.8	6.17	4.37	10.0	7.3	8.1	7.1	4.6	FGT
▲ MOLINA HEALTHCARE OF TEXAS INS CO	TX	C+	9.0	8.8	3.95	3.02	8.0	9.8	9.4	10.0	3.3	AT

See Page 27 for explanation of footnotes and Page 28 for explanation of stability factors.

Arrows denote recent upgrades ▲ or downgrades▼ (see Section VI for explanations)

44   www.weissratings.com

NET PREMIUM ($MIL)	IN-VESTED ASSETS ($MIL)	% OF INVESTED ASSETS IN:									INVEST. IN AFFIL	INSURANCE COMPANY NAME
		CASH	CMO & STRUCT. SECS.	OTH.INV. GRADE BONDS	NON-INV. GRADE BONDS	CMMON & PREF. STOCK	MORT IN GOOD STAND.	NON-PERF. MORT.	REAL ESTATE	OTHER INVEST-MENTS		
59.0	358.9 (*)	0.3	20.1	78.2	0.0	0.0	0.0	0.0	0.0	0.0	0.0 ●	LIFESECURE INS CO
42.9	68.9 (*)	4.2	52.7	-8.3	11.9	19.8	0.0	0.0	0.0	1.8	1.6 ●	LIFESHIELD NATIONAL INS CO
109.7	158.9 (*)	3.8	46.3	44.5	1.8	0.0	0.0	0.0	0.0	0.5	0.0 ●	LIFEWISE ASR CO
0.1	1.1 (*)	14.9	0.0	38.8	2.8	18.6	0.0	0.0	0.0	0.0	0.0	LILY LIFE INS CO
65.2	9,601.2	0.0	11.8	70.1	2.7	0.3	11.0	0.0	0.0	4.0	1.6 ●	LINCOLN BENEFIT LIFE CO
265.9	837.8	5.7	35.2	43.6	0.0	1.4	5.4	0.0	1.4	6.7	0.0 ●	LINCOLN HERITAGE LIFE INS CO
807.4	8,232.6	0.2	6.0	77.8	3.4	0.0	9.3	0.0	0.0	3.3	0.0 ●	LINCOLN LIFE & ANNUITY CO OF NY
21,334.5	95,685.1 (*)	-0.1	5.6	71.2	3.0	4.0	10.1	0.0	0.1	4.9	4.3 ●	LINCOLN NATIONAL LIFE INS CO
14.7	71.9 (*)	0.7	0.3	54.0	0.5	27.4	0.0	0.0	0.0	0.0	0.0 ●	LOCOMOTIVE ENGRS&COND MUT PROT ASSN
510.6	112.7 (*)	9.9	0.0	10.8	0.0	4.1	0.0	0.0	0.0	69.6	4.1 ●	LOMBARD INTL LIFE ASR CO
--	--	--	--	--	--	--	--	--	--	--	--	LOMBARD INTL LIFE ASR CO OF NY
0.8	19.7 (*)	0.8	4.5	92.8	0.0	0.0	0.0	0.0	0.0	0.0	0.0	LONDON LIFE INS CO
0.3	148.0 (*)	1.7	9.9	80.7	3.3	1.7	0.0	0.0	0.0	0.1	0.0 ●	LONDON LIFE REINSURANCE CO
--	--	--	--	--	--	--	--	--	--	--	--	LONE STAR LIFE INS CO
0.0	7.6 (*)	8.1	0.0	65.2	0.0	0.0	0.0	0.0	0.0	0.0	0.0	LONGEVITY INS CO
256.6	285.1	-2.7	0.7	80.0	1.1	20.9	0.0	0.0	0.0	0.0	20.9 ●	LOYAL AMERICAN LIFE INS CO
3.4	52.6	2.3	15.1	82.2	0.0	0.0	0.0	0.0	0.0	0.2	0.0 ●	LUMICO LIFE INSURANCE CO
304.6	149.2	2.4	21.6	71.6	0.2	0.0	0.0	0.0	0.0	3.3	0.0 ●	M LIFE INS CO
69.8	309.1	1.0	0.8	56.4	0.0	40.8	0.0	0.0	0.0	0.1	39.5 ●	MADISON NATIONAL LIFE INS CO INC
1.3	9.6	12.8	4.0	69.6	4.5	9.1	0.0	0.0	0.0	0.0	0.0	MAGNOLIA GUARANTY LIFE INS CO
0.7	12.6 (*)	0.5	0.0	17.5	0.0	68.5	0.3	0.0	0.2	10.1	0.0	MAJESTIC LIFE INS CO
63.0	570.6 (*)	0.7	11.3	65.7	2.4	6.1	8.2	0.0	0.0	3.2	5.5 ●	MANHATTAN LIFE INS CO
4.1	145.7	0.0	3.7	76.4	3.3	0.1	0.0	0.0	0.0	16.5	0.0	MANHATTAN NATIONAL LIFE INS CO
192.0	354.3 (*)	0.0	0.8	34.0	0.6	37.6	13.4	0.0	6.3	1.2	37.5 ●	MANHATTANLIFE ASSR CO OF AM
0.1	22.3	26.2	0.0	73.8	0.0	0.0	0.0	0.0	0.0	0.0	0.0 ●	MAPFRE LIFE INS CO
72.2	53.1	26.7	0.3	71.4	0.3	1.1	0.0	0.0	0.0	0.2	0.0 ●	MAPFRE LIFE INS CO OF PR
0.5	5.8 (*)	0.8	10.9	62.5	15.6	1.4	0.0	0.0	0.0	1.5	0.0	MARQUETTE INDEMNITY & LIFE INS CO
16,713.5	163,921.0 (*)	0.1	8.6	43.1	5.4	10.0	13.8	0.0	0.5	12.9	15.6 ●	MASSACHUSETTS MUTUAL LIFE INS CO
217.1	76.0	56.5	0.3	42.7	0.0	0.5	0.0	0.0	0.0	0.0	0.0 ●	MCS LIFE INS CO
41.3	933.4	0.0	3.5	82.0	5.5	1.3	0.0	0.0	0.0	6.8	0.5 ●	MEDAMERICA INS CO
2.8	41.0	9.1	0.4	88.6	0.1	0.0	0.0	0.0	0.0	0.8	0.0	MEDAMERICA INS CO OF FL
32.8	761.6 (*)	1.4	3.0	92.3	0.1	0.7	0.0	0.0	0.0	1.0	0.0	MEDAMERICA INS CO OF NEW YORK
0.8	13.1 (*)	0.9	8.0	30.3	0.0	46.6	0.0	0.0	10.4	0.0	18.1	MEDICAL BENEFITS MUTUAL LIFE INS CO
0.0	25.8 (*)	4.9	28.2	61.1	0.0	0.0	0.0	0.0	0.0	3.9	0.0 ●	MEDICO CORP LIFE INS CO
0.4	46.0	5.1	32.2	61.5	0.0	0.3	0.0	0.0	0.0	0.4	0.0 ●	MEDICO INS CO
0.0	13.3 (*)	7.2	24.3	63.3	0.0	0.0	0.0	0.0	0.0	3.6	0.0	MEDICO LIFE & HEALTH INS CO
0.5	10.3	6.5	0.0	49.8	5.3	30.5	7.1	0.0	0.6	0.1	7.1	MELANCON LIFE INS CO
--	--	--	--	--	--	--	--	--	--	--	--	MELLON LIFE INS CO
0.0	29.1 (*)	6.3	5.5	31.1	0.0	0.0	0.0	0.0	0.0	0.0	0.0	MEMBERS LIFE INS CO
0.0	1.0 (*)	39.4	0.0	36.5	0.0	0.0	0.0	0.0	9.9	0.0	0.0	MEMORIAL INS CO OF AMERICA
0.3	3.5	20.9	0.0	11.5	0.0	33.0	27.5	6.1	0.0	0.0	0.0	MEMORIAL LIFE INS CO
-18.1	441.9	0.8	22.2	71.9	1.8	1.0	0.9	0.0	0.0	1.1	0.0 ●	MERIT LIFE INS CO
--	--	--	--	--	--	--	--	--	--	--	--	METLIFE INSURANCE LTD
24,142.5	245,074.0 (*)	0.8	15.4	41.1	5.4	3.0	21.5	0.3	0.7	10.0	6.2 ●	METROPOLITAN LIFE INS CO
46.3	4,699.8	0.7	27.3	41.0	5.4	0.4	6.6	0.0	10.3	8.0	2.3 ●	METROPOLITAN TOWER LIFE INS CO
4.8	53.6 (*)	7.2	3.3	9.5	0.0	0.0	0.0	0.0	0.0	14.4	8.2 ●	MID-WEST NATIONAL LIFE INS CO OF TN
2,796.1	50,942.8	1.2	40.4	39.1	3.7	1.4	8.7	0.0	0.1	4.9	2.9 ●	MIDLAND NATIONAL LIFE INS CO
2.1	228.8	2.4	7.6	75.7	3.3	0.0	8.1	0.0	0.0	2.9	0.0 ●	MIDWESTERN UNITED LIFE INS CO
--	--	--	--	--	--	--	--	--	--	--	--	MILILANI LIFE INS CO
5,485.9	20,066.3 (*)	0.0	20.0	49.0	2.3	4.1	15.0	0.0	0.3	6.8	2.2 ●	MINNESOTA LIFE INS CO
2.0	465.3	0.0	34.8	43.8	1.2	0.0	0.7	0.0	0.0	20.3	1.5 ●	MML BAY STATE LIFE INS CO
0.0	8.4	64.1	0.0	35.9	0.0	0.0	0.0	0.0	0.0	0.0	0.0	MOLINA HEALTHCARE OF TEXAS INS CO

● Bullets denote a more detailed analysis is available in Section II.
(*) Asset category percentages do not add up to 100%

INSURANCE COMPANY NAME	DOM. STATE	RATING	TOTAL ASSETS ($MIL)	CAPITAL & SURPLUS ($MIL)	RISK ADJUSTED CAPITAL RATIO 1	RISK ADJUSTED CAPITAL RATIO 2	CAPITAL-IZATION INDEX (PTS)	INVEST. SAFETY INDEX (PTS)	PROFIT-ABILITY INDEX (PTS)	LIQUIDITY INDEX (PTS)	STAB. INDEX (PTS)	STABILITY FACTORS
MONARCH LIFE INS CO	MA	F (3)	669.5	4.3	0.41	0.22	0.0	0.0	2.0	2.5	0.0	CDFILT
MONITOR LIFE INS CO OF NEW YORK	NY	B	21.0	12.2	3.38	2.97	10.0	6.8	7.9	7.3	4.5	DFT
MONY LIFE INS CO	NY	B-	7114.0	420.8	2.30	1.22	7.3	6.2	3.8	4.4	5.0	AFL
MONY LIFE INS CO OF AMERICA	AZ	B	3981.0	266.5	2.03	1.36	7.5	5.7	1.9	5.3	5.8	IL
MOTORISTS LIFE INS CO	OH	B	491.5	70.9	3.57	1.98	8.5	6.7	6.1	5.6	4.4	ADT
MOUNTAIN LIFE INS CO	TN	C-	6.0	3.8	1.76	1.59	7.9	9.0	2.9	9.2	2.4	FGT
MULHEARN PROTECTIVE INS CO	LA	D	12.4	2.6	0.95	0.57	4.6	1.6	2.9	7.3	2.2	CDGI
MULTINATIONAL LIFE INS CO	PR	C-	118.1	19.6	2.00	1.11	7.2	4.9	3.0	6.7	2.9	CI
MUNICH AMERICAN REASSURANCE CO	GA	C	8459.3	659.8	2.33	1.51	7.8	7.4	2.0	5.9	4.1	F
MUNICH RE US LIFE CORP	GA	U (3)	--	--	--	--	--	--	--	--	--	Z
MUTUAL OF AMERICA LIFE INS CO	NY	A-	21758.9	956.0	2.92	1.39	7.6	5.4	5.8	7.6	6.9	I
MUTUAL OF OMAHA INS CO	NE	B	7924.2	3160.4	1.01	0.94	6.5	6.1	4.0	7.0	5.9	AI
MUTUAL SAVINGS LIFE INS CO	AL	B	480.7	54.7	2.99	1.82	8.2	7.2	6.4	5.6	5.6	AIT
MUTUAL TRUST LIFE INS CO	IL	B	2038.5	151.6	2.19	1.10	7.2	4.7	5.9	4.4	5.9	IL
▲ NASSAU LIFE & ANNUITY CO	CT	D	31.0	11.2	2.58	2.32	4.0	7.3	2.6	8.5	1.5	AFT
NASSAU LIFE INSURANCE CO	NY	D-	12246.6	532.6	1.72	0.87	6.1	5.0	5.5	4.5	1.1	CFILT
NATIONAL BENEFIT LIFE INS CO	NY	B+	564.7	150.4	6.46	3.47	10.0	6.6	6.8	6.9	6.6	ADI
NATIONAL FAMILY CARE LIFE INS CO	TX	C	16.0	9.3	3.00	2.70	9.6	9.6	3.8	8.6	3.5	DF
NATIONAL FARM LIFE INS CO	TX	B	417.6	46.2	3.08	1.86	8.3	7.2	5.7	4.0	5.5	DL
NATIONAL FARMERS UNION LIFE INS CO	TX	B+	193.3	47.6	4.46	2.29	8.9	5.4	6.9	6.3	6.5	ADFI
NATIONAL FOUNDATION LIFE INS CO	TX	B+	50.6	30.8	1.74	1.36	7.5	8.0	9.1	7.5	6.2	AG
NATIONAL GUARDIAN LIFE INS CO	WI	B-	4065.8	347.9	1.62	1.04	7.1	5.8	5.7	5.8	5.3	T
NATIONAL HEALTH INS CO	TX	C	54.5	16.0	1.90	0.80	6.4	9.7	5.7	8.2	3.5	AGT
NATIONAL INCOME LIFE INS CO	NY	B+	261.9	37.8	2.80	1.66	8.0	7.0	5.2	6.5	6.7	AD
NATIONAL INTEGRITY LIFE INS CO	NY	B-	4583.7	334.2	2.76	1.38	7.6	5.7	2.7	6.5	5.1	
NATIONAL LIFE INS CO	VT	B-	9786.2	2361.3	1.53	1.30	4.0	6.1	4.2	6.9	4.8	AT
NATIONAL PROSPERITY L&H INS CO	TX	U (3)	--	--	--	--	--	--	--	--	--	Z
NATIONAL SECURITY INS CO	AL	B	57.0	15.2	2.27	1.81	8.2	5.5	7.3	6.7	5.1	ADI
NATIONAL SECURITY LIFE & ANNUITY CO	NY	B	491.9	23.0	1.86	1.67	8.0	7.2	5.4	10.0	4.4	DT
NATIONAL TEACHERS ASSOCIATES L I C	TX	B	572.9	132.9	3.26	2.16	8.7	6.7	4.7	8.6	6.0	D
NATIONAL WESTERN LIFE INS CO	CO	A	11114.0	1441.0	4.25	2.24	8.9	6.4	7.8	6.0	7.4	I
NATIONWIDE LIFE & ANNUITY INS CO	OH	C	24689.8	1467.0	2.94	1.46	7.7	5.4	2.9	7.1	4.3	AG
NATIONWIDE LIFE INS CO	OH	B-	146933.0	6433.1	2.32	1.54	7.8	6.1	8.0	8.2	5.3	A
NETCARE LIFE & HEALTH INS CO	GU	E+ (4)	29.0	4.4	0.74	0.56	3.5	8.4	5.7	5.9	0.4	D
NEW ENGLAND LIFE INS CO	MA	B	9964.8	569.7	5.07	2.56	9.3	5.9	5.6	6.7	5.0	AIT
NEW ERA LIFE INS CO	TX	C	543.6	88.2	1.03	0.78	5.2	5.3	8.5	6.5	4.1	C
NEW ERA LIFE INS CO OF THE MIDWEST	TX	C+	138.4	13.5	1.36	0.86	5.9	3.7	9.0	6.5	4.8	ACDI
NEW YORK LIFE INS & ANNUITY CORP	DE	B+	156175.5	8695.0	3.57	1.75	8.1	6.0	7.9	6.5	6.8	I
NEW YORK LIFE INS CO	NY	A-	178706.9	20941.2	1.74	1.32	7.5	6.6	7.0	6.4	7.0	I
NIAGARA LIFE & HEALTH INS CO	NY	B	18.2	8.9	2.82	2.53	9.3	9.0	5.3	8.2	4.9	FGT
▲ NIPPON LIFE INS CO OF AMERICA	IA	A-	219.2	140.3	3.34	2.65	9.5	8.2	6.6	6.6	7.0	D
NORTH AMERICAN CO FOR LIFE & H INS	IA	B	27148.1	1423.0	1.81	0.84	6.2	4.0	8.0	5.9	5.8	CI
▲ NORTH AMERICAN INS CO	WI	B+	19.2	13.6	3.34	2.52	9.3	8.4	8.5	6.8	5.7	AD
NORTH AMERICAN NATIONAL RE INS CO	AZ	C	36.6	11.1	1.57	0.82	5.9	2.0	5.7	8.1	3.3	GIT
NORTH CAROLINA MUTUAL LIFE INS CO	NC	E-	26.7	-28.6	-2.05	-1.31	0.0	7.3	0.7	7.0	0.0	CDT
NORTHWESTERN LONG TERM CARE INS CO	WI	B	204.5	106.6	7.62	3.06	4.0	9.2	8.5	8.4	4.9	T
NORTHWESTERN MUTUAL LIFE INS CO	WI	B+	273304.0	22125.4	3.34	1.69	8.0	5.7	6.0	5.7	6.7	IL
NTA LIFE INS CO OF NEW YORK	NY	B	7.8	7.0	3.53	3.18	10.0	8.7	4.7	9.1	4.9	AD
NYLIFE INS CO OF ARIZONA	AZ	B	175.9	116.9	12.10	9.86	10.0	8.5	8.7	7.0	5.6	DFT
OCCIDENTAL LIFE INS CO OF NC	TX	C	258.8	25.1	2.52	1.50	7.8	7.2	2.9	4.8	4.2	ADL
OHIO NATIONAL LIFE ASR CORP	OH	B+	4098.9	288.3	2.08	1.09	7.1	5.6	6.2	5.4	5.9	AILT
OHIO NATIONAL LIFE INS CO	OH	B	32065.5	1058.1	1.32	0.86	5.9	5.7	6.4	7.2	5.8	ACI

See Page 27 for explanation of footnotes and Page 28 for explanation of stability factors.
Arrows denote recent upgrades ▲ or downgrades▼ (see Section VI for explanations)

46

www.weissratings.com

NET PREMIUM ($MIL)	IN-VESTED ASSETS ($MIL)	CASH	CMO & STRUCT. SECS.	OTH.INV. GRADE BONDS	NON-INV. GRADE BONDS	CMMON & PREF. STOCK	MORT IN GOOD STAND.	NON-PERF. MORT.	REAL ESTATE	OTHER INVEST-MENTS	INVEST. IN AFFIL		INSURANCE COMPANY NAME
						% OF INVESTED ASSETS IN:							
3.4	442.4	0.4	9.3	73.2	2.7	0.0	0.0	0.0	0.0	13.9	0.0		MONARCH LIFE INS CO
4.6	20.9 (*)	20.8	0.0	54.2	0.0	12.4	0.0	0.0	0.0	7.2	2.4		MONITOR LIFE INS CO OF NEW YORK
153.7	6,848.2	0.3	10.2	70.8	2.9	1.1	3.8	0.0	0.0	10.9	0.0	●	MONY LIFE INS CO
436.1	1,275.5 (*)	0.2	1.2	78.0	0.9	4.1	1.3	0.0	0.0	4.5	3.8	●	MONY LIFE INS CO OF AMERICA
35.7	444.3 (*)	1.2	18.0	65.3	3.4	3.6	0.0	0.0	0.0	3.6	0.0	●	MOTORISTS LIFE INS CO
1.1	7.5	34.1	0.0	66.0	0.0	0.0	0.0	0.0	0.0	0.0	0.0		MOUNTAIN LIFE INS CO
0.6	12.3	10.2	0.3	33.2	0.0	56.2	0.0	0.0	0.0	0.1	0.0		MULHEARN PROTECTIVE INS CO
24.0	105.1	5.7	19.9	58.9	3.4	0.1	1.2	0.0	8.9	1.8	0.0		MULTINATIONAL LIFE INS CO
878.6	6,843.6 (*)	0.3	2.5	94.8	0.1	0.5	0.0	0.0	0.0	0.1	0.5	●	MUNICH AMERICAN REASSURANCE CO
--	--	--	--	--	--	--	--	--	--	--	--		MUNICH RE US LIFE CORP
1,692.3	8,617.4	0.1	38.7	47.2	7.9	2.1	0.0	0.0	2.6	1.5	0.3	●	MUTUAL OF AMERICA LIFE INS CO
2,437.9	6,916.7	0.2	10.7	41.3	1.8	37.7	3.7	0.0	0.5	3.3	39.2	●	MUTUAL OF OMAHA INS CO
29.1	452.6	0.0	5.5	85.5	2.6	1.0	0.0	0.0	0.0	5.5	0.9	●	MUTUAL SAVINGS LIFE INS CO
126.1	1,953.1	0.2	19.9	57.2	3.6	0.7	2.6	0.0	0.4	15.3	0.0	●	MUTUAL TRUST LIFE INS CO
-0.2	22.9	20.8	20.2	53.3	2.2	0.0	0.0	0.0	0.0	3.5	0.0		NASSAU LIFE & ANNUITY CO
180.6	11,025.3	1.9	16.1	49.6	2.9	1.6	0.8	0.0	0.3	26.8	0.1	●	NASSAU LIFE INSURANCE CO
68.0	517.7 (*)	0.0	17.6	72.3	3.4	1.2	0.0	0.0	0.0	2.1	0.0	●	NATIONAL BENEFIT LIFE INS CO
4.8	15.9	15.7	0.0	84.3	0.0	0.0	0.0	0.0	0.0	0.0	0.0		NATIONAL FAMILY CARE LIFE INS CO
18.3	396.0	0.1	3.6	83.6	1.3	2.6	2.6	0.0	0.2	5.9	0.5	●	NATIONAL FARM LIFE INS CO
4.4	180.2	0.0	28.5	44.6	3.8	11.4	3.0	0.0	0.0	8.8	2.8	●	NATIONAL FARMERS UNION LIFE INS CO
58.0	36.4 (*)	28.6	18.8	42.8	3.0	0.0	0.0	0.0	0.0	0.0	0.0		NATIONAL FOUNDATION LIFE INS CO
514.2	3,746.4 (*)	0.2	5.7	77.9	2.4	3.9	2.7	0.1	0.2	3.7	2.3	●	NATIONAL GUARDIAN LIFE INS CO
10.1	29.9	83.4	0.0	16.6	0.0	0.0	0.0	0.0	0.0	0.0	0.0		NATIONAL HEALTH INS CO
64.4	205.6	5.4	1.0	84.3	2.1	0.0	0.0	0.0	0.0	7.2	0.0	●	NATIONAL INCOME LIFE INS CO
179.2	2,924.8	0.0	28.5	53.4	5.7	2.2	5.4	0.0	0.0	4.7	2.0	●	NATIONAL INTEGRITY LIFE INS CO
271.2	8,020.9	0.0	14.4	49.4	3.1	15.2	6.3	0.1	0.7	9.8	15.1	●	NATIONAL LIFE INS CO
--	--	--	--	--	--	--	--	--	--	--	--		NATIONAL PROSPERITY L&H INS CO
4.7	54.7	0.2	23.4	58.4	5.6	4.6	0.3	0.0	3.9	3.6	0.0		NATIONAL SECURITY INS CO
3.6	58.0	1.3	20.5	74.4	3.8	0.0	0.0	0.0	0.0	0.0	0.0		NATIONAL SECURITY LIFE & ANNUITY CO
97.7	527.5	2.4	31.7	52.0	4.5	3.9	4.2	0.4	0.0	0.1	1.3	●	NATIONAL TEACHERS ASSOCIATES L I C
539.2	11,021.1 (*)	0.0	11.9	78.7	1.2	2.8	1.7	0.0	0.0	2.0	2.8	●	NATIONAL WESTERN LIFE INS CO
4,725.7	18,728.3 (*)	0.0	5.0	61.4	4.0	0.0	18.2	0.0	0.0	6.6	0.8	●	NATIONWIDE LIFE & ANNUITY INS CO
6,548.2	42,506.6 (*)	0.0	10.6	58.9	3.9	3.9	17.5	0.0	0.0	3.9	4.5	●	NATIONWIDE LIFE INS CO
20.6	25.9	4.7	14.1	67.5	0.0	0.1	0.0	0.0	0.0	13.4	0.0		NETCARE LIFE & HEALTH INS CO
103.4	1,919.3	-0.1	16.6	48.5	6.7	0.0	5.3	0.0	0.0	22.5	0.0	●	NEW ENGLAND LIFE INS CO
115.7	528.1 (*)	5.8	5.6	50.1	5.1	10.2	20.5	0.0	0.7	0.1	9.4	●	NEW ERA LIFE INS CO
40.7	128.1 (*)	7.5	3.5	56.4	4.8	0.4	22.9	0.0	0.0	0.1	0.0		NEW ERA LIFE INS CO OF THE MIDWEST
9,462.7	102,038.0	0.0	28.2	50.3	4.4	1.4	13.4	0.0	0.1	2.2	2.6	●	NEW YORK LIFE INS & ANNUITY CORP
12,371.1	149,636.0	0.0	17.4	45.6	3.8	7.3	10.5	0.0	1.0	14.0	11.1	●	NEW YORK LIFE INS CO
4.3	10.6 (*)	47.4	11.9	36.2	0.0	0.0	0.0	0.0	0.0	0.0	0.0		NIAGARA LIFE & HEALTH INS CO
257.4	213.3 (*)	3.1	11.1	70.4	0.0	2.3	0.0	0.0	0.0	0.0	0.0	●	NIPPON LIFE INS CO OF AMERICA
2,063.8	25,062.1	1.1	39.3	42.1	3.6	0.8	8.1	0.0	0.0	4.1	2.5	●	NORTH AMERICAN CO FOR LIFE & H INS
9.0	17.4	6.4	6.9	86.3	0.3	0.0	0.0	0.0	0.0	0.0	0.0		NORTH AMERICAN INS CO
0.3	34.9	4.3	0.0	42.0	1.9	27.6	1.3	0.0	20.4	2.2	3.4		NORTH AMERICAN NATIONAL RE INS CO
12.8	21.8 (*)	10.1	0.0	28.9	0.0	3.6	24.7	0.1	0.3	30.3	18.7		NORTH CAROLINA MUTUAL LIFE INS CO
0.0	117.7	0.4	0.0	99.6	0.0	0.0	0.0	0.0	0.0	0.0	0.0	●	NORTHWESTERN LONG TERM CARE INS CO
13,247.4	225,535.0	0.0	19.6	40.4	6.1	2.6	15.9	0.0	1.0	14.0	3.8	●	NORTHWESTERN MUTUAL LIFE INS CO
1.0	7.5 (*)	3.8	69.7	23.7	0.0	0.0	0.0	0.0	0.0	0.0	0.0		NTA LIFE INS CO OF NEW YORK
9.3	149.6 (*)	0.0	20.9	79.9	0.3	0.0	0.0	0.0	0.0	0.0	0.0	●	NYLIFE INS CO OF ARIZONA
37.7	245.9 (*)	0.4	0.7	81.4	0.0	1.9	9.5	0.0	0.0	4.4	0.0	●	OCCIDENTAL LIFE INS CO OF NC
123.7	3,470.9	0.0	17.4	63.0	4.0	0.4	11.7	0.0	0.0	3.4	0.0	●	OHIO NATIONAL LIFE ASR CORP
1,204.3	8,293.4 (*)	4.1	19.2	50.6	2.4	4.9	9.7	0.0	0.3	7.5	4.2	●	OHIO NATIONAL LIFE INS CO

● Bullets denote a more detailed analysis is available in Section II.
(*) Asset category percentages do not add up to 100%

INSURANCE COMPANY NAME	DOM. STATE	RATING	TOTAL ASSETS ($MIL)	CAPITAL & SURPLUS ($MIL)	RISK ADJUSTED CAPITAL RATIO 1	RISK ADJUSTED CAPITAL RATIO 2	CAPITAL-IZATION INDEX (PTS)	INVEST. SAFETY INDEX (PTS)	PROFIT-ABILITY INDEX (PTS)	LIQUIDITY INDEX (PTS)	STAB. INDEX (PTS)	STABILIT FACTOR
OHIO STATE LIFE INS CO	TX	B-	13.2	10.3	20.28	10.78	8.0	7.9	4.4	7.0	5.3	AF
OLD AMERICAN INS CO	MO	B-	266.3	21.7	2.26	1.29	7.4	5.7	2.9	3.1	5.1	DIL
OLD REPUBLIC LIFE INS CO	IL	B-	113.7	33.9	3.60	2.24	8.9	5.4	2.8	6.9	4.9	FIT
OLD SPARTAN LIFE INS CO INC	SC	C	24.6	15.6	2.08	1.29	7.4	2.7	8.4	9.1	3.8	I
OLD SURETY LIFE INS CO	OK	C	29.5	12.3	0.71	0.53	3.2	6.1	4.3	5.9	3.2	CD
OLD UNITED LIFE INS CO	AZ	B	89.4	52.1	5.42	3.28	10.0	4.8	8.2	10.0	5.8	ADFIT
OMAHA HEALTH INS CO	NE	U (3)	--	--	--	--	--	--	--	--	--	Z
OMAHA INS CO	NE	B-	89.4	42.3	1.57	0.83	5.9	7.8	1.9	5.6	4.9	FT
OPTIMUM RE INS CO	TX	C+	191.2	40.5	2.64	1.65	8.0	7.6	2.5	9.1	4.6	
OPTUM INS OF OH INC	OH	B	264.1	55.7	5.77	5.19	8.0	9.8	7.6	9.0	5.8	AGT
OXFORD LIFE INS CO	AZ	B+	2192.1	196.9	1.92	1.20	7.3	6.3	6.9	6.5	6.5	I
OZARK NATIONAL LIFE INS CO	MO	B-	836.8	143.6	4.92	2.74	9.6	7.6	2.9	6.5	4.9	D
PACIFIC CENTURY LIFE INS CORP	AZ	U (3)	--	--	--	--	--	--	--	--	--	Z
PACIFIC GUARDIAN LIFE INS CO LTD	HI	A-	559.1	96.3	3.56	2.06	8.6	6.6	5.4	6.1	7.0	AI
PACIFIC LIFE & ANNUITY CO	AZ	B+	7409.8	587.6	4.68	2.27	8.9	6.4	7.0	7.3	6.7	AI
PACIFIC LIFE INS CO	NE	A-	133288.3	9884.7	3.73	2.04	8.6	5.5	6.4	6.2	6.9	AI
PACIFICARE LIFE & HEALTH INS CO	IN	B	186.3	181.3	18.59	16.73	10.0	8.2	6.2	9.2	5.8	ADT
PAN AMERICAN ASR CO	LA	B+	26.7	19.2	4.72	2.34	9.0	5.3	8.6	9.4	6.0	AIT
PAN AMERICAN ASR CO INTL INC	FL	U (3)	--	--	--	--	--	--	--	--	--	Z
PAN AMERICAN LIFE INS CO OF PR	PR	B	9.6	5.3	1.65	1.27	7.4	3.7	1.9	6.7	5.9	ADI
PAN-AMERICAN LIFE INS CO	LA	B	1215.8	243.9	2.51	1.61	7.9	5.4	5.9	6.4	6.0	AFI
PARK AVENUE LIFE INS CO	DE	B	234.6	48.7	1.26	1.08	7.1	6.2	6.6	6.0	6.0	DFIT
PARKER CENTENNIAL ASR CO	WI	A	96.0	48.1	5.62	5.05	10.0	8.6	7.7	10.0	6.9	ADG
PARTNERRE LIFE RE CO OF AM	AR	C	63.8	24.2	1.62	1.10	7.2	8.8	1.9	7.0	3.8	G
PATRIOT LIFE INS CO	MI	C+	21.9	17.3	4.81	4.18	10.0	5.9	2.0	7.2	4.8	DF
PAUL REVERE LIFE INS CO	MA	C+	3479.2	220.1	1.68	1.01	7.0	3.7	6.2	7.7	4.8	AFI
PAVONIA LIFE INS CO OF MICHIGAN	MI	C	1149.3	65.5	1.54	0.86	5.9	6.1	2.1	7.9	4.0	CFT
PAVONIA LIFE INS CO OF NEW YORK	NY	C	29.0	9.4	2.10	1.89	8.3	8.2	2.6	7.2	3.9	ADFT
PEKIN LIFE INS CO	IL	B	1496.7	128.6	2.03	1.20	7.3	6.5	5.7	5.7	6.2	A
PELLERIN LIFE INS CO	LA	D	11.8	1.5	0.67	0.60	3.8	4.2	2.5	5.8	1.7	CI
PENN INS & ANNUITY CO	DE	C+	6128.0	451.2	2.01	1.15	7.2	5.8	2.5	6.3	4.8	G
PENN MUTUAL LIFE INS CO	PA	B	21664.0	1757.4	1.81	1.22	7.3	5.9	6.0	6.2	4.8	IT
PERFORMANCE LIFE OF AMERICA	LA	B-	31.9	21.5	4.42	3.97	10.0	8.3	9.4	9.1	5.3	AD
PHILADELPHIA AMERICAN LIFE INS CO	TX	B	297.6	43.3	1.62	1.05	7.1	4.6	8.9	6.5	5.6	AI
PHL VARIABLE INS CO	CT	D	6103.7	133.9	1.17	0.62	5.3	4.4	1.9	2.0	1.9	ACFIL
PHYSICIANS BENEFITS TRUST LIFE INS	IL	C	6.2	5.9	2.96	2.67	9.5	9.0	1.5	7.5	3.4	DFT
PHYSICIANS LIFE INS CO	NE	A-	1664.1	161.2	3.13	1.58	7.9	6.3	6.0	5.4	6.9	IL
PHYSICIANS MUTUAL INS CO	NE	A+	2367.4	995.5	3.50	2.60	9.4	6.1	8.3	7.1	7.9	I
PINE BELT LIFE INS CO	MS	U (3)	--	--	--	--	--	--	--	--	--	Z
PIONEER AMERICAN INS CO	TX	C	68.4	16.9	2.25	2.02	8.5	8.1	1.8	6.4	3.8	DFT
PIONEER MILITARY INS CO	NV	U (5)	--	--	--	--	--	--	--	--	--	Z
PIONEER MUTUAL LIFE INS CO	ND	B	509.5	39.8	2.57	1.35	7.5	6.3	2.6	5.0	5.4	FIL
PIONEER SECURITY LIFE INS CO	TX	C	76.3	41.4	0.85	0.82	5.6	2.9	2.7	6.7	4.1	CDIT
PLATEAU INS CO	TN	C	27.4	14.8	3.40	2.69	9.5	8.7	2.8	7.8	4.3	ART
POPULAR LIFE RE	PR	B	69.3	39.6	5.27	4.74	10.0	8.9	9.1	9.2	5.7	I
PREFERRED SECURITY LIFE INS CO	TX	U (3)	--	--	--	--	--	--	--	--	--	Z
PRENEED REINS CO OF AMERICA	AZ	B	43.0	39.0	6.63	5.97	10.0	9.0	9.4	4.4	4.8	ALT
PRESIDENTIAL LIFE INS CO	TX	C	4.3	2.8	2.50	2.25	8.9	3.0	5.1	7.8	2.9	DFIT
PRIMERICA LIFE INS CO	TN	B	1617.7	682.4	1.48	1.27	7.4	4.3	9.0	6.9	5.8	I
PRINCIPAL LIFE INS CO	IA	B+	197908.3	5145.5	2.20	1.22	7.3	5.8	7.8	7.1	6.7	I
PRINCIPAL LIFE INS CO IOWA	IA	U (3)	--	--	--	--	--	--	--	--	--	Z
PRINCIPAL NATIONAL LIFE INS CO	IA	B	368.2	176.1	6.42	3.17	10.0	8.3	3.5	10.0	5.7	GT

See Page 27 for explanation of footnotes and Page 28 for explanation of stability factors.

Arrows denote recent upgrades ▲ or downgrades▼ (see Section VI for explanations)

48

www.weissratings.com

NET PREMIUM ($MIL)	IN-VESTED ASSETS ($MIL)	CASH	CMO & STRUCT. SECS.	OTH.INV. GRADE BONDS	NON-INV. GRADE BONDS	CMMON & PREF. STOCK	MORT IN GOOD STAND.	NON-PERF. MORT.	REAL ESTATE	OTHER INVEST-MENTS	INVEST. IN AFFIL	INSURANCE COMPANY NAME
					% OF INVESTED ASSETS IN:							
0.0	10.9 (*)	0.0	55.4	57.2	0.0	0.0	0.0	0.0	0.0	0.0	0.0	OHIO STATE LIFE INS CO
66.4	241.0	0.0	4.3	71.6	1.0	0.4	17.6	0.0	0.0	5.1	0.0	OLD AMERICAN INS CO
11.1	105.4 (*)	0.9	0.0	72.2	2.1	15.9	0.0	0.0	0.0	0.9	0.0 ●	OLD REPUBLIC LIFE INS CO
4.1	23.4 (*)	10.3	0.0	9.9	0.0	75.6	0.0	0.0	0.0	0.0	0.0	OLD SPARTAN LIFE INS CO INC
42.6	28.2 (*)	14.2	0.4	71.5	1.0	0.0	2.1	0.0	8.8	0.9	0.0	OLD SURETY LIFE INS CO
4.2	83.9 (*)	0.4	7.2	70.2	4.1	16.8	0.0	0.0	0.0	0.1	0.0 ●	OLD UNITED LIFE INS CO
--	--	--	--	--	--	--	--	--	--	--	--	OMAHA HEALTH INS CO
48.5	89.0	0.0	37.4	61.3	1.1	0.0	0.0	0.0	0.0	0.2	0.0 ●	OMAHA INS CO
35.1	174.0	3.0	0.0	91.2	1.6	0.6	0.0	0.0	1.7	1.8	1.8 ●	OPTIMUM RE INS CO
0.0	13.8 (*)	73.5	0.0	17.1	0.0	0.0	0.0	0.0	0.0	0.0	0.0 ●	OPTUM INS OF OH INC
347.5	1,927.2	2.3	7.5	70.1	1.9	2.3	13.8	0.0	1.0	0.9	2.9 ●	OXFORD LIFE INS CO
61.0	780.7	0.4	24.1	71.3	0.2	0.0	0.0	0.0	0.6	2.9	0.0 ●	OZARK NATIONAL LIFE INS CO
--	--	--	--	--	--	--	--	--	--	--	--	PACIFIC CENTURY LIFE INS CORP
61.1	529.2	2.1	19.1	35.2	0.6	0.6	36.3	0.0	0.0	5.8	0.0 ●	PACIFIC GUARDIAN LIFE INS CO LTD
453.9	4,132.1 (*)	0.6	5.9	76.4	3.4	0.1	10.9	0.0	0.0	1.0	0.0 ●	PACIFIC LIFE & ANNUITY CO
8,524.8	67,614.6 (*)	0.3	7.6	50.7	3.3	1.0	16.4	0.0	0.2	17.1	5.7 ●	PACIFIC LIFE INS CO
9.7	185.1	0.0	23.5	77.0	0.0	0.0	0.0	0.0	0.0	0.0	0.0 ●	PACIFICARE LIFE & HEALTH INS CO
0.0	24.1 (*)	20.9	2.0	55.8	10.7	7.0	0.0	0.0	0.0	0.0	0.0	PAN AMERICAN ASR CO
--	--	--	--	--	--	--	--	--	--	--	--	PAN AMERICAN ASR CO INTL INC
13.0	9.2	40.1	9.5	34.9	15.6	0.0	0.0	0.0	0.0	0.0	0.0	PAN AMERICAN LIFE INS CO OF PR
163.8	1,146.4	0.9	18.6	57.9	5.7	5.5	0.0	0.0	0.6	10.5	2.2 ●	PAN-AMERICAN LIFE INS CO
1.3	231.4	0.4	0.3	82.5	1.6	14.0	0.0	0.0	0.0	1.2	14.0 ●	PARK AVENUE LIFE INS CO
4.3	90.4	0.0	0.0	96.2	1.0	0.0	0.0	0.0	0.0	2.8	0.0 ●	PARKER CENTENNIAL ASR CO
6.2	48.1	8.8	8.8	81.9	0.0	0.0	0.0	0.0	0.0	0.0	0.0	PARTNERRE LIFE RE CO OF AM
1.1	21.0	3.5	14.4	65.1	0.0	17.0	0.0	0.0	0.0	0.0	0.0	PATRIOT LIFE INS CO
71.6	3,424.6	0.0	3.8	81.8	7.3	3.3	2.4	0.0	0.1	1.3	1.8 ●	PAUL REVERE LIFE INS CO
33.8	1,006.1 (*)	1.9	13.7	70.3	1.6	0.0	0.0	0.0	0.0	2.1	0.0 ●	PAVONIA LIFE INS CO OF MICHIGAN
2.5	27.5 (*)	8.7	8.5	65.8	2.8	0.0	0.0	0.0	0.0	0.0	0.0	PAVONIA LIFE INS CO OF NEW YORK
140.5	1,429.5	0.3	30.5	61.4	0.5	1.3	3.8	0.0	0.0	1.2	0.0 ●	PEKIN LIFE INS CO
1.0	8.7	4.3	0.6	54.9	0.0	10.6	17.1	0.0	11.9	0.6	14.8	PELLERIN LIFE INS CO
547.3	4,218.4 (*)	0.2	27.6	46.1	3.0	1.9	0.0	0.0	0.0	16.8	2.8 ●	PENN INS & ANNUITY CO
678.2	11,736.0 (*)	0.7	26.5	48.6	3.4	5.8	0.0	0.0	0.3	12.1	5.8 ●	PENN MUTUAL LIFE INS CO
4.2	32.2 (*)	1.1	0.0	89.2	1.6	0.0	0.0	0.0	0.0	0.0	0.0	PERFORMANCE LIFE OF AMERICA
139.8	262.5 (*)	4.0	8.7	71.4	8.6	0.7	4.3	0.0	0.0	0.1	0.0 ●	PHILADELPHIA AMERICAN LIFE INS CO
238.1	1,901.4	4.4	27.4	57.0	3.4	1.5	0.2	0.0	0.0	5.3	0.7 ●	PHL VARIABLE INS CO
0.1	6.5 (*)	4.5	0.0	92.4	0.0	0.0	0.0	0.0	0.0	0.0	0.0	PHYSICIANS BENEFITS TRUST LIFE INS
198.4	1,606.3	0.0	23.6	63.4	5.9	2.1	0.0	0.0	0.0	4.4	0.0 ●	PHYSICIANS LIFE INS CO
346.1	2,250.6 (*)	0.1	23.8	50.7	6.7	16.5	0.0	0.0	0.4	0.0	6.8 ●	PHYSICIANS MUTUAL INS CO
--	--	--	--	--	--	--	--	--	--	--	--	PINE BELT LIFE INS CO
24.3	63.2 (*)	1.3	0.0	85.2	2.0	0.4	3.1	0.0	0.0	5.0	0.0	PIONEER AMERICAN INS CO
--	--	--	--	--	--	--	--	--	--	--	--	PIONEER MILITARY INS CO
10.6	505.1	0.2	30.6	60.8	0.8	0.0	2.7	0.0	0.0	5.0	0.0 ●	PIONEER MUTUAL LIFE INS CO
16.7	74.8 (*)	0.5	0.0	29.1	0.0	62.1	0.4	0.0	0.0	2.9	62.1 ●	PIONEER SECURITY LIFE INS CO
12.0	23.7	37.6	0.0	59.1	0.0	1.6	0.0	0.0	0.7	0.8	1.2	PLATEAU INS CO
14.1	65.4	4.7	66.8	28.5	0.0	0.0	0.0	0.0	0.0	0.0	0.0 ●	POPULAR LIFE RE
--	--	--	--	--	--	--	--	--	--	--	--	PREFERRED SECURITY LIFE INS CO
7.6	36.6 (*)	1.3	0.0	95.7	0.0	0.0	0.0	0.0	0.0	0.0	0.0 ●	PRENEED REINS CO OF AMERICA
0.1	4.2 (*)	9.4	1.5	2.5	0.0	29.2	0.0	0.0	0.0	1.2	0.0	PRESIDENTIAL LIFE INS CO
237.7	1,629.7 (*)	0.0	13.3	49.9	2.5	28.5	0.0	0.0	0.0	1.4	26.3 ●	PRIMERICA LIFE INS CO
7,119.0	69,012.9 (*)	0.2	19.4	49.5	3.3	1.3	18.9	0.0	0.7	5.6	5.4 ●	PRINCIPAL LIFE INS CO
--	--	--	--	--	--	--	--	--	--	--	--	PRINCIPAL LIFE INS CO IOWA
0.0	144.4	9.2	7.9	81.2	1.8	0.0	0.0	0.0	0.0	0.0	0.0 ●	PRINCIPAL NATIONAL LIFE INS CO

● Bullets denote a more detailed analysis is available in Section II.
(*) Asset category percentages do not add up to 100%

INSURANCE COMPANY NAME	DOM. STATE	RATING	TOTAL ASSETS ($MIL)	CAPITAL & SURPLUS ($MIL)	RISK ADJUSTED CAPITAL RATIO 1	RISK ADJUSTED CAPITAL RATIO 2	CAPITAL-IZATION INDEX (PTS)	INVEST. SAFETY INDEX (PTS)	PROFIT-ABILITY INDEX (PTS)	LIQUIDITY INDEX (PTS)	STAB. INDEX (PTS)	STABILI FACTOR
PROFESSIONAL INS CO	TX	D	109.9	47.5	5.29	4.76	10.0	6.7	8.6	6.9	2.1	AD
PROFESSIONAL LIFE & CAS CO	IL	B-	180.9	61.2	3.23	1.80	8.2	3.2	8.9	5.6	4.9	DIT
PROTEC INS CO	IL	C+	5.1	4.6	3.21	2.89	9.8	9.8	8.5	8.2	4.2	T
PROTECTIVE LIFE & ANNUITY INS CO	AL	C+	5029.6	216.0	2.06	0.97	6.8	5.6	2.1	4.7	4.6	GL
PROTECTIVE LIFE INS CO	TN	B	59054.5	4000.5	1.54	1.06	7.1	5.7	6.3	6.3	5.8	AGI
PROVIDENT AMER LIFE & HEALTH INS CO	OH	B	9.0	7.7	1.51	1.36	7.5	7.3	6.2	6.9	4.5	ADT
PROVIDENT AMERICAN INS CO	TX	C	18.8	11.9	0.79	0.70	4.6	6.5	8.6	3.8	3.3	CDFL
PROVIDENT LIFE & ACCIDENT INS CO	TN	C+	8041.3	696.4	2.77	1.40	7.6	4.8	6.5	7.3	4.8	AI
PROVIDENT LIFE & CAS INS CO	TN	B-	746.1	142.7	4.42	2.49	9.2	4.6	7.6	7.5	4.9	ADI
PRUCO LIFE INS CO	AZ	C+	123473.2	1543.2	1.32	0.73	5.5	5.7	2.4	9.5	3.7	ACT
PRUCO LIFE INS CO OF NEW JERSEY	NJ	B-	16367.8	246.4	1.51	0.76	5.8	5.5	2.8	7.0	3.6	ACGT
PRUDENTIAL ANNUITIES LIFE ASR CORP	AZ	B-	53916.6	5994.9	11.37	8.36	10.0	6.4	5.8	10.0	4.2	AT
PRUDENTIAL INS CO OF AMERICA	NJ	B	269548.9	10538.2	1.52	1.08	7.1	6.3	5.4	7.6	5.5	AIT
PRUDENTIAL LEGACY INS CO OF NJ	NJ	D+ (3)	59813.8	258.1	0.47	0.39	1.7	9.5	5.5	0.0	1.7	CLT
PRUDENTIAL RETIREMENT INS & ANNUITY	CT	B-	75563.2	1128.3	1.97	0.91	6.5	3.7	5.9	6.6	5.1	AI
PURITAN LIFE INS CO	TX	C-	23.6	22.6	1.13	1.01	7.0	2.8	6.6	7.0	2.5	ADFG
PURITAN LIFE INS CO OF AMERICA	TX	D+	130.4	21.9	2.99	1.91	8.4	5.9	2.2	6.4	1.3	DFGT
PYRAMID LIFE INS CO	KS	D	72.6	16.8	2.31	1.94	8.4	6.9	4.2	7.9	1.8	ADFT
RABENHORST LIFE INS CO	LA	C-	30.7	4.2	1.04	0.86	5.9	3.9	2.4	6.3	2.9	DFI
REGAL LIFE OF AMERICA INS CO	TX	D-	7.4	4.9	1.10	1.06	7.1	5.3	2.3	7.0	1.1	ADFT
REGAL REINSURANCE COMPANY	MA	U (3)	--	--	--	--	--	--	--	--	--	Z
REINSURANCE CO OF MO INC	MO	C	1952.2	1743.7	1.10	0.98	6.8	1.4	3.5	6.9	3.8	FGIT
RELIABLE LIFE INS CO	MO	B-	21.2	11.8	2.00	0.99	6.9	8.6	6.7	10.0	5.2	A
RELIABLE LIFE INS CO	LA	E+ (3)	7.7	2.2	1.07	0.64	5.1	1.6	1.8	6.4	0.5	CFGIT
RELIABLE SERVICE INS CO	LA	U (3)	--	--	--	--	--	--	--	--	--	Z
RELIANCE STANDARD LIFE INS CO	IL	C+	13947.8	1257.6	1.86	1.03	7.0	3.5	8.3	6.5	4.5	I
RELIANCE STANDARD LIFE INS CO OF TX	TX	U (3)	--	--	--	--	--	--	--	--	--	Z
▲ RELIASTAR LIFE INS CO	MN	B-	20768.8	1599.4	2.01	1.19	7.3	6.0	2.8	4.5	5.0	FGL
RELIASTAR LIFE INS CO OF NEW YORK	NY	B	2927.2	276.6	3.11	1.68	8.0	6.5	3.5	5.8	5.8	
RESERVE NATIONAL INS CO	OK	B-	136.2	37.6	1.52	1.15	5.3	7.5	1.5	4.9	4.9	DFL
RESOURCE LIFE INS CO	IL	U (3)	--	--	--	--	--	--	--	--	--	Z
RGA REINSURANCE CO	MO	B-	37286.1	1771.9	1.75	0.92	6.4	5.2	7.7	4.9	4.5	AGILT
RHODES LIFE INS CO OF LA INC	LA	E-	3.8	-0.4	-0.14	-0.13	0.0	7.4	0.4	7.3	0.0	CDFI
RIVERMONT LIFE INS CO I	SC	C	610.3	127.3	3.60	2.04	8.6	7.3	1.6	7.0	3.7	D
RIVERSOURCE LIFE INS CO	MN	C+	106410.1	2838.6	1.63	1.00	7.0	5.9	5.0	7.8	4.7	T
RIVERSOURCE LIFE INS CO OF NY	NY	C	6891.0	245.0	2.60	1.31	7.5	6.0	2.9	7.6	4.3	
ROYAL STATE NATIONAL INS CO LTD	HI	C (2)	39.7	30.3	5.02	3.72	10.0	5.6	4.0	7.1	4.2	D
ROYALTY CAPITAL LIFE INS CO	MO	D	3.6	3.6	3.10	2.79	8.0	8.4	2.7	8.4	1.8	FGT
▼ RX LIFE INSURANCE CO	AZ	C+	9.3	9.0	4.16	3.74	10.0	6.6	6.1	0.0	3.4	ADFL
S USA LIFE INS CO INC	AZ	B	25.6	16.5	5.09	4.58	10.0	9.3	1.9	7.2	4.9	ADFG
SAGICOR LIFE INS CO	TX	C-	1419.5	77.2	1.08	0.55	5.1	3.7	1.9	3.8	3.1	CGILT
SB MUTL LIFE INS CO OF MA	MA	B+	3104.8	190.2	1.83	1.06	7.1	5.6	6.2	5.5	6.4	FIL
SBLI USA MUT LIFE INS CO INC	NY	B	1530.7	102.7	1.70	0.98	6.8	5.9	4.5	3.1	5.1	GIL
SCOR GLOBAL LIFE AMERICAS REIN CO	DE	B-	1057.7	231.1	1.12	0.82	5.6	7.1	3.0	6.7	5.0	AG
SCOR GLOBAL LIFE REINS CO OF DE	DE	C	452.8	121.9	4.22	2.55	9.3	8.5	2.9	6.5	4.3	AT
SCOR GLOBAL LIFE USA RE CO	DE	B-	836.9	251.1	3.72	2.21	8.8	7.4	3.4	7.0	5.0	AG
SCOTTISH RE US INC	DE	E+	1556.8	37.6	0.73	0.37	2.8	0.8	2.9	3.2	0.4	CFILT
SECU LIFE INS CO	NC	B	49.2	28.4	4.72	4.25	10.0	8.5	8.4	9.0	5.7	T
SECURIAN LIFE INS CO	MN	B	994.0	306.6	5.14	3.34	10.0	7.4	4.1	6.8	6.1	G
SECURICO LIFE INS CO	TX	D	2.3	2.0	2.44	2.20	8.8	5.9	1.4	7.2	2.0	DFGT
SECURITY BENEFIT LIFE INS CO	KS	B	33665.2	2051.6	2.60	1.19	7.3	3.9	6.6	7.6	4.9	IT
▲ SECURITY LIFE OF DENVER INS CO	CO	B-	14698.8	860.7	1.42	0.81	5.6	5.6	5.4	4.3	5.0	LT

See Page 27 for explanation of footnotes and Page 28 for explanation of stability factors.
Arrows denote recent upgrades ▲ or downgrades▼ (see Section VI for explanations)

50

www.weissratings.com

NET PREMIUM ($MIL)	IN-VESTED ASSETS ($MIL)	CASH	CMO & STRUCT. SECS.	OTH.INV. GRADE BONDS	NON-INV. GRADE BONDS	CMMON & PREF. STOCK	MORT IN GOOD STAND.	NON-PERF. MORT.	REAL ESTATE	OTHER INVEST-MENTS	INVEST. IN AFFIL		INSURANCE COMPANY NAME
14.4	104.2 (*)	0.3	15.0	76.9	0.0	0.0	0.0	0.0	0.0	4.3	0.0	●	PROFESSIONAL INS CO
3.1	172.3 (*)	0.8	0.0	48.0	13.5	27.0	0.0	0.0	0.0	8.8	0.0	●	PROFESSIONAL LIFE & CAS CO
0.2	4.3	65.0	0.0	35.0	0.0	0.0	0.0	0.0	0.0	0.0	0.0		PROTEC INS CO
3,045.4	1,838.3 (*)	0.2	17.2	67.4	4.6	1.6	5.7	0.0	0.0	1.7	0.0	●	PROTECTIVE LIFE & ANNUITY INS CO
13,207.5	30,631.5 (*)	0.0	14.9	54.1	3.6	5.6	16.3	0.0	0.1	3.3	6.8	●	PROTECTIVE LIFE INS CO
4.7	8.1	4.3	0.0	56.5	0.0	39.2	0.0	0.0	0.0	0.0	39.2		PROVIDENT AMER LIFE & HEALTH INS CO
46.3	18.2 (*)	35.1	2.2	47.1	7.6	0.1	0.0	0.0	0.0	1.8	0.0		PROVIDENT AMERICAN INS CO
609.1	7,498.5	0.0	5.6	75.7	6.7	1.4	5.9	0.0	1.0	3.8	0.0	●	PROVIDENT LIFE & ACCIDENT INS CO
71.3	727.0	0.0	5.3	81.5	7.0	0.0	4.8	0.0	0.0	1.6	0.0	●	PROVIDENT LIFE & CAS INS CO
1,014.4	6,065.9	0.0	13.1	43.9	5.0	4.0	15.3	0.0	0.0	19.2	6.5	●	PRUCO LIFE INS CO
207.0	1,604.1	0.0	19.4	51.4	6.7	0.2	7.6	0.0	0.0	14.6	2.0	●	PRUCO LIFE INS CO OF NEW JERSEY
5,421.1	18,691.9 (*)	2.2	6.7	53.2	2.0	0.1	6.7	0.0	0.0	1.0	0.6	●	PRUDENTIAL ANNUITIES LIFE ASR CORP
18,904.1	120,776.0 (*)	0.5	16.8	47.4	4.5	5.6	15.5	0.0	0.5	6.7	10.0	●	PRUDENTIAL INS CO OF AMERICA
2,513.3	263.6	0.0	0.0	99.9	0.0	0.0	0.0	0.0	0.0	0.1	0.0	●	PRUDENTIAL LEGACY INS CO OF NJ
825.9	26,610.9	0.2	20.5	51.2	6.3	0.4	20.0	0.0	0.0	0.8	0.6	●	PRUDENTIAL RETIREMENT INS & ANNUITY
0.0	20.1	1.0	4.2	3.3	0.0	91.2	0.0	0.0	0.0	0.0	91.2		PURITAN LIFE INS CO
18.9	112.1 (*)	4.6	15.6	52.0	4.3	1.5	14.0	0.0	0.5	5.4	0.0		PURITAN LIFE INS CO OF AMERICA
9.6	67.6	5.4	3.2	77.1	0.3	6.0	0.0	0.0	0.0	8.0	0.0		PYRAMID LIFE INS CO
2.1	21.6	0.4	8.8	55.4	0.5	24.1	9.5	0.0	0.0	0.6	9.5		RABENHORST LIFE INS CO
0.7	7.1	9.7	0.0	32.2	0.0	56.2	0.0	0.0	0.0	1.9	56.2		REGAL LIFE OF AMERICA INS CO
--	--	--	--	--	--	--	--	--	--	--	--		REGAL REINSURANCE COMPANY
25.3	1,746.6	0.1	2.1	7.1	0.0	90.7	0.0	0.0	0.0	0.0	90.7	●	REINSURANCE CO OF MO INC
0.0	24.6	0.0	0.0	89.3	0.0	0.0	0.0	0.0	0.0	10.7	0.0		RELIABLE LIFE INS CO
0.6	7.6 (*)	0.3	2.0	16.3	0.0	66.0	0.0	0.0	5.3	8.0	1.0		RELIABLE LIFE INS CO
--	--	--	--	--	--	--	--	--	--	--	--		RELIABLE SERVICE INS CO
2,224.5	11,732.5 (*)	0.5	30.8	28.8	9.1	2.5	22.7	0.5	0.0	2.4	1.6	●	RELIANCE STANDARD LIFE INS CO
--	--	--	--	--	--	--	--	--	--	--	--		RELIANCE STANDARD LIFE INS CO OF TX
1,809.3	17,038.9 (*)	1.0	11.0	59.8	3.6	2.0	12.7	0.0	0.0	7.0	3.7	●	RELIASTAR LIFE INS CO
101.0	2,184.8 (*)	2.3	9.1	66.4	3.1	0.2	9.1	0.0	0.0	5.4	0.0	●	RELIASTAR LIFE INS CO OF NEW YORK
121.3	101.8	0.0	6.8	86.2	2.4	0.0	0.0	0.0	0.0	4.6	0.2	●	RESERVE NATIONAL INS CO
--	--	--	--	--	--	--	--	--	--	--	--		RESOURCE LIFE INS CO
6,718.9	21,502.0 (*)	1.2	14.9	48.1	6.2	0.8	18.1	0.0	0.0	9.5	3.1	●	RGA REINSURANCE CO
0.5	3.9	13.7	0.5	66.8	0.6	0.0	4.7	0.0	4.7	8.9	0.0		RHODES LIFE INS CO OF LA INC
15.7	585.8	0.0	19.1	77.9	0.3	0.0	0.0	0.0	0.0	1.9	0.0	●	RIVERMONT LIFE INS CO I
4,004.5	28,174.6 (*)	0.0	25.1	42.0	5.1	2.8	8.8	0.0	0.3	2.9	2.7	●	RIVERSOURCE LIFE INS CO
278.2	2,098.8 (*)	0.0	26.7	54.1	3.4	0.0	7.2	0.0	0.0	2.5	0.0	●	RIVERSOURCE LIFE INS CO OF NY
1.2	45.8 (*)	3.0	14.1	63.9	0.0	16.5	0.0	0.0	0.0	0.6	0.0	●	ROYAL STATE NATIONAL INS CO LTD
0.0	3.6 (*)	0.8	0.0	35.1	0.7	0.0	0.0	0.0	0.0	0.0	0.0		ROYALTY CAPITAL LIFE INS CO
0.0	7.5 (*)	2.7	0.0	92.2	0.0	0.0	0.0	0.0	0.0	0.0	0.0		RX LIFE INSURANCE CO
4.9	14.9 (*)	38.5	5.7	50.8	0.0	0.0	0.0	0.0	0.0	2.5	0.0		S USA LIFE INS CO INC
237.6	1,073.1 (*)	0.6	23.2	63.3	0.9	2.7	3.2	0.0	0.0	3.0	0.0	●	SAGICOR LIFE INS CO
98.0	2,824.9	0.0	17.4	70.7	4.5	2.3	0.0	0.0	0.3	4.9	1.1	●	SB MUTL LIFE INS CO OF MA
111.4	1,439.6	0.6	16.4	72.3	0.0	1.2	0.2	0.0	0.0	8.3	0.8	●	SBLI USA MUT LIFE INS CO INC
139.1	838.7 (*)	0.5	12.1	64.0	0.4	11.6	0.0	0.0	0.0	1.8	11.6	●	SCOR GLOBAL LIFE AMERICAS REIN CO
67.7	282.6 (*)	0.4	32.9	55.7	0.0	0.0	0.0	0.0	0.0	4.9	0.0	●	SCOR GLOBAL LIFE REINS CO OF DE
187.8	645.4 (*)	0.4	19.5	59.9	0.0	0.0	0.0	0.0	0.0	16.1	13.9	●	SCOR GLOBAL LIFE USA RE CO
102.1	1,451.7 (*)	1.2	49.7	40.3	2.8	0.1	0.0	0.0	0.0	0.1	0.1	●	SCOTTISH RE US INC
7.3	42.4	23.3	0.0	39.2	0.0	0.0	37.5	0.0	0.0	0.0	0.0	●	SECU LIFE INS CO
328.5	629.3 (*)	1.3	18.7	68.1	1.9	0.9	6.0	0.0	0.2	0.5	0.0	●	SECURIAN LIFE INS CO
0.4	2.3 (*)	3.8	0.5	86.1	0.0	0.0	0.0	0.0	0.0	0.0	0.0		SECURICO LIFE INS CO
1,491.6	26,424.2 (*)	0.3	55.2	8.5	3.4	0.2	4.9	0.0	0.1	24.5	27.1	●	SECURITY BENEFIT LIFE INS CO
570.6	12,196.2 (*)	0.9	9.9	57.9	3.2	1.4	10.1	0.0	0.0	11.5	3.3	●	SECURITY LIFE OF DENVER INS CO

● Bullets denote a more detailed analysis is available in Section II.
(*) Asset category percentages do not add up to 100%

INSURANCE COMPANY NAME	DOM. STATE	RATING	TOTAL ASSETS ($MIL)	CAPITAL & SURPLUS ($MIL)	RISK ADJUSTED CAPITAL RATIO 1	RISK ADJUSTED CAPITAL RATIO 2	CAPITAL-IZATION INDEX (PTS)	INVEST. SAFETY INDEX (PTS)	PROFIT-ABILITY INDEX (PTS)	LIQUIDITY INDEX (PTS)	STAB. INDEX (PTS)	STABILITY FACTORS
SECURITY MUTUAL LIFE INS CO OF NY	NY	C	2766.8	164.5	1.66	0.90	6.2	6.2	5.4	0.7	2.9	L
SECURITY NATIONAL LIFE INS CO	UT	D	662.8	47.9	1.13	0.68	5.2	3.1	7.3	5.9	2.3	CI
SECURITY PLAN LIFE INS CO	LA	C-	307.0	17.5	0.86	0.58	3.9	4.0	1.7	6.0	2.9	ADT
SENIOR HEALTH INS CO OF PENNSYLVANIA	PA	E- (3)	2688.5	12.6	0.56	0.26	1.5	0.0	1.0	6.8	0.1	CFIT
SENIOR LIFE INS CO	GA	D+	63.6	13.4	1.84	0.92	6.4	3.3	2.0	6.6	2.6	DI
SENTINEL AMERICAN LIFE INS CO	TX	U (3)	--	--	--	--	--	--	--	--	--	Z
SENTINEL SECURITY LIFE INS CO	UT	C-	1103.6	41.7	0.81	0.37	3.4	1.7	2.2	7.6	2.9	ACFGIT
SENTRY LIFE INS CO	WI	A	7425.4	293.3	3.37	1.94	8.4	7.2	6.4	8.2	7.4	A
SENTRY LIFE INS CO OF NEW YORK	NY	B	118.6	10.1	1.13	1.02	7.0	8.3	5.8	9.5	6.2	DGT
SERVICE LIFE & CAS INS CO	TX	U (5)	--	--	--	--	--	--	--	--	--	Z
SETTLERS LIFE INS CO	WI	B	423.1	46.2	2.80	1.53	7.8	6.1	5.7	6.2	6.2	ADI
SHELTER LIFE INS CO	MO	B	1268.8	225.5	3.89	2.45	9.2	7.6	3.3	6.0	5.5	
SHELTERPOINT INS CO	FL	B	9.0	8.0	4.12	3.71	8.0	8.8	2.1	9.7	4.9	
SHELTERPOINT LIFE INS CO	NY	A	151.3	66.7	2.19	1.85	8.3	7.5	7.9	7.0	6.8	DG
SHENANDOAH LIFE INS CO	VA	B-	1003.5	105.7	2.73	1.49	7.7	6.6	5.4	3.8	4.9	FLT
SHERIDAN LIFE INS CO	OK	C-	2.2	2.1	2.72	2.45	9.2	9.8	6.9	10.0	3.3	AD
SMITH BURIAL & LIFE INS CO	AR	E	4.7	0.5	0.34	0.30	0.6	6.9	2.6	5.2	0.1	CD
SOUTHERN FARM BUREAU LIFE INS CO	MS	A	14356.8	2577.8	4.44	2.38	9.1	6.0	6.8	6.3	7.4	I
SOUTHERN FIDELITY LIFE INS CO	AR	U (3)	--	--	--	--	--	--	--	--	--	Z
SOUTHERN FINANCIAL LIFE INS CO	KY	C	9.8	3.0	1.36	1.23	7.3	8.3	2.4	7.9	3.2	GT
SOUTHERN FINANCIAL LIFE INS CO	LA	D+	128.2	42.0	3.09	1.71	8.1	2.8	8.4	6.7	2.8	DI
SOUTHERN LIFE & HEALTH INS CO	WI	B	71.2	32.0	1.74	1.65	8.0	7.2	6.4	6.9	4.9	DFT
SOUTHERN NATL LIFE INS CO INC	LA	B	16.9	13.4	2.40	1.88	8.3	5.9	4.8	7.5	5.5	IT
▼ SOUTHERN PIONEER LIFE INS CO	AR	A-	14.6	12.8	4.26	3.83	10.0	8.7	7.0	9.1	5.5	ADFT
SOUTHERN SECURITY LIFE INS CO INC	MS	D+	1.6	1.6	2.57	2.31	8.0	7.6	3.9	10.0	2.6	A
▼ SOUTHLAND NATIONAL INS CORP	NC	D+	360.7	30.4	2.19	1.07	7.1	3.8	3.0	6.9	1.8	FIT
SOUTHWEST CREDIT LIFE INC	NM	U (3)	--	--	--	--	--	--	--	--	--	Z
SOUTHWEST SERVICE LIFE INS CO	TX	D-	11.8	4.3	0.77	0.66	4.3	9.0	1.6	7.0	1.2	ACDT
SQUIRE REASSURANCE CO LLC	MI	U (5)	--	--	--	--	--	--	--	--	--	Z
STANDARD INS CO	OR	B+	24530.4	1258.7	2.31	1.19	7.3	5.1	6.3	6.8	6.5	AI
STANDARD LIFE & ACCIDENT INS CO	TX	A-	533.1	294.6	5.59	3.47	10.0	4.9	7.9	6.9	6.9	AFI
STANDARD LIFE & CAS INS CO	UT	D (1)	31.1	4.7	1.10	0.69	5.2	2.5	3.0	5.0	2.2	CIT
STANDARD LIFE INS CO OF NY	NY	A-	296.6	96.9	4.75	3.12	10.0	7.4	7.9	7.0	7.2	AD
STANDARD SECURITY LIFE INS CO OF NY	NY	B	138.0	71.5	6.45	5.00	10.0	8.3	5.3	6.9	5.6	AFT
STARMOUNT LIFE INS CO	LA	C+	82.6	43.5	1.24	0.97	5.7	7.8	2.5	2.1	4.1	FL
STATE FARM HEALTH INS CO	IL	U (3)	--	--	--	--	--	--	--	--	--	Z
STATE FARM LIFE & ACCIDENT ASR CO	IL	A+	3003.4	524.9	5.53	3.13	10.0	7.8	5.4	6.2	7.9	A
STATE FARM LIFE INS CO	IL	A+	74940.7	11502.7	4.51	2.54	9.3	6.5	5.5	6.0	7.9	AI
STATE LIFE INS CO	IN	B	8378.9	461.0	1.65	0.83	3.0	4.6	7.6	3.9	4.2	CGILT
STATE LIFE INS FUND	WI	B (3)	111.9	7.9	1.11	1.00	7.0	6.0	1.9	5.7	4.2	DFI
STATE MUTUAL INS CO	GA	D+	188.6	26.5	1.15	0.73	4.0	2.9	2.0	6.4	2.5	CFIT
STERLING INVESTORS LIFE INS CO	IN	B-	70.0	10.4	1.54	1.29	7.4	4.6	2.3	7.4	3.5	ADGIT
STERLING LIFE INS CO	IL	B-	39.9	20.4	1.17	0.90	5.7	8.0	6.0	5.8	4.6	DT
STRUCTURED ANNUITY RE CO	IA	U (3)	--	--	--	--	--	--	--	--	--	Z
SUN LIFE & HEALTH INS CO	MI	D	955.2	139.2	3.58	2.04	8.6	7.2	1.0	6.3	2.0	AFGT
▲ SUN LIFE ASR CO OF CANADA	MI	D	18767.4	1192.5	0.67	0.40	2.4	2.1	2.3	5.1	1.7	CGIT
SUNSET LIFE INS CO OF AMERICA	MO	B-	310.0	27.1	2.68	1.40	7.6	6.2	3.4	5.2	5.0	DF
SUPERIOR FUNERAL & LIFE INS CO	AR	C+	184.0	25.1	2.72	1.40	7.6	4.1	7.8	5.8	4.8	DI
SURENCY LIFE & HEALTH INS CO	KS	C	12.7	10.6	3.74	2.82	9.7	7.1	2.9	7.0	3.4	DF
SURETY LIFE & CASUALTY INS CO	ND	C-	12.6	5.0	2.02	1.82	8.2	3.8	8.6	9.0	2.8	DI
SURETY LIFE INS CO	NE	D	18.8	18.4	3.14	1.53	7.8	5.1	3.0	10.0	2.0	FT
SWBC LIFE INS CO	TX	B+	32.6	22.4	3.57	2.46	9.2	5.9	8.6	9.1	6.1	I

See Page 27 for explanation of footnotes and Page 28 for explanation of stability factors.

Arrows denote recent upgrades ▲ or downgrades▼ (see Section VI for explanations)

52   www.weissratings.com

NET PREMIUM ($MIL)	IN-VESTED ASSETS ($MIL)	% OF INVESTED ASSETS IN:									INVEST. IN AFFIL	INSURANCE COMPANY NAME
		CASH	CMO & STRUCT. SECS.	OTH.INV. GRADE BONDS	NON-INV. GRADE BONDS	CMMON & PREF. STOCK	MORT IN GOOD STAND.	NON-PERF. MORT.	REAL ESTATE	OTHER INVEST-MENTS		
150.2	2,589.2 (*)	0.1	3.3	71.1	0.5	0.1	7.5	0.1	0.4	15.6	0.1	● SECURITY MUTUAL LIFE INS CO OF NY
64.8	563.6 (*)	0.5	1.2	29.7	1.8	4.1	36.3	0.6	8.2	14.6	3.0	● SECURITY NATIONAL LIFE INS CO
33.2	295.4	2.1	2.0	79.6	4.5	8.1	0.0	0.0	1.0	2.9	3.5	SECURITY PLAN LIFE INS CO
45.5	2,594.1 (*)	-0.3	21.5	46.8	4.6	2.9	1.2	0.0	0.0	4.3	0.0	SENIOR HEALTH INS CO OF PENNSYLVANIA
19.3	46.5	17.4	0.6	30.4	0.2	17.6	0.0	0.0	24.8	9.0	0.0	SENIOR LIFE INS CO
--	--	--	--	--	--	--	--	--	--	--	--	SENTINEL AMERICAN LIFE INS CO
37.5	787.1 (*)	0.8	44.9	24.2	3.9	1.8	8.1	0.1	0.8	4.8	0.0	● SENTINEL SECURITY LIFE INS CO
628.9	2,698.9	0.0	5.8	90.3	2.5	0.4	0.0	0.0	0.0	0.4	0.4	● SENTRY LIFE INS CO
11.9	37.1 (*)	1.4	4.7	90.1	1.1	0.0	0.0	0.0	0.0	1.5	0.0	SENTRY LIFE INS CO OF NEW YORK
--	--	--	--	--	--	--	--	--	--	--	--	SERVICE LIFE & CAS INS CO
40.5	403.0	0.4	7.2	81.4	3.6	3.4	0.0	0.0	0.9	2.6	0.0	● SETTLERS LIFE INS CO
101.1	1,170.8	0.0	36.9	55.4	0.0	0.7	0.7	0.0	0.0	6.3	1.7	● SHELTER LIFE INS CO
0.0	8.4	11.8	20.6	66.9	0.0	0.0	0.0	0.0	0.0	0.0	0.0	SHELTERPOINT INS CO
149.2	100.0 (*)	4.3	16.0	68.8	0.7	8.9	0.0	0.0	0.0	0.0	8.9	● SHELTERPOINT LIFE INS CO
32.1	1,001.9	0.1	16.9	72.7	0.1	0.8	4.8	0.0	0.0	4.2	0.8	● SHENANDOAH LIFE INS CO
0.0	2.1	100.0	0.0	0.0	0.0	0.0	0.0	0.0	0.0	0.0	0.0	SHERIDAN LIFE INS CO
0.3	4.6	4.3	0.0	92.0	0.0	3.6	0.0	0.0	0.0	0.0	0.0	SMITH BURIAL & LIFE INS CO
658.0	13,643.8	0.3	17.4	53.2	2.5	5.2	13.1	0.0	0.1	8.3	0.5	● SOUTHERN FARM BUREAU LIFE INS CO
--	--	--	--	--	--	--	--	--	--	--	--	SOUTHERN FIDELITY LIFE INS CO
3.3	7.0 (*)	1.0	0.4	71.3	0.0	1.2	0.0	0.0	0.0	0.0	0.0	SOUTHERN FINANCIAL LIFE INS CO
9.6	116.0 (*)	1.2	0.0	47.9	11.5	31.5	0.0	0.0	0.0	6.0	0.0	● SOUTHERN FINANCIAL LIFE INS CO
-0.1	73.4 (*)	0.3	1.4	62.6	0.0	30.9	0.0	0.0	0.0	0.2	24.7	● SOUTHERN LIFE & HEALTH INS CO
4.5	15.5	4.6	10.5	50.8	0.0	33.9	0.0	0.0	0.0	0.2	14.9	SOUTHERN NATL LIFE INS CO INC
0.4	15.1	2.4	16.4	77.3	0.0	0.4	0.0	0.0	0.0	2.8	0.0	SOUTHERN PIONEER LIFE INS CO
0.0	1.6 (*)	18.1	23.4	15.3	2.6	3.4	0.0	0.0	0.0	0.0	0.0	SOUTHERN SECURITY LIFE INS CO INC
-38.3	354.9 (*)	9.6	28.0	43.2	2.0	9.1	0.8	0.2	0.3	4.0	13.4	● SOUTHLAND NATIONAL INS CORP
--	--	--	--	--	--	--	--	--	--	--	--	SOUTHWEST CREDIT LIFE INC
10.0	11.1	4.4	0.0	75.1	0.0	20.5	0.0	0.0	0.0	0.0	20.5	SOUTHWEST SERVICE LIFE INS CO
--	--	--	--	--	--	--	--	--	--	--	--	SQUIRE REASSURANCE CO LLC
3,002.2	15,173.5	0.8	5.6	45.1	3.7	0.2	40.8	0.0	0.4	4.3	0.0	● STANDARD INS CO
81.7	499.1	0.0	0.2	74.9	2.5	17.8	2.6	1.3	0.0	0.8	0.0	● STANDARD LIFE & ACCIDENT INS CO
5.3	24.1	2.1	0.1	63.0	10.7	0.0	10.9	0.0	7.5	5.7	0.0	STANDARD LIFE & CAS INS CO
76.3	279.7	2.2	0.0	48.3	0.5	0.0	49.0	0.0	0.0	0.0	0.0	● STANDARD LIFE INS CO OF NY
72.7	118.3 (*)	2.3	1.2	75.7	0.0	16.4	0.0	0.0	0.0	0.2	9.7	● STANDARD SECURITY LIFE INS CO OF NY
155.1	65.5 (*)	29.6	0.0	55.8	0.7	0.1	0.0	0.0	8.6	1.1	0.0	● STARMOUNT LIFE INS CO
--	--	--	--	--	--	--	--	--	--	--	--	STATE FARM HEALTH INS CO
181.3	2,818.7 (*)	0.0	23.0	68.8	0.7	0.0	0.0	0.0	0.0	5.9	1.5	● STATE FARM LIFE & ACCIDENT ASR CO
3,769.7	70,406.4	0.0	19.3	52.6	0.4	6.2	11.1	0.0	0.0	10.3	3.2	● STATE FARM LIFE INS CO
499.8	7,719.0 (*)	0.7	23.2	61.4	2.0	0.6	10.0	0.0	0.0	0.8	0.0	● STATE LIFE INS CO
1.2	110.5 (*)	0.1	0.0	94.4	1.5	0.0	0.0	0.0	0.0	2.9	0.0	STATE LIFE INS FUND
16.1	243.2 (*)	2.8	15.5	43.5	5.5	6.6	5.0	0.3	8.1	9.9	6.5	● STATE MUTUAL INS CO
18.8	51.5 (*)	4.6	5.5	77.3	6.4	0.0	0.0	0.0	0.0	0.4	0.0	STERLING INVESTORS LIFE INS CO
46.4	31.8	0.1	0.0	99.6	0.0	0.0	0.0	0.0	0.0	0.3	0.9	STERLING LIFE INS CO
--	--	--	--	--	--	--	--	--	--	--	--	STRUCTURED ANNUITY RE CO
86.5	726.2	1.4	21.7	65.9	1.1	0.7	7.3	0.0	0.0	1.9	0.0	● SUN LIFE & HEALTH INS CO
2,646.3	17,711.3 (*)	0.0	9.9	54.2	1.7	4.0	18.3	0.0	5.9	4.2	1.1	● SUN LIFE ASR CO OF CANADA
6.6	310.4	0.0	6.0	73.2	0.4	0.5	17.1	0.0	0.0	2.8	0.0	● SUNSET LIFE INS CO OF AMERICA
11.7	178.2	1.7	8.8	72.5	11.5	4.6	0.0	0.2	0.4	0.3	0.0	SUPERIOR FUNERAL & LIFE INS CO
9.0	11.6 (*)	33.4	7.1	46.0	0.0	11.8	0.0	0.0	0.0	0.0	0.0	SURENCY LIFE & HEALTH INS CO
1.1	11.9	19.6	0.0	46.1	13.3	18.3	0.0	0.0	0.7	2.1	0.0	SURETY LIFE & CASUALTY INS CO
0.0	15.3	0.0	0.0	45.2	0.0	0.0	0.0	0.0	15.7	39.1	0.0	SURETY LIFE INS CO
13.5	29.9	29.4	0.7	49.8	3.2	16.9	0.0	0.0	0.0	0.0	0.0	SWBC LIFE INS CO

● Bullets denote a more detailed analysis is available in Section II.
(*) Asset category percentages do not add up to 100%

INSURANCE COMPANY NAME	DOM. STATE	RATING	TOTAL ASSETS ($MIL)	CAPITAL & SURPLUS ($MIL)	RISK ADJUSTED CAPITAL RATIO 1	RISK ADJUSTED CAPITAL RATIO 2	CAPITAL-IZATION INDEX (PTS)	INVEST. SAFETY INDEX (PTS)	PROFIT-ABILITY INDEX (PTS)	LIQUIDITY INDEX (PTS)	STAB. INDEX (PTS)	STABILIT FACTOR
SWISS RE LIFE & HEALTH AMER INC	MO	C	15359.0	1569.5	1.83	1.15	7.2	6.6	1.7	5.8	3.8	G
SYMETRA LIFE INS CO	IA	B	37769.4	2158.0	1.76	0.94	6.5	5.2	5.6	6.2	6.3	IT
SYMETRA NATIONAL LIFE INS CO	IA	A-	18.6	11.1	3.48	3.13	10.0	8.7	7.1	9.2	6.5	ADG
T J M LIFE INS CO	TX	D+	17.2	1.7	0.63	0.57	3.6	3.6	3.3	3.7	2.7	CDIL
TALCOTT RESOLUTION INTL LIFE	CT	U (3)	--	--	--	--	--	--	--	--	--	Z
TALCOTT RESOLUTION LIFE	CT	B-	36933.6	969.3	2.15	1.07	7.1	6.2	5.1	9.5	4.3	FT
TALCOTT RESOLUTION LIFE INS CO	CT	C+	90215.7	3409.9	1.90	1.35	7.5	5.5	5.6	9.2	3.1	T
TEACHERS INS & ANNUITY ASN OF AM	NY	A+	302803.1	37328.4	3.83	2.24	8.9	6.5	8.1	7.0	7.9	I
TENNESSEE FARMERS LIFE INS CO	TN	B+	2318.6	465.9	2.58	1.66	8.0	5.7	4.2	6.2	6.6	AI
TEXAS DIRECTORS LIFE INS CO	TX	B (3)	5.5	1.1	0.74	0.66	4.3	6.7	8.0	6.3	4.4	CD
TEXAS LIFE INS CO	TX	B-	1204.2	86.2	1.69	0.91	6.3	3.8	3.0	5.9	4.7	AI
TEXAS REPUB LIFE INS CO	TX	D	7.2	3.7	2.89	2.60	9.4	8.3	1.5	9.3	1.4	DEG
TEXAS SERVICE LIFE INS CO	TX	C-	88.9	14.7	1.86	1.67	8.0	7.6	2.5	6.7	3.1	D
THE UNION LABOR LIFE INS CO	MD	B	3872.3	104.5	2.15	1.38	7.6	7.3	6.6	7.6	6.3	T
THRIVENT LIFE INS CO	WI	B	3939.4	167.2	1.88	0.93	6.4	4.5	3.0	4.7	5.5	CIL
TIAA-CREF LIFE INS CO	NY	B	13320.7	418.8	1.80	0.94	6.5	5.1	3.9	4.7	6.3	IL
TIER ONE INSURANCE CO	OK	U (3)	--	--	--	--	--	--	--	--	--	Z
TIME INS CO	WI	C+	62.3	36.7	5.19	3.24	10.0	6.1	3.0	1.4	3.0	AFLT
TOWN & COUNTRY LIFE INS CO	UT	C-	7.8	5.0	2.58	2.19	8.8	5.8	8.0	8.1	2.4	D
TPM LIFE INS CO	PA	B	18.9	5.0	1.51	1.13	7.2	6.9	1.8	8.8	4.7	ADGT
TRANS CITY LIFE INS CO	AZ	C-	19.4	9.2	3.28	2.95	9.9	7.5	2.7	9.6	2.9	D
TRANS OCEANIC LIFE INS CO	PR	A-	75.3	34.9	2.61	1.65	8.0	4.8	7.5	8.0	6.4	DI
TRANS WORLD ASR CO	CA	B+	344.9	86.3	2.49	1.90	8.4	6.0	6.8	6.5	6.7	ADI
TRANS-WESTERN LIFE INS CO	TX	U (3)	--	--	--	--	--	--	--	--	--	Z
TRANSAMERICA ADVISORS LIFE INS CO	AR	B-	7770.6	570.4	8.54	4.40	10.0	7.4	5.1	6.7	3.6	T
TRANSAMERICA FINANCIAL LIFE INS CO	NY	B	32230.0	1054.1	2.96	1.43	7.6	5.3	6.5	9.3	5.1	AI
TRANSAMERICA LIFE INS CO	IA	B	122998.5	5727.4	1.33	0.98	4.0	6.3	7.4	7.2	4.2	FIT
TRANSAMERICA PREMIER LIFE INS CO	IA	C+	50487.4	1821.9	1.59	0.91	6.3	5.4	3.6	6.4	3.3	GIT
TRINITY LIFE INS CO	OK	D-	230.9	12.5	0.63	0.44	2.3	2.3	6.8	2.3	1.3	CDGIL
TRIPLE S VIDA INC	PR	B-	650.2	60.7	1.12	0.73	5.2	4.1	6.5	3.9	5.2	ACIL
TRIPLE-S BLUE II	PR	D (2)	14.8	3.2	1.15	1.04	5.8	8.4	1.2	7.2	1.6	DFIT
TRUSTMARK INS CO	IL	B+	1606.0	342.6	2.83	1.60	7.9	4.8	6.9	6.9	6.8	I
TRUSTMARK LIFE INS CO	IL	B+	330.1	179.6	7.43	4.50	10.0	4.8	7.4	6.9	6.5	DIT
TRUSTMARK LIFE INS CO OF NEW YORK	NY	B	10.0	7.2	3.13	2.82	9.7	8.7	2.4	7.5	5.3	D
UBS LIFE INS CO USA	CA	U (3)	--	--	--	--	--	--	--	--	--	Z
UNICARE LIFE & HEALTH INS CO	IN	B-	282.8	79.7	1.89	1.43	5.9	3.8	6.2	4.5	5.2	DILT
UNIFIED LIFE INS CO	TX	B	210.9	26.7	2.15	1.30	7.5	4.6	6.8	5.1	6.3	FILT
UNIMERICA INS CO	WI	B	453.7	213.6	3.25	2.56	5.8	8.5	8.7	5.9	4.7	ADT
UNIMERICA LIFE INS CO OF NY	NY	B	41.0	22.8	4.62	4.16	10.0	8.6	6.8	9.1	5.7	AT
UNION FIDELITY LIFE INS CO	KS	E	20226.2	485.8	1.04	0.52	5.1	2.8	1.4	7.8	0.1	CFI
UNION NATIONAL LIFE INS CO	LA	B	21.0	16.7	5.06	2.53	8.0	9.0	9.0	10.0	5.5	A
UNION SECURITY INS CO	KS	B	2758.2	134.3	2.91	1.52	7.8	5.4	5.2	4.5	4.2	AFILT
UNION SECURITY LIFE INS CO OF NY	NY	C+	60.5	47.8	6.40	5.76	10.0	8.1	6.2	9.5	3.0	T
UNITED AMERICAN INS CO	NE	B-	731.5	94.8	0.98	0.74	4.9	6.2	6.6	5.6	4.4	CT
UNITED ASR LIFE INS CO	TX	D-	2.3	0.8	0.92	0.83	5.6	9.5	1.6	7.0	1.1	AD
UNITED BENEFIT LIFE INS CO	OH	U (3)	--	--	--	--	--	--	--	--	--	Z
UNITED FARM FAMILY LIFE INS CO	IN	A	2348.2	337.5	3.48	2.03	8.5	6.9	5.9	5.9	7.4	I
UNITED FIDELITY LIFE INS CO	TX	C	828.1	558.0	0.82	0.80	5.4	3.1	7.5	6.8	4.0	CDI
UNITED FUNERAL BENEFIT LIFE INS CO	OK	D	48.0	6.9	0.91	0.76	5.1	7.1	6.4	6.8	1.9	ACD
UNITED FUNERAL DIR BENEFIT LIC	TX	D	118.5	6.0	0.49	0.44	2.3	1.4	7.7	7.2	1.9	CDI
UNITED HEALTHCARE INS CO	CT	C	19448.9	6211.7	0.96	0.80	4.5	6.4	9.0	1.9	3.9	CL
UNITED HERITAGE LIFE INS CO	ID	B	597.7	65.9	2.38	1.15	7.2	4.0	7.7	4.7	5.7	IL

See Page 27 for explanation of footnotes and Page 28 for explanation of stability factors.
Arrows denote recent upgrades ▲ or downgrades▼ (see Section VI for explanations)

54

www.weissratings.com

NET PREMIUM ($MIL)	IN-VESTED ASSETS ($MIL)	% OF INVESTED ASSETS IN:									INVEST. IN AFFIL	INSURANCE COMPANY NAME
		CASH	CMO & STRUCT. SECS.	OTH.INV. GRADE BONDS	NON-INV. GRADE BONDS	CMMON & PREF. STOCK	MORT IN GOOD STAND.	NON-PERF. MORT.	REAL ESTATE	OTHER INVEST-MENTS		
5,106.8	12,312.0	-0.1	16.5	67.2	3.2	1.2	6.9	0.0	0.0	4.6	6.9 ●	SWISS RE LIFE & HEALTH AMER INC
-986.3	30,258.0 (*)	1.0	10.6	61.8	3.4	3.1	18.1	0.0	0.0	0.8	0.5 ●	SYMETRA LIFE INS CO
1.3	17.1	10.5	56.5	31.9	0.0	0.0	0.0	0.0	0.0	1.1	0.0	SYMETRA NATIONAL LIFE INS CO
0.8	16.6 (*)	3.3	9.3	66.8	1.5	0.0	0.0	0.0	12.5	3.4	0.0	T J M LIFE INS CO
--	--	--	--	--	--	--	--	--	--	--	--	TALCOTT RESOLUTION INTL LIFE
-1,648.4	5,224.9 (*)	7.5	20.2	50.7	2.2	1.5	8.9	0.0	0.0	3.4	0.3 ●	TALCOTT RESOLUTION LIFE
-5,367.0	19,014.8 (*)	0.7	16.1	46.2	3.4	7.3	9.1	0.0	0.4	13.0	6.3 ●	TALCOTT RESOLUTION LIFE INS CO
10,981.0	253,024.0	0.1	23.8	42.5	6.9	2.3	10.5	0.0	0.8	12.6	11.2 ●	TEACHERS INS & ANNUITY ASN OF AM
129.6	2,177.4	0.1	0.0	79.8	7.0	10.5	0.1	0.0	0.7	1.6	2.9 ●	TENNESSEE FARMERS LIFE INS CO
0.2	5.3 (*)	2.1	0.4	84.1	5.4	0.6	0.0	0.0	0.0	0.3	0.0	TEXAS DIRECTORS LIFE INS CO
192.6	1,132.6 (*)	1.6	35.8	51.6	3.1	1.2	0.0	0.0	0.2	5.4	0.0 ●	TEXAS LIFE INS CO
2.0	4.1 (*)	63.7	0.0	0.0	0.0	0.0	0.0	0.0	0.0	0.0	0.0	TEXAS REPUB LIFE INS CO
17.6	72.1 (*)	12.3	22.6	49.5	0.0	0.1	0.0	0.0	1.1	1.3	0.0	TEXAS SERVICE LIFE INS CO
113.6	308.8	0.0	25.7	54.7	0.8	6.4	3.3	0.0	0.0	9.1	3.5 ●	THE UNION LABOR LIFE INS CO
102.4	2,242.3	0.0	27.5	64.4	6.6	0.0	0.0	0.0	0.0	0.8	0.9 ●	THRIVENT LIFE INS CO
509.6	7,375.1	0.0	12.4	86.4	0.7	0.0	0.0	0.0	0.0	0.4	0.0 ●	TIAA-CREF LIFE INS CO
--	--	--	--	--	--	--	--	--	--	--	--	TIER ONE INSURANCE CO
0.4	56.7 (*)	1.3	31.0	43.5	1.1	2.0	0.0	0.0	17.2	0.3	0.0 ●	TIME INS CO
3.7	7.6	37.8	1.3	39.2	0.0	15.3	0.0	0.0	0.0	6.3	0.0	TOWN & COUNTRY LIFE INS CO
4.6	18.8 (*)	0.5	0.0	82.4	1.7	6.0	0.0	0.0	0.0	3.2	0.0	TPM LIFE INS CO
1.5	18.7 (*)	35.4	0.0	33.7	0.0	23.6	0.0	0.0	2.6	0.0	25.3	TRANS CITY LIFE INS CO
22.1	69.0	8.1	12.3	52.4	0.2	13.5	0.0	0.0	10.2	2.3	0.0 ●	TRANS OCEANIC LIFE INS CO
9.0	341.7	3.0	0.0	72.8	3.1	8.5	8.5	0.0	3.1	1.1	16.5 ●	TRANS WORLD ASR CO
--	--	--	--	--	--	--	--	--	--	--	--	TRANS-WESTERN LIFE INS CO
5.5	2,349.8 (*)	0.0	8.6	49.7	1.9	0.3	1.1	0.0	0.0	28.2	0.0 ●	TRANSAMERICA ADVISORS LIFE INS CO
4,294.2	8,728.7 (*)	0.4	13.7	50.2	5.0	0.1	15.5	0.0	0.0	5.0	3.8 ●	TRANSAMERICA FINANCIAL LIFE INS CO
8,535.5	41,556.0 (*)	0.2	10.1	50.4	4.7	7.4	10.1	0.0	0.5	5.5	8.8 ●	TRANSAMERICA LIFE INS CO
2,666.1	23,342.5 (*)	-0.1	10.1	60.5	4.6	0.6	9.4	0.0	1.0	7.3	3.3 ●	TRANSAMERICA PREMIER LIFE INS CO
14.0	200.9 (*)	7.5	0.1	58.3	4.8	4.5	20.0	1.0	1.0	1.2	4.4	TRINITY LIFE INS CO
136.0	578.7	1.7	0.1	79.2	0.0	17.4	0.0	0.0	0.0	1.6	0.7 ●	TRIPLE S VIDA INC
2.1	10.0	18.0	0.0	77.4	0.0	0.0	0.0	0.0	4.3	0.3	0.0	TRIPLE-S BLUE II
271.1	1,518.7 (*)	0.1	26.9	39.4	6.5	10.4	3.9	0.0	1.5	7.0	0.0 ●	TRUSTMARK INS CO
94.3	283.6	0.0	8.9	69.2	11.4	5.2	0.0	0.0	0.0	5.4	0.0 ●	TRUSTMARK LIFE INS CO
1.8	9.2 (*)	7.8	24.8	61.0	0.0	0.0	0.0	0.0	0.0	0.0	0.0	TRUSTMARK LIFE INS CO OF NEW YORK
--	--	--	--	--	--	--	--	--	--	--	--	UBS LIFE INS CO USA
255.2	237.3	0.0	0.5	85.9	13.3	0.3	0.0	0.0	0.0	0.0	0.0 ●	UNICARE LIFE & HEALTH INS CO
35.7	187.3 (*)	1.8	17.6	63.8	4.5	1.2	0.1	0.0	0.0	5.1	0.0 ●	UNIFIED LIFE INS CO
323.1	419.7 (*)	-0.6	15.2	82.5	0.0	0.0	0.0	0.0	0.0	0.0	0.0 ●	UNIMERICA INS CO
2.1	38.5 (*)	9.0	25.3	64.3	0.2	0.0	0.0	0.0	0.0	0.0	0.0	UNIMERICA LIFE INS CO OF NY
185.7	19,038.4	0.2	11.4	78.1	3.0	0.2	4.4	0.0	0.0	1.9	1.1 ●	UNION FIDELITY LIFE INS CO
0.0	22.1	0.0	0.0	97.9	0.0	0.0	0.0	0.0	0.0	2.1	0.0	UNION NATIONAL LIFE INS CO
2.9	1,004.0	0.2	8.5	66.2	4.5	6.6	7.9	0.0	0.0	5.7	0.0 ●	UNION SECURITY INS CO
0.6	54.2 (*)	1.9	21.8	71.0	1.7	0.2	0.0	0.0	0.0	0.0	0.0 ●	UNION SECURITY LIFE INS CO OF NY
364.6	613.3 (*)	-0.2	3.6	72.0	3.5	8.2	0.0	0.0	0.0	9.1	9.8 ●	UNITED AMERICAN INS CO
0.4	2.2	17.4	0.0	82.6	0.0	0.0	0.0	0.0	0.0	0.0	0.0	UNITED ASR LIFE INS CO
--	--	--	--	--	--	--	--	--	--	--	--	UNITED BENEFIT LIFE INS CO
100.9	2,253.1	0.5	8.9	66.8	0.0	2.9	14.9	0.0	0.2	6.0	1.6 ●	UNITED FARM FAMILY LIFE INS CO
4.6	795.3	0.0	6.5	6.2	0.4	81.9	1.2	0.0	0.3	3.7	78.6 ●	UNITED FIDELITY LIFE INS CO
1.2	47.3	6.8	60.1	16.9	0.7	14.7	0.0	0.0	0.0	0.7	12.6	UNITED FUNERAL BENEFIT LIFE INS CO
6.7	122.6	11.0	65.2	20.4	1.2	2.0	0.0	0.0	0.0	0.3	0.0	UNITED FUNERAL DIR BENEFIT LIC
40,911.5	13,797.3 (*)	-0.6	15.1	52.9	4.2	18.6	0.0	0.0	2.1	1.7	15.5 ●	UNITED HEALTHCARE INS CO
59.3	561.9	0.1	7.2	75.5	8.9	3.4	1.3	0.0	2.0	1.5	0.0 ●	UNITED HERITAGE LIFE INS CO

● Bullets denote a more detailed analysis is available in Section II.

(*) Asset category percentages do not add up to 100%

INSURANCE COMPANY NAME	DOM. STATE	RATING	TOTAL ASSETS ($MIL)	CAPITAL & SURPLUS ($MIL)	RISK ADJUSTED CAPITAL RATIO 1	RISK ADJUSTED CAPITAL RATIO 2	CAPITAL-IZATION INDEX (PTS)	INVEST. SAFETY INDEX (PTS)	PROFIT-ABILITY INDEX (PTS)	LIQUIDITY INDEX (PTS)	STAB. INDEX (PTS)	STABILIT FACTOR
UNITED HOME LIFE INS CO	IN	B	96.4	19.0	2.30	2.07	8.6	7.5	3.2	6.3	5.6	D
UNITED INS CO OF AMERICA	IL	B-	3905.4	453.9	1.93	1.14	7.2	5.1	6.5	5.0	5.3	AI
UNITED LIFE INS CO	IA	B	1549.3	143.4	2.66	1.38	7.6	5.9	4.2	5.5	5.9	FI
UNITED NATIONAL LIFE INS CO OF AM	IL	B	32.5	8.4	1.45	1.07	7.1	8.0	6.6	7.8	5.4	AC
UNITED OF OMAHA LIFE INS CO	NE	B	23546.4	1600.8	1.98	1.13	7.2	5.1	7.2	6.0	6.0	I
UNITED SECURITY ASR CO OF PA	PA	E+	26.4	11.1	2.81	2.02	8.5	8.7	1.5	7.0	0.7	T
UNITED STATES LIFE INS CO IN NYC	NY	B	28771.0	1902.2	2.69	1.28	7.4	5.1	6.4	5.7	4.7	AIT
UNITED WORLD LIFE INS CO	NE	B+	119.5	46.4	4.36	1.84	8.3	7.6	5.3	6.7	6.5	AF
UNITEDHEALTHCARE LIFE INS CO	WI	C	244.3	155.9	2.70	2.13	8.7	8.0	1.9	6.6	2.5	DFT
UNITY FINANCIAL LIFE INS CO	OH	C-	295.8	15.6	1.60	1.01	7.0	4.7	2.9	6.8	3.2	D
UNIVANTAGE INS CO	UT	U (3)	--	--	--	--	--	--	--	--	--	Z
UNIVERSAL FIDELITY LIFE INS CO	OK	D	15.5	5.3	1.73	1.23	7.3	6.5	2.9	6.0	1.8	T
UNIVERSAL GUARANTY LIFE INS CO	OH	C+	363.9	70.0	1.96	1.14	7.2	3.0	5.6	5.0	4.8	DFI
UNIVERSAL LIFE INS CO	PR	B+	1569.7	111.6	2.73	1.44	7.7	6.6	9.0	9.2	6.7	I
UNUM INS CO	ME	C	63.9	47.0	7.05	4.55	8.0	5.7	2.1	10.0	3.8	A
UNUM LIFE INS CO OF AMERICA	ME	C+	21839.2	1762.4	2.34	1.24	7.4	3.8	8.0	7.2	4.8	AI
▲ US ALLIANCE LIFE & SECURITY CO	KS	D	28.0	4.3	0.91	0.56	4.3	2.8	2.8	6.0	2.1	CGIT
US FINANCIAL LIFE INS CO	OH	B	543.6	74.6	3.15	1.71	8.1	7.5	3.7	5.1	5.8	DFLT
USA INS CO	MS	C-	3.9	3.1	2.66	2.40	9.1	4.0	8.9	7.0	2.1	DI
USA LIFE ONE INS CO OF INDIANA	IN	D+	33.8	13.8	2.73	2.46	9.2	7.4	2.9	6.7	2.5	DFT
USAA LIFE INS CO	TX	A	25292.8	2562.4	3.89	2.10	8.7	6.7	8.8	5.5	7.4	AI
USAA LIFE INS CO OF NEW YORK	NY	B+	780.2	84.5	2.68	1.41	7.6	5.9	8.4	4.9	6.6	AIL
USABLE LIFE	AR	A-	541.5	267.6	2.64	1.98	8.5	7.1	8.5	6.6	7.3	
USIC LIFE INS CO	PR	C+	10.8	8.3	2.09	1.51	7.8	6.5	7.0	8.2	4.4	AI
UTIC INS CO	AL	B+	102.4	24.0	2.62	1.65	8.0	5.1	8.3	7.4	6.0	AI
VANTIS LIFE INS CO	CT	C+	482.0	68.6	1.89	1.29	7.4	5.7	1.4	6.5	4.2	DGT
VANTISLIFE INS CO OF NEW YORK	NY	B	168.4	21.5	2.32	1.94	8.4	5.9	3.0	8.3	4.2	ADGIT
VARIABLE ANNUITY LIFE INS CO	TX	B	83441.4	2914.9	2.51	1.18	7.3	4.8	6.7	5.4	5.8	AIL
VERSANT LIFE INS CO	MS	B-	6.5	5.2	2.90	2.61	9.4	8.6	8.6	9.3	4.4	ADT
VOYA INS & ANNUITY CO	IA	B-	53491.6	2164.9	1.79	0.92	6.4	5.2	3.5	6.9	3.7	IT
VOYA RETIREMENT INS & ANNUITY CO	CT	B+	108678.3	1950.3	2.08	1.00	7.0	4.9	5.2	9.1	6.5	I
WASHINGTON NATIONAL INS CO	IN	D+	5465.1	361.4	1.62	0.91	6.3	4.7	5.6	6.5	2.7	AI
WEA INS CORP	WI	C	684.6	184.4	1.80	1.26	7.4	4.3	2.3	6.2	3.7	DFI
WEST COAST LIFE INS CO	NE	B-	5319.9	351.3	2.13	1.03	4.0	4.6	4.2	5.6	4.9	AI
WESTERN & SOUTHERN LIFE INS CO	OH	B	10735.7	5319.9	2.09	1.75	8.1	3.4	8.0	7.1	5.7	AI
▲ WESTERN AMERICAN LIFE INS CO	TX	D+	26.7	2.0	0.49	0.44	2.3	5.5	4.2	3.4	2.3	ACDL
WESTERN UNITED LIFE ASR CO	WA	B-	1217.0	80.0	1.64	0.79	6.0	3.5	8.7	3.4	5.0	CIL
WESTERN-SOUTHERN LIFE ASR CO	OH	B	12464.1	1010.8	1.99	1.09	7.1	5.2	6.5	6.0	4.6	AGIT
WICHITA NATIONAL LIFE INS CO	OK	C-	15.7	7.3	2.37	2.14	8.7	8.8	3.0	9.4	3.3	DF
WILCAC LIFE INS CO	IL	C	2279.6	121.3	4.85	2.22	4.0	6.2	5.9	9.3	2.6	AFT
WILCO LIFE INS CO	IN	C	2811.9	153.5	1.54	0.80	5.8	3.8	5.5	4.2	4.2	AFILT
WILLIAM PENN LIFE INS CO OF NEW YORK	NY	C	1190.2	89.1	1.98	0.94	6.5	4.0	1.7	6.4	3.6	IT
WILLIAMS PROGRESSIVE LIFE & ACC I C	LA	E	11.1	0.4	0.18	0.12	0.0	0.7	1.6	0.5	0.0	CDILT
WILTON REASSURANCE CO	MN	C	19124.8	1184.8	1.26	0.81	5.5	5.6	5.9	6.6	3.4	CGIT
WILTON REASSURANCE LIFE CO OF NY	NY	C+	879.3	98.2	2.63	1.32	7.5	5.7	4.3	5.2	4.7	AF
WINDSOR LIFE INS CO	TX	B-	3.2	3.0	2.86	2.57	9.4	7.8	4.3	10.0	3.8	ADG
ZURICH AMERICAN LIFE INS CO	IL	C	14241.3	110.9	1.56	0.89	6.1	7.9	1.6	9.5	2.7	T
ZURICH AMERICAN LIFE INS CO OF NY	NY	B-	78.2	21.6	2.80	2.52	9.3	9.6	4.1	9.2	3.6	AGT

See Page 27 for explanation of footnotes and Page 28 for explanation of stability factors.

Arrows denote recent upgrades ▲ or downgrades▼ (see Section VI for explanations)

56

www.weissratings.com

NET PREMIUM ($MIL)	IN-VESTED ASSETS ($MIL)	CASH	CMO & STRUCT. SECS.	OTH.INV. GRADE BONDS	NON-INV. GRADE BONDS	CMMON & PREF. STOCK	MORT IN GOOD STAND.	NON-PERF. MORT.	REAL ESTATE	OTHER INVEST-MENTS	INVEST. IN AFFIL	INSURANCE COMPANY NAME
16.7	74.1	2.0	11.2	79.7	0.0	2.8	0.0	0.0	0.0	4.4	0.0	UNITED HOME LIFE INS CO
274.8	3,567.8	0.0	8.4	62.5	9.6	3.5	0.0	0.0	3.3	12.3	2.8 ●	UNITED INS CO OF AMERICA
122.9	1,477.5	0.4	22.8	70.2	2.6	1.6	0.2	0.0	0.0	1.5	0.0 ●	UNITED LIFE INS CO
14.0	26.8 (*)	2.9	31.9	53.7	0.5	0.0	7.7	0.0	0.0	0.4	0.0	UNITED NATIONAL LIFE INS CO OF AM
3,165.1	18,126.6 (*)	-0.1	20.9	57.9	4.0	1.6	11.7	0.0	0.3	2.0	1.8 ●	UNITED OF OMAHA LIFE INS CO
6.0	21.8 (*)	4.5	4.1	82.7	0.0	0.0	0.0	0.0	0.0	0.3	0.0	UNITED SECURITY ASR CO OF PA
-4,021.0	23,299.3	0.1	27.2	48.3	5.4	0.1	12.1	0.0	0.0	5.8	1.1 ●	UNITED STATES LIFE INS CO IN NYC
0.8	120.0 (*)	4.6	26.8	64.9	0.9	0.0	0.0	0.0	0.0	0.6	0.0 ●	UNITED WORLD LIFE INS CO
354.0	201.0	0.0	40.8	58.7	0.0	0.0	0.0	0.0	0.0	0.0	0.0 ●	UNITEDHEALTHCARE LIFE INS CO
33.4	260.9 (*)	0.3	11.1	86.5	0.0	0.3	0.0	0.0	0.0	0.1	0.0	UNITY FINANCIAL LIFE INS CO
--	--	--	--	--	--	--	--	--	--	--	--	UNIVANTAGE INS CO
8.9	9.4 (*)	36.4	1.2	18.9	0.0	23.7	0.0	0.0	11.0	1.0	0.7	UNIVERSAL FIDELITY LIFE INS CO
4.1	338.9 (*)	2.5	0.0	44.0	3.2	15.9	4.5	0.6	5.8	18.7	4.9 ●	UNIVERSAL GUARANTY LIFE INS CO
86.5	719.7 (*)	1.6	19.3	70.7	1.1	2.9	0.0	0.0	0.0	1.5	0.0 ●	UNIVERSAL LIFE INS CO
3.3	56.5	0.5	14.8	82.3	0.0	0.0	0.0	0.0	0.0	2.5	0.0 ●	UNUM INS CO
2,709.5	20,370.9	0.0	6.8	72.8	11.5	0.3	5.4	0.0	0.3	2.9	0.1 ●	UNUM LIFE INS CO OF AMERICA
8.2	23.5	1.0	12.3	52.1	17.3	17.2	0.0	0.0	0.0	0.1	5.7	US ALLIANCE LIFE & SECURITY CO
24.3	467.3	0.0	0.2	93.3	0.9	0.9	0.0	0.0	0.0	4.7	0.0 ●	US FINANCIAL LIFE INS CO
0.3	2.8	0.1	0.0	0.0	0.0	17.1	52.9	0.0	27.8	2.1	5.1	USA INS CO
0.4	34.5	3.3	0.3	90.5	4.0	0.0	0.0	0.0	0.0	1.6	0.0	USA LIFE ONE INS CO OF INDIANA
1,300.0	24,187.2	-0.1	15.5	73.5	4.5	1.1	4.0	0.0	0.0	1.2	0.6 ●	USAA LIFE INS CO
26.0	739.4 (*)	0.5	14.6	77.2	4.8	0.7	0.0	0.0	0.0	0.9	0.0 ●	USAA LIFE INS CO OF NEW YORK
459.9	482.4	2.9	13.8	74.4	0.2	5.3	1.5	0.0	0.1	1.6	0.0 ●	USABLE LIFE
3.5	10.1	21.7	0.0	64.5	3.9	9.9	0.0	0.0	0.0	0.0	0.0	USIC LIFE INS CO
14.4	87.8 (*)	4.4	5.5	65.6	0.0	13.8	0.0	0.0	0.0	5.8	0.0	UTIC INS CO
66.8	349.7 (*)	0.8	16.1	69.9	1.6	7.1	0.0	0.0	1.6	1.8	6.1 ●	VANTIS LIFE INS CO
19.7	133.1 (*)	0.8	27.3	64.4	0.8	0.5	0.0	0.0	0.0	0.1	0.0	VANTISLIFE INS CO OF NEW YORK
3,546.6	44,278.4	0.2	36.9	38.7	4.8	0.3	13.2	0.0	0.1	4.9	7.2 ●	VARIABLE ANNUITY LIFE INS CO
0.4	6.2 (*)	6.9	0.0	86.6	0.0	0.0	0.0	0.0	0.0	0.0	0.0	VERSANT LIFE INS CO
-14,615.3	28,117.3 (*)	1.1	11.4	62.2	3.3	0.5	15.2	0.0	0.1	1.4	0.5 ●	VOYA INS & ANNUITY CO
8,719.0	30,188.3 (*)	0.6	14.6	56.6	4.1	0.5	16.3	0.0	0.2	3.6	1.8 ●	VOYA RETIREMENT INS & ANNUITY CO
527.1	5,273.8	1.2	20.6	61.3	3.7	2.8	4.9	0.1	1.0	4.3	1.3 ●	WASHINGTON NATIONAL INS CO
458.1	652.8 (*)	1.6	21.7	48.0	0.1	24.0	0.0	0.0	0.0	0.2	0.0 ●	WEA INS CORP
-12.9	4,758.0	0.1	4.4	72.9	5.8	3.1	12.0	0.0	0.0	0.9	0.0 ●	WEST COAST LIFE INS CO
173.5	9,339.1	0.1	6.2	31.1	3.0	38.8	0.5	0.0	0.3	19.8	38.1 ●	WESTERN & SOUTHERN LIFE INS CO
1.7	26.5	0.0	60.1	37.6	0.7	0.1	0.0	0.0	0.0	1.6	0.0	WESTERN AMERICAN LIFE INS CO
113.8	1,186.3 (*)	-0.1	20.8	69.3	4.1	0.8	1.5	0.0	1.3	0.1	0.0 ●	WESTERN UNITED LIFE ASR CO
493.1	11,606.5	0.5	29.0	50.5	6.6	3.2	7.6	0.0	0.0	2.5	2.6 ●	WESTERN-SOUTHERN LIFE ASR CO
2.4	15.9	78.5	1.4	0.3	0.0	12.9	0.0	0.0	1.2	5.7	12.9	WICHITA NATIONAL LIFE INS CO
0.1	1,930.6	0.4	22.5	70.3	2.1	2.7	0.0	0.0	0.0	1.1	0.0 ●	WILCAC LIFE INS CO
78.4	2,824.6 (*)	0.6	25.6	56.5	4.9	3.0	1.2	0.0	0.0	6.7	0.0 ●	WILCO LIFE INS CO
21.4	1,142.4	0.0	7.1	53.1	11.9	0.0	19.8	0.0	0.0	8.2	0.0 ●	WILLIAM PENN LIFE INS CO OF NEW YORK
0.9	11.0 (*)	2.3	3.5	18.5	1.8	31.0	30.3	3.8	2.1	4.3	0.9	WILLIAMS PROGRESSIVE LIFE & ACC I C
3,857.3	14,376.0	0.1	12.1	71.8	1.2	3.6	7.9	0.0	0.0	2.4	3.2 ●	WILTON REASSURANCE CO
9.6	864.3 (*)	1.4	37.7	53.3	2.2	1.3	0.0	0.0	0.0	2.8	0.0 ●	WILTON REASSURANCE LIFE CO OF NY
0.1	3.0	5.9	0.0	90.7	3.4	0.0	0.0	0.0	0.0	0.0	0.0	WINDSOR LIFE INS CO
-122.2	710.3 (*)	0.2	26.5	52.0	0.7	3.1	0.0	0.0	0.0	9.1	3.1 ●	ZURICH AMERICAN LIFE INS CO
5.1	25.1 (*)	1.9	0.0	86.7	0.0	0.0	0.0	0.0	0.0	0.1	0.0	ZURICH AMERICAN LIFE INS CO OF NY

● Bullets denote a more detailed analysis is available in Section II.
(*) Asset category percentages do not add up to 100%

Section II

Analysis of Largest Companies

A summary analysis of those

U.S. Life and Annuity Insurers

with capital in excess of $25 million.

Companies are listed in alphabetical order.

Section II Contents

This section contains rating factors, historical data and general information on each of the largest life and health insurers. Companies with capital and surplus of less than $25 million, Blue Cross Blue Shield plans and companies lacking year-end data do not appear in this section. You can find information on these firms in Section I.

1.	**Safety Rating**	The current rating appears to the right of the company name. Our ratings are designed to distinguish levels of insolvency risk and are measured on a scale from A (Excellent) to F (Failed). Highly rated companies are, in our opinion, less likely to experience financial difficulties than lower rated firms. See *About Weiss Safety Ratings* for more information.
2.	**Major Rating Factors**	A synopsis of the key indexes and sub-factors that have most influenced the rating of a particular insurer. Items are presented in the approximate order of their importance to the rating. There may be additional factors which have influenced the rating but do not appear due to space limitations or confidentiality agreements with insurers.
3.	**Other Rating Factors**	A summary of those Weiss Ratings indexes that were not included as Major Rating Factors, but nevertheless, may have had some impact on the final grade.
4.	**Principal Business**	The major types of policies written by an insurer along with the percentages for each line in relation to the entire book of business, including direct premium and deposit funds (from Exhibit 1 Part 1 of the annual statutory statement). Lines of business written by life, health and annuity insurers are individual life, individual health, individual annuities, group life, group health, group retirement contracts, credit life, credit health and reinsurance. The data used to calculate these amounts are the latest available from the National Association of Insurance Commissioners. Note: Percentages contained in this column may not agree with similar figures displayed in Section III which are based on net premium after reinsurance.
5.	**Principal Investments**	The major investments in an insurer's portfolio. These include non CMO Bonds (debt obligations which are rated Class 1 through Class 6 based on risk of default), CMOs and other structured securities, which consist primarily of mortgage-backed bonds, real estate, mortgages in good standing, nonperforming mortgages, common and preferred stocks, policy loans (which are loans given to policyholders), miscellaneous investments and cash.

6. Investments in Affiliates

The percentage of bonds, common and preferred stocks and other financial instruments an insurer has invested with affiliated companies. This is not a subcategory of "Principal Investments."

7. Group Affiliation

The name of the group of companies to which a particular insurer belongs.

8. Licensed in

List of the states in which an insurer is licensed to conduct business.

9. Commenced Business

The date when the company first opened for business.

10. Address

The address of an insurer's corporate headquarters. This location may differ from the company's state of domicile.

11. Phone

The telephone number of an insurer's corporate headquarters.

12. Domicile State

The state that has primary regulatory responsibility for this company. You do not have to live in the domicile state to do business with this firm, provided it is registered to do business in your state.

13. NAIC Code

The identification number assigned to an insurer by the National Association of Insurance Commissioners (NAIC).

14. Historical Data

Five years of background data for Weiss Safety Rating, risk-adjusted capital ratios (moderate and severe loss scenarios), total assets, capital (including capital stock and retained earnings), net premium and net income. See the following page for more details on how to read the historical data table.

15. Customized Graph (or Table)

A graph or table depicting one of the company's major strengths or weaknesses. See the following page for more details.

How to Read the Historical Data Table

| Data Date: The quarterly or annual date of the financial statements that provide the source of the data. | RACR#1: Ratio of the capital resources an insurer currently has to the resources that would be needed to deal with a modest loss scenario. | Total Assets: Total admitted assets in millions of dollars, including investments and other business assets. | Net Premiums: The total volume of premium dollars, in millions, retained by an insurer. This figure is equal to direct premiums written plus deposit funds, and reinsurance assumed, less reinsurance ceded. |

Data Date	Safety Rating	RACR #1	RACR #2	Total Assets ($mil)	Capital ($mil)	Net Premium ($mil)	Net Income ($mil)
9-18	B	6.56	4.32	190.1	84.8	53.4	3.5
9-17	B	5.46	3.55	217.2	86.6	59.0	3.5
2017	B	5.81	3.81	212.5	85.0	76.8	5.1
2016	B	5.21	3.36	207.5	82.6	72.9	0.6
2015	A	5.63	3.67	200.0	93.1	86.9	5.5
2014	A	3.89	2.72	198.5	92.3	151.8	7.3
2013	A	3.92	2.79	186.9	89.9	148.4	6.4

| Safety Rating: Our opinion of the financial risk of an insurer based on data from that time period. | RACR #2: Ratio of the capital resources an insurer currently has to the resources that would be needed to deal with a severe loss scenario. | Capital: The equity or net worth of an insurer in millions of dollars. | Net Income: Profit gained on operations and investments, after expenses and taxes. |

Row Descriptions:

Row 1 contains the most recent quarterly data as filed with state regulators and is presented on a year-to-date basis. For example, the figure for third quarter premiums includes premiums received through the third quarter. Row 2 consists of data from the same quarter of the prior year. Compare current quarterly results to those of a year ago.

Row 3 contains data from the most recent annual statutory filing. **Rows 4-7** include data from year-end statements going back four years from the most recent annual filing. Compare current year-end results to those of the previous four years. With the exception of Total Assets and Capital, quarterly data are not comparable with annual data.

Customized Graphs

In the lower right-hand corner of each company section, a customized graph or text block highlights a key factor affecting that company's financial strength. One of thirteen types of information is found, identified by one of the following headings:

Adverse Trends in Operations lists changes in key balance sheet and income statement items which may be leading indicators of deteriorating business performance.

Exposure to Withdrawals Without Penalty answers the question: For each dollar of capital and surplus, how much does the company have in annuity and deposit funds that can be withdrawn by policyholders with minimal or no penalty? The figures do not include the effects of reinsurance or funds subject to withdrawals from cash value life insurance policies.

Group Ratings shows the group name, a composite Weiss Safety Rating for the group, and a list of the largest members with their ratings. The composite Safety Rating is made up of the weighted average, by assets, of the individual ratings of each company in the group (including life/health companies, property/casualty companies or HMOs) plus a factor for the financial strength of the holding company, where applicable.

High Risk Assets as a % of Capital answers the question: For each dollar of capital and surplus, how much does the company have in junk bonds, nonperforming mortgages and repossessed real estate? Accumulations in the Asset Valuation Reserve or AVR, which provide some protection against investment losses, have not been included in the figure for capital. These figures are based on year-end data.

Investment Income Compared to Needs of Reserves answers the question: Is the company earning enough investment income to meet the expectations of actuaries when they priced their policies and set reserve levels? According to state insurance regulators, it would be "unusual" if an insurer were to have less than $1.25 in actual investment income for each dollar of investment income that it projected in its actuarial forecasts. This provides an excess margin of at least 25 cents on the dollar to cover any unexpected decline in income or increase in claims. This graph shows whether or not the company is maintaining the appropriate 25% margin and is based on year-end data.

Junk Bonds as a % of Capital answers the question: For each dollar of capital and surplus, how much does the company have in junk bonds? In addition, it shows a breakdown of the junk bond portfolio by bond rating – BB, B, CCC or in default. Accumulations in the Asset Valuation Reserve or AVR, which provide some protection against investment losses, have not been included in the figure for capital. These figures are based on year-end data.

Net Income History plots operating gains and losses over the most recent five-year period.

Policy Leverage answers the question: To what degree is this insurer capable of handling an unexpected spike in claims? Low leverage indicates low exposure; high leverage is high exposure.

Premium Growth History depicts the change in the insurer's net premiums written. Such changes may be the result of issuing more policies or changes in reinsurance arrangements. In either case, growth rates above 20% per year are considered excessive. "Standard" growth is under 20%; "shrinkage" refers to net declines.

Rating Indexes illustrate the score and range – strong, good, fair or weak – on each of the five Weiss Ratings indexes. The indexes are **capitalization**, **stability**, **investment safety**, **profitability** and **liquidity**.

Risk-Adjusted Capital Ratio #1 answers the question: In each of the past five years, does the insurer have sufficient capital to cover potential losses in its investments and business operations in a *moderate* loss scenario?

Risk-Adjusted Capital Ratio #2 answers the question: In each of the past five years, does the insurer have sufficient capital to cover potential losses in its investments and business operations in a *severe* loss scenario?

Risk-Adjusted Capital Ratios answers these questions for both a moderate loss scenario (RACR #1 shown by the dark bar) and a severe loss scenario (RACR #2, light bar).

4 EVER LIFE INSURANCE COMPANY

B　**Good**

Major Rating Factors: Good overall results on stability tests (5.0 on a scale of 0 to 10). Stability strengths include good operational trends and excellent risk diversification. Good quality investment portfolio (6.6) despite mixed results such as: no exposure to mortgages and substantial holdings of BBB bonds but minimal holdings in junk bonds. Good profitability (5.0).

Other Rating Factors: Good liquidity (6.8). Strong capitalization (10.0) based on excellent risk adjusted capital (severe loss scenario).

Principal Business: Group health insurance (67%), reinsurance (31%), and group life insurance (2%).

Principal Investments: NonCMO investment grade bonds (46%), CMOs and structured securities (24%), cash (11%), common & preferred stock (6%), and noninv. grade bonds (4%).

Investments in Affiliates: None

Group Affiliation: BCS Financial Corp

Licensed in: All states, the District of Columbia and Puerto Rico

Commenced Business: November 1949

Address: 2 Mid America Plaza Suite 200, Oakbrook Terrace, IL 60181

Phone: (630) 472-7700 **Domicile State:** IL **NAIC Code:** 80985

Data Date	Rating	RACR #1	RACR #2	Total Assets ($mil)	Capital ($mil)	Net Premium ($mil)	Net Income ($mil)
9-18	B	6.56	4.32	190.1	84.8	53.4	3.5
9-17	B	5.46	3.55	217.2	86.6	59.0	3.5
2017	B	5.81	3.83	212.5	85.0	76.8	5.1
2016	B	5.21	3.36	207.5	82.6	72.9	0.6
2015	A	5.63	3.67	200.0	93.1	86.9	5.5
2014	A	3.89	2.72	198.5	92.3	151.8	7.3
2013	A	3.92	2.79	186.9	89.9	148.4	6.4

Adverse Trends in Operations

Increase in policy surrenders from 2016 to 2017 (37%)
Decrease in premium volume from 2015 to 2016 (16%)
Decrease in capital during 2016 (11%)
Decrease in premium volume from 2014 to 2015 (43%)

AAA LIFE INSURANCE COMPANY

B　**Good**

Major Rating Factors: Good quality investment portfolio (6.4 on a scale of 0 to 10) despite mixed results such as: large holdings of BBB rated bonds but moderate junk bond exposure. Good overall profitability (6.7). Excellent expense controls. Good liquidity (6.5) with sufficient resources to handle a spike in claims as well as a significant increase in policy surrenders.

Other Rating Factors: Good overall results on stability tests (6.1) excellent operational trends and excellent risk diversification. Strong capitalization (8.3) based on excellent risk adjusted capital (severe loss scenario).

Principal Business: Individual life insurance (51%), group life insurance (26%), individual annuities (14%), group health insurance (8%), and individual health insurance (1%).

Principal Investments: NonCMO investment grade bonds (67%), CMOs and structured securities (18%), noninv. grade bonds (9%), common & preferred stock (2%), and misc. investments (2%).

Investments in Affiliates: 1%

Group Affiliation: ACLI Acquisition Co

Licensed in: All states except NY, PR

Commenced Business: July 1969

Address: 17900 N Laurel Park Drive, Livonia, MI 48152

Phone: (800) 684-4222 **Domicile State:** MI **NAIC Code:** 71854

Data Date	Rating	RACR #1	RACR #2	Total Assets ($mil)	Capital ($mil)	Net Premium ($mil)	Net Income ($mil)
9-18	B	3.30	1.88	677.0	170.5	90.3	13.3
9-17	B	3.15	1.82	652.5	157.6	86.8	7.9
2017	B	3.08	1.77	652.0	155.4	116.1	12.7
2016	B	3.09	1.80	629.2	152.7	114.6	13.1
2015	B	2.91	1.73	614.9	137.0	114.8	17.1
2014	B	2.68	1.61	575.1	122.7	112.2	15.6
2013	B	2.27	1.39	539.2	104.1	119.4	7.2

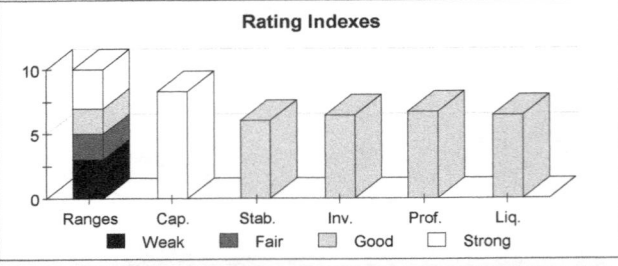

Rating Indexes

ACCORDIA LIFE & ANNUITY COMPANY

C　**Fair**

Major Rating Factors: Fair profitability (3.4 on a scale of 0 to 10). Fair overall results on stability tests (4.4) including weak risk adjusted capital in prior years. Good current capitalization (5.3) based on good risk adjusted capital (severe loss scenario) reflecting significant improvement over results in 2013.

Other Rating Factors: Good quality investment portfolio (5.1). Good liquidity (6.0).

Principal Business: Individual life insurance (81%) and reinsurance (19%).

Principal Investments: NonCMO investment grade bonds (46%), CMOs and structured securities (23%), mortgages in good standing (10%), common & preferred stock (6%), and misc. investments (11%).

Investments in Affiliates: 7%

Group Affiliation: Global Atlantic Financial Group

Licensed in: All states except NY, PR

Commenced Business: September 1967

Address: 215 10TH STREET SUITE 1100, DES MOINES, IA 50309

Phone: (855) 887-4487 **Domicile State:** IA **NAIC Code:** 62200

Data Date	Rating	RACR #1	RACR #2	Total Assets ($mil)	Capital ($mil)	Net Premium ($mil)	Net Income ($mil)
9-18	C	1.16	0.79	9,246.6	702.8	224.6	0.8
9-17	C	1.20	0.80	8,617.5	641.4	273.5	-48.7
2017	C	1.18	0.81	8,916.2	684.9	380.8	-114.3
2016	C	1.30	0.87	8,041.0	665.7	423.4	-89.2
2015	C	1.16	0.80	7,674.9	612.0	-468.0	48.1
2014	C-	1.08	0.74	7,754.8	496.7	438.6	97.4
2013	D	0.64	0.48	7,059.0	382.2	4,725.1	-112.1

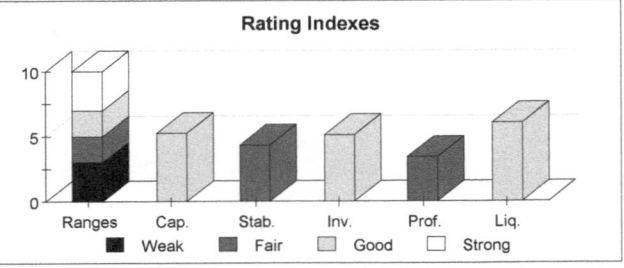

Rating Indexes

ADVANCE INSURANCE COMPANY OF KANSAS *   B+   Good

Major Rating Factors: Good overall results on stability tests (6.8 on a scale of 0 to 10). Stability strengths include excellent operational trends and excellent risk diversification. Fair quality investment portfolio (4.4). Strong capitalization (9.3) based on excellent risk adjusted capital (severe loss scenario). Moreover, capital levels have been consistently high over the last five years.

Other Rating Factors: Excellent profitability (8.4) with operating gains in each of the last five years. Excellent liquidity (7.0).

Principal Business: Group life insurance (54%), group health insurance (34%), and individual life insurance (12%).

Principal Investments: Common & preferred stock (32%), nonCMO investment grade bonds (32%), and CMOs and structured securities (32%).

Investments in Affiliates: 2%

Group Affiliation: Blue Cross Blue Shield Kansas

Licensed in: KS

Commenced Business: July 2004

Address: 1133 SW Topeka Blvd, Topeka, KS 66629-0001

Phone: (785) 273-9804 **Domicile State:** KS **NAIC Code:** 12143

Data Date	Rating	RACR #1	RACR #2	Total Assets ($mil)	Capital ($mil)	Net Premium ($mil)	Net Income ($mil)
9-18	B+	3.90	2.54	61.6	50.9	8.2	1.5
9-17	B+	3.89	2.56	58.6	48.5	8.2	2.2
2017	B+	3.95	2.59	59.7	49.7	10.9	2.7
2016	B+	4.01	2.67	56.0	46.8	10.8	1.3
2015	B+	3.91	2.59	54.0	45.3	10.6	2.2
2014	B+	3.64	2.40	53.5	44.0	9.9	2.9
2013	B+	3.51	2.32	51.4	41.5	9.6	1.6

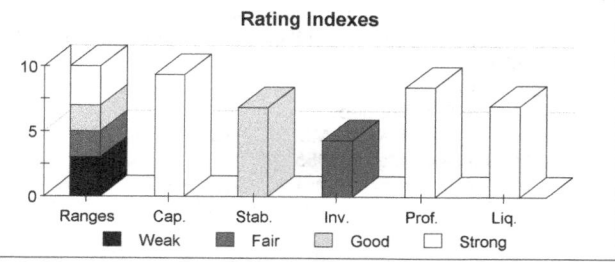

Rating Indexes

AETNA HEALTH & LIFE INSURANCE COMPANY   C   Fair

Major Rating Factors: Fair overall capitalization (4.0 on a scale of 0 to 10) based on mixed results -- excessive policy leverage mitigated by excellent risk adjusted capital (severe loss scenario). Nevertheless, capital levels have fluctuated during prior years. Fair quality investment portfolio (4.6). Good overall profitability (5.8) despite operating losses during the first nine months of 2018.

Other Rating Factors: Weak liquidity (0.0). Weak overall results on stability tests (2.9) including weak results on operational trends, negative cash flow from operations for 2017.

Principal Business: N/A

Principal Investments: NonCMO investment grade bonds (23%), CMOs and structured securities (14%), and noninv. grade bonds (4%).

Investments in Affiliates: 28%

Group Affiliation: Aetna Inc

Licensed in: All states except PR

Commenced Business: October 1971

Address: 151 FARMINGTON AVENUE, HARTFORD, CT 6156

Phone: (860) 273-0123 **Domicile State:** CT **NAIC Code:** 78700

Data Date	Rating	RACR #1	RACR #2	Total Assets ($mil)	Capital ($mil)	Net Premium ($mil)	Net Income ($mil)
9-18	C	9.72	5.45	175.2	106.0	270.6	-10.5
9-17	B+	1.88	1.17	2,403.1	262.1	671.5	12.2
2017	C+	5.60	3.55	388.4	307.3	-1,183.1	418.9
2016	B+	2.14	1.33	2,388.6	282.5	804.5	9.5
2015	B+	2.59	1.58	2,290.6	299.9	655.8	76.8
2014	B+	3.11	1.86	2,254.6	319.7	568.8	85.2
2013	B+	3.04	1.80	2,148.2	280.6	501.0	71.2

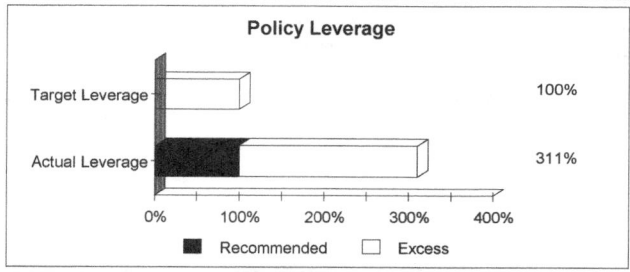

Policy Leverage

AETNA LIFE INSURANCE COMPANY   B   Good

Major Rating Factors: Good current capitalization (5.2 on a scale of 0 to 10) based on mixed results -- excessive policy leverage mitigated by excellent risk adjusted capital (severe loss scenario) reflecting improvement over results in 2017. Good quality investment portfolio (6.2) despite significant exposure to mortgages . Mortgage default rate has been low. large holdings of BBB rated bonds in addition to small junk bond holdings. Good overall profitability (6.7).

Other Rating Factors: Good liquidity (6.2). Good overall results on stability tests (5.4) excellent operational trends and excellent risk diversification.

Principal Business: Group health insurance (60%), individual health insurance (35%), group life insurance (3%), and reinsurance (1%).

Principal Investments: NonCMO investment grade bonds (57%), mortgages in good standing (13%), CMOs and structured securities (11%), noninv. grade bonds (8%), and misc. investments (12%).

Investments in Affiliates: 6%

Group Affiliation: Aetna Inc

Licensed in: All states, the District of Columbia and Puerto Rico

Commenced Business: December 1850

Address: 151 FARMINGTON AVENUE, HARTFORD, CT 6156

Phone: (860) 273-0123 **Domicile State:** CT **NAIC Code:** 60054

Data Date	Rating	RACR #1	RACR #2	Total Assets ($mil)	Capital ($mil)	Net Premium ($mil)	Net Income ($mil)
9-18	B	1.48	1.12	21,702.3	4,062.4	14,973.9	1,676.2
9-17	B	1.53	1.14	22,767.9	3,979.7	14,388.4	1,565.0
2017	B	1.12	0.84	19,894.8	2,904.0	17,984.7	1,339.4
2016	B	1.34	1.00	22,376.2	3,479.2	18,556.4	1,251.7
2015	B	1.57	1.15	21,214.1	3,770.8	17,155.4	1,211.9
2014	B+	1.72	1.25	22,795.4	3,871.9	15,544.4	1,321.7
2013	B+	1.76	1.25	21,793.1	3,199.9	12,354.0	911.1

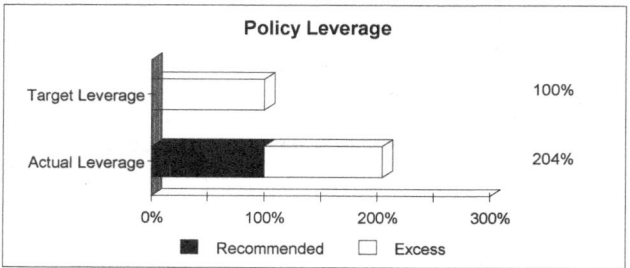

Policy Leverage

ALFA LIFE INSURANCE CORPORATION — B- — Good

Major Rating Factors: Good quality investment portfolio (5.0 on a scale of 0 to 10) despite mixed results such as: large holdings of BBB rated bonds but moderate junk bond exposure. Good liquidity (6.4) with sufficient resources to handle a spike in claims as well as a significant increase in policy surrenders. Good overall results on stability tests (5.2) excellent operational trends and excellent risk diversification.

Other Rating Factors: Fair profitability (4.3) with investment income below regulatory standards in relation to interest assumptions of reserves. Strong capitalization (7.8) based on excellent risk adjusted capital (severe loss scenario).

Principal Business: Individual life insurance (97%), individual annuities (2%), and group life insurance (1%).

Principal Investments: NonCMO investment grade bonds (61%), common & preferred stock (8%), policy loans (6%), noninv. grade bonds (6%), and misc. investments (15%).

Investments in Affiliates: None

Group Affiliation: Alfa Ins Group

Licensed in: AL, AR, FL, GA, LA, MS, MO, NC, SC, TN, VA

Commenced Business: March 1955

Address: 2108 East South Boulevard, Montgomery, AL 36116

Phone: (334) 288-3900 **Domicile State:** AL **NAIC Code:** 79049

Data Date	Rating	RACR #1	RACR #2	Total Assets ($mil)	Capital ($mil)	Net Premium ($mil)	Net Income ($mil)
9-18	B-	2.72	1.53	1,479.5	272.2	116.5	5.1
9-17	B-	2.97	1.66	1,422.9	264.0	115.1	7.4
2017	B-	3.02	1.69	1,430.2	269.0	151.8	16.5
2016	B-	2.83	1.56	1,375.5	249.5	151.1	8.9
2015	B-	2.78	1.58	1,377.1	235.6	151.2	11.8
2014	B-	2.89	1.66	1,318.0	226.9	143.3	23.3
2013	B-	3.00	1.69	1,357.2	218.0	134.1	25.8

Adverse Trends in Operations

Increase in policy surrenders from 2015 to 2016 (259%)
Increase in policy surrenders from 2013 to 2014 (329%)
Decrease in asset base during 2014 (3%)

ALL SAVERS INSURANCE COMPANY — C — Fair

Major Rating Factors: Weak profitability (2.8 on a scale of 0 to 10). Excellent expense controls. Weak overall results on stability tests (2.4) including weak results on operational trends. Strong current capitalization (10.0) based on excellent risk adjusted capital (severe loss scenario) reflecting improvement over results in 2013.

Other Rating Factors: High quality investment portfolio (8.1). Excellent liquidity (7.4).

Principal Business: Group health insurance (90%) and individual health insurance (10%).

Principal Investments: NonCMO investment grade bonds (61%), CMOs and structured securities (28%), and cash (1%).

Investments in Affiliates: None

Group Affiliation: UnitedHealth Group Inc

Licensed in: All states except CA, MA, MN, NJ, NY, PR

Commenced Business: February 1986

Address: 7440 WOODLAND DRIVE, INDIANAPOLIS, IN 46278-1719

Phone: (317) 290-8100 **Domicile State:** IN **NAIC Code:** 82406

Data Date	Rating	RACR #1	RACR #2	Total Assets ($mil)	Capital ($mil)	Net Premium ($mil)	Net Income ($mil)
9-18	C	8.56	6.29	703.8	557.0	353.7	35.3
9-17	C	11.79	8.41	1,368.8	1,240.2	382.0	183.9
2017	C	13.51	9.47	1,143.2	997.3	497.7	187.6
2016	C	5.31	3.99	1,551.5	1,054.2	1,603.1	-102.2
2015	C	5.60	4.41	1,067.5	600.8	891.4	-339.5
2014	B-	1.51	1.25	61.6	31.1	111.9	5.0
2013	B-	1.19	0.99	29.6	16.4	76.3	1.5

Adverse Trends in Operations

Decrease in capital during 2017 (5%)
Decrease in premium volume from 2016 to 2017 (69%)
Decrease in asset base during 2017 (26%)
Change in asset mix during 2016 (17%)
Change in premium mix from 2014 to 2015 (15.0%)

ALLIANZ LIFE INSURANCE COMPANY OF NEW YORK * — B+ — Good

Major Rating Factors: Good overall results on stability tests (5.3 on a scale of 0 to 10) despite fair financial strength of affiliated Allianz Ins Group. Other stability subfactors include excellent operational trends and excellent risk diversification. Good overall profitability (5.5) although investment income, in comparison to reserve requirements, is below regulatory standards. Strong capitalization (9.8) based on excellent risk adjusted capital (severe loss scenario).

Other Rating Factors: High quality investment portfolio (7.6). Excellent liquidity (9.3).

Principal Business: Individual annuities (98%) and individual health insurance (1%).

Principal Investments: NonCMO investment grade bonds (71%), CMOs and structured securities (24%), and noninv. grade bonds (1%).

Investments in Affiliates: None

Group Affiliation: Allianz Ins Group

Licensed in: CT, DC, IL, MN, MO, NY, ND

Commenced Business: April 1984

Address: 28 Liberty Street 38th Floor, New York, NY 10005-1422

Phone: (763) 765-2913 **Domicile State:** NY **NAIC Code:** 64190

Data Date	Rating	RACR #1	RACR #2	Total Assets ($mil)	Capital ($mil)	Net Premium ($mil)	Net Income ($mil)
9-18	B+	5.00	2.89	3,461.1	186.8	218.3	19.8
9-17	A	5.26	3.46	3,347.7	184.6	193.8	-0.1
2017	A	4.63	2.69	3,396.4	173.1	268.0	-5.3
2016	A	5.73	3.91	3,124.0	202.1	247.4	10.3
2015	B	5.88	4.15	2,943.5	198.8	280.8	34.3
2014	B	4.95	3.23	2,891.2	165.2	325.5	9.5
2013	B	3.07	1.60	2,668.0	97.8	317.4	7.4

Allianz Ins Group
Composite Group Rating: C
Largest Group Members

	Assets ($mil)	Rating
ALLIANZ LIFE INS CO OF NORTH AMERICA	138068	C
ALLIANZ GLOBAL RISKS US INS CO	7626	C
ALLIANZ LIFE INS CO OF NY	3396	B+
SAN FRANCISCO REINS CO	3390	C
FIREMANS FUND INS CO	2110	C+

ALLIANZ LIFE INSURANCE COMPANY OF NORTH AMERICA   C   Fair

Major Rating Factors: Fair overall results on stability tests (4.3 on a scale of 0 to 10). Good quality investment portfolio (6.0) despite large holdings of BBB rated bonds in addition to moderate junk bond exposure. Exposure to mortgages is significant, but the mortgage default rate has been low. Good liquidity (5.2) with sufficient resources to handle a spike in claims as well as a significant increase in policy surrenders.

Other Rating Factors: Weak profitability (2.7) with investment income below regulatory standards in relation to interest assumptions of reserves. Strong capitalization (7.3) based on excellent risk adjusted capital (severe loss scenario).

Principal Business: Individual annuities (91%), individual life insurance (7%), and individual health insurance (2%).

Principal Investments: NonCMO investment grade bonds (68%), CMOs and structured securities (14%), mortgages in good standing (11%), noninv. grade bonds (2%), and common & preferred stock (1%).

Investments in Affiliates: 1%
Group Affiliation: Allianz Ins Group
Licensed in: All states except NY
Commenced Business: December 1979
Address: 5701 Golden Hills Drive, Minneapolis, MN 55416-1297
Phone: (800) 328-5601 **Domicile State:** MN **NAIC Code:** 90611

Data Date	Rating	RACR #1	RACR #2	Total Assets ($mil)	Capital ($mil)	Net Premium ($mil)	Net Income ($mil)
9-18	C	2.20	1.23	147,320	6,683.6	8,547.1	180.4
9-17	B	2.86	1.61	136,207	6,031.4	7,776.4	431.1
2017	C	2.06	1.16	138,068	6,011.2	9,982.6	805.2
2016	B	2.94	1.65	127,558	6,165.3	12,642.9	1,011.3
2015	B	2.91	1.67	120,594	5,822.1	10,965.7	1,473.2
2014	C+	2.08	1.27	116,206	5,255.2	14,964.5	701.4
2013	C+	1.63	0.98	104,723	4,426.2	8,775.2	269.3

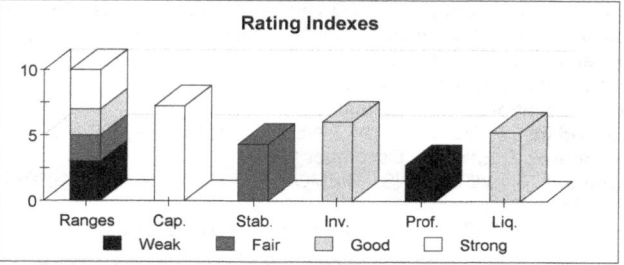

Rating Indexes

ALLSTATE ASSURANCE COMPANY   C+   Fair

Major Rating Factors: Fair overall results on stability tests (3.3 on a scale of 0 to 10). Good quality investment portfolio (6.5) despite large holdings of BBB rated bonds in addition to moderate junk bond exposure. Exposure to mortgages is significant, but the mortgage default rate has been low. Good liquidity (5.8) with sufficient resources to handle a spike in claims as well as a significant increase in policy surrenders.

Other Rating Factors: Weak profitability (1.8) with operating losses during the first nine months of 2018. Strong capitalization (8.9) based on excellent risk adjusted capital (severe loss scenario).

Principal Business: Individual life insurance (82%) and reinsurance (18%).

Principal Investments: NonCMO investment grade bonds (63%), mortgages in good standing (17%), noninv. grade bonds (7%), policy loans (6%), and CMOs and structured securities (6%).

Investments in Affiliates: None
Group Affiliation: Allstate Group
Licensed in: All states except NY, PR
Commenced Business: July 1967
Address: 3075 SANDERS ROAD SUITE I2W, NORTHBROOK, IL 60062-7127
Phone: (847) 402-5000 **Domicile State:** IL **NAIC Code:** 70866

Data Date	Rating	RACR #1	RACR #2	Total Assets ($mil)	Capital ($mil)	Net Premium ($mil)	Net Income ($mil)
9-18	C+	4.26	2.25	699.2	160.9	115.6	-31.7
9-17	C+	2.47	1.43	665.9	143.4	24.5	-3.6
2017	C+	3.55	1.88	674.1	135.8	57.6	-7.3
2016	C+	2.34	1.38	716.7	133.9	144.3	-57.8
2015	B-	3.18	1.79	634.3	105.2	557.5	-45.8
2014	A-	4.03	3.63	12.2	10.7	0.0	0.3
2013	B	4.03	3.62	12.2	10.8	0.0	0.2

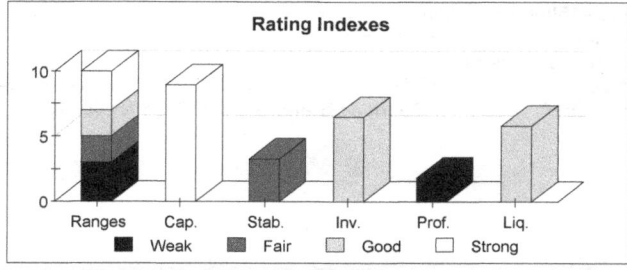

Rating Indexes

ALLSTATE LIFE INSURANCE COMPANY   B   Good

Major Rating Factors: Good liquidity (6.7 on a scale of 0 to 10) with sufficient resources to cover a large increase in policy surrenders. Fair quality investment portfolio (4.5) with large holdings of BBB rated bonds in addition to junk bond exposure equal to 78% of capital. Exposure to mortgages is significant, but the mortgage default rate has been low. Fair profitability (4.0) with investment income below regulatory standards in relation to interest assumptions of reserves.

Other Rating Factors: Fair overall results on stability tests (4.8) including excessive premium growth and negative cash flow from operations for 2017. Strong capitalization (7.4) based on excellent risk adjusted capital (severe loss scenario).

Principal Business: Reinsurance (72%), individual life insurance (23%), individual annuities (2%), group life insurance (1%), and group health insurance (1%).

Principal Investments: NonCMO investment grade bonds (51%), mortgages in good standing (12%), noninv. grade bonds (10%), common & preferred stock (7%), and misc. investments (19%).

Investments in Affiliates: 3%
Group Affiliation: Allstate Group
Licensed in: All states, the District of Columbia and Puerto Rico
Commenced Business: September 1957
Address: 3075 SANDERS ROAD SUITE I2W, NORTHBROOK, IL 60062-7127
Phone: (847) 402-5000 **Domicile State:** IL **NAIC Code:** 60186

Data Date	Rating	RACR #1	RACR #2	Total Assets ($mil)	Capital ($mil)	Net Premium ($mil)	Net Income ($mil)
9-18	B	2.17	1.27	30,993.3	3,680.8	703.8	323.6
9-17	B	2.00	1.16	31,602.0	3,373.3	494.2	760.0
2017	B	2.05	1.21	31,567.3	3,408.1	751.1	846.7
2016	B	1.83	1.06	32,127.0	3,046.6	1,212.2	231.9
2015	B	1.67	0.97	32,348.1	2,868.7	773.2	15.9
2014	B	1.70	1.00	34,120.9	2,712.3	-9,872.3	974.9
2013	B	1.31	0.80	47,858.5	2,875.1	2,377.5	425.1

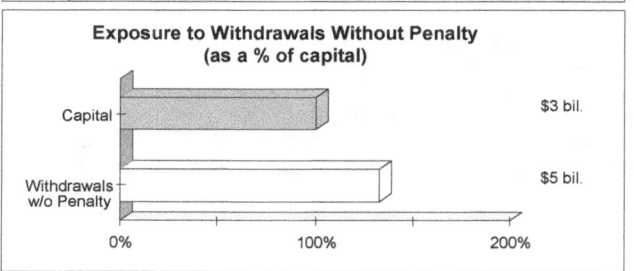

Exposure to Withdrawals Without Penalty
(as a % of capital)

ALLSTATE LIFE INSURANCE COMPANY OF NEW YORK B- Good

Major Rating Factors: Good quality investment portfolio (5.6 on a scale of 0 to 10) despite large holdings of BBB rated bonds in addition to moderate junk bond exposure. Exposure to mortgages is significant, but the mortgage default rate has been low. Good liquidity (6.5) with sufficient resources to cover a large increase in policy surrenders. Good overall results on stability tests (5.0) excellent operational trends and excellent risk diversification.

Other Rating Factors: Fair profitability (3.6) with investment income below regulatory standards in relation to interest assumptions of reserves. Strong capitalization (7.7) based on excellent risk adjusted capital (severe loss scenario).

Principal Business: Individual life insurance (78%), individual health insurance (16%), individual annuities (4%), and group health insurance (1%).

Principal Investments: NonCMO investment grade bonds (70%), mortgages in good standing (11%), noninv. grade bonds (5%), common & preferred stock (4%), and misc. investments (11%).

Investments in Affiliates: None

Group Affiliation: Allstate Group

Licensed in: CA, DC, DE, IL, MO, NE, NJ, NY, NC, PA, TX

Commenced Business: December 1967

Address: 878 VETERANS MEMORIAL HIGHWAY, HAUPPAUGE, NY 11788-5107

Phone: (631) 357-8920 **Domicile State:** NY **NAIC Code:** 70874

Data Date	Rating	RACR #1	RACR #2	Total Assets ($mil)	Capital ($mil)	Net Premium ($mil)	Net Income ($mil)
9-18	B-	2.74	1.45	6,223.9	685.3	142.8	107.1
9-17	C+	2.45	1.28	6,325.8	605.4	135.5	49.3
2017	C+	2.46	1.31	6,281.5	603.1	186.3	50.8
2016	C+	2.16	1.14	6,279.0	520.1	165.1	-12.6
2015	B-	2.07	1.09	6,410.3	507.6	157.2	-63.9
2014	B-	2.29	1.21	6,600.9	562.1	153.2	31.3
2013	B-	2.21	1.17	6,741.9	553.9	153.2	25.9

Adverse Trends in Operations

Decrease in asset base during 2016 (2%)
Decrease in capital during 2015 (10%)
Decrease in asset base during 2015 (3%)
Decrease in asset base during 2014 (2%)

AMALGAMATED LIFE INSURANCE COMPANY * A Excellent

Major Rating Factors: Good liquidity (6.3 on a scale of 0 to 10) with sufficient resources to handle a spike in claims. Strong capitalization (10.0) based on excellent risk adjusted capital (severe loss scenario). Furthermore, this high level of risk adjusted capital has been consistently maintained over the last five years. High quality investment portfolio (8.2).

Other Rating Factors: Excellent profitability (8.1). Excellent overall results on stability tests (7.1) excellent operational trends and excellent risk diversification.

Principal Business: Group life insurance (35%), reinsurance (35%), group health insurance (27%), and individual health insurance (3%).

Principal Investments: NonCMO investment grade bonds (61%) and CMOs and structured securities (27%).

Investments in Affiliates: None

Group Affiliation: National Retirement Fund

Licensed in: All states except PR

Commenced Business: February 1944

Address: 333 WESTCHESTER AVENUE, WHITE PLAINS, NY 10604

Phone: (914) 367-5000 **Domicile State:** NY **NAIC Code:** 60216

Data Date	Rating	RACR #1	RACR #2	Total Assets ($mil)	Capital ($mil)	Net Premium ($mil)	Net Income ($mil)
9-18	A	4.42	3.38	140.3	65.3	72.9	4.3
9-17	A-	5.10	3.93	124.9	61.4	62.8	5.1
2017	A	4.24	3.24	127.5	61.7	82.7	5.5
2016	A-	4.85	3.74	122.9	57.8	80.7	3.5
2015	A-	4.12	3.27	119.9	55.6	75.6	3.0
2014	A-	3.82	3.03	111.8	51.0	72.4	3.5
2013	A-	3.45	2.72	99.9	47.2	64.3	3.5

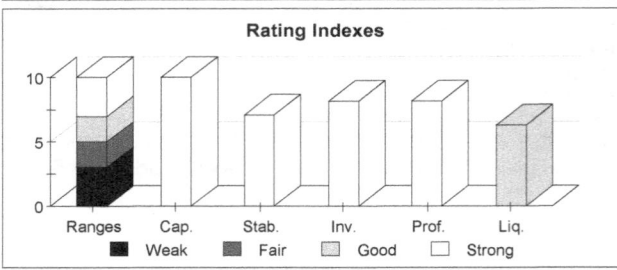

Rating Indexes

AMERICAN BANKERS LIFE ASSURANCE COMPANY OF FLORIDA C+ Fair

Major Rating Factors: Fair overall results on stability tests (3.6 on a scale of 0 to 10). Good quality investment portfolio (6.5) despite mixed results such as: minimal exposure to mortgages and substantial holdings of BBB bonds but minimal holdings in junk bonds. Strong overall capitalization (10.0) based on excellent risk adjusted capital (severe loss scenario). Nevertheless, capital levels have fluctuated during prior years.

Other Rating Factors: Excellent profitability (7.4). Excellent liquidity (7.4).

Principal Business: Credit life insurance (43%), credit health insurance (36%), reinsurance (14%), group health insurance (4%), and individual life insurance (2%).

Principal Investments: NonCMO investment grade bonds (56%), real estate (14%), CMOs and structured securities (9%), cash (9%), and misc. investments (7%).

Investments in Affiliates: None

Group Affiliation: Assurant Inc

Licensed in: All states except NY

Commenced Business: April 1952

Address: 11222 QUAIL ROOST DRIVE, MIAMI, FL 33157-6596

Phone: (305) 253-2244 **Domicile State:** FL **NAIC Code:** 60275

Data Date	Rating	RACR #1	RACR #2	Total Assets ($mil)	Capital ($mil)	Net Premium ($mil)	Net Income ($mil)
9-18	C+	5.45	3.05	334.1	56.1	68.5	18.4
9-17	C+	6.56	3.47	368.2	66.9	56.5	14.4
2017	C+	5.57	3.05	364.0	53.0	79.1	23.8
2016	C+	7.11	3.50	378.7	54.7	35.7	21.5
2015	C+	7.24	3.58	406.2	56.7	30.6	21.2
2014	B	5.37	2.87	489.6	55.9	67.9	18.6
2013	B	4.07	2.32	521.6	50.4	114.9	11.0

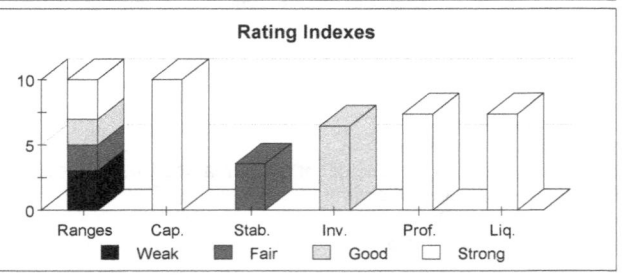

Rating Indexes

AMERICAN CONTINENTAL INSURANCE COMPANY   C+   Fair

Major Rating Factors: Fair overall results on stability tests (4.6 on a scale of 0 to 10). Good overall capitalization (5.9) based on mixed results -- excessive policy leverage mitigated by excellent risk adjusted capital (severe loss scenario). Capital levels have been relatively consistent over the last five years. Good liquidity (5.7) with sufficient resources to handle a spike in claims as well as a significant increase in policy surrenders.

Other Rating Factors: Weak profitability (2.9) with operating losses during the first nine months of 2018. High quality investment portfolio (7.7).

Principal Business: Individual health insurance (90%) and individual life insurance (10%).

Principal Investments: NonCMO investment grade bonds (74%), CMOs and structured securities (30%), mortgages in good standing (2%), and noninv. grade bonds (1%).

Investments in Affiliates: None

Group Affiliation: Aetna Inc

Licensed in: AL, AZ, AR, CO, FL, GA, IL, IN, IA, KS, KY, LA, MI, MN, MS, MO, MT, NE, NV, NM, NC, ND, OH, OK, PA, SC, SD, TN, TX, UT, VA, WV, WI, WY

Commenced Business: September 2005

Address: 800 CRESENT CENTRE DR STE 200, FRANKLIN, TN 37067

Phone: (800) 264-4000 **Domicile State:** TN **NAIC Code:** 12321

Data Date	Rating	RACR #1	RACR #2	Total Assets ($mil)	Capital ($mil)	Net Premium ($mil)	Net Income ($mil)
9-18	C+	1.74	1.31	268.1	109.9	377.1	-4.7
9-17	B-	1.62	1.22	253.8	100.7	381.2	-15.2
2017	B-	1.82	1.37	276.9	115.2	506.3	-15.0
2016	B-	1.60	1.21	229.0	94.0	472.9	-17.7
2015	B-	1.49	1.14	203.1	79.7	430.1	-15.3
2014	B	1.82	1.40	177.2	86.4	378.7	-12.7
2013	B	1.32	1.03	127.2	51.3	300.6	-13.5

Rating Indexes

AMERICAN EQUITY INVEST LIFE INSURANCE COMPANY   B-   Good

Major Rating Factors: Good quality investment portfolio (5.4 on a scale of 0 to 10) despite mixed results such as: large holdings of BBB rated bonds but moderate junk bond exposure. Good overall results on stability tests (5.3). Stability strengths include good operational trends and excellent risk diversification. Fair liquidity (4.7).

Other Rating Factors: Strong capitalization (7.4) based on excellent risk adjusted capital (severe loss scenario). Excellent profitability (8.6).

Principal Business: Individual annuities (90%) and reinsurance (10%).

Principal Investments: NonCMO investment grade bonds (65%), CMOs and structured securities (21%), mortgages in good standing (6%), noninv. grade bonds (3%), and common & preferred stock (1%).

Investments in Affiliates: None

Group Affiliation: American Equity Investment Group

Licensed in: All states except NY, PR

Commenced Business: January 1981

Address: 6000 WESTOWN PARKWAY, WEST DES MOINES, IA 50266-5921

Phone: (888) 222-1234 **Domicile State:** IA **NAIC Code:** 92738

Data Date	Rating	RACR #1	RACR #2	Total Assets ($mil)	Capital ($mil)	Net Premium ($mil)	Net Income ($mil)
9-18	B-	2.40	1.26	54,487.2	3,244.8	2,600.0	207.8
9-17	B-	2.24	1.20	50,728.9	2,948.6	2,636.2	269.2
2017	B-	2.32	1.23	51,891.7	3,005.7	3,393.5	375.9
2016	B-	2.14	1.15	47,580.2	2,726.7	5,160.1	75.0
2015	B	2.34	1.23	41,615.6	2,415.4	6,409.6	131.5
2014	B	2.77	1.43	36,129.7	2,172.5	3,866.6	340.0
2013	B	2.63	1.36	32,435.5	1,870.7	3,876.3	205.2

Adverse Trends in Operations

Decrease in premium volume from 2016 to 2017 (34%)
Decrease in premium volume from 2015 to 2016 (19%)

AMERICAN EQUITY INVESTMENT LIFE NEW YORK   B   Good

Major Rating Factors: Good overall results on stability tests (5.3 on a scale of 0 to 10) despite negative cash flow from operations for 2017. Other stability subfactors include good operational trends and excellent risk diversification. Good quality investment portfolio (6.7) despite mixed results such as: no exposure to mortgages and large holdings of BBB rated bonds but small junk bond holdings. Good overall profitability (6.4).

Other Rating Factors: Good liquidity (5.6). Strong capitalization (9.0) based on excellent risk adjusted capital (severe loss scenario).

Principal Business: Individual annuities (100%).

Principal Investments: NonCMO investment grade bonds (75%), CMOs and structured securities (18%), and noninv. grade bonds (4%).

Investments in Affiliates: None

Group Affiliation: American Equity Investment Group

Licensed in: NY

Commenced Business: July 2001

Address: 1979 MARCUS AVENUE STE 210, LAKE SUCCESS, NY 11042

Phone: (866) 233-6660 **Domicile State:** NY **NAIC Code:** 11135

Data Date	Rating	RACR #1	RACR #2	Total Assets ($mil)	Capital ($mil)	Net Premium ($mil)	Net Income ($mil)
9-18	B	3.82	2.35	201.4	36.7	0.1	1.7
9-17	B-	3.52	2.19	210.5	33.8	0.2	2.4
2017	B-	3.61	2.20	208.5	34.6	0.2	3.2
2016	B-	3.31	2.02	213.3	32.3	0.3	2.0
2015	B-	3.06	1.91	218.3	30.2	0.2	1.0
2014	B-	2.95	1.78	223.9	29.0	0.6	1.6
2013	B-	2.79	1.70	226.1	27.6	1.0	2.1

Rating Indexes

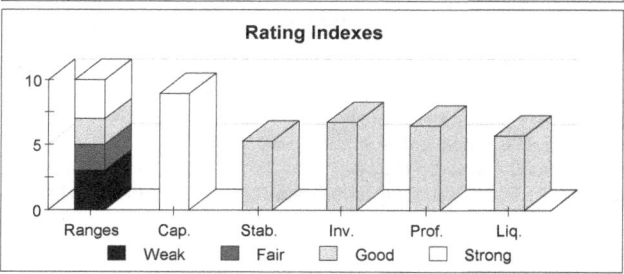

AMERICAN FAMILY LIFE ASSUR COMPANY OF NEW YORK * A- Excellent

Major Rating Factors: Excellent overall results on stability tests (7.2 on a scale of 0 to 10). Strengths that enhance stability include excellent operational trends and excellent risk diversification. Strong capitalization (10.0) based on excellent risk adjusted capital (severe loss scenario). Furthermore, this high level of risk adjusted capital has been consistently maintained over the last five years. High quality investment portfolio (8.0).

Other Rating Factors: Excellent profitability (9.0). Excellent liquidity (7.9).
Principal Business: Individual health insurance (94%), individual life insurance (4%), and group health insurance (2%).
Principal Investments: NonCMO investment grade bonds (90%), noninv. grade bonds (2%), and CMOs and structured securities (1%).
Investments in Affiliates: None
Group Affiliation: AFLAC Inc
Licensed in: CT, MA, NJ, NY, ND, VT
Commenced Business: December 1964
Address: 22 Corporate Woods Blvd Ste 2, Albany, NY 12211
Phone: (518) 438-0764 **Domicile State:** NY **NAIC Code:** 60526

Data Date	Rating	RACR #1	RACR #2	Total Assets ($mil)	Capital ($mil)	Net Premium ($mil)	Net Income ($mil)
9-18	A-	5.40	3.59	1,000.3	295.8	251.2	51.8
9-17	A-	5.56	3.70	945.4	298.3	244.7	43.9
2017	A-	5.60	3.74	915.6	300.6	326.8	58.9
2016	A-	5.91	3.97	870.1	304.3	315.9	51.6
2015	A-	6.11	4.20	817.9	298.5	304.2	47.4
2014	A-	5.39	3.76	735.9	250.1	293.5	26.8
2013	A-	4.96	3.49	645.3	221.8	285.5	45.4

Adverse Trends in Operations

Decrease in capital during 2017 (1%)
Increase in policy surrenders from 2014 to 2015 (30%)
Increase in policy surrenders from 2013 to 2014 (49%)

AMERICAN FAMILY LIFE INSURANCE COMPANY * A+ Excellent

Major Rating Factors: Good overall results on stability tests (6.3 on a scale of 0 to 10). Strengths that enhance stability include excellent risk diversification. Good quality investment portfolio (5.9) despite significant exposure to mortgages . Mortgage default rate has been low. large holdings of BBB rated bonds in addition to small junk bond holdings. Good overall profitability (6.5).

Other Rating Factors: Good liquidity (6.3). Strong capitalization (8.2) based on excellent risk adjusted capital (severe loss scenario).
Principal Business: Individual life insurance (95%), individual annuities (3%), group life insurance (1%), and reinsurance (1%).
Principal Investments: NonCMO investment grade bonds (56%), CMOs and structured securities (19%), mortgages in good standing (12%), policy loans (4%), and misc. investments (6%).
Investments in Affiliates: None
Group Affiliation: American Family Ins Group
Licensed in: All states except NY, PR
Commenced Business: December 1957
Address: 6000 AMERICAN PARKWAY, MADISON, WI 53783-0001
Phone: (608) 249-2111 **Domicile State:** WI **NAIC Code:** 60399

Data Date	Rating	RACR #1	RACR #2	Total Assets ($mil)	Capital ($mil)	Net Premium ($mil)	Net Income ($mil)
9-18	A+	3.27	1.78	5,269.9	644.4	276.3	88.1
9-17	A+	4.80	2.60	5,669.7	1,054.9	269.7	46.5
2017	A+	5.04	2.70	5,676.1	1,059.7	359.0	69.4
2016	A+	4.52	2.43	5,497.5	1,001.4	457.7	52.2
2015	A+	4.69	2.48	5,331.7	945.1	338.0	51.7
2014	A+	4.57	2.42	5,230.5	888.6	341.1	80.7
2013	A+	4.66	2.47	5,074.0	822.8	347.9	66.2

Rating Indexes

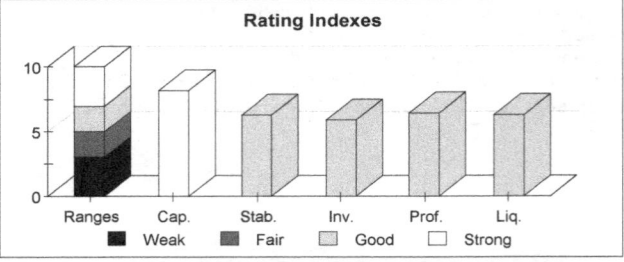

AMERICAN FIDELITY ASSURANCE COMPANY * B+ Good

Major Rating Factors: Good quality investment portfolio (6.0 on a scale of 0 to 10) despite mixed results such as: minimal exposure to mortgages and large holdings of BBB rated bonds but small junk bond holdings. Good liquidity (6.2) with sufficient resources to cover a large increase in policy surrenders. Good overall results on stability tests (6.8) excellent operational trends and excellent risk diversification.

Other Rating Factors: Strong capitalization (7.2) based on excellent risk adjusted capital (severe loss scenario). Excellent profitability (8.5).
Principal Business: Group health insurance (42%), individual health insurance (26%), individual life insurance (14%), individual annuities (13%), and reinsurance (4%).
Principal Investments: NonCMO investment grade bonds (63%), CMOs and structured securities (18%), mortgages in good standing (10%), cash (5%), and misc. investments (4%).
Investments in Affiliates: None
Group Affiliation: Cameron Associates Inc
Licensed in: All states except NY
Commenced Business: December 1960
Address: 9000 Cameron Parkway, Oklahoma City, OK 73114-3701
Phone: (405) 523-2000 **Domicile State:** OK **NAIC Code:** 60410

Data Date	Rating	RACR #1	RACR #2	Total Assets ($mil)	Capital ($mil)	Net Premium ($mil)	Net Income ($mil)
9-18	B+	1.90	1.11	6,090.1	471.9	757.4	75.1
9-17	B+	1.93	1.10	5,772.7	434.5	705.9	56.7
2017	B+	1.78	1.04	5,896.7	430.6	957.4	66.2
2016	B+	1.88	1.07	5,446.8	414.6	906.6	76.4
2015	B+	1.97	1.13	5,181.1	408.5	957.9	75.4
2014	B+	1.93	1.11	4,959.0	380.4	822.5	69.3
2013	B+	1.82	1.05	4,709.9	342.7	780.9	71.7

Adverse Trends in Operations

Decrease in premium volume from 2015 to 2016 (5%)

AMERICAN FIDELITY LIFE INSURANCE COMPANY　　　B　　Good

Major Rating Factors: Good quality investment portfolio (5.8 on a scale of 0 to 10) despite mixed results such as: minimal exposure to mortgages and large holdings of BBB rated bonds but minimal holdings in junk bonds. Good overall profitability (5.8). Good liquidity (6.0).

Other Rating Factors: Good overall results on stability tests (5.8) good operational trends and good risk diversification. Strong capitalization (7.4) based on excellent risk adjusted capital (severe loss scenario).

Principal Business: Individual life insurance (58%), individual annuities (27%), and reinsurance (15%).

Principal Investments: NonCMO investment grade bonds (71%), common & preferred stock (9%), mortgages in good standing (8%), real estate (7%), and misc. investments (6%).

Investments in Affiliates: 14%
Group Affiliation: AMFI Corp
Licensed in: All states except NY, VT, PR
Commenced Business: September 1956
Address: 500 So Palafox St Ste 200, Pensacola, FL 32502
Phone: (850) 456-7401　**Domicile State:** FL　**NAIC Code:** 60429

Data Date	Rating	RACR #1	RACR #2	Total Assets ($mil)	Capital ($mil)	Net Premium ($mil)	Net Income ($mil)
9-18	B	1.74	1.25	402.5	66.2	7.7	1.2
9-17	B	1.93	1.35	411.1	67.8	7.5	0.1
2017	B	1.78	1.29	410.2	67.3	9.6	1.3
2016	B-	1.96	1.37	422.5	68.9	10.1	3.5
2015	B-	2.03	1.40	426.4	67.7	10.3	2.4
2014	B-	2.23	1.54	433.1	68.1	10.6	-2.3
2013	B-	2.53	1.68	445.7	71.8	11.1	4.1

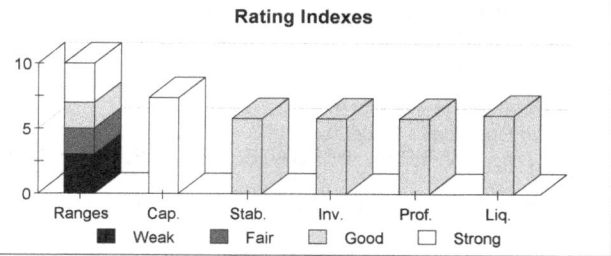

Rating Indexes

AMERICAN GENERAL LIFE INSURANCE COMPANY　　　B　　Good

Major Rating Factors: Good overall profitability (6.2 on a scale of 0 to 10). Good liquidity (5.9) with sufficient resources to cover a large increase in policy surrenders. Fair overall results on stability tests (4.0) including weak results on operational trends.

Other Rating Factors: Fair quality investment portfolio (3.9). Strong capitalization (7.2) based on excellent risk adjusted capital (severe loss scenario).

Principal Business: Individual annuities (59%), individual life insurance (23%), group retirement contracts (17%), and individual health insurance (1%).

Principal Investments: NonCMO investment grade bonds (47%), CMOs and structured securities (26%), mortgages in good standing (13%), noninv. grade bonds (5%), and policy loans (1%).

Investments in Affiliates: 5%
Group Affiliation: American International Group
Licensed in: All states except NY
Commenced Business: August 1960
Address: 2727-A Allen Parkway 3-D1, Houston, TX 77019
Phone: (713) 522-1111　**Domicile State:** TX　**NAIC Code:** 60488

Data Date	Rating	RACR #1	RACR #2	Total Assets ($mil)	Capital ($mil)	Net Premium ($mil)	Net Income ($mil)
9-18	B	2.48	1.16	179,039	6,273.9	-14,405.8	478.4
9-17	B	2.87	1.35	175,213	7,597.1	7,818.4	206.1
2017	B	2.98	1.40	178,705	7,983.6	10,972.7	612.3
2016	B	3.24	1.53	170,850	9,000.5	7,525.4	1,591.2
2015	B	3.07	1.51	166,711	8,893.8	15,632.0	1,412.9
2014	B	3.21	1.59	161,876	9,166.7	14,150.5	1,861.9
2013	B-	3.97	2.00	159,157	12,656.1	12,783.2	3,430.8

Adverse Trends in Operations

Decrease in capital during 2017 (11%)
Change in premium mix from 2015 to 2016 (15%)
Decrease in premium volume from 2015 to 2016 (52%)
Decrease in capital during 2015 (3%)
Decrease in capital during 2014 (28%)

AMERICAN HEALTH & LIFE INSURANCE COMPANY *　　　A-　　Excellent

Major Rating Factors: Good quality investment portfolio (6.3 on a scale of 0 to 10) despite mixed results such as: no exposure to mortgages and large holdings of BBB rated bonds but small junk bond holdings. Good overall profitability (6.3). Excellent expense controls. Good overall results on stability tests (5.8) despite excessive premium growth good operational trends and excellent risk diversification.

Other Rating Factors: Strong capitalization (8.1) based on excellent risk adjusted capital (severe loss scenario). Excellent liquidity (8.9).

Principal Business: Credit health insurance (38%), credit life insurance (36%), reinsurance (14%), group health insurance (5%), and other lines (8%).

Principal Investments: NonCMO investment grade bonds (74%), CMOs and structured securities (20%), noninv. grade bonds (3%), common & preferred stock (1%), and cash (1%).

Investments in Affiliates: None
Group Affiliation: Citigroup Inc
Licensed in: All states except NY, PR
Commenced Business: June 1954
Address: 3001 Meacham Blvd Ste 100, Fort Worth, TX 76137
Phone: (800) 316-5607　**Domicile State:** TX　**NAIC Code:** 60518

Data Date	Rating	RACR #1	RACR #2	Total Assets ($mil)	Capital ($mil)	Net Premium ($mil)	Net Income ($mil)
9-18	A-	2.74	1.74	1,018.0	155.6	272.1	22.1
9-17	A-	3.54	2.13	840.1	142.1	152.5	34.9
2017	A-	2.70	1.70	883.2	130.3	251.1	34.5
2016	A-	5.40	3.11	924.2	215.1	154.3	71.2
2015	A-	4.03	2.40	923.9	183.5	199.8	55.5
2014	B	2.88	1.96	912.8	188.6	209.9	70.0
2013	B-	3.08	2.11	941.1	208.6	221.8	84.1

Adverse Trends in Operations

Decrease in capital during 2017 (39%)
Decrease in premium volume from 2015 to 2016 (23%)
Increase in policy surrenders from 2014 to 2015 (126%)
Decrease in premium volume from 2013 to 2014 (5%)
Increase in policy surrenders from 2013 to 2014 (249%)

AMERICAN HERITAGE LIFE INSURANCE COMPANY · B · Good

Major Rating Factors: Good overall results on stability tests (5.9 on a scale of 0 to 10). Stability strengths include excellent operational trends and excellent risk diversification. Good overall capitalization (6.6) based on good risk adjusted capital (severe loss scenario). Nevertheless, capital levels have fluctuated during prior years. Good quality investment portfolio (5.4).

Other Rating Factors: Good overall profitability (5.4) although investment income, in comparison to reserve requirements, is below regulatory standards. Good liquidity (6.4).

Principal Business: Group health insurance (63%), individual health insurance (21%), individual life insurance (8%), group life insurance (7%), and reinsurance (1%).

Principal Investments: NonCMO investment grade bonds (47%), policy loans (18%), common & preferred stock (13%), mortgages in good standing (9%), and misc. investments (14%).

Investments in Affiliates: 8%

Group Affiliation: Allstate Group

Licensed in: All states except NY

Commenced Business: December 1956

Address: 1776 AMERICAN HERITAGE LIFE DR, JACKSONVILLE, FL 32224-6688

Phone: (904) 992-1776 **Domicile State:** FL **NAIC Code:** 60534

Data Date	Rating	RACR #1	RACR #2	Total Assets ($mil)	Capital ($mil)	Net Premium ($mil)	Net Income ($mil)
9-18	B	1.25	0.95	2,026.5	367.1	722.2	87.0
9-17	B	1.10	0.85	1,915.6	323.1	681.6	42.3
2017	B	1.08	0.82	1,922.0	306.0	905.3	55.3
2016	B	1.22	0.97	1,885.6	344.3	861.4	63.1
2015	B	1.19	0.96	1,830.9	329.7	785.9	56.3
2014	B	1.27	1.02	1,799.7	353.3	744.8	123.3
2013	B	1.18	0.97	1,770.2	337.7	707.7	57.0

Adverse Trends in Operations

Decrease in capital during 2017 (11%)
Decrease in capital during 2015 (7%)

AMERICAN INCOME LIFE INSURANCE COMPANY · B- · Good

Major Rating Factors: Good capitalization (6.0 on a scale of 0 to 10) based on good risk adjusted capital (severe loss scenario). Moreover, capital levels have been consistent over the last five years. Good overall profitability (5.1) although investment income, in comparison to reserve requirements, is below regulatory standards. Fair quality investment portfolio (4.6).

Other Rating Factors: Fair overall results on stability tests (4.2). Weak liquidity (2.2).

Principal Business: Individual life insurance (92%), individual health insurance (7%), and group health insurance (1%).

Principal Investments: NonCMO investment grade bonds (82%), noninv. grade bonds (5%), policy loans (5%), common & preferred stock (2%), and misc. investments (6%).

Investments in Affiliates: 3%

Group Affiliation: Torchmark Corp

Licensed in: All states except NY, PR

Commenced Business: August 1954

Address: 8604 ALLISONVILLE RD SUITE 151, INDIANAPOLIS, IN 46250

Phone: (254) 761-6400 **Domicile State:** IN **NAIC Code:** 60577

Data Date	Rating	RACR #1	RACR #2	Total Assets ($mil)	Capital ($mil)	Net Premium ($mil)	Net Income ($mil)
9-18	B-	1.49	0.87	4,094.0	307.6	635.7	147.2
9-17	B-	1.45	0.86	3,911.1	285.7	610.4	129.2
2017	B-	1.34	0.79	3,919.7	270.3	811.7	141.5
2016	B-	1.39	0.84	3,385.2	268.8	767.5	147.4
2015	B-	1.38	0.84	3,078.1	242.5	730.4	141.5
2014	B-	1.39	0.86	2,898.6	228.9	713.7	151.6
2013	B-	1.36	0.86	2,694.7	232.3	747.9	132.6

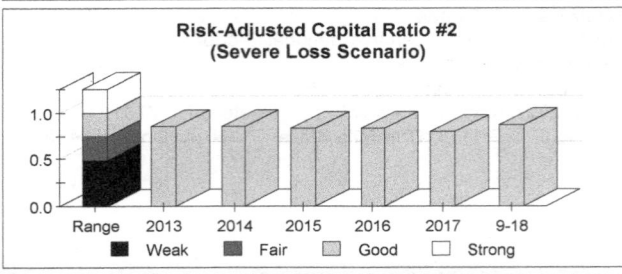

Risk-Adjusted Capital Ratio #2
(Severe Loss Scenario)

AMERICAN LIFE & ACCIDENT INSURANCE COMPANY OF KENTU · C · Fair

Major Rating Factors: Fair overall results on stability tests (3.5 on a scale of 0 to 10) including negative cash flow from operations for 2017. Good overall profitability (5.9). Excellent expense controls. Good liquidity (6.9) with sufficient resources to handle a spike in claims.

Other Rating Factors: Low quality investment portfolio (2.3). Strong capitalization (7.9) based on excellent risk adjusted capital (severe loss scenario).

Principal Business: Reinsurance (100%).

Principal Investments: Common & preferred stock (72%), nonCMO investment grade bonds (17%), real estate (7%), CMOs and structured securities (2%), and cash (2%).

Investments in Affiliates: None

Group Affiliation: Hardscuffle Inc

Licensed in: AR, GA, IN, KY, MD, OH, PA, TN

Commenced Business: July 1906

Address: 3 Riverfront Plz 471 W Main St, Louisville, KY 40202

Phone: (502) 585-5347 **Domicile State:** KY **NAIC Code:** 60666

Data Date	Rating	RACR #1	RACR #2	Total Assets ($mil)	Capital ($mil)	Net Premium ($mil)	Net Income ($mil)
9-18	C	2.62	1.59	252.6	138.6	47.5	18.7
9-17	C	2.66	1.56	242.6	114.2	68.0	1.9
2017	C	2.67	1.63	252.4	144.9	90.2	3.4
2016	C	2.74	1.62	237.1	113.2	176.2	-3.3
2015	C	3.37	1.94	216.1	114.3	198.7	22.9
2014	C	2.94	1.70	248.8	119.8	78.1	59.3
2013	C	2.08	1.25	358.7	95.9	83.3	-4.6

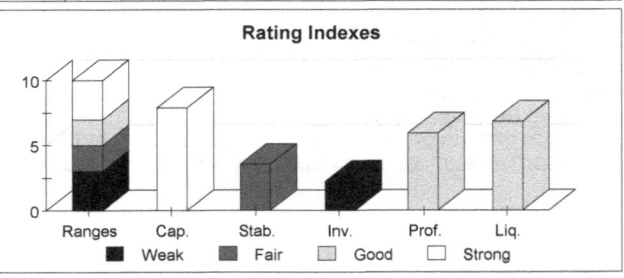

Rating Indexes

AMERICAN LIFE INSURANCE COMPANY | C | Fair

Major Rating Factors: Fair quality investment portfolio (3.0 on a scale of 0 to 10). Fair overall results on stability tests (3.4). Good current capitalization (6.3) based on good risk adjusted capital (severe loss scenario), although results have slipped from the excellent range during the last year.

Other Rating Factors: Good overall profitability (6.4). Excellent liquidity (9.2).

Principal Business: Individual life insurance (49%), group health insurance (22%), reinsurance (17%), individual health insurance (6%), and other lines (7%).

Principal Investments: Common & preferred stock (54%), nonCMO investment grade bonds (18%), noninv. grade bonds (13%), cash (7%), and misc. investments (9%).

Investments in Affiliates: 55%

Group Affiliation: MetLife Inc

Licensed in: DE

Commenced Business: August 1921

Address: 1209 Orange Street, Wilmington, DE 19801

Phone: (302) 594-2000 **Domicile State:** DE **NAIC Code:** 60690

Data Date	Rating	RACR #1	RACR #2	Total Assets ($mil)	Capital ($mil)	Net Premium ($mil)	Net Income ($mil)
9-18	C	0.94	0.91	10,706.5	5,037.1	1,188.3	1,204.4
9-17	C	1.30	1.24	12,555.4	6,472.0	1,041.2	1,165.1
2017	C	1.21	1.17	11,986.6	6,547.6	1,389.6	3,076.8
2016	C	1.03	0.99	10,377.8	5,235.3	1,373.6	341.5
2015	C	1.02	0.99	11,097.5	6,115.1	1,204.5	334.6
2014	C	0.93	0.89	8,215.9	3,358.5	1,409.1	-36.1
2013	C	0.92	0.88	7,296.4	2,711.2	1,140.4	630.5

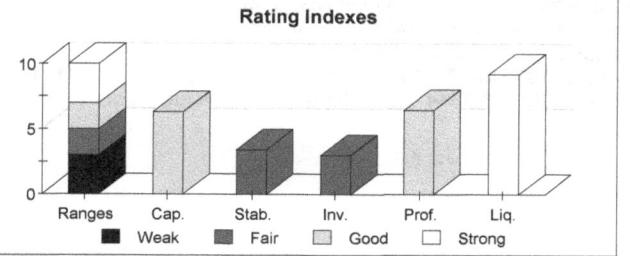

Rating Indexes

AMERICAN MATURITY LIFE INSURANCE COMPANY | B- | Good

Major Rating Factors: Fair profitability (4.2 on a scale of 0 to 10). Excellent expense controls. Fair overall results on stability tests (4.9) including excessive premium growth. Strong capitalization (10.0) based on excellent risk adjusted capital (severe loss scenario).

Other Rating Factors: High quality investment portfolio (9.5). Excellent liquidity (7.0).

Principal Business: Group retirement contracts (98%) and individual annuities (2%).

Principal Investments: NonCMO investment grade bonds (100%).

Investments in Affiliates: None

Group Affiliation: Hartford Financial Services Inc

Licensed in: All states except PR

Commenced Business: March 1973

Address: One Hartford Plaza, Windsor, CT 06095-1512

Phone: (860) 547-5000 **Domicile State:** CT **NAIC Code:** 81213

Data Date	Rating	RACR #1	RACR #2	Total Assets ($mil)	Capital ($mil)	Net Premium ($mil)	Net Income ($mil)
9-18	B-	6.69	6.02	63.1	48.6	0.1	0.4
9-17	B	6.72	6.05	62.0	48.3	0.0	0.2
2017	B	6.65	5.99	62.5	48.3	0.0	0.3
2016	B	6.69	6.02	60.6	48.1	0.0	0.6
2015	B	6.61	5.95	60.6	47.5	0.0	0.4
2014	B	6.54	5.88	61.7	47.3	0.0	0.0
2013	B	6.55	5.89	61.2	47.2	0.1	0.7

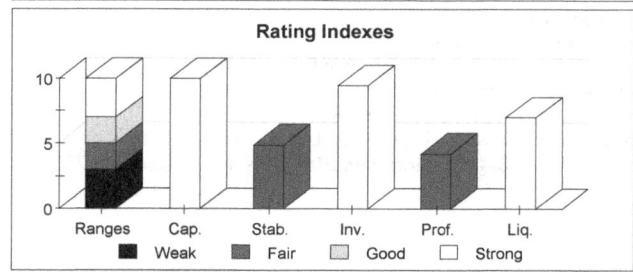

Rating Indexes

AMERICAN MEMORIAL LIFE INS CO | B- | Good

Major Rating Factors: Good current capitalization (5.8 on a scale of 0 to 10) based on good risk adjusted capital (moderate loss scenario) reflecting some improvement over results in 2016. Good liquidity (5.6) with sufficient resources to handle a spike in claims as well as a significant increase in policy surrenders. Fair quality investment portfolio (3.9).

Other Rating Factors: Fair overall results on stability tests (4.9) including fair risk adjusted capital in prior years. Excellent profitability (7.1).

Principal Business: Group life insurance (65%) and individual life insurance (35%).

Principal Investments: NonCMO investment grade bonds (70%), CMOs and structured securities (11%), mortgages in good standing (9%), noninv. grade bonds (5%), and common & preferred stock (1%).

Investments in Affiliates: None

Group Affiliation: Assurant Inc

Licensed in: All states except NY, PR

Commenced Business: October 1959

Address: 440 MOUNT RUSHMORE ROAD, RAPID CITY, SD 57701

Phone: (605) 719-0999 **Domicile State:** SD **NAIC Code:** 67989

Data Date	Rating	RACR #1	RACR #2	Total Assets ($mil)	Capital ($mil)	Net Premium ($mil)	Net Income ($mil)
9-18	B-	1.50	0.77	3,314.8	149.1	429.1	27.4
9-17	B-	1.51	0.76	3,127.0	140.9	413.3	27.2
2017	B-	1.35	0.69	3,166.4	128.5	544.3	32.0
2016	B-	1.33	0.67	2,962.1	115.5	530.5	34.5
2015	B-	1.41	0.71	2,761.6	115.7	495.6	26.5
2014	B-	1.45	0.73	2,655.5	112.4	489.9	26.7
2013	B-	1.48	0.75	2,493.7	103.5	483.2	20.4

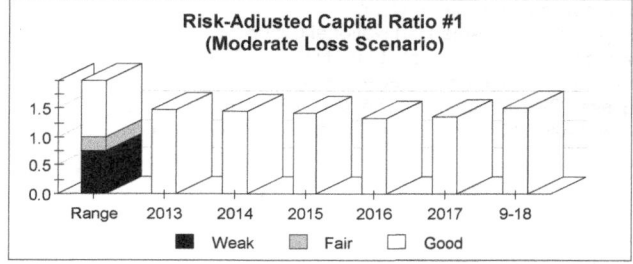

Risk-Adjusted Capital Ratio #1
(Moderate Loss Scenario)

AMERICAN MODERN LIFE INSURANCE COMPANY · B · Good

Major Rating Factors: Good liquidity (6.9 on a scale of 0 to 10) with sufficient resources to handle a spike in claims. Fair overall results on stability tests (4.1) including negative cash flow from operations for 2017. Strong capitalization (9.2) based on excellent risk adjusted capital (severe loss scenario). Moreover, capital levels have been consistently high over the last five years.

Other Rating Factors: High quality investment portfolio (8.0). Excellent profitability (9.0).

Principal Business: Credit life insurance (67%), credit health insurance (31%), and reinsurance (1%).

Principal Investments: NonCMO investment grade bonds (62%), common & preferred stock (33%), and CMOs and structured securities (4%).

Investments in Affiliates: 33%

Group Affiliation: Securian Financial Group

Licensed in: All states except NH, NJ, PR

Commenced Business: January 1957

Address: 1300 EAST NINTH STREET, CLEVELAND, OH 44114

Phone: (800) 543-2644 **Domicile State:** OH **NAIC Code:** 65811

Data Date	Rating	RACR #1	RACR #2	Total Assets ($mil)	Capital ($mil)	Net Premium ($mil)	Net Income ($mil)
9-18	B	2.57	2.48	38.3	32.9	0.4	0.6
9-17	B	2.45	2.33	40.2	31.7	0.1	1.2
2017	B	2.53	2.45	39.8	32.3	0.3	1.6
2016	B	2.31	2.19	44.7	30.5	3.1	1.2
2015	B	2.20	2.08	46.9	29.0	4.2	0.9
2014	B	2.09	1.96	47.8	27.9	5.1	2.1
2013	B	1.89	1.76	52.1	26.4	4.7	3.9

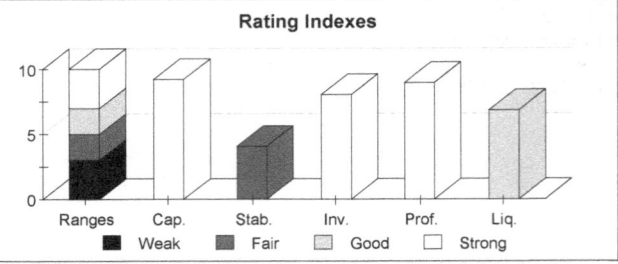

Rating Indexes

AMERICAN NATIONAL INSURANCE COMPANY · B · Good

Major Rating Factors: Good current capitalization (6.6 on a scale of 0 to 10) based on good risk adjusted capital (severe loss scenario), although results have slipped from the excellent range over the last two years. Good quality investment portfolio (5.3) despite significant exposure to mortgages . Mortgage default rate has been low. large holdings of BBB rated bonds in addition to small junk bond holdings. Good liquidity (6.6).

Other Rating Factors: Good overall results on stability tests (6.1) excellent operational trends and excellent risk diversification. Fair profitability (4.2).

Principal Business: Individual annuities (55%), individual life insurance (26%), group retirement contracts (11%), reinsurance (4%), and other lines (4%).

Principal Investments: NonCMO investment grade bonds (48%), mortgages in good standing (24%), common & preferred stock (14%), policy loans (2%), and misc. investments (10%).

Investments in Affiliates: 22%

Group Affiliation: American National Group Inc

Licensed in: All states except NY

Commenced Business: March 1905

Address: ONE MOODY PLAZA, GALVESTON, TX 77550

Phone: (409) 763-4661 **Domicile State:** TX **NAIC Code:** 60739

Data Date	Rating	RACR #1	RACR #2	Total Assets ($mil)	Capital ($mil)	Net Premium ($mil)	Net Income ($mil)
9-18	B	1.16	0.95	20,831.3	3,294.7	1,559.5	11.9
9-17	B	1.23	1.00	19,479.5	3,070.7	1,605.5	9.5
2017	B	1.16	0.97	20,146.6	3,293.5	2,131.3	20.1
2016	B	1.21	1.00	18,721.1	2,985.9	1,723.8	48.5
2015	B	1.22	1.01	18,342.1	2,925.9	1,645.2	118.6
2014	B	1.29	1.06	18,113.0	2,879.2	1,318.6	134.6
2013	B	1.27	1.03	18,036.2	2,667.9	1,146.3	149.1

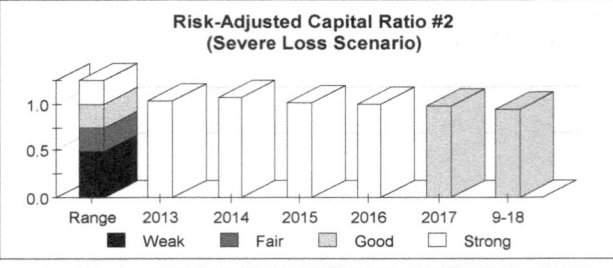

Risk-Adjusted Capital Ratio #2
(Severe Loss Scenario)

AMERICAN NATIONAL LIFE INSURANCE COMPANY OF TEXAS · B- · Good

Major Rating Factors: Good liquidity (6.4 on a scale of 0 to 10) with sufficient resources to handle a spike in claims. Good overall results on stability tests (5.0) despite negative cash flow from operations for 2017 and excessive premium growth. Strengths include good financial support from affiliation with American National Group Inc, excellent operational trends and excellent risk diversification. Weak profitability (2.3) with operating losses during the first nine months of 2018.

Other Rating Factors: Strong capitalization (9.7) based on excellent risk adjusted capital (severe loss scenario). High quality investment portfolio (7.1).

Principal Business: Group health insurance (46%), reinsurance (41%), individual health insurance (9%), and individual life insurance (4%).

Principal Investments: NonCMO investment grade bonds (93%), policy loans (3%), and noninv. grade bonds (2%).

Investments in Affiliates: None

Group Affiliation: American National Group Inc

Licensed in: All states except ME, NJ, NY, VT, PR

Commenced Business: December 1954

Address: ONE MOODY PLAZA, GALVESTON, TX 77550

Phone: (409) 763-4661 **Domicile State:** TX **NAIC Code:** 71773

Data Date	Rating	RACR #1	RACR #2	Total Assets ($mil)	Capital ($mil)	Net Premium ($mil)	Net Income ($mil)
9-18	B-	3.85	2.81	127.2	34.2	28.9	-0.5
9-17	B-	3.77	3.19	121.7	33.5	20.9	-0.9
2017	B-	3.85	2.99	123.7	34.2	28.8	-0.5
2016	B-	3.95	3.48	122.5	35.2	26.8	-0.8
2015	B-	4.01	3.16	127.5	35.9	35.5	-5.3
2014	B-	4.06	3.10	136.3	36.8	38.4	0.6
2013	B-	4.55	3.17	135.1	41.4	45.1	2.1

American National Group Inc Composite Group Rating: B Largest Group Members	Assets ($mil)	Rating
AMERICAN NATIONAL INS CO	20147	B
AMERICAN NATIONAL PROPERTY CAS CO	1418	B
FARM FAMILY LIFE INS CO	1370	B
FARM FAMILY CASUALTY INS CO	1242	B
STANDARD LIFE ACCIDENT INS CO	522	A-

AMERICAN PROGRESSIVE L&H INSURANCE COMPANY OF NY   C   Fair

Major Rating Factors: Fair profitability (3.5 on a scale of 0 to 10). Excellent expense controls. Good current capitalization (5.5) based on mixed results -- excessive policy leverage mitigated by good risk adjusted capital (severe loss scenario), although results have slipped from the excellent range over the last two years. Weak liquidity (0.8) as a spike in claims may stretch capacity.

Other Rating Factors: Weak overall results on stability tests (2.8) including negative cash flow from operations for 2017. High quality investment portfolio (7.4).

Principal Business: Individual health insurance (97%), individual life insurance (2%), and group health insurance (1%).

Principal Investments: NonCMO investment grade bonds (85%), CMOs and structured securities (8%), common & preferred stock (3%), and cash (2%).

Investments in Affiliates: None

Group Affiliation: WellCare Health Plans Inc

Licensed in: AL, AR, CO, CT, DC, DE, GA, HI, IL, IN, LA, ME, MD, MA, MN, MO, NH, NJ, NY, NC, OH, OK, OR, PA, RI, SC, TX, VT, VA, WV

Commenced Business: March 1946

Address: 44 South Broadway Suite 1200, White Plains, NY 10601-4411

Phone: (813) 290-6200 **Domicile State:** NY **NAIC Code:** 80624

Data Date	Rating	RACR #1	RACR #2	Total Assets ($mil)	Capital ($mil)	Net Premium ($mil)	Net Income ($mil)
9-18	C	1.12	0.91	259.4	121.4	456.0	15.6
9-17	C	1.09	0.89	269.8	104.2	400.4	-5.3
2017	C	1.04	0.84	222.9	102.1	535.7	-6.6
2016	C	1.25	1.02	215.0	109.3	463.9	10.0
2015	C	1.29	1.03	211.5	101.3	420.8	-13.0
2014	B	1.49	1.18	227.7	116.4	412.9	2.7
2013	B	1.39	1.10	235.7	122.3	469.8	13.5

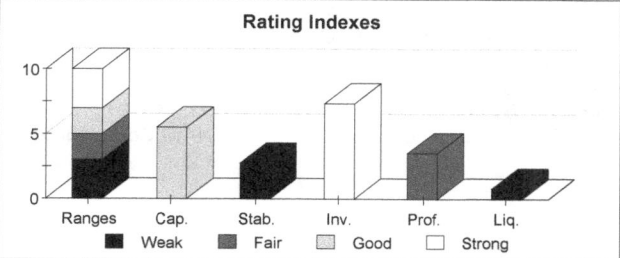

Rating Indexes

Ranges   Cap.   Stab.   Inv.   Prof.   Liq.
■ Weak   ■ Fair   ▨ Good   □ Strong

AMERICAN PUBLIC LIFE INSURANCE COMPANY   B   Good

Major Rating Factors: Good liquidity (6.9 on a scale of 0 to 10) with sufficient resources to handle a spike in claims. Good overall results on stability tests (5.9). Stability strengths include excellent operational trends and excellent risk diversification. Strong capitalization (7.9) based on excellent risk adjusted capital (severe loss scenario). Moreover, capital levels have been consistently high over the last five years.

Other Rating Factors: High quality investment portfolio (7.9). Excellent profitability (8.3).

Principal Business: Group health insurance (83%), individual health insurance (13%), reinsurance (2%), and individual life insurance (1%).

Principal Investments: NonCMO investment grade bonds (60%), CMOs and structured securities (24%), mortgages in good standing (8%), cash (5%), and misc. investments (3%).

Investments in Affiliates: None

Group Affiliation: Cameron Associates Inc

Licensed in: All states except NY, PR

Commenced Business: March 1946

Address: 9000 Cameron Parkway, Oklahoma City, OK 73114

Phone: (601) 936-6600 **Domicile State:** OK **NAIC Code:** 60801

Data Date	Rating	RACR #1	RACR #2	Total Assets ($mil)	Capital ($mil)	Net Premium ($mil)	Net Income ($mil)
9-18	B	2.15	1.63	99.1	33.3	73.8	2.0
9-17	B	1.95	1.47	98.4	29.9	67.5	3.0
2017	B	2.11	1.59	99.5	30.8	90.9	5.5
2016	B	1.96	1.47	90.3	26.4	74.4	5.9
2015	B	1.95	1.44	86.7	23.6	61.4	5.0
2014	B	1.92	1.41	83.2	21.6	52.8	4.4
2013	B	2.02	1.46	80.3	21.7	46.9	3.7

Adverse Trends in Operations

Increase in policy surrenders from 2014 to 2015 (36%)

AMERICAN REPUBLIC INSURANCE COMPANY   B-   Good

Major Rating Factors: Good quality investment portfolio (5.8 on a scale of 0 to 10) despite significant exposure to mortgages . Mortgage default rate has been low. large holdings of BBB rated bonds in addition to minimal holdings in junk bonds. Good overall profitability (6.8). Excellent expense controls. Good liquidity (6.9).

Other Rating Factors: Fair overall results on stability tests (4.8) including fair financial strength of affiliated American Enterprise Mutual Holding and excessive premium growth. Strong capitalization (9.3) based on excellent risk adjusted capital (severe loss scenario).

Principal Business: Reinsurance (69%), individual health insurance (18%), group health insurance (9%), individual life insurance (2%), and credit health insurance (1%).

Principal Investments: NonCMO investment grade bonds (55%), CMOs and structured securities (19%), mortgages in good standing (11%), real estate (4%), and misc. investments (10%).

Investments in Affiliates: 4%

Group Affiliation: American Enterprise Mutual Holding

Licensed in: All states except NY, PR

Commenced Business: May 1929

Address: 601 Sixth Avenue, Des Moines, IA 50309

Phone: (800) 247-2190 **Domicile State:** IA **NAIC Code:** 60836

Data Date	Rating	RACR #1	RACR #2	Total Assets ($mil)	Capital ($mil)	Net Premium ($mil)	Net Income ($mil)
9-18	B-	3.55	2.53	1,016.1	473.9	510.7	18.7
9-17	A-	4.74	3.38	933.1	502.9	329.1	15.5
2017	A-	4.18	2.99	937.4	445.0	442.0	23.3
2016	A-	5.06	3.60	937.6	511.1	392.1	33.1
2015	A-	5.21	3.70	820.0	477.9	328.1	21.6
2014	A-	5.26	3.89	802.5	468.1	297.9	34.1
2013	A-	4.85	3.67	801.4	437.5	325.1	40.5

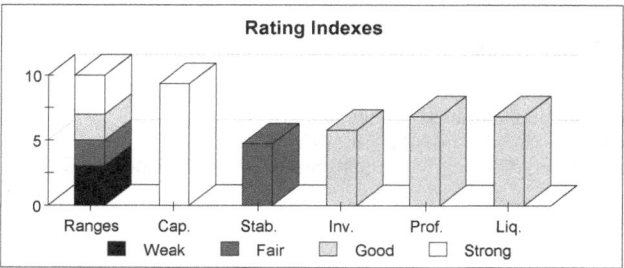

Rating Indexes

Ranges   Cap.   Stab.   Inv.   Prof.   Liq.
■ Weak   ■ Fair   ▨ Good   □ Strong

AMERICAN RETIREMENT LIFE INSURANCE COMPANY   C+   Fair

Major Rating Factors: Fair overall results on stability tests (3.3 on a scale of 0 to 10) including negative cash flow from operations for 2017, fair risk adjusted capital in prior years. Good current capitalization (5.3) based on mixed results -- excessive policy leverage mitigated by good risk adjusted capital (severe loss scenario) reflecting some improvement over results in 2016. Weak profitability (1.4) with operating losses during the first nine months of 2018.

Other Rating Factors: Weak liquidity (0.7). High quality investment portfolio (7.6).

Principal Business: Individual health insurance (100%).

Principal Investments: NonCMO investment grade bonds (114%).

Investments in Affiliates: None

Group Affiliation: CIGNA Corp

Licensed in: AL, AZ, AR, CA, CO, DE, FL, GA, IL, IN, IA, KS, KY, LA, MD, MN, MS, MO, MT, NE, NV, NH, NM, NC, ND, OH, OK, OR, PA, RI, SC, SD, TN, TX, UT, VA, WV, WI, WY

Commenced Business: November 1978

Address: 1300 East Ninth Street, Cleveland, OH 44114

Phone: (512) 451-2224 **Domicile State:** OH **NAIC Code:** 88366

Data Date	Rating	RACR #1	RACR #2	Total Assets ($mil)	Capital ($mil)	Net Premium ($mil)	Net Income ($mil)
9-18	C+	1.23	0.95	120.7	64.2	298.1	-28.1
9-17	C+	0.99	0.80	104.3	55.1	254.3	-28.4
2017	C+	1.27	0.99	112.2	59.7	345.2	-38.1
2016	C+	0.91	0.71	76.9	40.7	255.5	-26.4
2015	C+	1.36	1.05	77.4	47.3	192.2	-22.1
2014	B-	1.11	0.86	55.7	31.0	120.4	-17.7
2013	B-	1.61	1.25	18.0	8.4	16.7	-4.3

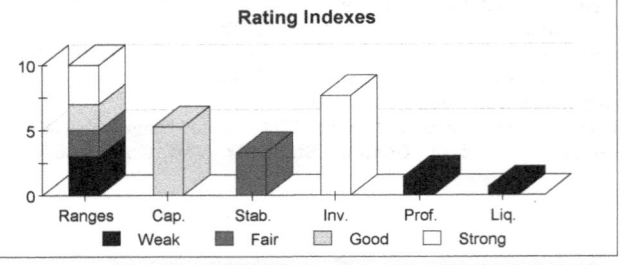

Rating Indexes

Ranges | Cap. | Stab. | Inv. | Prof. | Liq.
■ Weak   ■ Fair   □ Good   □ Strong

AMERICAN UNITED LIFE INSURANCE COMPANY *   B+   Good

Major Rating Factors: Good quality investment portfolio (5.4 on a scale of 0 to 10) despite large holdings of BBB rated bonds in addition to moderate junk bond exposure. Exposure to mortgages is significant, but the mortgage default rate has been low. Good overall profitability (6.9). Good overall results on stability tests (6.6) excellent operational trends and excellent risk diversification.

Other Rating Factors: Strong capitalization (7.2) based on excellent risk adjusted capital (severe loss scenario). Excellent liquidity (7.5).

Principal Business: Group retirement contracts (80%), individual life insurance (6%), reinsurance (5%), individual annuities (4%), and other lines (5%).

Principal Investments: NonCMO investment grade bonds (54%), CMOs and structured securities (21%), mortgages in good standing (14%), policy loans (3%), and misc. investments (6%).

Investments in Affiliates: None

Group Affiliation: American United Life Group

Licensed in: All states except PR

Commenced Business: November 1877

Address: ONE AMERICAN SQUARE, INDIANAPOLIS, IN 46282-0001

Phone: (317) 285-1877 **Domicile State:** IN **NAIC Code:** 60895

Data Date	Rating	RACR #1	RACR #2	Total Assets ($mil)	Capital ($mil)	Net Premium ($mil)	Net Income ($mil)
9-18	B+	2.30	1.14	29,575.8	1,029.1	2,836.4	32.9
9-17	B+	2.66	1.33	27,567.2	1,008.2	2,900.4	51.9
2017	B+	2.35	1.18	28,805.0	1,025.6	4,271.4	61.4
2016	B+	2.73	1.38	24,931.8	960.5	3,555.8	52.4
2015	B+	2.83	1.43	23,571.7	920.4	3,571.2	13.3
2014	B+	3.24	1.63	23,401.5	1,017.0	3,155.2	48.2
2013	B+	3.28	1.66	22,267.4	980.7	3,055.8	65.7

Adverse Trends in Operations

Decrease in capital during 2015 (10%)
Increase in policy surrenders from 2013 to 2014 (29%)

AMERICAN-AMICABLE LIFE INSURANCE COMPANY OF TEXAS   C   Fair

Major Rating Factors: Fair current capitalization (3.7 on a scale of 0 to 10) based on fair risk adjusted capital (severe loss scenario), although results have slipped from the good range over the last two years. Fair overall results on stability tests (3.7) including fair risk adjusted capital in prior years. Good quality investment portfolio (6.4).

Other Rating Factors: Good liquidity (5.2). Weak profitability (2.7) with investment income below regulatory standards in relation to interest assumptions of reserves.

Principal Business: Individual life insurance (93%), individual annuities (4%), and group life insurance (3%).

Principal Investments: NonCMO investment grade bonds (68%), common & preferred stock (18%), policy loans (6%), mortgages in good standing (5%), and misc. investments (2%).

Investments in Affiliates: 17%

Group Affiliation: Industrial Alliance Ins & Financial

Licensed in: All states except IA, MA, MI, NH, NJ, NY, RI, VT, PR

Commenced Business: December 1981

Address: 425 AUSTIN AVENUE, WACO, TX 76701

Phone: (254) 297-2777 **Domicile State:** TX **NAIC Code:** 68594

Data Date	Rating	RACR #1	RACR #2	Total Assets ($mil)	Capital ($mil)	Net Premium ($mil)	Net Income ($mil)
9-18	C	0.68	0.59	303.0	39.5	59.8	1.6
9-17	C	1.03	0.86	301.2	55.1	53.6	-1.2
2017	C	0.80	0.69	297.7	46.5	72.2	-1.7
2016	C	0.90	0.77	273.0	44.5	62.5	1.9
2015	C	1.28	1.13	287.0	78.4	50.2	11.3
2014	C	1.44	1.29	285.9	93.4	42.0	8.7
2013	C	1.31	1.16	258.6	79.0	44.7	4.0

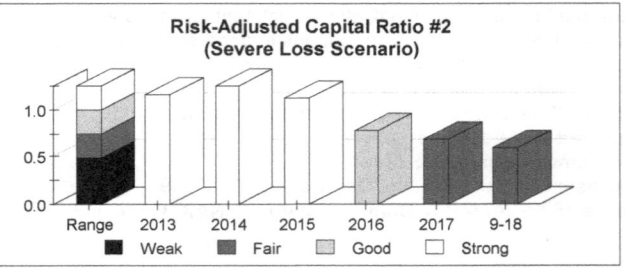

Risk-Adjusted Capital Ratio #2
(Severe Loss Scenario)

Range | 2013 | 2014 | 2015 | 2016 | 2017 | 9-18
■ Weak   ■ Fair   □ Good   □ Strong

AMERICO FINANCIAL LIFE & ANNUITY INSURANCE   B-   Good

Major Rating Factors: Good liquidity (6.1 on a scale of 0 to 10) with sufficient resources to cover a large increase in policy surrenders. Good overall results on stability tests (5.3). Stability strengths include excellent operational trends and excellent risk diversification. Fair quality investment portfolio (4.6) with large holdings of BBB rated bonds in addition to moderate junk bond exposure.

Other Rating Factors: Strong capitalization (7.2) based on excellent risk adjusted capital (severe loss scenario). Excellent profitability (8.1).

Principal Business: Individual annuities (52%), individual life insurance (30%), reinsurance (14%), group life insurance (3%), and individual health insurance (1%).

Principal Investments: NonCMO investment grade bonds (36%), CMOs and structured securities (33%), common & preferred stock (14%), mortgages in good standing (8%), and misc. investments (8%).

Investments in Affiliates: 3%
Group Affiliation: Americo Life Inc
Licensed in: All states except NY
Commenced Business: July 1946
Address: PO Box 139061, Dallas, TX 75313-9061
Phone: (816) 391-2000 **Domicile State:** TX **NAIC Code:** 61999

Data Date	Rating	RACR #1	RACR #2	Total Assets ($mil)	Capital ($mil)	Net Premium ($mil)	Net Income ($mil)
9-18	B-	1.89	1.10	4,642.1	534.2	399.7	49.9
9-17	B-	1.84	1.07	4,411.2	485.1	375.3	43.9
2017	B-	1.86	1.08	4,484.6	505.2	514.4	72.4
2016	B-	1.85	1.08	4,281.9	461.8	452.5	66.8
2015	B-	1.77	1.05	4,117.9	432.4	543.2	55.6
2014	B-	1.85	1.10	3,921.9	458.7	436.4	84.4
2013	B-	1.92	1.15	3,804.4	442.3	233.4	54.7

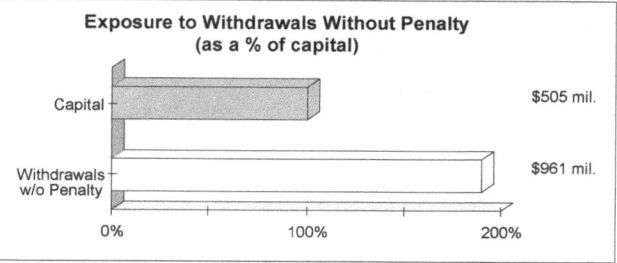

Exposure to Withdrawals Without Penalty (as a % of capital)

Capital — $505 mil.
Withdrawals w/o Penalty — $961 mil.

AMERITAS LIFE INSURANCE CORP OF NEW YORK   B-   Good

Major Rating Factors: Good quality investment portfolio (6.0 on a scale of 0 to 10) despite large holdings of BBB rated bonds in addition to moderate junk bond exposure. Exposure to mortgages is significant, but the mortgage default rate has been low. Good liquidity (5.0) with sufficient resources to cover a large increase in policy surrenders. Fair profitability (4.0) with investment income below regulatory standards in relation to interest assumptions of reserves.

Other Rating Factors: Fair overall results on stability tests (4.9). Strong capitalization (7.3) based on excellent risk adjusted capital (severe loss scenario).

Principal Business: Individual life insurance (38%), group retirement contracts (27%), group health insurance (17%), reinsurance (13%), and individual health insurance (4%).

Principal Investments: NonCMO investment grade bonds (64%), mortgages in good standing (15%), CMOs and structured securities (13%), noninv. grade bonds (3%), and policy loans (2%).

Investments in Affiliates: None
Group Affiliation: Ameritas Mutual Holding Co
Licensed in: NY
Commenced Business: May 1994
Address: 1350 Broadway Suite 2201, New York, NY 10018-7722
Phone: (845) 357-3816 **Domicile State:** NY **NAIC Code:** 60033

Data Date	Rating	RACR #1	RACR #2	Total Assets ($mil)	Capital ($mil)	Net Premium ($mil)	Net Income ($mil)
9-18	B-	2.34	1.23	1,316.4	108.7	96.2	2.3
9-17	B-	2.20	1.18	1,249.8	100.8	113.6	1.0
2017	B-	2.29	1.22	1,275.7	106.4	154.8	0.0
2016	B-	2.18	1.18	1,204.4	97.2	131.7	20.1
2015	B-	1.60	0.87	1,149.7	65.8	100.8	-17.1
2014	B-	2.15	1.18	1,128.8	86.9	95.3	-3.9
2013	B-	2.12	1.17	1,112.3	81.8	285.0	-45.8

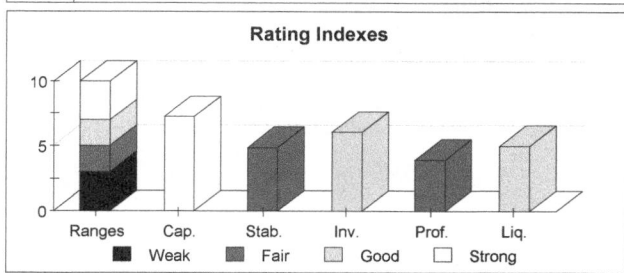

Rating Indexes

Ranges, Cap., Stab., Inv., Prof., Liq.
■ Weak ■ Fair ▢ Good ▢ Strong

AMERITAS LIFE INSURANCE CORPORATION   B   Good

Major Rating Factors: Good liquidity (6.1 on a scale of 0 to 10) with sufficient resources to cover a large increase in policy surrenders. Fair quality investment portfolio (4.9) with large holdings of BBB rated bonds in addition to moderate junk bond exposure. Exposure to mortgages is significant, but the mortgage default rate has been low. Fair profitability (4.9).

Other Rating Factors: Fair overall results on stability tests (4.4). Strong capitalization (7.5) based on excellent risk adjusted capital (severe loss scenario).

Principal Business: Group retirement contracts (30%), group health insurance (22%), individual life insurance (19%), individual annuities (12%), and other lines (17%).

Principal Investments: NonCMO investment grade bonds (53%), mortgages in good standing (15%), CMOs and structured securities (14%), common & preferred stock (5%), and misc. investments (10%).

Investments in Affiliates: 1%
Group Affiliation: Ameritas Mutual Holding Co
Licensed in: All states except NY, PR
Commenced Business: May 1887
Address: 5900 O Street, Lincoln, NE 68510-2234
Phone: (402) 467-1122 **Domicile State:** NE **NAIC Code:** 61301

Data Date	Rating	RACR #1	RACR #2	Total Assets ($mil)	Capital ($mil)	Net Premium ($mil)	Net Income ($mil)
9-18	B	2.23	1.32	21,881.9	1,584.6	2,094.8	47.5
9-17	B	2.39	1.42	19,676.1	1,575.8	2,016.3	92.6
2017	B	2.25	1.34	20,076.5	1,555.6	2,724.5	106.3
2016	B	2.22	1.34	18,696.6	1,484.1	4,421.9	-4.8
2015	B	2.40	1.45	18,148.8	1,511.5	3,359.6	-9.5
2014	B	2.67	1.67	16,822.0	1,623.5	2,119.7	129.8
2013	B	1.30	1.13	9,187.8	1,501.8	1,622.4	64.9

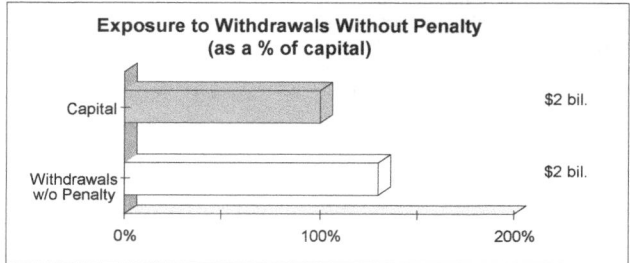

Exposure to Withdrawals Without Penalty (as a % of capital)

Capital — $2 bil.
Withdrawals w/o Penalty — $2 bil.

AMICA LIFE INSURANCE COMPANY *   B+   Good

Major Rating Factors: Good overall results on stability tests (6.5 on a scale of 0 to 10). Stability strengths include excellent operational trends and excellent risk diversification. Good overall profitability (5.7) although investment income, in comparison to reserve requirements, is below regulatory standards. Good liquidity (6.5).

Other Rating Factors: Strong capitalization (10.0) based on excellent risk adjusted capital (severe loss scenario). High quality investment portfolio (7.0).

Principal Business: Individual life insurance (87%), individual annuities (9%), and group life insurance (4%).

Principal Investments: NonCMO investment grade bonds (53%), CMOs and structured securities (30%), common & preferred stock (5%), mortgages in good standing (4%), and misc. investments (8%).

Investments in Affiliates: None

Group Affiliation: Amica Mutual Group

Licensed in: All states except PR

Commenced Business: May 1970

Address: 100 AMICA WAY, LINCOLN, RI 02865-1156

Phone: (800) 652-6422 **Domicile State:** RI **NAIC Code:** 72222

Data Date	Rating	RACR #1	RACR #2	Total Assets ($mil)	Capital ($mil)	Net Premium ($mil)	Net Income ($mil)
9-18	B+	5.28	3.05	1,302.6	330.3	53.4	5.8
9-17	B+	5.04	2.90	1,277.2	302.3	51.3	3.7
2017	B+	5.03	2.90	1,283.4	310.2	69.6	12.7
2016	B	4.95	2.91	1,240.7	278.8	67.4	10.3
2015	B	5.18	3.00	1,224.7	287.5	63.6	5.0
2014	B	4.77	2.78	1,196.4	260.3	62.2	4.5
2013	B	4.16	2.43	1,133.1	217.5	61.8	5.6

Adverse Trends in Operations

Decrease in capital during 2016 (3%)

ANNUITY INVESTORS LIFE INSURANCE COMPANY *   A-   Excellent

Major Rating Factors: Good overall results on stability tests (6.9 on a scale of 0 to 10). Strengths that enhance stability include excellent operational trends and excellent risk diversification. Good quality investment portfolio (6.4) despite mixed results such as: no exposure to mortgages and large holdings of BBB rated bonds but small junk bond holdings. Good liquidity (5.2).

Other Rating Factors: Strong capitalization (7.9) based on excellent risk adjusted capital (severe loss scenario). Excellent profitability (8.6).

Principal Business: Individual annuities (91%) and group retirement contracts (9%).

Principal Investments: NonCMO investment grade bonds (69%), CMOs and structured securities (23%), policy loans (2%), and noninv. grade bonds (1%).

Investments in Affiliates: None

Group Affiliation: American Financial Group Inc

Licensed in: All states except NY, VT, PR

Commenced Business: December 1981

Address: 301 East Fourth Street, Cincinnati, OH 45202

Phone: (513) 357-3300 **Domicile State:** OH **NAIC Code:** 93661

Data Date	Rating	RACR #1	RACR #2	Total Assets ($mil)	Capital ($mil)	Net Premium ($mil)	Net Income ($mil)
9-18	A-	3.21	1.62	3,232.6	315.1	148.7	22.6
9-17	A-	3.05	1.54	3,166.0	287.2	160.6	16.1
2017	A-	3.03	1.53	3,191.3	294.7	211.4	23.8
2016	A-	2.92	1.47	3,063.4	269.4	193.4	18.8
2015	B	2.82	1.42	3,014.1	245.6	215.6	25.0
2014	B	2.77	1.40	2,994.8	227.1	229.2	27.6
2013	B	2.68	1.35	2,892.9	203.2	232.4	23.2

Adverse Trends in Operations

Decrease in premium volume from 2015 to 2016 (10%)
Decrease in premium volume from 2014 to 2015 (6%)
Decrease in premium volume from 2013 to 2014 (1%)

ANTHEM LIFE INSURANCE COMPANY   B   Good

Major Rating Factors: Good liquidity (6.0 on a scale of 0 to 10) with sufficient resources to handle a spike in claims. Fair overall results on stability tests (4.7). Strong capitalization (7.9) based on excellent risk adjusted capital (severe loss scenario). Capital levels have been relatively consistent over the last five years.

Other Rating Factors: High quality investment portfolio (7.5). Excellent profitability (7.6).

Principal Business: Reinsurance (49%), group life insurance (29%), and group health insurance (22%).

Principal Investments: NonCMO investment grade bonds (59%), CMOs and structured securities (34%), and common & preferred stock (2%).

Investments in Affiliates: None

Group Affiliation: Anthem Inc

Licensed in: All states except NY, RI, VT, PR

Commenced Business: June 1956

Address: 120 MONUMENT CIRCLE, INDIANAPOLIS, IN 46204

Phone: (614) 433-8800 **Domicile State:** IN **NAIC Code:** 61069

Data Date	Rating	RACR #1	RACR #2	Total Assets ($mil)	Capital ($mil)	Net Premium ($mil)	Net Income ($mil)
9-18	B	2.31	1.59	720.0	131.9	324.4	13.7
9-17	A-	2.26	1.55	738.1	118.5	305.8	5.0
2017	B-	1.98	1.37	674.7	125.1	412.0	12.3
2016	A-	1.85	1.28	623.3	108.9	362.3	28.3
2015	A-	1.64	1.16	633.7	95.9	368.9	18.2
2014	A-	1.92	1.34	582.4	109.1	357.8	34.4
2013	A-	2.17	1.51	575.3	120.4	345.1	47.1

Rating Indexes

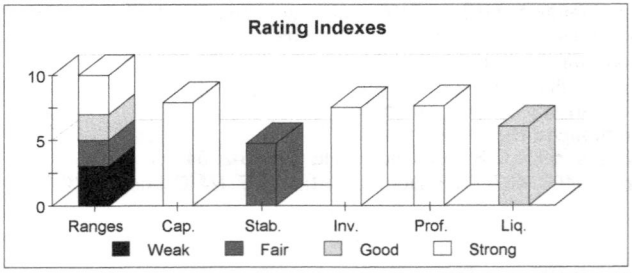

	Weak	Fair	Good	Strong

ASSURITY LIFE INSURANCE COMPANY * B+ Good

Major Rating Factors: Good quality investment portfolio (5.5 on a scale of 0 to 10) despite significant exposure to mortgages . Mortgage default rate has been low. large holdings of BBB rated bonds in addition to small junk bond holdings. Good overall profitability (5.9) although investment income, in comparison to reserve requirements, is below regulatory standards. Good liquidity (5.4).

Other Rating Factors: Good overall results on stability tests (6.6) excellent operational trends and excellent risk diversification. Strong capitalization (7.7) based on excellent risk adjusted capital (severe loss scenario).

Principal Business: Individual life insurance (47%), individual health insurance (28%), group health insurance (14%), individual annuities (4%), and other lines (7%).

Principal Investments: NonCMO investment grade bonds (56%), mortgages in good standing (16%), CMOs and structured securities (12%), policy loans (5%), and misc. investments (11%).

Investments in Affiliates: 1%
Group Affiliation: Assurity Security Group Inc
Licensed in: All states except NY, PR
Commenced Business: March 1964
Address: 2000 Q STREET, LINCOLN, NE 68503
Phone: (402) 476-6500 **Domicile State:** NE **NAIC Code:** 71439

Data Date	Rating	RACR #1	RACR #2	Total Assets ($mil)	Capital ($mil)	Net Premium ($mil)	Net Income ($mil)
9-18	B+	2.54	1.47	2,729.5	334.7	146.8	12.0
9-17	B+	2.76	1.54	2,726.8	332.2	142.1	9.5
2017	B+	2.54	1.47	2,632.3	334.7	189.2	16.8
2016	B+	2.70	1.51	2,605.0	324.9	193.3	12.0
2015	B+	2.71	1.51	2,472.0	318.1	189.5	20.8
2014	B+	3.03	1.61	2,463.6	300.5	189.7	19.2
2013	B+	3.17	1.69	2,449.3	306.4	191.2	14.6

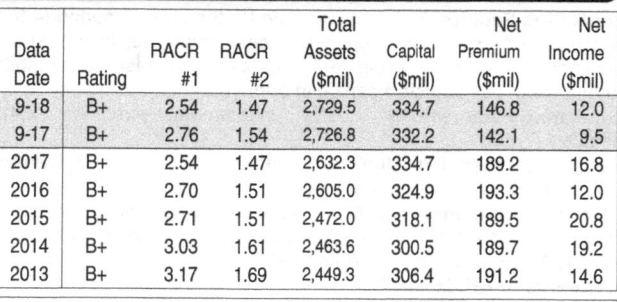
Rating Indexes
Ranges / Cap. / Stab. / Inv. / Prof. / Liq.
■ Weak ■ Fair □ Good □ Strong

ATHENE ANNUITY & LIFE ASSURANCE COMPANY C Fair

Major Rating Factors: Fair overall results on stability tests (3.7 on a scale of 0 to 10) including fair financial strength of affiliated BRH Holdings GP Ltd, negative cash flow from operations for 2017 and fair risk adjusted capital in prior years. Fair capitalization (4.7) based on fair risk adjusted capital (moderate loss scenario). Fair quality investment portfolio (3.6).

Other Rating Factors: Fair profitability (4.7) with operating losses during the first nine months of 2018. Good liquidity (6.4).

Principal Business: Reinsurance (69%), individual life insurance (26%), individual health insurance (2%), group health insurance (2%), and group life insurance (1%).

Principal Investments: CMOs and structured securities (31%), nonCMO investment grade bonds (26%), common & preferred stock (13%), mortgages in good standing (10%), and misc. investments (18%).

Investments in Affiliates: 23%
Group Affiliation: BRH Holdings GP Ltd
Licensed in: All states except NY
Commenced Business: July 1909
Address: 1209 ORANGE STREET, WILMINGTON, DE 19801
Phone: (864) 614-1000 **Domicile State:** DE **NAIC Code:** 61492

Data Date	Rating	RACR #1	RACR #2	Total Assets ($mil)	Capital ($mil)	Net Premium ($mil)	Net Income ($mil)
9-18	C	0.96	0.70	20,718.3	1,551.1	4,162.9	-26.9
9-17	C	0.94	0.72	13,029.6	1,320.0	19.0	13.0
2017	C	0.92	0.71	13,205.1	1,347.7	51.2	24.3
2016	C	0.94	0.75	10,350.7	1,272.4	24.3	71.3
2015	C	0.88	0.70	10,847.8	1,250.8	40.4	67.8
2014	C-	0.89	0.70	11,159.9	1,154.1	113.7	116.2
2013	D+	0.87	0.66	11,775.6	1,050.1	200.1	49.5

BRH Holdings GP Ltd Composite Group Rating: C Largest Group Members	Assets ($mil)	Rating
ATHENE ANNUITY LIFE CO	54933	C
ATHENE ANNUITY LIFE ASR CO	13205	C
ATHENE ANNUITY LIFE ASR CO OF NY	3165	C
ATHENE LIFE INS CO OF NEW YORK	968	C

ATHENE ANNUITY & LIFE ASSURANCE COMPANY OF NEW YOR C Fair

Major Rating Factors: Fair overall results on stability tests (4.0 on a scale of 0 to 10) including fair financial strength of affiliated BRH Holdings GP Ltd, excessive premium growth and fair risk adjusted capital in prior years. Fair quality investment portfolio (4.1) with large holdings of BBB rated bonds in addition to junk bond exposure equal to 77% of capital. Strong capitalization (7.2) based on excellent risk adjusted capital (severe loss scenario).

Other Rating Factors: Excellent profitability (8.5). Excellent liquidity (9.1).

Principal Business: Individual annuities (84%), individual life insurance (15%), and group retirement contracts (1%).

Principal Investments: NonCMO investment grade bonds (50%), CMOs and structured securities (34%), noninv. grade bonds (7%), mortgages in good standing (4%), and misc. investments (5%).

Investments in Affiliates: 2%
Group Affiliation: BRH Holdings GP Ltd
Licensed in: All states except PR
Commenced Business: October 1966
Address: 69 LYDECKER STREET, PEARL RIVER, NY 10965
Phone: (800) 926-7599 **Domicile State:** NY **NAIC Code:** 68039

Data Date	Rating	RACR #1	RACR #2	Total Assets ($mil)	Capital ($mil)	Net Premium ($mil)	Net Income ($mil)
9-18	C	1.97	1.10	3,174.7	293.8	15.6	6.5
9-17	C	1.78	0.95	3,191.0	257.2	9.0	9.9
2017	C	1.92	1.06	3,165.0	267.5	10.7	28.7
2016	C	1.58	0.81	3,261.2	231.0	24.3	1.3
2015	C	1.44	0.69	3,236.8	207.9	8.4	7.8
2014	C	1.42	0.64	3,382.9	168.1	11.5	7.1
2013	C	1.29	0.60	3,525.6	164.4	17.4	12.0

BRH Holdings GP Ltd Composite Group Rating: C Largest Group Members	Assets ($mil)	Rating
ATHENE ANNUITY LIFE CO	54933	C
ATHENE ANNUITY LIFE ASR CO	13205	C
ATHENE ANNUITY LIFE ASR CO OF NY	3165	C
ATHENE LIFE INS CO OF NEW YORK	968	C

ATHENE ANNUITY & LIFE COMPANY

C **Fair**

Major Rating Factors: Fair capitalization for the current period (4.9 on a scale of 0 to 10) based on fair risk adjusted capital (moderate loss scenario) reflecting some improvement over results in 2016. Fair overall results on stability tests (3.7) including weak risk adjusted capital in prior years. Good liquidity (6.4).
Other Rating Factors: Low quality investment portfolio (2.4). Excellent profitability (7.5).
Principal Business: Individual annuities (68%), group retirement contracts (29%), and individual life insurance (3%).
Principal Investments: NonCMO investment grade bonds (51%), CMOs and structured securities (28%), mortgages in good standing (10%), noninv. grade bonds (4%), and misc. investments (6%).
Investments in Affiliates: 3%
Group Affiliation: BRH Holdings GP Ltd
Licensed in: All states except NY
Commenced Business: February 1896
Address: 7700 MILLS CIVIC PARKWAY, WEST DES MOINES, IA 50266-3862

Phone: (888) 266-8489 **Domicile State:** IA **NAIC Code:** 61689

Data Date	Rating	RACR #1	RACR #2	Total Assets ($mil)	Capital ($mil)	Net Premium ($mil)	Net Income ($mil)
9-18	C	0.99	0.52	57,378.9	1,231.5	714.3	95.5
9-17	C	0.84	0.44	51,730.6	1,142.7	888.0	85.2
2017	C	0.97	0.51	54,933.3	1,164.2	1,533.9	239.3
2016	C	0.83	0.44	47,984.7	1,113.3	1,131.0	99.6
2015	C+	1.03	0.55	44,053.2	1,108.9	475.4	596.8
2014	C+	1.05	0.56	44,405.3	1,040.0	404.5	262.8
2013	C+	0.95	0.51	43,841.7	978.8	-25,903.0	43.1

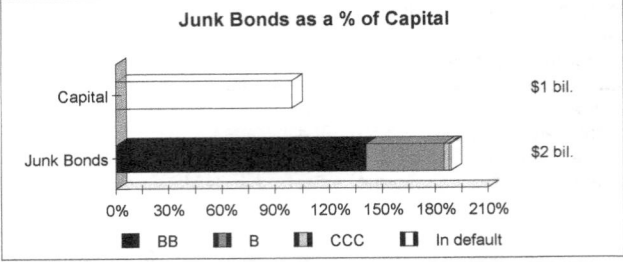

Junk Bonds as a % of Capital

ATLANTIC COAST LIFE INSURANCE COMPANY

B- **Good**

Major Rating Factors: Good capitalization (5.7 on a scale of 0 to 10) based on good risk adjusted capital (moderate loss scenario). Moreover, capital levels have been consistent over the last five years. Fair overall results on stability tests (3.5) including potential financial drain due to affiliation with Advantage Capital Partners LLC and weak results on operational trends. Fair quality investment portfolio (3.4).
Other Rating Factors: Weak profitability (2.7) with investment income below regulatory standards in relation to interest assumptions of reserves. Excellent liquidity (10.0).
Principal Business: Individual annuities (73%), individual life insurance (14%), group life insurance (12%), and group retirement contracts (1%).
Principal Investments: NonCMO investment grade bonds (57%), CMOs and structured securities (19%), mortgages in good standing (5%), noninv. grade bonds (4%), and misc. investments (9%).
Investments in Affiliates: None
Group Affiliation: Advantage Capital Partners LLC
Licensed in: AL, AZ, AR, CO, FL, GA, IL, IN, IA, KY, LA, MD, MS, MO, NE, NM, NC, OK, OR, PA, SC, TN, TX, UT, VA, WV
Commenced Business: March 1925
Address: 1565 SAM RITTENBERG BOULEVARD, CHARLESTON, SC 29407

Phone: (843) 763-8680 **Domicile State:** SC **NAIC Code:** 61115

Data Date	Rating	RACR #1	RACR #2	Total Assets ($mil)	Capital ($mil)	Net Premium ($mil)	Net Income ($mil)
9-18	B-	1.45	0.69	542.2	27.4	-38.6	5.3
9-17	B-	1.19	0.56	408.8	18.3	134.8	0.4
2017	B-	1.66	0.80	445.1	23.7	77.1	3.9
2016	B-	1.79	0.92	348.6	21.9	7.1	3.9
2015	B-	1.86	1.36	143.0	19.6	-35.7	2.2
2014	C+	1.81	1.63	129.1	14.9	23.8	2.5
2013	C+	1.52	1.37	116.5	12.1	24.0	0.1

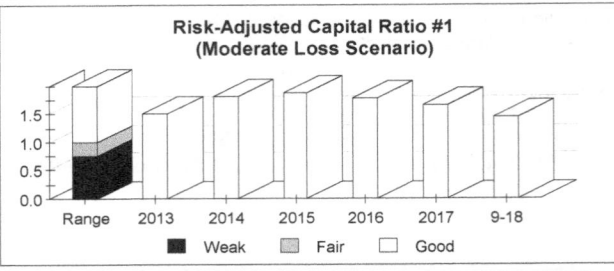

Risk-Adjusted Capital Ratio #1 (Moderate Loss Scenario)

AURORA NATIONAL LIFE ASSURANCE COMPANY

B **Good**

Major Rating Factors: Good overall results on stability tests (5.5 on a scale of 0 to 10) despite negative cash flow from operations for 2017. Other stability subfactors include good operational trends and excellent risk diversification. Good overall capitalization (6.0) based on good risk adjusted capital (severe loss scenario). Nevertheless, capital levels have fluctuated during prior years. Good quality investment portfolio (5.6).
Other Rating Factors: Good overall profitability (5.5) although investment income, in comparison to reserve requirements, is below regulatory standards. Good liquidity (6.8).
Principal Business: Individual life insurance (92%) and group life insurance (8%).
Principal Investments: NonCMO investment grade bonds (69%), mortgages in good standing (14%), CMOs and structured securities (8%), policy loans (4%), and misc. investments (4%).
Investments in Affiliates: None
Group Affiliation: Reinsurance Group of America Inc
Licensed in: All states except CT, ME, NH, NY, PR
Commenced Business: December 1961
Address: 818 WEST 7TH STREET, LOS ANGELES, CA 90017
Phone: (800) 265-2652 **Domicile State:** CA **NAIC Code:** 61182

Data Date	Rating	RACR #1	RACR #2	Total Assets ($mil)	Capital ($mil)	Net Premium ($mil)	Net Income ($mil)
9-18	B	1.69	0.88	3,097.8	145.4	0.4	7.0
9-17	B	1.43	0.73	3,097.5	119.6	0.5	6.0
2017	B	1.64	0.85	3,063.2	140.2	0.7	9.1
2016	B	1.58	0.80	2,935.4	126.5	0.6	16.6
2015	B	3.85	1.93	2,953.3	303.2	0.5	21.4
2014	B	4.27	2.22	3,061.6	321.1	0.6	18.0
2013	B-	4.39	2.27	3,143.7	341.5	0.6	17.8

Adverse Trends in Operations

Decrease in capital during 2016 (58%)
Decrease in premium volume from 2014 to 2015 (11%)
Decrease in asset base during 2015 (4%)
Decrease in capital during 2014 (6%)
Decrease in premium volume from 2013 to 2014 (8%)

AUTO CLUB LIFE INSURANCE COMPANY   C+   Fair

Major Rating Factors: Fair current capitalization (4.9 on a scale of 0 to 10) based on fair risk adjusted capital (moderate loss scenario), although results have slipped from the good range over the last two years. Fair overall results on stability tests (4.4) including fair risk adjusted capital in prior years. Good quality investment portfolio (5.6).

Other Rating Factors: Good liquidity (5.0). Weak profitability (2.6) with operating losses during the first nine months of 2018.

Principal Business: Reinsurance (95%), individual life insurance (4%), and individual annuities (1%).

Principal Investments: NonCMO investment grade bonds (62%), CMOs and structured securities (21%), noninv. grade bonds (8%), common & preferred stock (6%), and policy loans (2%).

Investments in Affiliates: 6%

Group Affiliation: Automobile Club of Michigan Group

Licensed in: AZ, AR, CA, CO, IL, IN, IA, KS, KY, MD, MI, MN, MO, NE, NM, NC, ND, OH, OK, PA, SC, SD, TX, VA, WA, WI

Commenced Business: August 1974

Address: 1 Auto Club Drive, Dearborn, MI 48126

Phone: (313) 336-1234 **Domicile State:** MI **NAIC Code:** 84522

Data Date	Rating	RACR #1	RACR #2	Total Assets ($mil)	Capital ($mil)	Net Premium ($mil)	Net Income ($mil)
9-18	C+	0.99	0.70	814.0	78.7	135.0	-4.9
9-17	C+	1.05	0.75	774.8	79.5	122.8	-8.2
2017	C+	0.98	0.70	760.8	76.4	162.2	-7.0
2016	C+	1.11	0.80	705.2	82.3	162.9	-5.3
2015	C+	1.15	0.83	623.7	77.1	141.1	-3.2
2014	C+	1.22	0.87	562.5	73.6	117.6	-8.0
2013	C+	1.14	0.81	503.6	59.6	89.0	-6.7

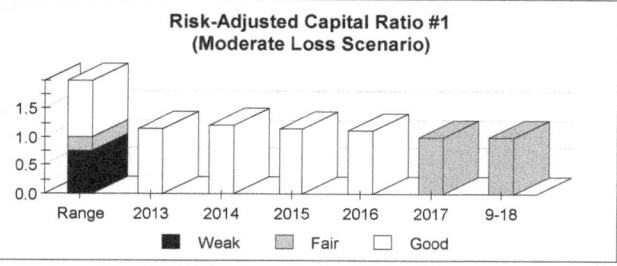

Risk-Adjusted Capital Ratio #1 (Moderate Loss Scenario)

AUTO-OWNERS LIFE INSURANCE COMPANY   B   Good

Major Rating Factors: Good quality investment portfolio (6.0 on a scale of 0 to 10) despite mixed results such as: minimal exposure to mortgages and substantial holdings of BBB bonds but small junk bond holdings. Good profitability (5.0) although investment income, in comparison to reserve requirements, is below regulatory standards. Good liquidity (6.4).

Other Rating Factors: Fair overall results on stability tests (4.4). Strong capitalization (8.0) based on excellent risk adjusted capital (severe loss scenario).

Principal Business: Group retirement contracts (47%), individual life insurance (27%), individual annuities (21%), and individual health insurance (4%).

Principal Investments: NonCMO investment grade bonds (67%), CMOs and structured securities (16%), real estate (4%), common & preferred stock (3%), and misc. investments (9%).

Investments in Affiliates: None

Group Affiliation: Auto-Owners Group

Licensed in: AL, AZ, AR, CO, FL, GA, ID, IL, IN, IA, KS, KY, ME, MA, MI, MN, MS, MO, NE, NV, NH, NM, NC, ND, OH, OR, PA, SC, SD, TN, UT, VT, VA, WA, WI

Commenced Business: January 1966

Address: 6101 ANACAPRI BOULEVARD, LANSING, MI 48917-3968

Phone: (517) 323-1200 **Domicile State:** MI **NAIC Code:** 61190

Data Date	Rating	RACR #1	RACR #2	Total Assets ($mil)	Capital ($mil)	Net Premium ($mil)	Net Income ($mil)
9-18	B	3.12	1.66	3,995.6	488.4	-89.5	22.4
9-17	A-	2.85	1.52	4,021.4	446.6	202.3	17.8
2017	B+	2.82	1.49	4,211.4	451.0	433.6	19.3
2016	A-	2.81	1.49	3,897.9	423.2	265.3	23.6
2015	A-	2.59	1.39	3,739.3	391.9	259.5	23.7
2014	A	2.41	1.28	3,632.3	344.0	257.2	16.0
2013	A	2.24	1.20	3,509.2	323.5	248.4	22.7

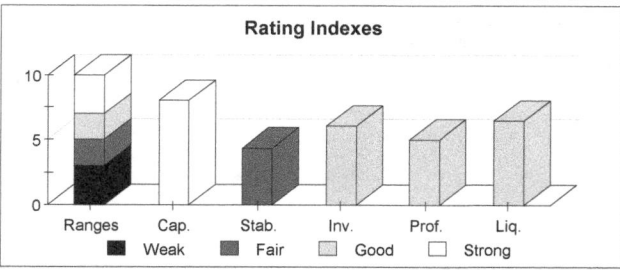

Rating Indexes

AUTOMOBILE CLUB OF SOUTHERN CALIFORNIA INSURANCE   B-   Good

Major Rating Factors: Good capitalization (5.1 on a scale of 0 to 10) based on good risk adjusted capital (moderate loss scenario). Good overall results on stability tests (5.1) despite fair risk adjusted capital in prior years. Strengths include good financial support from affiliation with Interins Exch Automobile Club, excellent operational trends and excellent risk diversification. Fair quality investment portfolio (3.2).

Other Rating Factors: Fair liquidity (3.6). Weak profitability (1.9) with operating losses during the first nine months of 2018.

Principal Business: Reinsurance (100%).

Principal Investments: NonCMO investment grade bonds (67%), CMOs and structured securities (23%), noninv. grade bonds (8%), and policy loans (1%).

Investments in Affiliates: None

Group Affiliation: Interins Exch Automobile Club

Licensed in: CA, MI

Commenced Business: December 1999

Address: 3333 Fairview Road, Costa Mesa, CA 92626-1698

Phone: (714) 850-5111 **Domicile State:** CA **NAIC Code:** 60256

Data Date	Rating	RACR #1	RACR #2	Total Assets ($mil)	Capital ($mil)	Net Premium ($mil)	Net Income ($mil)
9-18	B-	1.04	0.58	1,285.6	63.7	225.8	-14.7
9-17	B-	1.40	0.78	1,211.7	80.4	215.8	-12.4
2017	B-	1.19	0.67	1,199.0	72.9	282.2	-17.3
2016	B-	1.53	0.87	1,086.0	86.8	278.7	-10.4
2015	B-	1.68	0.96	947.3	82.1	228.3	-14.9
2014	B	1.68	0.95	841.8	74.4	193.7	-9.4
2013	B	1.39	0.78	746.9	53.7	140.6	-15.2

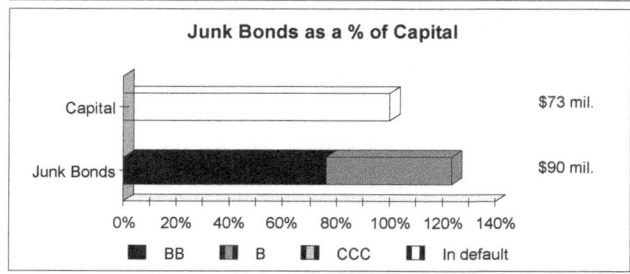

Junk Bonds as a % of Capital

AVIVA LIFE & ANNUITY COMPANY OF NEW YORK   C   Fair

Major Rating Factors: Good quality investment portfolio (5.6 on a scale of 0 to 10) despite mixed results such as: large holdings of BBB rated bonds but moderate junk bond exposure. Good overall profitability (6.5) despite operating losses during the first nine months of 2018. Weak overall results on stability tests (2.7) including fair financial strength of affiliated BRH Holdings GP Ltd and weak results on operational trends.

Other Rating Factors: Strong capitalization (7.4) based on excellent risk adjusted capital (severe loss scenario). Excellent liquidity (9.0).

Principal Business: Individual life insurance (93%), group life insurance (2%), reinsurance (2%), individual health insurance (2%), and group retirement contracts (1%).

Principal Investments: NonCMO investment grade bonds (81%), mortgages in good standing (8%), noninv. grade bonds (4%), CMOs and structured securities (4%), and cash (3%).

Investments in Affiliates: None

Group Affiliation: BRH Holdings GP Ltd

Licensed in: CT, FL, IL, IN, IA, KS, KY, MA, MI, MS, NV, NJ, NY, NC, PA, RI, VT

Commenced Business: November 1958

Address: 69 LYDECKER STREET, PEARL RIVER, NY 10965

Phone: (516) 364-5900 **Domicile State:** NY **NAIC Code:** 63932

Data Date	Rating	RACR #1	RACR #2	Total Assets ($mil)	Capital ($mil)	Net Premium ($mil)	Net Income ($mil)
9-18	C	2.58	1.25	970.0	83.9	1.1	-7.2
9-17	C	2.77	1.31	974.8	81.2	18.1	4.3
2017	C	2.41	1.17	967.9	75.5	19.1	6.3
2016	C	2.67	1.28	956.1	78.3	0.8	10.4
2015	C	2.72	1.30	945.1	72.9	1.4	14.4
2014	C	1.56	0.72	1,861.2	54.8	2.2	88.1
2013	C	1.76	0.83	1,727.8	64.0	-661.7	-114.9

BRH Holdings GP Ltd Composite Group Rating: C Largest Group Members	Assets ($mil)	Rating
ATHENE ANNUITY LIFE CO	54933	C
ATHENE ANNUITY LIFE ASR CO	13205	C
ATHENE ANNUITY LIFE ASR CO OF NY	3165	C
ATHENE LIFE INS CO OF NEW YORK	968	C

AXA CORPORATE SOLUTIONS LIFE REINSURANCE COMPANY   B   Good

Major Rating Factors: Fair quality investment portfolio (4.9 on a scale of 0 to 10). Fair profitability (3.4). Fair overall results on stability tests (4.9) including negative cash flow from operations for 2017.

Other Rating Factors: Strong overall capitalization (7.5) based on excellent risk adjusted capital (severe loss scenario). Nevertheless, capital levels have fluctuated during prior years. Excellent liquidity (9.1).

Principal Business: Reinsurance (100%).

Principal Investments: Common & preferred stock (49%), nonCMO investment grade bonds (44%), cash (4%), and CMOs and structured securities (1%).

Investments in Affiliates: 49%

Group Affiliation: AXA Financial Inc

Licensed in: All states except FL, PR

Commenced Business: January 1983

Address: 2711 Centerville Rd Ste 400, Wilmington, DE 19808

Phone: (201) 743-7217 **Domicile State:** DE **NAIC Code:** 68365

Data Date	Rating	RACR #1	RACR #2	Total Assets ($mil)	Capital ($mil)	Net Premium ($mil)	Net Income ($mil)
9-18	B	1.43	1.36	258.4	160.3	2.0	12.1
9-17	B	1.68	1.48	273.6	165.5	3.4	0.9
2017	B	1.44	1.37	259.9	160.0	4.6	54.2
2016	B	1.51	1.40	240.5	148.6	5.1	-20.7
2015	B-	2.04	1.83	255.2	154.1	6.4	-6.0
2014	B-	2.43	2.22	490.9	419.5	-536.1	95.1
2013	B-	8.09	5.47	978.0	253.9	52.4	57.8

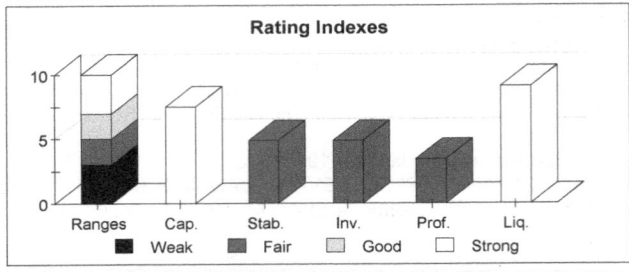

Rating Indexes

Ranges Cap. Stab. Inv. Prof. Liq.

■ Weak   ▨ Fair   ▢ Good   ▢ Strong

AXA EQUITABLE LIFE INSURANCE COMPANY *   B+   Good

Major Rating Factors: Good overall profitability (6.7 on a scale of 0 to 10) despite operating losses during the first three months of 2018. Good liquidity (6.2) with sufficient resources to cover a large increase in policy surrenders. Good overall results on stability tests (6.6) good operational trends, good risk adjusted capital for prior years and excellent risk diversification.

Other Rating Factors: Strong capitalization (8.4) based on excellent risk adjusted capital (severe loss scenario). High quality investment portfolio (7.1).

Principal Business: Individual annuities (57%), group retirement contracts (23%), individual life insurance (18%), and reinsurance (1%).

Principal Investments: NonCMO investment grade bonds (61%), mortgages in good standing (20%), policy loans (6%), noninv. grade bonds (2%), and misc. investments (8%).

Investments in Affiliates: 4%

Group Affiliation: AXA Financial Inc

Licensed in: All states, the District of Columbia and Puerto Rico

Commenced Business: July 1859

Address: 1290 Avenue of the Americas, New York, NY 10104

Phone: (212) 554-1234 **Domicile State:** NY **NAIC Code:** 62944

Data Date	Rating	RACR #1	RACR #2	Total Assets ($mil)	Capital ($mil)	Net Premium ($mil)	Net Income ($mil)
3-18	B+	3.79	1.95	191,807	7,320.1	2,422.7	-299.5
3-17	B+	1.77	1.11	179,286	4,912.4	3,430.9	-481.6
2017	B+	3.77	1.95	194,772	7,422.3	12,867.4	893.8
2016	B+	1.72	1.09	174,068	4,846.7	12,815.7	678.8
2015	B	2.29	1.39	164,668	5,422.6	12,220.2	2,038.0
2014	B	1.96	1.23	165,942	5,170.0	12,108.2	1,663.8
2013	B	1.49	0.90	158,658	3,825.5	11,934.6	-28.5

Adverse Trends in Operations

Decrease in capital during 2016 (11%)

BALTIMORE LIFE INSURANCE COMPANY   B   Good

Major Rating Factors: Good overall capitalization (5.9 on a scale of 0 to 10) based on good risk adjusted capital (moderate loss scenario). However, capital levels have fluctuated somewhat during past years. Good overall profitability (5.7). Good overall results on stability tests (5.1) excellent operational trends and good risk diversification.

Other Rating Factors: Fair quality investment portfolio (4.8). Fair liquidity (3.1).

Principal Business: Individual life insurance (87%), individual annuities (10%), reinsurance (1%), and group life insurance (1%).

Principal Investments: NonCMO investment grade bonds (77%), CMOs and structured securities (4%), policy loans (4%), noninv. grade bonds (4%), and misc. investments (10%).

Investments in Affiliates: None

Group Affiliation: Baltimore Life Holdings Inc

Licensed in: All states except NY, PR

Commenced Business: March 1882

Address: 10075 Red Run Boulevard, Owings Mills, MD 21117

Phone: (410) 581-6600 **Domicile State:** MD **NAIC Code:** 61212

Data Date	Rating	RACR #1	RACR #2	Total Assets ($mil)	Capital ($mil)	Net Premium ($mil)	Net Income ($mil)
9-18	B	1.62	0.85	1,286.6	83.3	91.1	2.0
9-17	B	1.74	0.90	1,263.8	83.2	94.7	1.2
2017	B	1.68	0.88	1,268.8	81.8	124.6	2.4
2016	B	1.67	0.85	1,241.7	81.3	134.0	3.2
2015	B	1.87	0.98	1,192.0	79.3	134.3	5.3
2014	B	1.87	0.98	1,140.4	74.7	139.1	4.5
2013	B	2.02	1.06	1,085.7	72.8	147.8	-2.6

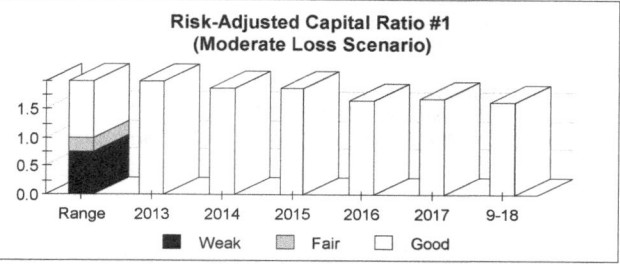

Risk-Adjusted Capital Ratio #1 (Moderate Loss Scenario)

BANKERS CONSECO LIFE INSURANCE COMPANY   D   Weak

Major Rating Factors: Weak profitability (2.2 on a scale of 0 to 10). Weak overall results on stability tests (1.8). Fair quality investment portfolio (4.4) with large holdings of BBB rated bonds in addition to moderate junk bond exposure.

Other Rating Factors: Good liquidity (6.8) with sufficient resources to handle a spike in claims as well as a significant increase in policy surrenders. Strong capitalization (8.0) based on excellent risk adjusted capital (severe loss scenario).

Principal Business: Individual life insurance (72%), individual health insurance (22%), individual annuities (5%), and reinsurance (1%).

Principal Investments: NonCMO investment grade bonds (60%), CMOs and structured securities (26%), cash (6%), noninv. grade bonds (3%), and misc. investments (5%).

Investments in Affiliates: None

Group Affiliation: CNO Financial Group Inc

Licensed in: NY

Commenced Business: July 1987

Address: 350 JERICHO TURNPIKE SUITE 304, JERICHO, NY 11753

Phone: (317) 817-6100 **Domicile State:** NY **NAIC Code:** 68560

Data Date	Rating	RACR #1	RACR #2	Total Assets ($mil)	Capital ($mil)	Net Premium ($mil)	Net Income ($mil)
9-18	D	3.34	1.66	494.3	60.2	46.9	1.0
9-17	D	3.77	1.80	475.5	57.4	45.1	-2.7
2017	D	3.31	1.67	478.1	58.2	58.3	-1.4
2016	D	2.66	1.23	449.7	41.2	54.2	-13.3
2015	D	4.81	2.98	218.1	47.5	49.6	5.6
2014	D	3.25	2.36	207.6	31.2	46.9	-6.8
2013	D	4.11	2.30	383.2	45.5	49.2	21.7

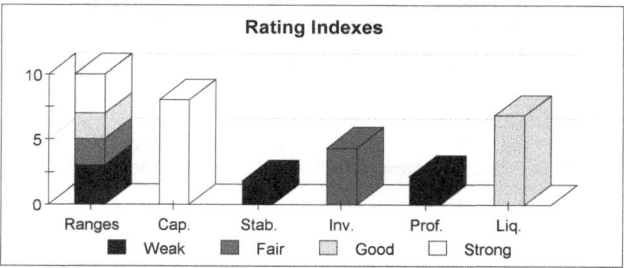

Rating Indexes

BANKERS FIDELITY LIFE INSURANCE COMPANY   C   Fair

Major Rating Factors: Fair quality investment portfolio (4.8 on a scale of 0 to 10) with large holdings of BBB rated bonds in addition to moderate junk bond exposure. Fair liquidity (4.5) as cash from operations and sale of marketable assets may not be adequate to cover a spike in claims or a run on policy withdrawals. Fair overall results on stability tests (3.8) including negative cash flow from operations for 2017.

Other Rating Factors: Good capitalization (5.6) based on good risk adjusted capital (severe loss scenario). Weak profitability (2.1) with operating losses during the first nine months of 2018.

Principal Business: Individual health insurance (76%), reinsurance (16%), individual life insurance (7%), and group health insurance (1%).

Principal Investments: NonCMO investment grade bonds (68%), common & preferred stock (12%), noninv. grade bonds (8%), CMOs and structured securities (5%), and misc. investments (6%).

Investments in Affiliates: 7%

Group Affiliation: Atlantic American Corp

Licensed in: All states except CA, CT, NY, VT, PR

Commenced Business: November 1955

Address: 4370 Peachtree Road NE, Atlanta, GA 30319

Phone: (800) 241-1439 **Domicile State:** GA **NAIC Code:** 61239

Data Date	Rating	RACR #1	RACR #2	Total Assets ($mil)	Capital ($mil)	Net Premium ($mil)	Net Income ($mil)
9-18	C	1.06	0.82	146.1	30.8	89.2	-3.6
9-17	B	1.07	0.82	140.6	29.7	83.1	-1.9
2017	B-	1.21	0.93	150.0	34.1	109.6	-2.9
2016	B	1.24	0.94	144.3	33.4	99.6	1.2
2015	B	1.28	0.96	143.9	35.3	96.1	4.0
2014	B	1.21	0.92	139.1	34.0	100.2	2.7
2013	B	1.58	1.14	138.8	34.5	99.6	3.0

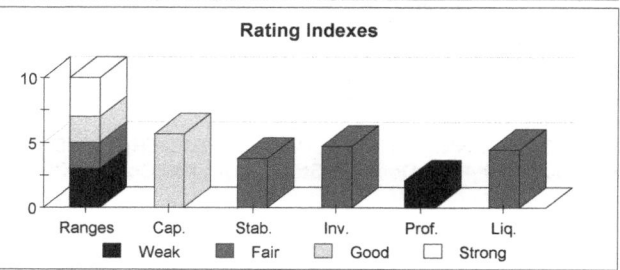

Rating Indexes

BANKERS LIFE & CASUALTY COMPANY

D+   **Weak**

Major Rating Factors: Weak overall results on stability tests (2.7 on a scale of 0 to 10). Fair quality investment portfolio (4.3) with large holdings of BBB rated bonds in addition to junk bond exposure equal to 59% of capital. Fair profitability (4.8) with operating losses during the first nine months of 2018.

Other Rating Factors: Good liquidity (5.6). Strong capitalization (7.1) based on excellent risk adjusted capital (severe loss scenario).

Principal Business: Individual annuities (39%), individual health insurance (29%), individual life insurance (17%), reinsurance (14%), and group health insurance (1%).

Principal Investments: NonCMO investment grade bonds (56%), CMOs and structured securities (26%), mortgages in good standing (6%), noninv. grade bonds (4%), and misc. investments (6%).

Investments in Affiliates: 1%

Group Affiliation: CNO Financial Group Inc

Licensed in: All states except NY, PR

Commenced Business: January 1879

Address: 111 EAST WACKER DRIVE STE 2100, CHICAGO, IL 60601-4508

Phone: (312) 396-6000 **Domicile State:** IL **NAIC Code:** 61263

Data Date	Rating	RACR #1	RACR #2	Total Assets ($mil)	Capital ($mil)	Net Premium ($mil)	Net Income ($mil)
9-18	D+	2.02	1.08	15,550.0	1,233.0	1,874.6	-321.8
9-17	D+	2.32	1.20	18,092.1	1,326.1	1,931.0	174.0
2017	D+	2.10	1.11	18,273.9	1,336.8	2,581.5	249.3
2016	D+	2.32	1.20	17,602.0	1,300.3	2,535.9	171.2
2015	D+	2.23	1.16	16,905.4	1,238.6	2,385.0	188.7
2014	D+	2.12	1.10	16,590.7	1,193.1	2,387.1	211.6
2013	D+	2.04	1.06	15,839.5	1,057.0	2,323.5	161.9

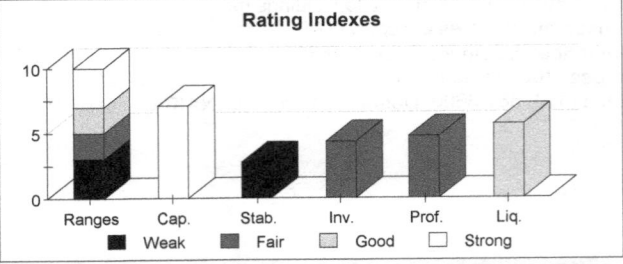

Rating Indexes

BANKERS LIFE INSURANCE COMPANY

C-   **Fair**

Major Rating Factors: Fair current capitalization (4.0 on a scale of 0 to 10) based on mixed results -- excessive policy leverage mitigated by excellent risk adjusted capital (severe loss scenario) reflecting significant improvement over results in 2015. Fair quality investment portfolio (3.5). Weak profitability (2.0) with operating losses during the first nine months of 2018.

Other Rating Factors: Weak overall results on stability tests (2.8) including weak results on operational trends and negative cash flow from operations for 2017. Good liquidity (5.9).

Principal Business: Individual annuities (99%) and reinsurance (1%).

Principal Investments: NonCMO investment grade bonds (61%), CMOs and structured securities (20%), cash (7%), and noninv. grade bonds (4%).

Investments in Affiliates: 2%

Group Affiliation: BLH Capital LLC

Licensed in: AL, AK, AZ, AR, CO, DC, DE, FL, GA, HI, ID, IL, IN, KS, KY, LA, MD, MI, MN, MS, MO, MT, NE, NV, NM, NC, ND, OH, OK, PA, SC, SD, TN, TX, UT, VA, WA, WV, WY

Commenced Business: May 1973

Address: 11101 Roosevelt Blvd N, Durham, NC 27713

Phone: (800) 839-2731 **Domicile State:** FL **NAIC Code:** 81043

Data Date	Rating	RACR #1	RACR #2	Total Assets ($mil)	Capital ($mil)	Net Premium ($mil)	Net Income ($mil)
9-18	C-	3.35	1.53	385.7	36.8	218.3	-9.8
9-17	C-	2.84	1.48	283.9	35.1	-184.0	-4.2
2017	C-	3.48	1.76	234.3	35.7	-176.6	-4.0
2016	C	1.67	0.82	447.4	27.4	57.5	0.6
2015	C	1.49	0.72	418.8	22.6	77.5	1.4
2014	C+	1.68	0.82	345.7	23.0	99.0	1.3
2013	C+	1.97	0.97	251.1	26.0	-85.0	4.2

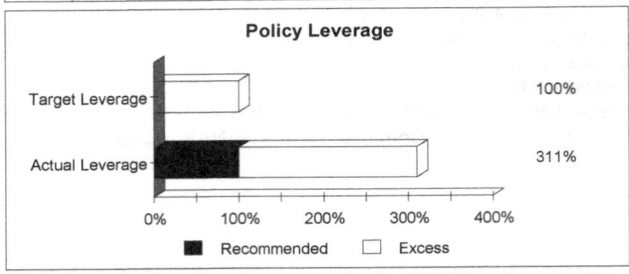

Policy Leverage

BANNER LIFE INSURANCE COMPANY

B-   **Good**

Major Rating Factors: Good quality investment portfolio (6.3 on a scale of 0 to 10) despite significant exposure to mortgages . Mortgage default rate has been low. substantial holdings of BBB bonds in addition to small junk bond holdings. Good overall profitability (5.3) despite operating losses during the first nine months of 2018. Fair overall results on stability tests (4.8) including excessive premium growth.

Other Rating Factors: Strong capitalization (8.1) based on excellent risk adjusted capital (severe loss scenario). Excellent liquidity (9.0).

Principal Business: Individual life insurance (59%) and group retirement contracts (41%).

Principal Investments: NonCMO investment grade bonds (64%), mortgages in good standing (11%), CMOs and structured securities (9%), noninv. grade bonds (4%), and misc. investments (5%).

Investments in Affiliates: 4%

Group Affiliation: Legal & General America Inc

Licensed in: All states except NY

Commenced Business: October 1981

Address: 3275 BENNETT CREEK AVENUE, FREDERICK, MD 21704

Phone: (301) 279-4800 **Domicile State:** MD **NAIC Code:** 94250

Data Date	Rating	RACR #1	RACR #2	Total Assets ($mil)	Capital ($mil)	Net Premium ($mil)	Net Income ($mil)
9-18	B-	2.61	1.76	4,020.8	496.0	598.6	-31.8
9-17	C+	1.74	1.26	3,034.8	354.4	441.1	46.3
2017	B-	3.96	2.72	3,850.8	751.6	967.6	65.5
2016	C+	2.32	1.71	2,881.9	481.7	720.1	157.6
2015	C	1.85	1.37	2,213.7	337.2	291.2	126.4
2014	D	1.35	1.09	1,818.6	369.1	219.8	-73.9
2013	D	1.84	1.44	1,687.7	450.0	324.1	-44.0

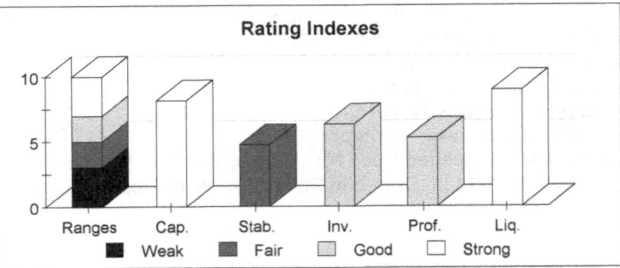

Rating Indexes

BENEFICIAL LIFE INSURANCE COMPANY

B **Good**

Major Rating Factors: Good quality investment portfolio (5.5 on a scale of 0 to 10) despite mixed results such as: no exposure to mortgages and large holdings of BBB rated bonds but small junk bond holdings. Good overall profitability (5.7). Good liquidity (5.6) with sufficient resources to handle a spike in claims as well as a significant increase in policy surrenders.

Other Rating Factors: Good overall results on stability tests (5.4) despite negative cash flow from operations for 2017 good operational trends and excellent risk diversification. Strong capitalization (7.2) based on excellent risk adjusted capital (severe loss scenario).

Principal Business: Individual life insurance (93%), individual annuities (5%), and reinsurance (2%).

Principal Investments: NonCMO investment grade bonds (74%), CMOs and structured securities (11%), common & preferred stock (5%), policy loans (4%), and misc. investments (4%).

Investments in Affiliates: None

Group Affiliation: DMC Reserve Trust

Licensed in: All states except NY, PR

Commenced Business: May 1905

Address: 55 North 300 West Suite 375, Salt Lake City, UT 84101

Phone: (801) 933-1100 **Domicile State:** UT **NAIC Code:** 61395

Data Date	Rating	RACR #1	RACR #2	Total Assets ($mil)	Capital ($mil)	Net Premium ($mil)	Net Income ($mil)
9-18	B	2.09	1.16	2,157.1	193.2	21.7	6.4
9-17	B	1.99	1.12	2,243.8	199.1	24.4	15.0
2017	B	2.36	1.31	2,251.3	205.7	32.2	13.4
2016	B	1.91	1.06	2,298.4	177.4	35.3	52.4
2015	B	5.11	2.77	2,796.0	585.1	40.0	39.3
2014	B	5.09	2.75	2,910.6	553.6	39.0	60.1
2013	B	6.14	3.22	3,011.2	579.1	43.0	44.9

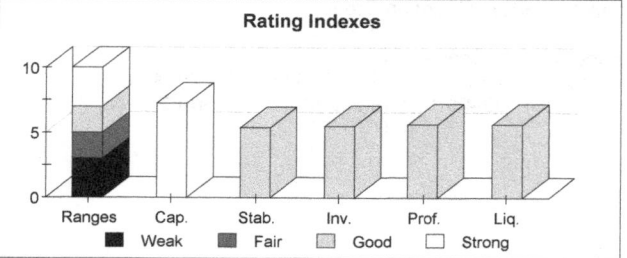

Rating Indexes

BERKLEY LIFE & HEALTH INSURANCE COMPANY *

A **Excellent**

Major Rating Factors: Good liquidity (6.8 on a scale of 0 to 10) with sufficient resources to handle a spike in claims. Excellent overall results on stability tests (7.8). Strengths that enhance stability include excellent operational trends and excellent risk diversification. Strong capitalization (10.0) based on excellent risk adjusted capital (severe loss scenario). Furthermore, this high level of risk adjusted capital has been consistently maintained over the last five years.

Other Rating Factors: High quality investment portfolio (7.8). Excellent profitability (8.7).

Principal Business: Group health insurance (99%) and reinsurance (1%).

Principal Investments: NonCMO investment grade bonds (56%) and CMOs and structured securities (45%).

Investments in Affiliates: None

Group Affiliation: W R Berkley Corp

Licensed in: All states except PR

Commenced Business: July 1963

Address: 11201 DOUGLAS AVE, URBANDALE, IA 50322

Phone: (609) 584-6990 **Domicile State:** IA **NAIC Code:** 64890

Data Date	Rating	RACR #1	RACR #2	Total Assets ($mil)	Capital ($mil)	Net Premium ($mil)	Net Income ($mil)
9-18	A	4.50	3.33	325.8	157.3	202.5	7.4
9-17	A	4.66	3.48	286.6	148.9	181.2	5.5
2017	A	4.73	3.50	277.3	150.7	238.1	8.2
2016	B	4.60	3.45	267.7	143.7	237.9	14.1
2015	B-	5.35	4.11	223.9	129.2	187.3	23.1
2014	B-	5.56	4.23	197.6	106.0	145.5	11.7
2013	B-	6.16	4.73	166.3	94.2	117.1	11.3

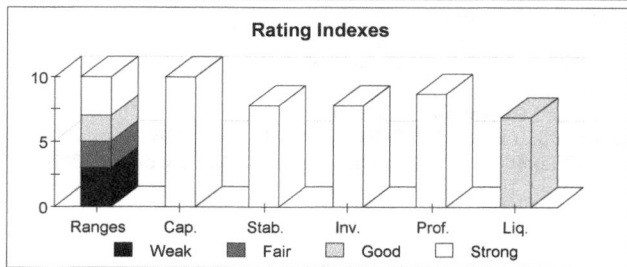

Rating Indexes

BERKSHIRE HATHAWAY LIFE INSURANCE COMPANY OF NEBR

C+ **Fair**

Major Rating Factors: Fair quality investment portfolio (3.7 on a scale of 0 to 10). Fair profitability (3.0) with investment income below regulatory standards in relation to interest assumptions of reserves. Fair overall results on stability tests (3.2) including weak results on operational trends.

Other Rating Factors: Strong capitalization (7.3) based on excellent risk adjusted capital (severe loss scenario). Excellent liquidity (10.0).

Principal Business: Reinsurance (65%), group retirement contracts (32%), and individual annuities (4%).

Principal Investments: NonCMO investment grade bonds (48%), common & preferred stock (20%), cash (5%), and CMOs and structured securities (2%).

Investments in Affiliates: 25%

Group Affiliation: Berkshire-Hathaway

Licensed in: All states except PR

Commenced Business: June 1993

Address: 1314 Douglas Street Suite 1400, Omaha, NE 68102-1944

Phone: (402) 916-3000 **Domicile State:** NE **NAIC Code:** 62345

Data Date	Rating	RACR #1	RACR #2	Total Assets ($mil)	Capital ($mil)	Net Premium ($mil)	Net Income ($mil)
9-18	C+	1.51	1.20	18,380.3	5,447.6	1,901.6	272.2
9-17	C+	1.82	1.53	18,746.1	4,735.0	1,707.5	267.8
2017	C+	1.52	1.31	19,610.1	4,816.0	225.2	437.6
2016	C+	1.70	1.44	17,969.6	4,398.4	2,735.0	425.7
2015	C+	1.56	1.31	16,287.3	3,684.5	2,943.9	406.4
2014	C+	1.42	1.21	14,786.4	3,283.3	1,693.6	361.1
2013	C+	1.35	1.19	13,768.3	2,701.4	4,073.2	1,527.4

Adverse Trends in Operations

Change in premium mix from 2016 to 2017 (124.7%)
Decrease in premium volume from 2016 to 2017 (92%)
Change in premium mix from 2013 to 2014 (19.6%)
Change in asset mix during 2014 (4.4%)
Decrease in premium volume from 2013 to 2014 (58%)

BERKSHIRE LIFE INSURANCE COMPANY OF AMERICA — B — Good

Major Rating Factors: Good overall profitability (5.5 on a scale of 0 to 10). Good overall results on stability tests (6.1). Strengths include potential support from affiliation with Guardian Group, excellent operational trends and excellent risk diversification. Fair quality investment portfolio (4.1) with large holdings of BBB rated bonds in addition to junk bond exposure equal to 71% of capital.

Other Rating Factors: Strong capitalization (7.3) based on excellent risk adjusted capital (severe loss scenario). Excellent liquidity (7.9).

Principal Business: Individual health insurance (75%), reinsurance (24%), and individual life insurance (1%).

Principal Investments: NonCMO investment grade bonds (91%), noninv. grade bonds (4%), CMOs and structured securities (1%), and real estate (1%).

Investments in Affiliates: None

Group Affiliation: Guardian Group

Licensed in: All states except PR

Commenced Business: July 2001

Address: 700 SOUTH STREET, PITTSFIELD, MA 1201

Phone: (413) 499-4321 **Domicile State:** MA **NAIC Code:** 71714

Data Date	Rating	RACR #1	RACR #2	Total Assets ($mil)	Capital ($mil)	Net Premium ($mil)	Net Income ($mil)
9-18	B	2.53	1.20	3,893.2	205.4	98.3	16.2
9-17	B	2.88	1.34	3,685.6	209.8	95.0	16.3
2017	B	2.57	1.20	3,717.7	189.1	126.9	10.2
2016	B	2.97	1.36	3,526.7	201.6	123.3	17.8
2015	B	3.34	1.58	3,381.4	207.9	118.2	14.2
2014	A-	4.53	2.24	3,377.3	269.5	114.0	16.9
2013	A	8.68	4.24	3,461.4	583.0	115.9	60.0

Rating Indexes

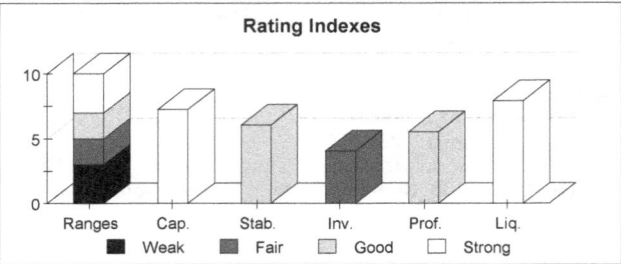

BEST MERIDIAN INSURANCE COMPANY — B- — Good

Major Rating Factors: Good quality investment portfolio (6.3 on a scale of 0 to 10) despite significant exposure to mortgages . Mortgage default rate has been low. substantial holdings of BBB bonds in addition to minimal holdings in junk bonds. Good overall profitability (5.2) although investment income, in comparison to reserve requirements, is below regulatory standards. Good liquidity (6.7).

Other Rating Factors: Fair overall results on stability tests (4.3). Strong capitalization (7.2) based on excellent risk adjusted capital (severe loss scenario).

Principal Business: Reinsurance (65%), individual life insurance (28%), and individual health insurance (6%).

Principal Investments: NonCMO investment grade bonds (40%), CMOs and structured securities (15%), cash (15%), mortgages in good standing (14%), and misc. investments (16%).

Investments in Affiliates: 1%

Group Affiliation: BMI Financial Group

Licensed in: FL

Commenced Business: August 1987

Address: 8950 SW 74TH COURT, MIAMI, FL 33156

Phone: (305) 443-2898 **Domicile State:** FL **NAIC Code:** 63886

Data Date	Rating	RACR #1	RACR #2	Total Assets ($mil)	Capital ($mil)	Net Premium ($mil)	Net Income ($mil)
9-18	B-	1.79	1.16	348.6	59.6	87.2	3.9
9-17	B-	1.88	1.20	334.7	58.6	83.4	1.5
2017	B-	1.64	1.06	336.9	54.2	111.5	1.1
2016	B-	1.64	1.07	317.2	56.5	158.2	0.6
2015	B-	1.94	1.25	303.2	60.8	142.6	8.0
2014	B-	1.77	1.13	277.8	53.0	138.9	7.2
2013	B-	2.02	1.33	254.5	47.9	100.8	7.0

Rating Indexes

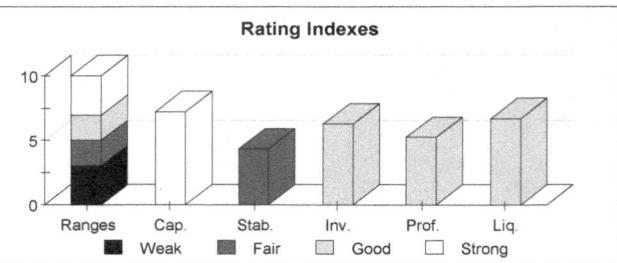

BLUE CROSS BLUE SHIELD OF KANSAS INCORPORATED — B — Good

Major Rating Factors: Good overall profitability (5.8 on a scale of 0 to 10). Excellent expense controls. Good liquidity (6.5) with sufficient resources to handle a spike in claims. Good overall results on stability tests (5.4) despite excessive premium growth. Other stability subfactors include excellent operational trends and excellent risk diversification.

Other Rating Factors: Fair quality investment portfolio (4.5). Strong capitalization (7.8) based on excellent risk adjusted capital (severe loss scenario).

Principal Business: Group health insurance (80%) and individual health insurance (20%).

Principal Investments: NonCMO investment grade bonds (31%), common & preferred stock (27%), CMOs and structured securities (19%), noninv. grade bonds (2%), and real estate (2%).

Investments in Affiliates: 6%

Group Affiliation: Blue Cross Blue Shield Kansas

Licensed in: KS

Commenced Business: July 1942

Address: 1133 SW Topeka Boulevard, Topeka, KS 66629-0001

Phone: (785) 291-4180 **Domicile State:** KS **NAIC Code:** 70729

Data Date	Rating	RACR #1	RACR #2	Total Assets ($mil)	Capital ($mil)	Net Premium ($mil)	Net Income ($mil)
9-18	B	2.01	1.50	1,791.6	874.2	1,691.4	71.4
9-17	B	2.00	1.54	1,571.6	821.1	1,329.1	75.1
2017	B	2.06	1.54	1,730.4	791.6	1,775.0	3.4
2016	B	1.74	1.35	1,452.3	728.9	1,899.8	59.1
2015	B	1.84	1.39	1,404.1	686.7	1,854.4	-30.8
2014	B	2.05	1.50	1,555.1	753.6	1,797.7	-11.5
2013	B	2.26	1.62	1,541.9	800.8	1,689.2	78.6

Adverse Trends in Operations

Decrease in premium volume from 2016 to 2017 (7%)
Decrease in asset base during 2015 (9%)
Decrease in capital during 2015 (9%)
Decrease in capital during 2014 (6%)

BLUE SHIELD OF CALIFORNIA LIFE & HEALTH INS COMPANY   B   Good

Major Rating Factors: Good overall profitability (5.8 on a scale of 0 to 10). Excellent expense controls. Fair overall results on stability tests (4.9) including weak results on operational trends. Strong current capitalization (10.0) based on excellent risk adjusted capital (severe loss scenario) reflecting improvement over results in 2013.

Other Rating Factors: High quality investment portfolio (8.1). Excellent liquidity (7.0).

Principal Business: Individual health insurance (63%), group health insurance (33%), and group life insurance (3%).

Principal Investments: NonCMO investment grade bonds (56%) and CMOs and structured securities (42%).

Investments in Affiliates: None

Group Affiliation: Blue Shield of California

Licensed in: CA

Commenced Business: July 1954

Address: 50 Beale Street, San Francisco, CA 94105-0000

Phone: (800) 642-5599 **Domicile State:** CA **NAIC Code:** 61557

Data Date	Rating	RACR #1	RACR #2	Total Assets ($mil)	Capital ($mil)	Net Premium ($mil)	Net Income ($mil)
9-18	B	5.05	3.74	303.9	189.5	182.0	10.7
9-17	B	3.14	2.43	338.4	164.0	191.6	-16.2
2017	B	4.61	3.41	303.5	179.2	253.4	9.7
2016	B	5.28	4.03	463.6	323.0	310.2	22.9
2015	B	2.98	2.37	665.2	481.1	1,249.2	39.5
2014	A-	1.93	1.53	743.7	444.3	1,794.5	78.5
2013	A-	1.22	0.97	890.7	367.1	2,381.3	12.3

Adverse Trends in Operations

Decrease in asset base during 2017 (34%)
Decrease in capital during 2017 (44%)
Decrease in premium volume from 2015 to 2016 (75%)
Decrease in capital during 2016 (33%)
Decrease in premium volume from 2014 to 2015 (30%)

BLUEBONNET LIFE INSURANCE COMPANY *   B+   Good

Major Rating Factors: Good overall results on stability tests (6.4 on a scale of 0 to 10). Stability strengths include excellent operational trends and good risk diversification. Strong capitalization (10.0) based on excellent risk adjusted capital (severe loss scenario). Moreover, capital levels have been consistently high over the last five years. High quality investment portfolio (8.1).

Other Rating Factors: Excellent profitability (9.4). Excellent liquidity (10.0).

Principal Business: Group life insurance (96%) and individual life insurance (4%).

Principal Investments: NonCMO investment grade bonds (57%), CMOs and structured securities (29%), noninv. grade bonds (1%), common & preferred stock (1%), and cash (1%).

Investments in Affiliates: None

Group Affiliation: Bl Cross & Bl Shield of Mississippi

Licensed in: AL, AR, LA, MS, TN

Commenced Business: June 1984

Address: 3545 Lakeland Dr, Flowood, MS 39232

Phone: (601) 664-4218 **Domicile State:** MS **NAIC Code:** 68535

Data Date	Rating	RACR #1	RACR #2	Total Assets ($mil)	Capital ($mil)	Net Premium ($mil)	Net Income ($mil)
9-18	B+	8.28	7.45	64.3	59.8	3.4	2.2
9-17	B+	8.02	7.22	62.2	57.4	3.4	1.9
2017	B+	7.91	7.12	61.3	57.2	4.6	2.6
2016	B+	7.76	6.98	59.5	55.5	4.7	2.5
2015	B+	7.53	6.78	57.0	53.0	4.8	2.6
2014	B+	7.22	6.50	54.3	49.9	5.0	2.5
2013	B+	6.99	6.29	52.0	47.7	5.5	2.4

Adverse Trends in Operations

Decrease in premium volume from 2016 to 2017 (2%)
Decrease in premium volume from 2015 to 2016 (3%)
Decrease in premium volume from 2014 to 2015 (4%)
Decrease in premium volume from 2013 to 2014 (8%)

BOSTON MUTUAL LIFE INSURANCE COMPANY *   B+   Good

Major Rating Factors: Good quality investment portfolio (6.2 on a scale of 0 to 10) despite significant exposure to mortgages . Mortgage default rate has been low. substantial holdings of BBB bonds in addition to minimal holdings in junk bonds. Good liquidity (6.0) with sufficient resources to handle a spike in claims as well as a significant increase in policy surrenders. Good overall results on stability tests (6.4) excellent operational trends and excellent risk diversification.

Other Rating Factors: Strong capitalization (7.6) based on excellent risk adjusted capital (severe loss scenario). Excellent profitability (7.2).

Principal Business: Individual life insurance (56%), group health insurance (23%), group life insurance (18%), and individual health insurance (4%).

Principal Investments: NonCMO investment grade bonds (56%), mortgages in good standing (15%), policy loans (12%), common & preferred stock (6%), and misc. investments (12%).

Investments in Affiliates: 2%

Group Affiliation: Boston Mutual Group

Licensed in: All states, the District of Columbia and Puerto Rico

Commenced Business: February 1892

Address: 120 Royall Street, Canton, MA 02021-1098

Phone: (781) 828-7000 **Domicile State:** MA **NAIC Code:** 61476

Data Date	Rating	RACR #1	RACR #2	Total Assets ($mil)	Capital ($mil)	Net Premium ($mil)	Net Income ($mil)
9-18	B+	2.20	1.42	1,461.7	221.7	152.1	10.7
9-17	B+	2.31	1.51	1,424.8	209.6	147.6	12.6
2017	B+	2.26	1.48	1,430.5	209.4	196.7	13.9
2016	B+	2.06	1.35	1,359.7	178.0	188.1	11.4
2015	B+	1.98	1.31	1,297.1	159.1	185.7	12.8
2014	B+	1.95	1.29	1,245.2	145.3	185.3	9.9
2013	B+	2.07	1.36	1,188.8	142.5	182.6	16.0

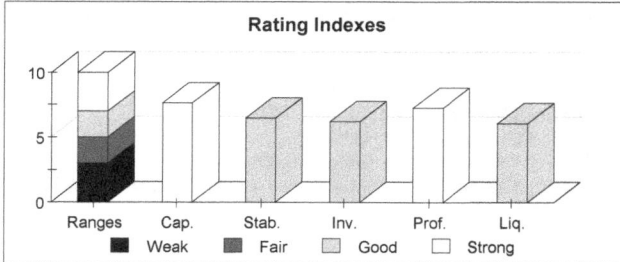

Rating Indexes

BROOKE LIFE INSURANCE COMPANY

B- **Good**

Major Rating Factors: Good overall profitability (6.8 on a scale of 0 to 10). Excellent expense controls. Fair overall results on stability tests (4.1). Low quality investment portfolio (1.2).
Other Rating Factors: Strong capitalization (7.2) based on excellent risk adjusted capital (severe loss scenario). Excellent liquidity (9.5).
Principal Business: Reinsurance (86%) and individual annuities (14%).
Principal Investments: Common & preferred stock (91%), nonCMO investment grade bonds (8%), and CMOs and structured securities (1%).
Investments in Affiliates: 91%
Group Affiliation: Prudential plc
Licensed in: MI
Commenced Business: August 1987
Address: 1 CORPORATE WAY, LANSING, MI 48951
Phone: (517) 381-5500 **Domicile State:** MI **NAIC Code:** 78620

Data Date	Rating	RACR #1	RACR #2	Total Assets ($mil)	Capital ($mil)	Net Premium ($mil)	Net Income ($mil)
9-18	B-	1.26	1.12	4,657.8	4,322.2	24.8	457.6
9-17	B	1.02	0.91	4,721.2	4,360.8	31.9	608.9
2017	B	1.15	1.02	4,299.7	3,936.5	39.3	604.7
2016	C+	1.17	1.04	5,326.7	4,966.8	9.2	557.8
2015	C+	1.16	1.03	5,131.1	4,765.0	10.6	716.0
2014	C+	1.15	1.02	4,914.3	4,526.6	9.1	655.7
2013	C+	1.06	0.94	4,783.6	4,042.2	14.8	408.4

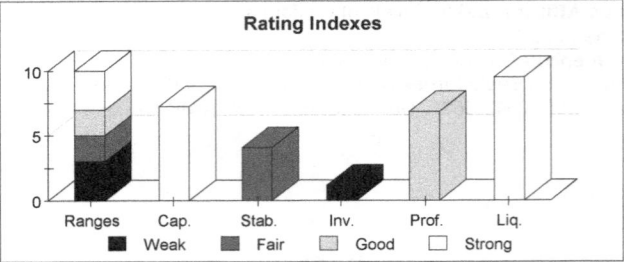

Rating Indexes

CANADA LIFE ASSURANCE COMPANY-US BRANCH

C **Fair**

Major Rating Factors: Fair profitability (4.0 on a scale of 0 to 10) with investment income below regulatory standards in relation to interest assumptions of reserves. Fair liquidity (4.9) as cash from operations and sale of marketable assets may not be adequate to cover a spike in claims or a run on policy withdrawals. Fair overall results on stability tests (3.7) including negative cash flow from operations for 2017, fair risk adjusted capital in prior years.
Other Rating Factors: Good capitalization (5.6) based on good risk adjusted capital (moderate loss scenario). Good quality investment portfolio (5.9).
Principal Business: Reinsurance (99%) and individual life insurance (1%).
Principal Investments: NonCMO investment grade bonds (66%), mortgages in good standing (11%), CMOs and structured securities (11%), policy loans (7%), and noninv. grade bonds (1%).
Investments in Affiliates: None
Group Affiliation: Great West Life Asr
Licensed in: All states except PR
Commenced Business: August 1847
Address: 330 University Avenue, Toronto, ON M5G 1R8
Phone: (303) 737-3000 **Domicile State:** MI **NAIC Code:** 80659

Data Date	Rating	RACR #1	RACR #2	Total Assets ($mil)	Capital ($mil)	Net Premium ($mil)	Net Income ($mil)
9-18	C	1.37	0.73	4,624.3	185.9	91.7	23.4
9-17	C	0.89	0.52	4,554.4	157.7	101.7	0.2
2017	C	1.18	0.63	4,581.8	147.1	134.6	-3.9
2016	C	0.91	0.52	4,567.2	157.0	211.1	11.9
2015	C	1.10	0.58	4,403.7	131.6	122.9	15.8
2014	C	1.14	0.60	4,425.1	136.2	132.2	5.7
2013	C	1.15	0.61	4,318.9	135.4	141.6	36.5

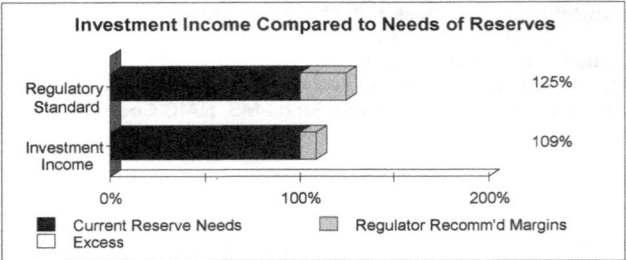

Investment Income Compared to Needs of Reserves

CAPITOL LIFE INSURANCE COMPANY

C **Fair**

Major Rating Factors: Fair overall results on stability tests (3.6 on a scale of 0 to 10) including fair financial strength of affiliated Liberty Life Group Trust. Fair quality investment portfolio (4.4) with large holdings of BBB rated bonds in addition to moderate junk bond exposure. Exposure to mortgages is significant, but the mortgage default rate has been low. Good overall profitability (5.5) although investment income, in comparison to reserve requirements, is below regulatory standards.
Other Rating Factors: Good liquidity (5.4). Strong capitalization (7.7) based on excellent risk adjusted capital (severe loss scenario).
Principal Business: Reinsurance (79%), individual annuities (15%), and individual life insurance (5%).
Principal Investments: NonCMO investment grade bonds (72%), mortgages in good standing (21%), noninv. grade bonds (3%), and CMOs and structured securities (3%).
Investments in Affiliates: None
Group Affiliation: Liberty Life Group Trust
Licensed in: All states except FL, NY, PR
Commenced Business: August 1905
Address: 1605 LBJ Freeway Suite 710, Dallas, TX 75234
Phone: (469) 522-4400 **Domicile State:** TX **NAIC Code:** 61581

Data Date	Rating	RACR #1	RACR #2	Total Assets ($mil)	Capital ($mil)	Net Premium ($mil)	Net Income ($mil)
9-18	C	2.88	1.44	299.9	28.0	14.1	2.6
9-17	C	2.89	1.58	245.0	27.0	11.9	1.9
2017	C	2.62	1.44	301.3	25.6	72.2	1.0
2016	C	2.70	1.55	241.5	25.4	28.0	2.0
2015	C	2.52	1.64	225.5	23.4	28.6	2.2
2014	C	2.36	1.59	214.4	21.7	7.3	2.7
2013	C-	2.29	1.35	210.0	21.0	7.7	2.1

Liberty Life Group Trust Composite Group Rating: C- Largest Group Members	Assets ($mil)	Rating
LIBERTY BANKERS LIFE INS CO	1712	D+
CAPITOL LIFE INS CO	301	C
AMERICAN BENEFIT LIFE INS CO	141	C
CONTINENTAL LIFE INS CO	27	D+
CONTINENTAL MUTUAL INS CO	2	D

CENTRAL STATES HEALTH & LIFE COMPANY OF OMAHA   B   Good

Major Rating Factors: Good quality investment portfolio (5.8 on a scale of 0 to 10) despite mixed results such as: minimal exposure to mortgages and substantial holdings of BBB bonds but minimal holdings in junk bonds. Good overall profitability (6.2) despite operating losses during the first nine months of 2018. Fair overall results on stability tests (4.7) including negative cash flow from operations for 2017.

Other Rating Factors: Strong capitalization (9.8) based on excellent risk adjusted capital (severe loss scenario). Excellent liquidity (7.3).

Principal Business: Credit life insurance (52%), credit health insurance (30%), individual health insurance (12%), group health insurance (3%), and individual life insurance (2%).

Principal Investments: NonCMO investment grade bonds (42%), CMOs and structured securities (24%), common & preferred stock (12%), mortgages in good standing (5%), and misc. investments (16%).

Investments in Affiliates: 7%

Group Affiliation: Central States Group

Licensed in: All states except NY, PR

Commenced Business: June 1932

Address: 1212 North 96th Street, Omaha, NE 68114

Phone: (402) 397-1111   **Domicile State:** NE   **NAIC Code:** 61751

Data Date	Rating	RACR #1	RACR #2	Total Assets ($mil)	Capital ($mil)	Net Premium ($mil)	Net Income ($mil)
9-18	B	3.94	2.87	389.7	131.9	84.7	-2.8
9-17	A-	4.51	3.21	411.0	146.7	30.1	10.6
2017	A-	4.58	3.30	407.5	151.9	37.8	13.0
2016	A-	4.28	3.06	420.0	134.3	51.3	10.5
2015	A-	3.99	2.88	419.9	122.9	66.1	6.4
2014	A-	3.79	2.71	414.7	119.6	72.7	5.5
2013	A-	3.98	2.85	395.5	119.6	77.1	0.2

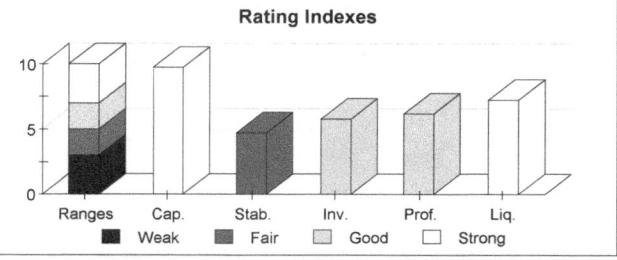

Rating Indexes

CENTRAL UNITED LIFE INSURANCE COMPANY   C   Fair

Major Rating Factors: Fair capitalization (3.2 on a scale of 0 to 10) based on fair risk adjusted capital (severe loss scenario). Fair overall results on stability tests (3.2) including fair risk adjusted capital in prior years. Good quality investment portfolio (5.2) despite significant exposure to mortgages . Mortgage default rate has been low. substantial holdings of BBB bonds in addition to minimal holdings in junk bonds.

Other Rating Factors: Good overall profitability (5.3) although investment income, in comparison to reserve requirements, is below regulatory standards. Good liquidity (5.8).

Principal Business: Individual health insurance (76%), reinsurance (17%), group health insurance (5%), and individual life insurance (2%).

Principal Investments: Common & preferred stock (38%), nonCMO investment grade bonds (34%), mortgages in good standing (13%), real estate (6%), and misc. investments (3%).

Investments in Affiliates: 38%

Group Affiliation: Manhattan Life Group Inc

Licensed in: All states except FL, NJ, NY, PR

Commenced Business: September 1963

Address: 425 W Capitol Ave Ste 1800, Little Rock, AR 72201

Phone: (713) 529-0045   **Domicile State:** AR   **NAIC Code:** 61883

Data Date	Rating	RACR #1	RACR #2	Total Assets ($mil)	Capital ($mil)	Net Premium ($mil)	Net Income ($mil)
9-18	C	0.59	0.52	675.1	107.8	192.0	8.9
9-17	C	0.64	0.58	390.7	102.0	84.0	5.5
2017	C	0.62	0.57	390.8	102.4	113.8	4.3
2016	C	0.61	0.55	385.0	95.6	99.9	-1.6
2015	C	0.64	0.59	327.0	92.9	100.0	2.6
2014	C	0.58	0.53	305.1	76.8	92.7	3.9
2013	C	0.59	0.54	307.2	76.6	88.8	3.8

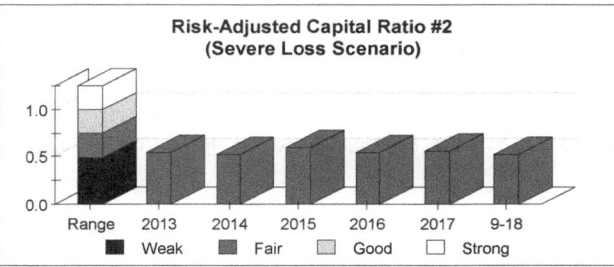

Risk-Adjusted Capital Ratio #2
(Severe Loss Scenario)

CENTRE LIFE INSURANCE COMPANY   B-   Good

Major Rating Factors: Good quality investment portfolio (6.7 on a scale of 0 to 10) with no exposure to mortgages and minimal holdings in junk bonds. Fair overall results on stability tests (4.7) including negative cash flow from operations for 2017. Weak profitability (2.8) with operating losses during the first nine months of 2018.

Other Rating Factors: Strong capitalization (9.3) based on excellent risk adjusted capital (severe loss scenario). Excellent liquidity (9.0).

Principal Business: Reinsurance (59%) and individual health insurance (41%).

Principal Investments: NonCMO investment grade bonds (82%) and CMOs and structured securities (18%).

Investments in Affiliates: None

Group Affiliation: Zurich Financial Services Group

Licensed in: All states except PR

Commenced Business: October 1927

Address: 1350 MAIN STREET SUITE 1600, SPRINGFIELD, MA 01103-1641

Phone: (212) 859-2640   **Domicile State:** MA   **NAIC Code:** 80896

Data Date	Rating	RACR #1	RACR #2	Total Assets ($mil)	Capital ($mil)	Net Premium ($mil)	Net Income ($mil)
9-18	B-	4.03	2.56	1,703.5	93.7	1.0	0.0
9-17	B-	4.01	2.49	1,834.2	93.3	1.0	-0.8
2017	B-	4.04	2.40	1,790.7	93.6	1.4	-1.7
2016	B-	4.03	2.48	1,809.8	93.8	1.4	-0.5
2015	B-	3.94	2.57	1,884.1	94.5	1.9	-3.7
2014	B-	4.03	2.54	1,926.1	98.0	0.0	-2.7
2013	B-	4.13	2.67	1,927.7	101.2	0.0	1.9

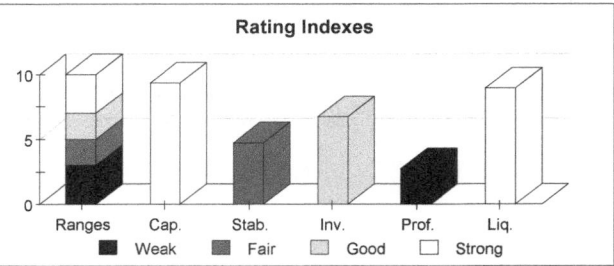

Rating Indexes

CENTURION LIFE INSURANCE COMPANY
C   Fair

Major Rating Factors: Fair overall results on stability tests (3.3 on a scale of 0 to 10) including negative cash flow from operations for 2017. Good quality investment portfolio (6.9) despite mixed results such as: no exposure to mortgages and large holdings of BBB rated bonds but minimal holdings in junk bonds. Good overall profitability (6.6). Excellent expense controls.
Other Rating Factors: Good liquidity (6.7). Strong capitalization (10.0) based on excellent risk adjusted capital (severe loss scenario).
Principal Business: Reinsurance (100%).
Principal Investments: NonCMO investment grade bonds (43%), CMOs and structured securities (28%), noninv. grade bonds (3%), and cash (2%).
Investments in Affiliates: None
Group Affiliation: Wells Fargo Group
Licensed in: All states except ME, NY, VT, PR
Commenced Business: July 1956
Address: 800 WALNUT STREET, DES MOINES, IA 50309
Phone: (515) 557-7321 **Domicile State:** IA **NAIC Code:** 62383

Data Date	Rating	RACR #1	RACR #2	Total Assets ($mil)	Capital ($mil)	Net Premium ($mil)	Net Income ($mil)
9-18	C	37.09	16.05	1,047.7	819.9	1.9	24.8
9-17	D+	4.40	2.57	1,267.7	368.1	160.7	50.7
2017	C	30.33	13.00	1,249.2	793.7	37.2	489.3
2016	D	3.82	2.23	1,288.2	317.7	172.8	22.5
2015	D	3.59	2.17	1,262.6	293.9	179.0	52.0
2014	D	2.64	1.59	1,259.3	251.2	314.0	-165.5
2013	D	4.92	2.88	1,209.0	397.3	204.6	-227.0

Rating Indexes

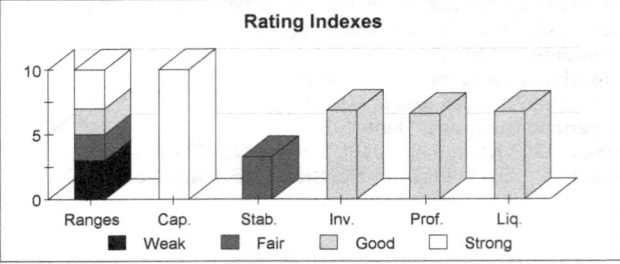

CHESAPEAKE LIFE INSURANCE COMPANY *
B+   Good

Major Rating Factors: Good overall results on stability tests (6.5 on a scale of 0 to 10) despite fair risk adjusted capital in prior years. Other stability subfactors include good operational trends and excellent risk diversification. Strong current capitalization (9.0) based on excellent risk adjusted capital (severe loss scenario) reflecting significant improvement over results in 2013. High quality investment portfolio (8.8).
Other Rating Factors: Excellent profitability (7.4) despite modest operating losses during 2013 and 2015. Excellent liquidity (7.5).
Principal Business: Individual health insurance (81%), individual life insurance (17%), and reinsurance (1%).
Principal Investments: NonCMO investment grade bonds (67%), CMOs and structured securities (8%), and cash (1%).
Investments in Affiliates: None
Group Affiliation: Blackstone Investor Group
Licensed in: All states except NJ, NY, VT, PR
Commenced Business: October 1956
Address: 1833 SOUTH MORGAN ROAD, OKLAHOMA CITY, OK 73128
Phone: (817) 255-3100 **Domicile State:** OK **NAIC Code:** 61832

Data Date	Rating	RACR #1	RACR #2	Total Assets ($mil)	Capital ($mil)	Net Premium ($mil)	Net Income ($mil)
9-18	B+	2.95	2.34	195.4	120.9	159.0	21.0
9-17	B	2.28	1.81	157.9	91.0	150.0	12.9
2017	B	2.21	1.76	158.7	86.7	200.8	16.6
2016	C+	1.85	1.47	133.3	69.7	184.3	11.6
2015	C+	1.38	1.11	99.8	46.8	159.6	-0.9
2014	C+	1.40	1.11	75.1	43.1	119.4	0.4
2013	C+	0.85	0.67	42.5	20.9	82.6	-3.2

Adverse Trends in Operations

Increase in policy surrenders from 2016 to 2017 (302%)
Change in asset mix during 2017 (5%)
Increase in policy surrenders from 2015 to 2016 (122%)
Change in asset mix during 2016 (5%)
Increase in policy surrenders from 2014 to 2015 (922%)

CHESTERFIELD REINS CO
C   Fair

Major Rating Factors: Good quality investment portfolio (6.8 on a scale of 0 to 10) despite mixed results such as: no exposure to mortgages and large holdings of BBB rated bonds but no exposure to junk bonds. Weak profitability (2.3) with investment income below regulatory standards in relation to interest assumptions of reserves. Weak liquidity (0.0).
Other Rating Factors: Weak overall results on stability tests (2.9) including lack of operational experience. Strong capitalization (7.2) based on excellent risk adjusted capital (severe loss scenario).
Principal Business: Reinsurance (100%).
Principal Investments: NonCMO investment grade bonds (81%), CMOs and structured securities (17%), and cash (1%).
Investments in Affiliates: None
Group Affiliation: Reinsurance Group of America Inc
Licensed in: MO
Commenced Business: October 2014
Address: 16600 Swingley Ridge Road, Chesterfield, MO 63017-1706
Phone: (636) 736-7000 **Domicile State:** MO **NAIC Code:** 15604

Data Date	Rating	RACR #1	RACR #2	Total Assets ($mil)	Capital ($mil)	Net Premium ($mil)	Net Income ($mil)
9-18	C	1.57	1.10	330.3	90.1	155.5	29.7
9-17	C	1.39	0.97	318.5	81.5	150.2	22.1
2017	C	1.67	1.17	326.1	95.3	201.1	40.6
2016	C	1.56	1.09	320.9	91.2	193.9	32.5
2015	C	1.46	1.02	332.9	106.9	191.2	35.0
2014	C+	1.63	1.14	311.0	98.8	244.3	-247.6
2013	N/A	N/A	N/A	0.0	0.0	0.0	0.0

Rating Indexes

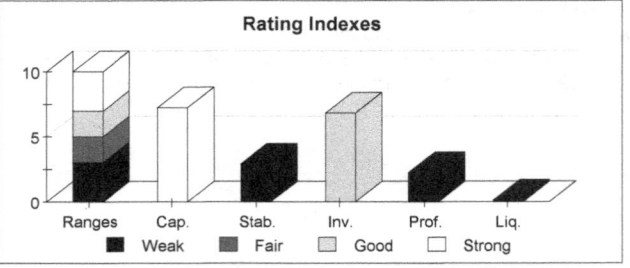

CHRISTIAN FIDELITY LIFE INSURANCE COMPANY *   B+   Good

Major Rating Factors: Good overall results on stability tests (6.5 on a scale of 0 to 10). Stability strengths include excellent operational trends and good risk diversification. Strong overall capitalization (9.7) based on excellent risk adjusted capital (severe loss scenario). Nevertheless, capital levels have fluctuated during prior years. High quality investment portfolio (7.9).

Other Rating Factors: Excellent profitability (7.3). Excellent liquidity (7.3).

Principal Business: Individual health insurance (88%), group health insurance (8%), and individual life insurance (5%).

Principal Investments: NonCMO investment grade bonds (84%), cash (6%), mortgages in good standing (4%), CMOs and structured securities (4%), and misc. investments (2%).

Investments in Affiliates: None

Group Affiliation: Amerco Corp

Licensed in: AL, AZ, AR, CO, FL, GA, ID, IL, IN, KS, KY, LA, MS, MO, MT, NE, NV, NM, ND, OH, OK, OR, SC, SD, TN, TX, UT, VA, WA, WV, WY

Commenced Business: December 1935

Address: 1999 Bryan Street Suite 900, Dallas, TX 75201

Phone: (602) 263-6666 **Domicile State:** TX **NAIC Code:** 61859

Data Date	Rating	RACR #1	RACR #2	Total Assets ($mil)	Capital ($mil)	Net Premium ($mil)	Net Income ($mil)
9-18	B+	3.78	2.77	64.2	32.9	20.5	6.3
9-17	B	3.53	2.58	67.6	34.0	23.3	6.0
2017	B	2.87	2.12	59.6	26.7	30.7	8.1
2016	B	2.75	2.03	63.9	28.0	34.5	8.1
2015	B	2.63	1.93	68.8	28.9	38.7	9.2
2014	B-	2.36	1.75	71.2	28.6	43.6	9.2
2013	B-	2.20	1.63	75.4	28.8	48.9	9.6

Adverse Trends in Operations

Decrease in premium volume from 2016 to 2017 (11%)
Decrease in premium volume from 2015 to 2016 (11%)
Decrease in premium volume from 2014 to 2015 (11%)
Decrease in premium volume from 2013 to 2014 (11%)
Increase in policy surrenders from 2013 to 2014 (138%)

CHURCH LIFE INSURANCE CORPORATION   B   Good

Major Rating Factors: Good quality investment portfolio (6.4 on a scale of 0 to 10) despite mixed results such as: no exposure to mortgages and large holdings of BBB rated bonds but small junk bond holdings. Good liquidity (6.5) with sufficient resources to handle a spike in claims as well as a significant increase in policy surrenders. Good overall results on stability tests (6.2) despite negative cash flow from operations for 2017 and excessive premium growth good operational trends and good risk diversification.

Other Rating Factors: Strong capitalization (9.5) based on excellent risk adjusted capital (severe loss scenario). Excellent profitability (7.7).

Principal Business: Group life insurance (55%), group retirement contracts (32%), individual annuities (11%), and individual life insurance (2%).

Principal Investments: NonCMO investment grade bonds (61%), CMOs and structured securities (26%), common & preferred stock (6%), and noninv. grade bonds (4%).

Investments in Affiliates: None

Group Affiliation: Church Pension Fund

Licensed in: All states except PR

Commenced Business: July 1922

Address: 19 East 34th Street, New York, NY 10016-4303

Phone: (212) 592-1800 **Domicile State:** NY **NAIC Code:** 61875

Data Date	Rating	RACR #1	RACR #2	Total Assets ($mil)	Capital ($mil)	Net Premium ($mil)	Net Income ($mil)
9-18	B	4.83	2.64	303.4	68.7	34.2	2.6
9-17	B	4.39	2.39	297.0	63.7	26.2	7.0
2017	B	4.72	2.58	294.2	64.7	34.6	8.1
2016	B	3.98	2.17	297.1	56.7	43.8	2.8
2015	B	3.91	2.14	291.7	53.3	35.4	2.0
2014	B	3.82	2.11	287.5	51.7	33.7	1.5
2013	B-	3.69	1.98	285.3	50.3	37.9	5.5

Adverse Trends in Operations

Decrease in premium volume from 2016 to 2017 (21%)
Increase in policy surrenders from 2015 to 2016 (31%)
Decrease in premium volume from 2013 to 2014 (11%)

CICA LIFE INSURANCE COMPANY OF AMERICA   D   Weak

Major Rating Factors: Weak overall results on stability tests (2.0 on a scale of 0 to 10) including weak risk adjusted capital in prior years. Fair quality investment portfolio (4.8) with large holdings of BBB rated bonds in addition to moderate junk bond exposure. Fair profitability (4.1) with investment income below regulatory standards in relation to interest assumptions of reserves.

Other Rating Factors: Fair liquidity (4.0). Good capitalization (6.8) based on good risk adjusted capital (severe loss scenario).

Principal Business: Individual life insurance (95%) and individual annuities (5%).

Principal Investments: NonCMO investment grade bonds (84%), policy loans (7%), common & preferred stock (3%), noninv. grade bonds (3%), and misc. investments (3%).

Investments in Affiliates: 3%

Group Affiliation: Citizens Inc

Licensed in: AL, AZ, AR, CO, DC, GA, HI, ID, IN, KS, KY, LA, MN, MS, MO, MT, NE, NV, NM, ND, OK, OR, PA, SC, SD, TN, TX, UT, WA, WV, WY

Commenced Business: June 1968

Address: 1560 Broadway Suite 2090, Denver, CO 80202

Phone: (512) 837-7100 **Domicile State:** CO **NAIC Code:** 71463

Data Date	Rating	RACR #1	RACR #2	Total Assets ($mil)	Capital ($mil)	Net Premium ($mil)	Net Income ($mil)
9-18	D	1.22	0.97	169.5	58.3	-723.9	26.9
9-17	D	0.76	0.55	989.6	46.7	112.2	9.4
2017	D	0.64	0.44	1,000.2	35.1	157.1	5.8
2016	D	0.60	0.43	932.7	34.9	156.7	14.5
2015	D	0.50	0.40	840.8	35.1	152.9	-5.0
2014	C-	0.65	0.51	773.3	42.0	146.8	-3.0
2013	C-	0.73	0.59	700.6	57.9	136.0	3.2

Rating Indexes

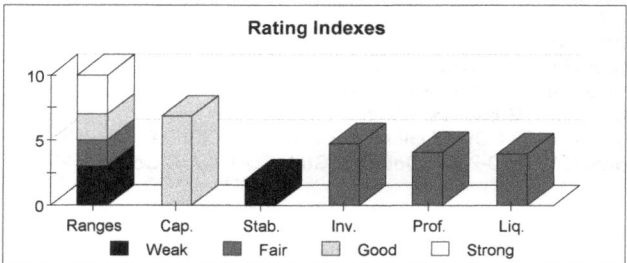

CIGNA HEALTH & LIFE INSURANCE COMPANY   B   Good

Major Rating Factors: Good overall results on stability tests (5.6 on a scale of 0 to 10). Stability strengths include excellent operational trends and excellent risk diversification. Fair quality investment portfolio (3.7). Fair liquidity (4.2) as cash from operations and sale of marketable assets may not be adequate to cover a spike in claims.

Other Rating Factors: Strong capitalization (7.1) based on excellent risk adjusted capital (severe loss scenario). Excellent profitability (9.9).

Principal Business: Group health insurance (84%), individual health insurance (14%), and reinsurance (2%).

Principal Investments: NonCMO investment grade bonds (50%), noninv. grade bonds (20%), mortgages in good standing (8%), common & preferred stock (7%), and CMOs and structured securities (2%).

Investments in Affiliates: 13%

Group Affiliation: CIGNA Corp

Licensed in: All states, the District of Columbia and Puerto Rico

Commenced Business: February 1964

Address: 900 COTTAGE GROVE ROAD, BLOOMFIELD, CT 6002

Phone: (860) 226-6000 **Domicile State:** CT **NAIC Code:** 67369

Data Date	Rating	RACR #1	RACR #2	Total Assets ($mil)	Capital ($mil)	Net Premium ($mil)	Net Income ($mil)
9-18	B	2.23	1.69	10,572.2	4,929.1	12,381.2	1,741.5
9-17	B	1.82	1.40	8,705.3	3,606.0	10,344.4	1,336.5
2017	B	1.86	1.42	9,002.2	3,680.6	13,779.7	1,569.1
2016	B	1.86	1.43	7,410.9	3,390.1	11,625.2	1,396.6
2015	B	1.66	1.31	6,559.9	3,008.9	11,457.7	1,187.2
2014	B	1.89	1.48	6,204.5	2,799.7	9,789.3	1,047.0
2013	B	1.68	1.37	4,139.3	1,713.2	6,456.2	489.1

Adverse Trends in Operations

Increase in policy surrenders from 2015 to 2016 (27%)
Change in asset mix during 2014 (5.3%)

CIGNA LIFE INSURANCE COMPANY OF NEW YORK *   A-   Excellent

Major Rating Factors: Good quality investment portfolio (6.3 on a scale of 0 to 10) despite mixed results such as: large holdings of BBB rated bonds but moderate junk bond exposure. Excellent overall results on stability tests (7.0). Strengths that enhance stability include excellent operational trends and excellent risk diversification. Strong capitalization (7.9) based on excellent risk adjusted capital (severe loss scenario).

Other Rating Factors: Excellent profitability (7.4). Excellent liquidity (7.0).

Principal Business: Group health insurance (68%) and group life insurance (32%).

Principal Investments: NonCMO investment grade bonds (88%), noninv. grade bonds (9%), and CMOs and structured securities (3%).

Investments in Affiliates: None

Group Affiliation: CIGNA Corp

Licensed in: AL, DC, MO, NY, PA, TN

Commenced Business: December 1965

Address: 140 EAST 45TH STREET, NEW YORK, NY 10017

Phone: (215) 761-1000 **Domicile State:** NY **NAIC Code:** 64548

Data Date	Rating	RACR #1	RACR #2	Total Assets ($mil)	Capital ($mil)	Net Premium ($mil)	Net Income ($mil)
9-18	A-	2.50	1.63	407.5	102.4	151.7	13.4
9-17	A-	2.47	1.61	403.0	95.7	134.4	10.1
2017	A-	2.71	1.77	403.7	109.0	178.7	22.9
2016	A-	2.41	1.58	383.4	92.0	164.4	5.1
2015	A-	2.69	1.78	364.4	97.4	150.3	18.9
2014	A-	3.25	2.08	368.1	102.8	128.0	24.7
2013	B+	3.21	2.03	375.9	93.5	119.9	16.9

Adverse Trends in Operations

Decrease in capital during 2016 (5%)
Decrease in capital during 2015 (5%)
Decrease in asset base during 2015 (1%)
Decrease in asset base during 2014 (2%)

CINCINNATI LIFE INSURANCE COMPANY   B-   Good

Major Rating Factors: Good capitalization (5.5 on a scale of 0 to 10) based on good risk adjusted capital (moderate loss scenario). Good overall results on stability tests (5.0) despite fair risk adjusted capital in prior years. Strengths include good financial support from affiliation with Cincinnati Financial Corp, excellent operational trends and excellent risk diversification. Fair quality investment portfolio (3.6).

Other Rating Factors: Fair profitability (3.6). Fair liquidity (4.6).

Principal Business: Individual life insurance (88%), individual annuities (9%), individual health insurance (1%), group life insurance (1%), and group health insurance (1%).

Principal Investments: NonCMO investment grade bonds (83%), CMOs and structured securities (6%), noninv. grade bonds (6%), policy loans (1%), and cash (1%).

Investments in Affiliates: 1%

Group Affiliation: Cincinnati Financial Corp

Licensed in: All states except NY, PR

Commenced Business: February 1988

Address: 6200 SOUTH GILMORE ROAD, FAIRFIELD, OH 45014-5141

Phone: (513) 870-2000 **Domicile State:** OH **NAIC Code:** 76236

Data Date	Rating	RACR #1	RACR #2	Total Assets ($mil)	Capital ($mil)	Net Premium ($mil)	Net Income ($mil)
9-18	B-	1.35	0.73	4,517.0	204.7	216.0	12.0
9-17	B	1.42	0.76	4,387.5	209.7	201.4	8.3
2017	B	1.31	0.70	4,407.2	195.1	272.8	12.4
2016	B	1.39	0.74	4,266.5	200.3	276.1	2.1
2015	B	1.45	0.77	4,066.8	208.4	250.1	-11.5
2014	B	1.65	0.89	3,916.0	223.5	243.8	-18.6
2013	B	1.94	1.06	3,737.5	247.0	235.3	-19.7

Junk Bonds as a % of Capital

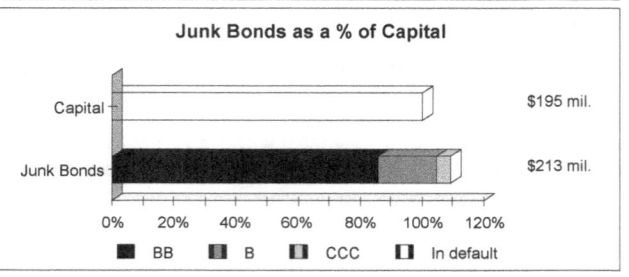

Capital — $195 mil.
Junk Bonds — $213 mil.

0% 20% 40% 60% 80% 100% 120%

■ BB ▨ B ▥ CCC ☐ In default

CM LIFE INSURANCE COMPANY   B   Good

Major Rating Factors: Good quality investment portfolio (5.3 on a scale of 0 to 10) despite large holdings of BBB rated bonds in addition to moderate junk bond exposure. Exposure to mortgages is significant, but the mortgage default rate has been low. Good liquidity (6.6) with sufficient resources to cover a large increase in policy surrenders. Fair overall results on stability tests (4.7).

Other Rating Factors: Strong capitalization (8.2) based on excellent risk adjusted capital (severe loss scenario). Excellent profitability (8.4).

Principal Business: Individual annuities (69%) and individual life insurance (31%).

Principal Investments: NonCMO investment grade bonds (47%), mortgages in good standing (14%), noninv. grade bonds (10%), CMOs and structured securities (10%), and misc. investments (13%).

Investments in Affiliates: 10%

Group Affiliation: Massachusetts Mutual Group

Licensed in: All states except NY

Commenced Business: May 1981

Address: 100 BRIGHT MEADOW BOULEVARD, ENFIELD, CT 6082

Phone: (413) 788-8411 **Domicile State:** CT **NAIC Code:** 93432

Data Date	Rating	RACR #1	RACR #2	Total Assets ($mil)	Capital ($mil)	Net Premium ($mil)	Net Income ($mil)
9-18	B	2.85	1.81	8,471.3	1,546.5	242.9	68.5
9-17	B	3.05	1.96	8,582.0	1,601.5	204.1	55.9
2017	B	2.93	1.86	8,657.3	1,573.2	283.4	67.1
2016	B	2.95	1.91	8,462.2	1,546.7	-79.9	61.7
2015	B	2.96	1.86	8,803.1	1,396.0	295.1	117.5
2014	B	2.85	1.75	8,792.5	1,304.8	316.1	160.4
2013	B	2.37	1.44	8,984.0	1,071.2	355.6	170.6

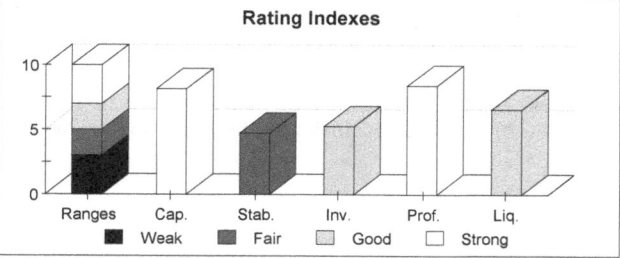

Rating Indexes

CMFG LIFE INSURANCE COMPANY   B-   Good

Major Rating Factors: Good liquidity (6.9 on a scale of 0 to 10) with sufficient resources to handle a spike in claims as well as a significant increase in policy surrenders. Good overall results on stability tests (5.0). Stability strengths include excellent operational trends, good risk adjusted capital for prior years and excellent risk diversification. Fair quality investment portfolio (4.8).

Other Rating Factors: Strong capitalization (7.4) based on excellent risk adjusted capital (severe loss scenario). Excellent profitability (8.0).

Principal Business: Group retirement contracts (28%), reinsurance (24%), individual life insurance (13%), credit health insurance (10%), and other lines (24%).

Principal Investments: NonCMO investment grade bonds (49%), mortgages in good standing (14%), CMOs and structured securities (13%), common & preferred stock (9%), and misc. investments (12%).

Investments in Affiliates: 15%

Group Affiliation: CUNA Mutual Ins Group

Licensed in: All states, the District of Columbia and Puerto Rico

Commenced Business: August 1935

Address: 2000 HERITAGE WAY, WAVERLY, IA 50677

Phone: (608) 238-5851 **Domicile State:** IA **NAIC Code:** 62626

Data Date	Rating	RACR #1	RACR #2	Total Assets ($mil)	Capital ($mil)	Net Premium ($mil)	Net Income ($mil)
9-18	B-	1.63	1.25	18,854.8	2,180.1	2,493.4	1.3
9-17	B-	1.64	1.27	17,660.7	2,154.5	2,340.2	130.8
2017	B-	1.59	1.24	18,078.3	2,107.2	3,130.1	227.3
2016	B-	1.53	1.19	16,573.5	2,002.7	3,139.4	195.2
2015	B-	1.47	1.16	15,475.9	1,858.4	3,110.2	256.2
2014	B-	1.33	1.04	15,490.1	1,632.9	2,479.9	106.9
2013	B-	1.26	0.98	15,659.8	1,553.5	1,923.4	101.9

Adverse Trends in Operations

Increase in policy surrenders from 2014 to 2015 (40%)
Increase in policy surrenders from 2013 to 2014 (49%)
Decrease in asset base during 2014 (1%)

COLONIAL LIFE & ACCIDENT INSURANCE COMPANY   C+   Fair

Major Rating Factors: Fair overall results on stability tests (4.4 on a scale of 0 to 10). Good quality investment portfolio (5.9) despite significant exposure to mortgages . Mortgage default rate has been low. large holdings of BBB rated bonds in addition to small junk bond holdings. Good liquidity (6.9) with sufficient resources to handle a spike in claims as well as a significant increase in policy surrenders.

Other Rating Factors: Strong capitalization (7.6) based on excellent risk adjusted capital (severe loss scenario). Excellent profitability (7.1).

Principal Business: Individual health insurance (66%), individual life insurance (21%), group health insurance (11%), and group life insurance (2%).

Principal Investments: NonCMO investment grade bonds (76%), mortgages in good standing (13%), noninv. grade bonds (3%), CMOs and structured securities (3%), and misc. investments (6%).

Investments in Affiliates: None

Group Affiliation: Unum Group

Licensed in: All states except NY

Commenced Business: September 1939

Address: 1200 COLONIAL LIFE BOULEVARD, COLUMBIA, SC 29210

Phone: (803) 798-7000 **Domicile State:** SC **NAIC Code:** 62049

Data Date	Rating	RACR #1	RACR #2	Total Assets ($mil)	Capital ($mil)	Net Premium ($mil)	Net Income ($mil)
9-18	C+	2.23	1.40	3,368.4	526.9	1,190.0	145.8
9-17	C+	2.54	1.59	3,274.2	580.7	1,129.7	116.8
2017	C+	2.14	1.35	3,220.0	490.4	1,503.0	157.9
2016	C+	2.53	1.57	3,143.9	562.1	1,414.5	151.5
2015	C+	2.65	1.64	3,018.8	566.0	1,333.8	157.8
2014	C+	2.44	1.53	2,922.0	567.1	1,277.5	160.9
2013	C+	2.71	1.66	2,752.7	538.2	1,238.8	134.4

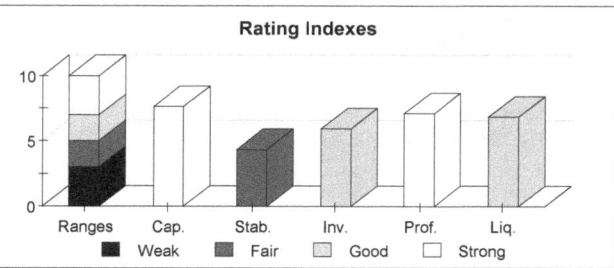

Rating Indexes

COLONIAL PENN LIFE INSURANCE COMPANY D+ Weak

Major Rating Factors: Weak overall results on stability tests (2.7 on a scale of 0 to 10) including potential financial drain due to affiliation with CNO Financial Group Inc. Weak profitability (1.9) with operating losses during the first nine months of 2018. Weak liquidity (2.5) as a spike in claims or a run on policy withdrawals may stretch capacity.
Other Rating Factors: Fair quality investment portfolio (4.0). Good capitalization (5.3) based on good risk adjusted capital (moderate loss scenario).
Principal Business: Individual health insurance (63%), individual life insurance (22%), and group life insurance (14%).
Principal Investments: NonCMO investment grade bonds (70%), CMOs and structured securities (17%), noninv. grade bonds (4%), policy loans (3%), and misc. investments (6%).
Investments in Affiliates: None
Group Affiliation: CNO Financial Group Inc
Licensed in: All states except NY
Commenced Business: September 1959
Address: 399 MARKET STREET, PHILADELPHIA, PA 19181
Phone: (215) 928-8000 **Domicile State:** PA **NAIC Code:** 62065

Data Date	Rating	RACR #1	RACR #2	Total Assets ($mil)	Capital ($mil)	Net Premium ($mil)	Net Income ($mil)
9-18	D+	1.23	0.71	871.8	97.1	294.5	-17.7
9-17	D+	1.27	0.73	860.4	97.4	285.7	-12.7
2017	D+	1.28	0.73	868.5	99.7	366.4	-11.7
2016	D+	1.27	0.72	854.7	95.8	352.5	-1.9
2015	D+	1.13	0.66	816.0	79.3	330.3	-18.8
2014	D+	1.16	0.67	742.8	73.3	303.7	-17.1
2013	D+	1.05	0.60	740.3	62.0	277.8	-19.1

CNO Financial Group Inc
Composite Group Rating: D+
Largest Group Members

	Assets ($mil)	Rating
BANKERS LIFE CAS CO	18274	D+
WASHINGTON NATIONAL INS CO	5418	D+
COLONIAL PENN LIFE INS CO	868	D+
BANKERS CONSECO LIFE INS CO	478	D

COLORADO BANKERS LIFE INSURANCE COMPANY C Fair

Major Rating Factors: Fair profitability (3.0 on a scale of 0 to 10) with operating losses during the first nine months of 2018. Good quality investment portfolio (5.5) despite mixed results such as: no exposure to mortgages and large holdings of BBB rated bonds but small junk bond holdings. Weak overall results on stability tests (2.1) including weak results on operational trends.
Other Rating Factors: Strong capitalization (7.1) based on excellent risk adjusted capital (severe loss scenario). Excellent liquidity (9.1).
Principal Business: Reinsurance (70%), individual annuities (24%), and individual life insurance (6%).
Principal Investments: NonCMO investment grade bonds (56%), CMOs and structured securities (11%), cash (11%), noninv. grade bonds (2%), and policy loans (1%).
Investments in Affiliates: 4%
Group Affiliation: SNA Capital LLC
Licensed in: All states except NY
Commenced Business: November 1974
Address: 2222 Sedwick Road, Durham, NC 27713
Phone: (919) 205-0713 **Domicile State:** NC **NAIC Code:** 84786

Data Date	Rating	RACR #1	RACR #2	Total Assets ($mil)	Capital ($mil)	Net Premium ($mil)	Net Income ($mil)
9-18	C	2.27	1.08	2,618.4	155.6	1,206.5	-42.4
9-17	B-	4.69	2.57	946.9	110.5	551.3	12.0
2017	B-	2.81	1.45	1,318.5	121.7	783.2	14.5
2016	B	4.73	2.54	354.1	58.5	61.7	5.0
2015	B	4.71	3.10	324.4	55.4	-72.2	9.6
2014	B+	2.72	1.57	284.2	33.9	90.2	3.9
2013	B+	2.49	1.46	256.9	28.9	89.4	3.2

Adverse Trends in Operations

Change in premium mix from 2016 to 2017 (19.8%)
Increase in policy surrenders from 2016 to 2017 (27%)
Change in premium mix from 2015 to 2016 (39%)
Change in asset mix during 2015 (9.8%)
Decrease in premium volume from 2014 to 2015 (180%)

COLUMBIAN LIFE INSURANCE COMPANY C Fair

Major Rating Factors: Fair liquidity (3.5 on a scale of 0 to 10) as cash from operations and sale of marketable assets may not be adequate to cover a spike in claims or a run on policy withdrawals. Fair overall results on stability tests (4.2). Weak profitability (2.5) with operating losses during the first nine months of 2018.
Other Rating Factors: Strong capitalization (7.6) based on excellent risk adjusted capital (severe loss scenario). High quality investment portfolio (7.4).
Principal Business: Individual life insurance (76%), group life insurance (20%), and individual annuities (4%).
Principal Investments: NonCMO investment grade bonds (62%), CMOs and structured securities (22%), policy loans (7%), mortgages in good standing (5%), and cash (2%).
Investments in Affiliates: None
Group Affiliation: Columbian Life Group
Licensed in: All states except AL, AK, ME, NY, ND, PR
Commenced Business: June 1988
Address: 111 South Wacker Drive, Chicago, IL 60602
Phone: (607) 724-2472 **Domicile State:** IL **NAIC Code:** 76023

Data Date	Rating	RACR #1	RACR #2	Total Assets ($mil)	Capital ($mil)	Net Premium ($mil)	Net Income ($mil)
9-18	C	2.57	1.42	342.1	34.3	44.6	-3.3
9-17	C	1.32	0.86	324.4	24.4	47.8	3.7
2017	C	1.99	1.11	335.8	26.3	61.2	4.0
2016	C	1.46	0.95	319.6	26.8	56.1	-3.3
2015	C	1.71	1.12	306.8	30.8	53.4	-2.3
2014	C	2.15	1.43	314.5	37.9	58.0	-0.9
2013	C+	1.48	0.99	292.7	24.3	58.0	-2.1

Rating Indexes

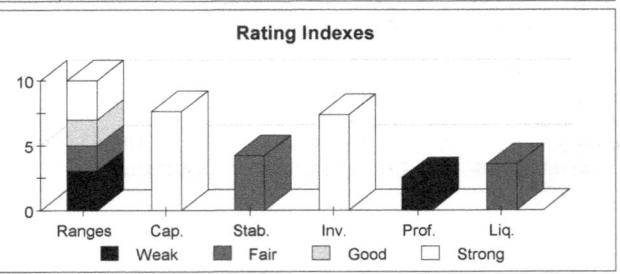

COLUMBIAN MUTUAL LIFE INSURANCE COMPANY　　　B　　Good

Major Rating Factors: Good quality investment portfolio (6.4 on a scale of 0 to 10) despite significant exposure to mortgages . Mortgage default rate has been low. large holdings of BBB rated bonds in addition to minimal holdings in junk bonds. Good profitability (5.0) although investment income, in comparison to reserve requirements, is below regulatory standards. Good overall results on stability tests (5.4) excellent operational trends, good risk adjusted capital for prior years and excellent risk diversification.

Other Rating Factors: Fair liquidity (3.6). Strong capitalization (7.0) based on excellent risk adjusted capital (severe loss scenario).

Principal Business: Reinsurance (68%), individual life insurance (30%), individual annuities (1%), and individual health insurance (1%).

Principal Investments: NonCMO investment grade bonds (64%), CMOs and structured securities (14%), mortgages in good standing (13%), policy loans (5%), and common & preferred stock (2%).

Investments in Affiliates: 2%

Group Affiliation: Columbian Life Group

Licensed in: All states except PR

Commenced Business: February 1883

Address: 4704 Vestal Pkwy E PO Box 1381, Binghamton, NY 13902-1381

Phone: (607) 724-2472 **Domicile State:** NY **NAIC Code:** 62103

Data Date	Rating	RACR #1	RACR #2	Total Assets ($mil)	Capital ($mil)	Net Premium ($mil)	Net Income ($mil)
9-18	B	1.60	1.02	1,454.3	105.2	136.7	4.1
9-17	B	1.62	1.04	1,445.0	102.6	138.9	6.7
2017	B	1.67	1.08	1,449.4	106.7	180.4	9.0
2016	B	1.55	1.01	1,398.0	96.2	183.2	9.2
2015	B	1.30	0.86	1,364.8	80.7	177.4	5.7
2014	B	1.19	0.82	1,326.3	79.2	175.3	5.6
2013	B	1.76	1.16	1,289.8	101.8	182.8	3.1

Adverse Trends in Operations

Decrease in premium volume from 2016 to 2017 (2%)
Decrease in premium volume from 2013 to 2014 (4%)
Decrease in capital during 2014 (22%)

COLUMBUS LIFE INSURANCE COMPANY　　　C+　　Fair

Major Rating Factors: Fair quality investment portfolio (4.8 on a scale of 0 to 10) with large holdings of BBB rated bonds in addition to junk bond exposure equal to 77% of capital. Fair overall results on stability tests (4.4). Good current capitalization (6.4) based on good risk adjusted capital (severe loss scenario), although results have slipped from the excellent range during the last year.

Other Rating Factors: Good liquidity (5.4). Weak profitability (1.9) with operating losses during the first nine months of 2018.

Principal Business: Individual life insurance (68%) and individual annuities (32%).

Principal Investments: NonCMO investment grade bonds (61%), CMOs and structured securities (16%), mortgages in good standing (6%), noninv. grade bonds (5%), and misc. investments (10%).

Investments in Affiliates: 3%

Group Affiliation: Western & Southern Group

Licensed in: All states except NY, PR

Commenced Business: July 1988

Address: 400 EAST 4TH STREET, CINCINNATI, OH 45202-3302

Phone: (513) 357-4000 **Domicile State:** OH **NAIC Code:** 99937

Data Date	Rating	RACR #1	RACR #2	Total Assets ($mil)	Capital ($mil)	Net Premium ($mil)	Net Income ($mil)
9-18	C+	1.80	0.93	4,144.8	257.5	244.4	-44.6
9-17	C+	1.97	1.03	4,095.0	290.7	196.2	-14.9
2017	C+	2.03	1.04	4,104.5	294.4	273.7	-39.5
2016	C+	2.04	1.06	3,769.2	290.1	268.6	-20.2
2015	C+	2.04	1.07	3,474.7	272.7	229.9	-13.3
2014	B-	1.85	0.98	3,337.3	222.6	249.5	-23.7
2013	B	2.05	1.09	3,198.9	250.8	228.6	-24.8

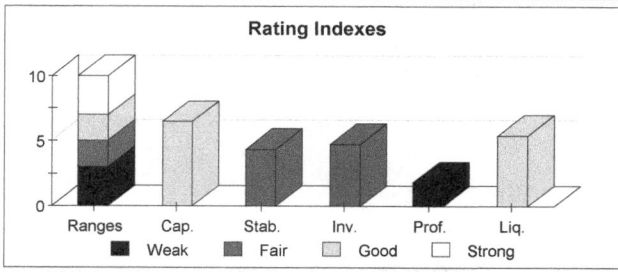

Rating Indexes

Ranges　Cap.　Stab.　Inv.　Prof.　Liq.

■ Weak　■ Fair　▨ Good　□ Strong

COMBINED INSURANCE COMPANY OF AMERICA　　　B-　　Good

Major Rating Factors: Good overall results on stability tests (5.3 on a scale of 0 to 10) despite fair risk adjusted capital in prior years. Other stability subfactors include excellent operational trends and excellent risk diversification. Good quality investment portfolio (5.5) despite mixed results such as: substantial holdings of BBB bonds but junk bond exposure equal to 57% of capital. Good liquidity (6.3).

Other Rating Factors: Fair profitability (4.7) with investment income below regulatory standards in relation to interest assumptions of reserves. Strong capitalization (7.3) based on excellent risk adjusted capital (severe loss scenario).

Principal Business: Individual health insurance (61%), group health insurance (26%), individual life insurance (7%), group life insurance (4%), and reinsurance (2%).

Principal Investments: NonCMO investment grade bonds (57%), CMOs and structured securities (19%), noninv. grade bonds (10%), common & preferred stock (3%), and misc. investments (4%).

Investments in Affiliates: 3%

Group Affiliation: Chubb Limited

Licensed in: All states except NY

Commenced Business: January 1922

Address: 111 E Wacker Drive, Chicago, IL 60601

Phone: (800) 225-4500 **Domicile State:** IL **NAIC Code:** 62146

Data Date	Rating	RACR #1	RACR #2	Total Assets ($mil)	Capital ($mil)	Net Premium ($mil)	Net Income ($mil)
9-18	B-	1.72	1.23	1,561.1	237.7	383.7	41.9
9-17	C+	1.30	0.90	1,507.0	159.5	358.2	23.1
2017	C+	1.37	0.97	1,495.7	178.7	480.2	33.4
2016	C+	1.15	0.80	1,432.1	131.5	447.5	30.7
2015	C	0.80	0.54	1,316.7	79.9	439.9	-14.1
2014	C+	1.10	0.78	1,378.3	134.4	434.5	60.1
2013	C+	1.99	1.54	1,588.9	324.6	428.1	71.8

Adverse Trends in Operations

Decrease in asset base during 2015 (4%)
Decrease in capital during 2015 (41%)
Decrease in capital during 2014 (59%)
Decrease in asset base during 2014 (13%)

COMBINED LIFE INSURANCE COMPANY OF NEW YORK — C+ — Fair

Major Rating Factors: Fair overall results on stability tests (4.5 on a scale of 0 to 10) including weak risk adjusted capital in prior years. Good current capitalization (6.7) based on good risk adjusted capital (severe loss scenario) reflecting significant improvement over results in 2015. Weak profitability (2.9) with investment income below regulatory standards in relation to interest assumptions of reserves.

Other Rating Factors: High quality investment portfolio (7.3). Excellent liquidity (7.1).

Principal Business: Individual health insurance (69%), individual life insurance (11%), reinsurance (10%), group health insurance (9%), and group life insurance (1%).

Principal Investments: CMOs and structured securities (49%), nonCMO investment grade bonds (47%), and policy loans (2%).

Investments in Affiliates: None

Group Affiliation: Chubb Limited

Licensed in: IL, NY

Commenced Business: June 1971

Address: 13 Cornell Road, Latham, NY 12110

Phone: (800) 951-6206 **Domicile State:** NY **NAIC Code:** 78697

Data Date	Rating	RACR #1	RACR #2	Total Assets ($mil)	Capital ($mil)	Net Premium ($mil)	Net Income ($mil)
9-18	C+	1.35	0.96	464.1	50.4	125.4	5.7
9-17	C+	1.16	0.82	442.6	42.8	122.7	7.3
2017	C+	1.21	0.86	441.6	44.3	163.4	10.0
2016	C+	0.95	0.67	420.3	33.4	155.2	7.6
2015	C	0.63	0.45	397.3	21.9	156.2	-9.7
2014	B	1.32	0.92	391.9	39.9	127.5	6.1
2013	B	1.85	1.29	402.9	56.4	126.0	3.7

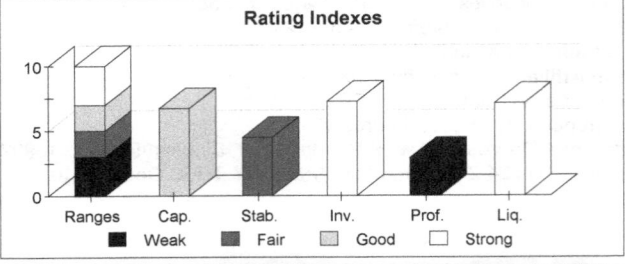

Rating Indexes

COMMONWEALTH ANNUITY & LIFE INSURANCE COMPANY — B- — Good

Major Rating Factors: Fair current capitalization (4.9 on a scale of 0 to 10) based on fair risk adjusted capital (severe loss scenario), although results have slipped from the good range during the last year. Fair quality investment portfolio (4.7). Fair overall results on stability tests (3.7) including negative cash flow from operations for 2017.

Other Rating Factors: Excellent profitability (7.8). Excellent liquidity (7.6).

Principal Business: Reinsurance (79%), individual life insurance (12%), and individual annuities (9%).

Principal Investments: NonCMO investment grade bonds (34%), common & preferred stock (26%), CMOs and structured securities (26%), policy loans (4%), and misc. investments (6%).

Investments in Affiliates: 30%

Group Affiliation: Global Atlantic Financial Group

Licensed in: All states except NY, PR

Commenced Business: January 1967

Address: 132 TURNPIKE ROAD SUITE 210, SOUTHBOROUGH, MA 2135

Phone: (508) 460-2400 **Domicile State:** MA **NAIC Code:** 84824

Data Date	Rating	RACR #1	RACR #2	Total Assets ($mil)	Capital ($mil)	Net Premium ($mil)	Net Income ($mil)
9-18	B-	0.87	0.74	19,628.2	2,465.7	1,326.0	45.2
9-17	B-	0.79	0.73	10,828.2	2,156.7	30.5	161.2
2017	B-	0.93	0.86	11,301.5	2,488.2	40.1	267.8
2016	B-	0.91	0.84	11,379.1	2,155.6	156.1	105.2
2015	B-	0.92	0.82	12,287.2	2,169.8	327.9	59.2
2014	C	0.91	0.82	10,497.0	1,646.0	552.4	215.5
2013	C	1.10	0.86	10,211.9	723.6	-637.5	-32.6

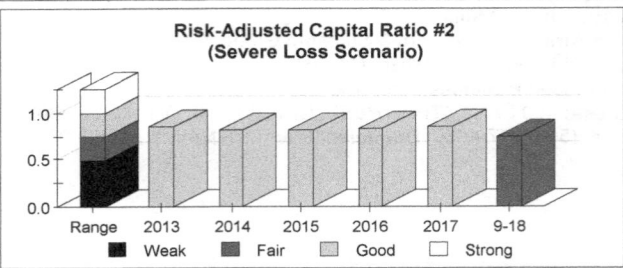

Risk-Adjusted Capital Ratio #2
(Severe Loss Scenario)

COMPANION LIFE INSURANCE COMPANY — B- — Good

Major Rating Factors: Good overall capitalization (5.8 on a scale of 0 to 10) based on good risk adjusted capital (moderate loss scenario). However, capital levels have fluctuated somewhat during past years. Fair quality investment portfolio (4.1). Fair liquidity (4.0).

Other Rating Factors: Fair overall results on stability tests (4.9). Weak profitability (2.0) with operating losses during the first nine months of 2018.

Principal Business: Individual life insurance (72%), group retirement contracts (14%), group life insurance (12%), and individual annuities (2%).

Principal Investments: NonCMO investment grade bonds (65%), CMOs and structured securities (22%), mortgages in good standing (9%), policy loans (3%), and noninv. grade bonds (1%).

Investments in Affiliates: None

Group Affiliation: Mutual Of Omaha Group

Licensed in: CT, NJ, NY

Commenced Business: July 1949

Address: 888 VETERANS MEM HWY STE 515, HAUPPAUGE, NY 11788

Phone: (800) 877-5399 **Domicile State:** NY **NAIC Code:** 62243

Data Date	Rating	RACR #1	RACR #2	Total Assets ($mil)	Capital ($mil)	Net Premium ($mil)	Net Income ($mil)
9-18	B-	1.54	0.81	1,170.0	55.0	69.6	-2.2
9-17	B-	1.58	0.83	1,084.6	53.8	71.7	6.7
2017	B-	1.64	0.87	1,130.4	57.4	99.7	-13.2
2016	C+	1.45	0.76	1,044.5	47.9	103.7	-0.9
2015	C+	1.59	0.84	1,013.4	50.9	98.8	-6.9
2014	B-	1.86	0.97	956.9	57.3	96.8	-5.5
2013	B-	1.61	0.84	883.2	47.0	84.5	0.3

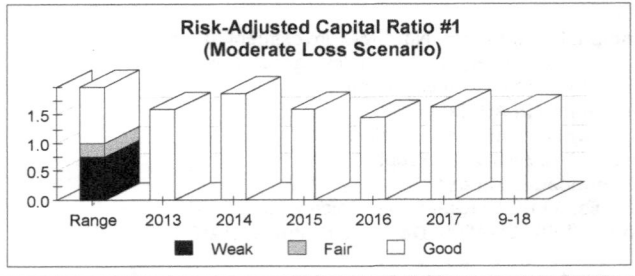

Risk-Adjusted Capital Ratio #1
(Moderate Loss Scenario)

COMPANION LIFE INSURANCE COMPANY *   B+   Good

Major Rating Factors: Good overall results on stability tests (6.6 on a scale of 0 to 10). Stability strengths include excellent operational trends and excellent risk diversification. Good liquidity (6.9) with sufficient resources to handle a spike in claims. Fair quality investment portfolio (4.4).

Other Rating Factors: Strong capitalization (8.7) based on excellent risk adjusted capital (severe loss scenario). Excellent profitability (8.6).

Principal Business: Group health insurance (76%), individual health insurance (12%), reinsurance (8%), and group life insurance (4%).

Principal Investments: NonCMO investment grade bonds (46%), common & preferred stock (37%), CMOs and structured securities (12%), and cash (4%).

Investments in Affiliates: 9%

Group Affiliation: Blue Cross Blue Shield of S Carolina

Licensed in: All states except CA, CT, HI, NJ, NY, PR

Commenced Business: July 1970

Address: 2501 Faraway Drive, Columbia, SC 29219

Phone: (800) 753-0404   **Domicile State:** SC   **NAIC Code:** 77828

Data Date	Rating	RACR #1	RACR #2	Total Assets ($mil)	Capital ($mil)	Net Premium ($mil)	Net Income ($mil)
9-18	B+	2.77	2.12	401.6	226.4	208.2	12.5
9-17	B+	2.68	2.07	359.8	206.2	185.7	13.9
2017	B+	2.71	2.08	373.6	212.4	253.2	19.4
2016	B+	2.55	1.99	338.7	186.2	237.4	16.4
2015	A-	3.15	2.44	300.4	160.4	221.6	13.7
2014	A-	2.95	2.30	284.9	149.0	220.5	15.6
2013	A-	2.92	2.31	251.7	138.0	202.8	14.5

Adverse Trends in Operations

Change in asset mix during 2015 (4.1%)

CONNECTICUT GENERAL LIFE INSURANCE COMPANY   B-   Good

Major Rating Factors: Good overall results on stability tests (5.2 on a scale of 0 to 10). Stability strengths include good operational trends and excellent risk diversification. Fair quality investment portfolio (4.4). Strong capitalization (7.5) based on excellent risk adjusted capital (severe loss scenario). Moreover, capital levels have been consistently high over the last five years.

Other Rating Factors: Excellent profitability (8.1). Excellent liquidity (7.3).

Principal Business: Individual life insurance (35%), group life insurance (32%), individual health insurance (24%), reinsurance (5%), and group health insurance (3%).

Principal Investments: Common & preferred stock (38%), nonCMO investment grade bonds (34%), policy loans (14%), mortgages in good standing (3%), and misc. investments (11%).

Investments in Affiliates: 40%

Group Affiliation: CIGNA Corp

Licensed in: All states, the District of Columbia and Puerto Rico

Commenced Business: October 1865

Address: 900 COTTAGE GROVE ROAD, BLOOMFIELD, CT 6002

Phone: (860) 226-6000   **Domicile State:** CT   **NAIC Code:** 62308

Data Date	Rating	RACR #1	RACR #2	Total Assets ($mil)	Capital ($mil)	Net Premium ($mil)	Net Income ($mil)
9-18	B-	1.48	1.31	19,355.3	5,637.9	268.5	698.6
9-17	B-	1.33	1.21	18,077.3	4,307.1	277.7	1,005.2
2017	B-	1.32	1.22	18,137.2	4,412.2	346.3	1,013.8
2016	B-	1.32	1.20	17,646.3	4,074.4	402.2	1,180.4
2015	B-	1.33	1.19	17,374.4	3,631.0	490.7	916.2
2014	B-	1.34	1.19	17,768.9	3,473.3	1,107.4	212.6
2013	B-	1.63	1.33	18,573.6	3,246.4	3,380.1	601.8

Adverse Trends in Operations

Decrease in premium volume from 2016 to 2017 (14%)
Decrease in premium volume from 2015 to 2016 (17%)
Decrease in premium volume from 2014 to 2015 (56%)
Change in premium mix from 2013 to 2014 (6.4%)
Decrease in premium volume from 2013 to 2014 (68%)

CONSTITUTION LIFE INSURANCE COMPANY   D   Weak

Major Rating Factors: Weak overall results on stability tests (2.3 on a scale of 0 to 10) including potential financial drain due to affiliation with Nassau Reinsurance Group Holdings LP and negative cash flow from operations for 2017. Weak profitability (2.2) with investment income below regulatory standards in relation to interest assumptions of reserves. Fair quality investment portfolio (4.3).

Other Rating Factors: Strong capitalization (7.5) based on excellent risk adjusted capital (severe loss scenario). Excellent liquidity (7.0).

Principal Business: Individual health insurance (48%), reinsurance (34%), group health insurance (9%), and individual life insurance (9%).

Principal Investments: NonCMO investment grade bonds (68%), CMOs and structured securities (26%), noninv. grade bonds (2%), and cash (2%).

Investments in Affiliates: 1%

Group Affiliation: Nassau Reinsurance Group Holdings LP

Licensed in: All states except NJ, NY, PR

Commenced Business: June 1929

Address: 4888 Loop Central Dr Ste 700, Houston, TX 77081

Phone: (407) 547-3800   **Domicile State:** TX   **NAIC Code:** 62359

Data Date	Rating	RACR #1	RACR #2	Total Assets ($mil)	Capital ($mil)	Net Premium ($mil)	Net Income ($mil)
9-18	D	2.37	1.30	393.5	35.0	32.9	0.7
9-17	D	2.74	1.59	438.3	45.7	38.6	2.5
2017	D	2.28	1.26	412.7	35.1	49.1	2.0
2016	D	2.71	1.71	444.1	55.6	90.0	-11.8
2015	C+	2.75	1.84	394.8	66.6	123.3	34.9
2014	C+	1.88	1.23	316.5	37.0	94.4	11.1
2013	C+	1.56	1.05	317.3	33.5	109.5	9.2

Nassau Reinsurance Group Holdings LP
Composite Group Rating: D-

Largest Group Members	Assets ($mil)	Rating
PHOENIX LIFE INS CO	12478	D-
PHL VARIABLE INS CO	6319	D
CONSTITUTION LIFE INS CO	413	D
PYRAMID LIFE INS CO	72	D
NASSAU LIFE ANNUITY CO	31	D-

CONSUMERS LIFE INSURANCE COMPANY   B   Good

Major Rating Factors: Good overall profitability (6.8 on a scale of 0 to 10). Excellent expense controls. Fair overall results on stability tests (4.9). Strong current capitalization (7.9) based on excellent risk adjusted capital (severe loss scenario) reflecting improvement over results in 2013.
Other Rating Factors: High quality investment portfolio (9.2). Excellent liquidity (7.1).
Principal Business: Group life insurance (51%), individual health insurance (34%), and group health insurance (14%).
Principal Investments: NonCMO investment grade bonds (58%) and cash (42%).
Investments in Affiliates: None
Group Affiliation: Medical Mutual of Ohio
Licensed in: AZ, AR, CO, DC, DE, GA, IL, IN, IA, KS, KY, LA, MD, MI, MN, MS, MO, MT, NE, NV, NJ, NM, ND, OH, OK, OR, PA, SC, SD, TX, UT, VA, WV, WI, WY
Commenced Business: October 1955
Address: 2060 East Ninth Street, Cleveland, OH 44115-1355
Phone: (216) 687-7000 **Domicile State:** OH **NAIC Code:** 62375

Data Date	Rating	RACR #1	RACR #2	Total Assets ($mil)	Capital ($mil)	Net Premium ($mil)	Net Income ($mil)
9-18	B	2.06	1.59	44.4	30.5	20.9	2.6
9-17	B	2.20	1.70	47.3	27.4	36.2	3.1
2017	B	1.61	1.25	44.9	27.6	47.3	4.9
2016	B	1.90	1.46	41.8	23.3	31.4	0.6
2015	C+	1.91	1.46	37.6	21.6	29.0	1.3
2014	C	1.89	1.45	36.4	19.7	25.9	-1.4
2013	C	1.17	0.92	39.7	19.7	60.9	1.2

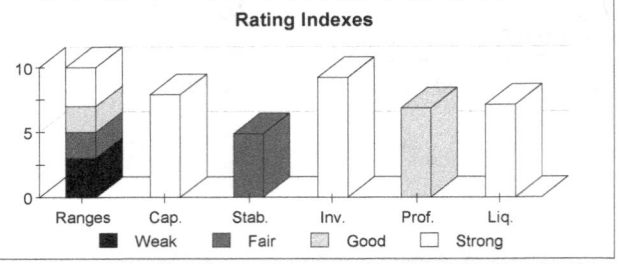

Rating Indexes

CONTINENTAL AMERICAN INSURANCE COMPANY   B   Good

Major Rating Factors: Good overall results on stability tests (5.7 on a scale of 0 to 10). Strengths include good financial support from affiliation with AFLAC Inc, excellent operational trends and excellent risk diversification. Fair profitability (4.5). Strong capitalization (7.4) based on excellent risk adjusted capital (severe loss scenario).
Other Rating Factors: High quality investment portfolio (7.6). Excellent liquidity (7.1).
Principal Business: Group health insurance (68%), reinsurance (30%), and group life insurance (2%).
Principal Investments: NonCMO investment grade bonds (91%), noninv. grade bonds (2%), and policy loans (1%).
Investments in Affiliates: None
Group Affiliation: AFLAC Inc
Licensed in: All states except NY, PR
Commenced Business: January 1969
Address: 1600 Williams Street, Omaha, NE 68114-3743
Phone: (888) 730-2244 **Domicile State:** SC **NAIC Code:** 71730

Data Date	Rating	RACR #1	RACR #2	Total Assets ($mil)	Capital ($mil)	Net Premium ($mil)	Net Income ($mil)
9-18	B	1.68	1.24	804.5	159.2	449.7	1.3
9-17	B	1.94	1.40	671.3	173.3	401.2	-14.4
2017	B	1.79	1.33	673.3	153.4	524.7	-21.7
2016	B	1.98	1.44	607.0	174.4	536.1	46.8
2015	B	1.84	1.37	512.3	138.0	436.8	26.2
2014	B	2.49	1.78	397.0	109.7	240.6	-17.3
2013	B	3.47	2.49	382.4	138.0	233.4	18.8

AFLAC Inc Composite Group Rating: B+ Largest Group Members	Assets ($mil)	Rating
AMERICAN FAMILY LIFE ASR CO OF NY	916	A-
CONTINENTAL AMERICAN INS CO	673	B

CONTINENTAL GENERAL INSURANCE COMPANY   C+   Fair

Major Rating Factors: Fair overall results on stability tests (4.7 on a scale of 0 to 10) including fair risk adjusted capital in prior years. Good capitalization (5.1) based on good risk adjusted capital (moderate loss scenario). Good overall profitability (5.9) despite operating losses during the first six months of 2018.
Other Rating Factors: Good liquidity (6.7). Low quality investment portfolio (2.8).
Principal Business: Individual health insurance (82%), group health insurance (9%), individual life insurance (5%), reinsurance (2%), and group retirement contracts (1%).
Principal Investments: NonCMO investment grade bonds (60%), CMOs and structured securities (20%), noninv. grade bonds (7%), common & preferred stock (5%), and misc. investments (5%).
Investments in Affiliates: 2%
Group Affiliation: HC2 Holdings Inc
Licensed in: All states except NY, PR
Commenced Business: July 1961
Address: 11001 Lakeline Blvd Ste 120, Austin, TX 78717
Phone: (866) 830-0607 **Domicile State:** OH **NAIC Code:** 71404

Data Date	Rating	RACR #1	RACR #2	Total Assets ($mil)	Capital ($mil)	Net Premium ($mil)	Net Income ($mil)
6-18	C+	1.05	0.63	1,407.1	68.4	41.1	-6.6
6-17	C+	0.94	0.61	1,373.3	69.3	41.4	-2.7
2017	C+	1.12	0.68	1,385.8	74.7	82.7	-0.1
2016	C+	1.10	0.72	1,344.1	76.9	82.2	-15.3
2015	C+	1.28	0.89	249.3	18.5	13.3	32.6
2014	C	2.35	1.38	242.4	21.5	14.3	1.9
2013	C	2.50	1.49	238.4	22.8	15.3	4.7

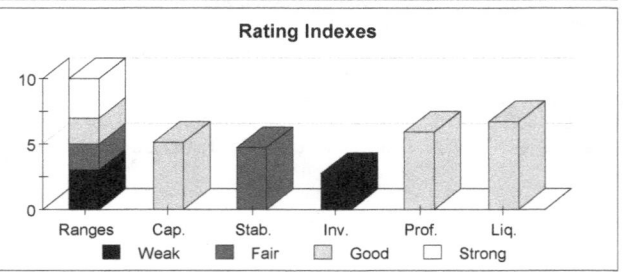

Rating Indexes

CONTINENTAL LIFE INSURANCE COMPANY OF BRENTWOOD   C+   Fair

Major Rating Factors: Fair overall results on stability tests (4.6 on a scale of 0 to 10). Good quality investment portfolio (5.4) despite mixed results such as: minimal exposure to mortgages and substantial holdings of BBB bonds but minimal holdings in junk bonds. Good liquidity (6.4) with sufficient resources to handle a spike in claims.

Other Rating Factors: Weak profitability (2.2) with operating losses during the first nine months of 2018. Strong capitalization (7.1) based on excellent risk adjusted capital (severe loss scenario).

Principal Business: Individual health insurance (98%), individual life insurance (1%), and group health insurance (1%).

Principal Investments: NonCMO investment grade bonds (41%), common & preferred stock (34%), CMOs and structured securities (26%), mortgages in good standing (3%), and noninv. grade bonds (1%).

Investments in Affiliates: 34%

Group Affiliation: Aetna Inc

Licensed in: All states except AK, DC, HI, ME, NY, PR

Commenced Business: December 1983

Address: 800 CRESCENT CENTRE DR STE 200, FRANKLIN, TN 37067

Phone: (800) 264-4000 **Domicile State:** TN **NAIC Code:** 68500

Data Date	Rating	RACR #1	RACR #2	Total Assets ($mil)	Capital ($mil)	Net Premium ($mil)	Net Income ($mil)
9-18	C+	1.19	1.07	376.4	214.9	377.2	-11.6
9-17	C+	1.21	1.07	336.0	190.1	349.7	-12.3
2017	C+	1.10	0.99	345.6	194.4	468.0	-9.5
2016	B	1.16	1.03	307.1	173.8	427.2	-7.8
2015	B	1.11	0.99	274.0	144.3	380.6	-1.2
2014	B	1.19	1.08	277.8	156.4	330.6	3.0
2013	B	1.12	1.01	205.6	97.0	256.6	3.2

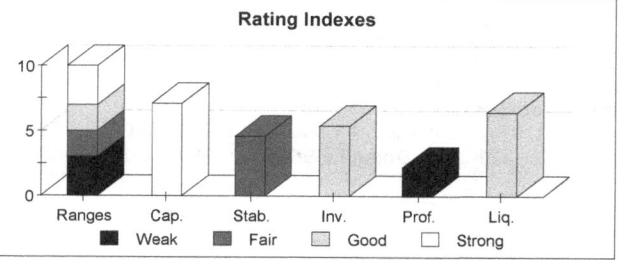

Rating Indexes

COTTON STATES LIFE INSURANCE COMPANY *   A-   Excellent

Major Rating Factors: Good quality investment portfolio (6.6 on a scale of 0 to 10) despite mixed results such as: no exposure to mortgages and large holdings of BBB rated bonds but small junk bond holdings. Good liquidity (6.2) with sufficient resources to handle a spike in claims as well as a significant increase in policy surrenders. Excellent overall results on stability tests (7.3) excellent operational trends and excellent risk diversification.

Other Rating Factors: Strong capitalization (9.4) based on excellent risk adjusted capital (severe loss scenario). Excellent profitability (7.3).

Principal Business: Individual life insurance (99%) and individual annuities (1%).

Principal Investments: NonCMO investment grade bonds (60%), CMOs and structured securities (22%), policy loans (5%), common & preferred stock (4%), and noninv. grade bonds (3%).

Investments in Affiliates: None

Group Affiliation: COUNTRY Financial

Licensed in: AL, FL, GA, KY, LA, MS, NC, SC, TN, VA

Commenced Business: December 1955

Address: 13560 MORRIS ROAD SUITE 4000, ALPHARETTA, GA 30004

Phone: (309) 821-3000 **Domicile State:** GA **NAIC Code:** 62537

Data Date	Rating	RACR #1	RACR #2	Total Assets ($mil)	Capital ($mil)	Net Premium ($mil)	Net Income ($mil)
9-18	A-	4.78	2.62	339.7	74.7	15.9	3.6
9-17	A-	4.68	2.60	336.1	71.2	16.7	2.3
2017	A-	4.64	2.56	335.9	71.0	21.9	2.8
2016	A-	4.54	2.50	336.2	68.3	23.8	3.1
2015	A-	4.46	2.51	333.9	66.1	25.3	4.0
2014	A-	4.11	2.32	332.3	62.8	27.6	6.4
2013	A-	3.82	2.15	329.6	58.2	29.7	5.2

Adverse Trends in Operations

Decrease in premium volume from 2016 to 2017 (8%)
Decrease in premium volume from 2015 to 2016 (6%)
Decrease in premium volume from 2014 to 2015 (8%)
Decrease in premium volume from 2013 to 2014 (7%)

COUNTRY INVESTORS LIFE ASSURANCE COMPANY *   A-   Excellent

Major Rating Factors: Strong capitalization (8.0 on a scale of 0 to 10) based on excellent risk adjusted capital (severe loss scenario). Furthermore, this high level of risk adjusted capital has been consistently maintained over the last five years. High quality investment portfolio (8.2) with no exposure to mortgages and minimal holdings in junk bonds. Excellent profitability (7.6).

Other Rating Factors: Excellent liquidity (7.4). Excellent overall results on stability tests (7.1) excellent operational trends and excellent risk diversification.

Principal Business: Individual annuities (72%) and individual life insurance (28%).

Principal Investments: NonCMO investment grade bonds (64%), CMOs and structured securities (25%), and noninv. grade bonds (2%).

Investments in Affiliates: None

Group Affiliation: COUNTRY Financial

Licensed in: All states except CA, DC, HI, NH, NJ, NY, UT, VT, PR

Commenced Business: November 1981

Address: 1701 N TOWANDA AVENUE, BLOOMINGTON, IL 61701-2090

Phone: (309) 821-3000 **Domicile State:** IL **NAIC Code:** 94218

Data Date	Rating	RACR #1	RACR #2	Total Assets ($mil)	Capital ($mil)	Net Premium ($mil)	Net Income ($mil)
9-18	A-	14.64	7.13	303.5	196.6	0.0	4.0
9-17	A-	13.93	6.79	303.0	192.2	0.0	3.0
2017	A-	14.39	7.03	299.2	193.1	0.0	4.1
2016	A-	14.41	7.05	297.3	188.9	0.0	4.7
2015	A-	14.70	7.21	292.9	184.2	0.0	5.6
2014	A-	15.10	7.48	286.5	178.3	0.0	4.7
2013	A-	14.95	7.35	286.9	173.4	0.0	4.8

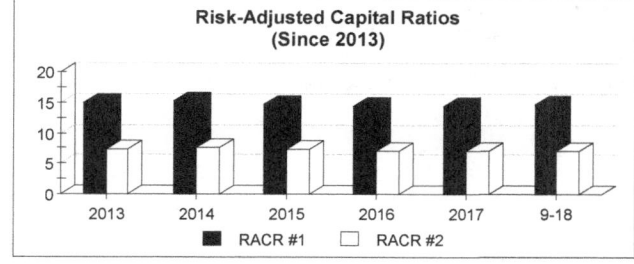

Risk-Adjusted Capital Ratios
(Since 2013)

COUNTRY LIFE INSURANCE COMPANY *   A+   Excellent

Major Rating Factors: Good quality investment portfolio (5.8 on a scale of 0 to 10) despite mixed results such as: large holdings of BBB rated bonds but moderate junk bond exposure. Good overall profitability (6.9). Good liquidity (5.8) with sufficient resources to handle a spike in claims as well as a significant increase in policy surrenders.

Other Rating Factors: Strong capitalization (7.6) based on excellent risk adjusted capital (severe loss scenario). Excellent overall results on stability tests (7.6) excellent operational trends and excellent risk diversification.

Principal Business: Individual life insurance (59%), reinsurance (24%), individual health insurance (15%), and group life insurance (1%).

Principal Investments: NonCMO investment grade bonds (59%), CMOs and structured securities (18%), common & preferred stock (7%), policy loans (4%), and misc. investments (9%).

Investments in Affiliates: 4%

Group Affiliation: COUNTRY Financial

Licensed in: All states except CA, DC, HI, NH, NJ, NY, VT, PR

Commenced Business: December 1928

Address: 1701 N TOWANDA AVENUE, BLOOMINGTON, IL 61701-2090

Phone: (309) 821-3000 **Domicile State:** IL **NAIC Code:** 62553

Data Date	Rating	RACR #1	RACR #2	Total Assets ($mil)	Capital ($mil)	Net Premium ($mil)	Net Income ($mil)
9-18	A+	2.11	1.39	9,673.9	1,223.6	458.6	40.2
9-17	A+	2.08	1.37	9,441.1	1,171.1	462.2	38.5
2017	A+	2.09	1.37	9,459.6	1,185.3	603.7	63.4
2016	A+	2.05	1.35	9,170.5	1,138.7	672.2	27.1
2015	A+	2.11	1.40	10,093.0	1,135.9	641.9	32.9
2014	A+	2.13	1.41	10,697.2	1,124.0	612.1	51.5
2013	A+	2.15	1.42	10,262.6	1,096.3	612.7	55.6

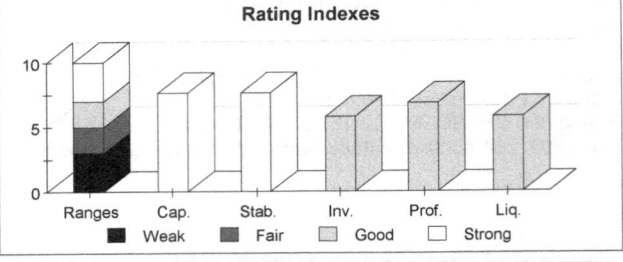

Rating Indexes (Ranges, Cap., Stab., Inv., Prof., Liq.)

Weak ■ Fair ■ Good ▨ Strong ☐

DEARBORN NATIONAL LIFE INSURANCE COMPANY *   B+   Good

Major Rating Factors: Good overall results on stability tests (6.5 on a scale of 0 to 10) despite negative cash flow from operations for 2017. Other stability subfactors include good operational trends and excellent risk diversification. Good quality investment portfolio (6.1) despite mixed results such as: large holdings of BBB rated bonds but moderate junk bond exposure. Good overall profitability (6.0).

Other Rating Factors: Good liquidity (6.3). Strong capitalization (8.7) based on excellent risk adjusted capital (severe loss scenario).

Principal Business: Group life insurance (65%), group health insurance (33%), individual life insurance (2%), and individual annuities (1%).

Principal Investments: NonCMO investment grade bonds (61%), CMOs and structured securities (19%), noninv. grade bonds (9%), mortgages in good standing (6%), and common & preferred stock (1%).

Investments in Affiliates: 1%

Group Affiliation: HCSC Group

Licensed in: All states except NY

Commenced Business: April 1969

Address: 300 East Randolph Street, Chicago, IL 60601-5099

Phone: (800) 633-3696 **Domicile State:** IL **NAIC Code:** 71129

Data Date	Rating	RACR #1	RACR #2	Total Assets ($mil)	Capital ($mil)	Net Premium ($mil)	Net Income ($mil)
9-18	B+	3.47	2.14	1,737.6	488.0	340.7	18.7
9-17	B+	3.42	2.15	1,849.7	510.9	328.1	14.8
2017	B+	3.40	2.09	1,785.1	474.3	437.9	34.0
2016	B+	3.36	2.11	1,872.5	497.0	408.0	19.7
2015	B+	3.63	2.25	1,990.5	522.1	382.5	59.1
2014	A-	2.86	1.91	2,145.5	514.7	379.9	54.8
2013	A-	2.27	1.52	2,324.1	439.7	495.5	42.3

Adverse Trends in Operations

Decrease in asset base during 2017 (5%)
Decrease in asset base during 2016 (6%)
Decrease in capital during 2016 (5%)
Decrease in asset base during 2014 (8%)
Decrease in premium volume from 2013 to 2014 (23%)

DELAWARE AMERICAN LIFE INSURANCE COMPANY *   B+   Good

Major Rating Factors: Good overall results on stability tests (6.1 on a scale of 0 to 10). Stability strengths include good operational trends and excellent risk diversification. Good overall profitability (6.3). Excellent expense controls. Good liquidity (6.8) with sufficient resources to handle a spike in claims.

Other Rating Factors: Strong capitalization (9.7) based on excellent risk adjusted capital (severe loss scenario). High quality investment portfolio (7.6).

Principal Business: Group health insurance (67%), reinsurance (23%), group life insurance (10%), and individual life insurance (1%).

Principal Investments: NonCMO investment grade bonds (67%), CMOs and structured securities (24%), and cash (5%).

Investments in Affiliates: 5%

Group Affiliation: MetLife Inc

Licensed in: All states except PR

Commenced Business: August 1966

Address: 1209 Orange Street, Wilmington, DE 19801

Phone: (302) 594-2000 **Domicile State:** DE **NAIC Code:** 62634

Data Date	Rating	RACR #1	RACR #2	Total Assets ($mil)	Capital ($mil)	Net Premium ($mil)	Net Income ($mil)
9-18	B+	3.79	2.83	122.9	68.7	72.5	9.4
9-17	B+	4.69	3.47	137.9	76.3	72.8	6.1
2017	B+	3.36	2.53	120.2	61.8	96.4	7.2
2016	B+	4.56	3.33	132.8	72.5	89.9	15.2
2015	A-	3.53	2.60	136.6	63.5	108.7	1.8
2014	A-	3.88	2.81	136.7	69.3	102.1	10.0
2013	B	4.89	3.54	137.1	74.3	91.1	17.1

Adverse Trends in Operations

Decrease in capital during 2017 (15%)
Decrease in asset base during 2017 (9%)
Change in premium mix from 2015 to 2016 (7%)
Decrease in premium volume from 2015 to 2016 (17%)
Decrease in capital during 2015 (8%)

DELAWARE LIFE INSURANCE COMPANY
C   Fair

Major Rating Factors: Fair quality investment portfolio (4.7 on a scale of 0 to 10) with large holdings of BBB rated bonds in addition to moderate junk bond exposure. Fair overall results on stability tests (4.1). Good overall capitalization (5.2) based on good risk adjusted capital (moderate loss scenario). Nevertheless, capital levels have fluctuated during prior years.

Other Rating Factors: Weak profitability (2.6) with investment income below regulatory standards in relation to interest assumptions of reserves. Excellent liquidity (8.1).

Principal Business: Individual annuities (94%), group retirement contracts (5%), and individual life insurance (1%).

Principal Investments: NonCMO investment grade bonds (47%), CMOs and structured securities (17%), common & preferred stock (6%), policy loans (5%), and misc. investments (14%).

Investments in Affiliates: 7%

Group Affiliation: Delaware Life Partners LLC

Licensed in: All states except NY

Commenced Business: January 1973

Address: 1209 Orange Street, Wilmington, DE 19801

Phone: (781) 790-8600 **Domicile State:** DE **NAIC Code:** 79065

Data Date	Rating	RACR #1	RACR #2	Total Assets ($mil)	Capital ($mil)	Net Premium ($mil)	Net Income ($mil)
9-18	C	1.13	0.70	37,022.2	1,481.5	-10,894.6	107.5
9-17	C	1.35	0.85	37,620.1	1,619.2	1,625.8	193.6
2017	C	1.20	0.75	37,207.3	1,463.4	2,033.4	281.4
2016	C	1.39	0.88	37,684.0	1,635.9	1,814.4	309.9
2015	C	1.67	1.07	36,876.9	1,635.9	1,321.2	348.8
2014	C	1.52	0.98	40,699.8	1,591.5	1,783.1	315.8
2013	D+	1.43	0.93	39,279.2	1,410.4	1,559.4	682.9

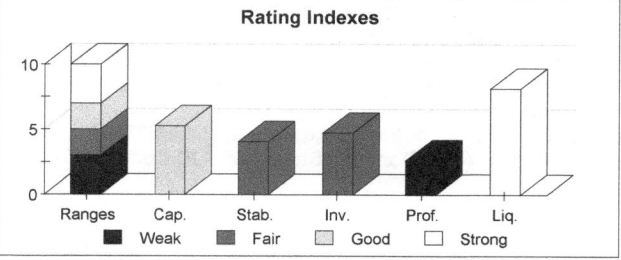
Rating Indexes

DELAWARE LIFE INSURANCE COMPANY OF NEW YORK
B-   Good

Major Rating Factors: Good quality investment portfolio (6.4 on a scale of 0 to 10) despite mixed results such as: minimal exposure to mortgages and large holdings of BBB rated bonds but minimal holdings in junk bonds. Good overall profitability (5.7). Good liquidity (6.9).

Other Rating Factors: Fair overall results on stability tests (4.6) including fair financial strength of affiliated Delaware Life Partners LLC. Strong capitalization (10.0) based on excellent risk adjusted capital (severe loss scenario).

Principal Business: Individual annuities (52%) and individual life insurance (47%).

Principal Investments: NonCMO investment grade bonds (62%), CMOs and structured securities (22%), common & preferred stock (3%), mortgages in good standing (3%), and misc. investments (2%).

Investments in Affiliates: None

Group Affiliation: Delaware Life Partners LLC

Licensed in: CT, NY, RI

Commenced Business: August 1985

Address: 1115 Broadway 12th Floor, New York, NY 10010

Phone: (781) 790-8600 **Domicile State:** NY **NAIC Code:** 72664

Data Date	Rating	RACR #1	RACR #2	Total Assets ($mil)	Capital ($mil)	Net Premium ($mil)	Net Income ($mil)
9-18	B-	9.41	4.50	2,382.2	378.7	10.9	33.5
9-17	C+	8.97	4.27	2,573.8	418.7	13.3	9.4
2017	B-	9.44	4.55	2,505.3	369.2	19.0	19.2
2016	C+	8.82	4.20	2,589.2	404.4	19.9	21.4
2015	C+	7.91	3.83	2,731.0	401.8	27.2	15.8
2014	C+	7.61	3.80	2,952.2	417.6	-16.3	37.5
2013	C	7.96	3.91	3,194.6	399.9	-8.7	16.9

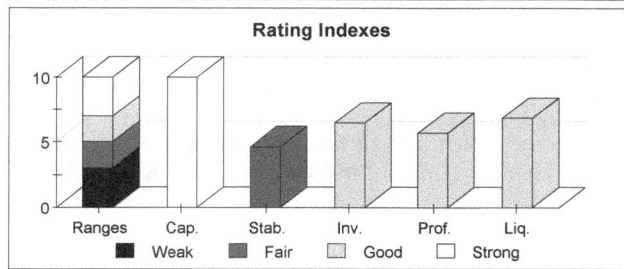
Rating Indexes

EAGLE LIFE INSURANCE COMPANY *
B+   Good

Major Rating Factors: Good overall results on stability tests (6.8 on a scale of 0 to 10) despite excessive premium growth. Other stability subfactors include excellent operational trends and excellent risk diversification. Good quality investment portfolio (6.5) despite mixed results such as: minimal exposure to mortgages and large holdings of BBB rated bonds but minimal holdings in junk bonds. Strong capitalization (8.2) based on excellent risk adjusted capital (severe loss scenario).

Other Rating Factors: Excellent profitability (7.7) despite modest operating losses during 2013. Excellent liquidity (7.8).

Principal Business: Individual annuities (100%).

Principal Investments: NonCMO investment grade bonds (45%), CMOs and structured securities (39%), mortgages in good standing (5%), noninv. grade bonds (2%), and cash (1%).

Investments in Affiliates: None

Group Affiliation: American Equity Investment Group

Licensed in: All states except ID, NY, PR

Commenced Business: August 2008

Address: 6000 WESTOWN PARKWAY, WEST DES MOINES, IA 50266-5921

Phone: (515) 221-0002 **Domicile State:** IA **NAIC Code:** 13183

Data Date	Rating	RACR #1	RACR #2	Total Assets ($mil)	Capital ($mil)	Net Premium ($mil)	Net Income ($mil)
9-18	B+	3.89	1.81	1,070.1	180.5	253.3	8.2
9-17	B	5.89	2.81	735.6	170.9	191.2	4.7
2017	B	4.37	2.08	810.3	172.4	284.3	7.2
2016	B	6.31	3.10	527.6	166.6	122.3	3.6
2015	B	4.75	2.41	313.9	62.9	74.8	0.3
2014	B	4.29	2.68	216.4	42.3	24.0	3.0
2013	B	4.10	2.87	188.7	39.5	22.9	-2.2

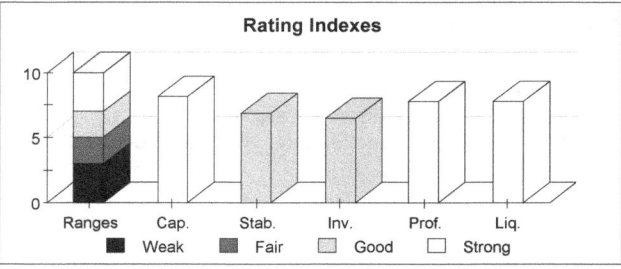
Rating Indexes

ELCO MUTUAL LIFE & ANNUITY

C+ **Fair**

Major Rating Factors: Fair quality investment portfolio (3.7 on a scale of 0 to 10) with large holdings of BBB rated bonds in addition to junk bond exposure equal to 60% of capital. Fair liquidity (4.4) due, in part, to cash value policies that are subject to withdrawals with minimal or no penalty. Fair overall results on stability tests (4.7).

Other Rating Factors: Good overall profitability (5.1) although investment income, in comparison to reserve requirements, is below regulatory standards. Strong capitalization (7.0) based on excellent risk adjusted capital (severe loss scenario).

Principal Business: Individual annuities (95%) and individual life insurance (5%).

Principal Investments: NonCMO investment grade bonds (79%), cash (6%), and noninv. grade bonds (5%).

Investments in Affiliates: None

Group Affiliation: None

Licensed in: All states except CT, DC, MA, NH, NJ, NY, RI, VT, PR

Commenced Business: May 1946

Address: 916 Sherwood Drive, Lake Bluff, IL 60044-2285

Phone: (888) 872-7954 **Domicile State:** IL **NAIC Code:** 84174

Data Date	Rating	RACR #1	RACR #2	Total Assets ($mil)	Capital ($mil)	Net Premium ($mil)	Net Income ($mil)
9-18	C+	2.10	1.00	821.4	63.0	162.5	4.6
9-17	C-	1.85	0.88	725.1	57.6	135.7	6.9
2017	C-	1.92	0.92	763.1	58.5	202.1	9.7
2016	C-	1.62	0.77	704.0	51.4	185.9	7.9
2015	C-	1.53	0.75	642.3	45.0	305.8	0.1
2014	C-	1.54	0.79	526.7	44.5	130.4	1.5
2013	B-	1.72	0.88	362.8	40.8	17.3	4.3

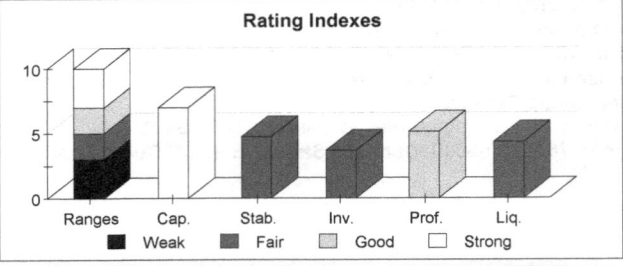

Rating Indexes

EMC NATIONAL LIFE COMPANY

B **Good**

Major Rating Factors: Good quality investment portfolio (6.7 on a scale of 0 to 10) despite mixed results such as: minimal exposure to mortgages and large holdings of BBB rated bonds but small junk bond holdings. Good liquidity (5.2) with sufficient resources to cover a large increase in policy surrenders. Good overall results on stability tests (6.0) despite negative cash flow from operations for 2017 excellent operational trends and excellent risk diversification.

Other Rating Factors: Strong capitalization (7.9) based on excellent risk adjusted capital (severe loss scenario). Excellent profitability (7.4).

Principal Business: Individual life insurance (64%), individual annuities (24%), group life insurance (6%), reinsurance (4%), and other lines (2%).

Principal Investments: NonCMO investment grade bonds (79%), CMOs and structured securities (7%), common & preferred stock (4%), mortgages in good standing (3%), and misc. investments (3%).

Investments in Affiliates: None

Group Affiliation: Employers Mutual Group

Licensed in: All states except NJ, NY, PR

Commenced Business: April 1963

Address: 699 WALNUT ST STE 1100, DES MOINES, IA 50309-3965

Phone: (515) 280-2511 **Domicile State:** IA **NAIC Code:** 62928

Data Date	Rating	RACR #1	RACR #2	Total Assets ($mil)	Capital ($mil)	Net Premium ($mil)	Net Income ($mil)
9-18	B	2.88	1.62	963.0	118.6	41.1	14.8
9-17	B	2.58	1.46	940.0	106.7	42.7	3.8
2017	B	2.64	1.49	954.8	105.6	56.6	6.3
2016	B	2.56	1.46	947.9	104.0	60.1	9.6
2015	B	2.47	1.41	978.9	99.5	60.9	4.5
2014	B	2.43	1.42	1,009.8	98.8	57.8	10.5
2013	B-	2.14	1.24	1,030.2	87.9	60.6	5.6

Adverse Trends in Operations

Decrease in premium volume from 2016 to 2017 (6%)
Decrease in asset base during 2016 (3%)
Decrease in asset base during 2015 (3%)
Decrease in asset base during 2014 (2%)
Decrease in premium volume from 2013 to 2014 (5%)

EMPIRE FIDELITY INVESTMENTS LIFE INSURANCE COMPANY *

B+ **Good**

Major Rating Factors: Good overall profitability (5.5 on a scale of 0 to 10) although investment income, in comparison to reserve requirements, is below regulatory standards. Good overall results on stability tests (6.7). Stability strengths include excellent operational trends and excellent risk diversification. Strong capitalization (8.7) based on excellent risk adjusted capital (severe loss scenario).

Other Rating Factors: High quality investment portfolio (8.1). Excellent liquidity (7.0).

Principal Business: Individual annuities (99%) and individual life insurance (1%).

Principal Investments: NonCMO investment grade bonds (96%) and CMOs and structured securities (1%).

Investments in Affiliates: None

Group Affiliation: FMR LLC

Licensed in: NY

Commenced Business: June 1992

Address: 640 Fifth Avenue 5th floor, New York, NY 10019

Phone: (401) 292-4616 **Domicile State:** NY **NAIC Code:** 71228

Data Date	Rating	RACR #1	RACR #2	Total Assets ($mil)	Capital ($mil)	Net Premium ($mil)	Net Income ($mil)
9-18	B+	2.62	2.10	3,035.0	88.5	93.3	5.9
9-17	B+	2.69	2.09	2,836.6	82.7	102.6	4.4
2017	B+	2.46	2.06	2,928.6	83.1	138.8	6.4
2016	B+	2.57	2.16	2,585.1	79.1	151.4	11.6
2015	B+	2.60	2.34	2,441.3	76.9	155.8	4.4
2014	B+	2.45	2.21	2,443.7	72.5	159.7	5.0
2013	B+	2.40	2.16	2,270.4	67.4	202.1	2.3

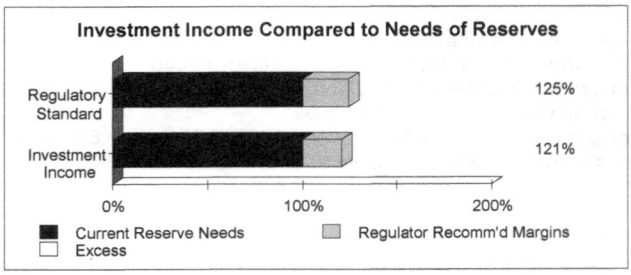

Investment Income Compared to Needs of Reserves

EMPLOYERS REASSURANCE CORPORATION

D   **Weak**

Major Rating Factors: Weak overall results on stability tests (1.9 on a scale of 0 to 10) including potential financial drain due to affiliation with GE Insurance Solutions and excessive premium growth. Weak profitability (1.8). Excellent expense controls. Good capitalization (5.5) based on good risk adjusted capital (severe loss scenario).

Other Rating Factors: Good quality investment portfolio (5.6). Good liquidity (6.6).

Principal Business: Reinsurance (100%).

Principal Investments: NonCMO investment grade bonds (68%), CMOs and structured securities (16%), mortgages in good standing (6%), common & preferred stock (5%), and noninv. grade bonds (2%).

Investments in Affiliates: 6%

Group Affiliation: GE Insurance Solutions

Licensed in: All states except NY

Commenced Business: November 1907

Address: 7101 College Blvd Ste 1400, Overland Park, KS 66210

Phone: (913) 982-3700   **Domicile State:** KS   **NAIC Code:** 68276

Data Date	Rating	RACR #1	RACR #2	Total Assets ($mil)	Capital ($mil)	Net Premium ($mil)	Net Income ($mil)
9-18	D	1.08	0.81	13,630.6	794.5	262.9	14.5
9-17	C	1.04	0.85	11,567.0	962.4	156.7	-17.3
2017	C-	1.16	0.91	14,815.8	816.5	236.7	-2,332.7
2016	C	1.05	0.86	11,334.9	978.4	317.2	-209.9
2015	C	1.28	0.99	10,708.7	775.8	366.1	63.9
2014	C	1.19	0.94	10,776.3	830.4	410.8	-44.5
2013	C	1.53	1.21	11,002.6	1,224.8	441.3	453.8

GE Insurance Solutions Composite Group Rating: E+ Largest Group Members	Assets ($mil)	Rating
UNION FIDELITY LIFE INS CO	20435	E
EMPLOYERS REASSURANCE CORP	14816	D
ELECTRIC INS CO	1424	C

ENTERPRISE LIFE INSURANCE COMPANY *

B+   **Good**

Major Rating Factors: Good overall results on stability tests (6.4 on a scale of 0 to 10) despite excessive premium growth and fair risk adjusted capital in prior years. Other stability subfactors include excellent operational trends and good risk diversification. Good quality investment portfolio (5.7) with no exposure to mortgages and minimal holdings in junk bonds. Strong capitalization (7.2) based on excellent risk adjusted capital (severe loss scenario).

Other Rating Factors: Excellent profitability (9.2). Excellent liquidity (7.5).

Principal Business: Reinsurance (99%) and group health insurance (1%).

Principal Investments: Common & preferred stock (47%), cash (26%), nonCMO investment grade bonds (15%), CMOs and structured securities (4%), and noninv. grade bonds (1%).

Investments in Affiliates: 47%

Group Affiliation: Credit Suisse Group

Licensed in: AZ, AR, IL, KS, LA, MS, NE, NM, OK, OR, TX, WI

Commenced Business: September 1978

Address: 300 Burnett Street Suite 200, Fort Worth, TX 76102-2734

Phone: (817) 878-3300   **Domicile State:** TX   **NAIC Code:** 89087

Data Date	Rating	RACR #1	RACR #2	Total Assets ($mil)	Capital ($mil)	Net Premium ($mil)	Net Income ($mil)
9-18	B+	1.29	1.15	73.7	49.3	105.8	10.5
9-17	B-	1.16	1.03	50.0	32.2	73.7	4.9
2017	C+	0.77	0.69	47.9	29.6	103.3	7.4
2016	B-	0.84	0.75	34.9	23.5	62.7	0.1
2015	C	0.88	0.79	28.2	19.9	38.9	0.0
2014	C	0.95	0.90	19.8	14.9	21.1	1.3
2013	C	1.10	1.05	17.0	13.9	10.7	0.6

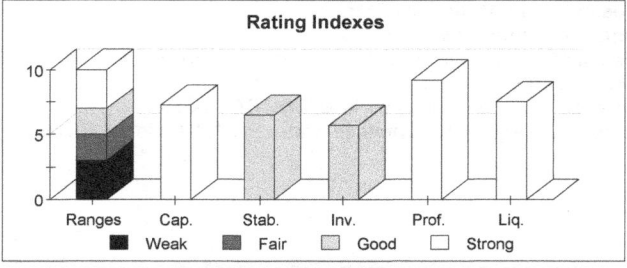

Rating Indexes

Ranges   Cap.   Stab.   Inv.   Prof.   Liq.

■ Weak   ■ Fair   □ Good   □ Strong

EQUITABLE LIFE & CASUALTY INSURANCE COMPANY

C+   **Fair**

Major Rating Factors: Fair current capitalization (4.3 on a scale of 0 to 10) based on fair risk adjusted capital (moderate loss scenario), although results have slipped from the good range over the last two years. Fair profitability (3.2) with operating losses during the first nine months of 2018. Fair overall results on stability tests (4.3) including excessive premium growth.

Other Rating Factors: Good quality investment portfolio (6.3). Excellent liquidity (7.2).

Principal Business: Individual health insurance (93%), individual life insurance (6%), and reinsurance (1%).

Principal Investments: NonCMO investment grade bonds (66%), CMOs and structured securities (10%), common & preferred stock (8%), mortgages in good standing (5%), and noninv. grade bonds (2%).

Investments in Affiliates: 8%

Group Affiliation: SILAC LLC

Licensed in: All states except CA, MN, NJ, NY, PR

Commenced Business: June 1935

Address: 3 TRIAD CENTER, SALT LAKE CITY, UT 84111

Phone: (801) 579-3400   **Domicile State:** UT   **NAIC Code:** 62952

Data Date	Rating	RACR #1	RACR #2	Total Assets ($mil)	Capital ($mil)	Net Premium ($mil)	Net Income ($mil)
9-18	C+	0.84	0.66	371.9	42.4	69.3	-1.3
9-17	B-	1.91	1.20	328.0	49.8	45.0	-8.7
2017	C+	0.98	0.80	351.6	43.3	59.7	-6.7
2016	B	2.86	1.90	313.6	44.8	64.7	-2.1
2015	B	2.94	1.96	306.4	46.2	69.7	9.5
2014	B	2.72	1.84	295.9	41.8	70.4	10.3
2013	D+	2.15	1.51	275.8	39.1	91.1	-0.3

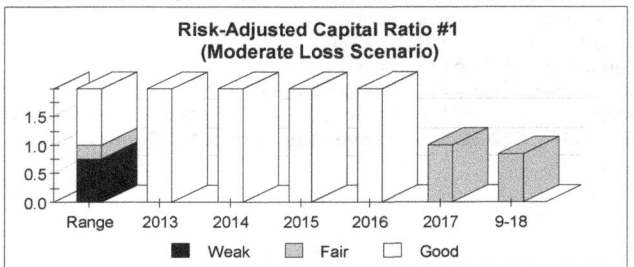

Risk-Adjusted Capital Ratio #1 (Moderate Loss Scenario)

Range   2013   2014   2015   2016   2017   9-18

■ Weak   ▨ Fair   □ Good

EQUITRUST LIFE INSURANCE COMPANY

B-   **Good**

Major Rating Factors: Good capitalization (5.6 on a scale of 0 to 10) based on good risk adjusted capital (moderate loss scenario). Good overall profitability (6.6). Good overall results on stability tests (5.0) despite fair risk adjusted capital in prior years. Other stability subfactors include good operational trends and excellent risk diversification.

Other Rating Factors: Fair quality investment portfolio (3.7). Excellent liquidity (7.5).

Principal Business: Individual annuities (74%), group retirement contracts (18%), and individual life insurance (7%).

Principal Investments: NonCMO investment grade bonds (46%), CMOs and structured securities (19%), mortgages in good standing (6%), noninv. grade bonds (4%), and misc. investments (17%).

Investments in Affiliates: 3%

Group Affiliation: Magic Johnson Enterprises Inc

Licensed in: All states except NY, PR

Commenced Business: July 1967

Address: 222 WEST ADAMS ST STE 2150, CHICAGO, IL 60606

Phone: (515) 225-5400 **Domicile State:** IL **NAIC Code:** 62510

Data Date	Rating	RACR #1	RACR #2	Total Assets ($mil)	Capital ($mil)	Net Premium ($mil)	Net Income ($mil)
9-18	B-	1.39	0.68	18,410.4	951.1	1,107.4	173.1
9-17	B-	1.19	0.60	17,814.5	819.5	1,314.3	108.1
2017	B-	1.24	0.62	18,168.7	872.7	1,671.3	210.7
2016	B-	1.43	0.71	17,268.0	931.6	1,951.3	227.4
2015	B-	1.32	0.66	15,881.3	819.0	2,099.1	164.7
2014	B-	1.63	0.87	14,454.7	897.0	2,205.2	179.6
2013	B-	2.33	1.07	12,615.5	846.2	2,131.9	203.6

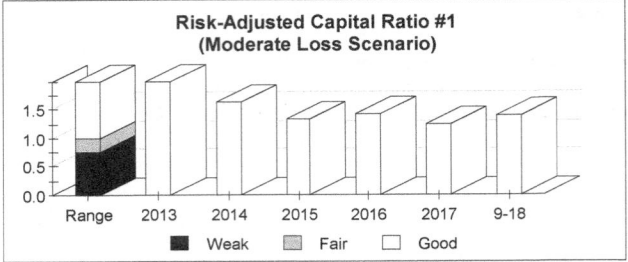

Risk-Adjusted Capital Ratio #1
(Moderate Loss Scenario)

ERIE FAMILY LIFE INSURANCE COMPANY *

A-   **Excellent**

Major Rating Factors: Good quality investment portfolio (5.9 on a scale of 0 to 10) despite mixed results such as: minimal exposure to mortgages and large holdings of BBB rated bonds but small junk bond holdings. Good overall profitability (6.3). Excellent expense controls. Good liquidity (6.1).

Other Rating Factors: Excellent overall results on stability tests (7.1) excellent operational trends and excellent risk diversification. Strong capitalization (7.9) based on excellent risk adjusted capital (severe loss scenario).

Principal Business: Individual life insurance (85%) and individual annuities (15%).

Principal Investments: NonCMO investment grade bonds (84%), CMOs and structured securities (3%), noninv. grade bonds (2%), common & preferred stock (2%), and misc. investments (3%).

Investments in Affiliates: None

Group Affiliation: Erie Ins Group

Licensed in: DC, IL, IN, KY, MD, MN, NC, OH, PA, TN, VA, WV, WI

Commenced Business: September 1967

Address: 100 Erie Insurance Place, Erie, PA 16530

Phone: (800) 458-0811 **Domicile State:** PA **NAIC Code:** 70769

Data Date	Rating	RACR #1	RACR #2	Total Assets ($mil)	Capital ($mil)	Net Premium ($mil)	Net Income ($mil)
9-18	A-	2.99	1.63	2,512.1	311.9	132.0	2.9
9-17	A-	3.17	1.73	2,448.7	315.7	127.5	8.3
2017	A-	2.91	1.59	2,433.1	303.6	170.8	7.5
2016	A-	3.14	1.72	2,247.0	310.7	162.2	0.3
2015	A-	3.29	1.81	2,169.0	310.8	151.1	8.7
2014	A-	3.43	1.90	2,096.9	303.5	150.3	10.1
2013	A-	3.36	1.86	2,021.4	290.7	137.2	14.9

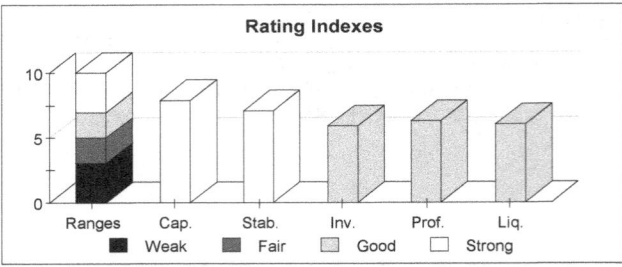

Rating Indexes

FAMILY HERITAGE LIFE INSURANCE COMPANY OF AMERICA *

B+   **Good**

Major Rating Factors: Good overall results on stability tests (6.5 on a scale of 0 to 10). Stability strengths include excellent operational trends and excellent risk diversification. Good quality investment portfolio (5.9) despite mixed results such as: minimal exposure to mortgages and large holdings of BBB rated bonds but small junk bond holdings. Good overall profitability (5.3) although investment income, in comparison to reserve requirements, is below regulatory standards.

Other Rating Factors: Strong capitalization (7.0) based on excellent risk adjusted capital (severe loss scenario). Excellent liquidity (7.6).

Principal Business: Individual health insurance (51%), reinsurance (45%), group health insurance (2%), and individual life insurance (1%).

Principal Investments: NonCMO investment grade bonds (92%), CMOs and structured securities (3%), and noninv. grade bonds (1%).

Investments in Affiliates: None

Group Affiliation: Torchmark Corp

Licensed in: All states except NY

Commenced Business: November 1989

Address: 6001 East Royalton Rd Ste 200, Cleveland, OH 44147-3529

Phone: (440) 922-5222 **Domicile State:** OH **NAIC Code:** 77968

Data Date	Rating	RACR #1	RACR #2	Total Assets ($mil)	Capital ($mil)	Net Premium ($mil)	Net Income ($mil)
9-18	B+	1.66	1.02	1,444.8	106.0	229.2	23.8
9-17	B+	1.82	1.15	1,249.5	103.8	214.4	13.6
2017	B+	1.65	1.01	1,290.4	100.3	284.3	23.0
2016	B+	1.96	1.25	1,108.8	104.2	264.6	23.8
2015	A-	1.92	1.27	921.0	78.3	254.1	19.1
2014	A-	1.87	1.27	775.2	67.4	237.0	18.1
2013	A-	2.09	1.48	641.5	66.9	192.7	17.0

Adverse Trends in Operations

Increase in policy surrenders from 2016 to 2017 (47%)
Decrease in capital during 2017 (4%)
Increase in policy surrenders from 2014 to 2015 (118%)

FAMILY LIFE INSURANCE COMPANY | C | Fair

Major Rating Factors: Fair profitability (3.0 on a scale of 0 to 10) with investment income below regulatory standards in relation to interest assumptions of reserves. Fair overall results on stability tests (4.2) including negative cash flow from operations for 2017. Good liquidity (5.8) with sufficient resources to handle a spike in claims as well as a significant increase in policy surrenders.

Other Rating Factors: Strong capitalization (9.4) based on excellent risk adjusted capital (severe loss scenario). High quality investment portfolio (8.2).

Principal Business: Individual health insurance (65%) and individual life insurance (35%).

Principal Investments: NonCMO investment grade bonds (72%), policy loans (10%), CMOs and structured securities (3%), mortgages in good standing (2%), and misc. investments (2%).

Investments in Affiliates: None

Group Affiliation: Manhattan Life Group Inc

Licensed in: All states except NY, PR

Commenced Business: June 1949

Address: 10777 Northwest Freeway, Houston, TX 77092

Phone: (713) 529-0045 **Domicile State:** TX **NAIC Code:** 63053

Data Date	Rating	RACR #1	RACR #2	Total Assets ($mil)	Capital ($mil)	Net Premium ($mil)	Net Income ($mil)
9-18	C	3.16	2.57	146.4	29.4	19.5	1.4
9-17	C	3.43	2.86	153.4	32.2	19.2	2.1
2017	C	3.33	2.72	150.8	31.1	25.6	2.7
2016	C	3.61	3.03	155.8	34.0	26.0	1.0
2015	C	3.79	3.13	158.7	35.8	26.5	2.7
2014	C	3.87	3.33	146.5	36.2	25.2	1.7
2013	C	3.41	2.69	147.6	31.9	26.0	3.5

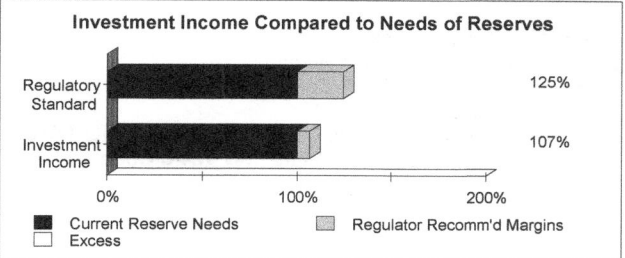

Investment Income Compared to Needs of Reserves

Regulatory Standard — 125%

Investment Income — 107%

■ Current Reserve Needs ■ Regulator Recomm'd Margins □ Excess

FARM BUREAU LIFE INSURANCE COMPANY * | B+ | Good

Major Rating Factors: Good quality investment portfolio (5.5 on a scale of 0 to 10) despite large holdings of BBB rated bonds in addition to moderate junk bond exposure. Exposure to mortgages is significant, but the mortgage default rate has been low. Good overall results on stability tests (6.0). Stability strengths include excellent operational trends and excellent risk diversification. Fair liquidity (4.0).

Other Rating Factors: Strong capitalization (7.2) based on excellent risk adjusted capital (severe loss scenario). Excellent profitability (8.0).

Principal Business: Individual life insurance (52%), individual annuities (43%), reinsurance (2%), group retirement contracts (1%), and individual health insurance (1%).

Principal Investments: NonCMO investment grade bonds (53%), CMOs and structured securities (25%), mortgages in good standing (12%), noninv. grade bonds (3%), and misc. investments (6%).

Investments in Affiliates: None

Group Affiliation: Iowa Farm Bureau

Licensed in: AZ, CO, ID, IA, KS, MN, MT, NE, NV, NM, ND, OK, OR, SD, UT, WA, WI, WY

Commenced Business: January 1945

Address: 5400 University Avenue, West Des Moines, IA 50266-5997

Phone: (515) 225-5400 **Domicile State:** IA **NAIC Code:** 63088

Data Date	Rating	RACR #1	RACR #2	Total Assets ($mil)	Capital ($mil)	Net Premium ($mil)	Net Income ($mil)
9-18	B+	2.17	1.13	9,267.1	634.1	471.4	93.0
9-17	B+	2.24	1.16	8,948.8	645.4	470.9	82.6
2017	B+	2.04	1.06	9,068.7	616.0	632.8	104.9
2016	B+	2.08	1.08	8,760.4	617.3	688.1	100.7
2015	B+	2.17	1.13	8,402.0	603.1	684.0	106.0
2014	B+	2.09	1.09	8,088.8	552.0	647.4	97.4
2013	B+	2.01	1.03	7,723.0	492.5	636.8	94.6

Adverse Trends in Operations

Decrease in premium volume from 2016 to 2017 (8%)

FARM BUREAU LIFE INSURANCE COMPANY OF MICHIGAN * | A- | Excellent

Major Rating Factors: Good quality investment portfolio (6.1 on a scale of 0 to 10) despite significant exposure to mortgages . Mortgage default rate has been low. substantial holdings of BBB bonds in addition to minimal holdings in junk bonds. Good liquidity (5.7) with sufficient resources to cover a large increase in policy surrenders. Good overall results on stability tests (6.9) excellent operational trends and excellent risk diversification.

Other Rating Factors: Strong capitalization (8.6) based on excellent risk adjusted capital (severe loss scenario). Excellent profitability (7.1).

Principal Business: Individual life insurance (52%), individual annuities (45%), group retirement contracts (1%), and group life insurance (1%).

Principal Investments: NonCMO investment grade bonds (70%), mortgages in good standing (17%), common & preferred stock (7%), policy loans (1%), and misc. investments (4%).

Investments in Affiliates: None

Group Affiliation: Michigan Farm Bureau

Licensed in: MI

Commenced Business: September 1951

Address: 7373 WEST SAGINAW HIGHWAY, LANSING, MI 48917

Phone: (517) 323-7000 **Domicile State:** MI **NAIC Code:** 63096

Data Date	Rating	RACR #1	RACR #2	Total Assets ($mil)	Capital ($mil)	Net Premium ($mil)	Net Income ($mil)
9-18	A-	3.70	2.06	2,502.3	458.6	80.6	22.2
9-17	A-	3.54	1.95	2,471.2	433.5	119.5	18.1
2017	A-	3.61	2.00	2,487.4	443.3	151.6	24.9
2016	A-	3.44	1.89	2,383.8	409.3	123.9	19.0
2015	A-	3.36	1.84	2,322.8	393.3	109.8	33.0
2014	A-	3.10	1.69	2,364.1	369.0	115.4	32.9
2013	A-	3.44	1.86	2,294.0	409.4	116.9	24.6

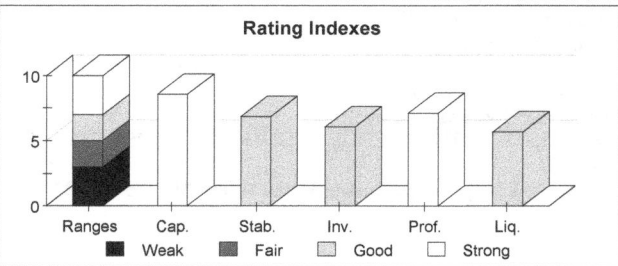

Rating Indexes

Ranges Cap. Stab. Inv. Prof. Liq.

■ Weak ■ Fair □ Good □ Strong

FARM BUREAU LIFE INSURANCE COMPANY OF MISSOURI * A- Excellent

Major Rating Factors: Good quality investment portfolio (5.2 on a scale of 0 to 10) despite mixed results such as: no exposure to mortgages and large holdings of BBB rated bonds but minimal holdings in junk bonds. Good overall profitability (5.3) although investment income, in comparison to reserve requirements, is below regulatory standards. Good liquidity (5.7).

Other Rating Factors: Good overall results on stability tests (6.9) excellent operational trends and excellent risk diversification. Strong capitalization (7.2) based on excellent risk adjusted capital (severe loss scenario).

Principal Business: Individual life insurance (85%), individual annuities (13%), group life insurance (1%), and group health insurance (1%).

Principal Investments: NonCMO investment grade bonds (67%), common & preferred stock (15%), CMOs and structured securities (13%), and policy loans (4%).

Investments in Affiliates: 3%

Group Affiliation: Missouri Farm Bureau

Licensed in: MO

Commenced Business: July 1950

Address: 701 South Country Club Drive, Jefferson City, MO 65109-4515

Phone: (573) 893-1400 **Domicile State:** MO **NAIC Code:** 63118

Data Date	Rating	RACR #1	RACR #2	Total Assets ($mil)	Capital ($mil)	Net Premium ($mil)	Net Income ($mil)
9-18	A-	1.68	1.11	604.4	71.1	32.2	2.1
9-17	A-	1.66	1.10	582.3	66.2	29.8	1.0
2017	A-	1.65	1.09	586.5	68.8	37.0	2.6
2016	A-	1.64	1.08	569.6	64.3	40.5	3.3
2015	A-	1.74	1.13	542.7	59.7	39.4	3.8
2014	A-	1.91	1.24	528.3	60.0	38.6	4.0
2013	A-	1.98	1.25	506.1	54.2	42.3	4.6

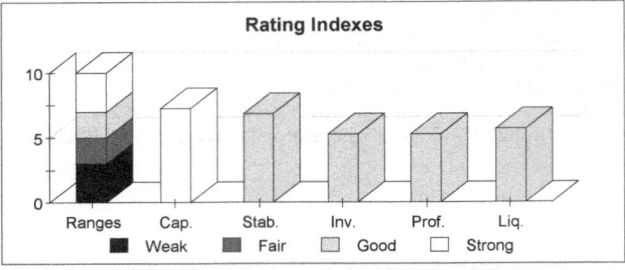

Rating Indexes

Ranges Cap. Stab. Inv. Prof. Liq.
■ Weak ■ Fair ▨ Good □ Strong

FARM FAMILY LIFE INSURANCE COMPANY B Good

Major Rating Factors: Good quality investment portfolio (5.0 on a scale of 0 to 10) despite mixed results such as: minimal exposure to mortgages and large holdings of BBB rated bonds but small junk bond holdings. Good overall profitability (6.0) although investment income, in comparison to reserve requirements, is below regulatory standards. Good liquidity (5.6).

Other Rating Factors: Good overall results on stability tests (6.0) excellent operational trends and excellent risk diversification. Strong capitalization (7.7) based on excellent risk adjusted capital (severe loss scenario).

Principal Business: Individual life insurance (82%), individual annuities (11%), and individual health insurance (8%).

Principal Investments: NonCMO investment grade bonds (71%), common & preferred stock (10%), mortgages in good standing (10%), noninv. grade bonds (4%), and misc. investments (4%).

Investments in Affiliates: None

Group Affiliation: American National Group Inc

Licensed in: CT, DE, ME, MD, MA, NH, NJ, NY, PA, RI, VT, VA, WV

Commenced Business: January 1954

Address: 344 ROUTE 9W, GLENMONT, NY 12077

Phone: (800) 392-0644 **Domicile State:** NY **NAIC Code:** 63126

Data Date	Rating	RACR #1	RACR #2	Total Assets ($mil)	Capital ($mil)	Net Premium ($mil)	Net Income ($mil)
3-18	B	2.61	1.44	2,259.2	253.2	73.2	2.2
3-17	B	2.50	1.39	1,348.8	179.9	15.8	0.6
2017	B	2.67	1.51	1,369.9	207.7	57.3	15.0
2016	B	2.53	1.42	1,343.4	179.1	69.1	13.4
2015	B	2.42	1.36	1,308.9	166.5	75.5	9.4
2014	B	2.43	1.35	1,284.6	160.5	70.8	10.2
2013	B	2.15	1.22	1,248.4	151.9	72.2	18.6

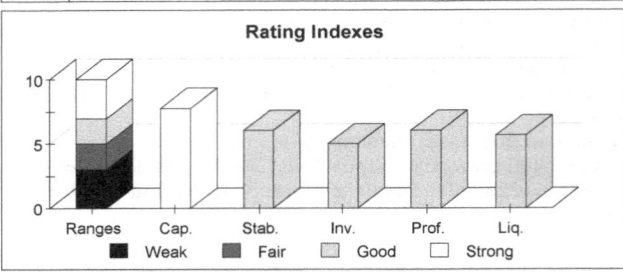

Rating Indexes

Ranges Cap. Stab. Inv. Prof. Liq.
■ Weak ■ Fair ▨ Good □ Strong

FARMERS NEW WORLD LIFE INSURANCE COMPANY B- Good

Major Rating Factors: Fair current capitalization (4.0 on a scale of 0 to 10) based on mixed results -- excessive policy leverage mitigated by excellent risk adjusted capital (severe loss scenario) reflecting improvement over results in 2015. Fair profitability (3.0) with investment income below regulatory standards in relation to interest assumptions of reserves. Fair liquidity (4.3).

Other Rating Factors: Fair overall results on stability tests (4.7) including negative cash flow from operations for 2017. Good quality investment portfolio (5.4).

Principal Business: Individual life insurance (95%), individual annuities (3%), and individual health insurance (2%).

Principal Investments: NonCMO investment grade bonds (55%), mortgages in good standing (14%), CMOs and structured securities (13%), policy loans (7%), and misc. investments (9%).

Investments in Affiliates: 3%

Group Affiliation: Zurich Financial Services Group

Licensed in: All states except NY, PR

Commenced Business: May 1911

Address: 3003 77TH AVENUE SOUTHEAST, MERCER ISLAND, WA 98040-2837

Phone: (206) 232-8400 **Domicile State:** WA **NAIC Code:** 63177

Data Date	Rating	RACR #1	RACR #2	Total Assets ($mil)	Capital ($mil)	Net Premium ($mil)	Net Income ($mil)
9-18	B-	2.14	1.18	5,159.1	480.9	398.5	95.9
9-17	B-	2.39	1.27	5,171.5	563.4	-1,881.1	120.6
2017	B-	2.06	1.13	5,127.3	468.9	-1,738.6	148.9
2016	B-	2.08	1.10	7,155.3	527.7	592.6	137.9
2015	B-	1.38	0.82	7,048.9	481.5	600.0	101.4
2014	B-	1.66	0.98	7,063.7	497.6	588.9	117.0
2013	B-	2.39	1.33	7,141.0	566.6	469.3	79.8

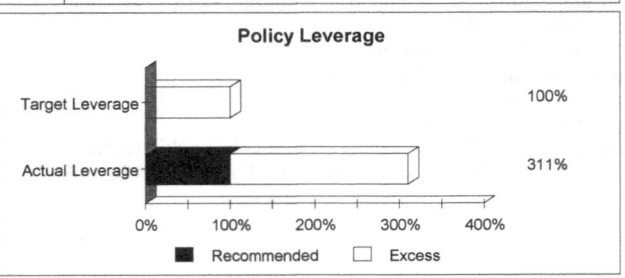

Policy Leverage

Target Leverage — 100%

Actual Leverage — 311%

0% 100% 200% 300% 400%
■ Recommended □ Excess

FEDERATED LIFE INSURANCE COMPANY *   A   Excellent

Major Rating Factors: Good quality investment portfolio (6.7 on a scale of 0 to 10) despite mixed results such as: no exposure to mortgages and large holdings of BBB rated bonds but small junk bond holdings. Good liquidity (6.4) with sufficient resources to handle a spike in claims as well as a significant increase in policy surrenders. Excellent overall results on stability tests (7.4) excellent operational trends and excellent risk diversification.

Other Rating Factors: Strong capitalization (9.5) based on excellent risk adjusted capital (severe loss scenario). Excellent profitability (8.8).

Principal Business: Individual life insurance (73%), individual health insurance (14%), individual annuities (10%), and group life insurance (3%).

Principal Investments: NonCMO investment grade bonds (76%), CMOs and structured securities (14%), noninv. grade bonds (4%), common & preferred stock (1%), and policy loans (1%).

Investments in Affiliates: None

Group Affiliation: Federated Mutual Ins Group

Licensed in: All states except AK, DC, HI, PR

Commenced Business: January 1959

Address: 121 EAST PARK SQUARE, OWATONNA, MN 55060

Phone: (507) 455-5200 **Domicile State:** MN **NAIC Code:** 63258

Data Date	Rating	RACR #1	RACR #2	Total Assets ($mil)	Capital ($mil)	Net Premium ($mil)	Net Income ($mil)
9-18	A	4.96	2.68	1,969.7	411.9	138.7	28.2
9-17	A	4.59	2.45	1,849.9	381.0	137.4	23.4
2017	A	4.39	2.35	1,877.4	382.4	192.7	32.6
2016	A	4.39	2.36	1,776.8	359.8	195.8	24.3
2015	A	4.56	2.53	1,648.9	335.5	180.9	22.7
2014	A	4.47	2.49	1,526.3	308.1	168.9	19.3
2013	A	4.42	2.46	1,435.5	293.5	179.5	13.9

Adverse Trends in Operations

Decrease in premium volume from 2016 to 2017 (2%)
Decrease in premium volume from 2013 to 2014 (6%)

FIDELITY & GUARANTY LIFE INSURANCE COMPANY   C+   Fair

Major Rating Factors: Fair overall results on stability tests (4.6 on a scale of 0 to 10) including fair risk adjusted capital in prior years. Good capitalization (5.1) based on good risk adjusted capital (moderate loss scenario). Good overall profitability (5.8) despite operating losses during the first nine months of 2018.

Other Rating Factors: Good liquidity (6.0). Low quality investment portfolio (2.6).

Principal Business: Individual annuities (85%) and individual life insurance (15%).

Principal Investments: NonCMO investment grade bonds (56%), CMOs and structured securities (24%), noninv. grade bonds (6%), common & preferred stock (5%), and misc. investments (9%).

Investments in Affiliates: 2%

Group Affiliation: FGL Holdings

Licensed in: All states except NY

Commenced Business: November 1960

Address: 601 Locust Street, Des Moines, IA 50309

Phone: (410) 895-0100 **Domicile State:** IA **NAIC Code:** 63274

Data Date	Rating	RACR #1	RACR #2	Total Assets ($mil)	Capital ($mil)	Net Premium ($mil)	Net Income ($mil)
9-18	C+	1.09	0.58	24,281.8	946.4	2,201.5	-24.5
9-17	C+	1.57	0.86	22,577.8	1,528.5	1,870.6	145.4
2017	C+	1.15	0.61	22,380.8	919.0	2,392.4	222.4
2016	C+	1.40	0.77	21,414.2	1,323.0	2,705.0	20.9
2015	C+	1.31	0.73	19,810.1	1,239.0	2,185.6	-52.9
2014	C+	1.31	0.73	18,973.2	1,211.6	2,526.1	104.6
2013	C+	1.36	0.77	17,422.5	1,108.3	1,363.8	118.2

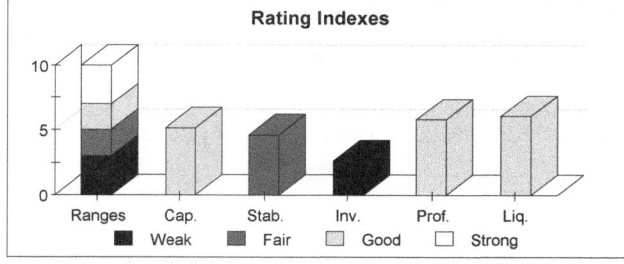

Rating Indexes — Ranges, Cap., Stab., Inv., Prof., Liq. — Weak, Fair, Good, Strong

FIDELITY & GUARANTY LIFE INSURANCE COMPANY OF NEW Y(B-   Good

Major Rating Factors: Good quality investment portfolio (5.2 on a scale of 0 to 10) despite mixed results such as: no exposure to mortgages and large holdings of BBB rated bonds but small junk bond holdings. Good liquidity (6.1) with sufficient resources to cover a large increase in policy surrenders. Fair overall results on stability tests (4.8) including fair financial strength of affiliated FGL Holdings and negative cash flow from operations for 2017.

Other Rating Factors: Strong capitalization (9.0) based on excellent risk adjusted capital (severe loss scenario). Excellent profitability (7.1) despite modest operating losses during 2015.

Principal Business: Individual annuities (80%) and individual life insurance (20%).

Principal Investments: NonCMO investment grade bonds (65%), CMOs and structured securities (16%), common & preferred stock (6%), and noninv. grade bonds (4%).

Investments in Affiliates: None

Group Affiliation: FGL Holdings

Licensed in: NY

Commenced Business: November 1962

Address: 445 Park Avenue 9th Floor, New York, NY 10022

Phone: (888) 697-5433 **Domicile State:** NY **NAIC Code:** 69434

Data Date	Rating	RACR #1	RACR #2	Total Assets ($mil)	Capital ($mil)	Net Premium ($mil)	Net Income ($mil)
9-18	B-	4.62	2.36	539.9	94.4	8.5	5.6
9-17	B-	3.59	1.80	526.1	70.0	8.1	4.4
2017	B-	4.44	2.23	548.9	88.6	9.6	41.0
2016	B-	3.29	1.62	520.4	64.2	13.6	4.1
2015	B-	3.29	1.63	526.0	59.5	27.0	-1.2
2014	B-	3.18	1.63	522.1	61.2	31.5	1.9
2013	B-	3.55	1.82	504.3	61.9	33.5	1.3

FGL Holdings
Composite Group Rating: C+
Largest Group Members

	Assets ($mil)	Rating
FIDELITY GUARANTY LIFE INS CO	22381	C+
FIDELITY GUARANTY LIFE INS CO NY	549	B-

FIDELITY INVESTMENTS LIFE INSURANCE COMPANY *   A-   Excellent

Major Rating Factors: Good quality investment portfolio (6.6 on a scale of 0 to 10) despite mixed results such as: no exposure to mortgages and large holdings of BBB rated bonds but minimal holdings in junk bonds. Strong capitalization (8.5) based on excellent risk adjusted capital (severe loss scenario). Furthermore, this high level of risk adjusted capital has been consistently maintained over the last five years. Excellent profitability (9.2).

Other Rating Factors: Excellent liquidity (7.0). Excellent overall results on stability tests (7.0) excellent operational trends and excellent risk diversification.

Principal Business: Individual annuities (99%) and individual life insurance (1%).

Principal Investments: NonCMO investment grade bonds (75%), common & preferred stock (8%), noninv. grade bonds (7%), and CMOs and structured securities (1%).

Investments in Affiliates: 8%

Group Affiliation: FMR LLC

Licensed in: All states except NY, PR

Commenced Business: December 1981

Address: 49 North 400 West 6th Floor, Salt Lake City, UT 84101

Phone: (401) 292-4616 **Domicile State:** UT **NAIC Code:** 93696

Data Date	Rating	RACR #1	RACR #2	Total Assets ($mil)	Capital ($mil)	Net Premium ($mil)	Net Income ($mil)
9-18	A-	3.39	2.03	30,960.8	934.0	1,094.1	66.2
9-17	A-	3.43	2.07	28,629.5	873.1	1,042.1	55.6
2017	A-	3.23	2.02	29,539.9	876.1	1,384.4	73.6
2016	A-	3.48	2.12	25,859.6	830.0	1,275.8	82.4
2015	A-	3.23	1.96	24,854.3	750.9	1,836.4	62.3
2014	A-	3.03	1.83	24,504.3	685.8	1,874.6	66.0
2013	A-	2.90	1.75	22,477.4	614.7	1,871.3	56.1

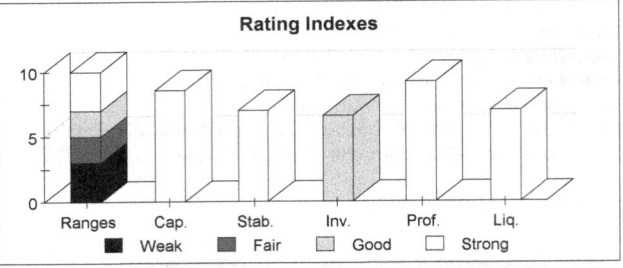

Rating Indexes

FIDELITY LIFE ASSOCIATION   C+   Fair

Major Rating Factors: Fair profitability (3.7 on a scale of 0 to 10) with operating losses during the first nine months of 2018. Fair overall results on stability tests (4.8). Good quality investment portfolio (6.3) despite substantial holdings of BBB bonds in addition to moderate junk bond exposure. Exposure to mortgages is significant, but the mortgage default rate has been low.

Other Rating Factors: Good liquidity (6.7). Strong capitalization (10.0) based on excellent risk adjusted capital (severe loss scenario).

Principal Business: Individual life insurance (74%), group life insurance (13%), reinsurance (12%), and group health insurance (1%).

Principal Investments: NonCMO investment grade bonds (48%), CMOs and structured securities (26%), mortgages in good standing (11%), noninv. grade bonds (8%), and misc. investments (8%).

Investments in Affiliates: None

Group Affiliation: Vericity Inc

Licensed in: All states except NY, PR

Commenced Business: February 1896

Address: 8700 W Bryn Mawr Ave Suite 900, Chicago, IL 60631

Phone: (630) 522-0392 **Domicile State:** IL **NAIC Code:** 63290

Data Date	Rating	RACR #1	RACR #2	Total Assets ($mil)	Capital ($mil)	Net Premium ($mil)	Net Income ($mil)
9-18	C+	5.99	3.20	404.2	118.0	45.6	-4.1
9-17	C+	6.55	3.41	400.7	123.6	44.7	-4.0
2017	C+	6.25	3.29	406.3	127.6	61.1	1.0
2016	C+	7.00	3.65	405.0	132.2	60.3	5.2
2015	C	6.62	3.54	421.2	134.6	70.0	13.1
2014	C	7.19	3.87	411.9	134.7	59.9	30.2
2013	C	5.12	2.88	414.6	124.1	44.3	-22.8

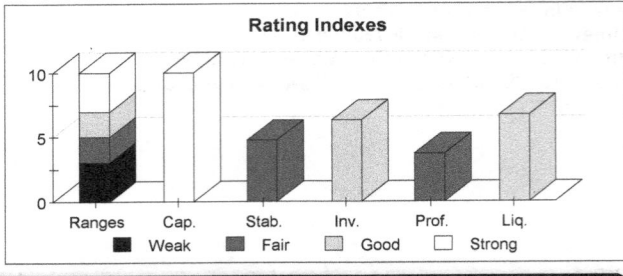

Rating Indexes

FIDELITY SECURITY LIFE INSURANCE COMPANY   B   Good

Major Rating Factors: Good quality investment portfolio (6.7 on a scale of 0 to 10) despite mixed results such as: minimal exposure to mortgages and large holdings of BBB rated bonds but minimal holdings in junk bonds. Good liquidity (6.6) with sufficient resources to cover a large increase in policy surrenders. Good overall results on stability tests (5.5) despite negative cash flow from operations for 2017 good operational trends and excellent risk diversification.

Other Rating Factors: Strong capitalization (9.6) based on excellent risk adjusted capital (severe loss scenario). Excellent profitability (7.6).

Principal Business: Group health insurance (90%), reinsurance (5%), individual health insurance (2%), group life insurance (1%), and other lines (3%).

Principal Investments: NonCMO investment grade bonds (51%), CMOs and structured securities (36%), cash (3%), common & preferred stock (3%), and misc. investments (4%).

Investments in Affiliates: 2%

Group Affiliation: Fidelity Security Group

Licensed in: All states except PR

Commenced Business: July 1969

Address: 3130 Broadway, Kansas City, MO 64111-2452

Phone: (816) 750-1060 **Domicile State:** MO **NAIC Code:** 71870

Data Date	Rating	RACR #1	RACR #2	Total Assets ($mil)	Capital ($mil)	Net Premium ($mil)	Net Income ($mil)
9-18	B	4.44	2.70	931.6	234.7	91.5	31.4
9-17	B	3.66	2.18	930.2	201.8	87.4	18.0
2017	B	3.87	2.36	949.5	204.4	115.0	22.8
2016	B	3.46	2.07	875.1	186.8	121.6	17.5
2015	B	2.02	1.44	864.2	169.0	420.4	18.1
2014	B-	2.65	1.73	831.7	151.9	204.6	18.4
2013	B-	2.99	1.83	819.5	135.3	109.2	13.9

Adverse Trends in Operations

Decrease in premium volume from 2016 to 2017 (5%)
Change in premium mix from 2015 to 2016 (6%)
Decrease in premium volume from 2015 to 2016 (71%)
Change in premium mix from 2013 to 2014 (5.7%)

FIRST ALLMERICA FINANCIAL LIFE INSURANCE   B   Good

Major Rating Factors: Good overall results on stability tests (5.8 on a scale of 0 to 10) despite negative cash flow from operations for 2017. Other stability subfactors include good operational trends and excellent risk diversification. Good quality investment portfolio (6.6) despite mixed results such as: minimal exposure to mortgages and large holdings of BBB rated bonds but minimal holdings in junk bonds. Good overall profitability (6.0).

Other Rating Factors: Good liquidity (5.9). Strong capitalization (9.2) based on excellent risk adjusted capital (severe loss scenario).

Principal Business: Individual life insurance (54%), reinsurance (43%), group retirement contracts (2%), and group life insurance (1%).

Principal Investments: NonCMO investment grade bonds (71%), CMOs and structured securities (19%), policy loans (2%), cash (2%), and misc. investments (3%).

Investments in Affiliates: 1%
Group Affiliation: Global Atlantic Financial Group
Licensed in: All states except PR
Commenced Business: June 1845
Address: 132 TURNPIKE ROAD SUITE 210, SOUTHBOROUGH, MA 2135
Phone: (508) 460-2400 **Domicile State:** MA **NAIC Code:** 69140

Data Date	Rating	RACR #1	RACR #2	Total Assets ($mil)	Capital ($mil)	Net Premium ($mil)	Net Income ($mil)
9-18	B	5.16	2.45	3,333.8	236.8	21.4	10.8
9-17	B-	4.34	2.03	3,380.8	199.2	19.9	21.0
2017	B-	5.18	2.44	3,420.3	240.3	28.6	28.7
2016	C+	4.18	1.95	3,435.0	184.8	28.4	8.6
2015	C	4.56	2.11	3,559.5	237.6	-535.1	22.3
2014	C	4.40	2.09	4,240.5	216.4	78.8	73.8
2013	D	3.47	1.65	4,206.0	154.7	-313.6	-38.7

Adverse Trends in Operations

Decrease in capital during 2016 (22%)
Decrease in asset base during 2016 (3%)
Decrease in asset base during 2015 (16%)
Decrease in premium volume from 2014 to 2015 (779%)
Change in premium mix from 2013 to 2014 (86.1%)

FIRST ASSURANCE LIFE OF AMERICA   B   Good

Major Rating Factors: Good overall results on stability tests (5.9 on a scale of 0 to 10) despite fair financial strength of affiliated LDS Group. Other stability subfactors include good operational trends and good risk diversification. Strong capitalization (10.0) based on excellent risk adjusted capital (severe loss scenario). Capital levels have been relatively consistent over the last five years. High quality investment portfolio (8.4).

Other Rating Factors: Excellent profitability (8.3). Excellent liquidity (8.4).

Principal Business: Credit life insurance (85%) and credit health insurance (15%).

Principal Investments: NonCMO investment grade bonds (67%), common & preferred stock (25%), noninv. grade bonds (1%), and cash (1%).

Investments in Affiliates: 25%
Group Affiliation: LDS Group
Licensed in: AL, LA, MS, TN
Commenced Business: September 1981
Address: 9016 BLUEBONNET BOULEVARD, BATON ROUGE, LA 70810-2810

Phone: (225) 769-9923 **Domicile State:** LA **NAIC Code:** 94579

Data Date	Rating	RACR #1	RACR #2	Total Assets ($mil)	Capital ($mil)	Net Premium ($mil)	Net Income ($mil)
9-18	B	3.35	3.12	41.6	36.9	1.4	0.8
9-17	B	3.31	3.07	40.7	35.1	2.1	0.7
2017	B	3.28	3.08	41.0	35.8	1.9	1.2
2016	B	3.24	3.01	39.9	34.2	2.8	0.8
2015	B	3.21	3.02	39.0	33.3	3.1	0.8
2014	B	3.17	3.01	37.8	32.4	3.5	0.6
2013	B	3.14	2.98	36.8	31.7	3.0	0.7

LDS Group
Composite Group Rating: C+

Largest Group Members	Assets ($mil)	Rating
VERSANT CASUALTY INS CO	51	C
FIRST ASR LIFE OF AMERICA	41	B
PERFORMANCE LIFE OF AMERICA	33	B-
VERSANT LIFE INS CO	7	B-

FIRST BERKSHIRE HATHAWAY LIFE INSURANCE COMPANY   C+   Fair

Major Rating Factors: Fair quality investment portfolio (3.7 on a scale of 0 to 10) with substantial holdings of BBB bonds in addition to moderate junk bond exposure. Fair overall results on stability tests (4.4). Weak profitability (2.8) with investment income below regulatory standards in relation to interest assumptions of reserves.

Other Rating Factors: Strong capitalization (10.0) based on excellent risk adjusted capital (severe loss scenario). Excellent liquidity (10.0).

Principal Business: Group retirement contracts (100%).

Principal Investments: NonCMO investment grade bonds (51%), noninv. grade bonds (18%), cash (17%), CMOs and structured securities (11%), and common & preferred stock (5%).

Investments in Affiliates: 4%
Group Affiliation: Berkshire-Hathaway
Licensed in: MO, NE, NY
Commenced Business: March 2003
Address: Marine Air Terminal LaGuardia, Flushing, NY 11371
Phone: (402) 916-3000 **Domicile State:** NY **NAIC Code:** 11591

Data Date	Rating	RACR #1	RACR #2	Total Assets ($mil)	Capital ($mil)	Net Premium ($mil)	Net Income ($mil)
9-18	C+	12.05	6.26	215.8	119.0	4.0	2.3
9-17	C+	12.61	6.54	213.5	119.7	5.3	0.7
2017	C+	11.80	6.75	228.6	116.1	6.8	-3.6
2016	C	11.54	6.85	186.1	109.6	3.5	2.5
2015	C	10.67	6.03	159.9	99.6	2.0	2.4
2014	C+	10.08	6.34	386.4	114.6	-79.4	80.3
2013	C	2.48	2.23	286.6	25.5	80.1	-87.3

Rating Indexes

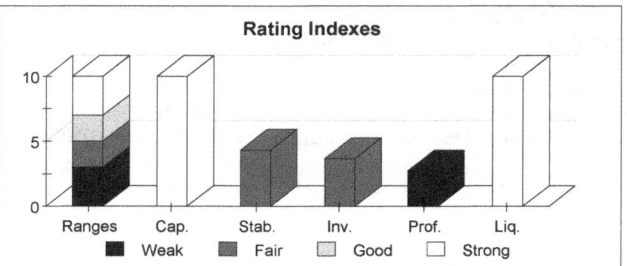

FIRST HEALTH LIFE & HEALTH INSURANCE COMPANY | C+ | Fair

Major Rating Factors: Fair profitability (3.9 on a scale of 0 to 10). Excellent expense controls. Fair overall results on stability tests (3.2) including negative cash flow from operations for 2017. Good quality investment portfolio (5.4) despite mixed results such as: no exposure to mortgages and substantial holdings of BBB bonds but minimal holdings in junk bonds.

Other Rating Factors: Weak liquidity (1.8). Strong capitalization (7.5) based on excellent risk adjusted capital (severe loss scenario).

Principal Business: Individual health insurance (98%) and group health insurance (2%).

Principal Investments: NonCMO investment grade bonds (38%), cash (34%), CMOs and structured securities (15%), and noninv. grade bonds (11%).

Investments in Affiliates: None

Group Affiliation: Aetna Inc

Licensed in: All states except PR

Commenced Business: June 1979

Address: DOWNERS GROVE, IL 60515

Phone: (630) 737-7900 **Domicile State:** TX **NAIC Code:** 90328

Data Date	Rating	RACR #1	RACR #2	Total Assets ($mil)	Capital ($mil)	Net Premium ($mil)	Net Income ($mil)
9-18	C+	1.61	1.33	420.1	166.9	427.1	13.4
9-17	B-	1.49	1.22	515.7	207.8	587.1	-3.6
2017	B-	1.70	1.39	400.7	227.8	761.1	16.5
2016	B-	1.50	1.24	454.9	211.1	798.3	-1.7
2015	B-	2.24	1.85	581.8	289.2	700.0	16.1
2014	B	1.15	0.96	475.0	226.0	925.3	-6.6
2013	B	1.02	0.85	505.6	233.3	1,420.5	-175.3

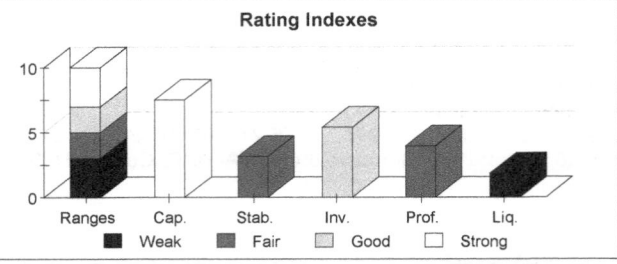

Rating Indexes

FIRST METLIFE INVESTORS INSURANCE COMPANY | C+ | Fair

Major Rating Factors: Fair overall results on stability tests (4.4 on a scale of 0 to 10) including excessive premium growth. Good quality investment portfolio (6.5) despite large holdings of BBB rated bonds in addition to moderate junk bond exposure. Exposure to mortgages is significant, but the mortgage default rate has been low. Good liquidity (6.3) with sufficient resources to handle a spike in claims as well as a significant increase in policy surrenders.

Other Rating Factors: Weak profitability (2.0) with operating losses during the first nine months of 2018. Strong capitalization (7.3) based on excellent risk adjusted capital (severe loss scenario).

Principal Business: Individual annuities (78%) and individual life insurance (22%).

Principal Investments: NonCMO investment grade bonds (58%), CMOs and structured securities (19%), mortgages in good standing (16%), noninv. grade bonds (5%), and cash (1%).

Investments in Affiliates: None

Group Affiliation: Brighthouse Financial Inc

Licensed in: NY

Commenced Business: March 1993

Address: 200 Park Avenue, New York, NY 10017

Phone: (212) 578-9500 **Domicile State:** NY **NAIC Code:** 60992

Data Date	Rating	RACR #1	RACR #2	Total Assets ($mil)	Capital ($mil)	Net Premium ($mil)	Net Income ($mil)
9-18	C+	2.33	1.20	8,005.3	274.0	325.9	-5.0
9-17	C+	1.95	1.00	7,606.9	222.0	184.0	25.3
2017	C+	2.50	1.27	7,834.7	294.3	285.4	22.2
2016	C+	1.74	0.87	6,967.4	195.8	1,286.8	-87.3
2015	C+	4.29	2.14	6,115.2	320.7	53.9	17.2
2014	C	3.81	1.89	6,504.7	297.4	-4,181.7	10.6
2013	C	2.12	1.07	6,244.5	124.4	295.6	-23.8

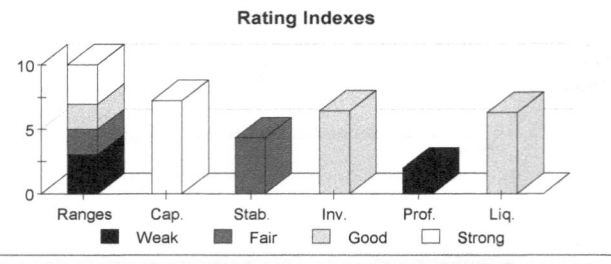

Rating Indexes

FIRST PENN-PACIFIC LIFE INSURANCE COMPANY | B | Good

Major Rating Factors: Good overall results on stability tests (5.1 on a scale of 0 to 10) despite negative cash flow from operations for 2017. Other stability subfactors include good operational trends and excellent risk diversification. Good quality investment portfolio (6.0) despite mixed results such as: large holdings of BBB rated bonds but moderate junk bond exposure. Fair profitability (4.4) with operating losses during the first nine months of 2018.

Other Rating Factors: Fair liquidity (4.0). Strong capitalization (7.6) based on excellent risk adjusted capital (severe loss scenario).

Principal Business: Individual life insurance (53%) and reinsurance (47%).

Principal Investments: NonCMO investment grade bonds (77%), CMOs and structured securities (10%), mortgages in good standing (6%), noninv. grade bonds (4%), and policy loans (2%).

Investments in Affiliates: 1%

Group Affiliation: Lincoln National Corp

Licensed in: All states except NY, PR

Commenced Business: June 1964

Address: 1300 South Clinton Street, Fort Wayne, IN 46802-3518

Phone: (800) 444-2363 **Domicile State:** IN **NAIC Code:** 67652

Data Date	Rating	RACR #1	RACR #2	Total Assets ($mil)	Capital ($mil)	Net Premium ($mil)	Net Income ($mil)
9-18	B	2.53	1.37	1,418.1	163.5	96.0	-25.0
9-17	B	2.44	1.32	1,487.9	162.8	95.8	-16.7
2017	B	2.87	1.54	1,504.1	189.0	130.2	16.0
2016	B	2.92	1.57	1,578.9	201.7	124.9	20.6
2015	B	2.77	1.48	1,609.3	201.3	112.8	51.6
2014	B	2.75	1.50	1,741.8	208.4	145.7	54.2
2013	B	2.95	1.60	1,817.4	235.6	129.8	64.1

Adverse Trends in Operations

Decrease in asset base during 2017 (5%)
Decrease in capital during 2015 (3%)
Decrease in premium volume from 2014 to 2015 (23%)
Decrease in capital during 2014 (12%)
Decrease in asset base during 2014 (4%)

FIRST RELIANCE STANDARD LIFE INSURANCE COMPANY *   A-   Excellent

Major Rating Factors: Good overall results on stability tests (5.7 on a scale of 0 to 10) despite fair financial strength of affiliated Tokio Marine Holdings Inc. Strengths that enhance stability include excellent operational trends and excellent risk diversification. Good quality investment portfolio (6.6) despite mixed results such as: no exposure to mortgages and large holdings of BBB rated bonds but small junk bond holdings. Fair profitability (3.6) with operating losses during the first nine months of 2018.

Other Rating Factors: Strong capitalization (10.0) based on excellent risk adjusted capital (severe loss scenario). Excellent liquidity (7.0).

Principal Business: Group health insurance (60%) and group life insurance (40%).

Principal Investments: NonCMO investment grade bonds (73%), CMOs and structured securities (17%), and noninv. grade bonds (7%).

Investments in Affiliates: None
Group Affiliation: Tokio Marine Holdings Inc
Licensed in: DC, DE, NY
Commenced Business: October 1984
Address: 590 Madison Avenue 29th Floor, New York, NY 10022
Phone: (215) 787-4000 **Domicile State:** NY **NAIC Code:** 71005

Data Date	Rating	RACR #1	RACR #2	Total Assets ($mil)	Capital ($mil)	Net Premium ($mil)	Net Income ($mil)
9-18	A-	4.77	3.16	208.0	59.6	54.9	-1.3
9-17	A	5.84	3.71	197.5	66.7	45.5	-0.9
2017	A	5.19	3.33	199.1	61.2	61.8	-5.8
2016	A	6.14	4.05	188.9	68.3	63.0	9.5
2015	A	5.72	3.61	184.0	65.5	57.9	6.5
2014	A	5.62	3.53	184.1	66.4	57.0	7.8
2013	A	5.71	3.72	182.7	64.2	56.8	5.9

Tokio Marine Holdings Inc Composite Group Rating: C+ Largest Group Members	Assets ($mil)	Rating
RELIANCE STANDARD LIFE INS CO	12173	C+
PHILADELPHIA INDEMNITY INS CO	8653	B-
SAFETY NATIONAL CASUALTY CORP	7224	C
HOUSTON CASUALTY CO	3383	B-
US SPECIALTY INS CO	1888	B

FIRST SECURITY BENEFIT LIFE & ANNUITY   B   Good

Major Rating Factors: Good current capitalization (6.0 on a scale of 0 to 10) based on good risk adjusted capital (moderate loss scenario) reflecting some improvement over results in 2015. Good overall profitability (6.0). Fair liquidity (3.6) as cash from operations and sale of marketable assets may not be adequate to cover a spike in claims or a run on policy withdrawals.

Other Rating Factors: Fair overall results on stability tests (4.0) including negative cash flow from operations for 2017, weak results on operational trends, fair risk adjusted capital in prior years. Low quality investment portfolio (2.8).

Principal Business: Group retirement contracts (51%) and individual annuities (49%).

Principal Investments: CMOs and structured securities (45%), nonCMO investment grade bonds (44%), and noninv. grade bonds (4%).

Investments in Affiliates: None
Group Affiliation: NZC Capital LLC
Licensed in: KS, NY
Commenced Business: July 1995
Address: 350 Park Avenue 14th Floor, New York, NY 10022
Phone: (785) 431-3000 **Domicile State:** NY **NAIC Code:** 60084

Data Date	Rating	RACR #1	RACR #2	Total Assets ($mil)	Capital ($mil)	Net Premium ($mil)	Net Income ($mil)
9-18	B	1.66	0.79	599.1	31.4	12.0	1.8
9-17	B	1.29	0.60	696.5	28.6	10.7	0.3
2017	B	1.49	0.70	675.0	30.2	14.1	1.4
2016	B	1.23	0.56	686.8	29.0	13.1	0.8
2015	B	1.13	0.51	684.2	27.1	23.5	2.5
2014	B	1.22	0.58	691.3	25.6	97.3	-3.8
2013	B	1.92	0.96	617.1	30.6	216.9	-3.8

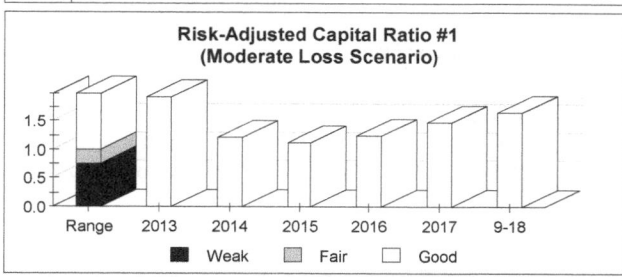

Risk-Adjusted Capital Ratio #1 (Moderate Loss Scenario)

Range / 2013 / 2014 / 2015 / 2016 / 2017 / 9-18
■ Weak   ▨ Fair   ☐ Good

FIRST SYMETRA NATIONAL LIFE INSURANCE COMPANY OF NE   B+   Good

Major Rating Factors: Good overall results on stability tests (6.3 on a scale of 0 to 10). Stability strengths include excellent operational trends and excellent risk diversification. Good current capitalization (6.3) based on good risk adjusted capital (severe loss scenario), although results have slipped from the excellent range over the last two years. Good liquidity (5.1).

Other Rating Factors: Fair quality investment portfolio (4.6). Excellent profitability (7.8) despite modest operating losses during 2016.

Principal Business: Individual annuities (93%), group health insurance (5%), and group life insurance (2%).

Principal Investments: NonCMO investment grade bonds (78%), mortgages in good standing (13%), CMOs and structured securities (8%), and noninv. grade bonds (1%).

Investments in Affiliates: None
Group Affiliation: Sumitomo Life Ins Company
Licensed in: NY
Commenced Business: January 1990
Address: 420 LEXINGTON AVE SUITE 300, NEW YORK, NY 10170
Phone: (425) 256-8000 **Domicile State:** NY **NAIC Code:** 78417

Data Date	Rating	RACR #1	RACR #2	Total Assets ($mil)	Capital ($mil)	Net Premium ($mil)	Net Income ($mil)
9-18	B+	1.80	0.91	2,070.2	115.3	352.3	2.1
9-17	B+	2.47	1.19	1,776.8	116.9	282.7	7.1
2017	B+	1.87	0.95	1,803.0	114.7	355.8	9.3
2016	B+	2.54	1.23	1,572.1	112.6	396.2	-1.5
2015	A	3.20	1.57	1,261.0	113.7	386.5	8.2
2014	A-	3.96	1.97	962.4	106.1	218.0	9.1
2013	A-	4.03	2.02	813.2	96.7	154.6	11.9

Adverse Trends in Operations
Increase in policy surrenders from 2016 to 2017 (26%)
Decrease in premium volume from 2016 to 2017 (10%)

FIRST UNITED AMERICAN LIFE INSURANCE COMPANY — B — Good

Major Rating Factors: Good overall results on stability tests (6.0 on a scale of 0 to 10). Stability strengths include excellent operational trends and excellent risk diversification. Good overall profitability (6.1). Excellent expense controls. Fair quality investment portfolio (4.5).

Other Rating Factors: Fair liquidity (4.2). Strong capitalization (7.1) based on excellent risk adjusted capital (severe loss scenario).

Principal Business: N/A

Principal Investments: NonCMO investment grade bonds (79%), noninv. grade bonds (6%), CMOs and structured securities (5%), policy loans (4%), and cash (2%).

Investments in Affiliates: None

Group Affiliation: Torchmark Corp

Licensed in: NY

Commenced Business: December 1984

Address: 1020 SEVENTH NORTH ST STE 130, LIVERPOOL, NY 13212

Phone: (315) 451-2544 **Domicile State:** NY **NAIC Code:** 74101

Data Date	Rating	RACR #1	RACR #2	Total Assets ($mil)	Capital ($mil)	Net Premium ($mil)	Net Income ($mil)
9-18	B	1.73	1.07	248.9	28.4	53.2	1.3
9-17	B+	2.17	1.36	237.8	36.3	52.9	3.4
2017	B	1.87	1.16	238.8	30.3	68.6	0.2
2016	B+	2.25	1.41	229.1	39.0	76.7	6.2
2015	B+	2.26	1.43	209.7	35.6	72.9	3.0
2014	B+	2.40	1.54	194.7	35.9	72.7	4.9
2013	B+	2.18	1.42	178.0	34.2	78.7	3.1

Adverse Trends in Operations

Decrease in premium volume from 2016 to 2017 (11%)
Increase in policy surrenders from 2016 to 2017 (27%)
Decrease in capital during 2017 (22%)
Decrease in premium volume from 2013 to 2014 (8%)

FIRST UNUM LIFE INSURANCE COMPANY — C+ — Fair

Major Rating Factors: Fair overall results on stability tests (4.8 on a scale of 0 to 10) including fair financial strength of affiliated Unum Group. Fair quality investment portfolio (3.6) with large holdings of BBB rated bonds in addition to significant exposure to junk bonds. Good overall profitability (5.5) despite operating losses during the first nine months of 2018.

Other Rating Factors: Strong capitalization (7.1) based on excellent risk adjusted capital (severe loss scenario). Excellent liquidity (7.6).

Principal Business: Group health insurance (54%), individual health insurance (23%), group life insurance (20%), individual life insurance (2%), and reinsurance (1%).

Principal Investments: NonCMO investment grade bonds (80%), noninv. grade bonds (9%), mortgages in good standing (5%), and CMOs and structured securities (5%).

Investments in Affiliates: None

Group Affiliation: Unum Group

Licensed in: NY

Commenced Business: January 1960

Address: 666 THIRD AVENUE SUITE 301, NEW YORK, NY 10017

Phone: (212) 328-8830 **Domicile State:** NY **NAIC Code:** 64297

Data Date	Rating	RACR #1	RACR #2	Total Assets ($mil)	Capital ($mil)	Net Premium ($mil)	Net Income ($mil)
9-18	C+	2.02	1.04	3,656.0	234.1	340.3	-15.8
9-17	C+	2.76	1.39	3,352.5	306.9	296.5	25.6
2017	C+	2.66	1.36	3,457.4	299.1	392.7	27.4
2016	C+	2.63	1.32	3,260.8	282.4	375.7	82.4
2015	C+	2.54	1.27	3,130.4	263.5	363.2	26.5
2014	C+	2.63	1.33	2,976.2	272.1	360.0	-5.4
2013	C+	2.75	1.42	2,704.1	266.3	348.7	20.4

Unum Group
Composite Group Rating: C+

Largest Group Members	Assets ($mil)	Rating
UNUM LIFE INS CO OF AMERICA	21455	C+
PROVIDENT LIFE ACCIDENT INS CO	8034	C+
PAUL REVERE LIFE INS CO	3571	C+
FIRST UNUM LIFE INS CO	3457	C+
COLONIAL LIFE ACCIDENT INS CO	3220	C+

FIVE STAR LIFE INSURANCE COMPANY — C — Fair

Major Rating Factors: Fair overall results on stability tests (3.9 on a scale of 0 to 10) including negative cash flow from operations for 2017. Good quality investment portfolio (6.7) despite mixed results such as: large holdings of BBB rated bonds but moderate junk bond exposure. Good liquidity (5.0) with sufficient resources to handle a spike in claims as well as a significant increase in policy surrenders.

Other Rating Factors: Weak profitability (1.4) with operating losses during the first nine months of 2018. Strong capitalization (7.2) based on excellent risk adjusted capital (severe loss scenario).

Principal Business: Group life insurance (70%) and individual life insurance (30%).

Principal Investments: NonCMO investment grade bonds (70%), CMOs and structured securities (19%), policy loans (3%), noninv. grade bonds (3%), and cash (3%).

Investments in Affiliates: None

Group Affiliation: 5 Star Financial LLC

Licensed in: All states except NY

Commenced Business: May 1943

Address: 8440 Jefferson Highway Ste 301, Lincoln, NE 68516

Phone: (800) 776-2322 **Domicile State:** NE **NAIC Code:** 77879

Data Date	Rating	RACR #1	RACR #2	Total Assets ($mil)	Capital ($mil)	Net Premium ($mil)	Net Income ($mil)
9-18	C	1.79	1.12	294.2	27.4	98.6	-0.8
9-17	C+	2.16	1.34	290.7	30.9	93.7	-7.5
2017	C	1.86	1.16	291.2	28.9	126.1	-10.0
2016	C+	2.72	1.68	286.6	40.2	125.6	-6.2
2015	C+	2.69	1.64	273.6	38.5	124.2	-5.8
2014	C+	2.93	1.82	268.6	40.8	124.2	-9.6
2013	B-	2.98	1.87	248.7	40.5	116.0	-6.2

Rating Indexes

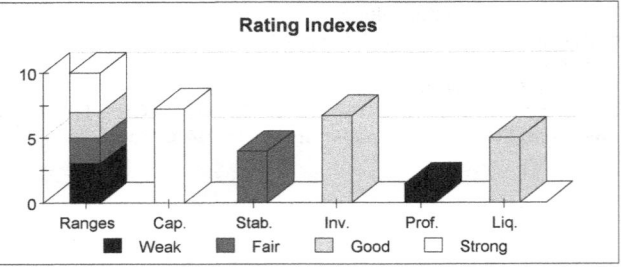

FLORIDA COMBINED LIFE INSURANCE COMPANY INCORPORA⁻   C   Fair

Major Rating Factors: Fair quality investment portfolio (4.8 on a scale of 0 to 10). Fair overall results on stability tests (4.3). Weak profitability (2.8) with operating losses during the first nine months of 2018.
Other Rating Factors: Strong capitalization (8.0) based on excellent risk adjusted capital (severe loss scenario). Excellent liquidity (7.8) with ample cash flow from premiums and investment income.
Principal Business: Group health insurance (46%), individual health insurance (37%), group life insurance (15%), and individual life insurance (2%).
Principal Investments: NonCMO investment grade bonds (16%), cash (5%), and CMOs and structured securities (2%).
Investments in Affiliates: 75%
Group Affiliation: Blue Cross Blue Shield of Florida
Licensed in: AL, FL, GA, NC, SC
Commenced Business: May 1988
Address: 4800 Deerwood Campus Parkway, Jacksonville, FL 32246
Phone: (800) 333-3256 **Domicile State:** FL **NAIC Code:** 76031

Data Date	Rating	RACR #1	RACR #2	Total Assets ($mil)	Capital ($mil)	Net Premium ($mil)	Net Income ($mil)
9-18	C	6.73	3.36	70.5	43.6	0.0	-3.6
9-17	C	5.24	3.24	52.4	31.0	0.0	0.6
2017	C	5.64	3.45	59.8	35.3	0.0	0.5
2016	C	4.94	3.29	50.7	28.9	0.0	0.1
2015	C	4.60	3.45	50.2	27.1	0.0	0.3
2014	B	4.59	3.64	46.9	25.8	0.0	0.1
2013	B+	4.40	3.96	42.8	23.4	0.0	0.2

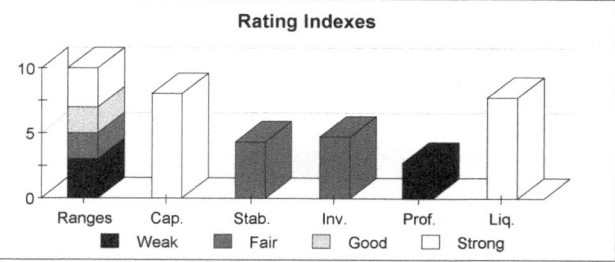

Rating Indexes

FORESTERS LIFE INSURANCE & ANNUITY COMPANY   C+   Fair

Major Rating Factors: Fair profitability (3.0 on a scale of 0 to 10) with investment income below regulatory standards in relation to interest assumptions of reserves. Fair overall results on stability tests (4.5) including excessive premium growth. Good capitalization (6.6) based on good risk adjusted capital (severe loss scenario). Capital levels have been relatively consistent over the last five years.
Other Rating Factors: Good quality investment portfolio (6.1). Good liquidity (6.0).
Principal Business: Individual annuities (68%) and individual life insurance (32%).
Principal Investments: NonCMO investment grade bonds (84%), policy loans (11%), noninv. grade bonds (4%), and cash (1%).
Investments in Affiliates: None
Group Affiliation: Independent Order of Foresters
Licensed in: All states except SD, PR
Commenced Business: December 1962
Address: 40 Wall Street, New York, NY 10005
Phone: (800) 832-7783 **Domicile State:** NY **NAIC Code:** 63495

Data Date	Rating	RACR #1	RACR #2	Total Assets ($mil)	Capital ($mil)	Net Premium ($mil)	Net Income ($mil)
9-18	C+	1.78	0.95	2,619.6	72.1	211.0	6.7
9-17	C+	1.67	0.88	2,360.8	65.5	142.1	7.3
2017	C+	1.62	0.86	2,463.4	63.4	209.3	12.7
2016	C+	1.57	0.82	2,142.2	60.1	217.7	7.0
2015	C+	1.91	1.01	1,932.9	60.3	203.7	8.3
2014	B-	2.08	1.10	1,852.8	58.7	240.4	8.0
2013	B	2.23	1.19	1,641.4	51.8	182.1	9.9

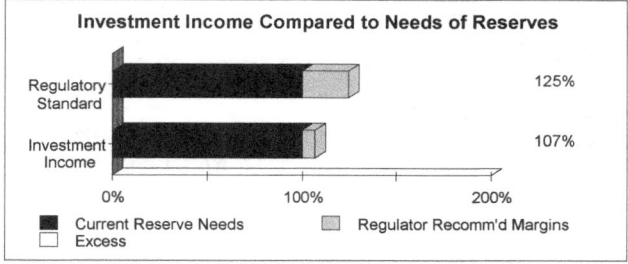

Investment Income Compared to Needs of Reserves

FORETHOUGHT LIFE INSURANCE COMPANY   B   Good

Major Rating Factors: Fair current capitalization (4.0 on a scale of 0 to 10) based on mixed results -- excessive policy leverage mitigated by excellent risk adjusted capital (severe loss scenario) reflecting improvement over results in 2016. Fair quality investment portfolio (4.7) with significant exposure to mortgages . Mortgage default rate has been low. Fair overall results on stability tests (4.4).
Other Rating Factors: Excellent profitability (7.1). Excellent liquidity (7.3).
Principal Business: Individual annuities (91%), group retirement contracts (4%), group life insurance (3%), individual health insurance (1%), and individual life insurance (1%).
Principal Investments: CMOs and structured securities (52%), nonCMO investment grade bonds (30%), mortgages in good standing (14%), noninv. grade bonds (1%), and common & preferred stock (1%).
Investments in Affiliates: None
Group Affiliation: Global Atlantic Financial Group
Licensed in: All states except NY
Commenced Business: September 1980
Address: 300 NORTH MERIDIAN ST STE 1800, INDIANAPOLIS, IN 46204
Phone: (317) 223-2700 **Domicile State:** IN **NAIC Code:** 91642

Data Date	Rating	RACR #1	RACR #2	Total Assets ($mil)	Capital ($mil)	Net Premium ($mil)	Net Income ($mil)
9-18	B	2.20	1.05	30,391.4	1,693.7	3,349.0	117.7
9-17	B	1.31	0.72	30,543.9	1,683.7	-5,371.6	278.9
2017	B	2.03	0.96	31,431.3	1,595.9	-4,463.2	352.1
2016	B	1.51	0.83	24,911.0	1,632.2	5,416.2	83.9
2015	B	2.70	1.32	18,822.8	1,194.1	6,772.9	83.7
2014	B-	2.64	1.31	12,583.9	805.0	4,907.9	170.3
2013	B	2.73	1.38	7,957.2	522.5	2,331.0	23.0

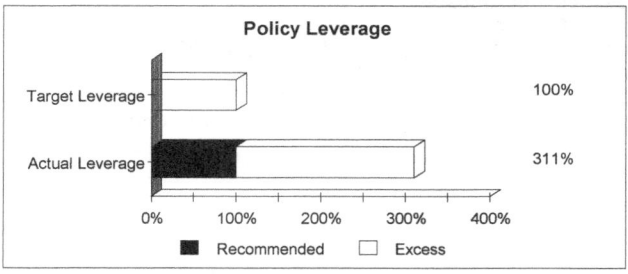

Policy Leverage

FRANDISCO LIFE INSURANCE COMPANY *

A   **Excellent**

Major Rating Factors: Good overall results on stability tests (6.9 on a scale of 0 to 10) despite excessive premium growth. Strengths that enhance stability include excellent operational trends and good risk diversification. Strong capitalization (10.0) based on excellent risk adjusted capital (severe loss scenario). Furthermore, this high level of risk adjusted capital has been consistently maintained over the last five years. High quality investment portfolio (8.9).

Other Rating Factors: Excellent profitability (9.7). Excellent liquidity (9.1).
Principal Business: Reinsurance (100%).
Principal Investments: NonCMO investment grade bonds (98%).
Investments in Affiliates: None
Group Affiliation: 1st Franklin Financial Corp
Licensed in: GA
Commenced Business: November 1977
Address: 135 East Tugalo Street, Toccoa, GA 30577
Phone: (706) 886-7571 **Domicile State:** GA **NAIC Code:** 89079

Data Date	Rating	RACR #1	RACR #2	Total Assets ($mil)	Capital ($mil)	Net Premium ($mil)	Net Income ($mil)
9-18	A	9.51	8.56	93.8	79.8	13.3	3.6
9-17	A	9.25	8.33	85.0	75.2	9.5	3.3
2017	A	9.06	8.16	87.0	76.1	13.9	4.3
2016	A	8.84	7.96	81.1	71.9	12.2	4.4
2015	A-	8.51	7.66	76.2	67.3	18.9	5.4
2014	A-	8.33	7.50	66.4	62.3	14.6	5.6
2013	A-	7.86	7.07	60.5	56.7	14.5	5.0

Adverse Trends in Operations

Decrease in premium volume from 2015 to 2016 (36%)

FREEDOM LIFE INSURANCE COMPANY OF AMERICA *

B+   **Good**

Major Rating Factors: Good quality investment portfolio (6.7 on a scale of 0 to 10) with no exposure to mortgages and minimal holdings in junk bonds. Good overall results on stability tests (6.5) despite excessive premium growth and fair risk adjusted capital in prior years. Other stability subfactors include good operational trends and excellent risk diversification. Strong capitalization (7.3) based on excellent risk adjusted capital (severe loss scenario).

Other Rating Factors: Excellent profitability (8.4). Excellent liquidity (7.1).
Principal Business: Group health insurance (68%), individual health insurance (22%), and individual life insurance (11%).
Principal Investments: NonCMO investment grade bonds (44%), common & preferred stock (24%), cash (14%), and CMOs and structured securities (13%).
Investments in Affiliates: 24%
Group Affiliation: Credit Suisse Group
Licensed in: AL, AZ, AR, CO, DE, FL, GA, IL, IN, IA, KS, KY, LA, MD, MI, MN, MS, MO, NE, NV, NM, NC, OH, OK, OR, PA, SC, SD, TN, TX, UT, VA, WA, WV, WY
Commenced Business: June 1956
Address: 300 Burnett Street Suite 200, Fort Worth, TX 76102-2734
Phone: (817) 878-3300 **Domicile State:** TX **NAIC Code:** 62324

Data Date	Rating	RACR #1	RACR #2	Total Assets ($mil)	Capital ($mil)	Net Premium ($mil)	Net Income ($mil)
9-18	B+	1.47	1.22	213.2	127.9	306.2	24.2
9-17	C+	0.95	0.79	132.9	71.1	202.6	10.4
2017	C+	1.11	0.96	148.3	76.4	282.2	19.4
2016	C+	0.83	0.71	100.2	51.1	196.9	12.0
2015	C+	0.75	0.65	77.3	37.0	140.1	14.9
2014	C	0.69	0.60	59.9	25.7	109.7	10.1
2013	C	0.67	0.59	56.2	22.6	98.1	12.3

Adverse Trends in Operations

Change in asset mix during 2017 (6%)

FUNERAL DIRECTORS LIFE INSURANCE COMPANY

B-   **Good**

Major Rating Factors: Good quality investment portfolio (6.3 on a scale of 0 to 10) despite mixed results such as: minimal exposure to mortgages and large holdings of BBB rated bonds but small junk bond holdings. Fair overall results on stability tests (4.7). Weak liquidity (2.7) as a spike in claims may stretch capacity.

Other Rating Factors: Strong capitalization (7.5) based on excellent risk adjusted capital (severe loss scenario). Excellent profitability (7.9).
Principal Business: Individual annuities (63%), group life insurance (27%), and individual life insurance (10%).
Principal Investments: NonCMO investment grade bonds (84%), mortgages in good standing (8%), CMOs and structured securities (3%), noninv. grade bonds (2%), and real estate (1%).
Investments in Affiliates: 1%
Group Affiliation: Directors Investment Group
Licensed in: All states except DC, ME, MA, NH, NY, WY, PR
Commenced Business: April 1981
Address: 6550 Directors Parkway, Abilene, TX 79606
Phone: (915) 695-3412 **Domicile State:** TX **NAIC Code:** 99775

Data Date	Rating	RACR #1	RACR #2	Total Assets ($mil)	Capital ($mil)	Net Premium ($mil)	Net Income ($mil)
9-18	B-	2.42	1.30	1,386.8	126.9	174.0	10.7
9-17	B-	2.40	1.29	1,305.9	118.0	163.1	7.9
2017	B-	2.30	1.24	1,320.3	116.3	212.4	8.4
2016	B-	2.28	1.24	1,248.0	110.4	225.2	12.5
2015	B-	2.20	1.20	1,159.1	99.1	218.1	8.0
2014	B-	2.23	1.23	1,068.9	91.9	209.0	7.1
2013	B-	2.26	1.26	978.5	85.6	205.5	6.0

Rating Indexes

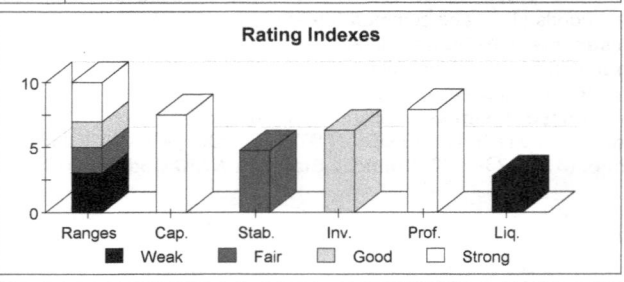

	Ranges	Cap.	Stab.	Inv.	Prof.	Liq.
■ Weak	■ Fair	□ Good	□ Strong			

GARDEN STATE LIFE INSURANCE COMPANY *

A   **Excellent**

Major Rating Factors: Good quality investment portfolio (6.7 on a scale of 0 to 10) despite mixed results such as: no exposure to mortgages and large holdings of BBB rated bonds but minimal holdings in junk bonds. Good liquidity (6.9) with sufficient resources to handle a spike in claims. Excellent overall results on stability tests (7.8) excellent operational trends and excellent risk diversification.

Other Rating Factors: Strong capitalization (10.0) based on excellent risk adjusted capital (severe loss scenario). Excellent profitability (8.8).

Principal Business: Individual life insurance (77%) and reinsurance (22%).

Principal Investments: NonCMO investment grade bonds (94%), policy loans (3%), noninv. grade bonds (2%), and CMOs and structured securities (1%).

Investments in Affiliates: None

Group Affiliation: American National Group Inc

Licensed in: All states except PR

Commenced Business: November 1956

Address: 2450 SOUTH SHORE BOULEVARD, GALVESTON, TX 77550

Phone: (409) 763-4661 **Domicile State:** TX **NAIC Code:** 63657

Data Date	Rating	RACR #1	RACR #2	Total Assets ($mil)	Capital ($mil)	Net Premium ($mil)	Net Income ($mil)
9-18	A	8.68	7.81	135.5	79.3	16.5	6.6
9-17	A-	8.09	7.28	131.8	73.8	16.0	4.3
2017	A-	8.04	7.23	131.3	73.4	21.3	5.7
2016	A-	7.59	6.83	129.6	69.2	21.9	7.0
2015	A-	6.83	6.15	127.2	62.1	22.6	6.9
2014	A-	6.13	5.52	121.5	55.3	24.2	5.8
2013	A-	5.42	4.88	117.1	48.5	26.2	5.6

Adverse Trends in Operations

Decrease in premium volume from 2016 to 2017 (2%)
Decrease in premium volume from 2015 to 2016 (3%)
Decrease in premium volume from 2014 to 2015 (7%)
Decrease in premium volume from 2013 to 2014 (8%)

GENERAL RE LIFE CORPORATION

C   **Fair**

Major Rating Factors: Fair quality investment portfolio (4.1 on a scale of 0 to 10). Fair overall results on stability tests (3.0) including negative cash flow from operations for 2017 and excessive premium growth. Poor current capitalization (0.8) based on excessive policy leverage and weak risk adjusted capital (severe loss scenario), although results have slipped from the excellent range during the last year.

Other Rating Factors: Weak profitability (2.9) with investment income below regulatory standards in relation to interest assumptions of reserves. Excellent liquidity (7.9).

Principal Business: Reinsurance (100%).

Principal Investments: NonCMO investment grade bonds (67%), common & preferred stock (12%), and noninv. grade bonds (2%).

Investments in Affiliates: 15%

Group Affiliation: Berkshire-Hathaway

Licensed in: All states except PR

Commenced Business: August 1967

Address: 120 Long Ridge Rd, Stamford, CT 6902

Phone: (203) 352-3000 **Domicile State:** CT **NAIC Code:** 86258

Data Date	Rating	RACR #1	RACR #2	Total Assets ($mil)	Capital ($mil)	Net Premium ($mil)	Net Income ($mil)
9-18	C	0.41	0.32	4,272.2	931.7	995.3	177.1
9-17	B	2.20	1.39	3,584.2	636.1	777.5	47.0
2017	C+	4.62	2.45	4,066.3	746.8	-59.4	-608.3
2016	B	2.23	1.40	3,504.6	644.3	1,022.8	34.4
2015	B	2.08	1.30	3,351.9	594.5	1,040.3	49.9
2014	B+	2.39	1.49	3,422.2	702.5	1,055.6	140.0
2013	B	2.31	1.44	3,337.4	667.2	1,047.7	121.2

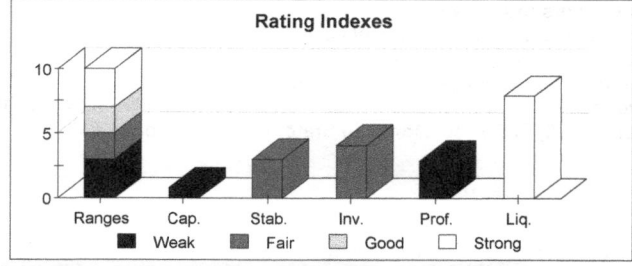

Rating Indexes

GENERATION LIFE INSURANCE COMPANY

C   **Fair**

Major Rating Factors: Fair overall results on stability tests (4.0 on a scale of 0 to 10) including excessive premium growth. Weak profitability (2.5). Strong capitalization (10.0) based on excellent risk adjusted capital (severe loss scenario). Capital levels have been relatively consistent over the last five years.

Other Rating Factors: High quality investment portfolio (7.9). Excellent liquidity (8.2).

Principal Business: Individual life insurance (100%).

Principal Investments: NonCMO investment grade bonds (82%), CMOs and structured securities (15%), and cash (2%).

Investments in Affiliates: None

Group Affiliation: Swiss Re Limited

Licensed in: All states except NY, PR

Commenced Business: May 1966

Address: 5025 N CENTRAL AVE SUITE 546, JEFFERSON CITY, MO 65101

Phone: (877) 794-7773 **Domicile State:** MO **NAIC Code:** 73504

Data Date	Rating	RACR #1	RACR #2	Total Assets ($mil)	Capital ($mil)	Net Premium ($mil)	Net Income ($mil)
9-18	C	6.50	5.85	58.4	44.5	3.4	2.4
9-17	C	6.11	5.50	52.9	41.8	2.7	-1.6
2017	C	6.15	5.53	53.1	42.2	3.6	-1.2
2016	B	6.33	5.70	52.6	43.3	3.8	-4.6
2015	B	6.23	5.60	32.2	30.0	4.4	-0.5
2014	B	6.36	5.73	32.3	30.6	3.2	-3.6
2013	B	6.40	5.76	32.6	31.1	1.1	-4.2

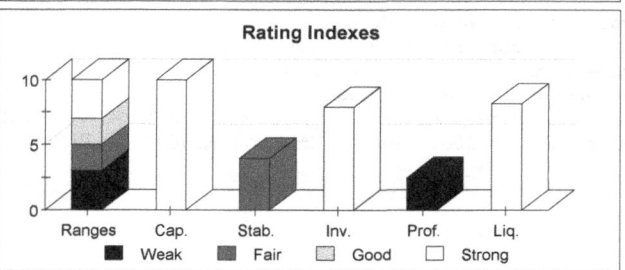

Rating Indexes

GENWORTH LIFE & ANNUITY INSURANCE COMPANY   C-   Fair

Major Rating Factors: Weak profitability (2.5 on a scale of 0 to 10) with investment income below regulatory standards in relation to interest assumptions of reserves. Weak overall results on stability tests (2.0) including weak results on operational trends. Good quality investment portfolio (6.0).

Other Rating Factors: Good liquidity (6.0). Strong capitalization (7.1) based on excellent risk adjusted capital (severe loss scenario).

Principal Business: Individual life insurance (74%), reinsurance (21%), individual health insurance (3%), and individual annuities (2%).

Principal Investments: NonCMO investment grade bonds (56%), CMOs and structured securities (19%), mortgages in good standing (12%), policy loans (4%), and misc. investments (7%).

Investments in Affiliates: 1%

Group Affiliation: Genworth Financial

Licensed in: All states except NY, PR

Commenced Business: April 1871

Address: 6610 WEST BROAD STREET, RICHMOND, VA 23230

Phone: (804) 662-2400 **Domicile State:** VA **NAIC Code:** 65536

Data Date	Rating	RACR #1	RACR #2	Total Assets ($mil)	Capital ($mil)	Net Premium ($mil)	Net Income ($mil)
9-18	C-	1.82	1.05	22,016.7	1,315.4	261.6	180.8
9-17	B-	2.13	1.27	22,616.8	1,586.6	9,547.3	145.2
2017	C	1.82	1.05	22,444.5	1,288.8	520.7	-32.1
2016	B-	2.00	1.19	22,447.8	1,487.5	-2,356.6	-301.2
2015	B-	1.71	1.08	23,410.5	1,668.8	328.8	-283.1
2014	B-	1.51	1.09	24,242.0	2,148.2	1,638.6	199.8
2013	B-	1.51	1.11	24,161.7	2,235.0	1,893.8	343.9

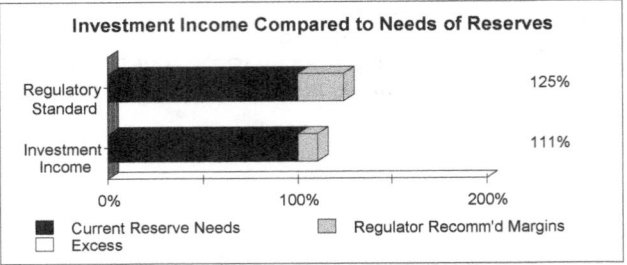

Investment Income Compared to Needs of Reserves

GENWORTH LIFE INSURANCE COMPANY   C+   Fair

Major Rating Factors: Fair quality investment portfolio (4.8 on a scale of 0 to 10) with large holdings of BBB rated bonds in addition to junk bond exposure equal to 66% of capital. Exposure to mortgages is significant, but the mortgage default rate has been low. Fair overall results on stability tests (4.7). Good capitalization (5.3) based on good risk adjusted capital (severe loss scenario).

Other Rating Factors: Weak profitability (2.5) with operating losses during the first nine months of 2018. Excellent liquidity (7.0).

Principal Business: Individual health insurance (69%), reinsurance (13%), individual life insurance (9%), and group health insurance (9%).

Principal Investments: NonCMO investment grade bonds (61%), CMOs and structured securities (13%), mortgages in good standing (10%), noninv. grade bonds (4%), and misc. investments (8%).

Investments in Affiliates: 4%

Group Affiliation: Genworth Financial

Licensed in: All states except NY

Commenced Business: October 1956

Address: 2711 CENTERVILLE ROAD STE 400, WILMINGTON, DE 19808

Phone: (800) 255-7836 **Domicile State:** DE **NAIC Code:** 70025

Data Date	Rating	RACR #1	RACR #2	Total Assets ($mil)	Capital ($mil)	Net Premium ($mil)	Net Income ($mil)
9-18	C+	1.12	0.79	39,956.4	2,514.7	1,712.7	-231.3
9-17	C+	1.36	1.00	40,425.9	3,257.4	-7,422.9	-74.6
2017	C+	1.20	0.86	40,012.0	2,727.7	2,308.7	-39.1
2016	C+	1.17	0.87	40,225.8	3,152.9	2,084.8	-39.1
2015	B-	1.02	0.78	38,504.3	2,740.7	1,587.2	35.2
2014	B-	1.02	0.81	38,163.2	3,224.4	1,713.3	-179.7
2013	C+	1.06	0.85	36,445.4	3,487.2	2,569.0	329.8

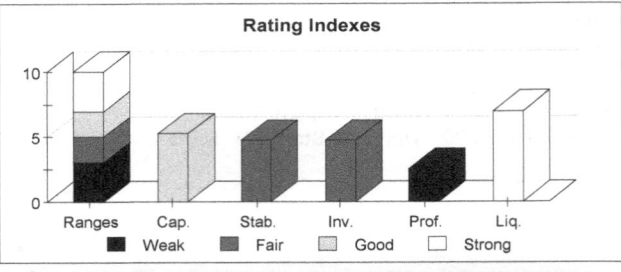

Rating Indexes

GENWORTH LIFE INSURANCE COMPANY OF NEW YORK   C   Fair

Major Rating Factors: Fair quality investment portfolio (4.0 on a scale of 0 to 10) with large holdings of BBB rated bonds in addition to junk bond exposure equal to 63% of capital. Fair overall results on stability tests (3.7) including negative cash flow from operations for 2017, fair risk adjusted capital in prior years. Good capitalization (5.8) based on good risk adjusted capital (moderate loss scenario).

Other Rating Factors: Good liquidity (6.0). Weak profitability (1.5).

Principal Business: Individual health insurance (61%), reinsurance (17%), individual life insurance (17%), group health insurance (3%), and individual annuities (1%).

Principal Investments: NonCMO investment grade bonds (59%), CMOs and structured securities (23%), mortgages in good standing (9%), noninv. grade bonds (3%), and common & preferred stock (1%).

Investments in Affiliates: None

Group Affiliation: Genworth Financial

Licensed in: CT, DC, DE, FL, IL, NJ, NY, RI, VA

Commenced Business: October 1988

Address: 600 THIRD AVENUE SUITE 2400, NEW YORK, NY 10016

Phone: (800) 357-1066 **Domicile State:** NY **NAIC Code:** 72990

Data Date	Rating	RACR #1	RACR #2	Total Assets ($mil)	Capital ($mil)	Net Premium ($mil)	Net Income ($mil)
9-18	C	1.53	0.78	7,736.8	311.4	185.6	29.3
9-17	C	2.17	1.10	8,167.4	473.5	190.7	9.3
2017	C	1.41	0.72	7,985.9	288.4	260.0	-168.1
2016	C	2.20	1.12	8,495.5	481.2	276.9	-20.0
2015	C+	2.22	1.12	8,372.2	494.8	356.1	-39.8
2014	B-	2.14	1.08	8,474.6	481.1	521.7	-93.3
2013	B	2.29	1.15	8,139.0	527.3	610.9	13.1

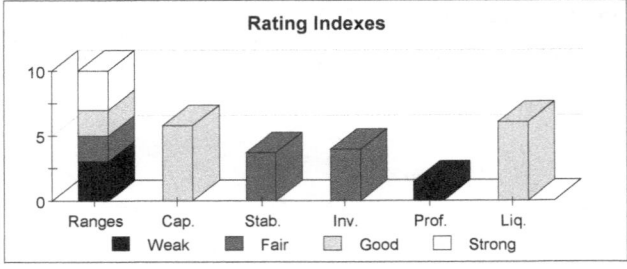

Rating Indexes

GERBER LIFE INSURANCE COMPANY *   B+   Good

Major Rating Factors: Good quality investment portfolio (6.0 on a scale of 0 to 10) despite mixed results such as: large holdings of BBB rated bonds but moderate junk bond exposure. Good overall results on stability tests (6.4). Stability strengths include excellent operational trends and excellent risk diversification. Fair profitability (4.8) with investment income below regulatory standards in relation to interest assumptions of reserves.

Other Rating Factors: Fair liquidity (4.8). Strong capitalization (7.1) based on excellent risk adjusted capital (severe loss scenario).

Principal Business: Individual life insurance (46%), group health insurance (35%), individual health insurance (11%), and reinsurance (8%).

Principal Investments: NonCMO investment grade bonds (67%), CMOs and structured securities (23%), policy loans (5%), and noninv. grade bonds (4%).

Investments in Affiliates: None

Group Affiliation: Nestle SA

Licensed in: All states, the District of Columbia and Puerto Rico

Commenced Business: September 1968

Address: 1311 Mamaroneck Avenue, White Plains, NY 10605

Phone: (914) 272-4000 **Domicile State:** NY **NAIC Code:** 70939

Data Date	Rating	RACR #1	RACR #2	Total Assets ($mil)	Capital ($mil)	Net Premium ($mil)	Net Income ($mil)
9-18	B+	1.79	1.05	3,909.7	297.1	565.9	0.9
9-17	B+	1.74	1.04	3,650.7	311.4	554.5	-10.2
2017	B+	1.83	1.07	3,703.2	300.7	727.1	-2.7
2016	B+	1.78	1.06	3,397.6	307.0	690.0	15.3
2015	B+	1.90	1.14	3,088.3	295.8	604.2	18.5
2014	A-	1.97	1.20	2,812.2	285.3	565.3	24.2
2013	A-	2.00	1.21	2,548.1	263.5	506.8	22.7

Adverse Trends in Operations

Decrease in capital during 2017 (2%)

GLOBE LIFE & ACCIDENT INSURANCE COMPANY   C+   Fair

Major Rating Factors: Fair quality investment portfolio (4.1 on a scale of 0 to 10) with large holdings of BBB rated bonds in addition to junk bond exposure equal to 66% of capital. Fair overall results on stability tests (3.8) including fair risk adjusted capital in prior years. Good capitalization (5.2) based on good risk adjusted capital (moderate loss scenario).

Other Rating Factors: Good overall profitability (5.2) although investment income, in comparison to reserve requirements, is below regulatory standards. Weak liquidity (1.8).

Principal Business: Individual life insurance (49%), group life insurance (47%), and individual health insurance (4%).

Principal Investments: NonCMO investment grade bonds (85%), noninv. grade bonds (5%), common & preferred stock (2%), CMOs and structured securities (2%), and misc. investments (6%).

Investments in Affiliates: 5%

Group Affiliation: Torchmark Corp

Licensed in: All states except NY, PR

Commenced Business: September 1980

Address: 10306 REGENCY PARKWAY DRIVE, OMAHA, NE 68114-3743

Phone: (972) 569-3744 **Domicile State:** NE **NAIC Code:** 91472

Data Date	Rating	RACR #1	RACR #2	Total Assets ($mil)	Capital ($mil)	Net Premium ($mil)	Net Income ($mil)
9-18	C+	1.11	0.70	4,652.8	318.2	555.8	67.6
9-17	B-	1.28	0.68	4,416.0	223.8	542.1	23.0
2017	C+	1.00	0.63	4,485.1	280.2	694.0	51.8
2016	B-	1.57	0.85	3,955.3	260.6	679.0	81.1
2015	B-	1.57	0.86	3,733.3	243.7	657.2	84.0
2014	B	1.60	0.89	3,519.4	239.4	630.4	82.3
2013	B	1.74	0.95	3,363.5	258.3	618.0	314.8

Rating Indexes

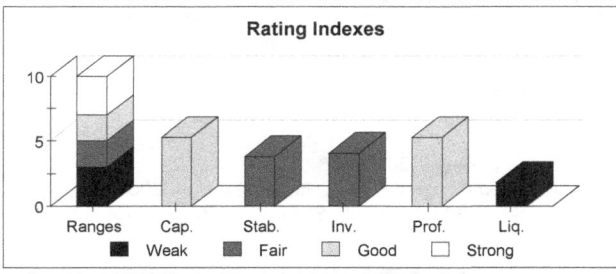

Ranges | Cap. | Stab. | Inv. | Prof. | Liq.

■ Weak   ■ Fair   ▤ Good   □ Strong

GOLDEN RULE INSURANCE COMPANY   B   Good

Major Rating Factors: Good overall results on stability tests (5.4 on a scale of 0 to 10) despite fair financial strength of affiliated UnitedHealth Group Inc. Other stability subfactors include good operational trends and excellent risk diversification. Good current capitalization (5.1) based on mixed results -- excessive policy leverage mitigated by excellent risk adjusted capital (severe loss scenario) reflecting improvement over results in 2016. Good overall profitability (6.8).

Other Rating Factors: Good liquidity (6.2). High quality investment portfolio (8.0).

Principal Business: Group health insurance (81%), individual health insurance (16%), and individual life insurance (2%).

Principal Investments: NonCMO investment grade bonds (76%), CMOs and structured securities (19%), cash (1%), and real estate (1%).

Investments in Affiliates: None

Group Affiliation: UnitedHealth Group Inc

Licensed in: All states except NY, PR

Commenced Business: June 1961

Address: 7440 WOODLAND DRIVE, INDIANAPOLIS, IN 46278

Phone: (317) 290-8100 **Domicile State:** IN **NAIC Code:** 62286

Data Date	Rating	RACR #1	RACR #2	Total Assets ($mil)	Capital ($mil)	Net Premium ($mil)	Net Income ($mil)
9-18	B	1.67	1.31	534.7	283.1	935.2	128.8
9-17	B	1.28	1.01	508.5	222.7	1,010.9	105.6
2017	B	1.14	0.89	499.2	198.6	1,338.1	82.6
2016	B	0.99	0.78	529.5	170.1	1,354.2	65.2
2015	B	1.37	1.07	635.6	268.0	1,501.3	106.8
2014	B	1.30	1.03	718.2	313.2	1,850.6	76.7
2013	B	1.12	0.89	759.8	293.5	2,020.6	129.4

UnitedHealth Group Inc Composite Group Rating: C+ Largest Group Members	Assets ($mil)	Rating
UNITED HEALTHCARE INS CO	19618	C
SIERRA HEALTH AND LIFE INS CO INC	3270	B
OXFORD HEALTH INS INC	2570	B
UNITED HEALTHCARE OF WISCONSIN INC	1760	B+
UNITED HEALTHCARE INS CO OF NY	1262	B-

GOVERNMENT PERSONNEL MUTUAL LIFE INSURANCE CO   B   Good

Major Rating Factors: Good quality investment portfolio (6.6 on a scale of 0 to 10) despite significant exposure to mortgages . Mortgage default rate has been low. substantial holdings of BBB bonds in addition to small junk bond holdings. Good overall profitability (5.9) despite operating losses during the first nine months of 2018. Good liquidity (5.6).

Other Rating Factors: Good overall results on stability tests (5.8) excellent operational trends and excellent risk diversification. Strong capitalization (8.0) based on excellent risk adjusted capital (severe loss scenario).

Principal Business: Individual life insurance (60%), individual health insurance (38%), reinsurance (1%), and individual annuities (1%).

Principal Investments: NonCMO investment grade bonds (63%), mortgages in good standing (16%), policy loans (8%), common & preferred stock (3%), and misc. investments (8%).

Investments in Affiliates: 2%

Group Affiliation: GPM Life Group

Licensed in: All states except NJ, NY, PR

Commenced Business: October 1934

Address: 2211 NE Loop 410, San Antonio, TX 78217

Phone: (800) 938-9765 **Domicile State:** TX **NAIC Code:** 63967

Data Date	Rating	RACR #1	RACR #2	Total Assets ($mil)	Capital ($mil)	Net Premium ($mil)	Net Income ($mil)
9-18	B	2.58	1.65	821.2	114.8	34.8	-1.3
9-17	B+	2.50	1.62	832.3	122.3	33.9	3.0
2017	B+	2.64	1.69	825.7	116.8	44.2	5.3
2016	B+	2.51	1.62	835.1	120.9	44.9	4.0
2015	B+	2.81	1.76	836.1	116.2	46.3	2.6
2014	B+	2.72	1.73	837.5	112.4	46.2	3.3
2013	B+	2.69	1.72	830.9	109.2	46.9	4.1

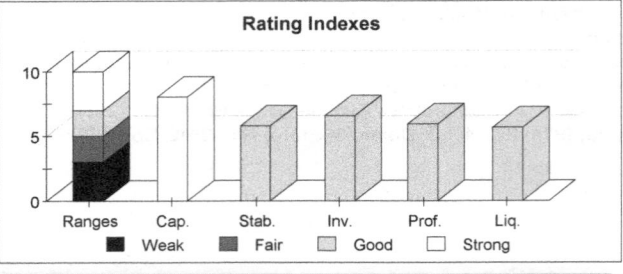

Rating Indexes

GRANGE LIFE INSURANCE COMPANY   C   Fair

Major Rating Factors: Good quality investment portfolio (6.5 on a scale of 0 to 10) despite mixed results such as: substantial holdings of BBB bonds but junk bond exposure equal to 52% of capital. Good liquidity (5.9) with sufficient resources to handle a spike in claims as well as a significant increase in policy surrenders. Weak profitability (1.8) with operating losses during the first nine months of 2018.

Other Rating Factors: Weak overall results on stability tests (2.9) including negative cash flow from operations for 2017, weak results on operational trends. Strong capitalization (7.9) based on excellent risk adjusted capital (severe loss scenario).

Principal Business: Individual life insurance (93%), reinsurance (3%), group life insurance (2%), and individual annuities (1%).

Principal Investments: NonCMO investment grade bonds (58%), CMOs and structured securities (28%), noninv. grade bonds (6%), cash (5%), and policy loans (3%).

Investments in Affiliates: None

Group Affiliation: Grange Mutual Casualty Group

Licensed in: GA, IL, IN, IA, KS, KY, MI, MN, MO, OH, PA, SC, TN, VA, WI

Commenced Business: July 1968

Address: 671 South High Street, Columbus, OH 43206-1066

Phone: (614) 445-2900 **Domicile State:** OH **NAIC Code:** 71218

Data Date	Rating	RACR #1	RACR #2	Total Assets ($mil)	Capital ($mil)	Net Premium ($mil)	Net Income ($mil)
9-18	C	2.65	1.59	390.8	41.1	40.0	-2.6
9-17	C	2.50	1.69	406.6	73.1	-12.1	-1.2
2017	C	4.34	2.42	412.2	72.5	1.8	-1.3
2016	C	2.52	1.70	452.3	71.3	68.3	-37.4
2015	B-	1.75	1.17	393.2	42.5	56.6	-1.6
2014	B-	2.61	1.67	370.7	56.1	49.9	2.0
2013	B-	2.51	1.63	353.4	51.0	46.4	3.0

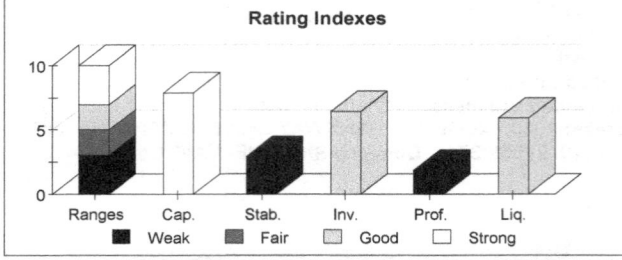

Rating Indexes

GREAT AMERICAN LIFE INSURANCE COMPANY   B-   Good

Major Rating Factors: Good capitalization (6.8 on a scale of 0 to 10) based on good risk adjusted capital (severe loss scenario). Moreover, capital levels have been consistent over the last five years. Good quality investment portfolio (5.2) despite mixed results such as: large holdings of BBB rated bonds but moderate junk bond exposure. Good liquidity (5.5).

Other Rating Factors: Good overall results on stability tests (5.3) excellent operational trends and excellent risk diversification. Excellent profitability (8.8).

Principal Business: Individual annuities (98%) and individual life insurance (1%).

Principal Investments: NonCMO investment grade bonds (57%), CMOs and structured securities (28%), common & preferred stock (3%), mortgages in good standing (3%), and noninv. grade bonds (2%).

Investments in Affiliates: 1%

Group Affiliation: American Financial Group Inc

Licensed in: All states except NY, PR

Commenced Business: August 1963

Address: 301 East Fourth Street, Cincinnati, OH 45202

Phone: (800) 854-3649 **Domicile State:** OH **NAIC Code:** 63312

Data Date	Rating	RACR #1	RACR #2	Total Assets ($mil)	Capital ($mil)	Net Premium ($mil)	Net Income ($mil)
9-18	B-	1.75	0.97	35,805.2	2,333.2	3,780.9	348.3
9-17	B-	1.79	0.99	32,146.2	2,128.1	3,273.8	200.7
2017	B-	1.66	0.93	32,576.6	2,131.5	4,134.9	263.2
2016	B-	1.74	0.97	29,301.5	1,976.4	4,241.8	147.9
2015	B-	1.61	0.91	25,936.0	1,721.3	3,963.1	375.3
2014	B-	1.74	0.99	22,772.6	1,636.0	3,469.4	356.0
2013	B-	1.82	1.04	20,182.2	1,511.8	3,801.6	262.2

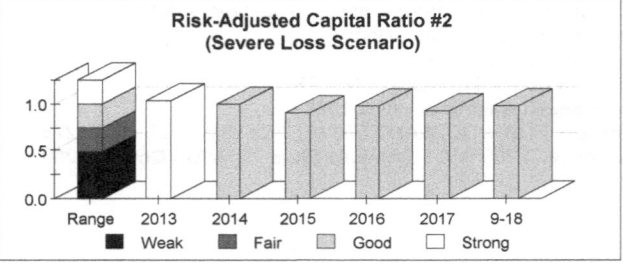

Risk-Adjusted Capital Ratio #2
(Severe Loss Scenario)

GREAT SOUTHERN LIFE INSURANCE COMPANY | B | Good

Major Rating Factors: Good overall results on stability tests (6.3 on a scale of 0 to 10). Stability strengths include good operational trends and excellent risk diversification. Good quality investment portfolio (6.5) despite mixed results such as: minimal exposure to mortgages and substantial holdings of BBB bonds but minimal holdings in junk bonds. Strong capitalization (10.0) based on excellent risk adjusted capital (severe loss scenario).

Other Rating Factors: Excellent profitability (9.3). Excellent liquidity (7.0).

Principal Business: Individual life insurance (87%), group life insurance (7%), group health insurance (3%), individual annuities (1%), and reinsurance (1%).

Principal Investments: CMOs and structured securities (50%), nonCMO investment grade bonds (39%), common & preferred stock (6%), and noninv. grade bonds (2%).

Investments in Affiliates: None
Group Affiliation: Americo Life Inc
Licensed in: All states except NH, NY, RI, VT, PR
Commenced Business: November 1909
Address: PO Box 139061, Dallas, TX 75313-9061
Phone: (816) 391-2000 **Domicile State:** TX **NAIC Code:** 90212

Data Date	Rating	RACR #1	RACR #2	Total Assets ($mil)	Capital ($mil)	Net Premium ($mil)	Net Income ($mil)
9-18	B	5.75	3.17	212.0	53.1	0.1	1.7
9-17	B	5.39	2.79	215.2	49.6	0.1	2.3
2017	B	5.59	2.93	211.9	51.5	0.2	3.2
2016	B	5.18	2.65	216.6	47.5	0.2	2.9
2015	B+	4.96	2.63	220.1	45.3	0.3	3.1
2014	B	4.72	2.42	224.8	42.9	0.2	2.9
2013	B	4.43	2.29	231.9	40.3	0.8	2.3

Adverse Trends in Operations

Decrease in asset base during 2017 (2%)
Decrease in premium volume from 2016 to 2017 (14%)
Decrease in premium volume from 2015 to 2016 (30%)
Increase in policy surrenders from 2014 to 2015 (79%)
Decrease in premium volume from 2013 to 2014 (72%)

GREAT WEST LIFE ASSURANCE COMPANY | C+ | Fair

Major Rating Factors: Fair profitability (3.0 on a scale of 0 to 10) with investment income below regulatory standards in relation to interest assumptions of reserves. Fair overall results on stability tests (4.8) including negative cash flow from operations for 2017. Good liquidity (6.6) with sufficient resources to handle a spike in claims as well as a significant increase in policy surrenders.

Other Rating Factors: Strong capitalization (9.7) based on excellent risk adjusted capital (severe loss scenario). High quality investment portfolio (7.5).

Principal Business: Individual life insurance (85%), individual health insurance (11%), and reinsurance (4%).

Principal Investments: NonCMO investment grade bonds (70%), CMOs and structured securities (22%), policy loans (2%), real estate (2%), and cash (1%).

Investments in Affiliates: None
Group Affiliation: Great West Life Asr
Licensed in: All states except NY, PR
Commenced Business: August 1892
Address: 100 Osborne Street North, Winnipeg, MB R3C 3A5
Phone: (303) 737-3000 **Domicile State:** MI **NAIC Code:** 80705

Data Date	Rating	RACR #1	RACR #2	Total Assets ($mil)	Capital ($mil)	Net Premium ($mil)	Net Income ($mil)
9-18	C+	3.33	2.83	73.3	25.9	1.9	0.8
9-17	C+	3.17	2.69	75.8	24.9	2.0	2.2
2017	C+	3.09	2.59	75.0	24.0	2.8	2.6
2016	C+	2.87	2.43	77.0	22.6	2.7	2.1
2015	C+	2.53	2.01	77.3	19.9	2.7	1.1
2014	B-	2.33	1.92	77.6	18.4	2.8	1.9
2013	B-	1.91	1.43	78.6	15.1	3.4	-1.3

Investment Income Compared to Needs of Reserves

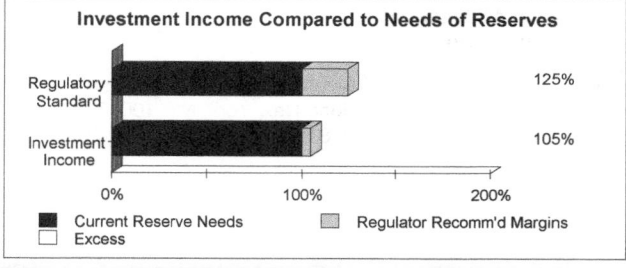

GREAT WESTERN INSURANCE COMPANY | C- | Fair

Major Rating Factors: Poor current capitalization (1.3 on a scale of 0 to 10) based on weak risk adjusted capital (moderate loss scenario), although results have slipped from the good range over the last two years. Low quality investment portfolio (0.5) containing large holdings of BBB rated bonds in addition to junk bond exposure equal to 55% of capital. Exposure to mortgages is significant, but the mortgage default rate has been low. Weak profitability (0.9) with operating losses during the first nine months of 2018.

Other Rating Factors: Weak overall results on stability tests (1.5) including weak risk adjusted capital in prior years. Good liquidity (5.4).

Principal Business: Group life insurance (69%), individual life insurance (28%), individual annuities (2%), and reinsurance (1%).

Principal Investments: NonCMO investment grade bonds (72%), mortgages in good standing (12%), CMOs and structured securities (11%), noninv. grade bonds (1%), and common & preferred stock (1%).

Investments in Affiliates: None
Group Affiliation: JAMEL Ltd
Licensed in: All states except AK, CT, HI, NY, PR
Commenced Business: May 1983
Address: 3434 Washington Blvd Ste 300, Ogden, UT 84401
Phone: (801) 621-5688 **Domicile State:** UT **NAIC Code:** 71480

Data Date	Rating	RACR #1	RACR #2	Total Assets ($mil)	Capital ($mil)	Net Premium ($mil)	Net Income ($mil)
9-18	C-	0.54	0.28	1,402.4	27.5	-8.8	-1.5
9-17	B	1.98	1.01	1,321.4	83.9	158.3	7.3
2017	D	0.61	0.31	1,388.0	32.4	213.4	-99.6
2016	B	1.96	1.01	1,214.6	77.1	194.6	7.9
2015	B	2.06	1.08	1,051.5	71.7	181.4	8.0
2014	B	2.09	1.10	900.0	66.3	415.9	5.7
2013	B-	2.78	1.54	496.5	60.6	39.0	14.2

Risk-Adjusted Capital Ratio #1
(Moderate Loss Scenario)

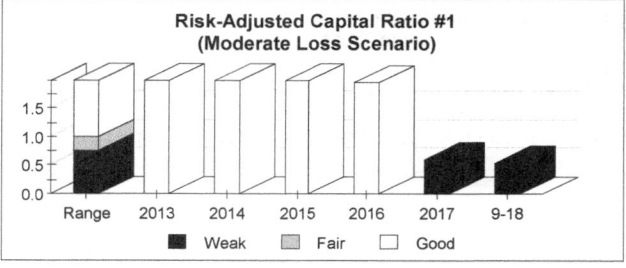

GREAT-WEST LIFE & ANNUITY INSURANCE COMPANY

B-   **Good**

Major Rating Factors: Good capitalization (5.5 on a scale of 0 to 10) based on good risk adjusted capital (moderate loss scenario). Good quality investment portfolio (5.5) despite significant exposure to mortgages . Mortgage default rate has been low. large holdings of BBB rated bonds in addition to small junk bond holdings. Good overall profitability (6.2).

Other Rating Factors: Good liquidity (5.7). Fair overall results on stability tests (4.2) including fair risk adjusted capital in prior years.

Principal Business: Group retirement contracts (69%), individual life insurance (18%), individual annuities (10%), group life insurance (2%), and group health insurance (1%).

Principal Investments: NonCMO investment grade bonds (50%), CMOs and structured securities (18%), policy loans (14%), mortgages in good standing (13%), and noninv. grade bonds (1%).

Investments in Affiliates: 1%

Group Affiliation: Great West Life Asr

Licensed in: All states, the District of Columbia and Puerto Rico

Commenced Business: April 1907

Address: 8515 East Orchard Road, Greenwood Village, CO 80111

Phone: (800) 537-2033 **Domicile State:** CO **NAIC Code:** 68322

Data Date	Rating	RACR #1	RACR #2	Total Assets ($mil)	Capital ($mil)	Net Premium ($mil)	Net Income ($mil)
9-18	B-	1.32	0.71	57,765.4	1,270.0	10,500.9	236.1
9-17	B-	1.24	0.67	59,394.3	1,054.9	4,018.7	106.2
2017	B-	1.23	0.67	58,010.2	1,129.5	5,270.5	170.0
2016	B-	1.18	0.64	56,436.0	1,053.3	-397.8	100.7
2015	B-	1.29	0.71	54,460.5	1,114.8	5,729.5	187.2
2014	B-	1.19	0.64	54,523.5	1,000.9	5,634.0	134.1
2013	B-	1.33	0.75	52,282.0	1,200.6	5,610.4	175.3

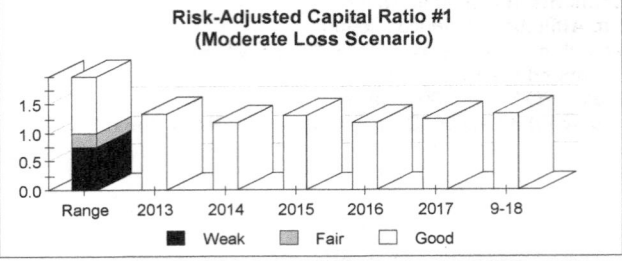

Risk-Adjusted Capital Ratio #1 (Moderate Loss Scenario)

■ Weak   ▨ Fair   ☐ Good

GREAT-WEST LIFE & ANNUITY INSURANCE COMPANY OF NEW

B   **Good**

Major Rating Factors: Good overall results on stability tests (5.9 on a scale of 0 to 10). Stability strengths include excellent operational trends and excellent risk diversification. Good quality investment portfolio (5.9) despite mixed results such as: minimal exposure to mortgages and large holdings of BBB rated bonds but small junk bond holdings. Fair profitability (4.4).

Other Rating Factors: Fair liquidity (4.4). Strong capitalization (7.2) based on excellent risk adjusted capital (severe loss scenario).

Principal Business: Group retirement contracts (58%), individual life insurance (30%), and individual annuities (11%).

Principal Investments: NonCMO investment grade bonds (72%), CMOs and structured securities (16%), mortgages in good standing (6%), policy loans (2%), and noninv. grade bonds (1%).

Investments in Affiliates: None

Group Affiliation: Great West Life Asr

Licensed in: NY

Commenced Business: January 1972

Address: 489 5th Avenue 28th Floor, New York, NY 10017

Phone: (303) 737-3000 **Domicile State:** NY **NAIC Code:** 79359

Data Date	Rating	RACR #1	RACR #2	Total Assets ($mil)	Capital ($mil)	Net Premium ($mil)	Net Income ($mil)
9-18	B	2.14	1.13	2,258.1	89.0	187.1	1.9
9-17	B	2.24	1.20	2,173.4	85.3	258.3	-1.5
2017	B	2.16	1.16	2,198.5	87.5	328.5	3.1
2016	B	2.36	1.27	1,968.7	86.7	371.1	-1.9
2015	B	2.83	1.53	1,718.6	89.7	301.6	6.3
2014	B	2.79	1.48	1,594.6	82.9	272.8	1.5
2013	B	2.91	1.52	1,456.3	79.5	248.1	-4.5

Adverse Trends in Operations

Increase in policy surrenders from 2016 to 2017 (28%)
Decrease in premium volume from 2016 to 2017 (11%)
Decrease in capital during 2016 (3%)
Increase in policy surrenders from 2013 to 2014 (44%)

GUARANTEE TRUST LIFE INSURANCE COMPANY

B   **Good**

Major Rating Factors: Good quality investment portfolio (6.5 on a scale of 0 to 10) despite mixed results such as: minimal exposure to mortgages and large holdings of BBB rated bonds but small junk bond holdings. Good overall results on stability tests (5.4). Stability strengths include excellent operational trends and excellent risk diversification. Strong capitalization (7.5) based on excellent risk adjusted capital (severe loss scenario).

Other Rating Factors: Excellent profitability (7.8). Excellent liquidity (7.2).

Principal Business: Individual health insurance (75%), group health insurance (17%), individual life insurance (7%), and reinsurance (1%).

Principal Investments: NonCMO investment grade bonds (51%), CMOs and structured securities (31%), mortgages in good standing (9%), noninv. grade bonds (3%), and misc. investments (4%).

Investments in Affiliates: 1%

Group Affiliation: Guarantee Trust

Licensed in: All states except NY

Commenced Business: June 1936

Address: 1275 Milwaukee Avenue, Glenview, IL 60025

Phone: (847) 699-0600 **Domicile State:** IL **NAIC Code:** 64211

Data Date	Rating	RACR #1	RACR #2	Total Assets ($mil)	Capital ($mil)	Net Premium ($mil)	Net Income ($mil)
9-18	B	2.07	1.35	637.7	94.9	177.6	14.6
9-17	B	1.83	1.20	592.0	79.6	166.8	7.3
2017	B	1.84	1.21	594.8	79.2	218.7	12.4
2016	B	1.85	1.23	550.7	77.0	219.2	9.1
2015	B	1.75	1.18	495.8	70.0	221.4	8.7
2014	B	1.67	1.15	433.3	62.3	210.7	9.7
2013	B	1.49	1.03	366.1	54.3	196.4	7.1

Adverse Trends in Operations

Increase in policy surrenders from 2016 to 2017 (32%)
Increase in policy surrenders from 2015 to 2016 (46%)

GUARANTY INCOME LIFE INSURANCE COMPANY — B — Good

Major Rating Factors: Good liquidity (5.5 on a scale of 0 to 10) with sufficient resources to cover a large increase in policy surrenders. Good overall results on stability tests (5.4) despite excessive premium growth. Other stability subfactors include good operational trends and good risk diversification. Fair quality investment portfolio (4.5).

Other Rating Factors: Strong capitalization (7.7) based on excellent risk adjusted capital (severe loss scenario). Excellent profitability (8.9).

Principal Business: Individual annuities (95%), individual health insurance (3%), and individual life insurance (2%).

Principal Investments: NonCMO investment grade bonds (53%), CMOs and structured securities (38%), noninv. grade bonds (2%), common & preferred stock (2%), and real estate (2%).

Investments in Affiliates: None

Group Affiliation: Kuvare US Holdings Inc

Licensed in: AL, AZ, AR, CA, CO, FL, GA, IL, IN, IA, KS, KY, LA, MI, MS, MO, MT, NE, NV, NM, NC, ND, OH, OK, OR, SC, TN, TX, UT, WA, WY

Commenced Business: February 1926

Address: 929 Government Street, Baton Rouge, LA 70802-6089

Phone: (225) 383-0355 **Domicile State:** LA **NAIC Code:** 64238

Data Date	Rating	RACR #1	RACR #2	Total Assets ($mil)	Capital ($mil)	Net Premium ($mil)	Net Income ($mil)
9-18	B	3.31	1.48	812.7	66.5	159.8	2.5
9-17	C+	3.34	1.58	610.3	55.2	88.2	2.9
2017	C+	3.39	1.52	664.5	56.6	116.9	3.9
2016	C	3.61	1.69	503.7	50.8	44.8	5.4
2015	C	2.45	1.21	483.4	39.7	37.1	4.8
2014	C	2.45	1.18	479.5	34.0	32.8	5.4
2013	C-	2.35	1.13	477.9	31.0	26.7	5.2

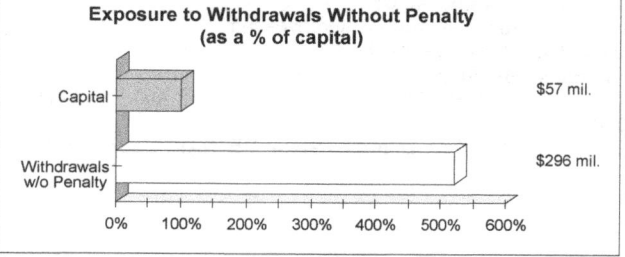

Exposure to Withdrawals Without Penalty (as a % of capital)

Capital — $57 mil.

Withdrawals w/o Penalty — $296 mil.

GUARDIAN INSURANCE & ANNUITY COMPANY INCORPORATED — B — Good

Major Rating Factors: Good current capitalization (6.7 on a scale of 0 to 10) based on good risk adjusted capital (severe loss scenario) reflecting some improvement over results in 2016. Good quality investment portfolio (5.4) despite large holdings of BBB rated bonds in addition to moderate junk bond exposure. Exposure to mortgages is significant, but the mortgage default rate has been low. Fair profitability (3.5) with investment income below regulatory standards in relation to interest assumptions of reserves.

Other Rating Factors: Fair overall results on stability tests (4.7) including fair risk adjusted capital in prior years. Excellent liquidity (9.0).

Principal Business: Individual annuities (59%), group retirement contracts (37%), and individual life insurance (4%).

Principal Investments: NonCMO investment grade bonds (78%), mortgages in good standing (11%), noninv. grade bonds (3%), CMOs and structured securities (3%), and policy loans (2%).

Investments in Affiliates: 1%

Group Affiliation: Guardian Group

Licensed in: All states except PR

Commenced Business: December 1971

Address: 2711 CENTERVILLE ROAD STE 400, WILMINGTON, DE 19808

Phone: (212) 598-8000 **Domicile State:** DE **NAIC Code:** 78778

Data Date	Rating	RACR #1	RACR #2	Total Assets ($mil)	Capital ($mil)	Net Premium ($mil)	Net Income ($mil)
9-18	B	1.89	0.96	15,824.8	342.0	1,233.9	70.0
9-17	B	1.62	0.83	17,327.5	320.5	387.7	112.7
2017	B	1.72	0.88	17,357.0	310.2	449.4	26.3
2016	B	1.37	0.71	16,780.9	260.4	-963.3	-139.7
2015	B	1.65	0.84	15,883.4	259.8	1,678.6	-23.6
2014	B	1.61	0.82	15,656.2	227.2	1,504.4	-0.4
2013	B	1.62	0.85	14,529.6	180.9	1,420.3	-82.5

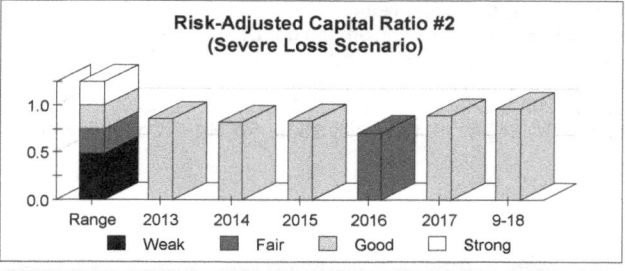

Risk-Adjusted Capital Ratio #2 (Severe Loss Scenario)

Range 2013 2014 2015 2016 2017 9-18

■ Weak ■ Fair ▨ Good ☐ Strong

GUARDIAN LIFE INSURANCE COMPANY OF AMERICA * — A — Excellent

Major Rating Factors: Good quality investment portfolio (6.6 on a scale of 0 to 10) despite mixed results such as: large holdings of BBB rated bonds but moderate junk bond exposure. Good liquidity (6.1) with sufficient resources to handle a spike in claims as well as a significant increase in policy surrenders. Strong capitalization (8.3) based on excellent risk adjusted capital (severe loss scenario).

Other Rating Factors: Excellent profitability (7.2). Excellent overall results on stability tests (7.5) excellent operational trends and excellent risk diversification.

Principal Business: Individual life insurance (50%), group health insurance (35%), group life insurance (7%), reinsurance (6%), and individual health insurance (2%).

Principal Investments: NonCMO investment grade bonds (65%), mortgages in good standing (8%), CMOs and structured securities (8%), policy loans (7%), and misc. investments (13%).

Investments in Affiliates: 4%

Group Affiliation: Guardian Group

Licensed in: All states except PR

Commenced Business: July 1860

Address: 7 HANOVER SQUARE, NEW YORK, NY 10004-4025

Phone: (212) 598-8000 **Domicile State:** NY **NAIC Code:** 64246

Data Date	Rating	RACR #1	RACR #2	Total Assets ($mil)	Capital ($mil)	Net Premium ($mil)	Net Income ($mil)
9-18	A	2.89	1.84	57,852.7	7,110.3	6,222.0	300.9
9-17	A	2.87	1.84	55,226.5	6,864.6	6,027.9	269.8
2017	A	2.84	1.83	55,568.8	6,683.7	8,116.1	423.1
2016	A	2.77	1.79	51,883.7	6,172.5	7,772.7	367.7
2015	A	2.55	1.66	48,120.9	6,089.7	7,337.7	433.1
2014	A	2.76	1.80	45,297.4	5,691.6	7,000.0	711.8
2013	A	2.64	1.73	42,066.0	5,011.9	6,705.6	285.5

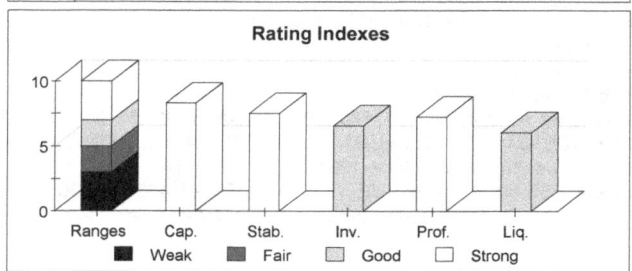

Rating Indexes

Ranges Cap. Stab. Inv. Prof. Liq.

■ Weak ■ Fair ▨ Good ☐ Strong

GUGGENHEIM LIFE & ANNUITY COMPANY

B- | Good

Major Rating Factors: Good current capitalization (5.9 on a scale of 0 to 10) based on good risk adjusted capital (moderate loss scenario) reflecting some improvement over results in 2015. Good overall profitability (6.9). Good liquidity (6.2) with sufficient resources to handle a spike in claims as well as a significant increase in policy surrenders.

Other Rating Factors: Fair quality investment portfolio (4.1). Fair overall results on stability tests (4.2) including fair risk adjusted capital in prior years.

Principal Business: Individual annuities (82%), reinsurance (18%), and individual life insurance (1%).

Principal Investments: NonCMO investment grade bonds (50%), CMOs and structured securities (23%), policy loans (8%), mortgages in good standing (3%), and misc. investments (12%).

Investments in Affiliates: 6%

Group Affiliation: Sammons Enterprises Inc

Licensed in: All states except NY

Commenced Business: October 1985

Address: 2711 CENTERVILLE ROAD STE 400, WILMINGTON, DE 19808-1645

Phone: (317) 396-9960 **Domicile State:** DE **NAIC Code:** 83607

Data Date	Rating	RACR #1	RACR #2	Total Assets ($mil)	Capital ($mil)	Net Premium ($mil)	Net Income ($mil)
3-18	B-	1.57	0.79	13,884.9	606.4	137.2	5.9
3-17	B-	1.08	0.64	13,826.9	533.8	215.4	9.9
2017	B-	1.61	0.82	14,353.5	608.6	804.5	155.5
2016	B-	1.27	0.76	13,716.2	651.1	957.8	205.4
2015	B-	1.19	0.71	13,333.2	599.9	1,162.6	128.6
2014	B-	1.32	0.74	12,812.4	646.0	1,674.3	146.7
2013	B-	1.34	0.75	11,101.8	550.8	1,726.0	107.8

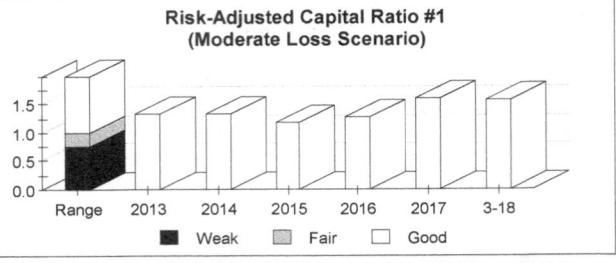

Risk-Adjusted Capital Ratio #1
(Moderate Loss Scenario)

HANNOVER LIFE REASSURANCE COMPANY OF AMERICA *

B+ | Good

Major Rating Factors: Good current capitalization (6.7 on a scale of 0 to 10) based on good risk adjusted capital (severe loss scenario), although results have slipped from the excellent range during the last year. Good quality investment portfolio (6.8) despite mixed results such as: minimal exposure to mortgages and large holdings of BBB rated bonds but small junk bond holdings. Good liquidity (6.7).

Other Rating Factors: Good overall results on stability tests (6.5) despite excessive premium growth and fair risk adjusted capital in prior years good operational trends and excellent risk diversification. Excellent profitability (7.6).

Principal Business: Reinsurance (100%).

Principal Investments: NonCMO investment grade bonds (87%), CMOs and structured securities (6%), and noninv. grade bonds (3%).

Investments in Affiliates: None

Group Affiliation: Haftpflichtverband der Deutschen Ind

Licensed in: All states, the District of Columbia and Puerto Rico

Commenced Business: October 1988

Address: 200 S Orange Ave Ste 1900, Orlando, FL 32801

Phone: (407) 649-8411 **Domicile State:** FL **NAIC Code:** 88340

Data Date	Rating	RACR #1	RACR #2	Total Assets ($mil)	Capital ($mil)	Net Premium ($mil)	Net Income ($mil)
9-18	B+	1.75	0.96	16,338.8	442.5	289.0	0.2
9-17	B	1.87	1.01	14,906.5	355.5	170.8	23.6
2017	B+	2.10	1.14	15,439.3	411.2	232.7	45.6
2016	B	1.70	0.96	14,998.5	331.2	242.3	25.0
2015	B-	1.46	0.81	4,251.0	229.5	281.0	16.7
2014	C	1.21	0.71	4,346.7	212.1	287.6	26.9
2013	C	1.03	0.60	4,528.0	196.9	412.4	23.2

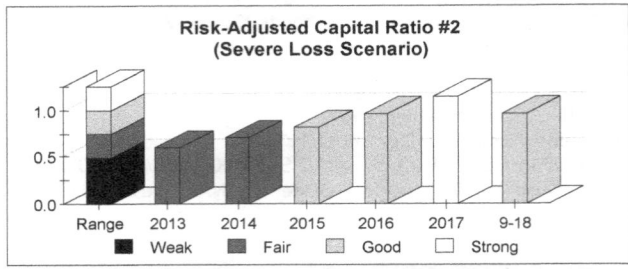

Risk-Adjusted Capital Ratio #2
(Severe Loss Scenario)

HARLEYSVILLE LIFE INSURANCE COMPANY

B | Good

Major Rating Factors: Good overall results on stability tests (5.4 on a scale of 0 to 10) despite negative cash flow from operations for 2017. Other stability subfactors include good operational trends, good risk adjusted capital for prior years and excellent risk diversification. Good quality investment portfolio (6.4) despite mixed results such as: no exposure to mortgages and large holdings of BBB rated bonds but minimal holdings in junk bonds. Good overall profitability (5.6) although investment income, in comparison to reserve requirements, is below regulatory standards.

Other Rating Factors: Good liquidity (5.2). Strong capitalization (8.1) based on excellent risk adjusted capital (severe loss scenario).

Principal Business: Individual life insurance (89%) and individual annuities (11%).

Principal Investments: NonCMO investment grade bonds (85%), CMOs and structured securities (9%), policy loans (1%), and noninv. grade bonds (1%).

Investments in Affiliates: None

Group Affiliation: Nationwide Corp

Licensed in: AL, AZ, AR, CT, DC, DE, FL, GA, IL, IN, IA, KY, MD, MA, MI, MN, NE, NH, NJ, NM, NC, ND, OH, PA, RI, SC, SD, TN, TX, UT, VA, WV, WI

Commenced Business: June 1961

Address: 355 MAPLE AVENUE, COLUMBUS, OH 43215-2220

Phone: (215) 256-5000 **Domicile State:** OH **NAIC Code:** 64327

Data Date	Rating	RACR #1	RACR #2	Total Assets ($mil)	Capital ($mil)	Net Premium ($mil)	Net Income ($mil)
9-18	B	3.20	1.71	401.8	50.1	11.1	3.6
9-17	B	2.99	1.61	406.1	47.0	12.8	2.6
2017	B	3.04	1.64	406.5	46.7	16.7	3.0
2016	B	2.86	1.55	411.8	44.2	17.7	3.0
2015	B	2.60	1.43	410.4	40.7	19.4	6.8
2014	B	1.86	1.08	415.1	34.1	34.8	7.9
2013	B	1.39	0.80	415.0	26.0	37.6	3.2

Adverse Trends in Operations

Decrease in asset base during 2017 (1%)
Decrease in premium volume from 2014 to 2015 (44%)
Decrease in asset base during 2015 (1%)
Increase in policy surrenders from 2013 to 2014 (261%)
Decrease in premium volume from 2013 to 2014 (7%)

HARTFORD LIFE & ACCIDENT INSURANCE COMPANY   C   Fair

Major Rating Factors: Fair overall results on stability tests (3.9 on a scale of 0 to 10) including excessive premium growth and negative cash flow from operations for 2017. Good liquidity (6.3) with sufficient resources to handle a spike in claims as well as a significant increase in policy surrenders. Weak profitability (2.0).

Other Rating Factors: Strong capitalization (9.3) based on excellent risk adjusted capital (severe loss scenario). High quality investment portfolio (7.0).

Principal Business: Reinsurance (53%), group health insurance (27%), and group life insurance (20%).

Principal Investments: NonCMO investment grade bonds (68%), CMOs and structured securities (15%), mortgages in good standing (7%), noninv. grade bonds (3%), and common & preferred stock (1%).

Investments in Affiliates: None

Group Affiliation: Hartford Financial Services Inc

Licensed in: All states, the District of Columbia and Puerto Rico

Commenced Business: February 1967

Address: One Hartford Plaza, Hartford, CT 06155-0001

Phone: (860) 547-5000 **Domicile State:** CT **NAIC Code:** 70815

Data Date	Rating	RACR #1	RACR #2	Total Assets ($mil)	Capital ($mil)	Net Premium ($mil)	Net Income ($mil)
9-18	C	4.01	2.53	12,962.6	2,267.8	3,406.3	257.8
9-17	B-	4.00	2.53	9,168.5	1,624.3	1,790.6	185.3
2017	C	3.42	2.19	12,935.8	2,028.5	5,777.5	-1,065.7
2016	B-	4.15	2.61	8,785.9	1,623.8	2,241.9	208.3
2015	C	3.96	2.47	8,992.2	1,651.4	2,296.5	168.1
2014	C	3.43	2.15	9,086.9	1,592.3	2,486.3	-331.3
2013	B-	1.05	1.00	13,890.8	5,595.2	1,974.0	-174.0

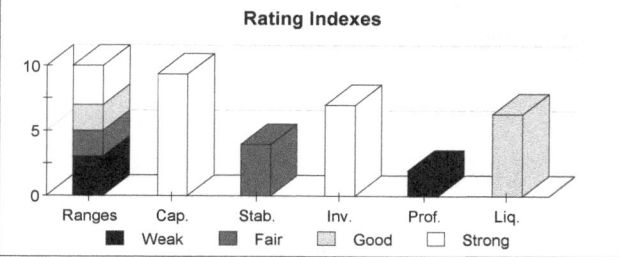

Rating Indexes

HARTFORD LIFE & ANNUITY INSURANCE COMPANY   B-   Good

Major Rating Factors: Good quality investment portfolio (6.2 on a scale of 0 to 10) despite mixed results such as: minimal exposure to mortgages and large holdings of BBB rated bonds but small junk bond holdings. Good overall profitability (5.1). Fair overall results on stability tests (4.3) including negative cash flow from operations for 2017.

Other Rating Factors: Strong capitalization (7.1) based on excellent risk adjusted capital (severe loss scenario). Excellent liquidity (9.5).

Principal Business: Individual life insurance (71%), individual annuities (21%), and reinsurance (8%).

Principal Investments: NonCMO investment grade bonds (51%), CMOs and structured securities (20%), mortgages in good standing (9%), cash (8%), and misc. investments (6%).

Investments in Affiliates: None

Group Affiliation: Hartford Financial Services Inc

Licensed in: All states except NY

Commenced Business: July 1965

Address: One Hartford Plaza, Windsor, CT 06095-1512

Phone: (860) 547-5000 **Domicile State:** CT **NAIC Code:** 71153

Data Date	Rating	RACR #1	RACR #2	Total Assets ($mil)	Capital ($mil)	Net Premium ($mil)	Net Income ($mil)
9-18	B-	2.15	1.07	36,933.6	969.3	-1,648.4	149.0
9-17	B-	4.16	2.08	36,874.4	1,456.7	192.5	95.0
2017	B-	3.40	1.71	36,378.6	1,139.0	229.9	170.8
2016	B-	5.53	2.74	36,793.2	1,913.8	283.3	146.1
2015	B-	5.83	3.06	40,189.1	2,625.3	313.1	80.9
2014	B-	6.70	3.51	47,246.3	3,408.9	41,392.8	95.2
2013	B-	6.35	3.36	54,556.9	3,080.6	-2,982.6	721.8

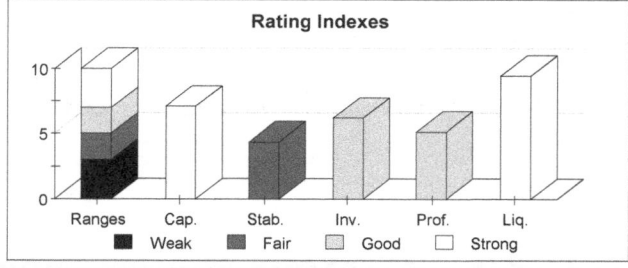

Rating Indexes

HARTFORD LIFE INSURANCE COMPANY   C+   Fair

Major Rating Factors: Fair overall results on stability tests (3.1 on a scale of 0 to 10) including weak results on operational trends. Good quality investment portfolio (5.5) despite mixed results such as: minimal exposure to mortgages and substantial holdings of BBB bonds but small junk bond holdings. Good overall profitability (5.6).

Other Rating Factors: Strong capitalization (7.5) based on excellent risk adjusted capital (severe loss scenario). Excellent liquidity (9.2).

Principal Business: Group retirement contracts (77%), individual annuities (11%), individual life insurance (7%), group health insurance (4%), and group life insurance (1%).

Principal Investments: NonCMO investment grade bonds (46%), CMOs and structured securities (16%), mortgages in good standing (9%), policy loans (7%), and misc. investments (17%).

Investments in Affiliates: 6%

Group Affiliation: Hartford Financial Services Inc

Licensed in: All states except PR

Commenced Business: January 1979

Address: One Hartford Plaza, Windsor, CT 06095-1512

Phone: (800) 862-6668 **Domicile State:** CT **NAIC Code:** 88072

Data Date	Rating	RACR #1	RACR #2	Total Assets ($mil)	Capital ($mil)	Net Premium ($mil)	Net Income ($mil)
9-18	C+	1.90	1.35	90,215.7	3,409.9	-5,367.0	246.2
9-17	C+	1.60	1.20	110,132	4,100.6	359.2	553.6
2017	C+	1.88	1.28	109,357	3,552.5	433.0	1,197.6
2016	C+	1.68	1.25	111,450	4,397.9	542.6	951.9
2015	C+	1.47	1.12	114,421	4,939.5	1,406.9	295.2
2014	C+	1.32	1.06	123,445	5,564.4	-1,087.6	35.4
2013	C+	1.28	0.99	128,074	5,005.0	-7,168.0	549.9

Adverse Trends in Operations

Decrease in premium volume from 2016 to 2017 (20%)
Increase in policy surrenders from 2016 to 2017 (71%)
Decrease in capital during 2017 (19%)
Decrease in capital during 2016 (11%)
Decrease in premium volume from 2015 to 2016 (61%)

HAYMARKET INS CO | D | Weak

Major Rating Factors: Weak liquidity (0.0 on a scale of 0 to 10) as a spike in claims or a run on policy withdrawals may stretch capacity. Weak overall results on stability tests (2.0) including lack of operational experience. Fair quality investment portfolio (3.8).

Other Rating Factors: Fair profitability (3.0). Good capitalization (5.4) based on good risk adjusted capital (moderate loss scenario).

Principal Business: Reinsurance (100%).

Principal Investments: CMOs and structured securities (51%), nonCMO investment grade bonds (26%), cash (10%), and mortgages in good standing (7%).

Investments in Affiliates: None

Group Affiliation: Advantage Capital Partners LLC

Licensed in: NE, SC, UT

Commenced Business: September 2015

Address: 222 South 15th Street 1202S, Omaha, NE 68102

Phone: (914) 579-2929 **Domicile State:** NE **NAIC Code:** 15828

Data Date	Rating	RACR #1	RACR #2	Total Assets ($mil)	Capital ($mil)	Net Premium ($mil)	Net Income ($mil)
9-18	D	1.24	0.71	1,016.4	41.3	67.9	3.8
9-17	D	1.12	0.66	801.6	27.7	56.6	1.1
2017	D	1.01	0.58	858.8	27.9	69.1	1.6
2016	D	1.15	0.70	593.2	27.3	55.9	-4.5
2015	E+	0.80	0.72	334.5	17.2	112.4	-13.0
2014	N/A	N/A	N/A	0.0	0.0	0.0	0.0
2013	N/A	N/A	N/A	0.0	0.0	0.0	0.0

Rating Indexes

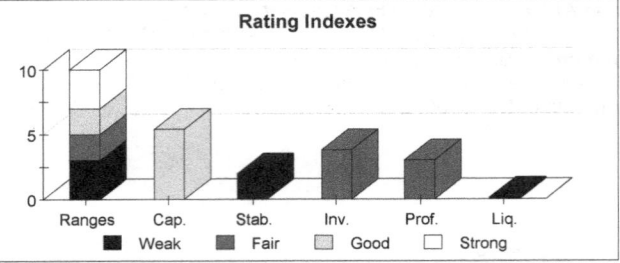

(Ranges, Cap., Stab., Inv., Prof., Liq. — Weak, Fair, Good, Strong)

HCC LIFE INSURANCE COMPANY | B | Good

Major Rating Factors: Good overall results on stability tests (5.7 on a scale of 0 to 10) despite fair financial strength of affiliated HCC Ins Holdings Inc and excessive premium growth. Other stability subfactors include excellent operational trends and excellent risk diversification. Good overall profitability (6.8). Excellent expense controls. Good liquidity (6.6).

Other Rating Factors: Strong capitalization (9.5) based on excellent risk adjusted capital (severe loss scenario). High quality investment portfolio (8.4).

Principal Business: Group health insurance (90%), reinsurance (7%), and individual health insurance (2%).

Principal Investments: NonCMO investment grade bonds (62%) and CMOs and structured securities (38%).

Investments in Affiliates: None

Group Affiliation: HCC Ins Holdings Inc

Licensed in: All states except PR

Commenced Business: March 1981

Address: 150 West Market Street Ste 800, Indianapolis, IN 46204

Phone: (770) 973-9851 **Domicile State:** IN **NAIC Code:** 92711

Data Date	Rating	RACR #1	RACR #2	Total Assets ($mil)	Capital ($mil)	Net Premium ($mil)	Net Income ($mil)
9-18	B	3.37	2.66	1,086.9	516.9	1,021.5	111.2
9-17	B	5.38	4.15	1,058.7	689.6	767.1	89.1
2017	B	3.06	2.40	994.8	406.2	1,095.5	90.9
2016	B	4.81	3.71	981.6	601.8	987.7	104.8
2015	B	4.44	3.40	921.5	552.7	973.3	112.1
2014	B	4.61	3.60	923.5	554.3	956.4	116.1
2013	B	3.61	2.96	750.2	436.9	854.6	142.1

HCC Ins Holdings Inc
Composite Group Rating: C+
Largest Group Members

	Assets ($mil)	Rating
RELIANCE STANDARD LIFE INS CO	12173	C+
PHILADELPHIA INDEMNITY INS CO	8653	B-
SAFETY NATIONAL CASUALTY CORP	7224	C
HOUSTON CASUALTY CO	3383	B-
US SPECIALTY INS CO	1888	B

HEALTH NET LIFE INSURANCE COMPANY | C | Fair

Major Rating Factors: Fair overall results on stability tests (3.9 on a scale of 0 to 10) including fair financial strength of affiliated Centene Corporation. Good liquidity (6.8) with sufficient resources to handle a spike in claims. Weak profitability (1.9) with operating losses during the first nine months of 2018.

Other Rating Factors: Strong capitalization (9.3) based on excellent risk adjusted capital (severe loss scenario). High quality investment portfolio (8.5).

Principal Business: Group health insurance (50%) and individual health insurance (49%).

Principal Investments: NonCMO investment grade bonds (37%), cash (30%), and CMOs and structured securities (13%).

Investments in Affiliates: None

Group Affiliation: Centene Corporation

Licensed in: All states except MI, NY, PR

Commenced Business: January 1987

Address: 21281 Burbank Boulevard B3, Woodland Hills, CA 91367

Phone: (314) 725-4477 **Domicile State:** CA **NAIC Code:** 66141

Data Date	Rating	RACR #1	RACR #2	Total Assets ($mil)	Capital ($mil)	Net Premium ($mil)	Net Income ($mil)
9-18	C	3.22	2.56	748.8	391.3	591.7	-14.9
9-17	C	3.78	3.10	748.6	423.9	594.2	6.3
2017	C	3.44	2.79	691.4	399.9	763.3	-16.4
2016	C	3.59	2.94	727.2	410.0	809.8	-171.8
2015	C	1.84	1.52	618.5	331.3	1,181.3	-93.2
2014	C	2.26	1.84	624.0	363.9	1,040.9	-9.3
2013	B	1.88	1.52	485.1	257.2	916.1	22.9

Centene Corporation
Composite Group Rating: C
Largest Group Members

	Assets ($mil)	Rating
SUPERIOR HEALTHPLAN INC	754	C+
SUNSHINE HEALTH	736	D+
HEALTH NET LIFE INS CO	691	C
CELTIC INS CO	593	C+
LOUISIANA HEALTHCARE CONNECTIONS INC	486	E

HERITAGE LIFE INSURANCE COMPANY   C+   Fair

Major Rating Factors: Fair quality investment portfolio (3.7 on a scale of 0 to 10) with large holdings of BBB rated bonds in addition to junk bond exposure equal to 52% of capital. Fair overall results on stability tests (4.2) including negative cash flow from operations for 2017. Good overall profitability (6.7).
Other Rating Factors: Strong capitalization (8.1) based on excellent risk adjusted capital (severe loss scenario). Excellent liquidity (8.0).
Principal Business: Reinsurance (100%).
Principal Investments: NonCMO investment grade bonds (41%), CMOs and structured securities (24%), noninv. grade bonds (12%), and common & preferred stock (2%).
Investments in Affiliates: 2%
Group Affiliation: Calton Holdings LLC
Licensed in: All states except NY, PR
Commenced Business: August 1957
Address: 8601 N SCOTTSDALE RD STE 300, SCOTTSDALE, AZ 85253
Phone: (312) 977-0904 **Domicile State:** AZ **NAIC Code:** 64394

Data Date	Rating	RACR #1	RACR #2	Total Assets ($mil)	Capital ($mil)	Net Premium ($mil)	Net Income ($mil)
9-18	C+	3.76	1.73	3,923.4	937.5	30.3	68.0
9-17	C+	4.06	1.77	4,223.1	945.9	81.0	63.3
2017	C+	3.75	1.72	4,212.9	958.7	105.7	87.5
2016	C+	4.06	1.75	4,472.0	983.9	109.6	87.1
2015	C	3.95	1.68	4,508.2	992.4	46.1	65.0
2014	C	3.97	1.62	4,685.9	1,027.6	36.8	57.6
2013	C-	4.49	1.94	4,872.4	1,018.0	85.8	34.0

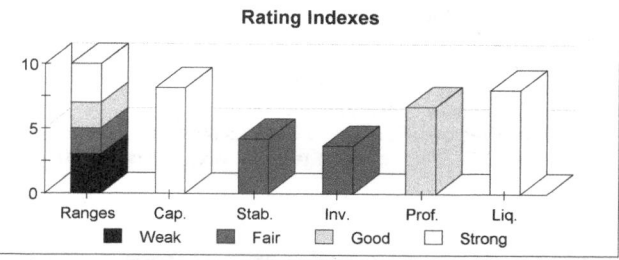

Rating Indexes

Ranges Cap. Stab. Inv. Prof. Liq.
■ Weak ■ Fair □ Good □ Strong

HM LIFE INSURANCE COMPANY   B   Good

Major Rating Factors: Good overall results on stability tests (5.4 on a scale of 0 to 10) despite fair financial strength of affiliated Highmark Inc. Other stability subfactors include good operational trends and excellent risk diversification. Good overall profitability (6.8). Good liquidity (6.2).
Other Rating Factors: Fair quality investment portfolio (4.8). Strong capitalization (9.4) based on excellent risk adjusted capital (severe loss scenario).
Principal Business: Group health insurance (88%) and reinsurance (12%).
Principal Investments: NonCMO investment grade bonds (41%), CMOs and structured securities (13%), noninv. grade bonds (11%), and common & preferred stock (11%).
Investments in Affiliates: None
Group Affiliation: Highmark Inc
Licensed in: All states except NY, PR
Commenced Business: May 1981
Address: Fifth AvePlace 120 Fifth Ave, Pittsburgh, PA 15222-3099
Phone: (800) 328-5433 **Domicile State:** PA **NAIC Code:** 93440

Data Date	Rating	RACR #1	RACR #2	Total Assets ($mil)	Capital ($mil)	Net Premium ($mil)	Net Income ($mil)
9-18	B	3.91	2.63	721.2	396.5	325.4	38.1
9-17	B-	3.33	2.39	687.4	377.1	554.9	-2.8
2017	B-	3.20	2.29	674.0	360.1	720.9	-23.8
2016	B-	3.39	2.43	643.3	360.7	673.4	17.8
2015	B	3.73	2.73	620.8	348.6	640.3	37.3
2014	B	3.28	2.49	574.5	309.2	647.9	24.1
2013	B	3.07	2.35	557.9	284.6	634.0	35.5

Highmark Inc Composite Group Rating: C+ Largest Group Members	Assets ($mil)	Rating
HIGHMARK INC	6922	C
HIGHMARK WEST VIRGINIA INC	762	B
HM LIFE INS CO	674	B
GATEWAY HEALTH PLAN INC	653	B-
HIGHMARK BCBSD INC	443	B

HM LIFE INSURANCE COMPANY OF NEW YORK   B   Good

Major Rating Factors: Good overall results on stability tests (5.4 on a scale of 0 to 10) despite fair financial strength of affiliated Highmark Inc. Other stability subfactors include good operational trends and excellent risk diversification. Good overall profitability (6.4) despite operating losses during the first nine months of 2018. Good liquidity (6.9).
Other Rating Factors: Strong capitalization (10.0) based on excellent risk adjusted capital (severe loss scenario). High quality investment portfolio (8.8).
Principal Business: Group health insurance (96%) and reinsurance (4%).
Principal Investments: NonCMO investment grade bonds (43%), CMOs and structured securities (20%), and cash (2%).
Investments in Affiliates: None
Group Affiliation: Highmark Inc
Licensed in: DC, NY, RI
Commenced Business: March 1997
Address: 420 Fifth Avenue 3rd Floor, New York, NY 10119
Phone: (800) 328-5433 **Domicile State:** NY **NAIC Code:** 60213

Data Date	Rating	RACR #1	RACR #2	Total Assets ($mil)	Capital ($mil)	Net Premium ($mil)	Net Income ($mil)
9-18	B	5.54	4.28	67.2	44.4	27.2	-0.8
9-17	B	3.53	2.81	69.1	45.2	56.6	5.2
2017	B	3.64	2.90	67.3	45.1	72.8	5.1
2016	B	3.23	2.57	67.0	40.2	72.4	1.7
2015	B	3.33	2.64	65.7	38.9	66.2	-1.1
2014	B+	3.12	2.47	71.4	39.2	75.4	8.0
2013	B+	2.28	1.81	76.1	31.9	85.4	-0.4

Highmark Inc Composite Group Rating: C+ Largest Group Members	Assets ($mil)	Rating
HIGHMARK INC	6922	C
HIGHMARK WEST VIRGINIA INC	762	B
HM LIFE INS CO	674	B
GATEWAY HEALTH PLAN INC	653	B-
HIGHMARK BCBSD INC	443	B

HOMESTEADERS LIFE COMPANY

B   **Good**

Major Rating Factors: Good quality investment portfolio (6.1 on a scale of 0 to 10) despite mixed results such as: large holdings of BBB rated bonds but moderate junk bond exposure. Good overall profitability (5.5) although investment income, in comparison to reserve requirements, is below regulatory standards. Good overall results on stability tests (5.5) excellent operational trends and excellent risk diversification.

Other Rating Factors: Strong capitalization (7.3) based on excellent risk adjusted capital (severe loss scenario). Excellent liquidity (7.1).

Principal Business: Group life insurance (93%), individual life insurance (4%), and individual annuities (3%).

Principal Investments: NonCMO investment grade bonds (75%), CMOs and structured securities (19%), noninv. grade bonds (3%), cash (1%), and mortgages in good standing (1%).

Investments in Affiliates: None

Group Affiliation: None

Licensed in: All states except NY, PR

Commenced Business: February 1906

Address: 5700 Westown Parkway, West Des Moines, IA 50266-8221

Phone: (515) 440-7777   **Domicile State:** IA   **NAIC Code:** 64505

Data Date	Rating	RACR #1	RACR #2	Total Assets ($mil)	Capital ($mil)	Net Premium ($mil)	Net Income ($mil)
9-18	B	2.26	1.20	3,035.3	202.0	376.9	9.8
9-17	B	2.30	1.22	2,887.9	191.6	364.8	12.3
2017	B	2.27	1.21	2,921.3	193.2	480.0	16.3
2016	B	2.20	1.18	2,771.5	180.5	456.8	14.8
2015	B	2.22	1.24	2,623.9	168.7	422.3	10.5
2014	B	2.19	1.24	2,500.8	161.1	399.8	12.4
2013	B	2.02	1.16	2,378.1	149.6	396.7	12.6

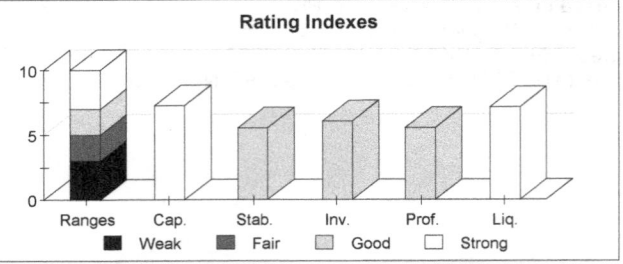

Rating Indexes

HORACE MANN LIFE INSURANCE COMPANY

B   **Good**

Major Rating Factors: Good capitalization (6.3 on a scale of 0 to 10) based on good risk adjusted capital (severe loss scenario). Moreover, capital levels have been consistent over the last five years. Good quality investment portfolio (5.3) despite mixed results such as: minimal exposure to mortgages and large holdings of BBB rated bonds but small junk bond holdings. Good overall results on stability tests (5.4) excellent operational trends and excellent risk diversification.

Other Rating Factors: Fair liquidity (4.3). Excellent profitability (8.1).

Principal Business: Individual annuities (68%), individual life insurance (20%), and group retirement contracts (11%).

Principal Investments: NonCMO investment grade bonds (59%), CMOs and structured securities (31%), policy loans (2%), common & preferred stock (2%), and noninv. grade bonds (2%).

Investments in Affiliates: None

Group Affiliation: Horace Mann Educators Corp

Licensed in: All states except NJ, NY, PR

Commenced Business: September 1949

Address: #1 HORACE MANN PLAZA, SPRINGFIELD, IL 62715

Phone: (800) 999-1030   **Domicile State:** IL   **NAIC Code:** 64513

Data Date	Rating	RACR #1	RACR #2	Total Assets ($mil)	Capital ($mil)	Net Premium ($mil)	Net Income ($mil)
9-18	B	1.76	0.91	9,548.2	479.7	407.7	46.1
9-17	B	1.73	0.87	9,154.5	455.3	427.1	34.7
2017	B	1.77	0.91	9,262.8	473.2	562.4	59.0
2016	B	1.73	0.87	8,845.2	447.0	625.8	51.7
2015	B	1.74	0.88	8,358.8	421.9	648.8	43.2
2014	B	1.80	0.90	7,894.0	398.7	580.3	46.8
2013	B	1.90	0.96	7,281.4	372.4	520.1	54.1

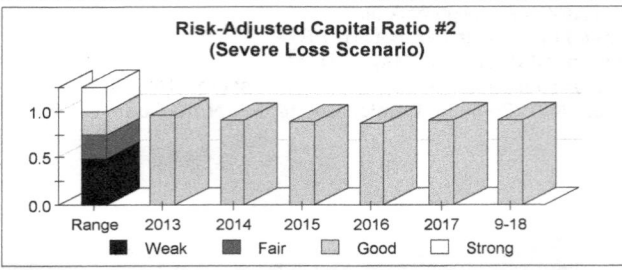

Risk-Adjusted Capital Ratio #2
(Severe Loss Scenario)

HUMANA INSURANCE COMPANY OF KENTUCKY

B   **Good**

Major Rating Factors: Good overall profitability (6.9 on a scale of 0 to 10). Excellent expense controls. Fair overall results on stability tests (4.5). Strong capitalization (10.0) based on excellent risk adjusted capital (severe loss scenario). Moreover, capital levels have been consistently high over the last five years.

Other Rating Factors: High quality investment portfolio (7.3). Excellent liquidity (7.3).

Principal Business: Reinsurance (56%), individual health insurance (28%), group life insurance (15%), and group health insurance (1%).

Principal Investments: NonCMO investment grade bonds (69%), CMOs and structured securities (26%), and noninv. grade bonds (4%).

Investments in Affiliates: None

Group Affiliation: Humana Inc

Licensed in: CA, CO, KY, TX

Commenced Business: January 2001

Address: 500 WEST MAIN STREET, LOUISVILLE, KY 40202

Phone: (502) 580-1000   **Domicile State:** KY   **NAIC Code:** 60219

Data Date	Rating	RACR #1	RACR #2	Total Assets ($mil)	Capital ($mil)	Net Premium ($mil)	Net Income ($mil)
9-18	B	6.80	5.00	209.8	180.8	102.3	15.9
9-17	C	6.51	4.69	214.6	169.2	94.2	19.3
2017	B-	6.34	4.65	215.3	164.9	126.5	17.3
2016	C	6.43	4.69	204.5	149.9	90.9	37.4
2015	C	2.61	1.95	432.9	122.2	269.9	-2.8
2014	B-	2.71	2.11	418.0	107.6	157.8	-5.8
2013	B-	2.03	1.57	108.6	61.1	111.5	15.7

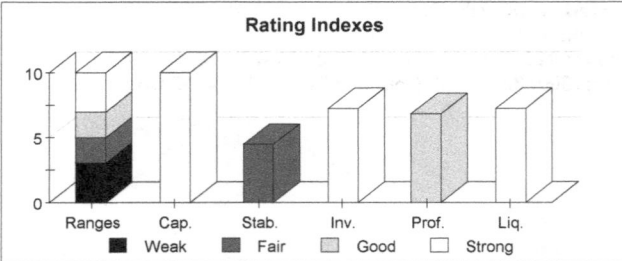

Rating Indexes

HUMANA INSURANCE COMPANY OF PUERTO RICO INCORPOR/   C+   Fair

Major Rating Factors: Fair overall results on stability tests (4.8 on a scale of 0 to 10). Good liquidity (6.6) with sufficient resources to handle a spike in claims. Weak profitability (2.5) with operating losses during the first nine months of 2018.
Other Rating Factors: Strong capitalization (8.1) based on excellent risk adjusted capital (severe loss scenario). High quality investment portfolio (8.3).
Principal Business: Group health insurance (89%) and individual health insurance (11%).
Principal Investments: NonCMO investment grade bonds (51%), CMOs and structured securities (32%), and noninv. grade bonds (3%).
Investments in Affiliates: None
Group Affiliation: Humana Inc
Licensed in: PR
Commenced Business: September 1971
Address: 383 FD ROOSEVELT AVENUE, SAN JUAN, PR 00918-2131
Phone: (787) 282-7900   **Domicile State:** PR   **NAIC Code:** 84603

Data Date	Rating	RACR #1	RACR #2	Total Assets ($mil)	Capital ($mil)	Net Premium ($mil)	Net Income ($mil)
9-18	C+	2.12	1.70	77.8	46.1	98.5	-4.4
9-17	B-	2.28	1.82	73.9	50.9	97.7	5.0
2017	B-	2.18	1.74	77.0	49.4	130.9	4.4
2016	C+	2.29	1.84	67.3	46.2	110.8	-4.4
2015	B-	2.85	2.28	69.3	51.2	96.9	1.5
2014	B-	2.80	2.22	70.2	49.8	93.3	-6.6
2013	B-	3.20	2.52	73.3	57.0	93.2	4.7

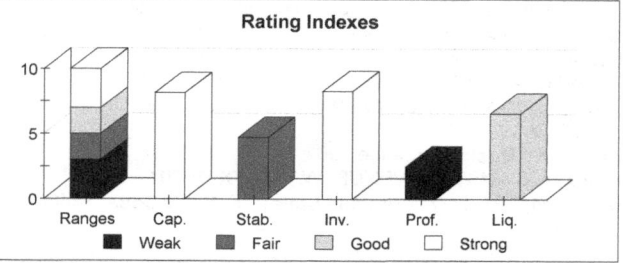

Rating Indexes

ILLINOIS MUTUAL LIFE INSURANCE COMPANY   B   Good

Major Rating Factors: Good quality investment portfolio (6.5 on a scale of 0 to 10) despite mixed results such as: minimal exposure to mortgages and large holdings of BBB rated bonds but small junk bond holdings. Good overall profitability (5.9). Good liquidity (6.5) with sufficient resources to handle a spike in claims as well as a significant increase in policy surrenders.
Other Rating Factors: Good overall results on stability tests (6.2) excellent operational trends and excellent risk diversification. Strong capitalization (8.7) based on excellent risk adjusted capital (severe loss scenario).
Principal Business: Individual life insurance (50%), individual health insurance (47%), group health insurance (2%), and individual annuities (1%).
Principal Investments: NonCMO investment grade bonds (62%), CMOs and structured securities (24%), common & preferred stock (4%), noninv. grade bonds (3%), and misc. investments (5%).
Investments in Affiliates: None
Group Affiliation: None
Licensed in: All states except AK, DC, HI, NY, PR
Commenced Business: July 1912
Address: 300 SW Adams Street, Peoria, IL 61634
Phone: (309) 674-8255   **Domicile State:** IL   **NAIC Code:** 64580

Data Date	Rating	RACR #1	RACR #2	Total Assets ($mil)	Capital ($mil)	Net Premium ($mil)	Net Income ($mil)
9-18	B	3.82	2.14	1,447.8	240.3	77.2	14.3
9-17	B	3.77	2.13	1,444.5	232.7	80.2	9.3
2017	B	3.74	2.12	1,442.3	229.8	105.4	12.7
2016	B	3.70	2.08	1,434.3	226.0	102.8	9.4
2015	A-	3.53	1.99	1,388.9	211.7	100.3	14.8
2014	A-	3.27	1.84	1,367.7	196.3	100.5	28.2
2013	A-	3.57	2.05	1,329.4	173.7	104.2	26.7

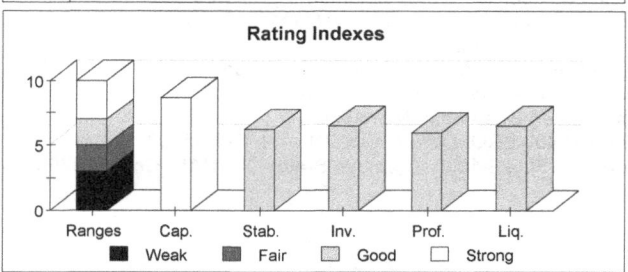

Rating Indexes

INDEPENDENCE LIFE & ANNUITY COMPANY   D   Weak

Major Rating Factors: Weak overall results on stability tests (2.1 on a scale of 0 to 10) including potential financial drain due to affiliation with Sun Life Assurance Group. Fair overall capitalization (4.0) based on mixed results -- excessive policy leverage mitigated by excellent risk adjusted capital (severe loss scenario). However, capital levels have fluctuated somewhat during past years. Good overall profitability (6.5).
Other Rating Factors: Good liquidity (6.9). High quality investment portfolio (7.9).
Principal Business: Reinsurance (100%).
Principal Investments: NonCMO investment grade bonds (48%), CMOs and structured securities (40%), policy loans (7%), and noninv. grade bonds (1%).
Investments in Affiliates: None
Group Affiliation: Sun Life Assurance Group
Licensed in: All states except NY, PR
Commenced Business: November 1945
Address: 1209 Orange Street, Wilmington, DE 19801
Phone: (781) 237-6030   **Domicile State:** DE   **NAIC Code:** 64602

Data Date	Rating	RACR #1	RACR #2	Total Assets ($mil)	Capital ($mil)	Net Premium ($mil)	Net Income ($mil)
9-18	D	4.55	3.51	3,172.7	164.5	-0.3	3.1
9-17	D	5.29	4.01	3,139.9	185.6	-0.3	2.8
2017	D	4.47	3.19	3,144.3	161.3	-0.4	3.8
2016	D-	5.21	3.69	3,028.0	182.8	-0.4	3.6
2015	C	5.33	3.55	2,862.7	179.3	-0.4	3.0
2014	C	4.01	2.60	2,639.5	126.5	-0.4	-1.3
2013	C	4.48	2.72	2,284.3	127.3	-0.4	1.2

Sun Life Assurance Group Composite Group Rating: D- Largest Group Members	Assets ($mil)	Rating
SUN LIFE ASR CO OF CANADA	19086	D-
INDEPENDENCE LIFE ANNUITY CO	3144	D
SUN LIFE HEALTH INS CO	943	D
PROFESSIONAL INS CO	110	D

INDUSTRIAL ALLIANCE INS & FIN SERV   C   Fair

Major Rating Factors: Fair overall results on stability tests (4.0 on a scale of 0 to 10). Good quality investment portfolio (5.8) despite mixed results such as: minimal exposure to mortgages and large holdings of BBB rated bonds but no exposure to junk bonds. Good liquidity (5.7) with sufficient resources to cover a large increase in policy surrenders.

Other Rating Factors: Weak profitability (2.9) with investment income below regulatory standards in relation to interest assumptions of reserves. Strong capitalization (10.0) based on excellent risk adjusted capital (severe loss scenario).

Principal Business: Reinsurance (86%), individual life insurance (9%), and individual annuities (5%).

Principal Investments: NonCMO investment grade bonds (91%), real estate (4%), policy loans (2%), nonperforming mortgages (2%), and cash (1%).

Investments in Affiliates: None

Group Affiliation: Industrial Alliance Ins & Financial

Licensed in: AK, AZ, AR, CA, CO, GA, HI, ID, IL, IN, IA, KS, KY, LA, ME, MD, MA, MI, MS, MO, MT, NE, NV, NH, NJ, NM, OH, OK, OR, PA, SC, TN, TX, UT, VA, WA, WV, WI, WY

Commenced Business: June 1967

Address: 425 AUSTIN AVENUE, WACO, TX 76701

Phone: (254) 297-2777 **Domicile State:** TX **NAIC Code:** 14406

Data Date	Rating	RACR #1	RACR #2	Total Assets ($mil)	Capital ($mil)	Net Premium ($mil)	Net Income ($mil)
9-18	C	5.69	3.33	272.5	65.7	54.6	11.4
9-17	C-	3.85	2.26	239.7	48.1	53.8	5.1
2017	C-	4.15	2.44	246.9	52.0	70.2	7.4
2016	C-	3.51	2.05	220.7	43.0	70.3	-2.3
2015	C-	3.67	2.18	202.4	44.8	71.4	-10.0
2014	C	4.59	2.73	193.7	59.6	54.4	-0.7
2013	C	5.59	3.22	200.7	73.2	31.7	-18.5

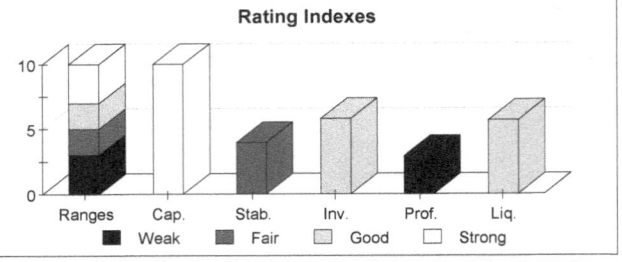

Rating Indexes

INTEGRITY LIFE INSURANCE COMPANY   B-   Good

Major Rating Factors: Good quality investment portfolio (5.0 on a scale of 0 to 10) despite mixed results such as: large holdings of BBB rated bonds but moderate junk bond exposure. Good overall results on stability tests (5.0). Strengths include good financial support from affiliation with Western & Southern Group, good operational trends and excellent risk diversification. Weak profitability (2.9) with investment income below regulatory standards in relation to interest assumptions of reserves.

Other Rating Factors: Strong capitalization (7.3) based on excellent risk adjusted capital (severe loss scenario). Excellent liquidity (7.5).

Principal Business: Individual annuities (100%).

Principal Investments: NonCMO investment grade bonds (43%), CMOs and structured securities (29%), common & preferred stock (9%), mortgages in good standing (7%), and misc. investments (11%).

Investments in Affiliates: 6%

Group Affiliation: Western & Southern Group

Licensed in: All states except NY, PR

Commenced Business: May 1966

Address: 400 BROADWAY, CINCINNATI, OH 45202

Phone: (513) 629-1800 **Domicile State:** OH **NAIC Code:** 74780

Data Date	Rating	RACR #1	RACR #2	Total Assets ($mil)	Capital ($mil)	Net Premium ($mil)	Net Income ($mil)
9-18	B-	1.82	1.19	9,713.5	1,147.9	481.5	4.8
9-17	B-	1.54	1.06	8,960.3	905.7	653.9	20.6
2017	B-	1.58	1.05	9,210.2	875.8	845.7	21.1
2016	B-	1.46	1.03	7,999.6	808.3	1,201.8	115.9
2015	B-	1.36	1.00	6,844.3	678.6	1,101.2	67.2
2014	B-	1.35	1.03	6,107.1	663.8	407.5	57.0
2013	B-	1.52	1.12	6,056.7	668.0	249.8	42.2

Western Southern Group Composite Group Rating: B Largest Group Members	Assets ($mil)	Rating
WESTERN-SOUTHERN LIFE ASR CO	12452	B
WESTERN SOUTHERN LIFE INS CO	10551	B
INTEGRITY LIFE INS CO	9210	B-
LAFAYETTE LIFE INS CO	5436	B
NATIONAL INTEGRITY LIFE INS CO	4641	B-

INVESTORS HERITAGE LIFE INSURANCE COMPANY   C+   Fair

Major Rating Factors: Fair quality investment portfolio (4.9 on a scale of 0 to 10). Fair profitability (4.2) with investment income below regulatory standards in relation to interest assumptions of reserves. Fair liquidity (3.2) as cash from operations and sale of marketable assets may not be adequate to cover a spike in claims or a run on policy withdrawals.

Other Rating Factors: Fair overall results on stability tests (4.6) including fair risk adjusted capital in prior years. Strong capitalization (7.0) based on excellent risk adjusted capital (severe loss scenario).

Principal Business: Individual life insurance (80%), individual annuities (7%), credit life insurance (7%), credit health insurance (5%), and reinsurance (1%).

Principal Investments: NonCMO investment grade bonds (68%), CMOs and structured securities (15%), mortgages in good standing (9%), common & preferred stock (3%), and misc. investments (5%).

Investments in Affiliates: 2%

Group Affiliation: Investors Heritage Capital Corp

Licensed in: AL, AZ, AR, CA, CO, FL, GA, IL, IN, IA, KS, KY, LA, ME, MD, MA, MI, MN, MS, MO, MT, NE, NH, NM, NC, ND, OH, OK, PA, SC, SD, TN, TX, UT, VT, VA, WV, WI

Commenced Business: March 1961

Address: 200 CAPITAL AVENUE, FRANKFORT, KY 40601

Phone: (502) 223-2361 **Domicile State:** KY **NAIC Code:** 64904

Data Date	Rating	RACR #1	RACR #2	Total Assets ($mil)	Capital ($mil)	Net Premium ($mil)	Net Income ($mil)
9-18	C+	1.56	1.01	466.9	39.3	33.2	9.5
9-17	C	1.35	0.78	453.0	26.7	32.5	0.3
2017	C	1.22	0.79	454.2	29.4	42.7	1.3
2016	C	1.33	0.78	449.0	26.0	44.8	2.1
2015	C	1.06	0.62	485.7	21.2	48.8	1.3
2014	C	1.05	0.63	482.8	20.9	52.4	0.8
2013	C	1.01	0.60	471.9	20.2	60.7	1.2

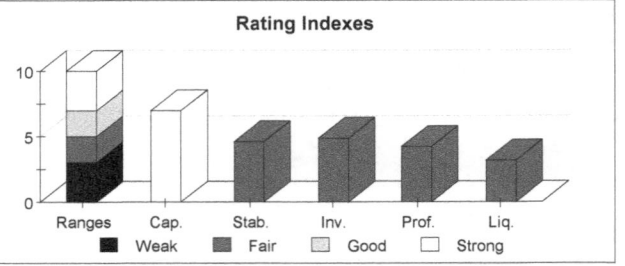

Rating Indexes

INVESTORS LIFE INSURANCE COMPANY NORTH AMERICA — B — Good

Major Rating Factors: Good overall results on stability tests (6.1 on a scale of 0 to 10) despite negative cash flow from operations for 2017. Other stability subfactors include good operational trends, excellent risk adjusted capital for prior years and excellent risk diversification. Good quality investment portfolio (5.2) despite mixed results such as: large holdings of BBB rated bonds but moderate junk bond exposure. Good liquidity (5.9).

Other Rating Factors: Fair overall capitalization (4.0) based on mixed results -- excessive policy leverage mitigated by excellent risk adjusted capital (severe loss scenario). Excellent profitability (7.4).

Principal Business: Individual life insurance (99%) and individual annuities (1%).

Principal Investments: NonCMO investment grade bonds (48%), CMOs and structured securities (35%), common & preferred stock (7%), policy loans (4%), and noninv. grade bonds (4%).

Investments in Affiliates: 1%

Group Affiliation: Americo Life Inc

Licensed in: All states except NY, PR

Commenced Business: December 1963

Address: PO Box 139061, Dallas, TX 75313-9061

Phone: (816) 391-2000 **Domicile State:** TX **NAIC Code:** 63487

Data Date	Rating	RACR #1	RACR #2	Total Assets ($mil)	Capital ($mil)	Net Premium ($mil)	Net Income ($mil)
9-18	B	2.99	1.62	597.6	58.8	0.0	0.7
9-17	B	2.97	1.62	606.7	56.7	-0.1	-0.1
2017	B	2.97	1.60	609.4	56.1	-0.1	1.0
2016	B	2.96	1.58	614.8	54.9	-0.1	0.4
2015	B	2.88	1.54	648.2	54.2	-0.1	1.7
2014	B	2.84	1.54	680.7	53.3	-0.1	2.8
2013	B-	2.45	1.25	691.3	49.2	-0.1	1.9

Adverse Trends in Operations

Increase in policy surrenders from 2016 to 2017 (35%)
Decrease in asset base during 2016 (5%)
Decrease in premium volume from 2015 to 2016 (9%)
Decrease in asset base during 2015 (5%)
Decrease in asset base during 2014 (2%)

IOWA AMERICAN LIFE INSURANCE COMPANY — C+ — Fair

Major Rating Factors: Fair overall results on stability tests (4.8 on a scale of 0 to 10) including fair financial strength of affiliated Industrial Alliance Ins & Financial. Fair current capitalization (4.8) based on fair risk adjusted capital (severe loss scenario), although results have slipped from the good range during the last year. Fair quality investment portfolio (4.5).

Other Rating Factors: Fair profitability (3.5) with operating losses during the first nine months of 2018. Good liquidity (6.5).

Principal Business: Individual life insurance (84%), reinsurance (12%), individual health insurance (2%), and individual annuities (2%).

Principal Investments: NonCMO investment grade bonds (53%), common & preferred stock (39%), policy loans (4%), cash (2%), and mortgages in good standing (1%).

Investments in Affiliates: 47%

Group Affiliation: Industrial Alliance Ins & Financial

Licensed in: All states except NY, PR

Commenced Business: May 1980

Address: 425 AUSTIN AVENUE, WACO, TX 76701

Phone: (254) 297-2777 **Domicile State:** TX **NAIC Code:** 91693

Data Date	Rating	RACR #1	RACR #2	Total Assets ($mil)	Capital ($mil)	Net Premium ($mil)	Net Income ($mil)
9-18	C+	0.81	0.73	140.8	40.0	19.5	-0.2
9-17	C+	1.06	0.97	159.9	62.9	16.2	0.9
2017	C+	0.82	0.79	148.4	50.1	21.6	0.8
2016	C	0.95	0.94	165.4	69.2	17.7	35.2
2015	C	0.86	0.86	229.2	133.2	15.0	9.4
2014	C	0.85	0.86	241.4	141.1	11.4	-4.3
2013	C-	0.75	0.78	218.1	124.6	10.6	0.6

Industrial Alliance Ins Financial
Composite Group Rating: C

Largest Group Members	Assets ($mil)	Rating
AMERICAN-AMICABLE LIFE INS CO OF TX	298	C
OCCIDENTAL LIFE INS CO OF NC	258	C
INDUSTRIAL ALLIANCE INS FIN SERV	247	C
IA AMERICAN LIFE INS CO	148	C+
PIONEER SECURITY LIFE INS CO	81	C

JACKSON NATIONAL LIFE INSURANCE CO OF NEW YORK — B — Good

Major Rating Factors: Good overall results on stability tests (6.0 on a scale of 0 to 10) despite negative cash flow from operations for 2017. Other stability subfactors include excellent operational trends and excellent risk diversification. Good quality investment portfolio (5.4) despite mixed results such as: no exposure to mortgages and large holdings of BBB rated bonds but minimal holdings in junk bonds. Strong capitalization (10.0) based on excellent risk adjusted capital (severe loss scenario).

Other Rating Factors: Excellent profitability (8.4). Excellent liquidity (7.0).

Principal Business: Individual annuities (100%).

Principal Investments: NonCMO investment grade bonds (62%), CMOs and structured securities (25%), and noninv. grade bonds (4%).

Investments in Affiliates: None

Group Affiliation: Prudential plc

Licensed in: DE, MI, NY

Commenced Business: August 1996

Address: 2900 WESTCHESTER AVE STE 305, PURCHASE, NY 10577

Phone: (517) 381-5500 **Domicile State:** NY **NAIC Code:** 60140

Data Date	Rating	RACR #1	RACR #2	Total Assets ($mil)	Capital ($mil)	Net Premium ($mil)	Net Income ($mil)
9-18	B	4.73	2.97	13,730.6	580.6	105.7	28.4
9-17	B	4.85	2.79	12,328.7	544.9	107.7	51.3
2017	B	4.54	2.98	12,922.1	557.1	142.6	69.8
2016	B	4.29	2.28	11,769.9	475.7	132.3	23.6
2015	B	4.47	2.55	10,434.7	443.5	1,658.1	30.7
2014	B	4.46	2.55	9,608.5	409.8	1,766.8	32.7
2013	B	4.75	2.33	8,079.2	370.9	1,317.3	57.6

Adverse Trends in Operations

Decrease in premium volume from 2015 to 2016 (92%)
Decrease in premium volume from 2014 to 2015 (6%)

JACKSON NATIONAL LIFE INSURANCE COMPANY | B | Good

Major Rating Factors: Good current capitalization (6.3 on a scale of 0 to 10) based on good risk adjusted capital (severe loss scenario), although results have slipped from the excellent range over the last two years. Good quality investment portfolio (5.7) despite large holdings of BBB rated bonds in addition to moderate junk bond exposure. Exposure to mortgages is significant, but the mortgage default rate has been low. Good overall profitability (6.1).

Other Rating Factors: Good overall results on stability tests (6.0) good operational trends and excellent risk diversification. Excellent liquidity (7.7).

Principal Business: Individual annuities (76%), group retirement contracts (12%), reinsurance (7%), and individual life insurance (4%).

Principal Investments: NonCMO investment grade bonds (57%), mortgages in good standing (14%), CMOs and structured securities (12%), policy loans (7%), and misc. investments (5%).

Investments in Affiliates: 2%

Group Affiliation: Prudential plc

Licensed in: All states except NY, PR

Commenced Business: August 1961

Address: 1 CORPORATE WAY, LANSING, MI 48951

Phone: (517) 381-5500 **Domicile State:** MI **NAIC Code:** 65056

Data Date	Rating	RACR #1	RACR #2	Total Assets ($mil)	Capital ($mil)	Net Premium ($mil)	Net Income ($mil)
9-18	B	1.64	0.91	237,904	4,262.1	13,799.6	838.7
9-17	B+	1.76	0.97	222,617	4,304.2	14,000.1	380.0
2017	B	1.60	0.88	228,788	3,884.1	19,004.5	168.4
2016	B+	2.06	1.14	204,781	4,918.9	18,631.4	-563.8
2015	B+	2.07	1.13	189,097	4,718.5	23,650.6	627.0
2014	B+	2.00	1.08	180,834	4,486.1	23,578.6	878.3
2013	B+	2.00	1.06	163,834	4,353.8	22,736.2	741.3

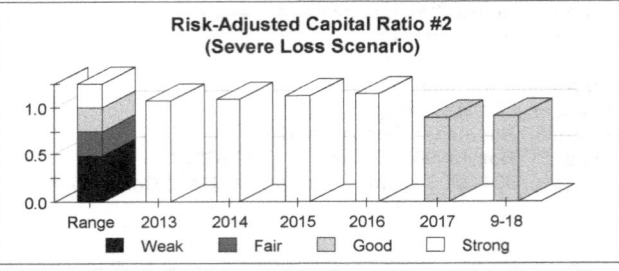

Risk-Adjusted Capital Ratio #2
(Severe Loss Scenario)

Range 2013 2014 2015 2016 2017 9-18
■ Weak ■ Fair ▨ Good ☐ Strong

JAMESTOWN LIFE INSURANCE COMPANY | B- | Good

Major Rating Factors: Good overall results on stability tests (5.1 on a scale of 0 to 10) despite fair financial strength of affiliated Genworth Financial. Other stability subfactors include good operational trends and excellent risk diversification. Strong capitalization (10.0) based on excellent risk adjusted capital (severe loss scenario). Capital levels have been relatively consistent over the last five years. High quality investment portfolio (7.3).

Other Rating Factors: Excellent profitability (7.0) despite modest operating losses during 2015 and 2017. Excellent liquidity (8.2).

Principal Business: Reinsurance (100%).

Principal Investments: NonCMO investment grade bonds (45%), CMOs and structured securities (26%), cash (10%), and noninv. grade bonds (1%).

Investments in Affiliates: None

Group Affiliation: Genworth Financial

Licensed in: VA

Commenced Business: December 1982

Address: 700 MAIN STREET, LYNCHBURG, VA 24504

Phone: (434) 845-0911 **Domicile State:** VA **NAIC Code:** 97144

Data Date	Rating	RACR #1	RACR #2	Total Assets ($mil)	Capital ($mil)	Net Premium ($mil)	Net Income ($mil)
9-18	B-	6.26	5.64	127.3	57.7	0.8	2.0
9-17	B	6.72	6.04	128.0	61.6	0.9	1.0
2017	B	6.51	5.86	128.7	59.9	1.1	-0.6
2016	B	6.60	5.94	125.5	60.5	1.3	25.1
2015	B	3.87	2.81	148.3	36.0	4.9	-1.3
2014	B	3.97	2.89	145.0	36.7	5.1	3.1
2013	B	3.59	2.68	141.1	33.0	5.5	2.2

Genworth Financial
Composite Group Rating: C

Largest Group Members	Assets ($mil)	Rating
GENWORTH LIFE INS CO	40012	C+
GENWORTH LIFE ANNUITY INS CO	22445	C-
GENWORTH LIFE INS CO OF NEW YORK	7986	C
GENWORTH MORTGAGE INS CORP	3346	C
RIVERMONT LIFE INS CO I	594	C

JEFFERSON NATIONAL LIFE INSURANCE COMPANY | C | Fair

Major Rating Factors: Fair current capitalization (4.7 on a scale of 0 to 10) based on mixed results -- excessive policy leverage mitigated by fair risk adjusted capital (moderate loss scenario), although results have slipped from the good range over the last two years. Fair profitability (4.6). Excellent expense controls. Fair overall results on stability tests (4.2) including negative cash flow from operations for 2017, fair risk adjusted capital in prior years.

Other Rating Factors: Good quality investment portfolio (6.1). Excellent liquidity (7.0).

Principal Business: Individual annuities (98%) and individual life insurance (1%).

Principal Investments: NonCMO investment grade bonds (52%), CMOs and structured securities (33%), common & preferred stock (4%), noninv. grade bonds (3%), and misc. investments (6%).

Investments in Affiliates: 1%

Group Affiliation: Nationwide Mutual Group

Licensed in: All states except NY, PR

Commenced Business: February 1937

Address: 350 NORTH ST PAUL STREET, DALLAS, TX 75201

Phone: (866) 667-0561 **Domicile State:** TX **NAIC Code:** 64017

Data Date	Rating	RACR #1	RACR #2	Total Assets ($mil)	Capital ($mil)	Net Premium ($mil)	Net Income ($mil)
9-18	C	0.96	0.57	6,534.9	42.4	900.0	6.4
9-17	C	1.08	0.58	5,474.3	38.2	757.4	-0.8
2017	C	0.84	0.52	5,816.9	34.7	1,049.4	-0.2
2016	C-	1.10	0.64	4,610.6	39.0	713.5	0.3
2015	C-	1.18	0.63	4,058.0	38.3	789.0	-0.8
2014	C-	1.33	0.71	3,714.0	39.8	795.2	-2.9
2013	C-	1.55	0.78	3,053.5	39.4	740.9	-1.1

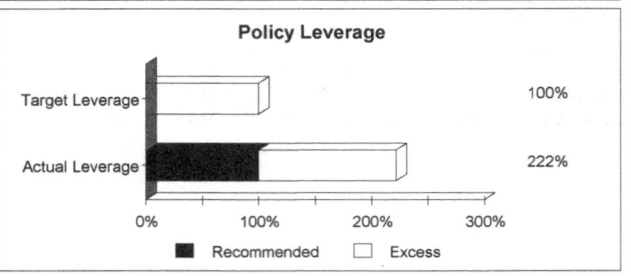

Policy Leverage

Target Leverage — 100%
Actual Leverage — 222%

0% 100% 200% 300%
■ Recommended ☐ Excess

JOHN HANCOCK LIFE & HEALTH INSURANCE COMPANY ‎ B ‎ Good

Major Rating Factors: Good quality investment portfolio (5.2 on a scale of 0 to 10) with minimal exposure to mortgages and minimal holdings in junk bonds. Fair overall results on stability tests (4.0). Strong capitalization (8.4) based on excellent risk adjusted capital (severe loss scenario). Capital levels have been relatively consistent over the last five years.

Other Rating Factors: Excellent profitability (8.9). Excellent liquidity (9.1).

Principal Business: Group health insurance (76%), individual health insurance (21%), and reinsurance (4%).

Principal Investments: NonCMO investment grade bonds (57%), mortgages in good standing (7%), CMOs and structured securities (5%), real estate (3%), and misc. investments (20%).

Investments in Affiliates: 1%

Group Affiliation: Manulife Financial Group

Licensed in: All states, the District of Columbia and Puerto Rico

Commenced Business: October 1981

Address: 197 Clarendon Street, Boston, MA 02116-5010

Phone: (617) 572-6000 **Domicile State:** MA **NAIC Code:** 93610

Data Date	Rating	RACR #1	RACR #2	Total Assets ($mil)	Capital ($mil)	Net Premium ($mil)	Net Income ($mil)
9-18	B	3.54	1.91	13,974.9	929.6	515.4	104.7
9-17	B	2.90	1.65	12,953.4	805.5	513.9	90.2
2017	B	3.56	1.95	14,006.8	891.9	686.5	104.6
2016	B	3.12	1.71	11,875.2	723.6	351.9	101.6
2015	B	3.22	1.76	11,150.5	704.6	575.4	40.3
2014	B	3.85	2.14	10,700.1	745.8	576.0	2.8
2013	B	3.05	1.81	9,737.6	682.7	565.5	82.4

Rating Indexes

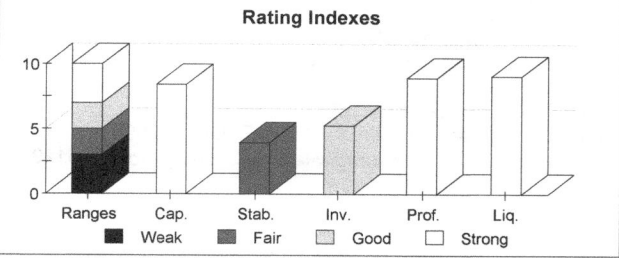

JOHN HANCOCK LIFE INSURANCE COMPANY (USA) ‎ B ‎ Good

Major Rating Factors: Good overall profitability (6.1 on a scale of 0 to 10). Good overall results on stability tests (6.1) despite fair risk adjusted capital in prior years. Other stability subfactors include good operational trends and excellent risk diversification. Fair quality investment portfolio (4.4) with significant exposure to mortgages . Mortgage default rate has been low.

Other Rating Factors: Strong capitalization (7.1) based on excellent risk adjusted capital (severe loss scenario). Excellent liquidity (7.2).

Principal Business: Group retirement contracts (68%), individual life insurance (21%), individual health insurance (6%), reinsurance (3%), and group health insurance (2%).

Principal Investments: NonCMO investment grade bonds (46%), mortgages in good standing (12%), CMOs and structured securities (7%), real estate (6%), and misc. investments (19%).

Investments in Affiliates: 5%

Group Affiliation: Manulife Financial Group

Licensed in: All states except NY

Commenced Business: January 1956

Address: 201 Townsend Street Suite 900, Lansing, MI 48933

Phone: (617) 663-3000 **Domicile State:** MI **NAIC Code:** 65838

Data Date	Rating	RACR #1	RACR #2	Total Assets ($mil)	Capital ($mil)	Net Premium ($mil)	Net Income ($mil)
9-18	B	1.76	1.08	240,601	9,115.0	7,405.7	2,141.3
9-17	B	1.33	0.85	240,367	7,581.6	10,866.5	1,073.2
2017	B	1.60	0.98	242,823	8,109.4	18,286.5	1,898.9
2016	B	1.16	0.74	229,892	6,153.7	13,226.6	29.3
2015	B	0.87	0.58	227,843	5,443.8	16,323.5	694.1
2014	B	1.11	0.71	245,892	5,328.3	12,738.4	-2,464.4
2013	B	0.97	0.62	239,096	5,809.2	12,881.7	3,015.4

Adverse Trends in Operations

Increase in policy surrenders from 2016 to 2017 (26%)
Decrease in premium volume from 2015 to 2016 (19%)
Decrease in asset base during 2015 (7%)
Decrease in premium volume from 2013 to 2014 (1%)
Decrease in capital during 2014 (8%)

JOHN HANCOCK LIFE INSURANCE COMPANY OF NEW YORK ‎ B ‎ Good

Major Rating Factors: Good quality investment portfolio (5.9 on a scale of 0 to 10) with minimal exposure to mortgages and small junk bond holdings. Good liquidity (6.6) with sufficient resources to handle a spike in claims as well as a significant increase in policy surrenders. Fair profitability (3.0) with investment income below regulatory standards in relation to interest assumptions of reserves.

Other Rating Factors: Fair overall results on stability tests (4.3). Strong capitalization (8.6) based on excellent risk adjusted capital (severe loss scenario).

Principal Business: Group retirement contracts (58%), individual life insurance (25%), reinsurance (16%), and individual annuities (1%).

Principal Investments: NonCMO investment grade bonds (57%), mortgages in good standing (10%), CMOs and structured securities (5%), real estate (3%), and misc. investments (16%).

Investments in Affiliates: None

Group Affiliation: Manulife Financial Group

Licensed in: MI, NY

Commenced Business: July 1992

Address: 100 Summit Lake Drive 2nd Fl, Valhalla, NY 10595

Phone: (800) 344-1029 **Domicile State:** NY **NAIC Code:** 86375

Data Date	Rating	RACR #1	RACR #2	Total Assets ($mil)	Capital ($mil)	Net Premium ($mil)	Net Income ($mil)
9-18	B	4.03	2.07	17,266.2	1,474.5	810.7	223.9
9-17	B	3.51	1.89	17,497.1	1,479.9	786.5	97.2
2017	B	4.08	2.10	17,574.1	1,482.5	1,072.9	84.7
2016	B	3.40	1.83	16,707.1	1,404.9	1,529.9	80.2
2015	B+	4.21	2.16	16,390.2	1,310.3	1,751.4	-18.2
2014	A-	4.27	2.08	17,475.5	1,215.7	1,041.4	-232.1
2013	A-	2.77	1.62	17,315.6	1,284.3	1,043.3	465.8

Rating Indexes

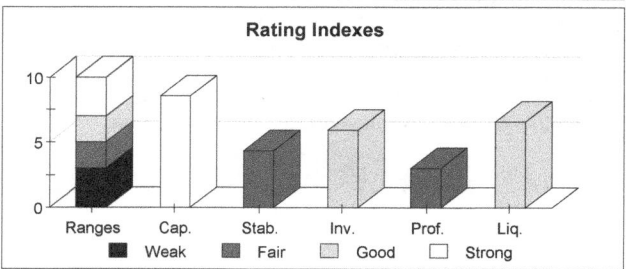

KANSAS CITY LIFE INSURANCE COMPANY | B | Good

Major Rating Factors: Good overall profitability (5.6 on a scale of 0 to 10). Good liquidity (5.7) with sufficient resources to cover a large increase in policy surrenders. Good overall results on stability tests (5.9). Stability strengths include excellent operational trends, good risk adjusted capital for prior years and excellent risk diversification.

Other Rating Factors: Fair quality investment portfolio (4.5). Strong capitalization (7.1) based on excellent risk adjusted capital (severe loss scenario).

Principal Business: Individual life insurance (38%), individual annuities (33%), group health insurance (16%), reinsurance (8%), and group life insurance (4%).

Principal Investments: NonCMO investment grade bonds (63%), mortgages in good standing (19%), real estate (5%), CMOs and structured securities (4%), and misc. investments (8%).

Investments in Affiliates: 2%
Group Affiliation: Kansas City Life Group
Licensed in: All states except NY, VT, PR
Commenced Business: May 1895
Address: 3520 Broadway, Kansas City, MO 64111-2565
Phone: (816) 753-7000 **Domicile State:** MO **NAIC Code:** 65129

Data Date	Rating	RACR #1	RACR #2	Total Assets ($mil)	Capital ($mil)	Net Premium ($mil)	Net Income ($mil)
9-18	B	1.80	1.04	3,401.6	289.8	214.0	8.3
9-17	B	1.44	0.88	3,415.5	323.1	222.9	13.4
2017	B	1.88	1.07	3,411.3	307.5	300.7	16.0
2016	B	1.50	0.92	3,359.1	323.3	287.6	12.5
2015	B	1.86	1.09	3,324.3	297.6	282.8	29.1
2014	B	1.51	0.94	3,402.1	338.4	303.4	26.7
2013	B	1.74	1.08	3,386.4	330.6	329.4	0.3

Adverse Trends in Operations

Decrease in capital during 2017 (5%)
Decrease in premium volume from 2014 to 2015 (7%)
Decrease in asset base during 2015 (2%)
Decrease in capital during 2015 (12%)
Decrease in premium volume from 2013 to 2014 (8%)

LAFAYETTE LIFE INSURANCE COMPANY | B | Good

Major Rating Factors: Good overall results on stability tests (5.6 on a scale of 0 to 10). Stability strengths include excellent operational trends and excellent risk diversification. Good capitalization (6.1) based on good risk adjusted capital (moderate loss scenario). Moreover, capital levels have been consistent over the last five years. Good overall profitability (6.1).

Other Rating Factors: Good liquidity (5.4). Fair quality investment portfolio (4.6).

Principal Business: Individual life insurance (73%), individual annuities (24%), and group retirement contracts (3%).

Principal Investments: NonCMO investment grade bonds (49%), CMOs and structured securities (17%), policy loans (10%), mortgages in good standing (9%), and misc. investments (12%).

Investments in Affiliates: 1%
Group Affiliation: Western & Southern Group
Licensed in: All states except NY, PR
Commenced Business: December 1905
Address: 301 EAST 4TH STREET, CINCINNATI, OH 45202
Phone: (513) 362-4900 **Domicile State:** OH **NAIC Code:** 65242

Data Date	Rating	RACR #1	RACR #2	Total Assets ($mil)	Capital ($mil)	Net Premium ($mil)	Net Income ($mil)
9-18	B	1.75	0.87	5,572.4	318.2	421.7	8.5
9-17	B	1.88	0.94	5,367.2	303.4	418.1	8.3
2017	B	1.80	0.90	5,435.9	318.0	558.4	3.3
2016	B	1.87	0.93	4,911.4	288.7	569.5	2.9
2015	B	1.85	0.93	4,548.1	261.4	532.9	32.9
2014	B	1.67	0.85	4,067.8	204.4	536.8	8.9
2013	B	1.70	0.88	3,836.5	193.7	593.3	-7.8

Adverse Trends in Operations

Decrease in premium volume from 2016 to 2017 (2%)
Increase in policy surrenders from 2013 to 2014 (26%)
Decrease in premium volume from 2013 to 2014 (10%)

LIBERTY BANKERS LIFE INSURANCE COMPANY | D+ | Weak

Major Rating Factors: Weak overall results on stability tests (2.8 on a scale of 0 to 10). Fair quality investment portfolio (3.7) with significant exposure to mortgages. Mortgage default rate has been low. Good overall capitalization (5.1) based on good risk adjusted capital (moderate loss scenario). However, capital levels have fluctuated somewhat during past years.

Other Rating Factors: Good overall profitability (6.6). Good liquidity (6.3).

Principal Business: Individual annuities (67%), reinsurance (20%), individual life insurance (12%), and individual health insurance (1%).

Principal Investments: NonCMO investment grade bonds (53%), mortgages in good standing (22%), common & preferred stock (10%), real estate (4%), and misc. investments (11%).

Investments in Affiliates: 7%
Group Affiliation: Liberty Life Group Trust
Licensed in: All states except AL, MN, NY, PR
Commenced Business: February 1958
Address: 1605 LBJ Freeway Suite 710, Dallas, TX 75234
Phone: (469) 522-4400 **Domicile State:** OK **NAIC Code:** 68543

Data Date	Rating	RACR #1	RACR #2	Total Assets ($mil)	Capital ($mil)	Net Premium ($mil)	Net Income ($mil)
9-18	D+	1.08	0.73	1,974.6	203.8	207.2	8.7
9-17	D+	1.20	0.79	1,678.4	203.1	189.8	7.4
2017	D+	1.14	0.80	1,711.6	201.9	305.5	9.2
2016	D+	1.29	0.90	1,547.6	204.9	280.6	6.6
2015	D+	1.30	0.91	1,356.1	197.9	326.4	9.0
2014	D+	1.47	1.01	1,141.4	195.5	234.5	11.5
2013	D+	1.23	0.84	1,035.3	168.0	205.5	10.3

Rating Indexes

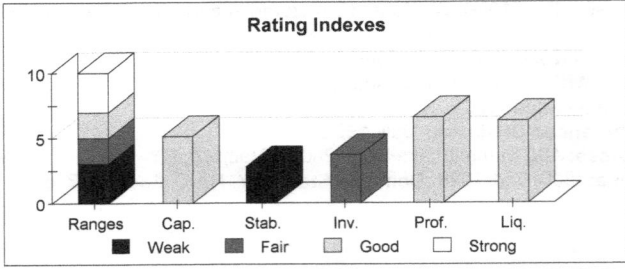

LIBERTY LIFE ASSURANCE COMPANY OF BOSTON B- Good

Major Rating Factors: Good overall profitability (5.2 on a scale of 0 to 10) although investment income, in comparison to reserve requirements, is below regulatory standards. Good liquidity (6.1) with sufficient resources to cover a large increase in policy surrenders. Fair quality investment portfolio (3.1).

Other Rating Factors: Fair overall results on stability tests (4.7). Strong capitalization (7.1) based on excellent risk adjusted capital (severe loss scenario).

Principal Business: Group health insurance (37%), individual annuities (25%), group life insurance (19%), and individual life insurance (19%).

Principal Investments: NonCMO investment grade bonds (77%), CMOs and structured securities (8%), mortgages in good standing (6%), noninv. grade bonds (3%), and policy loans (1%).

Investments in Affiliates: None

Group Affiliation: Liberty Mutual Group

Licensed in: All states except PR

Commenced Business: January 1964

Address: 175 Berkeley Street, Radnor, PA 19087

Phone: (484) 583-1400 **Domicile State:** NH **NAIC Code:** 65315

Data Date	Rating	RACR #1	RACR #2	Total Assets ($mil)	Capital ($mil)	Net Premium ($mil)	Net Income ($mil)
9-18	B-	1.80	1.07	4,034.0	526.3	-14,185.6	141.6
9-17	B	1.88	1.09	18,681.2	1,174.7	2,272.4	21.4
2017	B	1.96	1.14	19,045.9	1,336.7	2,929.6	50.6
2016	B	1.90	1.11	17,479.3	1,161.0	2,714.5	5.3
2015	B	1.77	1.04	16,054.1	966.4	2,501.1	69.9
2014	B	1.88	1.09	14,628.8	902.4	2,410.6	37.0
2013	B	1.83	1.07	13,115.1	716.9	2,095.9	39.2

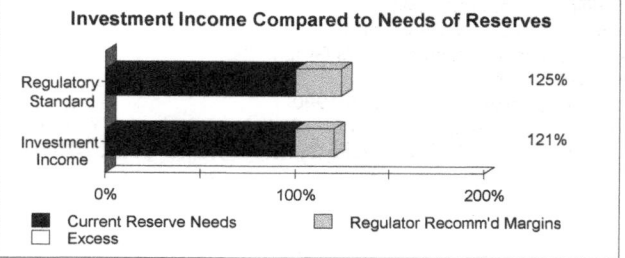

Investment Income Compared to Needs of Reserves

Regulatory Standard — 125%

Investment Income — 121%

0%   100%   200%

■ Current Reserve Needs   ■ Regulator Recomm'd Margins
□ Excess

LIBERTY NATIONAL LIFE INSURANCE COMPANY B Good

Major Rating Factors: Good overall results on stability tests (5.7 on a scale of 0 to 10). Stability strengths include excellent operational trends, excellent risk adjusted capital for prior years and excellent risk diversification. Good current capitalization (6.4) based on good risk adjusted capital (severe loss scenario), although results have slipped from the excellent range during the last year. Good overall profitability (6.0) although investment income, in comparison to reserve requirements, is below regulatory standards.

Other Rating Factors: Fair quality investment portfolio (4.2). Fair liquidity (4.4).

Principal Business: Individual life insurance (39%), reinsurance (37%), individual health insurance (15%), group life insurance (7%), and individual annuities (1%).

Principal Investments: NonCMO investment grade bonds (77%), noninv. grade bonds (6%), common & preferred stock (4%), policy loans (4%), and CMOs and structured securities (1%).

Investments in Affiliates: 8%

Group Affiliation: Torchmark Corp

Licensed in: All states except NY, PR

Commenced Business: July 1929

Address: 10306 REGENCY PARKWAY DR, OMAHA, NE 68114

Phone: (205) 325-4918 **Domicile State:** NE **NAIC Code:** 65331

Data Date	Rating	RACR #1	RACR #2	Total Assets ($mil)	Capital ($mil)	Net Premium ($mil)	Net Income ($mil)
9-18	B	1.75	0.92	7,484.1	477.6	661.7	85.4
9-17	B	1.89	0.98	7,474.5	551.7	609.0	90.1
2017	B	1.91	1.00	7,411.6	542.3	819.7	132.8
2016	B	1.96	1.02	7,820.8	573.7	761.9	131.3
2015	B	1.90	1.00	7,559.6	525.8	626.5	73.9
2014	B	2.13	1.13	7,419.6	578.5	575.3	164.7
2013	B	2.16	1.13	7,257.9	589.7	565.9	151.1

Adverse Trends in Operations

Decrease in asset base during 2017 (5%)
Decrease in capital during 2017 (5%)
Decrease in capital during 2015 (9%)
Decrease in capital during 2014 (2%)

LIFE INSURANCE COMPANY OF ALABAMA B Good

Major Rating Factors: Good overall profitability (6.7 on a scale of 0 to 10) despite operating losses during the first nine months of 2018. Good liquidity (6.4) with sufficient resources to handle a spike in claims. Good overall results on stability tests (5.7). Stability strengths include excellent operational trends and good risk diversification.

Other Rating Factors: Fair quality investment portfolio (4.2). Strong capitalization (9.0) based on excellent risk adjusted capital (severe loss scenario).

Principal Business: Individual health insurance (73%), individual life insurance (19%), and group health insurance (8%).

Principal Investments: NonCMO investment grade bonds (79%), noninv. grade bonds (9%), common & preferred stock (6%), policy loans (3%), and misc. investments (2%).

Investments in Affiliates: None

Group Affiliation: None

Licensed in: AL, AR, FL, GA, KY, LA, MS, NC, OK, SC, TN

Commenced Business: August 1952

Address: 302 Broad Street, Gadsden, AL 35901

Phone: (256) 543-2022 **Domicile State:** AL **NAIC Code:** 65412

Data Date	Rating	RACR #1	RACR #2	Total Assets ($mil)	Capital ($mil)	Net Premium ($mil)	Net Income ($mil)
9-18	B	3.50	2.32	124.2	42.3	27.9	-0.4
9-17	B	3.56	2.22	126.5	41.9	27.6	1.4
2017	B	3.52	2.17	124.8	42.5	36.7	2.2
2016	B	3.39	2.03	120.8	40.6	36.0	2.2
2015	A-	3.37	2.10	116.6	38.7	36.3	2.8
2014	A-	3.33	2.22	113.5	37.3	37.4	7.0
2013	A-	2.88	1.95	108.0	33.0	37.2	2.7

Adverse Trends in Operations

Decrease in premium volume from 2014 to 2015 (3%)

LIFE INSURANCE COMPANY OF BOSTON & NEW YORK *   A-   Excellent

Major Rating Factors: Good quality investment portfolio (6.8 on a scale of 0 to 10) despite mixed results such as: no exposure to mortgages and large holdings of BBB rated bonds but minimal holdings in junk bonds. Good overall profitability (6.1). Good liquidity (6.6) with sufficient resources to handle a spike in claims as well as a significant increase in policy surrenders.

Other Rating Factors: Excellent overall results on stability tests (7.0) excellent operational trends and good risk diversification. Strong capitalization (8.9) based on excellent risk adjusted capital (severe loss scenario).

Principal Business: Individual life insurance (61%), group health insurance (20%), and individual health insurance (19%).

Principal Investments: NonCMO investment grade bonds (63%), policy loans (21%), CMOs and structured securities (9%), common & preferred stock (3%), and misc. investments (4%).

Investments in Affiliates: None

Group Affiliation: Boston Mutual Group

Licensed in: NY

Commenced Business: March 1990

Address: 4300 Camp Road PO Box 331, Athol Springs, NY 14010

Phone: (212) 684-2000 **Domicile State:** NY **NAIC Code:** 78140

Data Date	Rating	RACR #1	RACR #2	Total Assets ($mil)	Capital ($mil)	Net Premium ($mil)	Net Income ($mil)
9-18	A-	3.56	2.26	157.5	32.2	16.5	2.0
9-17	A-	3.33	2.50	148.4	30.3	16.1	1.5
2017	A-	3.30	2.36	150.4	30.1	22.6	1.5
2016	A-	3.15	2.49	141.4	28.9	22.0	1.5
2015	A-	2.91	2.40	130.4	26.6	21.5	3.3
2014	A-	2.64	2.07	124.1	23.9	24.8	1.8
2013	A-	2.42	2.00	117.3	21.8	23.9	-1.4

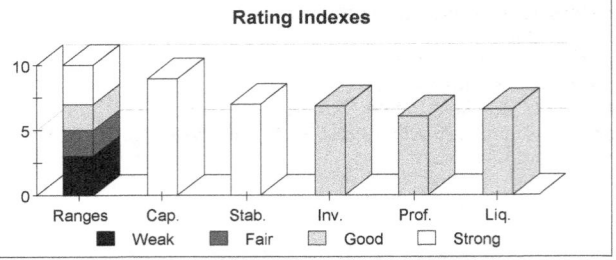

Rating Indexes

LIFE INSURANCE COMPANY OF NORTH AMERICA   B   Good

Major Rating Factors: Good overall results on stability tests (5.8 on a scale of 0 to 10). Stability strengths include good operational trends and excellent risk diversification. Good quality investment portfolio (5.4) despite large holdings of BBB rated bonds in addition to moderate junk bond exposure. Exposure to mortgages is significant, but the mortgage default rate has been low. Good liquidity (6.7).

Other Rating Factors: Strong capitalization (8.1) based on excellent risk adjusted capital (severe loss scenario). Excellent profitability (8.0).

Principal Business: Group health insurance (57%), group life insurance (39%), and reinsurance (3%).

Principal Investments: NonCMO investment grade bonds (73%), mortgages in good standing (11%), noninv. grade bonds (8%), and CMOs and structured securities (2%).

Investments in Affiliates: 7%

Group Affiliation: CIGNA Corp

Licensed in: All states, the District of Columbia and Puerto Rico

Commenced Business: September 1957

Address: 2 LIBERTY PLC 1601 CHESTNUT ST, PHILADELPHIA, PA 19192-2362

Phone: (215) 761-1000 **Domicile State:** PA **NAIC Code:** 65498

Data Date	Rating	RACR #1	RACR #2	Total Assets ($mil)	Capital ($mil)	Net Premium ($mil)	Net Income ($mil)
9-18	B	2.66	1.71	8,743.9	1,846.5	2,798.4	213.3
9-17	B	2.52	1.62	8,856.7	1,728.4	2,793.7	234.6
2017	B	2.62	1.69	8,900.7	1,798.2	3,730.5	334.4
2016	B	2.20	1.41	8,604.4	1,477.8	3,751.3	111.9
2015	B	2.34	1.51	8,141.6	1,495.3	3,674.5	236.6
2014	B	2.42	1.54	7,562.6	1,346.0	3,192.3	287.8
2013	B	2.20	1.39	6,711.9	1,103.5	3,232.7	173.3

Adverse Trends in Operations

Decrease in capital during 2016 (1%)
Increase in policy surrenders from 2015 to 2016 (392%)
Increase in policy surrenders from 2014 to 2015 (994%)
Decrease in premium volume from 2013 to 2014 (1%)
Change in premium mix from 2013 to 2014 (5.7%)

LIFE INSURANCE COMPANY OF THE SOUTHWEST   B   Good

Major Rating Factors: Good quality investment portfolio (5.1 on a scale of 0 to 10) despite large holdings of BBB rated bonds in addition to junk bond exposure equal to 53% of capital. Exposure to mortgages is significant, but the mortgage default rate has been low. Good overall results on stability tests (5.5). Stability strengths include good operational trends, good risk adjusted capital for prior years and excellent risk diversification. Fair liquidity (4.4).

Other Rating Factors: Strong capitalization (7.3) based on excellent risk adjusted capital (severe loss scenario). Excellent profitability (8.3).

Principal Business: Individual annuities (58%), individual life insurance (39%), and group retirement contracts (3%).

Principal Investments: NonCMO investment grade bonds (52%), CMOs and structured securities (17%), mortgages in good standing (15%), noninv. grade bonds (4%), and policy loans (2%).

Investments in Affiliates: None

Group Affiliation: National Life Group

Licensed in: All states except NY, PR

Commenced Business: January 1956

Address: 15455 Dallas Parkway, Addison, TX 75001

Phone: (800) 579-2878 **Domicile State:** TX **NAIC Code:** 65528

Data Date	Rating	RACR #1	RACR #2	Total Assets ($mil)	Capital ($mil)	Net Premium ($mil)	Net Income ($mil)
9-18	B	2.50	1.21	19,754.5	1,346.7	1,558.4	7.4
9-17	B	2.20	1.08	18,030.6	1,168.7	1,253.6	124.5
2017	B	2.33	1.14	18,743.4	1,207.6	1,769.3	61.2
2016	B	2.07	1.02	16,805.4	1,067.9	1,261.4	168.7
2015	B	1.70	0.85	14,681.0	840.9	1,583.6	35.9
2014	B	1.87	0.93	13,382.0	779.0	1,577.7	105.6
2013	B	2.10	1.03	12,354.9	720.2	1,329.9	142.5

Adverse Trends in Operations

Change in premium mix from 2016 to 2017 (4.9%)
Change in premium mix from 2015 to 2016 (7%)
Decrease in premium volume from 2015 to 2016 (20%)

LIFECARE ASSURANCE COMPANY   C   Fair

Major Rating Factors: Fair overall results on stability tests (3.2 on a scale of 0 to 10) including fair risk adjusted capital in prior years. Good capitalization (5.2) based on good risk adjusted capital (moderate loss scenario). Low quality investment portfolio (1.8) containing large holdings of BBB rated bonds in addition to significant exposure to junk bonds.

Other Rating Factors: Weak profitability (1.8) with operating losses during the first nine months of 2018. Excellent liquidity (8.9).

Principal Business: Reinsurance (100%).

Principal Investments: NonCMO investment grade bonds (62%), CMOs and structured securities (32%), and noninv. grade bonds (3%).

Investments in Affiliates: None

Group Affiliation: 21st Century Life & Health Co Inc

Licensed in: All states except CT, FL, MA, MN, NH, NY, RI, SC, WY, PR

Commenced Business: July 1980

Address: 8601 N Scottsdale Road Ste 300, Scottsdale, AZ 85253

Phone: (818) 887-4436 **Domicile State:** AZ **NAIC Code:** 91898

Data Date	Rating	RACR #1	RACR #2	Total Assets ($mil)	Capital ($mil)	Net Premium ($mil)	Net Income ($mil)
9-18	C	1.13	0.58	2,516.7	60.6	127.9	-3.9
9-17	B-	1.36	0.71	2,421.9	84.4	178.1	-14.9
2017	C	1.07	0.57	2,438.4	64.5	238.4	-18.7
2016	B-	1.67	0.89	2,282.5	102.4	233.3	5.5
2015	B-	1.79	0.96	2,113.1	107.2	231.6	10.0
2014	B-	1.83	0.99	1,945.6	107.1	230.3	21.0
2013	B-	1.71	0.94	1,780.0	95.7	233.9	17.7

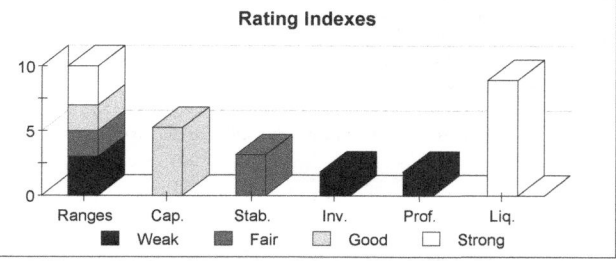

Rating Indexes

Ranges / Cap. / Stab. / Inv. / Prof. / Liq.
■ Weak ■ Fair □ Good □ Strong

LIFEMAP ASSURANCE COMPANY   B-   Good

Major Rating Factors: Good quality investment portfolio (5.0 on a scale of 0 to 10) with no exposure to mortgages and minimal holdings in junk bonds. Good liquidity (6.8) with sufficient resources to handle a spike in claims. Good overall results on stability tests (5.0). Strengths include good financial support from affiliation with Regence Group, excellent operational trends and excellent risk diversification.

Other Rating Factors: Fair profitability (3.4) with operating losses during the first nine months of 2018. Strong capitalization (7.7) based on excellent risk adjusted capital (severe loss scenario).

Principal Business: Group health insurance (65%), group life insurance (28%), and individual health insurance (6%).

Principal Investments: CMOs and structured securities (39%), nonCMO investment grade bonds (31%), common & preferred stock (22%), and cash (6%).

Investments in Affiliates: 2%

Group Affiliation: Regence Group

Licensed in: AK, AZ, CA, ID, MT, OR, RI, UT, WA, WY

Commenced Business: July 1966

Address: 100 SW MARKET STREET, PORTLAND, OR 97201

Phone: (503) 225-6069 **Domicile State:** OR **NAIC Code:** 97985

Data Date	Rating	RACR #1	RACR #2	Total Assets ($mil)	Capital ($mil)	Net Premium ($mil)	Net Income ($mil)
9-18	B-	1.99	1.45	100.7	49.5	59.9	0.0
9-17	B-	1.72	1.26	97.5	45.7	63.6	0.3
2017	B-	1.92	1.40	97.2	47.6	84.3	-0.2
2016	B-	1.50	1.11	84.0	38.4	81.0	-0.3
2015	B-	1.55	1.14	83.1	39.4	76.4	-1.4
2014	B	1.80	1.32	85.1	43.1	68.9	-0.1
2013	B	1.96	1.41	89.6	45.3	64.1	-0.5

Regence Group
Composite Group Rating: B

Largest Group Members	Assets ($mil)	Rating
REGENCE BLUESHIELD	1731	B
REGENCE BL CROSS BL SHIELD OREGON	1195	B+
REGENCE BLUE CROSS BLUE SHIELD OF UT	646	B
REGENCE BLUESHIELD OF IDAHO INC	302	B
ASURIS NORTHWEST HEALTH	99	B-

LIFESECURE INSURANCE COMPANY   D   Weak

Major Rating Factors: Weak profitability (1.9 on a scale of 0 to 10) with investment income below regulatory standards in relation to interest assumptions of reserves. Weak overall results on stability tests (1.9). Strong current capitalization (8.0) based on excellent risk adjusted capital (severe loss scenario) reflecting improvement over results in 2015.

Other Rating Factors: High quality investment portfolio (7.3). Excellent liquidity (9.0).

Principal Business: Individual health insurance (63%), reinsurance (29%), individual life insurance (7%), and individual annuities (1%).

Principal Investments: NonCMO investment grade bonds (78%) and CMOs and structured securities (20%).

Investments in Affiliates: None

Group Affiliation: Blue Cross Blue Shield of Michigan

Licensed in: All states except ME, MA, NY, PR

Commenced Business: July 1954

Address: 10559 Citation Drive Suite 300, Brighton, MI 48116

Phone: (810) 220-7700 **Domicile State:** MI **NAIC Code:** 77720

Data Date	Rating	RACR #1	RACR #2	Total Assets ($mil)	Capital ($mil)	Net Premium ($mil)	Net Income ($mil)
9-18	D	2.55	1.66	404.4	47.7	59.0	1.6
9-17	D	1.82	1.20	353.9	31.1	54.1	-3.0
2017	D	2.66	1.75	366.3	46.3	72.5	-3.4
2016	D	2.05	1.33	309.2	32.5	61.9	-0.5
2015	D	1.32	0.85	262.3	18.0	50.4	-10.3
2014	D-	1.76	1.16	226.9	20.4	42.5	-13.0
2013	D-	2.10	1.34	189.7	20.2	33.4	-3.9

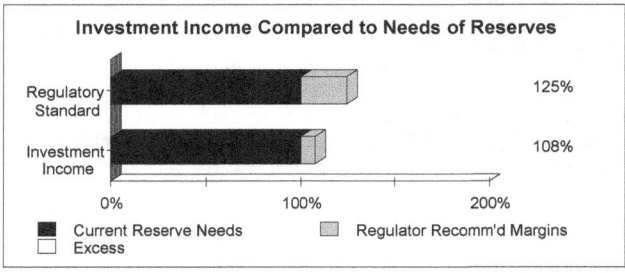

Investment Income Compared to Needs of Reserves

Regulatory Standard — 125%
Investment Income — 108%

0%   100%   200%

■ Current Reserve Needs   □ Regulator Recomm'd Margins
□ Excess

LIFESHIELD NATIONAL INSURANCE COMPANY | B- | Good

Major Rating Factors: Good liquidity (6.7 on a scale of 0 to 10) with sufficient resources to handle a spike in claims. Good overall results on stability tests (5.0) despite excessive premium growth. Other stability subfactors include excellent operational trends and good risk diversification. Fair quality investment portfolio (3.9).

Other Rating Factors: Strong capitalization (7.5) based on excellent risk adjusted capital (severe loss scenario). Excellent profitability (7.9).

Principal Business: Group health insurance (46%), reinsurance (44%), individual life insurance (9%), and group life insurance (1%).

Principal Investments: CMOs and structured securities (53%), common & preferred stock (20%), noninv. grade bonds (12%), cash (4%), and policy loans (1%).

Investments in Affiliates: 2%
Group Affiliation: Homeshield Capital Group
Licensed in: All states except AK, HI, ME, NH, NY, RI, VT, WI, PR
Commenced Business: May 1982
Address: 5701 N Shartel 1st Floor, Oklahoma City, OK 73118
Phone: (405) 236-2640 **Domicile State:** OK **NAIC Code:** 99724

Data Date	Rating	RACR #1	RACR #2	Total Assets ($mil)	Capital ($mil)	Net Premium ($mil)	Net Income ($mil)
9-18	B-	1.97	1.35	86.1	28.8	42.9	1.0
9-17	B-	2.08	1.25	73.7	24.9	25.4	-0.2
2017	B-	2.03	1.23	78.7	26.2	36.8	1.4
2016	B-	2.30	1.34	69.8	24.5	24.4	1.3
2015	B-	2.17	1.26	69.4	23.8	21.6	0.6
2014	B-	2.13	1.23	67.8	23.3	20.0	0.5
2013	B-	2.17	1.25	66.9	22.4	18.9	1.8

Adverse Trends in Operations

Increase in policy surrenders from 2013 to 2014 (67%)

LIFEWISE ASSURANCE COMPANY * | A | Excellent

Major Rating Factors: Excellent overall results on stability tests (7.1 on a scale of 0 to 10). Strengths that enhance stability include excellent operational trends and excellent risk diversification. Strong capitalization (10.0) based on excellent risk adjusted capital (severe loss scenario). Furthermore, this high level of risk adjusted capital has been consistently maintained over the last five years. High quality investment portfolio (8.0).

Other Rating Factors: Excellent profitability (9.3). Excellent liquidity (7.1).

Principal Business: Group health insurance (100%).

Principal Investments: CMOs and structured securities (46%), nonCMO investment grade bonds (45%), cash (4%), and noninv. grade bonds (2%).

Investments in Affiliates: None
Group Affiliation: PREMERA
Licensed in: AK, CA, ID, MD, OR, WA
Commenced Business: November 1981
Address: 7001 220th Street SW, Mountlake Terrace, WA 98043
Phone: (425) 918-4575 **Domicile State:** WA **NAIC Code:** 94188

Data Date	Rating	RACR #1	RACR #2	Total Assets ($mil)	Capital ($mil)	Net Premium ($mil)	Net Income ($mil)
9-18	A	7.52	5.54	193.1	148.0	109.7	19.9
9-17	A	7.11	5.27	166.6	123.1	96.7	15.2
2017	A	7.25	5.38	168.2	128.2	130.0	20.4
2016	A	6.77	5.05	142.7	108.1	118.3	11.6
2015	A	6.80	5.11	133.5	96.5	105.7	6.7
2014	A	7.38	5.56	127.0	89.9	90.9	9.3
2013	A	6.19	4.70	119.4	81.1	85.4	9.5

Rating Indexes

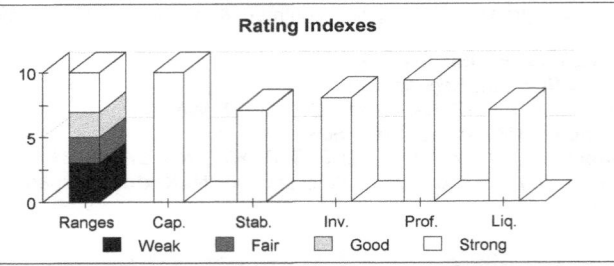

LINCOLN BENEFIT LIFE COMPANY | C+ | Fair

Major Rating Factors: Fair quality investment portfolio (3.9 on a scale of 0 to 10) with large holdings of BBB rated bonds in addition to junk bond exposure equal to 57% of capital. Exposure to mortgages is significant, but the mortgage default rate has been low. Fair overall results on stability tests (4.8) including negative cash flow from operations for 2017, fair risk adjusted capital in prior years. Good capitalization (5.6) based on good risk adjusted capital (moderate loss scenario).

Other Rating Factors: Good overall profitability (6.0). Good liquidity (5.4).

Principal Business: Individual life insurance (88%), individual annuities (5%), individual health insurance (4%), group life insurance (2%), and group retirement contracts (1%).

Principal Investments: NonCMO investment grade bonds (70%), CMOs and structured securities (12%), mortgages in good standing (11%), noninv. grade bonds (3%), and policy loans (1%).

Investments in Affiliates: 2%
Group Affiliation: Resolution Life Holdings Inc
Licensed in: All states except NY, PR
Commenced Business: October 1938
Address: 1221 N STREET SUITE 200, LINCOLN, NE 68508
Phone: (800) 525-9287 **Domicile State:** NE **NAIC Code:** 65595

Data Date	Rating	RACR #1	RACR #2	Total Assets ($mil)	Capital ($mil)	Net Premium ($mil)	Net Income ($mil)
9-18	C+	1.39	0.70	10,952.9	446.1	65.2	34.6
9-17	C+	1.48	0.74	11,535.0	499.9	84.0	45.3
2017	C+	1.04	0.60	11,231.3	425.8	111.0	64.5
2016	C+	1.50	0.79	11,517.6	559.5	102.1	51.5
2015	C+	1.34	0.72	11,701.1	555.2	82.2	74.1
2014	B	1.53	0.84	12,651.3	719.0	7,038.0	226.0
2013	B+	3.75	1.87	2,070.9	332.5	0.0	7.7

Rating Indexes

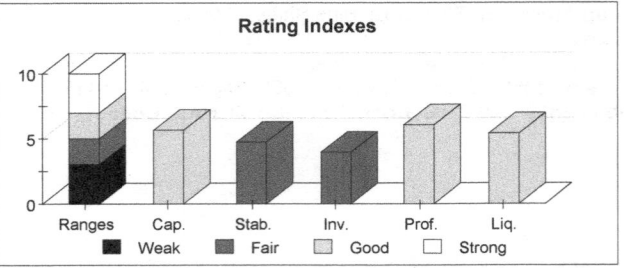

LINCOLN HERITAGE LIFE INSURANCE COMPANY   B-   Good

Major Rating Factors: Good quality investment portfolio (6.5 on a scale of 0 to 10) despite mixed results such as: minimal exposure to mortgages and substantial holdings of BBB bonds but minimal holdings in junk bonds. Good liquidity (6.1) with sufficient resources to handle a spike in claims as well as a significant increase in policy surrenders. Good overall results on stability tests (5.1) excellent operational trends and excellent risk diversification.

Other Rating Factors: Weak profitability (2.7) with investment income below regulatory standards in relation to interest assumptions of reserves. Strong capitalization (7.5) based on excellent risk adjusted capital (severe loss scenario).

Principal Business: Individual life insurance (96%), reinsurance (2%), group life insurance (1%), and individual health insurance (1%).

Principal Investments: NonCMO investment grade bonds (44%), CMOs and structured securities (35%), policy loans (7%), cash (6%), and misc. investments (7%).

Investments in Affiliates: None
Group Affiliation: Londen Ins Group
Licensed in: All states except NY, PR
Commenced Business: October 1963
Address: 920 S Spring St, Springfield, IL 62704
Phone: (602) 957-1650   **Domicile State:** IL   **NAIC Code:** 65927

Data Date	Rating	RACR #1	RACR #2	Total Assets ($mil)	Capital ($mil)	Net Premium ($mil)	Net Income ($mil)
9-18	B-	2.42	1.31	1,018.0	97.2	265.9	7.3
9-17	B-	3.13	1.70	981.3	114.4	260.3	3.9
2017	B-	2.24	1.22	970.0	88.0	340.5	1.8
2016	B-	3.24	1.78	935.4	111.5	319.2	2.7
2015	B-	3.52	1.91	873.4	110.0	311.4	3.1
2014	B-	3.78	2.06	805.2	109.0	314.9	4.7
2013	B-	3.71	1.96	740.8	101.2	259.8	3.9

Adverse Trends in Operations

Decrease in capital during 2017 (21%)
Decrease in premium volume from 2014 to 2015 (1%)

LINCOLN LIFE & ANNUITY COMPANY OF NEW YORK   B   Good

Major Rating Factors: Good quality investment portfolio (5.9 on a scale of 0 to 10) despite mixed results such as: minimal exposure to mortgages and large holdings of BBB rated bonds but small junk bond holdings. Good overall profitability (6.5). Excellent expense controls. Good liquidity (6.5).

Other Rating Factors: Fair overall results on stability tests (4.1). Strong capitalization (8.9) based on excellent risk adjusted capital (severe loss scenario).

Principal Business: Individual life insurance (36%), individual annuities (28%), group retirement contracts (21%), reinsurance (10%), and other lines (5%).

Principal Investments: NonCMO investment grade bonds (78%), mortgages in good standing (9%), CMOs and structured securities (6%), policy loans (3%), and noninv. grade bonds (3%).

Investments in Affiliates: None
Group Affiliation: Lincoln National Corp
Licensed in: All states except PR
Commenced Business: December 1897
Address: 100 Madison Street Suite 1860, Syracuse, NY 13202-2802
Phone: (336) 691-3000   **Domicile State:** NY   **NAIC Code:** 62057

Data Date	Rating	RACR #1	RACR #2	Total Assets ($mil)	Capital ($mil)	Net Premium ($mil)	Net Income ($mil)
9-18	B	4.46	2.26	15,062.1	1,191.5	807.4	137.9
9-17	B	4.79	2.36	14,347.2	1,215.2	800.7	145.7
2017	B	4.41	2.20	14,783.9	1,187.3	1,338.2	236.7
2016	B	4.57	2.28	13,729.8	1,207.4	-720.8	378.8
2015	B	1.97	1.02	13,176.6	512.2	1,263.5	-55.2
2014	B	2.49	1.29	12,840.2	652.5	1,291.4	39.4
2013	B-	2.76	1.43	12,046.4	713.0	1,229.4	161.2

Rating Indexes

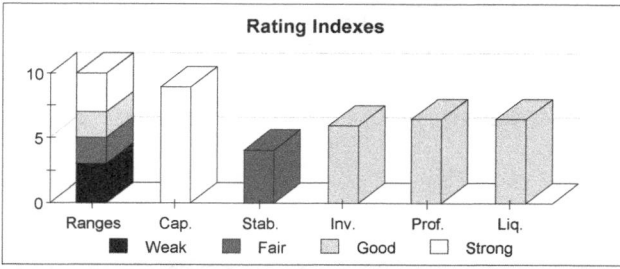

Ranges Cap. Stab. Inv. Prof. Liq.
■ Weak ■ Fair ☐ Good ☐ Strong

LINCOLN NATIONAL LIFE INSURANCE COMPANY   B   Good

Major Rating Factors: Good capitalization (6.3 on a scale of 0 to 10) based on good risk adjusted capital (severe loss scenario). Capital levels have been relatively consistent over the last five years. Good quality investment portfolio (6.2) despite large holdings of BBB rated bonds in addition to moderate junk bond exposure. Exposure to mortgages is significant, but the mortgage default rate has been low. Good liquidity (6.1).

Other Rating Factors: Good overall results on stability tests (5.8) despite excessive premium growth excellent operational trends and excellent risk diversification. Excellent profitability (7.6).

Principal Business: Individual annuities (40%), individual life insurance (29%), group retirement contracts (16%), group health insurance (6%), and other lines (9%).

Principal Investments: NonCMO investment grade bonds (71%), mortgages in good standing (10%), CMOs and structured securities (6%), common & preferred stock (4%), and misc. investments (8%).

Investments in Affiliates: 4%
Group Affiliation: Lincoln National Corp
Licensed in: All states except NY
Commenced Business: September 1905
Address: 1300 South Clinton Street, Fort Wayne, IN 46802
Phone: (260) 455-2000   **Domicile State:** IN   **NAIC Code:** 65676

Data Date	Rating	RACR #1	RACR #2	Total Assets ($mil)	Capital ($mil)	Net Premium ($mil)	Net Income ($mil)
9-18	B	1.31	0.91	249,329	7,941.7	21,334.5	633.8
9-17	B	1.47	0.99	235,288	7,707.3	12,354.2	1,118.7
2017	B	1.32	0.92	239,826	7,845.4	17,337.1	1,390.1
2016	B	1.41	0.95	221,259	7,473.0	17,172.0	789.9
2015	B	1.55	1.01	213,891	7,117.1	19,605.3	1,056.9
2014	B	1.57	1.05	213,625	7,526.3	22,068.4	1,520.3
2013	B-	1.40	0.93	200,018	6,836.1	21,752.4	577.6

Risk-Adjusted Capital Ratio #2
(Severe Loss Scenario)

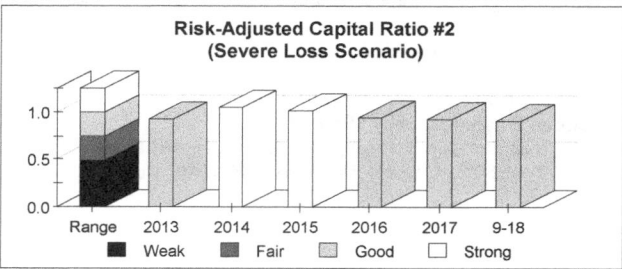

Range 2013 2014 2015 2016 2017 9-18
■ Weak ■ Fair ☐ Good ☐ Strong

LOCOMOTIVE ENGINEERS & CONDUCTORS MUTUAL PROTECT   B+   Good

Major Rating Factors: Good quality investment portfolio (5.2 on a scale of 0 to 10) with no exposure to mortgages and minimal holdings in junk bonds. Good overall results on stability tests (6.0). Stability strengths include excellent operational trends and good risk diversification. Strong capitalization (10.0) based on excellent risk adjusted capital (severe loss scenario).
Other Rating Factors: Excellent profitability (7.4). Excellent liquidity (7.0).
Principal Business: Individual life insurance (100%).
Principal Investments: NonCMO investment grade bonds (54%), common & preferred stock (27%), and cash (1%).
Investments in Affiliates: None
Group Affiliation: None
Licensed in: MI, NE, NM, TX
Commenced Business: July 1910
Address: 4000 Town Center Suite 1250, Southfield, MI 48075-1407
Phone: (800) 514-0010 **Domicile State:** MI **NAIC Code:** 87920

Data Date	Rating	RACR #1	RACR #2	Total Assets ($mil)	Capital ($mil)	Net Premium ($mil)	Net Income ($mil)
9-18	B+	8.21	4.83	73.6	62.7	14.7	2.3
9-17	B+	8.12	4.96	71.4	58.9	14.5	1.0
2017	B+	7.98	4.90	72.2	59.3	19.4	0.7
2016	B+	7.77	5.53	66.4	56.2	19.4	4.6
2015	B+	7.27	5.93	59.9	50.8	20.0	4.1
2014	B+	6.89	5.92	56.2	47.0	19.9	3.3
2013	B+	6.50	5.85	52.1	43.2	19.9	5.5

Adverse Trends in Operations

Decrease in premium volume from 2015 to 2016 (3%)

LONDON LIFE REINSURANCE COMPANY   C+   Fair

Major Rating Factors: Fair overall results on stability tests (4.0 on a scale of 0 to 10). Good overall profitability (5.6) although investment income, in comparison to reserve requirements, is below regulatory standards. Strong overall capitalization (10.0) based on excellent risk adjusted capital (severe loss scenario). However, capital levels have fluctuated somewhat during past years.
Other Rating Factors: High quality investment portfolio (7.7). Excellent liquidity (7.2).
Principal Business: Reinsurance (100%).
Principal Investments: NonCMO investment grade bonds (81%), CMOs and structured securities (10%), noninv. grade bonds (3%), common & preferred stock (2%), and cash (2%).
Investments in Affiliates: None
Group Affiliation: Great West Life Asr
Licensed in: All states, the District of Columbia and Puerto Rico
Commenced Business: December 1969
Address: 1787 Sentry Pkwy W Bldg 16, Blue Bell, PA 19422-2240
Phone: (215) 542-7200 **Domicile State:** PA **NAIC Code:** 76694

Data Date	Rating	RACR #1	RACR #2	Total Assets ($mil)	Capital ($mil)	Net Premium ($mil)	Net Income ($mil)
9-18	C+	6.42	4.27	200.0	60.4	0.3	2.0
9-17	C+	5.82	3.59	201.2	58.5	0.9	0.5
2017	C+	5.97	3.66	204.0	58.3	1.1	0.9
2016	C+	5.58	3.21	289.3	58.5	1.5	2.3
2015	C+	5.43	2.91	301.3	57.4	1.9	2.1
2014	C+	5.29	2.81	316.2	56.6	2.2	4.2
2013	C+	4.74	2.39	344.1	52.9	-8.1	2.3

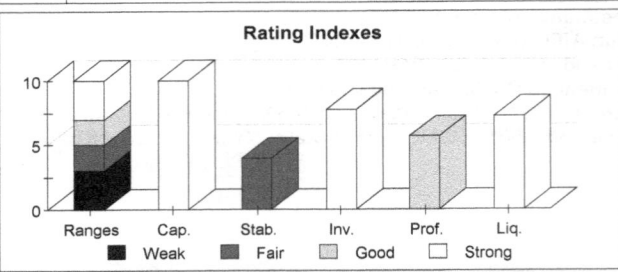

Rating Indexes

LOYAL AMERICAN LIFE INSURANCE COMPANY   B-   Good

Major Rating Factors: Good capitalization (6.5 on a scale of 0 to 10) based on good risk adjusted capital (severe loss scenario). Moreover, capital levels have been consistent over the last five years. Good quality investment portfolio (6.1) despite mixed results such as: no exposure to mortgages and large holdings of BBB rated bonds but minimal holdings in junk bonds. Good overall profitability (6.2).
Other Rating Factors: Good liquidity (6.6). Fair overall results on stability tests (4.9).
Principal Business: Individual health insurance (66%), reinsurance (30%), individual life insurance (2%), and group health insurance (2%).
Principal Investments: NonCMO investment grade bonds (80%), common & preferred stock (21%), noninv. grade bonds (1%), and CMOs and structured securities (1%).
Investments in Affiliates: 21%
Group Affiliation: CIGNA Corp
Licensed in: All states except NY, PR
Commenced Business: July 1955
Address: 1300 East Ninth Street, Cleveland, OH 44114
Phone: (512) 451-2224 **Domicile State:** OH **NAIC Code:** 65722

Data Date	Rating	RACR #1	RACR #2	Total Assets ($mil)	Capital ($mil)	Net Premium ($mil)	Net Income ($mil)
9-18	B-	1.10	0.94	334.0	117.7	256.6	9.8
9-17	B-	1.20	0.99	304.3	104.9	232.2	5.6
2017	B-	0.95	0.82	303.7	96.6	311.5	9.1
2016	C+	1.08	0.91	272.9	86.3	281.7	15.6
2015	C+	1.00	0.86	266.7	85.6	278.5	16.5
2014	C	1.11	0.93	249.3	73.5	243.7	20.2
2013	C	1.53	1.18	244.0	71.5	260.0	14.3

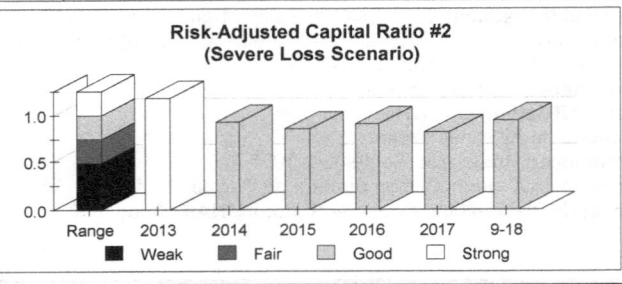

Risk-Adjusted Capital Ratio #2
(Severe Loss Scenario)

M LIFE INSURANCE COMPANY *   B+   Good

Major Rating Factors: Good liquidity (6.7 on a scale of 0 to 10) with sufficient resources to handle a spike in claims as well as a significant increase in policy surrenders. Good overall results on stability tests (5.3). Stability strengths include good operational trends and excellent risk diversification. Strong capitalization (10.0) based on excellent risk adjusted capital (severe loss scenario).

Other Rating Factors: High quality investment portfolio (7.8). Excellent profitability (7.2).

Principal Business: Reinsurance (100%).

Principal Investments: NonCMO investment grade bonds (71%), CMOs and structured securities (22%), and cash (2%).

Investments in Affiliates: None

Group Affiliation: M Financial Holdings Inc

Licensed in: AZ, CO, DE, MI, NE, NJ, OH

Commenced Business: December 1981

Address: The Corp Co 1675 Broadway, Centennial, CO 80112

Phone: (503) 414-7336 **Domicile State:** CO **NAIC Code:** 93580

Data Date	Rating	RACR #1	RACR #2	Total Assets ($mil)	Capital ($mil)	Net Premium ($mil)	Net Income ($mil)
9-18	B+	7.89	5.22	307.3	129.0	304.6	47.4
9-17	B	6.04	3.96	297.0	106.8	321.8	21.0
2017	B	6.48	4.29	330.4	107.0	473.0	37.9
2016	B-	5.14	3.40	286.3	89.5	400.2	4.8
2015	C	4.60	3.03	252.6	74.4	420.6	11.3
2014	C	4.84	3.19	285.4	74.2	403.2	10.0
2013	C	6.05	4.02	257.0	87.0	347.6	39.5

Adverse Trends in Operations

Increase in policy surrenders from 2016 to 2017 (109%)
Decrease in premium volume from 2015 to 2016 (5%)
Decrease in asset base during 2015 (11%)
Decrease in capital during 2014 (15%)

MADISON NATIONAL LIFE INSURANCE COMPANY INCORPORA   B   Good

Major Rating Factors: Good quality investment portfolio (5.9 on a scale of 0 to 10) with no exposure to mortgages and no exposure to junk bonds. Good overall results on stability tests (6.3). Stability strengths include good operational trends and excellent risk diversification. Strong capitalization (7.8) based on excellent risk adjusted capital (severe loss scenario).

Other Rating Factors: Excellent profitability (8.1). Excellent liquidity (7.0).

Principal Business: Group health insurance (59%), group life insurance (20%), individual life insurance (8%), individual annuities (8%), and reinsurance (4%).

Principal Investments: NonCMO investment grade bonds (56%), common & preferred stock (41%), cash (1%), and CMOs and structured securities (1%).

Investments in Affiliates: 40%

Group Affiliation: Geneve Holdings Inc

Licensed in: All states except NY, PR

Commenced Business: March 1962

Address: 1241 John Q Hammons Drive, Madison, WI 53717-1929

Phone: (608) 830-2000 **Domicile State:** WI **NAIC Code:** 65781

Data Date	Rating	RACR #1	RACR #2	Total Assets ($mil)	Capital ($mil)	Net Premium ($mil)	Net Income ($mil)
9-18	B	1.62	1.51	339.1	202.0	69.8	13.5
9-17	C+	1.53	1.46	335.6	185.8	64.9	8.2
2017	B-	1.48	1.41	326.3	179.6	87.9	12.8
2016	C+	1.48	1.41	329.7	179.0	86.9	-1.6
2015	B-	1.95	1.71	256.9	116.7	126.4	20.3
2014	C+	1.26	1.06	496.7	81.5	147.5	9.9
2013	C+	1.20	1.00	488.6	78.0	168.8	11.7

Adverse Trends in Operations

Change in asset mix during 2016 (5%)
Decrease in premium volume from 2015 to 2016 (31%)
Decrease in premium volume from 2014 to 2015 (14%)
Decrease in asset base during 2015 (48%)
Decrease in premium volume from 2013 to 2014 (13%)

MANHATTAN LIFE INSURANCE COMPANY   B   Good

Major Rating Factors: Good overall results on stability tests (5.4 on a scale of 0 to 10) despite fair financial strength of affiliated Manhattan Life Group Inc. Other stability subfactors include good operational trends and good risk diversification. Good capitalization (6.8) based on good risk adjusted capital (severe loss scenario). Moreover, capital levels have been consistent over the last five years. Good quality investment portfolio (6.1).

Other Rating Factors: Good overall profitability (5.1) although investment income, in comparison to reserve requirements, is below regulatory standards. Good liquidity (5.5).

Principal Business: Individual health insurance (64%), individual annuities (29%), individual life insurance (5%), group health insurance (2%), and reinsurance (1%).

Principal Investments: NonCMO investment grade bonds (66%), CMOs and structured securities (11%), mortgages in good standing (8%), common & preferred stock (6%), and misc. investments (6%).

Investments in Affiliates: 5%

Group Affiliation: Manhattan Life Group Inc

Licensed in: All states, the District of Columbia and Puerto Rico

Commenced Business: August 1850

Address: 225 Community Drive Suite 11, Great Neck, NY 11021

Phone: (713) 529-0045 **Domicile State:** NY **NAIC Code:** 65870

Data Date	Rating	RACR #1	RACR #2	Total Assets ($mil)	Capital ($mil)	Net Premium ($mil)	Net Income ($mil)
9-18	B	1.37	0.98	623.8	58.0	63.0	9.5
9-17	B	1.28	0.93	577.7	53.0	73.1	7.4
2017	B	1.30	0.94	581.1	54.1	90.1	8.6
2016	B	1.26	0.94	543.1	51.1	125.6	13.9
2015	B	1.18	0.91	484.6	47.1	152.1	11.2
2014	B	1.17	0.96	362.4	41.0	71.1	2.8
2013	B	1.23	1.03	310.4	36.9	12.1	3.7

Manhattan Life Group Inc Composite Group Rating: C+ Largest Group Members	Assets ($mil)	Rating
WESTERN UNITED LIFE ASR CO	1201	B-
MANHATTAN LIFE INS CO	581	B
MANHATTANLIFE ASSR CO OF AM	391	C
FAMILY LIFE INS CO	151	C

MAPFRE LIFE INSURANCE COMPANY

C **Fair**

Major Rating Factors: Fair profitability (3.1 on a scale of 0 to 10) with operating losses during the first nine months of 2018. Fair overall results on stability tests (4.1) including negative cash flow from operations for 2017. Strong overall capitalization (10.0) based on excellent risk adjusted capital (severe loss scenario). However, capital levels have fluctuated somewhat during past years.

Other Rating Factors: High quality investment portfolio (9.2). Excellent liquidity (9.6).

Principal Business: Reinsurance (91%), individual life insurance (6%), group health insurance (2%), and individual health insurance (1%).

Principal Investments: NonCMO investment grade bonds (74%) and cash (26%).

Investments in Affiliates: None

Group Affiliation: MAPFRE Ins Group

Licensed in: All states except NY, PR

Commenced Business: October 1975

Address: 116 WEST WATER STREET, DOVER, DE 19903

Phone: (847) 273-1261 **Domicile State:** DE **NAIC Code:** 85561

Data Date	Rating	RACR #1	RACR #2	Total Assets ($mil)	Capital ($mil)	Net Premium ($mil)	Net Income ($mil)
9-18	C	10.53	9.48	40.7	39.9	0.1	-0.4
9-17	C	4.77	4.29	20.3	17.5	0.3	-1.6
2017	C	5.39	4.85	22.6	20.4	0.4	-1.7
2016	C	4.94	4.44	21.6	18.1	1.0	-1.0
2015	C-	5.30	4.77	23.5	20.6	0.0	-1.0
2014	C+	5.48	4.93	26.0	22.8	0.0	-1.3
2013	C+	4.89	4.40	20.9	17.6	0.0	2.8

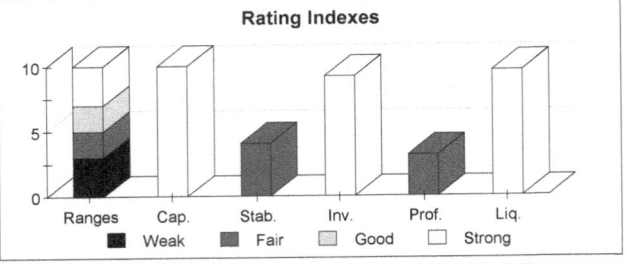

Rating Indexes

Weak ■ Fair ■ Good ■ Strong □

MASSACHUSETTS MUTUAL LIFE INSURANCE COMPANY *

A- **Excellent**

Major Rating Factors: Good capitalization (6.8 on a scale of 0 to 10) based on good risk adjusted capital (severe loss scenario). Furthermore, this high level of risk adjusted capital has been consistently maintained over the last five years. Good quality investment portfolio (6.1) despite large holdings of BBB rated bonds in addition to junk bond exposure equal to 61% of capital. Exposure to mortgages is significant, but the mortgage default rate has been low. Good overall profitability (6.3) despite operating losses during the first nine months of 2018.

Other Rating Factors: Good liquidity (6.7). Good overall results on stability tests (6.6) good operational trends, excellent risk adjusted capital for prior years and excellent risk diversification.

Principal Business: Group retirement contracts (44%), individual life insurance (31%), individual annuities (10%), group life insurance (6%), and other lines (9%).

Principal Investments: NonCMO investment grade bonds (43%), mortgages in good standing (14%), common & preferred stock (10%), CMOs and structured securities (9%), and misc. investments (20%).

Investments in Affiliates: 16%

Group Affiliation: Massachusetts Mutual Group

Licensed in: All states, the District of Columbia and Puerto Rico

Commenced Business: August 1851

Address: 1295 STATE STREET, SPRINGFIELD, MA 1111

Phone: (413) 788-8411 **Domicile State:** MA **NAIC Code:** 65935

Data Date	Rating	RACR #1	RACR #2	Total Assets ($mil)	Capital ($mil)	Net Premium ($mil)	Net Income ($mil)
9-18	A-	1.30	0.97	245,872	14,722.1	16,713.5	-1,299.1
9-17	A-	1.45	1.09	235,570	16,152.4	15,022.7	193.1
2017	A-	1.42	1.05	240,063	15,705.2	17,461.6	52.1
2016	A-	1.42	1.07	223,670	15,423.5	21,408.4	-13.9
2015	A-	1.76	1.26	210,359	14,982.5	21,530.4	412.2
2014	A-	1.77	1.27	197,189	14,231.3	18,377.0	623.1
2013	A-	1.80	1.28	182,776	12,524.4	20,418.8	-285.6

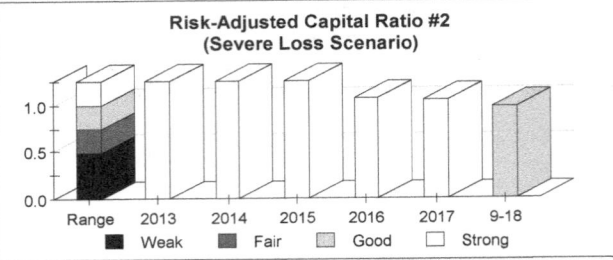

Risk-Adjusted Capital Ratio #2
(Severe Loss Scenario)

Weak ■ Fair ■ Good ■ Strong □

MCS LIFE INSURANCE COMPANY

D- **Weak**

Major Rating Factors: Weak overall results on stability tests (1.0 on a scale of 0 to 10) including potential financial drain due to affiliation with Medical Card System Inc and weak risk adjusted capital in prior years. Fair current capitalization (4.8) based on mixed results -- excessive policy leverage mitigated by good risk adjusted capital (severe loss scenario) reflecting significant improvement over results in 2016. Fair liquidity (4.6).

Other Rating Factors: Good overall profitability (5.3). High quality investment portfolio (9.4).

Principal Business: Group health insurance (92%), individual health insurance (7%), and group life insurance (1%).

Principal Investments: Cash (57%) and nonCMO investment grade bonds (43%).

Investments in Affiliates: None

Group Affiliation: Medical Card System Inc

Licensed in: PR

Commenced Business: January 1996

Address: Ste 900 255 Ponce de Leon Ave, San Juan, PR 917

Phone: (787) 758-2500 **Domicile State:** PR **NAIC Code:** 60030

Data Date	Rating	RACR #1	RACR #2	Total Assets ($mil)	Capital ($mil)	Net Premium ($mil)	Net Income ($mil)
9-18	D-	0.96	0.79	92.7	45.0	217.1	1.5
9-17	D-	0.56	0.49	83.9	30.3	233.3	9.1
2017	D-	0.89	0.73	97.5	43.6	310.0	22.4
2016	E	0.38	0.34	68.7	20.6	308.4	9.2
2015	E	0.18	0.16	71.7	10.4	306.4	-10.7
2014	E+	0.42	0.37	60.9	20.2	277.5	-1.7
2013	D-	0.44	0.36	67.3	22.2	252.4	1.2

Medical Card System Inc Composite Group Rating: E+ Largest Group Members	Assets ($mil)	Rating
MCS ADVANTAGE INC	252	E+
MCS LIFE INS CO	98	D-

MEDICO CORP LIFE INSURANCE COMPANY   B-   Good

Major Rating Factors: Fair overall results on stability tests (4.8 on a scale of 0 to 10) including fair financial strength of affiliated American Enterprise Mutual Holding. Strong capitalization (8.0) based on excellent risk adjusted capital (severe loss scenario). High quality investment portfolio (8.3).
Other Rating Factors: Excellent profitability (7.0). Excellent liquidity (7.0).
Principal Business: Individual health insurance (100%).
Principal Investments: NonCMO investment grade bonds (61%), CMOs and structured securities (28%), and cash (5%).
Investments in Affiliates: None
Group Affiliation: American Enterprise Mutual Holding
Licensed in: All states except CA, CT, MA, NH, NJ, NY, PR
Commenced Business: May 1960
Address: 1010 North 102nd St Ste 201, Des Moines, IA 50309
Phone: (804) 354-7000 **Domicile State:** NE **NAIC Code:** 79987

Data Date	Rating	RACR #1	RACR #2	Total Assets ($mil)	Capital ($mil)	Net Premium ($mil)	Net Income ($mil)
9-18	B-	3.53	3.17	70.6	26.1	0.0	0.4
9-17	A-	3.32	2.99	63.9	22.8	0.0	0.2
2017	A-	3.01	2.71	65.6	22.3	0.0	0.3
2016	B+	3.16	2.85	53.7	21.8	0.0	0.4
2015	B+	4.07	3.66	36.0	21.2	0.0	0.4
2014	B+	5.68	5.12	27.5	24.4	0.0	0.6
2013	B+	6.02	5.42	25.3	24.4	0.0	0.7

American Enterprise Mutual Holding
Composite Group Rating: C
Largest Group Members

	Assets ($mil)	Rating
GREAT WESTERN INS CO	1388	C-
AMERICAN REPUBLIC INS CO	937	B-
MEDICO INS CO	82	B-
MEDICO CORP LIFE INS CO	66	B-
AMERICAN REPUBLIC CORP INS CO	23	C

MEDICO INSURANCE COMPANY   B-   Good

Major Rating Factors: Good overall profitability (6.3 on a scale of 0 to 10). Good liquidity (6.8) with sufficient resources to handle a spike in claims. Fair overall results on stability tests (4.8) including fair financial strength of affiliated American Enterprise Mutual Holding.
Other Rating Factors: Strong capitalization (10.0) based on excellent risk adjusted capital (severe loss scenario). High quality investment portfolio (7.7).
Principal Business: Individual health insurance (80%), group health insurance (18%), individual life insurance (1%), and reinsurance (1%).
Principal Investments: NonCMO investment grade bonds (62%), CMOs and structured securities (32%), and cash (5%).
Investments in Affiliates: None
Group Affiliation: American Enterprise Mutual Holding
Licensed in: All states except CT, NJ, NY, PR
Commenced Business: April 1930
Address: 1010 North 102nd St Ste 201, Des Moines, IA 50309
Phone: (800) 228-6080 **Domicile State:** NE **NAIC Code:** 31119

Data Date	Rating	RACR #1	RACR #2	Total Assets ($mil)	Capital ($mil)	Net Premium ($mil)	Net Income ($mil)
9-18	B-	4.95	4.46	84.6	40.3	0.4	5.1
9-17	B	4.13	3.72	82.1	34.6	0.4	1.0
2017	B	4.28	3.85	81.9	34.8	0.5	1.3
2016	B	4.63	4.16	87.3	38.8	0.6	1.8
2015	B	4.12	3.71	74.3	31.9	0.7	2.1
2014	B	4.14	3.73	69.1	30.9	0.9	-0.2
2013	B	4.06	3.66	65.7	29.7	0.9	0.8

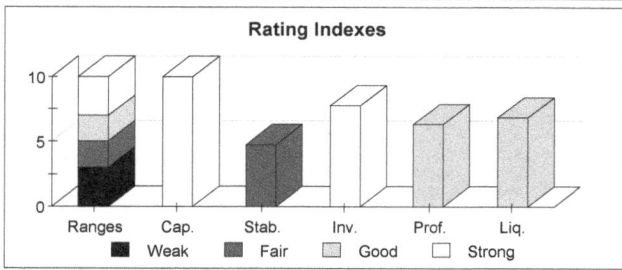

Rating Indexes

MERIT LIFE INSURANCE COMPANY   B   Good

Major Rating Factors: Good quality investment portfolio (6.7 on a scale of 0 to 10) despite mixed results such as: minimal exposure to mortgages and large holdings of BBB rated bonds but minimal holdings in junk bonds. Good overall profitability (5.1). Excellent expense controls. Fair overall results on stability tests (4.1) including negative cash flow from operations for 2017.
Other Rating Factors: Strong capitalization (10.0) based on excellent risk adjusted capital (severe loss scenario). Excellent liquidity (7.9).
Principal Business: Credit life insurance (38%), individual life insurance (37%), credit health insurance (23%), and individual health insurance (1%).
Principal Investments: NonCMO investment grade bonds (72%), CMOs and structured securities (22%), noninv. grade bonds (2%), common & preferred stock (1%), and misc. investments (3%).
Investments in Affiliates: None
Group Affiliation: Fortress Investment Group LLC
Licensed in: All states except AK, MA, NY, VT, PR
Commenced Business: October 1957
Address: 601 NW 2ND ST, EVANSVILLE, IN 47708-1013
Phone: (800) 325-2147 **Domicile State:** IN **NAIC Code:** 65951

Data Date	Rating	RACR #1	RACR #2	Total Assets ($mil)	Capital ($mil)	Net Premium ($mil)	Net Income ($mil)
9-18	B	8.66	4.45	386.6	111.9	-18.1	35.8
9-17	B	6.19	3.63	560.7	155.6	61.3	22.7
2017	B	4.95	2.70	442.2	79.1	49.6	36.6
2016	B	4.82	2.90	559.3	133.4	127.4	19.8
2015	B	4.11	2.56	588.8	122.8	150.1	-0.9
2014	B+	5.53	3.47	588.2	171.4	157.1	-2.4
2013	B+	6.34	4.09	532.0	184.5	128.1	3.3

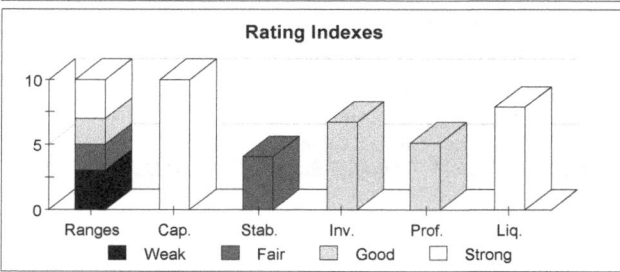

Rating Indexes

METLIFE INSURANCE COMPANY USA — B — Good

Major Rating Factors: Good quality investment portfolio (6.2 on a scale of 0 to 10) despite substantial holdings of BBB bonds in addition to junk bond exposure equal to 51% of capital. Exposure to mortgages is significant, but the mortgage default rate has been low. Good overall profitability (5.4) despite operating losses during the first nine months of 2018. Fair overall results on stability tests (4.5).

Other Rating Factors: Strong capitalization (7.6) based on excellent risk adjusted capital (severe loss scenario). Excellent liquidity (7.4).

Principal Business: Reinsurance (52%), individual annuities (27%), individual life insurance (18%), individual health insurance (2%), and group retirement contracts (2%).

Principal Investments: NonCMO investment grade bonds (51%), CMOs and structured securities (18%), mortgages in good standing (15%), noninv. grade bonds (4%), and misc. investments (8%).

Investments in Affiliates: 1%

Group Affiliation: Brighthouse Financial Inc

Licensed in: All states except NY

Commenced Business: April 1864

Address: 1209 Orange Street, Wilmington, DE 19801

Phone: (212) 578-9500 **Domicile State:** DE **NAIC Code:** 87726

Data Date	Rating	RACR #1	RACR #2	Total Assets ($mil)	Capital ($mil)	Net Premium ($mil)	Net Income ($mil)
9-18	B	2.65	1.38	172,097	5,033.3	4,420.0	-356.2
9-17	B	3.38	1.65	175,382	5,510.3	9,952.9	-644.1
2017	B	3.06	1.61	176,052	5,594.3	11,351.1	-424.8
2016	B	2.54	1.24	170,910	4,374.5	8,528.5	1,186.1
2015	B	3.37	1.66	173,762	5,942.0	7,568.0	-1,022.5
2014	B	3.15	1.57	174,606	6,041.5	-1,076.6	1,543.5
2013	B	1.52	1.09	60,275.2	4,794.6	1,361.1	789.5

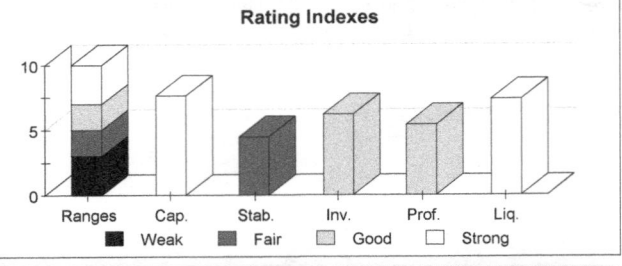

Rating Indexes (Ranges, Cap., Stab., Inv., Prof., Liq.) — Weak, Fair, Good, Strong

METROPOLITAN LIFE INSURANCE COMPANY — B- — Good

Major Rating Factors: Good overall capitalization (5.1 on a scale of 0 to 10) based on good risk adjusted capital (moderate loss scenario). Nevertheless, capital levels have fluctuated during prior years. Good overall profitability (6.3). Fair quality investment portfolio (4.1).

Other Rating Factors: Fair overall results on stability tests (3.8) including excessive premium growth. Excellent liquidity (7.0).

Principal Business: N/A

Principal Investments: NonCMO investment grade bonds (42%), mortgages in good standing (22%), CMOs and structured securities (15%), noninv. grade bonds (5%), and misc. investments (15%).

Investments in Affiliates: 6%

Group Affiliation: MetLife Inc

Licensed in: All states, the District of Columbia and Puerto Rico

Commenced Business: May 1867

Address: 200 Park Avenue, New York, NY 10166-0188

Phone: (212) 578-9500 **Domicile State:** NY **NAIC Code:** 65978

Data Date	Rating	RACR #1	RACR #2	Total Assets ($mil)	Capital ($mil)	Net Premium ($mil)	Net Income ($mil)
9-18	B-	1.08	0.71	389,583	10,506.8	24,142.5	2,811.3
9-17	B-	1.31	0.83	401,351	10,422.8	12,515.7	1,449.5
2017	B-	1.17	0.77	396,508	10,384.5	18,256.1	1,982.0
2016	B-	1.33	0.85	396,367	11,194.8	24,891.2	3,444.2
2015	B-	1.43	0.96	390,843	14,485.0	28,388.6	3,703.3
2014	B-	1.24	0.82	391,925	12,007.9	41,932.0	1,487.1
2013	B-	1.24	0.82	373,393	12,428.1	30,808.0	369.0

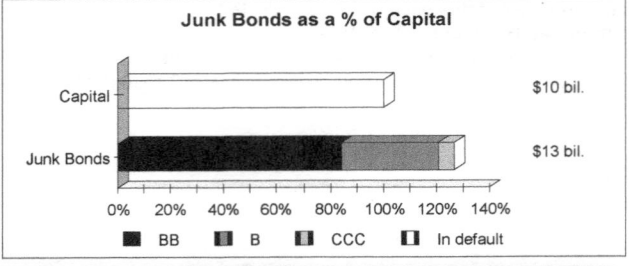

Junk Bonds as a % of Capital — Capital $10 bil., Junk Bonds $13 bil. — BB, B, CCC, In default

METROPOLITAN TOWER LIFE INSURANCE COMPANY — B- — Good

Major Rating Factors: Good overall profitability (6.1 on a scale of 0 to 10) although investment income, in comparison to reserve requirements, is below regulatory standards. Good liquidity (6.3) with sufficient resources to handle a spike in claims as well as a significant increase in policy surrenders. Fair quality investment portfolio (3.3).

Other Rating Factors: Fair overall results on stability tests (4.6). Strong capitalization (7.7) based on excellent risk adjusted capital (severe loss scenario).

Principal Business: Individual annuities (61%) and individual life insurance (38%).

Principal Investments: NonCMO investment grade bonds (41%), CMOs and structured securities (27%), real estate (10%), mortgages in good standing (7%), and misc. investments (14%).

Investments in Affiliates: 2%

Group Affiliation: MetLife Inc

Licensed in: All states except PR

Commenced Business: February 1983

Address: 1209 Orange Street, Lincoln, NE 68516

Phone: (212) 578-2211 **Domicile State:** NE **NAIC Code:** 97136

Data Date	Rating	RACR #1	RACR #2	Total Assets ($mil)	Capital ($mil)	Net Premium ($mil)	Net Income ($mil)
3-18	B-	3.30	1.47	5,013.0	733.8	46.3	2.0
3-17	B-	3.08	1.38	4,471.9	671.8	7.3	7.8
2017	B-	3.39	1.53	4,921.8	733.3	200.3	73.9
2016	B-	3.07	1.38	4,403.7	668.7	19.4	8.5
2015	B-	3.22	1.45	4,665.6	709.8	20.5	-41.5
2014	B-	3.10	1.37	4,999.2	767.2	23.8	51.1
2013	B-	2.55	1.08	4,942.8	735.5	27.6	51.5

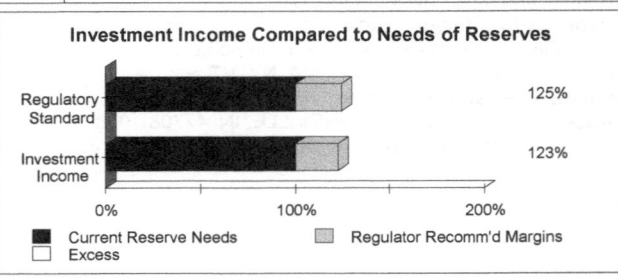

Investment Income Compared to Needs of Reserves — Regulatory Standard 125%, Investment Income 123% — Current Reserve Needs, Excess, Regulator Recomm'd Margins

MID-WEST NATIONAL LIFE INSURANCE COMPANY OF TENNES\   C+   Fair

Major Rating Factors: Fair overall results on stability tests (3.4 on a scale of 0 to 10) including negative cash flow from operations for 2017. Good overall profitability (5.8). Strong overall capitalization (10.0) based on excellent risk adjusted capital (severe loss scenario). Nevertheless, capital levels have fluctuated during prior years.

Other Rating Factors: High quality investment portfolio (8.0). Excellent liquidity (8.0).

Principal Business: Individual life insurance (50%), group health insurance (30%), individual health insurance (12%), group life insurance (4%), and individual annuities (4%).

Principal Investments: NonCMO investment grade bonds (10%), cash (7%), and CMOs and structured securities (3%).

Investments in Affiliates: 8%

Group Affiliation: Blackstone Investor Group

Licensed in: All states except NY, VT, PR

Commenced Business: May 1965

Address: 9151 BOULEVARD 26, NORTH RICHLAND HILLS, TX 76180

Phone: (817) 255-3100 **Domicile State:** TX **NAIC Code:** 66087

Data Date	Rating	RACR #1	RACR #2	Total Assets ($mil)	Capital ($mil)	Net Premium ($mil)	Net Income ($mil)
9-18	C+	3.89	3.50	62.6	28.2	4.8	2.2
9-17	C	2.34	2.11	63.6	18.6	5.6	6.4
2017	C	3.74	3.36	63.8	26.9	7.3	9.4
2016	C-	2.17	1.95	86.1	17.1	8.8	-18.0
2015	C+	7.62	6.21	166.2	71.5	32.2	17.8
2014	B-	2.91	2.07	291.8	90.6	194.1	19.0
2013	B-	4.24	3.34	92.0	51.7	80.4	6.4

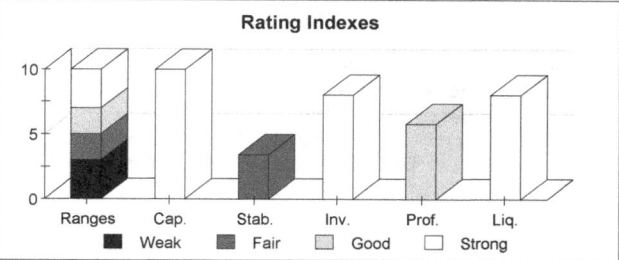

Rating Indexes

MIDLAND NATIONAL LIFE INSURANCE COMPANY *   B+   Good

Major Rating Factors: Good liquidity (5.9 on a scale of 0 to 10) with sufficient resources to cover a large increase in policy surrenders. Good overall results on stability tests (6.5). Stability strengths include excellent operational trends and excellent risk diversification. Fair quality investment portfolio (4.6).

Other Rating Factors: Strong capitalization (7.0) based on excellent risk adjusted capital (severe loss scenario). Excellent profitability (9.1).

Principal Business: Individual annuities (56%), individual life insurance (38%), group retirement contracts (4%), and reinsurance (2%).

Principal Investments: CMOs and structured securities (40%), nonCMO investment grade bonds (39%), mortgages in good standing (9%), noninv. grade bonds (4%), and misc. investments (7%).

Investments in Affiliates: 3%

Group Affiliation: Sammons Enterprises Inc

Licensed in: All states except NY

Commenced Business: September 1906

Address: 4350 Westown Parkway, West Des Moines, IA 50266

Phone: (605) 335-5700 **Domicile State:** IA **NAIC Code:** 66044

Data Date	Rating	RACR #1	RACR #2	Total Assets ($mil)	Capital ($mil)	Net Premium ($mil)	Net Income ($mil)
9-18	B+	2.00	1.01	58,240.4	3,510.9	2,796.1	417.4
9-17	B+	2.29	1.17	55,140.0	3,549.7	2,938.0	362.5
2017	B+	1.97	1.00	56,495.2	3,414.1	4,043.4	545.8
2016	B+	2.15	1.11	51,098.3	3,099.1	4,954.4	546.4
2015	B+	1.92	1.00	44,729.3	2,857.0	4,264.1	271.3
2014	B+	1.94	1.03	41,138.7	2,794.0	3,276.2	203.4
2013	B+	2.16	1.11	37,441.0	2,563.1	3,631.9	455.7

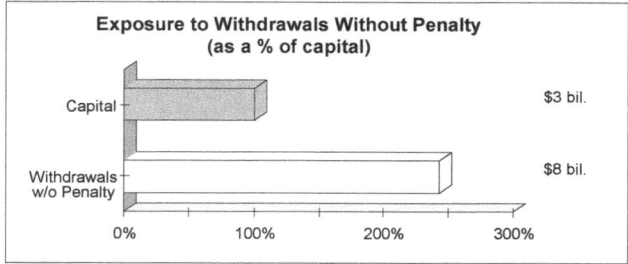

Exposure to Withdrawals Without Penalty
(as a % of capital)

MIDWESTERN UNITED LIFE INSURANCE COMPANY   B   Good

Major Rating Factors: Good liquidity (6.9 on a scale of 0 to 10) with sufficient resources to handle a spike in claims as well as a significant increase in policy surrenders. Good overall results on stability tests (5.8) despite negative cash flow from operations for 2017. Other stability subfactors include excellent operational trends and excellent risk diversification. Fair profitability (4.0).

Other Rating Factors: Strong capitalization (10.0) based on excellent risk adjusted capital (severe loss scenario). High quality investment portfolio (7.8).

Principal Business: Individual life insurance (100%).

Principal Investments: NonCMO investment grade bonds (75%), mortgages in good standing (8%), CMOs and structured securities (8%), policy loans (3%), and misc. investments (5%).

Investments in Affiliates: None

Group Affiliation: Voya Financial Inc

Licensed in: All states except NY, PR

Commenced Business: August 1948

Address: 8761 BUFFETT PARKWAY, INDIANAPOLIS, IN 46204

Phone: (303) 860-1290 **Domicile State:** IN **NAIC Code:** 66109

Data Date	Rating	RACR #1	RACR #2	Total Assets ($mil)	Capital ($mil)	Net Premium ($mil)	Net Income ($mil)
9-18	B	12.87	11.31	234.5	127.3	2.1	2.9
9-17	A	13.49	12.14	233.4	133.9	2.3	3.2
2017	B	12.57	11.17	232.4	124.2	2.9	-6.0
2016	A	13.23	11.91	234.4	131.4	3.1	3.7
2015	A-	12.85	11.56	234.9	127.7	3.2	3.5
2014	A-	12.53	11.27	236.5	124.8	3.6	2.7
2013	B	12.23	11.01	238.7	122.0	3.7	1.9

Adverse Trends in Operations

Decrease in premium volume from 2016 to 2017 (6%)
Decrease in capital during 2017 (5%)
Decrease in premium volume from 2015 to 2016 (3%)
Decrease in premium volume from 2014 to 2015 (10%)
Decrease in premium volume from 2013 to 2014 (2%)

MINNESOTA LIFE INSURANCE COMPANY *   B+   Good

Major Rating Factors: Good quality investment portfolio (5.6 on a scale of 0 to 10) despite significant exposure to mortgages . Mortgage default rate has been low. large holdings of BBB rated bonds in addition to small junk bond holdings. Good overall profitability (6.7). Good liquidity (6.6).

Other Rating Factors: Good overall results on stability tests (6.5) excellent operational trends and excellent risk diversification. Strong capitalization (7.6) based on excellent risk adjusted capital (severe loss scenario).

Principal Business: Group retirement contracts (40%), individual life insurance (21%), group life insurance (18%), individual annuities (9%), and other lines (12%).

Principal Investments: NonCMO investment grade bonds (49%), CMOs and structured securities (20%), mortgages in good standing (15%), common & preferred stock (4%), and misc. investments (8%).

Investments in Affiliates: 2%

Group Affiliation: Securian Financial Group

Licensed in: All states except NY

Commenced Business: August 1880

Address: 400 ROBERT STREET NORTH, ST. PAUL, MN 55101-2098

Phone: (612) 665-3500 **Domicile State:** MN **NAIC Code:** 66168

Data Date	Rating	RACR #1	RACR #2	Total Assets ($mil)	Capital ($mil)	Net Premium ($mil)	Net Income ($mil)
9-18	B+	2.25	1.40	49,271.3	3,054.8	5,485.9	117.8
9-17	B+	2.40	1.51	44,369.0	3,045.1	5,282.6	237.9
2017	B+	2.31	1.46	46,433.6	3,059.9	7,586.6	277.9
2016	B+	2.40	1.51	40,438.1	2,971.6	6,239.2	82.3
2015	B+	2.36	1.49	36,910.4	2,766.4	6,040.7	212.8
2014	B+	2.38	1.50	35,716.0	2,600.4	5,597.8	204.0
2013	B+	2.29	1.44	33,154.4	2,329.7	5,261.5	118.9

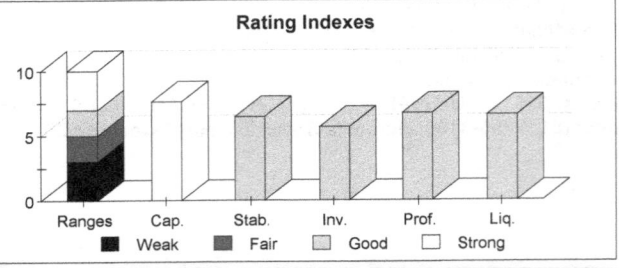

Rating Indexes

MML BAY STATE LIFE INSURANCE COMPANY   B   Good

Major Rating Factors: Fair overall results on stability tests (4.6 on a scale of 0 to 10) including negative cash flow from operations for 2017. Strong capitalization (10.0) based on excellent risk adjusted capital (severe loss scenario). Moreover, capital levels have been consistently high over the last five years. High quality investment portfolio (7.3).

Other Rating Factors: Excellent profitability (8.1). Excellent liquidity (7.1).

Principal Business: Individual life insurance (95%), group life insurance (5%), and individual annuities (1%).

Principal Investments: NonCMO investment grade bonds (44%), CMOs and structured securities (35%), policy loans (20%), noninv. grade bonds (1%), and mortgages in good standing (1%).

Investments in Affiliates: 2%

Group Affiliation: Massachusetts Mutual Group

Licensed in: All states except NY, PR

Commenced Business: July 1894

Address: 100 BRIGHT MEADOW BOULEVARD, ENFIELD, CT 6082

Phone: (413) 788-8411 **Domicile State:** CT **NAIC Code:** 70416

Data Date	Rating	RACR #1	RACR #2	Total Assets ($mil)	Capital ($mil)	Net Premium ($mil)	Net Income ($mil)
9-18	B	6.17	4.37	5,026.5	310.8	2.0	16.1
9-17	B+	5.98	4.19	4,899.6	292.9	1.6	7.3
2017	B	5.70	4.06	4,960.5	295.3	1.6	14.8
2016	B+	5.70	3.98	4,814.3	288.3	-105.9	20.3
2015	A	4.68	3.37	4,700.1	231.3	24.5	20.7
2014	A-	4.31	2.99	4,671.0	211.7	24.1	15.8
2013	A-	4.06	2.80	4,587.9	196.0	28.5	22.3

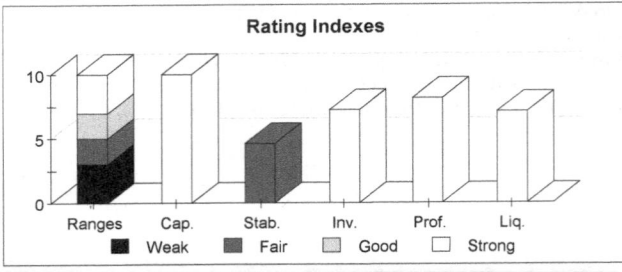

Rating Indexes

MONY LIFE INSURANCE COMPANY   B-   Good

Major Rating Factors: Good quality investment portfolio (6.2 on a scale of 0 to 10) despite mixed results such as: large holdings of BBB rated bonds but moderate junk bond exposure. Good overall results on stability tests (5.0) despite negative cash flow from operations for 2017. Other stability subfactors include good operational trends, good risk adjusted capital for prior years and excellent risk diversification. Fair profitability (3.8) with investment income below regulatory standards in relation to interest assumptions of reserves.

Other Rating Factors: Fair liquidity (4.4). Strong capitalization (7.3) based on excellent risk adjusted capital (severe loss scenario).

Principal Business: Individual life insurance (88%), individual health insurance (9%), and individual annuities (2%).

Principal Investments: NonCMO investment grade bonds (71%), policy loans (11%), CMOs and structured securities (10%), mortgages in good standing (4%), and misc. investments (4%).

Investments in Affiliates: None

Group Affiliation: Dai-ichi Life Holdings Inc

Licensed in: All states, the District of Columbia and Puerto Rico

Commenced Business: February 1843

Address: 5788 WIDEWATERS PARKWAY 2ND FL, SYRACUSE, NY 13214

Phone: (800) 487-6669 **Domicile State:** NY **NAIC Code:** 66370

Data Date	Rating	RACR #1	RACR #2	Total Assets ($mil)	Capital ($mil)	Net Premium ($mil)	Net Income ($mil)
9-18	B-	2.30	1.22	7,114.0	420.8	153.7	45.9
9-17	B-	2.49	1.32	7,266.9	454.8	163.7	47.7
2017	B-	2.39	1.26	7,224.2	433.8	231.1	60.1
2016	B-	2.49	1.32	7,386.9	465.0	239.8	59.3
2015	B-	2.41	1.30	7,482.7	455.9	269.2	59.1
2014	B-	2.52	1.34	7,674.5	490.6	281.8	137.8
2013	B-	1.60	0.84	7,683.1	309.2	305.0	-567.1

Adverse Trends in Operations

Decrease in capital during 2017 (7%)
Decrease in asset base during 2017 (2%)
Decrease in premium volume from 2015 to 2016 (11%)
Decrease in capital during 2015 (7%)
Decrease in premium volume from 2013 to 2014 (8%)

MONY LIFE INSURANCE COMPANY OF AMERICA   B   Good

Major Rating Factors: Good quality investment portfolio (5.7 on a scale of 0 to 10) despite mixed results such as: minimal exposure to mortgages and large holdings of BBB rated bonds but minimal holdings in junk bonds. Good liquidity (5.3) with sufficient resources to cover a large increase in policy surrenders. Good overall results on stability tests (5.8) excellent operational trends and excellent risk diversification.

Other Rating Factors: Weak profitability (1.9) with operating losses during the first nine months of 2018. Strong capitalization (7.5) based on excellent risk adjusted capital (severe loss scenario).

Principal Business: Individual life insurance (92%), individual annuities (4%), group life insurance (2%), and group health insurance (2%).

Principal Investments: NonCMO investment grade bonds (78%), common & preferred stock (4%), policy loans (4%), mortgages in good standing (1%), and misc. investments (2%).

Investments in Affiliates: 4%
Group Affiliation: AXA Financial Inc
Licensed in: All states except NY
Commenced Business: June 1969
Address: 3030 N Third Street Suite 790, Phoenix, AZ 85012
Phone: (212) 554-1234 **Domicile State:** AZ **NAIC Code:** 78077

Data Date	Rating	RACR #1	RACR #2	Total Assets ($mil)	Capital ($mil)	Net Premium ($mil)	Net Income ($mil)
9-18	B	2.03	1.36	3,981.0	266.5	436.1	-6.3
9-17	B	2.76	1.85	3,638.0	316.7	378.2	0.5
2017	B	2.38	1.62	3,735.1	302.7	519.4	-12.5
2016	B	2.84	1.95	3,155.6	318.6	457.9	-14.4
2015	B	3.39	2.34	2,912.8	352.8	446.2	-3.6
2014	B-	3.80	2.63	2,830.6	384.9	298.0	11.7
2013	B-	4.02	2.70	2,794.3	356.7	-1,140.4	33.6

Adverse Trends in Operations

Decrease in capital during 2017 (5%)
Increase in policy surrenders from 2015 to 2016 (237%)
Decrease in capital during 2015 (8%)
Increase in policy surrenders from 2014 to 2015 (53%)
Change in premium mix from 2013 to 2014 (10.9%)

MOTORISTS LIFE INSURANCE COMPANY   B   Good

Major Rating Factors: Good quality investment portfolio (6.7 on a scale of 0 to 10) with no exposure to mortgages and small junk bond holdings. Good overall profitability (6.1). Good liquidity (5.6) with sufficient resources to cover a large increase in policy surrenders.

Other Rating Factors: Fair overall results on stability tests (4.4). Strong capitalization (8.5) based on excellent risk adjusted capital (severe loss scenario).

Principal Business: Individual life insurance (81%), individual annuities (18%), and group life insurance (1%).

Principal Investments: NonCMO investment grade bonds (65%), CMOs and structured securities (18%), policy loans (4%), common & preferred stock (4%), and misc. investments (4%).

Investments in Affiliates: None
Group Affiliation: The Motorists Group
Licensed in: AR, FL, GA, IL, IN, IA, KY, MA, MI, MN, MO, NE, NH, OH, PA, RI, SC, TN, VA, WV, WI
Commenced Business: January 1967
Address: 471 EAST BROAD STREET, COLUMBUS, OH 43215
Phone: (888) 876-6542 **Domicile State:** OH **NAIC Code:** 66311

Data Date	Rating	RACR #1	RACR #2	Total Assets ($mil)	Capital ($mil)	Net Premium ($mil)	Net Income ($mil)
9-18	B	3.57	1.98	491.5	70.9	35.7	2.7
9-17	B	3.01	1.60	589.1	64.3	141.5	1.5
2017	B	3.53	1.95	471.7	68.6	36.7	3.2
2016	B	3.10	1.67	467.4	62.2	53.1	-1.2
2015	B	3.08	1.65	490.0	61.8	-53.8	4.0
2014	B	2.47	1.37	523.6	56.4	64.8	2.4
2013	B	2.54	1.42	495.3	54.7	70.7	3.6

Rating Indexes

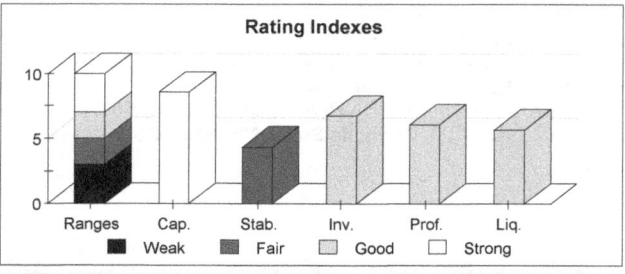

MUNICH AMERICAN REASSURANCE COMPANY   C   Fair

Major Rating Factors: Fair overall results on stability tests (4.1 on a scale of 0 to 10) including excessive premium growth and negative cash flow from operations for 2017. Good liquidity (5.9) with sufficient resources to handle a spike in claims as well as a significant increase in policy surrenders. Weak profitability (2.0) with investment income below regulatory standards in relation to interest assumptions of reserves.

Other Rating Factors: Strong capitalization (7.8) based on excellent risk adjusted capital (severe loss scenario). High quality investment portfolio (7.4).

Principal Business: Reinsurance (100%).

Principal Investments: NonCMO investment grade bonds (94%), CMOs and structured securities (3%), and common & preferred stock (1%).

Investments in Affiliates: None
Group Affiliation: Munchener R-G AG
Licensed in: All states, the District of Columbia and Puerto Rico
Commenced Business: November 1959
Address: 56 Perimeter Center East NE, Atlanta, GA 30346-2290
Phone: (770) 350-3200 **Domicile State:** GA **NAIC Code:** 66346

Data Date	Rating	RACR #1	RACR #2	Total Assets ($mil)	Capital ($mil)	Net Premium ($mil)	Net Income ($mil)
9-18	C	2.33	1.51	8,459.3	659.8	878.6	74.5
9-17	C	2.53	1.72	7,572.6	685.5	594.0	-67.8
2017	C	2.61	1.76	7,622.7	718.5	849.3	-48.4
2016	C	2.37	1.63	7,663.9	670.2	865.0	-99.1
2015	C	2.27	1.56	7,599.4	583.1	991.6	-74.8
2014	C+	2.41	1.68	7,289.5	737.9	1,451.5	-59.2
2013	B-	2.05	1.43	6,981.2	789.9	261.1	-29.0

Rating Indexes

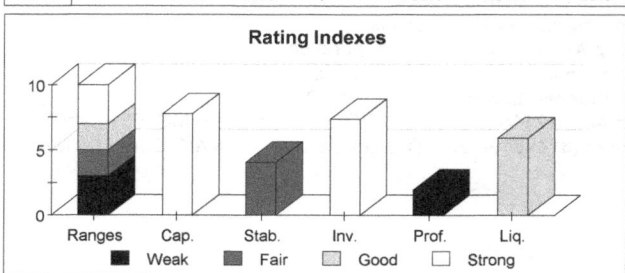

MUTUAL OF AMERICA LIFE INSURANCE COMPANY *

A- **Excellent**

Major Rating Factors: Good quality investment portfolio (5.4 on a scale of 0 to 10) despite mixed results such as: large holdings of BBB rated bonds but junk bond exposure equal to 71% of capital. Good overall profitability (5.8). Good overall results on stability tests (6.9) excellent operational trends and excellent risk diversification.

Other Rating Factors: Strong capitalization (7.6) based on excellent risk adjusted capital (severe loss scenario). Excellent liquidity (7.6).

Principal Business: Group retirement contracts (77%) and individual annuities (23%).

Principal Investments: NonCMO investment grade bonds (47%), CMOs and structured securities (39%), noninv. grade bonds (8%), real estate (3%), and misc. investments (3%).

Investments in Affiliates: None

Group Affiliation: None

Licensed in: All states except PR

Commenced Business: October 1945

Address: 320 Park Avenue, New York, NY 10022

Phone: (212) 224-1600 **Domicile State:** NY **NAIC Code:** 88668

Data Date	Rating	RACR #1	RACR #2	Total Assets ($mil)	Capital ($mil)	Net Premium ($mil)	Net Income ($mil)
9-18	A-	2.92	1.39	21,758.9	956.0	1,692.3	9.1
9-17	A-	3.07	1.45	20,499.3	986.1	1,834.7	9.5
2017	A-	3.03	1.43	21,184.9	983.3	2,710.1	25.7
2016	A-	3.28	1.52	19,041.8	993.4	2,263.9	16.4
2015	A-	3.70	1.75	17,865.4	1,032.2	2,043.3	64.5
2014	A-	3.57	1.68	17,790.9	997.7	1,963.7	59.2
2013	A-	3.41	1.62	16,666.7	951.2	1,771.8	49.4

Adverse Trends in Operations

Decrease in capital during 2017 (1%)
Decrease in capital during 2016 (4%)

MUTUAL OF OMAHA INSURANCE COMPANY

B **Good**

Major Rating Factors: Good overall results on stability tests (5.9 on a scale of 0 to 10). Stability strengths include excellent operational trends and excellent risk diversification. Good capitalization (6.5) based on good risk adjusted capital (severe loss scenario). Capital levels have been relatively consistent over the last five years. Good quality investment portfolio (6.1).

Other Rating Factors: Fair profitability (4.0) with operating losses during the first nine months of 2018. Excellent liquidity (7.0).

Principal Business: Reinsurance (54%), individual health insurance (39%), and group health insurance (6%).

Principal Investments: NonCMO investment grade bonds (41%), common & preferred stock (38%), CMOs and structured securities (11%), mortgages in good standing (4%), and misc. investments (6%).

Investments in Affiliates: 39%

Group Affiliation: Mutual Of Omaha Group

Licensed in: All states, the District of Columbia and Puerto Rico

Commenced Business: January 1910

Address: MUTUAL OF OMAHA PLAZA, OMAHA, NE 68175

Phone: (402) 342-7600 **Domicile State:** NE **NAIC Code:** 71412

Data Date	Rating	RACR #1	RACR #2	Total Assets ($mil)	Capital ($mil)	Net Premium ($mil)	Net Income ($mil)
9-18	B	1.01	0.94	7,924.2	3,160.4	2,437.9	-69.8
9-17	B+	1.07	0.99	7,661.2	3,083.3	2,256.0	-19.9
2017	B+	1.03	0.96	7,824.4	3,189.6	3,036.5	-7.1
2016	B+	1.07	0.99	7,278.9	3,048.3	2,726.5	103.4
2015	B+	1.02	0.95	6,945.1	2,862.8	2,411.8	11.2
2014	B+	1.02	0.96	6,426.8	2,795.7	2,186.3	30.4
2013	B+	1.11	1.04	5,795.4	2,674.5	2,071.2	105.8

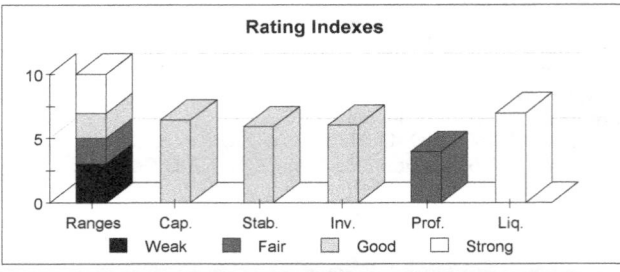

Rating Indexes

MUTUAL SAVINGS LIFE INSURANCE COMPANY

B **Good**

Major Rating Factors: Good overall results on stability tests (5.6 on a scale of 0 to 10). Stability strengths include good operational trends and excellent risk diversification. Good overall profitability (6.4). Excellent expense controls. Good liquidity (5.6) with sufficient resources to handle a spike in claims as well as a significant increase in policy surrenders.

Other Rating Factors: Strong capitalization (8.2) based on excellent risk adjusted capital (severe loss scenario). High quality investment portfolio (7.2).

Principal Business: Individual life insurance (86%), individual health insurance (11%), and reinsurance (3%).

Principal Investments: NonCMO investment grade bonds (85%), CMOs and structured securities (6%), policy loans (5%), noninv. grade bonds (3%), and common & preferred stock (1%).

Investments in Affiliates: 1%

Group Affiliation: Kemper Corporation

Licensed in: AL, FL, GA, IN, LA, MS, TN

Commenced Business: January 1927

Address: 12115 LACKLAND ROAD, ST. LOUIS, MO 63146-4003

Phone: (314) 819-4300 **Domicile State:** AL **NAIC Code:** 66397

Data Date	Rating	RACR #1	RACR #2	Total Assets ($mil)	Capital ($mil)	Net Premium ($mil)	Net Income ($mil)
9-18	B	2.99	1.82	480.7	54.7	29.1	12.6
9-17	B	2.36	1.42	468.6	42.3	29.5	6.0
2017	B	2.34	1.41	467.9	41.6	38.0	7.9
2016	B	2.07	1.24	462.4	36.3	38.4	1.2
2015	B	2.06	1.26	450.3	35.4	38.9	6.4
2014	B	1.88	1.15	445.1	31.6	39.9	10.2
2013	B+	2.80	1.76	464.3	57.3	41.6	6.7

Adverse Trends in Operations

Decrease in premium volume from 2016 to 2017 (1%)
Decrease in asset base during 2014 (4%)
Change in premium mix from 2013 to 2014 (9.5%)
Decrease in premium volume from 2013 to 2014 (4%)
Decrease in capital during 2014 (45%)

MUTUAL TRUST LIFE INSURANCE COMPANY B Good

Major Rating Factors: Good overall profitability (5.9 on a scale of 0 to 10). Good overall results on stability tests (5.9). Stability strengths include excellent operational trends and excellent risk diversification. Fair quality investment portfolio (4.7) with large holdings of BBB rated bonds in addition to moderate junk bond exposure.

Other Rating Factors: Fair liquidity (4.4). Strong capitalization (7.2) based on excellent risk adjusted capital (severe loss scenario).

Principal Business: Individual life insurance (99%) and individual annuities (1%).

Principal Investments: NonCMO investment grade bonds (57%), CMOs and structured securities (20%), policy loans (14%), noninv. grade bonds (4%), and misc. investments (5%).

Investments in Affiliates: None

Group Affiliation: Pan-American Life

Licensed in: All states except NY, PR

Commenced Business: April 1905

Address: 1200 Jorie Boulevard, Oak Brook, IL 60523-2269

Phone: (800) 323-7320 **Domicile State:** IL **NAIC Code:** 66427

Data Date	Rating	RACR #1	RACR #2	Total Assets ($mil)	Capital ($mil)	Net Premium ($mil)	Net Income ($mil)
9-18	B	2.19	1.10	2,038.5	151.6	126.1	6.1
9-17	B	2.28	1.16	1,998.7	150.6	132.4	3.7
2017	B	2.10	1.05	2,015.5	145.0	186.1	5.7
2016	B	2.24	1.15	1,959.8	144.8	159.7	3.4
2015	B	2.27	1.18	1,931.1	138.0	156.2	3.8
2014	B	2.13	1.12	1,928.0	132.0	174.4	7.5
2013	B	2.04	1.09	1,894.9	127.8	201.2	2.0

Adverse Trends in Operations

Decrease in premium volume from 2014 to 2015 (10%)
Decrease in premium volume from 2013 to 2014 (13%)
Increase in policy surrenders from 2013 to 2014 (39%)

NATIONAL BENEFIT LIFE INSURANCE COMPANY * B+ Good

Major Rating Factors: Good overall results on stability tests (6.6 on a scale of 0 to 10). Stability strengths include excellent operational trends and excellent risk diversification. Good quality investment portfolio (6.6) despite mixed results such as: no exposure to mortgages and large holdings of BBB rated bonds but small junk bond holdings. Good overall profitability (6.8). Excellent expense controls.

Other Rating Factors: Good liquidity (6.9). Strong capitalization (10.0) based on excellent risk adjusted capital (severe loss scenario).

Principal Business: Individual life insurance (99%) and group life insurance (1%).

Principal Investments: NonCMO investment grade bonds (72%), CMOs and structured securities (18%), noninv. grade bonds (3%), common & preferred stock (1%), and policy loans (1%).

Investments in Affiliates: None

Group Affiliation: Primerica Inc

Licensed in: All states except PR

Commenced Business: May 1963

Address: One Court Square, Long Island City, NY 11120-0001

Phone: (718) 361-3636 **Domicile State:** NY **NAIC Code:** 61409

Data Date	Rating	RACR #1	RACR #2	Total Assets ($mil)	Capital ($mil)	Net Premium ($mil)	Net Income ($mil)
9-18	B+	6.46	3.47	564.7	150.4	68.0	16.3
9-17	B+	6.96	3.70	537.3	156.7	61.4	11.3
2017	B+	6.61	3.53	539.5	155.3	82.8	14.9
2016	B+	7.27	3.85	513.9	164.3	74.0	16.4
2015	B	7.68	4.07	493.8	169.7	65.9	14.1
2014	B	8.00	4.28	481.6	171.9	60.9	20.3
2013	B+	7.13	4.02	484.0	174.5	88.8	22.3

Adverse Trends in Operations

Decrease in capital during 2016 (3%)
Increase in policy surrenders from 2015 to 2016 (50%)
Decrease in capital during 2014 (1%)
Change in premium mix from 2013 to 2014 (8.6%)
Decrease in premium volume from 2013 to 2014 (31%)

NATIONAL FARM LIFE INSURANCE COMPANY B Good

Major Rating Factors: Good overall profitability (5.7 on a scale of 0 to 10). Good overall results on stability tests (5.5). Stability strengths include excellent operational trends and good risk diversification. Fair liquidity (4.0) due, in part, to cash value policies that are subject to withdrawals with minimal or no penalty.

Other Rating Factors: Strong capitalization (8.3) based on excellent risk adjusted capital (severe loss scenario). High quality investment portfolio (7.2).

Principal Business: Individual life insurance (97%) and individual annuities (3%).

Principal Investments: NonCMO investment grade bonds (83%), policy loans (6%), CMOs and structured securities (4%), common & preferred stock (3%), and misc. investments (4%).

Investments in Affiliates: None

Group Affiliation: National Farm Group

Licensed in: TX

Commenced Business: May 1946

Address: 6001 Bridge Street, Fort Worth, TX 76112

Phone: (817) 451-9550 **Domicile State:** TX **NAIC Code:** 66532

Data Date	Rating	RACR #1	RACR #2	Total Assets ($mil)	Capital ($mil)	Net Premium ($mil)	Net Income ($mil)
9-18	B	3.08	1.86	417.6	46.2	18.3	2.7
9-17	B	2.80	1.67	406.3	41.5	18.1	1.9
2017	B	2.87	1.71	410.1	43.1	25.3	3.3
2016	B	2.67	1.59	399.6	39.3	25.3	3.0
2015	B	2.60	1.55	390.2	36.6	26.8	2.6
2014	B-	2.57	1.53	378.0	33.9	26.6	2.8
2013	B-	2.48	1.47	366.3	32.6	26.1	2.9

Adverse Trends in Operations

Decrease in premium volume from 2015 to 2016 (5%)

NATIONAL FARMERS UNION LIFE INSURANCE COMPANY * B+ Good

Major Rating Factors: Good overall results on stability tests (6.5 on a scale of 0 to 10) despite negative cash flow from operations for 2017. Other stability subfactors include good operational trends and excellent risk diversification. Good quality investment portfolio (5.4) despite mixed results such as: minimal exposure to mortgages and large holdings of BBB rated bonds but small junk bond holdings. Good overall profitability (6.9).

Other Rating Factors: Good liquidity (6.3). Strong capitalization (8.9) based on excellent risk adjusted capital (severe loss scenario).

Principal Business: Individual life insurance (71%), reinsurance (27%), individual annuities (1%), and group life insurance (1%).

Principal Investments: NonCMO investment grade bonds (45%), CMOs and structured securities (28%), common & preferred stock (11%), policy loans (4%), and misc. investments (11%).

Investments in Affiliates: 3%

Group Affiliation: Americo Life Inc

Licensed in: AK, AZ, AR, CA, CO, DC, ID, IL, IN, IA, KS, KY, MI, MN, MS, MO, MT, NE, NV, NM, ND, OH, OK, OR, PA, SD, TX, UT, VA, WA, WI, WY

Commenced Business: April 1938

Address: PO Box 139061, Dallas, TX 75313-9061

Phone: (816) 391-2000 **Domicile State:** TX **NAIC Code:** 66540

Data Date	Rating	RACR #1	RACR #2	Total Assets ($mil)	Capital ($mil)	Net Premium ($mil)	Net Income ($mil)
9-18	B+	4.46	2.29	193.3	47.6	4.4	4.3
9-17	B+	4.58	2.43	199.1	45.8	4.8	3.1
2017	B+	4.45	2.34	199.0	44.6	6.3	4.9
2016	B+	4.26	2.25	203.2	42.5	7.1	3.5
2015	B+	4.28	2.24	206.7	43.4	6.1	4.5
2014	B+	4.13	2.17	216.6	43.7	4.9	4.7
2013	B	4.09	2.17	221.6	43.2	4.8	3.8

Adverse Trends in Operations

Decrease in premium volume from 2016 to 2017 (11%)
Decrease in asset base during 2017 (2%)
Decrease in capital during 2016 (2%)
Decrease in asset base during 2015 (5%)
Decrease in asset base during 2014 (2%)

NATIONAL FOUNDATION LIFE INSURANCE COMPANY * B+ Good

Major Rating Factors: Good overall results on stability tests (6.2 on a scale of 0 to 10) despite excessive premium growth. Other stability subfactors include excellent operational trends, good risk adjusted capital for prior years and good risk diversification. Strong current capitalization (7.5) based on excellent risk adjusted capital (severe loss scenario) reflecting improvement over results in 2013. High quality investment portfolio (8.0).

Other Rating Factors: Excellent profitability (9.1). Excellent liquidity (7.5).

Principal Business: Individual health insurance (50%), group health insurance (37%), reinsurance (7%), and individual life insurance (6%).

Principal Investments: NonCMO investment grade bonds (43%), cash (29%), CMOs and structured securities (19%), and noninv. grade bonds (3%).

Investments in Affiliates: None

Group Affiliation: Credit Suisse Group

Licensed in: AL, AK, AZ, AR, CA, CO, DC, DE, GA, ID, IN, IA, KS, KY, LA, ME, MS, MO, MT, NE, NV, NM, NC, ND, OH, OK, OR, PA, SC, SD, TN, TX, UT, VA, WA, WY

Commenced Business: November 1983

Address: 300 Burnett Street Suite 200, Fort Worth, TX 76102-2734

Phone: (817) 878-3300 **Domicile State:** TX **NAIC Code:** 98205

Data Date	Rating	RACR #1	RACR #2	Total Assets ($mil)	Capital ($mil)	Net Premium ($mil)	Net Income ($mil)
9-18	B+	1.74	1.36	50.6	30.8	58.0	8.7
9-17	B	2.09	1.64	39.6	23.8	38.5	3.8
2017	B	1.61	1.25	38.9	21.7	53.7	5.4
2016	B	2.10	1.63	33.8	19.9	40.1	5.4
2015	B-	2.08	1.61	29.9	16.5	34.9	6.0
2014	C	1.38	1.06	25.1	11.5	37.3	2.3
2013	C+	1.06	0.82	26.7	10.5	45.3	2.3

Adverse Trends in Operations

Change in asset mix during 2016 (5%)
Decrease in premium volume from 2014 to 2015 (6%)
Decrease in asset base during 2014 (6%)
Decrease in premium volume from 2013 to 2014 (18%)

NATIONAL GUARDIAN LIFE INSURANCE COMPANY B- Good

Major Rating Factors: Good quality investment portfolio (5.8 on a scale of 0 to 10) despite mixed results such as: large holdings of BBB rated bonds but moderate junk bond exposure. Good overall profitability (5.7). Good liquidity (5.8) with sufficient resources to handle a spike in claims as well as a significant increase in policy surrenders.

Other Rating Factors: Good overall results on stability tests (5.3) good operational trends, good risk adjusted capital for prior years and excellent risk diversification. Strong capitalization (7.1) based on excellent risk adjusted capital (severe loss scenario).

Principal Business: Group health insurance (38%), group life insurance (33%), individual life insurance (19%), reinsurance (6%), and other lines (4%).

Principal Investments: NonCMO investment grade bonds (78%), CMOs and structured securities (6%), common & preferred stock (4%), mortgages in good standing (3%), and misc. investments (6%).

Investments in Affiliates: 2%

Group Affiliation: NGL Ins Group

Licensed in: All states except NY, PR

Commenced Business: October 1910

Address: 2 East Gilman Street, Madison, WI 53703-1494

Phone: (608) 257-5611 **Domicile State:** WI **NAIC Code:** 66583

Data Date	Rating	RACR #1	RACR #2	Total Assets ($mil)	Capital ($mil)	Net Premium ($mil)	Net Income ($mil)
9-18	B-	1.62	1.04	4,065.8	347.9	514.2	22.6
9-17	B-	1.67	1.04	3,859.7	336.0	467.3	18.9
2017	B-	1.53	0.98	3,884.4	322.6	603.4	28.8
2016	B-	1.52	0.95	3,657.9	293.3	553.0	18.1
2015	B-	1.45	0.91	3,422.2	271.1	790.0	-4.5
2014	B	1.47	0.96	2,948.3	250.1	476.1	24.4
2013	B	1.51	0.99	2,730.8	241.3	416.1	28.8

Rating Indexes

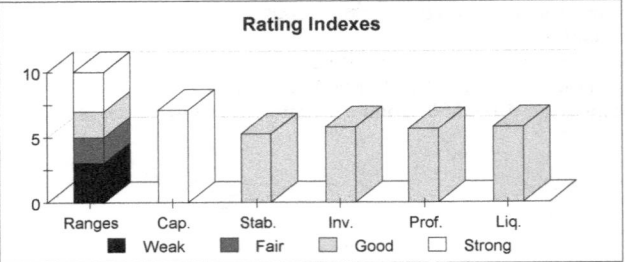

NATIONAL INCOME LIFE INSURANCE COMPANY *   B+   Good

Major Rating Factors: Good overall results on stability tests (6.7 on a scale of 0 to 10). Stability strengths include excellent operational trends and excellent risk diversification. Good overall profitability (5.2) although investment income, in comparison to reserve requirements, is below regulatory standards. Good liquidity (6.5).

Other Rating Factors: Strong capitalization (8.0) based on excellent risk adjusted capital (severe loss scenario). High quality investment portfolio (7.0).

Principal Business: Individual life insurance (92%) and individual health insurance (8%).

Principal Investments: NonCMO investment grade bonds (84%), cash (5%), policy loans (4%), noninv. grade bonds (2%), and CMOs and structured securities (1%).

Investments in Affiliates: None
Group Affiliation: Torchmark Corp
Licensed in: NY
Commenced Business: November 2000
Address: 1020 SEVENTH NORTH ST STE 130, LIVERPOOL, NY 13212
Phone: (315) 451-8180 **Domicile State:** NY **NAIC Code:** 10093

Data Date	Rating	RACR #1	RACR #2	Total Assets ($mil)	Capital ($mil)	Net Premium ($mil)	Net Income ($mil)
9-18	B+	2.80	1.66	261.9	37.8	64.4	10.0
9-17	B+	3.26	1.98	223.3	37.4	60.8	8.4
2017	B+	2.85	1.72	233.3	37.0	80.7	9.1
2016	B+	3.55	2.18	203.4	40.1	73.3	10.9
2015	B+	3.47	2.14	171.7	34.1	64.9	8.1
2014	B+	3.27	2.21	145.5	30.1	58.4	5.8
2013	B+	3.90	2.76	132.5	35.7	53.9	5.0

Rating Indexes

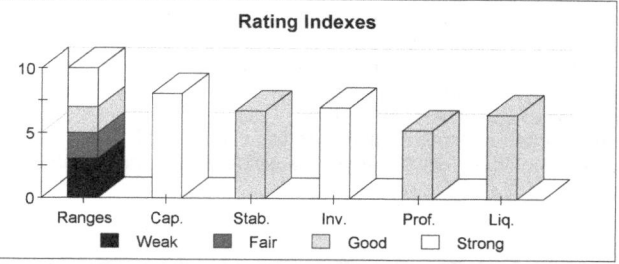

NATIONAL INTEGRITY LIFE INSURANCE COMPANY   B-   Good

Major Rating Factors: Good quality investment portfolio (5.7 on a scale of 0 to 10) despite mixed results such as: large holdings of BBB rated bonds but moderate junk bond exposure. Good liquidity (6.5) with sufficient resources to cover a large increase in policy surrenders. Good overall results on stability tests (5.1) good operational trends and excellent risk diversification.

Other Rating Factors: Weak profitability (2.7) with investment income below regulatory standards in relation to interest assumptions of reserves. Strong capitalization (7.6) based on excellent risk adjusted capital (severe loss scenario).

Principal Business: Individual annuities (89%) and individual life insurance (11%).

Principal Investments: NonCMO investment grade bonds (54%), CMOs and structured securities (28%), noninv. grade bonds (6%), mortgages in good standing (5%), and misc. investments (7%).

Investments in Affiliates: 2%
Group Affiliation: Western & Southern Group
Licensed in: CT, DC, FL, ME, NH, NY, OH, RI, VT
Commenced Business: December 1968
Address: 14 MAIN STREET SUITE 100, GREENWICH, NY 12834
Phone: (513) 629-1402 **Domicile State:** NY **NAIC Code:** 75264

Data Date	Rating	RACR #1	RACR #2	Total Assets ($mil)	Capital ($mil)	Net Premium ($mil)	Net Income ($mil)
9-18	B-	2.76	1.38	4,583.7	334.2	179.2	22.4
9-17	B-	3.24	1.62	4,722.6	390.7	165.9	22.6
2017	B-	2.71	1.36	4,640.5	315.9	224.4	-14.1
2016	B-	3.22	1.58	4,692.8	359.3	279.8	33.8
2015	B-	3.24	1.60	4,739.0	356.6	255.1	34.3
2014	B-	3.46	1.71	4,777.0	377.5	247.1	48.3
2013	B-	3.07	1.50	4,767.1	321.0	215.3	34.4

Adverse Trends in Operations

Decrease in capital during 2017 (12%)
Decrease in premium volume from 2016 to 2017 (20%)
Decrease in asset base during 2017 (1%)
Decrease in capital during 2015 (6%)

NATIONAL LIFE INSURANCE COMPANY   B-   Good

Major Rating Factors: Fair overall capitalization (4.0 on a scale of 0 to 10) based on mixed results -- excessive policy leverage mitigated by excellent risk adjusted capital (severe loss scenario). Moreover, capital levels have been consistently high over the last five years. Fair profitability (4.2). Fair overall results on stability tests (4.8).

Other Rating Factors: Good quality investment portfolio (6.1). Good liquidity (6.9).

Principal Business: Individual life insurance (87%), individual annuities (6%), individual health insurance (4%), and group retirement contracts (3%).

Principal Investments: NonCMO investment grade bonds (50%), common & preferred stock (15%), CMOs and structured securities (14%), policy loans (7%), and misc. investments (13%).

Investments in Affiliates: 15%
Group Affiliation: National Life Group
Licensed in: All states except PR
Commenced Business: January 1850
Address: 1 National Life Drive, Montpelier, VT 5604
Phone: (802) 229-3333 **Domicile State:** VT **NAIC Code:** 66680

Data Date	Rating	RACR #1	RACR #2	Total Assets ($mil)	Capital ($mil)	Net Premium ($mil)	Net Income ($mil)
9-18	B-	1.53	1.30	9,786.2	2,361.3	271.2	14.7
9-17	B	1.56	1.30	9,442.4	1,986.3	252.5	-22.9
2017	B	1.45	1.25	9,500.0	2,015.6	-43.2	14.9
2016	B	1.54	1.29	9,276.9	1,925.2	331.1	-51.1
2015	B	1.72	1.37	9,148.7	1,778.0	-2,919.0	12.0
2014	B	1.50	1.18	9,209.9	1,541.2	411.8	19.1
2013	B	1.52	1.19	9,091.3	1,413.1	418.3	88.5

Policy Leverage

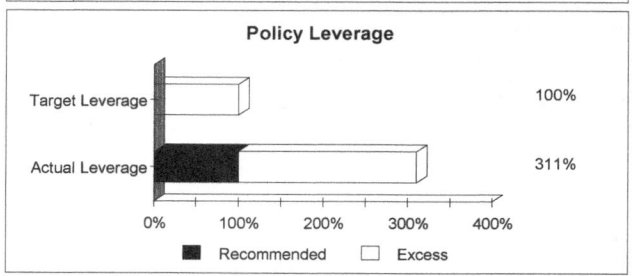

NATIONAL TEACHERS ASSOCIATES LIFE INSURANCE COMPAN   B   Good

Major Rating Factors: Good quality investment portfolio (6.7 on a scale of 0 to 10) despite mixed results such as: minimal exposure to mortgages and large holdings of BBB rated bonds but small junk bond holdings. Good overall results on stability tests (6.0). Stability strengths include excellent operational trends and excellent risk diversification. Fair profitability (4.7) with investment income below regulatory standards in relation to interest assumptions of reserves.

Other Rating Factors: Strong capitalization (8.7) based on excellent risk adjusted capital (severe loss scenario). Excellent liquidity (8.6).

Principal Business: Individual health insurance (98%) and individual life insurance (2%).

Principal Investments: NonCMO investment grade bonds (52%), CMOs and structured securities (32%), noninv. grade bonds (5%), mortgages in good standing (5%), and misc. investments (6%).

Investments in Affiliates: 1%

Group Affiliation: Ellard Family Holdings Inc

Licensed in: All states except NY, PR

Commenced Business: July 1938

Address: 4949 Keller Springs Rd, Addison, TX 75001

Phone: (972) 532-2100 **Domicile State:** TX **NAIC Code:** 87963

Data Date	Rating	RACR #1	RACR #2	Total Assets ($mil)	Capital ($mil)	Net Premium ($mil)	Net Income ($mil)
9-18	B	3.26	2.16	572.9	132.9	97.7	22.6
9-17	B	3.03	2.03	535.3	110.4	98.1	13.4
2017	B	2.89	1.95	544.9	115.9	130.7	20.3
2016	B	2.86	1.94	510.5	102.4	129.2	11.2
2015	B	N/A	N/A	464.1	92.1	123.6	11.1
2014	B	2.47	1.73	422.9	80.9	117.5	7.8
2013	B	2.55	1.84	381.8	73.1	108.1	7.0

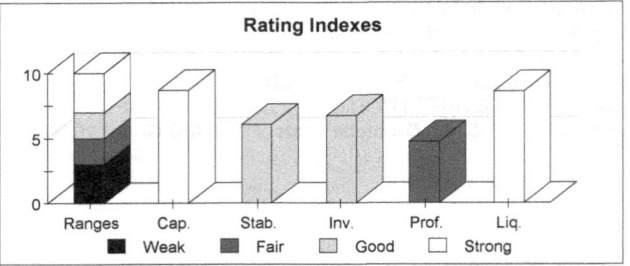

Rating Indexes

NATIONAL WESTERN LIFE INSURANCE COMPANY *   A   Excellent

Major Rating Factors: Good quality investment portfolio (6.4 on a scale of 0 to 10) despite mixed results such as: minimal exposure to mortgages and large holdings of BBB rated bonds but minimal holdings in junk bonds. Good liquidity (6.0) with sufficient resources to handle a spike in claims as well as a significant increase in policy surrenders. Strong capitalization (8.9) based on excellent risk adjusted capital (severe loss scenario).

Other Rating Factors: Excellent profitability (7.8). Excellent overall results on stability tests (7.4) excellent operational trends and excellent risk diversification.

Principal Business: Individual annuities (69%) and individual life insurance (31%).

Principal Investments: NonCMO investment grade bonds (79%), CMOs and structured securities (12%), common & preferred stock (3%), mortgages in good standing (2%), and misc. investments (3%).

Investments in Affiliates: 3%

Group Affiliation: None

Licensed in: All states except NY

Commenced Business: June 1957

Address: 1675 Broadway #1200, Centennial, CO 80112

Phone: (512) 719-2240 **Domicile State:** CO **NAIC Code:** 66850

Data Date	Rating	RACR #1	RACR #2	Total Assets ($mil)	Capital ($mil)	Net Premium ($mil)	Net Income ($mil)
9-18	A	4.25	2.24	11,114.0	1,441.0	539.2	85.2
9-17	A	4.32	2.24	11,058.8	1,341.4	647.4	88.0
2017	A	4.09	2.16	11,149.8	1,374.6	863.1	126.9
2016	A	4.11	2.13	10,820.6	1,251.4	980.2	88.7
2015	A	3.81	2.05	10,544.6	1,171.2	1,051.5	7.1
2014	A	4.60	2.37	10,262.7	1,185.6	1,109.9	77.2
2013	B+	4.35	2.38	9,771.2	1,126.2	1,105.4	106.2

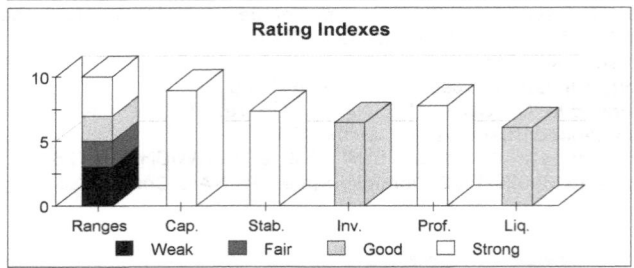

Rating Indexes

NATIONWIDE LIFE & ANNUITY INSURANCE COMPANY   C   Fair

Major Rating Factors: Fair overall results on stability tests (4.3 on a scale of 0 to 10). Good quality investment portfolio (5.4) despite large holdings of BBB rated bonds in addition to junk bond exposure equal to 51% of capital. Exposure to mortgages is significant, but the mortgage default rate has been low. Weak profitability (2.9).

Other Rating Factors: Strong capitalization (7.7) based on excellent risk adjusted capital (severe loss scenario). Excellent liquidity (7.1).

Principal Business: N/A

Principal Investments: NonCMO investment grade bonds (61%), mortgages in good standing (18%), CMOs and structured securities (5%), and noninv. grade bonds (4%).

Investments in Affiliates: 1%

Group Affiliation: Nationwide Corp

Licensed in: All states except NY, PR

Commenced Business: May 1981

Address: ONE WEST NATIONWIDE BLVD, COLUMBUS, OH 43215-2220

Phone: (614) 249-5227 **Domicile State:** OH **NAIC Code:** 92657

Data Date	Rating	RACR #1	RACR #2	Total Assets ($mil)	Capital ($mil)	Net Premium ($mil)	Net Income ($mil)
9-18	C	2.94	1.46	24,689.8	1,467.0	4,725.7	164.7
9-17	C	2.97	1.42	18,807.0	1,147.9	4,279.6	-100.7
2017	C	3.06	1.57	20,608.3	1,339.6	5,655.3	-276.3
2016	C	2.95	1.44	14,466.2	968.2	3,563.7	-226.6
2015	C	2.74	1.37	10,757.6	735.0	3,314.9	-99.5
2014	C	3.37	1.73	7,896.7	690.6	1,086.7	-122.4
2013	B-	3.13	1.60	6,901.6	534.1	84.3	-103.3

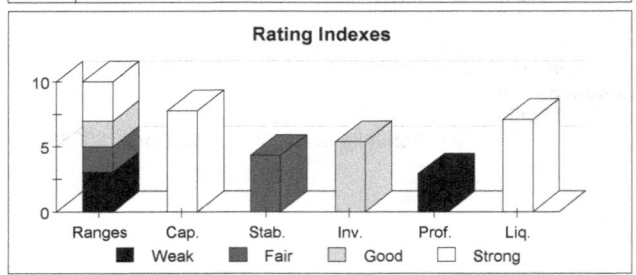

Rating Indexes

NATIONWIDE LIFE INSURANCE COMPANY

B-   **Good**

Major Rating Factors: Good quality investment portfolio (6.1 on a scale of 0 to 10) despite large holdings of BBB rated bonds in addition to moderate junk bond exposure. Exposure to mortgages is significant, but the mortgage default rate has been low. Good overall results on stability tests (5.3). Stability strengths include excellent operational trends and excellent risk diversification. Strong capitalization (7.8) based on excellent risk adjusted capital (severe loss scenario).

Other Rating Factors: Excellent profitability (8.0). Excellent liquidity (8.2).

Principal Business: Individual annuities (42%), group retirement contracts (37%), group life insurance (12%), individual life insurance (6%), and group health insurance (2%).

Principal Investments: NonCMO investment grade bonds (58%), mortgages in good standing (17%), CMOs and structured securities (11%), noninv. grade bonds (4%), and misc. investments (8%).

Investments in Affiliates: 4%

Group Affiliation: Nationwide Corp

Licensed in: All states, the District of Columbia and Puerto Rico

Commenced Business: January 1931

Address: ONE WEST NATIONWIDE BLVD, COLUMBUS, OH 43215-2220

Phone: (614) 249-5227 **Domicile State:** OH **NAIC Code:** 66869

Data Date	Rating	RACR #1	RACR #2	Total Assets ($mil)	Capital ($mil)	Net Premium ($mil)	Net Income ($mil)
9-18	B-	2.32	1.54	146,933	6,433.1	6,548.2	408.6
9-17	B-	2.51	1.53	141,988	5,682.6	7,249.5	631.6
2017	B-	2.19	1.46	145,670	5,949.3	10,402.4	1,038.7
2016	B-	2.45	1.50	133,345	5,208.4	9,868.1	751.0
2015	B-	2.48	1.47	126,861	4,566.5	11,305.1	166.8
2014	B-	2.50	1.48	128,585	4,408.0	11,645.4	341.5
2013	B	2.30	1.34	120,676	3,550.0	11,604.5	262.2

Adverse Trends in Operations

Decrease in premium volume from 2015 to 2016 (13%)
Decrease in asset base during 2015 (1%)
Decrease in premium volume from 2014 to 2015 (3%)
Increase in policy surrenders from 2013 to 2014 (1434%)

NEW ENGLAND LIFE INSURANCE COMPANY

B   **Good**

Major Rating Factors: Good overall results on stability tests (5.0 on a scale of 0 to 10). Stability strengths include good operational trends and excellent risk diversification. Good quality investment portfolio (5.9) despite mixed results such as: minimal exposure to mortgages and large holdings of BBB rated bonds but small junk bond holdings. Good overall profitability (5.6).

Other Rating Factors: Good liquidity (6.7). Strong capitalization (9.3) based on excellent risk adjusted capital (severe loss scenario).

Principal Business: Individual life insurance (86%), individual annuities (12%), and individual health insurance (3%).

Principal Investments: NonCMO investment grade bonds (48%), policy loans (22%), CMOs and structured securities (17%), noninv. grade bonds (7%), and mortgages in good standing (5%).

Investments in Affiliates: None

Group Affiliation: Brighthouse Financial Inc

Licensed in: All states except PR

Commenced Business: December 1980

Address: One Financial Plaza, Boston, MA 2111

Phone: (617) 578-2000 **Domicile State:** MA **NAIC Code:** 91626

Data Date	Rating	RACR #1	RACR #2	Total Assets ($mil)	Capital ($mil)	Net Premium ($mil)	Net Income ($mil)
9-18	B	5.07	2.56	9,964.8	569.7	103.4	102.0
9-17	B	4.91	2.47	10,196.3	572.5	111.2	40.2
2017	B	4.27	2.15	10,160.6	482.5	153.8	68.0
2016	B	3.97	1.98	9,801.7	454.8	187.9	108.8
2015	B	5.02	2.48	10,172.8	631.9	204.0	156.8
2014	B	5.04	2.48	11,179.5	675.2	-3,295.8	303.2
2013	B	3.73	2.01	11,640.2	571.1	260.1	102.7

Adverse Trends in Operations

Decrease in premium volume from 2016 to 2017 (18%)
Decrease in capital during 2016 (28%)
Change in premium mix from 2014 to 2015 (22.0%)
Decrease in asset base during 2014 (4%)
Decrease in premium volume from 2013 to 2014 (1367%)

NEW ERA LIFE INSURANCE COMPANY

C   **Fair**

Major Rating Factors: Fair overall results on stability tests (4.1 on a scale of 0 to 10) including fair risk adjusted capital in prior years. Good current capitalization (5.2) based on good risk adjusted capital (severe loss scenario) reflecting some improvement over results in 2013. Good quality investment portfolio (5.3).

Other Rating Factors: Good liquidity (6.5). Excellent profitability (8.5).

Principal Business: Individual health insurance (57%), individual annuities (41%), and individual life insurance (1%).

Principal Investments: NonCMO investment grade bonds (50%), mortgages in good standing (21%), common & preferred stock (10%), cash (6%), and misc. investments (12%).

Investments in Affiliates: 9%

Group Affiliation: New Era Life Group

Licensed in: AL, AZ, AR, CA, CO, DE, FL, GA, IN, KS, KY, LA, MI, MS, MO, MT, NE, NM, NC, ND, OH, OK, PA, SC, SD, TN, TX, UT, WA, WV

Commenced Business: June 1924

Address: 11720 Katy Freeway Suite 1700, Houston, TX 77079

Phone: (281) 368-7200 **Domicile State:** TX **NAIC Code:** 78743

Data Date	Rating	RACR #1	RACR #2	Total Assets ($mil)	Capital ($mil)	Net Premium ($mil)	Net Income ($mil)
9-18	C	1.03	0.78	543.6	88.2	115.7	1.4
9-17	C	0.99	0.75	533.5	79.9	138.8	3.0
2017	C	0.94	0.73	538.3	79.3	181.4	3.5
2016	C	0.94	0.72	504.2	75.1	190.3	4.5
2015	C	0.95	0.73	463.5	70.7	111.2	5.1
2014	C	0.95	0.73	402.5	66.2	99.3	4.3
2013	C	0.90	0.69	371.3	58.0	77.3	4.6

Rating Indexes

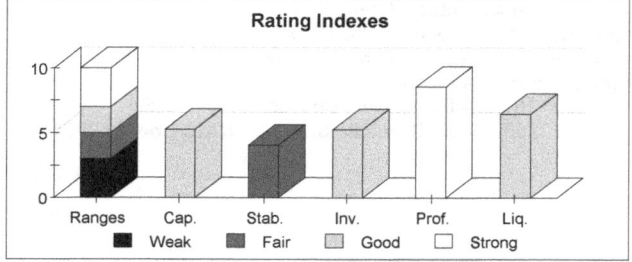

NEW YORK LIFE INSURANCE & ANNUITY CORPORATION *   B+   Good

Major Rating Factors: Good quality investment portfolio (6.0 on a scale of 0 to 10) despite large holdings of BBB rated bonds in addition to junk bond exposure equal to 50% of capital. Exposure to mortgages is significant, but the mortgage default rate has been low. Good liquidity (6.5) with sufficient resources to cover a large increase in policy surrenders. Good overall results on stability tests (6.8) excellent operational trends and excellent risk diversification.

Other Rating Factors: Strong capitalization (8.1) based on excellent risk adjusted capital (severe loss scenario). Excellent profitability (7.9).

Principal Business: Individual annuities (83%), individual life insurance (16%), group life insurance (1%), and group retirement contracts (1%).

Principal Investments: NonCMO investment grade bonds (50%), CMOs and structured securities (28%), mortgages in good standing (13%), noninv. grade bonds (4%), and misc. investments (3%).

Investments in Affiliates: 3%

Group Affiliation: New York Life Group

Licensed in: All states except PR

Commenced Business: December 1980

Address: 200 CONTINENTAL DRIVE STE 306, NEWARK, DE 19713

Phone: (212) 576-7000 **Domicile State:** DE **NAIC Code:** 91596

Data Date	Rating	RACR #1	RACR #2	Total Assets ($mil)	Capital ($mil)	Net Premium ($mil)	Net Income ($mil)
9-18	B+	3.57	1.75	156,175	8,695.0	9,462.7	302.8
9-17	B+	3.69	1.81	149,883	8,983.7	10,493.7	494.4
2017	B+	3.81	1.87	152,851	9,186.9	13,315.8	652.2
2016	B+	3.70	1.81	141,353	8,724.5	12,732.1	777.7
2015	B+	3.80	1.85	132,239	8,145.8	12,674.2	396.8
2014	B+	3.46	1.70	126,837	7,668.5	12,028.2	742.7
2013	B+	3.15	1.53	119,947	6,748.1	10,411.6	798.0

Adverse Trends in Operations

Increase in policy surrenders from 2013 to 2014 (45%)

NEW YORK LIFE INSURANCE COMPANY *   A-   Excellent

Major Rating Factors: Good quality investment portfolio (6.6 on a scale of 0 to 10) despite substantial holdings of BBB bonds in addition to moderate junk bond exposure. Exposure to mortgages is significant, but the mortgage default rate has been low. Good liquidity (6.4) with sufficient resources to handle a spike in claims as well as a significant increase in policy surrenders. Strong capitalization (7.5) based on excellent risk adjusted capital (severe loss scenario).

Other Rating Factors: Excellent profitability (7.0). Excellent overall results on stability tests (7.0) excellent operational trends and excellent risk diversification.

Principal Business: Individual life insurance (49%), group retirement contracts (28%), group life insurance (12%), reinsurance (6%), and other lines (5%).

Principal Investments: NonCMO investment grade bonds (46%), CMOs and structured securities (17%), mortgages in good standing (10%), policy loans (7%), and misc. investments (18%).

Investments in Affiliates: 11%

Group Affiliation: New York Life Group

Licensed in: All states, the District of Columbia and Puerto Rico

Commenced Business: April 1845

Address: 51 MADISON AVENUE, NEW YORK, NY 10010

Phone: (212) 576-7000 **Domicile State:** NY **NAIC Code:** 66915

Data Date	Rating	RACR #1	RACR #2	Total Assets ($mil)	Capital ($mil)	Net Premium ($mil)	Net Income ($mil)
9-18	A-	1.74	1.32	178,707	20,941.2	12,371.1	988.5
9-17	A-	1.80	1.37	176,417	21,012.4	10,619.6	724.3
2017	A-	1.70	1.30	176,766	20,357.0	15,070.0	1,479.9
2016	A-	1.72	1.32	170,762	20,107.6	15,440.1	298.0
2015	A-	1.62	1.23	163,554	19,495.9	20,396.0	-152.2
2014	A-	1.75	1.34	146,267	18,606.0	13,931.9	848.3
2013	A-	1.55	1.22	139,198	17,853.8	13,047.8	520.3

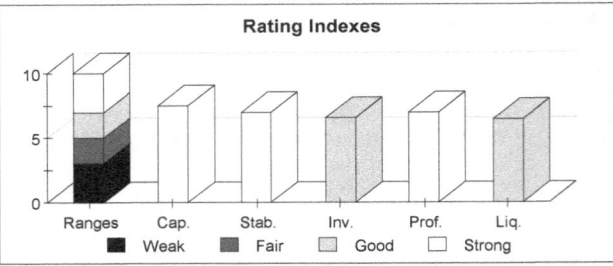

Rating Indexes

Ranges | Cap. | Stab. | Inv. | Prof. | Liq.
■ Weak ■ Fair ▨ Good □ Strong

NIPPON LIFE INSURANCE COMPANY OF AMERICA *   A-   Excellent

Major Rating Factors: Good overall profitability (6.6 on a scale of 0 to 10). Good liquidity (6.6) with sufficient resources to handle a spike in claims. Strong capitalization (9.5) based on excellent risk adjusted capital (severe loss scenario). Furthermore, this high level of risk adjusted capital has been consistently maintained over the last five years.

Other Rating Factors: High quality investment portfolio (8.2). Excellent overall results on stability tests (7.0) excellent operational trends and excellent risk diversification.

Principal Business: Group health insurance (99%) and group life insurance (1%).

Principal Investments: NonCMO investment grade bonds (70%), CMOs and structured securities (11%), cash (3%), and common & preferred stock (2%).

Investments in Affiliates: None

Group Affiliation: Nippon Life Ins Co Japan

Licensed in: All states except ME, NH, WY, PR

Commenced Business: July 1973

Address: 7115 Vista Drive, West Des Moines, IA 50266

Phone: (212) 682-3000 **Domicile State:** IA **NAIC Code:** 81264

Data Date	Rating	RACR #1	RACR #2	Total Assets ($mil)	Capital ($mil)	Net Premium ($mil)	Net Income ($mil)
9-18	A-	3.34	2.65	219.2	140.3	257.4	0.8
9-17	A-	3.78	2.99	219.6	141.7	231.0	2.0
2017	A-	3.42	2.71	220.7	139.7	311.5	1.5
2016	A-	3.73	2.96	212.3	139.6	285.7	0.5
2015	A-	3.92	3.11	212.6	140.8	277.0	4.6
2014	A-	3.39	2.71	216.4	141.1	315.7	8.2
2013	A-	2.96	2.35	225.1	136.7	351.2	6.7

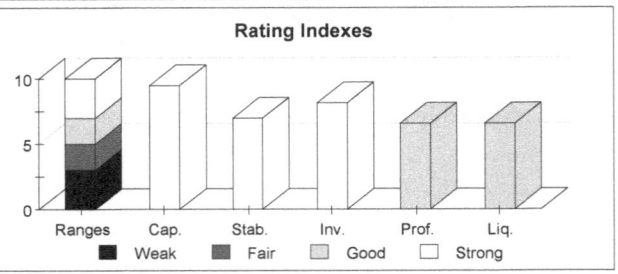

Rating Indexes

Ranges | Cap. | Stab. | Inv. | Prof. | Liq.
■ Weak ■ Fair ▨ Good □ Strong

NORTH AMERICAN COMPANY FOR LIFE & HEALTH INSURANCE   B   Good

Major Rating Factors: Good capitalization (6.2 on a scale of 0 to 10) based on good risk adjusted capital (moderate loss scenario). Capital levels have been relatively consistent over the last five years. Good liquidity (5.9) with sufficient resources to cover a large increase in policy surrenders. Good overall results on stability tests (5.8) excellent operational trends and excellent risk diversification.

Other Rating Factors: Fair quality investment portfolio (4.0). Excellent profitability (8.0).

Principal Business: Individual annuities (64%), individual life insurance (30%), group retirement contracts (4%), reinsurance (1%), and group life insurance (1%).

Principal Investments: NonCMO investment grade bonds (42%), CMOs and structured securities (39%), mortgages in good standing (8%), noninv. grade bonds (4%), and misc. investments (6%).

Investments in Affiliates: 3%
Group Affiliation: Sammons Enterprises Inc
Licensed in: All states except NY
Commenced Business: June 1886
Address: 4350 Westown Parkway, West Des Moines, IA 50266
Phone: (515) 226-7100   **Domicile State:** IA   **NAIC Code:** 66974

Data Date	Rating	RACR #1	RACR #2	Total Assets ($mil)	Capital ($mil)	Net Premium ($mil)	Net Income ($mil)
9-18	B	1.81	0.84	27,148.1	1,423.0	2,063.8	131.5
9-17	B	2.42	1.16	24,509.7	1,645.6	1,755.4	147.0
2017	B	1.77	0.83	25,607.5	1,361.4	2,443.5	147.4
2016	B	2.28	1.10	22,182.3	1,410.1	2,993.0	97.4
2015	B	1.92	0.88	18,900.2	1,129.3	2,317.2	-44.8
2014	B	2.29	1.06	16,970.0	1,176.7	1,653.4	85.4
2013	B	2.38	1.09	15,021.7	1,065.1	1,713.6	121.9

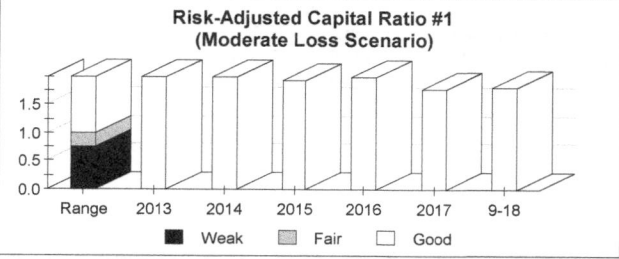

Risk-Adjusted Capital Ratio #1
(Moderate Loss Scenario)

■ Weak   ▨ Fair   □ Good

NORTHWESTERN LONG TERM CARE INSURANCE COMPANY   B   Good

Major Rating Factors: Fair current capitalization (4.0 on a scale of 0 to 10) based on mixed results -- excessive policy leverage mitigated by excellent risk adjusted capital (severe loss scenario) reflecting improvement over results in 2013. Fair overall results on stability tests (4.9). High quality investment portfolio (9.2).

Other Rating Factors: Excellent profitability (8.5) despite modest operating losses during 2013. Excellent liquidity (8.4).

Principal Business: Individual health insurance (100%).
Principal Investments: NonCMO investment grade bonds (100%).
Investments in Affiliates: None
Group Affiliation: Northwestern Mutual Group
Licensed in: All states except PR
Commenced Business: October 1953
Address: 720 EAST WISCONSIN AVENUE, MILWAUKEE, WI 53202
Phone: (414) 271-1444   **Domicile State:** WI   **NAIC Code:** 69000

Data Date	Rating	RACR #1	RACR #2	Total Assets ($mil)	Capital ($mil)	Net Premium ($mil)	Net Income ($mil)
9-18	B	7.62	3.06	204.5	106.6	0.0	2.4
9-17	B	7.89	3.17	196.0	104.8	-0.1	6.7
2017	B	8.03	3.23	200.6	104.1	-0.1	7.5
2016	B	6.46	2.60	172.7	82.2	0.2	2.6
2015	B	6.57	2.65	166.0	79.5	0.3	2.5
2014	B	8.08	7.27	161.4	77.2	-1,548.3	403.6
2013	B	1.76	0.99	2,220.1	213.8	457.3	-84.2

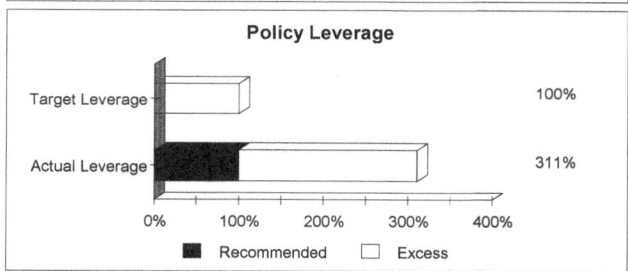

Policy Leverage

Target Leverage — 100%
Actual Leverage — 311%

■ Recommended   □ Excess

NORTHWESTERN MUTUAL LIFE INSURANCE COMPANY *   B+   Good

Major Rating Factors: Good quality investment portfolio (5.7 on a scale of 0 to 10) despite substantial holdings of BBB bonds in addition to junk bond exposure equal to 63% of capital. Exposure to mortgages is significant, but the mortgage default rate has been low. Good overall profitability (6.0) although investment income, in comparison to reserve requirements, is below regulatory standards. Good liquidity (5.7).

Other Rating Factors: Good overall results on stability tests (6.7) excellent operational trends and excellent risk diversification. Strong capitalization (8.0) based on excellent risk adjusted capital (severe loss scenario).

Principal Business: Individual life insurance (77%), individual annuities (11%), individual health insurance (6%), reinsurance (4%), and group retirement contracts (1%).

Principal Investments: NonCMO investment grade bonds (40%), CMOs and structured securities (20%), mortgages in good standing (16%), policy loans (8%), and misc. investments (16%).

Investments in Affiliates: 4%
Group Affiliation: Northwestern Mutual Group
Licensed in: All states except PR
Commenced Business: November 1858
Address: 720 EAST WISCONSIN AVENUE, MILWAUKEE, WI 53202-4797
Phone: (414) 271-1444   **Domicile State:** WI   **NAIC Code:** 67091

Data Date	Rating	RACR #1	RACR #2	Total Assets ($mil)	Capital ($mil)	Net Premium ($mil)	Net Income ($mil)
9-18	B+	3.34	1.69	273,304	22,125.4	13,247.4	737.9
9-17	A-	3.47	1.75	264,165	22,027.5	13,212.5	787.1
2017	B+	3.27	1.66	265,049	20,850.2	17,698.7	1,017.0
2016	A-	3.42	1.72	250,507	20,229.6	17,660.6	810.1
2015	A-	3.57	1.81	238,544	19,659.6	17,581.3	801.2
2014	A-	3.59	1.83	230,004	19,055.1	18,362.1	330.9
2013	A-	3.60	1.84	215,165	17,198.8	15,995.2	886.4

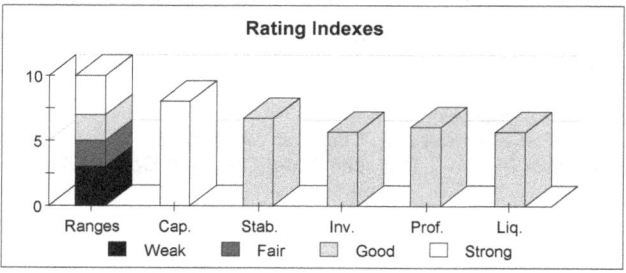

Rating Indexes

■ Weak   ▨ Fair   ▨ Good   □ Strong

NYLIFE INSURANCE COMPANY OF ARIZONA — B — Good

Major Rating Factors: Good overall results on stability tests (5.6 on a scale of 0 to 10) despite negative cash flow from operations for 2017. Other stability subfactors include good operational trends and excellent risk diversification. Strong capitalization (10.0) based on excellent risk adjusted capital (severe loss scenario). Moreover, capital levels have been consistently high over the last five years. High quality investment portfolio (8.5).

Other Rating Factors: Excellent profitability (8.7). Excellent liquidity (7.0).

Principal Business: Individual life insurance (99%) and reinsurance (1%).

Principal Investments: NonCMO investment grade bonds (80%) and CMOs and structured securities (21%).

Investments in Affiliates: None

Group Affiliation: New York Life Group

Licensed in: All states except ME, NY, PR

Commenced Business: December 1987

Address: 14850 N SCOTTSDALE RD STE 400, SCOTTSDALE, AZ 85254

Phone: (212) 576-7000 **Domicile State:** AZ **NAIC Code:** 81353

Data Date	Rating	RACR #1	RACR #2	Total Assets ($mil)	Capital ($mil)	Net Premium ($mil)	Net Income ($mil)
9-18	B	12.10	9.86	175.9	116.9	9.3	6.1
9-17	B	11.55	8.22	182.0	112.1	10.7	8.6
2017	B	11.43	9.28	177.2	110.3	14.8	9.9
2016	B	10.71	7.61	182.9	103.9	18.5	12.4
2015	B	8.61	5.63	200.5	91.2	23.3	12.0
2014	B	6.39	4.20	199.8	79.6	33.0	11.0
2013	B	6.08	3.94	194.9	68.2	24.9	8.1

Adverse Trends in Operations

Decrease in premium volume from 2016 to 2017 (20%)
Decrease in asset base during 2017 (3%)
Decrease in premium volume from 2015 to 2016 (21%)
Decrease in asset base during 2016 (9%)
Decrease in premium volume from 2014 to 2015 (29%)

OCCIDENTAL LIFE INSURANCE COMPANY OF NORTH CAROLIN — C — Fair

Major Rating Factors: Fair overall results on stability tests (4.2 on a scale of 0 to 10) including fair financial strength of affiliated Industrial Alliance Ins & Financial. Fair liquidity (4.8) due, in part, to cash value policies that are subject to withdrawals with minimal or no penalty. Weak profitability (2.9) with investment income below regulatory standards in relation to interest assumptions of reserves.

Other Rating Factors: Strong capitalization (7.8) based on excellent risk adjusted capital (severe loss scenario). High quality investment portfolio (7.2).

Principal Business: Individual life insurance (88%), individual annuities (11%), and group life insurance (1%).

Principal Investments: NonCMO investment grade bonds (81%), mortgages in good standing (10%), policy loans (4%), common & preferred stock (2%), and CMOs and structured securities (1%).

Investments in Affiliates: None

Group Affiliation: Industrial Alliance Ins & Financial

Licensed in: All states except NY

Commenced Business: November 1906

Address: 425 AUSTIN AVENUE, WACO, TX 76701

Phone: (254) 297-2777 **Domicile State:** TX **NAIC Code:** 67148

Data Date	Rating	RACR #1	RACR #2	Total Assets ($mil)	Capital ($mil)	Net Premium ($mil)	Net Income ($mil)
9-18	C	2.52	1.50	258.8	25.1	37.7	1.6
9-17	C	2.78	1.71	256.3	27.7	32.2	0.5
2017	C	2.70	1.61	257.6	27.0	43.2	0.5
2016	C	2.86	1.74	254.6	28.6	36.3	1.3
2015	C	3.17	1.93	256.7	31.7	34.6	7.6
2014	C	3.66	2.19	261.4	36.9	34.0	3.7
2013	C	3.30	2.01	249.9	33.0	37.1	5.3

Industrial Alliance Ins Financial
Composite Group Rating: C
Largest Group Members

	Assets ($mil)	Rating
AMERICAN-AMICABLE LIFE INS CO OF TX	298	C
OCCIDENTAL LIFE INS CO OF NC	258	C
INDUSTRIAL ALLIANCE INS FIN SERV	247	C
IA AMERICAN LIFE INS CO	148	C+
PIONEER SECURITY LIFE INS CO	81	C

OHIO NATIONAL LIFE ASSURANCE CORPORATION * — B+ — Good

Major Rating Factors: Good overall results on stability tests (5.9 on a scale of 0 to 10). Stability strengths include good operational trends and excellent risk diversification. Good quality investment portfolio (5.6) despite large holdings of BBB rated bonds in addition to moderate junk bond exposure. Exposure to mortgages is significant, but the mortgage default rate has been low. Good overall profitability (6.2).

Other Rating Factors: Good liquidity (5.4). Strong capitalization (7.1) based on excellent risk adjusted capital (severe loss scenario).

Principal Business: Individual life insurance (94%) and individual health insurance (5%).

Principal Investments: NonCMO investment grade bonds (63%), CMOs and structured securities (17%), mortgages in good standing (12%), noninv. grade bonds (4%), and policy loans (3%).

Investments in Affiliates: None

Group Affiliation: Ohio Natonal Mutual Inc

Licensed in: All states except NY

Commenced Business: August 1979

Address: One Financial Way, Cincinnati, OH 45242

Phone: (513) 794-6100 **Domicile State:** OH **NAIC Code:** 89206

Data Date	Rating	RACR #1	RACR #2	Total Assets ($mil)	Capital ($mil)	Net Premium ($mil)	Net Income ($mil)
9-18	B+	2.08	1.09	4,098.9	288.3	123.7	15.3
9-17	B+	2.23	1.15	4,048.6	292.7	121.3	24.3
2017	B+	2.03	1.06	3,978.3	283.9	158.3	43.7
2016	B+	2.10	1.08	3,957.0	278.0	253.4	14.1
2015	B+	2.33	1.22	3,688.5	281.5	238.1	20.8
2014	B+	2.30	1.23	3,605.8	296.0	281.2	18.1
2013	B+	2.82	1.45	3,408.1	316.8	278.6	13.6

Adverse Trends in Operations

Decrease in premium volume from 2016 to 2017 (38%)
Decrease in capital during 2016 (1%)
Decrease in premium volume from 2014 to 2015 (15%)
Change in premium mix from 2014 to 2015 (4.2%)
Change in premium mix from 2013 to 2014 (4.7%)

OHIO NATIONAL LIFE INSURANCE COMPANY   B   Good

Major Rating Factors: Good overall capitalization (5.9 on a scale of 0 to 10) based on good risk adjusted capital (severe loss scenario). However, capital levels have fluctuated somewhat during past years. Good quality investment portfolio (5.7) despite mixed results such as: minimal exposure to mortgages and large holdings of BBB rated bonds but small junk bond holdings. Good overall profitability (6.4).

Other Rating Factors: Good overall results on stability tests (5.8) good operational trends and excellent risk diversification. Excellent liquidity (7.2).

Principal Business: Individual annuities (54%), individual life insurance (29%), group retirement contracts (12%), reinsurance (4%), and individual health insurance (1%).

Principal Investments: NonCMO investment grade bonds (51%), CMOs and structured securities (19%), mortgages in good standing (10%), policy loans (7%), and misc. investments (12%).

Investments in Affiliates: 4%

Group Affiliation: Ohio Natonal Mutual Inc

Licensed in: All states except NY

Commenced Business: October 1910

Address: One Financial Way, Cincinnati, OH 45242

Phone: (513) 794-6100   **Domicile State:** OH   **NAIC Code:** 67172

Data Date	Rating	RACR #1	RACR #2	Total Assets ($mil)	Capital ($mil)	Net Premium ($mil)	Net Income ($mil)
9-18	B	1.32	0.86	32,065.5	1,058.1	1,204.3	20.8
9-17	B	1.40	0.92	31,141.3	1,053.0	1,350.7	27.4
2017	B	1.41	0.93	31,676.7	1,101.6	1,841.2	71.0
2016	B	1.46	0.96	29,061.7	1,082.1	2,180.8	36.4
2015	B	1.52	1.03	27,589.8	1,087.2	2,538.3	62.7
2014	B	1.59	1.07	27,449.3	1,097.1	2,758.9	90.4
2013	B	1.38	0.97	25,381.8	1,002.7	2,830.6	61.6

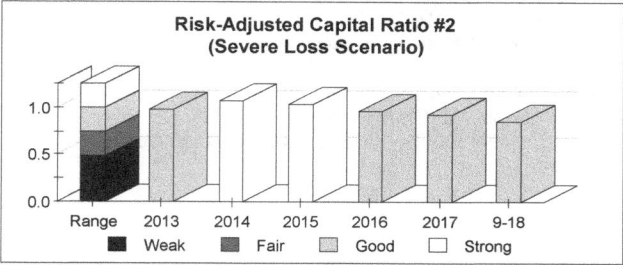

Risk-Adjusted Capital Ratio #2 (Severe Loss Scenario)

OLD REPUBLIC LIFE INSURANCE COMPANY   B-   Good

Major Rating Factors: Good quality investment portfolio (5.4 on a scale of 0 to 10) despite mixed results such as: no exposure to mortgages and substantial holdings of BBB bonds but minimal holdings in junk bonds. Good liquidity (6.9) with sufficient resources to handle a spike in claims. Fair overall results on stability tests (4.9) including negative cash flow from operations for 2017.

Other Rating Factors: Weak profitability (2.8) with operating losses during the first nine months of 2018. Strong capitalization (8.9) based on excellent risk adjusted capital (severe loss scenario).

Principal Business: Group health insurance (57%), individual life insurance (28%), and reinsurance (15%).

Principal Investments: NonCMO investment grade bonds (72%), common & preferred stock (16%), noninv. grade bonds (2%), policy loans (1%), and cash (1%).

Investments in Affiliates: None

Group Affiliation: Old Republic Group

Licensed in: All states except NY

Commenced Business: April 1923

Address: 307 NORTH MICHIGAN AVENUE, CHICAGO, IL 60601

Phone: (312) 346-8100   **Domicile State:** IL   **NAIC Code:** 67261

Data Date	Rating	RACR #1	RACR #2	Total Assets ($mil)	Capital ($mil)	Net Premium ($mil)	Net Income ($mil)
9-18	B-	3.60	2.24	113.7	33.9	11.1	-0.5
9-17	B-	3.52	2.19	120.8	33.1	13.9	-0.2
2017	B-	3.66	2.28	122.7	34.8	18.2	1.7
2016	B-	3.43	2.12	125.0	31.4	19.4	2.3
2015	B-	2.84	1.77	126.9	27.0	18.1	-0.3
2014	B-	3.22	2.02	125.1	30.6	20.1	0.8
2013	B-	4.30	2.81	131.7	36.4	21.2	2.2

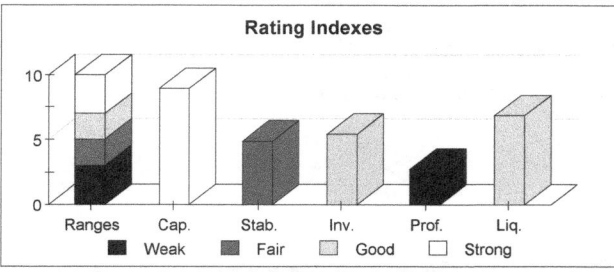

Rating Indexes

OLD UNITED LIFE INSURANCE COMPANY   B   Good

Major Rating Factors: Good overall results on stability tests (5.8 on a scale of 0 to 10) despite negative cash flow from operations for 2017. Other stability subfactors include good operational trends and excellent risk diversification. Fair quality investment portfolio (4.8). Strong capitalization (10.0) based on excellent risk adjusted capital (severe loss scenario).

Other Rating Factors: Excellent profitability (8.2). Excellent liquidity (10.0).

Principal Business: Credit life insurance (50%) and credit health insurance (50%).

Principal Investments: NonCMO investment grade bonds (70%), common & preferred stock (17%), CMOs and structured securities (7%), and noninv. grade bonds (4%).

Investments in Affiliates: None

Group Affiliation: Berkshire Hathaway Inc

Licensed in: All states except ME, NH, NY, PR

Commenced Business: January 1964

Address: 3800 N Central Ave Ste 460, Phoenix, AZ 85012

Phone: (913) 895-0200   **Domicile State:** AZ   **NAIC Code:** 76007

Data Date	Rating	RACR #1	RACR #2	Total Assets ($mil)	Capital ($mil)	Net Premium ($mil)	Net Income ($mil)
9-18	B	5.42	3.28	89.4	52.1	4.2	3.4
9-17	B	6.41	4.32	83.3	46.6	4.6	2.4
2017	B	6.47	4.50	84.7	47.8	6.1	2.9
2016	B	5.88	4.49	81.6	43.9	7.9	1.8
2015	B	5.56	5.01	82.5	42.0	6.2	4.2
2014	B	6.13	3.70	91.4	46.3	8.2	2.4
2013	B	6.08	3.55	87.4	44.9	8.5	0.4

Adverse Trends in Operations

Increase in policy surrenders from 2016 to 2017 (120%)
Decrease in premium volume from 2016 to 2017 (22%)
Change in asset mix during 2016 (6%)
Increase in policy surrenders from 2015 to 2016 (152%)
Decrease in premium volume from 2014 to 2015 (24%)

OMAHA INS CO
B- **Good**

Major Rating Factors: Good overall capitalization (5.9 on a scale of 0 to 10) based on good risk adjusted capital (moderate loss scenario). However, capital levels have fluctuated somewhat during past years. Good liquidity (5.6) with sufficient resources to handle a spike in claims. Fair overall results on stability tests (4.9) including negative cash flow from operations for 2017.

Other Rating Factors: Weak profitability (1.9) with operating losses during the first nine months of 2018. High quality investment portfolio (7.8).

Principal Business: Individual health insurance (100%).

Principal Investments: NonCMO investment grade bonds (62%), CMOs and structured securities (37%), and noninv. grade bonds (1%).

Investments in Affiliates: None

Group Affiliation: Mutual Of Omaha Group

Licensed in: AK, AZ, AR, CT, DC, DE, GA, HI, IN, IA, KS, KY, ME, MD, MA, MI, MN, MS, MO, MT, NE, NJ, NM, ND, OH, OK, OR, PA, SC, SD, TN, TX, UT, VT, VA, WA, WV, WY

Commenced Business: November 2006

Address: MUTUAL OF OMAHA PLAZA, OMAHA, NE 68175

Phone: (402) 342-7600 **Domicile State:** NE **NAIC Code:** 13100

Data Date	Rating	RACR #1	RACR #2	Total Assets ($mil)	Capital ($mil)	Net Premium ($mil)	Net Income ($mil)
9-18	B-	1.57	0.83	89.4	42.3	48.5	-4.3
9-17	B-	2.10	1.11	95.3	48.4	41.5	-3.3
2017	B-	1.84	0.97	98.3	45.2	56.2	-5.3
2016	C+	2.48	1.31	99.2	49.2	44.4	-5.4
2015	C+	3.70	1.97	88.2	54.1	29.3	-5.4
2014	B-	2.47	1.33	43.8	21.1	14.3	-3.9
2013	B-	4.16	2.72	22.9	15.9	5.1	-2.0

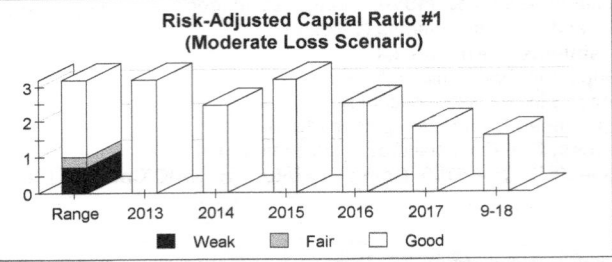

Risk-Adjusted Capital Ratio #1
(Moderate Loss Scenario)

■ Weak ▨ Fair □ Good

OPTIMUM RE INSURANCE COMPANY
C+ **Fair**

Major Rating Factors: Fair overall results on stability tests (4.6 on a scale of 0 to 10). Weak profitability (2.5) with investment income below regulatory standards in relation to interest assumptions of reserves. Strong capitalization (8.0) based on excellent risk adjusted capital (severe loss scenario). Moreover, capital levels have been consistently high over the last five years.

Other Rating Factors: High quality investment portfolio (7.6). Excellent liquidity (9.1).

Principal Business: Reinsurance (100%).

Principal Investments: NonCMO investment grade bonds (91%), cash (3%), noninv. grade bonds (2%), real estate (2%), and common & preferred stock (1%).

Investments in Affiliates: 2%

Group Affiliation: Optimum Group Inc

Licensed in: All states except NY

Commenced Business: June 1978

Address: 1345 River Bend Drive Ste 100, DALLAS, TX 75247

Phone: (214) 528-2020 **Domicile State:** TX **NAIC Code:** 88099

Data Date	Rating	RACR #1	RACR #2	Total Assets ($mil)	Capital ($mil)	Net Premium ($mil)	Net Income ($mil)
9-18	C+	2.64	1.65	191.2	40.5	35.1	4.2
9-17	C+	2.54	1.59	173.0	36.1	31.7	2.9
2017	C+	2.53	1.57	183.4	37.5	42.7	5.2
2016	C+	2.40	1.51	170.1	34.0	47.8	3.5
2015	C+	2.46	1.52	145.9	31.5	38.1	4.4
2014	C+	2.25	1.42	132.7	29.2	44.2	2.2
2013	B-	2.36	1.51	114.9	27.9	44.3	2.0

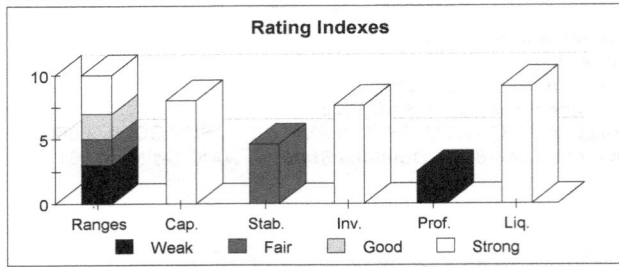

Rating Indexes

Ranges Cap. Stab. Inv. Prof. Liq.

■ Weak ▨ Fair ▤ Good □ Strong

OPTUM INSURANCE OF OHIO INC
B **Good**

Major Rating Factors: Good overall results on stability tests (5.8 on a scale of 0 to 10) despite fair financial strength of affiliated UnitedHealth Group Inc. Other stability subfactors include excellent operational trends and excellent risk diversification. Strong capitalization (8.0) based on excellent risk adjusted capital (severe loss scenario). Moreover, capital levels have been consistently high over the last five years. High quality investment portfolio (9.8).

Other Rating Factors: Excellent profitability (7.6). Excellent liquidity (9.0).

Principal Business: Individual life insurance (91%) and individual annuities (9%).

Principal Investments: Cash (74%) and nonCMO investment grade bonds (17%).

Investments in Affiliates: None

Group Affiliation: UnitedHealth Group Inc

Licensed in: All states except ME, NY, PR

Commenced Business: December 1978

Address: 50 W Broad Street Suite 1800, Columbus, OH 43215

Phone: (800) 282-3232 **Domicile State:** OH **NAIC Code:** 69647

Data Date	Rating	RACR #1	RACR #2	Total Assets ($mil)	Capital ($mil)	Net Premium ($mil)	Net Income ($mil)
9-18	B	5.77	5.19	264.1	55.7	0.0	26.8
9-17	B	5.38	4.84	159.9	44.7	0.0	11.2
2017	B	4.96	4.47	185.9	47.9	0.0	14.4
2016	B	4.88	4.39	87.1	40.4	0.0	7.3
2015	B+	3.41	3.07	151.9	33.1	0.0	12.2
2014	C+	2.00	1.80	52.3	20.9	0.0	12.0
2013	C+	4.16	3.75	9.2	8.9	0.0	0.3

UnitedHealth Group Inc Composite Group Rating: C+ Largest Group Members	Assets ($mil)	Rating
UNITED HEALTHCARE INS CO	19618	C
SIERRA HEALTH AND LIFE INS CO INC	3270	B
OXFORD HEALTH INS INC	2570	B
UNITED HEALTHCARE OF WISCONSIN INC	1760	B+
UNITED HEALTHCARE INS CO OF NY	1262	B-

OXFORD LIFE INSURANCE COMPANY *   B+   Good

Major Rating Factors: Good quality investment portfolio (6.3 on a scale of 0 to 10) despite significant exposure to mortgages . Mortgage default rate has been low. large holdings of BBB rated bonds in addition to small junk bond holdings. Good overall profitability (6.9) despite operating losses during the first nine months of 2018. Good liquidity (6.5).

Other Rating Factors: Good overall results on stability tests (6.5) excellent operational trends and excellent risk diversification. Strong capitalization (7.3) based on excellent risk adjusted capital (severe loss scenario).

Principal Business: Individual annuities (73%), individual life insurance (12%), individual health insurance (11%), and reinsurance (3%).

Principal Investments: NonCMO investment grade bonds (71%), mortgages in good standing (14%), CMOs and structured securities (7%), noninv. grade bonds (2%), and misc. investments (6%).

Investments in Affiliates: 3%

Group Affiliation: Amerco Corp

Licensed in: All states except NY, VT, PR

Commenced Business: June 1968

Address: 2721 North Central Avenue, Phoenix, AZ 85004

Phone: (602) 263-6666 **Domicile State:** AZ **NAIC Code:** 76112

Data Date	Rating	RACR #1	RACR #2	Total Assets ($mil)	Capital ($mil)	Net Premium ($mil)	Net Income ($mil)
9-18	B+	1.92	1.20	2,192.1	196.9	347.5	-4.9
9-17	B	1.71	1.15	1,907.3	197.9	324.9	1.8
2017	B+	2.01	1.27	1,954.6	195.9	405.0	10.4
2016	B	1.81	1.24	1,684.3	189.3	314.7	17.5
2015	B	2.00	1.39	1,490.4	172.3	372.2	12.2
2014	B-	1.64	1.19	1,197.5	158.5	191.4	12.1
2013	B-	2.05	1.42	1,097.7	148.5	197.1	11.1

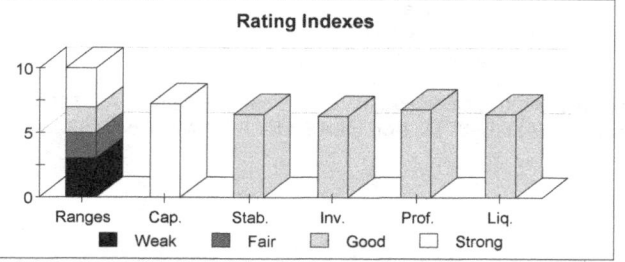

OZARK NATIONAL LIFE INSURANCE COMPANY   B-   Good

Major Rating Factors: Good liquidity (6.5 on a scale of 0 to 10) with sufficient resources to handle a spike in claims as well as a significant increase in policy surrenders. Fair overall results on stability tests (4.9). Weak profitability (2.9) with investment income below regulatory standards in relation to interest assumptions of reserves.

Other Rating Factors: Strong capitalization (9.6) based on excellent risk adjusted capital (severe loss scenario). High quality investment portfolio (7.6).

Principal Business: Individual life insurance (99%).

Principal Investments: NonCMO investment grade bonds (71%), CMOs and structured securities (24%), policy loans (3%), and real estate (1%).

Investments in Affiliates: None

Group Affiliation: CNS Corp

Licensed in: AL, AZ, AR, CA, CO, FL, GA, IL, IN, IA, KS, KY, LA, MI, MN, MS, MO, MT, NE, NV, NM, ND, OH, OK, SD, TN, TX, UT, WI, WY

Commenced Business: June 1964

Address: 500 East Ninth Street, Kansas City, MO 64106-2627

Phone: (816) 842-6300 **Domicile State:** MO **NAIC Code:** 67393

Data Date	Rating	RACR #1	RACR #2	Total Assets ($mil)	Capital ($mil)	Net Premium ($mil)	Net Income ($mil)
9-18	B-	4.92	2.74	836.8	143.6	61.0	15.2
9-17	B-	4.91	2.75	816.3	139.4	61.8	11.3
2017	B-	4.82	2.69	820.9	138.8	82.6	15.8
2016	B-	4.83	2.72	801.9	136.3	82.7	14.8
2015	B-	4.92	2.83	775.2	130.6	82.8	15.7
2014	B-	4.91	2.88	750.2	124.5	82.8	13.2
2013	B-	5.07	3.02	730.6	123.4	82.3	14.9

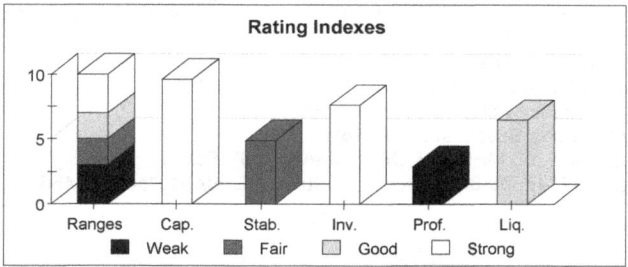

PACIFIC GUARDIAN LIFE INSURANCE COMPANY LIMITED *   A-   Excellent

Major Rating Factors: Good quality investment portfolio (6.6 on a scale of 0 to 10) despite large exposure to mortgages . Mortgage default rate has been low. substantial holdings of BBB bonds in addition to minimal holdings in junk bonds. Good overall profitability (5.4) although investment income, in comparison to reserve requirements, is below regulatory standards. Good liquidity (6.1).

Other Rating Factors: Excellent overall results on stability tests (7.0) excellent operational trends and excellent risk diversification. Strong capitalization (8.6) based on excellent risk adjusted capital (severe loss scenario).

Principal Business: Group health insurance (52%), individual life insurance (37%), and group life insurance (11%).

Principal Investments: Mortgages in good standing (36%), nonCMO investment grade bonds (35%), CMOs and structured securities (19%), policy loans (6%), and misc. investments (4%).

Investments in Affiliates: None

Group Affiliation: Meiji Yasuda Life Ins Co

Licensed in: AK, AZ, CA, CO, HI, ID, IA, LA, MO, MT, NE, NV, NM, OK, OR, SD, TX, UT, WA, WY

Commenced Business: June 1962

Address: 1440 Kapiolani Blvd Ste 1600, Honolulu, HI 96814-3698

Phone: (808) 955-2236 **Domicile State:** HI **NAIC Code:** 64343

Data Date	Rating	RACR #1	RACR #2	Total Assets ($mil)	Capital ($mil)	Net Premium ($mil)	Net Income ($mil)
9-18	A-	3.56	2.06	559.1	96.3	61.1	3.4
9-17	A-	4.03	2.33	552.3	103.7	57.4	3.1
2017	A-	3.96	2.31	553.9	102.4	74.4	4.0
2016	A-	4.30	2.51	543.1	107.1	74.3	5.2
2015	A-	4.52	2.62	528.4	108.5	70.2	6.7
2014	A-	4.72	2.73	515.6	108.8	68.4	8.1
2013	A-	5.09	2.93	504.7	108.0	69.8	6.9

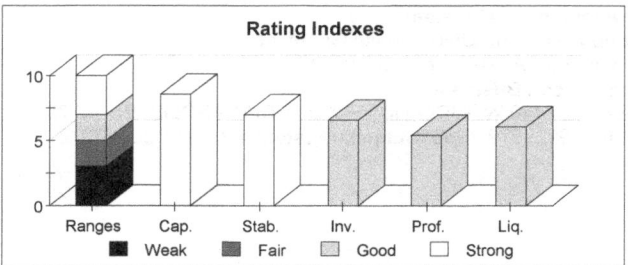

PACIFIC LIFE & ANNUITY COMPANY * B+ Good

Major Rating Factors: Good quality investment portfolio (6.4 on a scale of 0 to 10) despite significant exposure to mortgages . Mortgage default rate has been low. large holdings of BBB rated bonds in addition to small junk bond holdings. Good overall results on stability tests (6.7). Stability strengths include excellent operational trends and excellent risk diversification. Strong capitalization (8.9) based on excellent risk adjusted capital (severe loss scenario).

Other Rating Factors: Excellent profitability (7.0). Excellent liquidity (7.3).

Principal Business: Individual annuities (95%), individual life insurance (4%), and reinsurance (2%).

Principal Investments: NonCMO investment grade bonds (76%), mortgages in good standing (11%), CMOs and structured securities (6%), noninv. grade bonds (3%), and cash (1%).

Investments in Affiliates: None

Group Affiliation: Pacific LifeCorp

Licensed in: All states except PR

Commenced Business: July 1983

Address: 3800 N CENTRAL AVE STE 460, PHOENIX, AZ 85012

Phone: (714) 640-3011 **Domicile State:** AZ **NAIC Code:** 97268

Data Date	Rating	RACR #1	RACR #2	Total Assets ($mil)	Capital ($mil)	Net Premium ($mil)	Net Income ($mil)
9-18	B+	4.68	2.27	7,409.8	587.6	453.9	49.1
9-17	B+	5.11	2.42	7,035.9	571.4	400.8	35.9
2017	B+	4.61	2.24	7,125.3	540.6	520.6	46.0
2016	B+	5.37	2.58	6,582.8	539.4	463.5	41.2
2015	B+	6.09	2.91	6,217.1	531.5	341.6	53.7
2014	B+	5.58	2.71	6,151.1	512.6	469.0	53.1
2013	B+	5.06	2.49	5,819.5	495.4	455.5	45.8

Adverse Trends in Operations

Decrease in premium volume from 2014 to 2015 (27%)

PACIFIC LIFE INSURANCE COMPANY * A- Excellent

Major Rating Factors: Good quality investment portfolio (5.5 on a scale of 0 to 10) despite significant exposure to mortgages . Mortgage default rate has been low. large holdings of BBB rated bonds in addition to small junk bond holdings. Good overall profitability (6.4) although investment income, in comparison to reserve requirements, is below regulatory standards. Good liquidity (6.2).

Other Rating Factors: Good overall results on stability tests (6.9) despite excessive premium growth excellent operational trends and excellent risk diversification. Strong capitalization (8.6) based on excellent risk adjusted capital (severe loss scenario).

Principal Business: Individual annuities (50%), individual life insurance (32%), reinsurance (10%), and group retirement contracts (8%).

Principal Investments: NonCMO investment grade bonds (50%), mortgages in good standing (16%), policy loans (11%), CMOs and structured securities (8%), and misc. investments (10%).

Investments in Affiliates: 6%

Group Affiliation: Pacific LifeCorp

Licensed in: All states except NY, PR

Commenced Business: May 1868

Address: 6750 MERCY ROAD, OMAHA, NE 68106

Phone: (714) 630-3011 **Domicile State:** NE **NAIC Code:** 67466

Data Date	Rating	RACR #1	RACR #2	Total Assets ($mil)	Capital ($mil)	Net Premium ($mil)	Net Income ($mil)
9-18	A-	3.73	2.04	133,288	9,884.7	8,524.8	679.8
9-17	A-	2.17	1.47	125,502	9,114.6	6,461.6	592.9
2017	A-	3.57	2.00	128,652	9,312.9	9,267.9	1,201.4
2016	A-	2.12	1.47	118,628	8,548.4	8,300.5	850.0
2015	A-	2.06	1.43	113,242	7,762.5	9,039.7	519.8
2014	A-	2.00	1.39	112,503	7,171.6	8,573.9	634.8
2013	A-	2.01	1.36	109,065	6,502.9	8,702.0	521.4

Rating Indexes

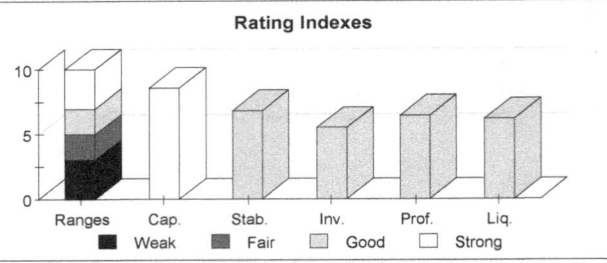

Weak | Fair | Good | Strong

Ranges | Cap. | Stab. | Inv. | Prof. | Liq.

PACIFICARE LIFE & HEALTH INSURANCE COMPANY B Good

Major Rating Factors: Good overall results on stability tests (5.8 on a scale of 0 to 10) despite fair financial strength of affiliated UnitedHealth Group Inc. Other stability subfactors include good operational trends and excellent risk diversification. Good overall profitability (6.2). Excellent expense controls. Strong capitalization (10.0) based on excellent risk adjusted capital (severe loss scenario).

Other Rating Factors: High quality investment portfolio (8.2). Excellent liquidity (9.2).

Principal Business: Individual health insurance (73%) and group health insurance (27%).

Principal Investments: NonCMO investment grade bonds (77%) and CMOs and structured securities (23%).

Investments in Affiliates: None

Group Affiliation: UnitedHealth Group Inc

Licensed in: All states except NY, PR

Commenced Business: September 1967

Address: 7440 WOODLAND DRIVE, INDIANAPOLIS, IN 46278

Phone: (952) 979-7959 **Domicile State:** IN **NAIC Code:** 70785

Data Date	Rating	RACR #1	RACR #2	Total Assets ($mil)	Capital ($mil)	Net Premium ($mil)	Net Income ($mil)
9-18	B	18.59	16.73	186.3	181.3	9.7	3.2
9-17	C+	18.46	16.62	187.0	180.4	10.4	2.3
2017	B	18.62	16.75	187.3	181.5	13.6	3.4
2016	C+	18.52	16.67	189.2	180.8	14.3	3.2
2015	C+	19.90	17.91	205.7	197.4	15.8	4.1
2014	C+	19.49	17.54	204.8	193.3	36.3	7.9
2013	C+	29.46	19.62	616.2	592.6	104.7	13.2

UnitedHealth Group Inc
Composite Group Rating: C+
Largest Group Members

	Assets ($mil)	Rating
UNITED HEALTHCARE INS CO	19618	C
SIERRA HEALTH AND LIFE INS CO INC	3270	B
OXFORD HEALTH INS INC	2570	B
UNITED HEALTHCARE OF WISCONSIN INC	1760	B+
UNITED HEALTHCARE INS CO OF NY	1262	B-

PAN-AMERICAN LIFE INSURANCE COMPANY

B   **Good**

Major Rating Factors: Good overall results on stability tests (6.0 on a scale of 0 to 10) despite negative cash flow from operations for 2017. Other stability subfactors include excellent operational trends and excellent risk diversification. Good quality investment portfolio (5.4) despite mixed results such as: large holdings of BBB rated bonds but moderate junk bond exposure. Good overall profitability (5.9).

Other Rating Factors: Good liquidity (6.4). Strong capitalization (7.9) based on excellent risk adjusted capital (severe loss scenario).

Principal Business: Group health insurance (70%), reinsurance (11%), individual life insurance (10%), individual health insurance (6%), and group life insurance (4%).

Principal Investments: NonCMO investment grade bonds (57%), CMOs and structured securities (19%), noninv. grade bonds (6%), common & preferred stock (6%), and misc. investments (11%).

Investments in Affiliates: 2%

Group Affiliation: Pan-American Life

Licensed in: All states except ME, NY, VT

Commenced Business: March 1912

Address: PAN-AMERICAN LIFE CENTER, NEW ORLEANS, LA 70130-6060

Phone: (504) 566-3554 **Domicile State:** LA **NAIC Code:** 67539

Data Date	Rating	RACR #1	RACR #2	Total Assets ($mil)	Capital ($mil)	Net Premium ($mil)	Net Income ($mil)
9-18	B	2.51	1.61	1,215.8	243.9	163.8	12.1
9-17	B	2.73	1.74	1,249.1	261.0	160.9	19.2
2017	B	2.41	1.53	1,221.1	234.1	212.9	14.5
2016	B	2.53	1.60	1,260.9	244.6	226.5	21.3
2015	B	2.52	1.62	1,293.7	244.9	237.9	22.0
2014	B	2.20	1.40	1,345.4	237.5	238.9	23.8
2013	B	2.29	1.43	1,425.5	244.6	270.3	27.3

Adverse Trends in Operations

Decrease in premium volume from 2016 to 2017 (6%)
Decrease in asset base during 2017 (3%)
Decrease in asset base during 2016 (3%)
Decrease in asset base during 2014 (6%)
Decrease in premium volume from 2013 to 2014 (12%)

PARK AVENUE LIFE INSURANCE COMPANY

B   **Good**

Major Rating Factors: Good quality investment portfolio (6.2 on a scale of 0 to 10) despite mixed results such as: no exposure to mortgages and large holdings of BBB rated bonds but minimal holdings in junk bonds. Good overall profitability (6.6). Excellent expense controls. Good liquidity (6.0) with sufficient resources to handle a spike in claims.

Other Rating Factors: Good overall results on stability tests (6.0) despite negative cash flow from operations for 2017 good operational trends, good risk adjusted capital for prior years and excellent risk diversification. Strong capitalization (7.1) based on excellent risk adjusted capital (severe loss scenario).

Principal Business: Reinsurance (76%) and individual life insurance (24%).

Principal Investments: NonCMO investment grade bonds (83%), common & preferred stock (14%), noninv. grade bonds (2%), and policy loans (1%).

Investments in Affiliates: 14%

Group Affiliation: Guardian Group

Licensed in: All states except HI, NY, PR

Commenced Business: April 1965

Address: 2711 CENTERVILLE ROAD STE 400, WILMINGTON, DE 19808

Phone: (800) 538-6203 **Domicile State:** DE **NAIC Code:** 60003

Data Date	Rating	RACR #1	RACR #2	Total Assets ($mil)	Capital ($mil)	Net Premium ($mil)	Net Income ($mil)
9-18	B	1.26	1.08	234.6	48.7	1.3	5.2
9-17	B	1.66	1.41	265.2	69.3	1.4	3.7
2017	B	1.09	0.93	236.5	41.2	1.8	5.0
2016	B	1.55	1.32	267.6	63.5	2.2	5.7
2015	B	1.49	1.22	268.8	50.7	2.3	4.9
2014	B+	1.89	1.56	305.3	75.7	2.7	2.2
2013	B	1.94	1.54	305.8	67.8	3.0	6.7

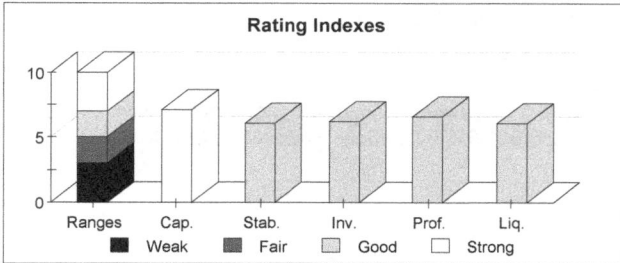

Rating Indexes

Ranges — Cap. — Stab. — Inv. — Prof. — Liq.
■ Weak ■ Fair ☐ Good ☐ Strong

PARKER CENTENNIAL ASSURANCE COMPANY *

A   **Excellent**

Major Rating Factors: Good overall results on stability tests (6.9 on a scale of 0 to 10). Strengths that enhance stability include good operational trends and excellent risk diversification. Strong capitalization (10.0) based on excellent risk adjusted capital (severe loss scenario). Furthermore, this high level of risk adjusted capital has been consistently maintained over the last five years. High quality investment portfolio (8.6).

Other Rating Factors: Excellent profitability (7.7). Excellent liquidity (10.0).

Principal Business: Group retirement contracts (100%).

Principal Investments: NonCMO investment grade bonds (96%) and noninv. grade bonds (1%).

Investments in Affiliates: None

Group Affiliation: Sentry Ins Group

Licensed in: All states except NY, PR

Commenced Business: August 1973

Address: 1800 NORTH POINT DRIVE, STEVENS POINT, WI 54481

Phone: (715) 346-6000 **Domicile State:** WI **NAIC Code:** 71099

Data Date	Rating	RACR #1	RACR #2	Total Assets ($mil)	Capital ($mil)	Net Premium ($mil)	Net Income ($mil)
9-18	A	5.62	5.05	96.0	48.1	4.3	1.3
9-17	A	5.62	5.06	92.4	47.9	1.6	1.5
2017	A	5.46	4.92	91.8	46.8	2.3	1.9
2016	A	5.45	4.91	90.8	46.5	1.1	1.7
2015	A	5.40	4.86	91.3	46.2	4.2	1.6
2014	A	5.44	4.89	89.4	46.0	5.1	1.8
2013	A	5.55	5.00	84.4	45.8	5.0	1.6

Adverse Trends in Operations

Decrease in premium volume from 2015 to 2016 (73%)
Decrease in premium volume from 2014 to 2015 (18%)

PAUL REVERE LIFE INSURANCE COMPANY

C+   **Fair**

Major Rating Factors: Fair overall results on stability tests (4.8 on a scale of 0 to 10) including fair financial strength of affiliated Unum Group and negative cash flow from operations for 2017. Fair quality investment portfolio (3.7) with large holdings of BBB rated bonds in addition to significant exposure to junk bonds. Good overall profitability (6.2).

Other Rating Factors: Strong capitalization (7.0) based on excellent risk adjusted capital (severe loss scenario). Excellent liquidity (7.7).

Principal Business: Individual health insurance (67%), reinsurance (24%), group health insurance (5%), individual life insurance (4%), and group life insurance (1%).

Principal Investments: NonCMO investment grade bonds (82%), noninv. grade bonds (7%), CMOs and structured securities (4%), common & preferred stock (3%), and mortgages in good standing (2%).

Investments in Affiliates: 2%

Group Affiliation: Unum Group

Licensed in: All states except PR

Commenced Business: July 1930

Address: 1 MERCANTILE STREET, WORCESTER, MA 1608

Phone: (423) 294-1011 **Domicile State:** MA **NAIC Code:** 67598

Data Date	Rating	RACR #1	RACR #2	Total Assets ($mil)	Capital ($mil)	Net Premium ($mil)	Net Income ($mil)
9-18	C+	1.68	1.01	3,479.2	220.1	71.6	54.1
9-17	C+	1.49	0.90	3,653.7	213.5	71.2	31.2
2017	C+	1.40	0.82	3,570.6	177.3	93.8	55.4
2016	C+	1.71	1.01	3,790.4	251.4	95.2	65.6
2015	C+	1.72	1.02	3,977.0	257.7	96.8	63.1
2014	C+	1.85	1.09	4,145.1	278.0	91.0	76.5
2013	C+	1.78	1.13	4,301.8	336.1	90.4	66.5

Unum Group
Composite Group Rating: C+
Largest Group Members

	Assets ($mil)	Rating
UNUM LIFE INS CO OF AMERICA	21455	C+
PROVIDENT LIFE ACCIDENT INS CO	8034	C+
PAUL REVERE LIFE INS CO	3571	C+
FIRST UNUM LIFE INS CO	3457	C+
COLONIAL LIFE ACCIDENT INS CO	3220	C+

PAVONIA LIFE INSURANCE COMPANY OF MICHIGAN

C   **Fair**

Major Rating Factors: Fair overall results on stability tests (4.0 on a scale of 0 to 10) including negative cash flow from operations for 2017, fair risk adjusted capital in prior years. Good current capitalization (5.9) based on good risk adjusted capital (severe loss scenario) reflecting some improvement over results in 2016. Good quality investment portfolio (6.1).

Other Rating Factors: Weak profitability (2.1) with operating losses during the first nine months of 2018. Excellent liquidity (7.9).

Principal Business: Individual life insurance (40%), reinsurance (35%), credit life insurance (16%), credit health insurance (8%), and group life insurance (1%).

Principal Investments: NonCMO investment grade bonds (70%), CMOs and structured securities (14%), policy loans (2%), noninv. grade bonds (2%), and cash (2%).

Investments in Affiliates: None

Group Affiliation: SNA Capital LLC

Licensed in: All states except NY, PR

Commenced Business: January 1981

Address: 500 Woodward Avenue Suite 4000, SouthField, MI 48034

Phone: (201) 651-5167 **Domicile State:** MI **NAIC Code:** 93777

Data Date	Rating	RACR #1	RACR #2	Total Assets ($mil)	Capital ($mil)	Net Premium ($mil)	Net Income ($mil)
9-18	C	1.54	0.86	1,149.3	65.5	33.8	-6.2
9-17	C	1.30	0.78	1,039.7	70.5	38.6	4.7
2017	C	1.63	0.91	1,034.5	66.6	51.6	2.5
2016	C	1.15	0.69	1,057.4	63.2	64.6	4.3
2015	C	1.53	0.90	1,069.7	55.4	76.5	-8.6
2014	C	2.38	1.72	405.9	82.3	96.4	11.3
2013	C	2.39	1.77	445.9	99.8	112.0	25.1

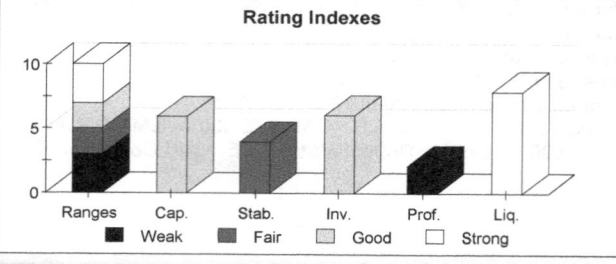

Rating Indexes — Ranges, Cap., Stab., Inv., Prof., Liq. — Weak, Fair, Good, Strong

PEKIN LIFE INSURANCE COMPANY

B   **Good**

Major Rating Factors: Good overall results on stability tests (6.2 on a scale of 0 to 10). Stability strengths include excellent operational trends and excellent risk diversification. Good quality investment portfolio (6.5) despite mixed results such as: minimal exposure to mortgages and substantial holdings of BBB bonds but minimal holdings in junk bonds. Good overall profitability (5.7) although investment income, in comparison to reserve requirements, is below regulatory standards.

Other Rating Factors: Good liquidity (5.7). Strong capitalization (7.3) based on excellent risk adjusted capital (severe loss scenario).

Principal Business: Individual life insurance (39%), group life insurance (21%), individual health insurance (16%), group health insurance (8%), and other lines (16%).

Principal Investments: NonCMO investment grade bonds (62%), CMOs and structured securities (30%), mortgages in good standing (4%), policy loans (1%), and common & preferred stock (1%).

Investments in Affiliates: None

Group Affiliation: Farmers Automobile Ins Assn

Licensed in: AL, AZ, AR, GA, IL, IN, IA, KS, KY, LA, MI, MN, MS, MO, NE, NV, NC, OH, PA, TN, TX, UT, VA, WI

Commenced Business: September 1965

Address: 2505 COURT STREET, PEKIN, IL 61558-0001

Phone: (309) 346-1161 **Domicile State:** IL **NAIC Code:** 67628

Data Date	Rating	RACR #1	RACR #2	Total Assets ($mil)	Capital ($mil)	Net Premium ($mil)	Net Income ($mil)
9-18	B	2.03	1.20	1,496.7	128.6	140.5	1.5
9-17	B	2.09	1.24	1,465.6	129.3	152.1	5.2
2017	B	2.03	1.20	1,475.0	127.6	199.3	7.4
2016	B	2.03	1.21	1,459.6	124.6	222.5	-1.0
2015	B	1.98	1.19	1,393.6	120.2	215.7	-1.3
2014	B	2.11	1.28	1,324.1	120.3	206.2	5.9
2013	B	2.24	1.37	1,301.6	122.7	227.0	2.4

Adverse Trends in Operations

Decrease in premium volume from 2016 to 2017 (10%)
Decrease in premium volume from 2013 to 2014 (9%)
Decrease in capital during 2014 (2%)

PENN INSURANCE & ANNUITY COMPANY   C+   Fair

Major Rating Factors: Fair overall results on stability tests (4.8 on a scale of 0 to 10). Good quality investment portfolio (5.8) despite mixed results such as: large holdings of BBB rated bonds but moderate junk bond exposure. Good liquidity (6.3) with sufficient resources to handle a spike in claims as well as a significant increase in policy surrenders.

Other Rating Factors: Weak profitability (2.5) with operating losses during the first nine months of 2018. Strong capitalization (7.2) based on excellent risk adjusted capital (severe loss scenario).

Principal Business: Individual life insurance (56%), reinsurance (38%), and individual annuities (6%).

Principal Investments: NonCMO investment grade bonds (46%), CMOs and structured securities (28%), policy loans (12%), noninv. grade bonds (3%), and common & preferred stock (2%).

Investments in Affiliates: 3%
Group Affiliation: Penn Mutual Group
Licensed in: All states except NY, PR
Commenced Business: April 1981
Address: 1209 Orange Street, Wilmington, DE 19801
Phone: (215) 956-8000 **Domicile State:** DE **NAIC Code:** 93262

Data Date	Rating	RACR #1	RACR #2	Total Assets ($mil)	Capital ($mil)	Net Premium ($mil)	Net Income ($mil)
9-18	C+	2.01	1.15	6,128.0	451.2	547.3	-3.8
9-17	B-	1.78	1.10	5,037.5	399.3	490.2	4.1
2017	C+	1.85	1.16	5,321.0	431.5	701.2	-15.9
2016	B-	1.88	1.18	4,371.8	393.9	427.3	-4.2
2015	B-	2.03	1.29	3,780.5	363.1	488.3	-32.9
2014	B	2.81	1.84	3,254.7	417.2	211.1	25.4
2013	B	2.73	1.73	2,307.3	310.7	-108.0	-2.4

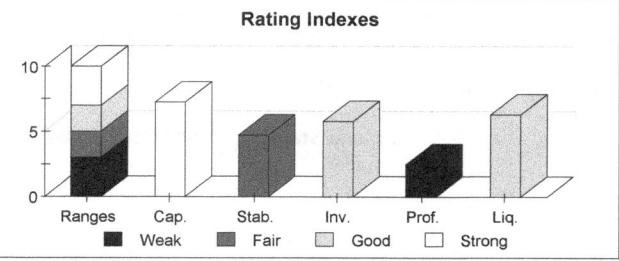

Rating Indexes

PENN MUTUAL LIFE INSURANCE COMPANY   B   Good

Major Rating Factors: Good quality investment portfolio (5.9 on a scale of 0 to 10) despite mixed results such as: no exposure to mortgages and large holdings of BBB rated bonds but small junk bond holdings. Good overall profitability (6.0). Good liquidity (6.2) with sufficient resources to handle a spike in claims as well as a significant increase in policy surrenders.

Other Rating Factors: Fair overall results on stability tests (4.8). Strong capitalization (7.3) based on excellent risk adjusted capital (severe loss scenario).

Principal Business: Individual life insurance (75%) and individual annuities (24%).

Principal Investments: NonCMO investment grade bonds (48%), CMOs and structured securities (27%), common & preferred stock (6%), policy loans (3%), and misc. investments (13%).

Investments in Affiliates: 6%
Group Affiliation: Penn Mutual Group
Licensed in: All states except PR
Commenced Business: May 1847
Address: The Penn Mutual Life Ins Co, Philadelphia, PA 19172
Phone: (215) 956-8000 **Domicile State:** PA **NAIC Code:** 67644

Data Date	Rating	RACR #1	RACR #2	Total Assets ($mil)	Capital ($mil)	Net Premium ($mil)	Net Income ($mil)
9-18	B	1.81	1.22	21,664.0	1,757.4	678.2	64.7
9-17	B	1.87	1.25	20,377.0	1,734.7	-30.8	-25.1
2017	B	1.80	1.22	20,669.4	1,697.4	821.8	-40.5
2016	B	1.88	1.26	19,105.8	1,740.6	1,260.8	99.4
2015	B	2.22	1.46	18,235.0	1,787.7	1,192.2	101.3
2014	B	2.21	1.52	17,270.8	1,799.8	657.2	9.3
2013	B	2.19	1.48	15,945.2	1,490.7	1,483.0	-34.4

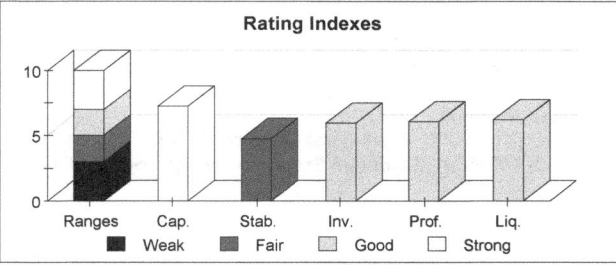

Rating Indexes

PHILADELPHIA AMERICAN LIFE INSURANCE COMPANY   B   Good

Major Rating Factors: Good overall results on stability tests (5.6 on a scale of 0 to 10) despite fair financial strength of affiliated New Era Life Group. Other stability subfactors include excellent operational trends, good risk adjusted capital for prior years and good risk diversification. Good liquidity (6.5) with sufficient resources to handle a spike in claims as well as a significant increase in policy surrenders. Fair quality investment portfolio (4.6).

Other Rating Factors: Strong capitalization (7.1) based on excellent risk adjusted capital (severe loss scenario). Excellent profitability (8.9).

Principal Business: Individual health insurance (83%), individual annuities (13%), group health insurance (2%), and individual life insurance (2%).

Principal Investments: NonCMO investment grade bonds (71%), CMOs and structured securities (9%), noninv. grade bonds (9%), cash (4%), and misc. investments (5%).

Investments in Affiliates: None
Group Affiliation: New Era Life Group
Licensed in: All states except NY, RI, PR
Commenced Business: March 1978
Address: 11720 Katy Freeway Suite 1700, Houston, TX 77079
Phone: (281) 368-7200 **Domicile State:** TX **NAIC Code:** 67784

Data Date	Rating	RACR #1	RACR #2	Total Assets ($mil)	Capital ($mil)	Net Premium ($mil)	Net Income ($mil)
9-18	B	1.62	1.05	297.6	43.3	139.8	6.4
9-17	B	1.59	1.02	290.6	35.5	115.5	3.1
2017	B	1.51	0.97	284.8	35.5	157.2	3.9
2016	B	1.62	1.03	263.3	34.2	141.1	1.4
2015	B	1.46	0.95	235.2	33.9	160.1	1.1
2014	B-	1.50	0.96	220.2	33.2	144.1	5.9
2013	B-	1.38	0.88	205.7	29.0	120.4	3.1

New Era Life Group Composite Group Rating: C+ Largest Group Members	Assets ($mil)	Rating
NEW ERA LIFE INS CO	538	C
PHILADELPHIA AMERICAN LIFE INS CO	285	B
NEW ERA LIFE INS CO OF THE MIDWEST	133	C+
LIFE OF AMERICA INS CO	12	C

PHL VARIABLE INSURANCE COMPANY

D — Weak

Major Rating Factors: Weak overall results on stability tests (1.9 on a scale of 0 to 10) including potential financial drain due to affiliation with Nassau Reinsurance Group Holdings LP and negative cash flow from operations for 2017. Weak profitability (1.9) with operating losses during the first nine months of 2018. Weak liquidity (2.0).

Other Rating Factors: Fair quality investment portfolio (4.4). Good capitalization (5.3) based on good risk adjusted capital (moderate loss scenario).

Principal Business: Individual life insurance (58%), individual annuities (41%), and reinsurance (1%).

Principal Investments: NonCMO investment grade bonds (57%), CMOs and structured securities (27%), policy loans (4%), cash (4%), and misc. investments (6%).

Investments in Affiliates: 1%

Group Affiliation: Nassau Reinsurance Group Holdings LP

Licensed in: All states except ME, NY

Commenced Business: July 1981

Address: One American Row, Hartford, CT 6103

Phone: (860) 403-5000 **Domicile State:** CT **NAIC Code:** 93548

Data Date	Rating	RACR #1	RACR #2	Total Assets ($mil)	Capital ($mil)	Net Premium ($mil)	Net Income ($mil)
9-18	D	1.17	0.62	6,103.7	133.9	238.1	-41.6
9-17	D-	1.33	0.72	6,378.8	165.4	248.0	1.8
2017	D-	1.62	0.86	6,319.3	184.1	320.9	-56.2
2016	D-	1.34	0.73	6,386.8	166.7	-1,057.8	-69.9
2015	E+	1.92	0.99	6,397.8	194.5	1,749.4	-14.0
2014	C-	1.91	0.99	6,533.9	198.6	927.0	-41.1
2013	C	2.29	1.18	6,163.6	222.9	854.8	-86.1

Nassau Reinsurance Group Holdings LP Composite Group Rating: D- Largest Group Members	Assets ($mil)	Rating
PHOENIX LIFE INS CO	12478	D-
PHL VARIABLE INS CO	6319	D
CONSTITUTION LIFE INS CO	413	D
PYRAMID LIFE INS CO	72	D
NASSAU LIFE ANNUITY CO	31	D-

PHOENIX LIFE INSURANCE COMPANY

D- — Weak

Major Rating Factors: Weak overall results on stability tests (1.1 on a scale of 0 to 10) including negative cash flow from operations for 2017. Fair liquidity (4.5) due, in part, to cash value policies that are subject to withdrawals with minimal or no penalty. Good current capitalization (6.1) based on good risk adjusted capital (moderate loss scenario) reflecting some improvement over results in 2013.

Other Rating Factors: Good quality investment portfolio (5.0). Good overall profitability (5.5) although investment income, in comparison to reserve requirements, is below regulatory standards.

Principal Business: Individual life insurance (87%), reinsurance (12%), and individual annuities (1%).

Principal Investments: NonCMO investment grade bonds (50%), policy loans (21%), CMOs and structured securities (16%), noninv. grade bonds (3%), and misc. investments (11%).

Investments in Affiliates: None

Group Affiliation: Nassau Reinsurance Group Holdings LP

Licensed in: All states, the District of Columbia and Puerto Rico

Commenced Business: May 1851

Address: 15 Tech Valley Drive, East Greenbush, NY 12061-4137

Phone: (860) 403-5000 **Domicile State:** NY **NAIC Code:** 67814

Data Date	Rating	RACR #1	RACR #2	Total Assets ($mil)	Capital ($mil)	Net Premium ($mil)	Net Income ($mil)
9-18	D-	1.72	0.87	12,246.6	532.6	180.6	96.2
9-17	E	1.53	0.77	12,519.3	449.7	220.8	49.7
2017	D-	1.55	0.78	12,478.2	449.2	289.7	68.4
2016	E	1.38	0.69	12,450.8	393.2	299.7	51.9
2015	E	1.40	0.70	12,716.8	382.0	-516.8	-660.7
2014	C	1.23	0.74	13,249.3	609.2	314.5	132.5
2013	C	1.12	0.68	13,564.2	597.0	330.1	-21.0

Rating Indexes

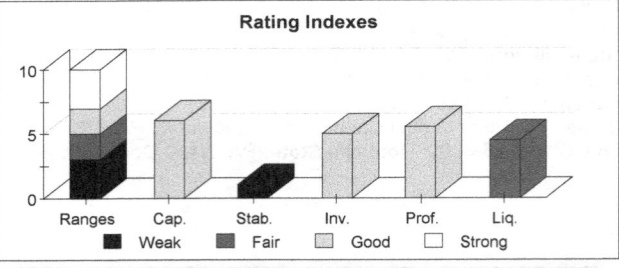

PHYSICIANS LIFE INSURANCE COMPANY *

A- — Excellent

Major Rating Factors: Good quality investment portfolio (6.3 on a scale of 0 to 10) despite mixed results such as: large holdings of BBB rated bonds but junk bond exposure equal to 58% of capital. Good overall profitability (6.0) although investment income, in comparison to reserve requirements, is below regulatory standards. Good liquidity (5.4).

Other Rating Factors: Good overall results on stability tests (6.9) excellent operational trends and excellent risk diversification. Strong capitalization (7.9) based on excellent risk adjusted capital (severe loss scenario).

Principal Business: Individual life insurance (49%), individual health insurance (20%), group life insurance (17%), individual annuities (13%), and reinsurance (1%).

Principal Investments: NonCMO investment grade bonds (63%), CMOs and structured securities (24%), noninv. grade bonds (6%), common & preferred stock (2%), and policy loans (2%).

Investments in Affiliates: None

Group Affiliation: Physicians Mutual Group

Licensed in: All states except NY, PR

Commenced Business: January 1970

Address: 2600 Dodge Street, Omaha, NE 68131-2671

Phone: (402) 633-1000 **Domicile State:** NE **NAIC Code:** 72125

Data Date	Rating	RACR #1	RACR #2	Total Assets ($mil)	Capital ($mil)	Net Premium ($mil)	Net Income ($mil)
9-18	A-	3.13	1.58	1,664.1	161.2	198.4	10.5
9-17	A-	3.21	1.65	1,625.7	160.2	206.3	10.7
2017	A-	3.01	1.53	1,632.1	151.4	268.1	8.7
2016	A-	3.04	1.55	1,596.4	150.8	296.5	13.2
2015	A-	2.93	1.50	1,490.7	137.9	275.0	6.4
2014	A-	2.77	1.36	1,430.5	130.1	262.4	7.0
2013	A-	2.94	1.45	1,378.7	122.7	248.6	8.3

Rating Indexes

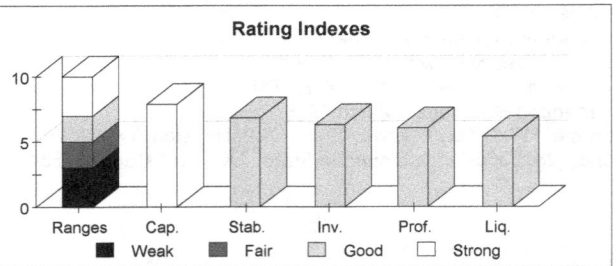

PHYSICIANS MUTUAL INSURANCE COMPANY *   A+   Excellent

Major Rating Factors: Good quality investment portfolio (6.1 on a scale of 0 to 10) despite mixed results such as: no exposure to mortgages and large holdings of BBB rated bonds but small junk bond holdings. Strong capitalization (9.4) based on excellent risk adjusted capital (severe loss scenario). Furthermore, this high level of risk adjusted capital has been consistently maintained over the last five years. Excellent profitability (8.3).

Other Rating Factors: Excellent liquidity (7.1). Excellent overall results on stability tests (7.9) excellent operational trends and excellent risk diversification.

Principal Business: Individual health insurance (72%), reinsurance (16%), and group health insurance (12%).

Principal Investments: NonCMO investment grade bonds (50%), CMOs and structured securities (24%), common & preferred stock (16%), and noninv. grade bonds (7%).

Investments in Affiliates: 7%

Group Affiliation: Physicians Mutual Group

Licensed in: All states except PR

Commenced Business: February 1902

Address: 2600 Dodge Street, Omaha, NE 68131-2671

Phone: (402) 633-1000   **Domicile State:** NE   **NAIC Code:** 80578

Data Date	Rating	RACR #1	RACR #2	Total Assets ($mil)	Capital ($mil)	Net Premium ($mil)	Net Income ($mil)
9-18	A+	3.50	2.60	2,367.4	995.5	346.1	40.0
9-17	A+	3.48	2.62	2,289.0	957.4	325.5	31.0
2017	A+	3.43	2.56	2,291.9	951.2	436.2	39.8
2016	A+	3.41	2.58	2,208.6	919.2	454.5	29.1
2015	A+	3.51	2.65	2,106.2	885.5	454.2	39.6
2014	A+	3.67	2.78	2,026.2	845.5	424.5	42.8
2013	A+	4.23	3.22	1,920.5	931.1	453.9	33.6

Rating Indexes

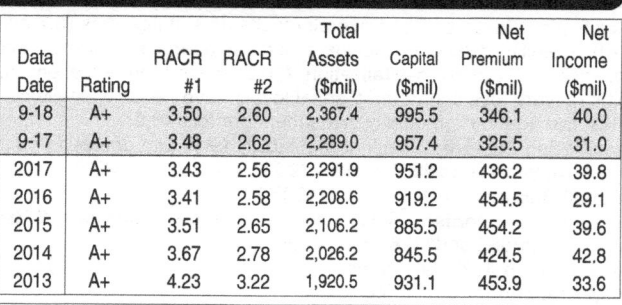

PIONEER MUTUAL LIFE INSURANCE COMPANY   B   Good

Major Rating Factors: Good quality investment portfolio (6.3 on a scale of 0 to 10) despite mixed results such as: minimal exposure to mortgages and large holdings of BBB rated bonds but small junk bond holdings. Good liquidity (5.0) with sufficient resources to cover a large increase in policy surrenders. Good overall results on stability tests (5.4) despite negative cash flow from operations for 2017 good operational trends and excellent risk diversification.

Other Rating Factors: Weak profitability (2.6). Strong capitalization (7.5) based on excellent risk adjusted capital (severe loss scenario).

Principal Business: Individual life insurance (92%) and individual annuities (8%).

Principal Investments: NonCMO investment grade bonds (60%), CMOs and structured securities (31%), policy loans (5%), mortgages in good standing (3%), and noninv. grade bonds (1%).

Investments in Affiliates: None

Group Affiliation: American United Life Group

Licensed in: All states except AK, NY, PR

Commenced Business: November 1947

Address: P O BOX 2167, FARGO, ND 58107

Phone: (701) 277-2300   **Domicile State:** ND   **NAIC Code:** 67911

Data Date	Rating	RACR #1	RACR #2	Total Assets ($mil)	Capital ($mil)	Net Premium ($mil)	Net Income ($mil)
9-18	B	2.57	1.35	509.5	39.8	10.6	2.6
9-17	B	3.38	1.83	519.7	50.9	15.1	2.9
2017	B	2.44	1.28	517.9	37.5	19.1	-6.6
2016	B	3.16	1.70	517.3	46.5	23.5	-1.7
2015	B	3.18	1.70	516.9	47.5	24.1	9.8
2014	B	2.66	1.42	511.4	38.3	26.4	-2.5
2013	B+	2.76	1.46	500.1	39.9	24.7	-1.4

Adverse Trends in Operations

Decrease in premium volume from 2016 to 2017 (19%)
Decrease in capital during 2017 (19%)
Decrease in capital during 2016 (2%)
Decrease in premium volume from 2014 to 2015 (9%)
Decrease in capital during 2014 (4%)

PIONEER SECURITY LIFE INSURANCE COMPANY   C   Fair

Major Rating Factors: Fair overall results on stability tests (4.1 on a scale of 0 to 10). Good current capitalization (5.6) based on good risk adjusted capital (severe loss scenario), although results have slipped from the excellent range over the last two years. Good liquidity (6.7) with sufficient resources to handle a spike in claims.

Other Rating Factors: Low quality investment portfolio (2.9). Weak profitability (2.7) with operating losses during the first nine months of 2018.

Principal Business: Individual life insurance (100%).

Principal Investments: Common & preferred stock (62%), nonCMO investment grade bonds (29%), and policy loans (3%).

Investments in Affiliates: 62%

Group Affiliation: Industrial Alliance Ins & Financial

Licensed in: AL, AR, CA, CO, DC, DE, FL, GA, HI, ID, IL, IN, KS, KY, LA, MD, MN, MS, MO, MT, NE, NM, NC, ND, OK, OR, PA, SC, SD, TN, TX, UT, VA, WA, WV, WI

Commenced Business: November 1956

Address: 425 AUSTIN AVENUE, WACO, TX 76701

Phone: (254) 297-2777   **Domicile State:** TX   **NAIC Code:** 67946

Data Date	Rating	RACR #1	RACR #2	Total Assets ($mil)	Capital ($mil)	Net Premium ($mil)	Net Income ($mil)
9-18	C	0.85	0.82	76.3	41.4	16.7	-0.5
9-17	C	1.13	1.04	88.5	58.2	14.2	-2.0
2017	C	1.00	0.97	80.6	49.0	19.3	-2.2
2016	C	1.18	1.15	82.9	55.2	14.5	23.8
2015	C+	1.26	1.24	125.5	101.4	7.7	23.6
2014	C+	1.16	1.14	132.2	109.7	8.0	4.5
2013	C+	1.11	1.10	109.7	89.3	10.1	2.0

Rating Indexes

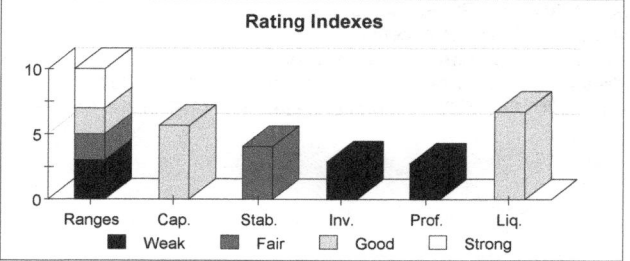

POPULAR LIFE RE

B **Good**

Major Rating Factors: Good overall results on stability tests (5.7 on a scale of 0 to 10). Stability strengths include excellent operational trends and good risk diversification. Strong capitalization (10.0) based on excellent risk adjusted capital (severe loss scenario). Capital levels have been relatively consistent over the last five years. High quality investment portfolio (8.9).

Other Rating Factors: Excellent profitability (9.1) with operating gains in each of the last five years. Excellent liquidity (9.2).

Principal Business: Reinsurance (100%).

Principal Investments: CMOs and structured securities (67%), nonCMO investment grade bonds (28%), and cash (5%).

Investments in Affiliates: None

Group Affiliation: Popular Inc

Licensed in: (No states)

Commenced Business: December 2003

Address: CORPORATE OFFICE PARK SOLAR A, GUAYNABO, PR 966

Phone: (787) 706-4111 **Domicile State:** PR **NAIC Code:** 11876

Data Date	Rating	RACR #1	RACR #2	Total Assets ($mil)	Capital ($mil)	Net Premium ($mil)	Net Income ($mil)
9-18	B	5.27	4.74	69.3	39.6	14.1	3.6
9-17	C+	4.91	4.42	65.8	36.1	13.7	2.9
2017	B	5.05	4.54	67.0	37.9	17.3	4.7
2016	C+	4.54	3.61	63.4	33.4	18.9	5.1
2015	C+	4.03	3.31	58.2	28.7	19.3	2.4
2014	C+	4.14	3.72	56.8	29.2	19.2	2.0
2013	C+	3.96	3.26	52.6	27.2	18.0	3.4

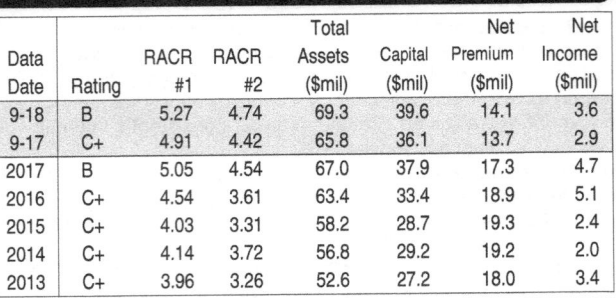

Rating Indexes

PRENEED REINSURANCE COMPANY OF AMERICA

B **Good**

Major Rating Factors: Fair overall results on stability tests (4.8 on a scale of 0 to 10). Fair liquidity (4.4) as cash from operations and sale of marketable assets may not be adequate to cover a spike in claims. Strong capitalization (10.0) based on excellent risk adjusted capital (severe loss scenario). Capital levels have been relatively consistent over the last five years.

Other Rating Factors: High quality investment portfolio (9.0). Excellent profitability (9.4) with operating gains in each of the last five years.

Principal Business: Reinsurance (100%).

Principal Investments: NonCMO investment grade bonds (96%) and cash (1%).

Investments in Affiliates: None

Group Affiliation: NGL Ins Group

Licensed in: AZ

Commenced Business: October 2001

Address: 2999 North 44th St Ste 250, Phoenix, AZ 85018

Phone: (608) 257-5611 **Domicile State:** AZ **NAIC Code:** 11155

Data Date	Rating	RACR #1	RACR #2	Total Assets ($mil)	Capital ($mil)	Net Premium ($mil)	Net Income ($mil)
9-18	B	6.63	5.97	43.0	39.0	7.6	2.9
9-17	B	7.14	6.43	43.2	41.8	31.8	4.6
2017	B	6.90	6.21	42.1	40.6	34.3	6.4
2016	B	6.70	6.03	41.8	39.2	104.3	5.5
2015	B	6.61	5.94	38.6	36.4	105.2	5.5
2014	B	6.36	5.72	34.5	32.2	101.2	5.1
2013	B	6.03	5.43	29.3	27.2	99.6	5.2

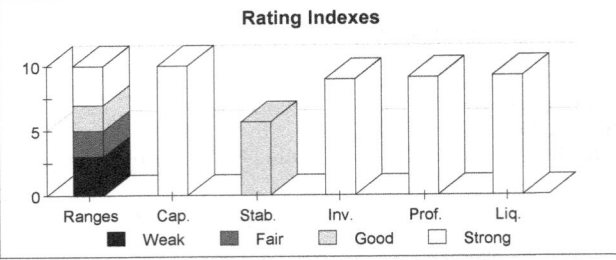

Rating Indexes

PRIMERICA LIFE INSURANCE COMPANY

B **Good**

Major Rating Factors: Good liquidity (6.9 on a scale of 0 to 10) with sufficient resources to handle a spike in claims as well as a significant increase in policy surrenders. Good overall results on stability tests (5.8). Stability strengths include excellent operational trends and excellent risk diversification. Fair quality investment portfolio (4.3).

Other Rating Factors: Strong capitalization (7.4) based on excellent risk adjusted capital (severe loss scenario). Excellent profitability (9.0).

Principal Business: Individual life insurance (100%).

Principal Investments: NonCMO investment grade bonds (50%), common & preferred stock (29%), CMOs and structured securities (13%), and noninv. grade bonds (3%).

Investments in Affiliates: 26%

Group Affiliation: Primerica Inc

Licensed in: All states except NY

Commenced Business: January 1903

Address: 33 Arch Street - 26th Floor, Nashville, TN 37201

Phone: (770) 381-1000 **Domicile State:** TN **NAIC Code:** 65919

Data Date	Rating	RACR #1	RACR #2	Total Assets ($mil)	Capital ($mil)	Net Premium ($mil)	Net Income ($mil)
9-18	B	1.48	1.27	1,617.7	682.4	237.7	405.2
9-17	B	1.34	1.13	1,457.4	586.2	228.5	280.0
2017	B	1.32	1.13	1,493.8	598.0	291.0	398.2
2016	B	1.34	1.13	1,431.6	572.7	250.1	392.9
2015	B	1.29	1.11	1,320.9	560.9	116.3	435.4
2014	B	1.35	1.13	1,279.4	499.0	277.1	268.3
2013	B	1.54	1.27	1,479.8	563.3	255.7	307.1

Adverse Trends in Operations

Decrease in premium volume from 2014 to 2015 (58%)
Decrease in asset base during 2014 (14%)
Decrease in capital during 2014 (11%)

PRINCIPAL LIFE INSURANCE COMPANY *   B+   Good

Major Rating Factors: Good quality investment portfolio (5.8 on a scale of 0 to 10) despite large holdings of BBB rated bonds in addition to moderate junk bond exposure. Exposure to mortgages is significant, but the mortgage default rate has been low. Good overall results on stability tests (6.7). Stability strengths include excellent operational trends and excellent risk diversification. Strong capitalization (7.3) based on excellent risk adjusted capital (severe loss scenario).

Other Rating Factors: Excellent profitability (7.8). Excellent liquidity (7.1).

Principal Business: Group retirement contracts (30%), individual annuities (28%), group health insurance (14%), individual life insurance (11%), and other lines (17%).

Principal Investments: NonCMO investment grade bonds (50%), mortgages in good standing (19%), CMOs and structured securities (19%), noninv. grade bonds (3%), and misc. investments (8%).

Investments in Affiliates: 5%

Group Affiliation: Principal Financial Group

Licensed in: All states, the District of Columbia and Puerto Rico

Commenced Business: September 1879

Address: 711 HIGH STREET, DES MOINES, IA 50392-2300

Phone: (800) 986-3343 **Domicile State:** IA **NAIC Code:** 61271

Data Date	Rating	RACR #1	RACR #2	Total Assets ($mil)	Capital ($mil)	Net Premium ($mil)	Net Income ($mil)
9-18	B+	2.20	1.22	197,908	5,145.5	7,119.0	849.7
9-17	B+	2.22	1.22	185,959	5,318.8	6,435.3	1,523.7
2017	B+	2.19	1.22	189,004	4,946.8	8,339.6	1,976.7
2016	B+	2.03	1.12	171,338	4,643.8	7,808.5	996.7
2015	B+	2.13	1.14	157,775	4,496.7	7,693.4	948.6
2014	B+	1.99	1.08	154,074	4,202.1	5,533.2	535.5
2013	B+	2.05	1.09	143,742	4,142.2	5,267.0	607.9

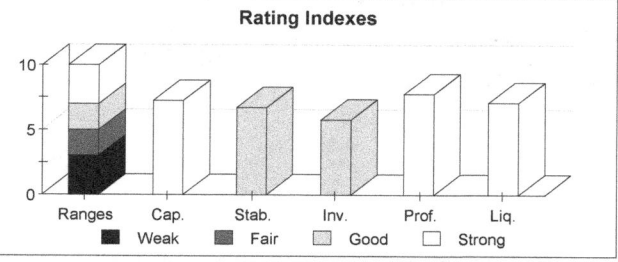

Rating Indexes

PRINCIPAL NATIONAL LIFE INSURANCE CO   B   Good

Major Rating Factors: Good overall results on stability tests (5.7 on a scale of 0 to 10). Strengths include good financial support from affiliation with Principal Financial Group, good operational trends and excellent risk diversification. Fair profitability (3.5) with operating losses during the first nine months of 2018. Strong capitalization (10.0) based on excellent risk adjusted capital (severe loss scenario).

Other Rating Factors: High quality investment portfolio (8.3). Excellent liquidity (10.0).

Principal Business: Individual life insurance (100%).

Principal Investments: NonCMO investment grade bonds (81%), cash (9%), CMOs and structured securities (8%), and noninv. grade bonds (2%).

Investments in Affiliates: None

Group Affiliation: Principal Financial Group

Licensed in: All states except NY, PR

Commenced Business: March 1968

Address: 711 HIGH STREET, DES MOINES, IA 50392-2300

Phone: (515) 247-5111 **Domicile State:** IA **NAIC Code:** 71161

Data Date	Rating	RACR #1	RACR #2	Total Assets ($mil)	Capital ($mil)	Net Premium ($mil)	Net Income ($mil)
9-18	B	6.42	3.17	368.2	176.1	0.0	-2.5
9-17	B	6.40	3.16	300.4	147.4	0.0	-2.6
2017	B	5.70	2.82	316.9	148.9	0.0	-3.9
2016	B	6.23	3.07	239.8	127.9	0.0	-4.4
2015	B	5.85	2.89	185.1	103.7	0.0	-4.5
2014	B	4.88	2.42	141.2	84.8	0.0	-4.5
2013	B	6.16	3.04	110.4	84.2	0.0	-6.4

Principal Financial Group Composite Group Rating: B+ Largest Group Members	Assets ($mil)	Rating
PRINCIPAL LIFE INS CO	189004	B+
PRINCIPAL NATIONAL LIFE INS CO	317	B

PROFESSIONAL INSURANCE COMPANY   D   Weak

Major Rating Factors: Weak overall results on stability tests (2.1 on a scale of 0 to 10) including potential financial drain due to affiliation with Sun Life Assurance Group. Good quality investment portfolio (6.7) despite mixed results such as: no exposure to mortgages and large holdings of BBB rated bonds but no exposure to junk bonds. Good liquidity (6.9) with sufficient resources to handle a spike in claims.

Other Rating Factors: Strong capitalization (10.0) based on excellent risk adjusted capital (severe loss scenario). Excellent profitability (8.6).

Principal Business: Individual health insurance (93%) and individual life insurance (7%).

Principal Investments: NonCMO investment grade bonds (77%), CMOs and structured securities (15%), and policy loans (3%).

Investments in Affiliates: None

Group Affiliation: Sun Life Assurance Group

Licensed in: All states except AK, DE, ME, NH, NJ, NY, RI, VT, PR

Commenced Business: September 1937

Address: 350 North St Paul Street, Dallas, TX 75201

Phone: (781) 237-6030 **Domicile State:** TX **NAIC Code:** 68047

Data Date	Rating	RACR #1	RACR #2	Total Assets ($mil)	Capital ($mil)	Net Premium ($mil)	Net Income ($mil)
9-18	D	5.29	4.76	109.9	47.5	14.4	3.0
9-17	D	5.21	4.69	111.4	46.7	16.1	3.7
2017	D	5.02	4.51	109.6	45.0	21.6	4.4
2016	D-	4.68	4.11	110.0	42.0	24.5	4.5
2015	C	4.32	3.34	109.2	38.6	27.7	2.7
2014	C	4.02	2.88	108.9	35.9	31.6	1.8
2013	C-	3.16	2.21	105.1	29.5	37.1	3.4

Sun Life Assurance Group Composite Group Rating: D- Largest Group Members	Assets ($mil)	Rating
SUN LIFE ASR CO OF CANADA	19086	D-
INDEPENDENCE LIFE ANNUITY CO	3144	D
SUN LIFE HEALTH INS CO	943	D
PROFESSIONAL INS CO	110	D

PROFESSIONAL LIFE & CASUALTY COMPANY

B-   **Good**

Major Rating Factors: Good liquidity (5.6 on a scale of 0 to 10) with sufficient resources to cover a large increase in policy surrenders. Fair quality investment portfolio (3.2) with substantial holdings of BBB bonds in addition to moderate junk bond exposure. Fair overall results on stability tests (4.9).

Other Rating Factors: Strong capitalization (8.2) based on excellent risk adjusted capital (severe loss scenario). Excellent profitability (8.9).

Principal Business: Individual annuities (99%) and individual life insurance (1%).

Principal Investments: NonCMO investment grade bonds (48%), common & preferred stock (27%), noninv. grade bonds (13%), and cash (1%).

Investments in Affiliates: None

Group Affiliation: None

Licensed in: IL, IN, MT, ND, OK

Commenced Business: September 1957

Address: 20 N WACKER DR STE 3110, CHICAGO, IL 60606-3182

Phone: (312) 220-0655 **Domicile State:** IL **NAIC Code:** 68063

Data Date	Rating	RACR #1	RACR #2	Total Assets ($mil)	Capital ($mil)	Net Premium ($mil)	Net Income ($mil)
9-18	B-	3.23	1.80	180.9	61.2	3.1	4.4
9-17	B-	2.67	1.41	169.7	47.1	4.9	4.2
2017	B-	2.75	1.46	173.3	52.1	5.8	6.8
2016	B-	3.22	1.71	164.3	46.1	9.6	4.1
2015	C	2.96	1.58	158.2	42.8	7.5	4.3
2014	C	2.68	1.45	154.2	41.8	6.4	5.1
2013	C	2.66	1.39	144.3	33.3	9.6	6.5

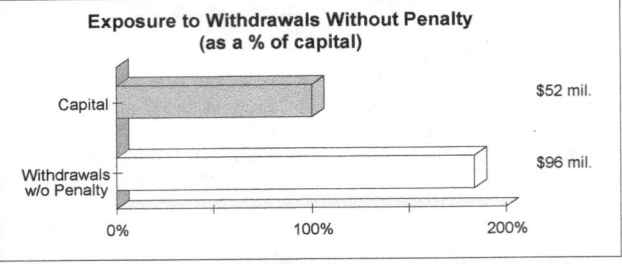

Exposure to Withdrawals Without Penalty
(as a % of capital)

Capital — $52 mil.
Withdrawals w/o Penalty — $96 mil.

PROTECTIVE LIFE & ANNUITY INSURANCE COMPANY

C+   **Fair**

Major Rating Factors: Fair liquidity (4.7 on a scale of 0 to 10) due, in part, to cash value policies that are subject to withdrawals with minimal or no penalty. Fair overall results on stability tests (4.6). Good current capitalization (6.8) based on good risk adjusted capital (severe loss scenario), although results have slipped from the excellent range during the last year.

Other Rating Factors: Good quality investment portfolio (5.6). Weak profitability (2.1) with operating losses during the first nine months of 2018.

Principal Business: Individual annuities (86%), individual life insurance (7%), and reinsurance (7%).

Principal Investments: NonCMO investment grade bonds (68%), CMOs and structured securities (17%), mortgages in good standing (6%), noninv. grade bonds (5%), and misc. investments (4%).

Investments in Affiliates: None

Group Affiliation: Dai-ichi Life Holdings Inc

Licensed in: All states except MN, PR

Commenced Business: December 1978

Address: 2801 HIGHWAY 280 SOUTH, BIRMINGHAM, AL 35223

Phone: (205) 268-1000 **Domicile State:** AL **NAIC Code:** 88536

Data Date	Rating	RACR #1	RACR #2	Total Assets ($mil)	Capital ($mil)	Net Premium ($mil)	Net Income ($mil)
9-18	C+	2.06	0.97	5,029.6	216.0	3,045.4	-123.7
9-17	B	2.46	1.24	2,028.3	162.1	161.9	18.9
2017	B	2.28	1.15	2,076.5	155.9	248.7	23.3
2016	B	2.63	1.32	1,959.8	172.0	55.1	34.7
2015	B	2.62	1.34	2,007.6	173.6	47.5	26.7
2014	B	2.70	1.39	2,093.7	183.4	49.0	33.6
2013	B	2.79	1.44	2,162.7	193.6	156.6	27.7

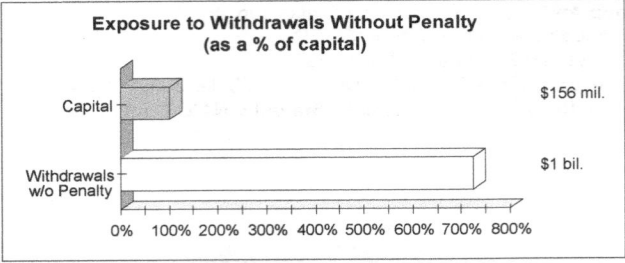

Exposure to Withdrawals Without Penalty
(as a % of capital)

Capital — $156 mil.
Withdrawals w/o Penalty — $1 bil.

PROTECTIVE LIFE INSURANCE COMPANY

B   **Good**

Major Rating Factors: Good quality investment portfolio (5.7 on a scale of 0 to 10) despite large holdings of BBB rated bonds in addition to moderate junk bond exposure. Exposure to mortgages is significant, but the mortgage default rate has been low. Good overall profitability (6.3). Good liquidity (6.3).

Other Rating Factors: Good overall results on stability tests (5.8) excellent operational trends, good risk adjusted capital for prior years and excellent risk diversification. Strong capitalization (7.1) based on excellent risk adjusted capital (severe loss scenario).

Principal Business: Individual life insurance (47%), individual annuities (37%), and reinsurance (15%).

Principal Investments: NonCMO investment grade bonds (54%), mortgages in good standing (16%), CMOs and structured securities (15%), common & preferred stock (6%), and misc. investments (7%).

Investments in Affiliates: 7%

Group Affiliation: Dai-ichi Life Holdings Inc

Licensed in: All states except NY

Commenced Business: September 1907

Address: 1620 WESTGATE CIRCLE SUITE 200, BRENTWOOD, TN 37027-8035

Phone: (205) 268-1000 **Domicile State:** TN **NAIC Code:** 68136

Data Date	Rating	RACR #1	RACR #2	Total Assets ($mil)	Capital ($mil)	Net Premium ($mil)	Net Income ($mil)
9-18	B	1.54	1.06	59,054.5	4,000.5	13,207.5	119.7
9-17	B	1.78	1.28	47,125.6	4,451.2	1,806.5	648.0
2017	B	1.54	1.19	47,662.8	4,282.3	2,409.9	731.2
2016	B	1.43	1.12	44,644.9	4,236.9	2,378.8	-391.6
2015	B	1.27	1.01	41,809.7	3,781.9	2,682.3	440.0
2014	B	1.20	0.98	41,231.7	3,498.9	2,359.8	554.2
2013	B	1.03	0.83	41,027.0	2,917.7	4,589.6	165.5

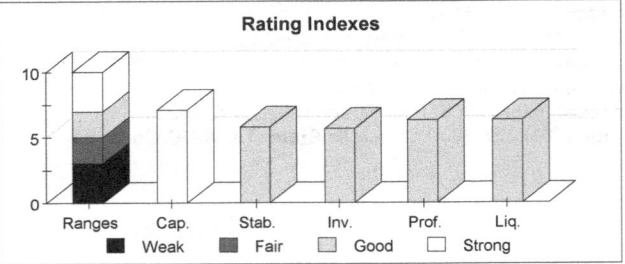

Rating Indexes

Ranges | Cap. | Stab. | Inv. | Prof. | Liq.

■ Weak ▨ Fair ▢ Good □ Strong

PROVIDENT LIFE & ACCIDENT INSURANCE COMPANY   C+   Fair

Major Rating Factors: Fair overall results on stability tests (4.8 on a scale of 0 to 10) including fair financial strength of affiliated Unum Group. Fair quality investment portfolio (4.8) with large holdings of BBB rated bonds in addition to junk bond exposure equal to 71% of capital. Good overall profitability (6.5). Excellent expense controls.

Other Rating Factors: Strong capitalization (7.6) based on excellent risk adjusted capital (severe loss scenario). Excellent liquidity (7.3).

Principal Business: Individual health insurance (69%), individual life insurance (30%), and reinsurance (1%).

Principal Investments: NonCMO investment grade bonds (75%), noninv. grade bonds (7%), mortgages in good standing (6%), CMOs and structured securities (6%), and misc. investments (6%).

Investments in Affiliates: None
Group Affiliation: Unum Group
Licensed in: All states except NY
Commenced Business: May 1887
Address: 1 FOUNTAIN SQUARE, CHATTANOOGA, TN 37402-1330
Phone: (423) 294-1011 **Domicile State:** TN **NAIC Code:** 68195

Data Date	Rating	RACR #1	RACR #2	Total Assets ($mil)	Capital ($mil)	Net Premium ($mil)	Net Income ($mil)
9-18	C+	2.77	1.40	8,041.3	696.4	609.1	188.0
9-17	C+	2.81	1.41	8,207.4	738.0	600.2	128.5
2017	C+	2.44	1.22	8,034.0	605.0	769.3	163.5
2016	C+	2.76	1.38	8,272.6	728.2	840.8	191.7
2015	C+	2.74	1.38	8,325.3	727.5	869.4	178.9
2014	C+	2.72	1.37	8,297.3	720.0	889.8	187.1
2013	C+	2.55	1.28	8,347.6	699.7	898.5	166.4

Unum Group
Composite Group Rating: C+

Largest Group Members	Assets ($mil)	Rating
UNUM LIFE INS CO OF AMERICA	21455	C+
PROVIDENT LIFE ACCIDENT INS CO	8034	C+
PAUL REVERE LIFE INS CO	3571	C+
FIRST UNUM LIFE INS CO	3457	C+
COLONIAL LIFE ACCIDENT INS CO	3220	C+

PROVIDENT LIFE & CASUALTY INSURANCE COMPANY   B-   Good

Major Rating Factors: Fair overall results on stability tests (4.9 on a scale of 0 to 10) including fair financial strength of affiliated Unum Group. Fair quality investment portfolio (4.6) with large holdings of BBB rated bonds in addition to moderate junk bond exposure. Strong capitalization (9.2) based on excellent risk adjusted capital (severe loss scenario).

Other Rating Factors: Excellent profitability (7.6). Excellent liquidity (7.5).

Principal Business: Individual health insurance (94%), reinsurance (4%), and individual life insurance (2%).

Principal Investments: NonCMO investment grade bonds (82%), noninv. grade bonds (7%), mortgages in good standing (5%), and CMOs and structured securities (5%).

Investments in Affiliates: None
Group Affiliation: Unum Group
Licensed in: AK, AR, CO, CT, DC, DE, GA, HI, ID, IL, IA, KY, LA, MA, MS, MO, NE, NH, NJ, NM, NY, NC, ND, OH, OK, PA, RI, SC, SD, TN, VA, WA
Commenced Business: January 1952
Address: 1 FOUNTAIN SQUARE, CHATTANOOGA, TN 37402-1330
Phone: (423) 294-1011 **Domicile State:** TN **NAIC Code:** 68209

Data Date	Rating	RACR #1	RACR #2	Total Assets ($mil)	Capital ($mil)	Net Premium ($mil)	Net Income ($mil)
9-18	B-	4.42	2.49	746.1	142.7	71.3	3.0
9-17	B-	4.96	2.72	760.2	165.3	69.9	23.0
2017	B-	4.75	2.63	746.7	150.2	92.2	26.0
2016	B-	4.43	2.38	753.2	141.7	90.3	13.7
2015	B-	4.65	2.50	755.8	147.2	87.0	21.3
2014	B-	4.38	2.32	767.2	139.4	84.5	6.8
2013	B-	4.65	2.46	764.1	150.9	86.2	18.3

Unum Group
Composite Group Rating: C+

Largest Group Members	Assets ($mil)	Rating
UNUM LIFE INS CO OF AMERICA	21455	C+
PROVIDENT LIFE ACCIDENT INS CO	8034	C+
PAUL REVERE LIFE INS CO	3571	C+
FIRST UNUM LIFE INS CO	3457	C+
COLONIAL LIFE ACCIDENT INS CO	3220	C+

PRUCO LIFE INSURANCE COMPANY   C+   Fair

Major Rating Factors: Fair overall results on stability tests (3.7 on a scale of 0 to 10) including fair risk adjusted capital in prior years. Good capitalization (5.5) based on good risk adjusted capital (moderate loss scenario). Good quality investment portfolio (5.7) despite significant exposure to mortgages . Mortgage default rate has been low. large holdings of BBB rated bonds in addition to small junk bond holdings.

Other Rating Factors: Weak profitability (2.4) with investment income below regulatory standards in relation to interest assumptions of reserves. Excellent liquidity (9.5).

Principal Business: Individual annuities (54%), individual life insurance (42%), and reinsurance (5%).

Principal Investments: NonCMO investment grade bonds (44%), policy loans (16%), mortgages in good standing (15%), CMOs and structured securities (13%), and misc. investments (12%).

Investments in Affiliates: 6%
Group Affiliation: Prudential of America
Licensed in: All states except NY, PR
Commenced Business: December 1971
Address: 2929 N CENTRAL AVE STE 1700, PHOENIX, AZ 85253-2738
Phone: (973) 802-6000 **Domicile State:** AZ **NAIC Code:** 79227

Data Date	Rating	RACR #1	RACR #2	Total Assets ($mil)	Capital ($mil)	Net Premium ($mil)	Net Income ($mil)
9-18	C+	1.32	0.73	123,473	1,543.2	1,014.4	154.7
9-17	C+	1.23	0.71	119,224	1,401.5	1,351.0	-658.2
2017	C+	1.22	0.68	122,428	1,364.9	1,770.7	-457.4
2016	C+	1.12	0.64	111,524	1,250.1	-821.4	738.0
2015	C+	2.27	1.36	107,815	2,795.6	7,918.6	530.9
2014	C+	2.33	1.38	106,838	2,656.5	8,744.8	108.9
2013	C+	2.18	1.32	98,541.3	2,386.9	11,307.7	553.1

Rating Indexes

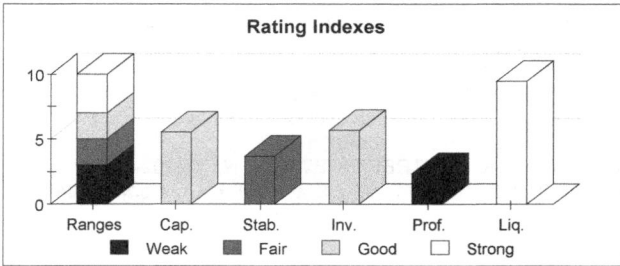

PRUCO LIFE INSURANCE COMPANY OF NEW JERSEY — B- — Good

Major Rating Factors: Good current capitalization (5.8 on a scale of 0 to 10) based on good risk adjusted capital (moderate loss scenario) reflecting some improvement over results in 2017. Good quality investment portfolio (5.5) despite mixed results such as: substantial holdings of BBB bonds but moderate junk bond exposure. Fair overall results on stability tests (3.6) including fair financial strength of affiliated Prudential of America and fair risk adjusted capital in prior years.

Other Rating Factors: Weak profitability (2.8) with investment income below regulatory standards in relation to interest assumptions of reserves. Excellent liquidity (7.0).

Principal Business: Individual life insurance (52%) and individual annuities (48%).

Principal Investments: NonCMO investment grade bonds (52%), CMOs and structured securities (19%), policy loans (12%), mortgages in good standing (8%), and noninv. grade bonds (7%).

Investments in Affiliates: 2%

Group Affiliation: Prudential of America

Licensed in: NJ, NY

Commenced Business: December 1982

Address: 213 WASHINGTON STREET, NEWARK, NJ 07102-2992

Phone: (973) 802-6000 **Domicile State:** NJ **NAIC Code:** 97195

Data Date	Rating	RACR #1	RACR #2	Total Assets ($mil)	Capital ($mil)	Net Premium ($mil)	Net Income ($mil)
9-18	B-	1.51	0.76	16,367.8	246.4	207.0	34.2
9-17	B-	1.57	0.78	15,679.7	235.0	181.8	25.4
2017	B-	1.42	0.71	15,975.5	223.0	219.8	33.3
2016	B-	2.11	1.06	14,457.0	313.3	61.9	81.3
2015	B-	2.87	1.44	13,487.2	409.6	1,087.4	61.7
2014	B-	2.60	1.32	13,037.5	352.4	1,143.5	58.7
2013	B-	3.11	1.57	11,810.8	379.7	1,078.5	81.2

Risk-Adjusted Capital Ratio #1
(Moderate Loss Scenario)

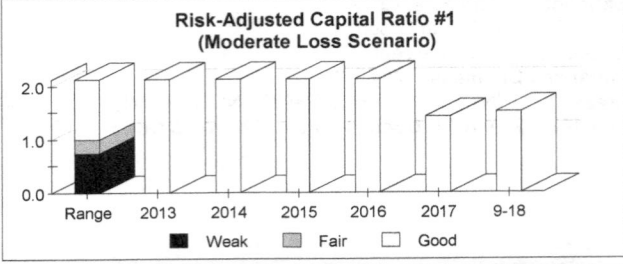

Range 2013 2014 2015 2016 2017 9-18
■ Weak   ▨ Fair   □ Good

PRUDENTIAL ANNUITIES LIFE ASSURANCE CORPORATION — B- — Good

Major Rating Factors: Good quality investment portfolio (6.4 on a scale of 0 to 10) with minimal exposure to mortgages and minimal holdings in junk bonds. Good overall profitability (5.8). Fair overall results on stability tests (4.2) including fair financial strength of affiliated Prudential of America and excessive premium growth.

Other Rating Factors: Strong capitalization (10.0) based on excellent risk adjusted capital (severe loss scenario). Excellent liquidity (10.0).

Principal Business: Reinsurance (99%) and individual annuities (1%).

Principal Investments: NonCMO investment grade bonds (53%), mortgages in good standing (7%), CMOs and structured securities (7%), noninv. grade bonds (2%), and cash (2%).

Investments in Affiliates: 1%

Group Affiliation: Prudential of America

Licensed in: All states except NY

Commenced Business: May 1988

Address: 2929 N CENTRAL AVE STE 1700, PHOENIX, AZ 85253-2738

Phone: (203) 926-1888 **Domicile State:** AZ **NAIC Code:** 86630

Data Date	Rating	RACR #1	RACR #2	Total Assets ($mil)	Capital ($mil)	Net Premium ($mil)	Net Income ($mil)
9-18	B-	11.37	8.36	53,916.6	5,994.9	5,421.1	905.0
9-17	B-	15.66	10.87	60,038.4	8,357.4	3,790.6	2,623.3
2017	B-	15.11	11.06	58,738.7	8,058.9	5,247.4	3,910.5
2016	C	10.82	7.80	58,775.7	5,718.2	15,511.7	-2,017.6
2015	C+	1.29	0.98	42,821.4	482.1	-230.8	340.0
2014	C	1.44	1.11	47,706.6	605.7	-145.1	392.6
2013	C	1.01	0.81	50,649.1	443.5	-127.6	406.1

Prudential of America
Composite Group Rating: C+
Largest Group Members / Assets ($mil) / Rating

Largest Group Members	Assets ($mil)	Rating
PRUDENTIAL INS CO OF AMERICA	266164	B
PRUCO LIFE INS CO	122428	C+
PRUDENTIAL RETIREMENT INS ANNUITY	75338	B-
PRUDENTIAL LEGACY INS CO OF NJ	59814	D+
PRUDENTIAL ANNUITIES LIFE ASR CORP	58739	B-

PRUDENTIAL INSURANCE COMPANY OF AMERICA — B — Good

Major Rating Factors: Good overall results on stability tests (5.5 on a scale of 0 to 10) despite fair financial strength of affiliated Prudential of America. Other stability subfactors include good operational trends, good risk adjusted capital for prior years and excellent risk diversification. Good quality investment portfolio (6.3) despite substantial holdings of BBB bonds in addition to junk bond exposure equal to 51% of capital. Exposure to mortgages is significant, but the mortgage default rate has been low. Good overall profitability (5.4).

Other Rating Factors: Strong capitalization (7.1) based on excellent risk adjusted capital (severe loss scenario). Excellent liquidity (7.6).

Principal Business: Group retirement contracts (44%), reinsurance (27%), group life insurance (14%), individual life insurance (10%), and other lines (5%).

Principal Investments: NonCMO investment grade bonds (47%), CMOs and structured securities (17%), mortgages in good standing (16%), common & preferred stock (6%), and misc. investments (10%).

Investments in Affiliates: 10%

Group Affiliation: Prudential of America

Licensed in: All states, the District of Columbia and Puerto Rico

Commenced Business: October 1875

Address: 751 BROAD STREET, NEWARK, NJ 07102-3777

Phone: (973) 802-6000 **Domicile State:** NJ **NAIC Code:** 68241

Data Date	Rating	RACR #1	RACR #2	Total Assets ($mil)	Capital ($mil)	Net Premium ($mil)	Net Income ($mil)
9-18	B	1.52	1.08	269,549	10,538.2	18,904.1	162.8
9-17	B	1.76	1.26	263,146	11,589.0	17,521.4	714.3
2017	B	1.45	1.04	266,164	9,948.3	25,303.8	-216.7
2016	B	1.71	1.23	260,294	11,173.7	25,550.2	5,213.3
2015	B	1.53	1.15	244,996	11,543.7	-29,033.9	5,252.8
2014	B	1.35	0.93	309,102	10,331.0	22,557.6	901.1
2013	B	1.29	0.88	296,637	9,382.6	21,059.8	1,357.8

Prudential of America
Composite Group Rating: C+
Largest Group Members / Assets ($mil) / Rating

Largest Group Members	Assets ($mil)	Rating
PRUDENTIAL INS CO OF AMERICA	266164	B
PRUCO LIFE INS CO	122428	C+
PRUDENTIAL RETIREMENT INS ANNUITY	75338	B-
PRUDENTIAL LEGACY INS CO OF NJ	59814	D+
PRUDENTIAL ANNUITIES LIFE ASR CORP	58739	B-

PRUDENTIAL LEGACY INS CO OF NJ — D+ — Weak

Major Rating Factors: Poor overall capitalization (1.7 on a scale of 0 to 10) based on excessive policy leverage and weak risk adjusted capital (moderate loss scenario). Weak liquidity (0.0) based on large exposure to policies that are subject to policyholder withdrawals with minimal or no penalty. Weak overall results on stability tests (1.7) including weak risk adjusted capital in prior years.

Other Rating Factors: Good overall profitability (5.5). High quality investment portfolio (9.5).

Principal Business: Reinsurance (100%).

Principal Investments: NonCMO investment grade bonds (100%).

Investments in Affiliates: None

Group Affiliation: Prudential of America

Licensed in: NJ

Commenced Business: October 2010

Address: 751 Broad St, Newark, NJ 07102-3777

Phone: (877) 301-1212 **Domicile State:** NJ **NAIC Code:** 13809

Data Date	Rating	RACR #1	RACR #2	Total Assets ($mil)	Capital ($mil)	Net Premium ($mil)	Net Income ($mil)
2017	D+	0.47	0.39	59,813.8	258.1	2,513.3	427.7
2016	D+	0.45	0.37	60,142.6	245.9	2,609.5	488.1
2015	C	0.64	0.53	61,222.1	359.2	55,309.0	1,468.5
2014	U	3.50	3.15	6.0	6.0	0.0	0.0

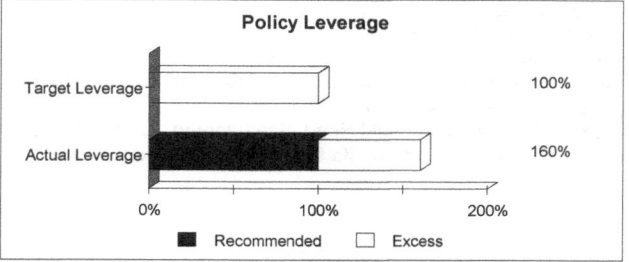

Policy Leverage

Target Leverage — 100%
Actual Leverage — 160%

0% 100% 200%

■ Recommended □ Excess

PRUDENTIAL RETIREMENT INSURANCE & ANNUITY — B- — Good

Major Rating Factors: Good overall results on stability tests (5.1 on a scale of 0 to 10) despite fair financial strength of affiliated Prudential of America and excessive premium growth. Other stability subfactors include excellent operational trends and excellent risk diversification. Good overall capitalization (6.5) based on good risk adjusted capital (moderate loss scenario). However, capital levels have fluctuated somewhat during past years. Good overall profitability (5.9) although investment income, in comparison to reserve requirements, is below regulatory standards.

Other Rating Factors: Good liquidity (6.6). Fair quality investment portfolio (3.7).

Principal Business: Reinsurance (58%) and group retirement contracts (42%).

Principal Investments: NonCMO investment grade bonds (51%), CMOs and structured securities (21%), mortgages in good standing (20%), and noninv. grade bonds (6%).

Investments in Affiliates: 1%

Group Affiliation: Prudential of America

Licensed in: All states, the District of Columbia and Puerto Rico

Commenced Business: October 1981

Address: 280 TRUMBULL STREET, HARTFORD, CT 06103-3509

Phone: (860) 534-2000 **Domicile State:** CT **NAIC Code:** 93629

Data Date	Rating	RACR #1	RACR #2	Total Assets ($mil)	Capital ($mil)	Net Premium ($mil)	Net Income ($mil)
9-18	B-	1.97	0.91	75,563.2	1,128.3	825.9	127.2
9-17	B-	2.04	0.90	73,547.4	1,114.6	645.7	88.9
2017	B-	1.88	0.86	75,337.8	1,056.8	884.3	100.5
2016	B-	1.86	0.83	71,588.0	1,020.5	862.4	172.4
2015	B-	1.89	0.86	75,576.9	1,080.4	749.7	114.9
2014	B-	1.60	0.76	78,877.5	932.7	568.4	191.0
2013	B-	1.66	0.79	78,046.5	941.0	583.1	313.0

Prudential of America Composite Group Rating: C+ Largest Group Members	Assets ($mil)	Rating
PRUDENTIAL INS CO OF AMERICA	266164	B
PRUCO LIFE INS CO	122428	C+
PRUDENTIAL RETIREMENT INS ANNUITY	75338	B-
PRUDENTIAL LEGACY INS CO OF NJ	59814	D+
PRUDENTIAL ANNUITIES LIFE ASR CORP	58739	B-

REINSURANCE COMPANY OF MISSOURI INCORPORATED — C — Fair

Major Rating Factors: Fair profitability (3.5 on a scale of 0 to 10) with operating losses during the first nine months of 2018. Fair overall results on stability tests (3.8) including negative cash flow from operations for 2017. Good overall capitalization (6.8) based on good risk adjusted capital (severe loss scenario). Nevertheless, capital levels have fluctuated during prior years.

Other Rating Factors: Good liquidity (6.9). Low quality investment portfolio (1.4).

Principal Business: Reinsurance (100%).

Principal Investments: Common & preferred stock (91%), nonCMO investment grade bonds (7%), and CMOs and structured securities (2%).

Investments in Affiliates: 91%

Group Affiliation: Reinsurance Group of America Inc

Licensed in: MO

Commenced Business: December 1998

Address: 16600 Swingley Ridge Road, Chesterfield, MO 63017-1706

Phone: (636) 736-7000 **Domicile State:** MO **NAIC Code:** 89004

Data Date	Rating	RACR #1	RACR #2	Total Assets ($mil)	Capital ($mil)	Net Premium ($mil)	Net Income ($mil)
9-18	C	1.10	0.98	1,952.2	1,743.7	25.3	-1.4
9-17	C	0.97	0.86	1,726.9	1,491.2	34.7	-174.2
2017	C	0.98	0.87	1,765.8	1,557.5	16.3	-183.1
2016	C	1.09	0.97	1,687.0	1,651.3	-17.1	272.0
2015	C	1.01	0.94	1,761.0	1,598.3	65.2	51.0
2014	C+	1.02	0.95	1,773.1	1,625.3	5.7	126.3
2013	C+	1.04	0.94	1,746.6	1,633.4	30.9	109.1

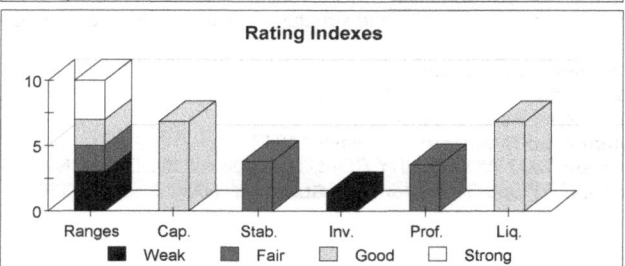

Rating Indexes

Ranges Cap. Stab. Inv. Prof. Liq.

■ Weak ▨ Fair ▤ Good □ Strong

RELIANCE STANDARD LIFE INSURANCE COMPANY — C+ — Fair

Major Rating Factors: Fair quality investment portfolio (3.5 on a scale of 0 to 10) with large holdings of BBB rated bonds in addition to junk bond exposure equal to 84% of capital. Exposure to mortgages is significant, but the mortgage default rate has been low. Fair overall results on stability tests (4.5) including excessive premium growth. Good liquidity (6.5).

Other Rating Factors: Strong capitalization (7.0) based on excellent risk adjusted capital (severe loss scenario). Excellent profitability (8.3).

Principal Business: Individual annuities (45%), group health insurance (31%), group life insurance (17%), group retirement contracts (3%), and reinsurance (3%).

Principal Investments: CMOs and structured securities (31%), nonCMO investment grade bonds (29%), mortgages in good standing (23%), noninv. grade bonds (9%), and misc. investments (6%).

Investments in Affiliates: 2%

Group Affiliation: Tokio Marine Holdings Inc

Licensed in: All states, the District of Columbia and Puerto Rico

Commenced Business: April 1907

Address: 1100 East Woodfield Road, Schaumburg, IL 60173

Phone: (215) 787-4000 **Domicile State:** IL **NAIC Code:** 68381

Data Date	Rating	RACR #1	RACR #2	Total Assets ($mil)	Capital ($mil)	Net Premium ($mil)	Net Income ($mil)
9-18	C+	1.86	1.03	13,947.8	1,257.6	2,224.5	207.4
9-17	B	1.84	0.99	11,909.1	1,089.1	1,678.6	118.0
2017	B	1.87	1.06	12,172.5	1,152.0	2,202.8	118.3
2016	B	1.91	1.06	10,889.4	1,066.1	1,801.1	166.0
2015	B	1.64	0.89	9,580.8	923.9	1,536.0	124.5
2014	B	1.70	0.92	7,583.8	713.3	1,787.2	166.9
2013	B	1.78	1.06	5,980.4	598.4	1,642.5	134.6

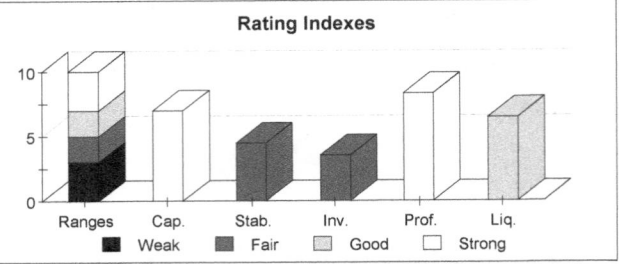

Rating Indexes — Ranges, Cap., Stab., Inv., Prof., Liq. — Weak, Fair, Good, Strong

RELIASTAR LIFE INSURANCE COMPANY — B- — Good

Major Rating Factors: Good quality investment portfolio (6.0 on a scale of 0 to 10) despite large holdings of BBB rated bonds in addition to moderate junk bond exposure. Exposure to mortgages is significant, but the mortgage default rate has been low. Good overall results on stability tests (5.0) despite negative cash flow from operations for 2017. Strengths include good financial support from affiliation with Voya Financial Inc, good operational trends and excellent risk diversification. Fair liquidity (4.5).

Other Rating Factors: Weak profitability (2.8). Strong capitalization (7.3) based on excellent risk adjusted capital (severe loss scenario).

Principal Business: Group health insurance (39%), individual life insurance (34%), group life insurance (15%), individual annuities (8%), and other lines (5%).

Principal Investments: NonCMO investment grade bonds (60%), mortgages in good standing (13%), CMOs and structured securities (11%), noninv. grade bonds (4%), and misc. investments (9%).

Investments in Affiliates: 4%

Group Affiliation: Voya Financial Inc

Licensed in: All states, the District of Columbia and Puerto Rico

Commenced Business: September 1885

Address: 20 WASHINGTON AVENUE SOUTH, MINNEAPOLIS, MN 55401

Phone: (770) 980-5100 **Domicile State:** MN **NAIC Code:** 67105

Data Date	Rating	RACR #1	RACR #2	Total Assets ($mil)	Capital ($mil)	Net Premium ($mil)	Net Income ($mil)
9-18	B-	2.01	1.19	20,768.8	1,599.4	1,809.3	79.0
9-17	C+	1.96	1.18	20,125.4	1,547.1	533.6	182.3
2017	C+	1.98	1.18	19,910.1	1,483.1	633.1	234.3
2016	C+	2.09	1.26	19,828.5	1,662.0	777.1	-506.6
2015	C+	2.03	1.23	19,805.1	1,609.2	740.9	74.2
2014	C+	2.40	1.42	21,468.7	1,944.7	-149.0	103.9
2013	C	2.29	1.38	21,621.2	1,942.5	840.3	215.9

Voya Financial Inc
Composite Group Rating: B

Largest Group Members	Assets ($mil)	Rating
VOYA RETIREMENT INS ANNUITY CO	104543	B+
RELIASTAR LIFE INS CO	19910	C+
SECURITY LIFE OF DENVER INS CO	14548	C+
RELIASTAR LIFE INS CO OF NEW YORK	3017	B
MIDWESTERN UNITED LIFE INS CO	232	B

RELIASTAR LIFE INSURANCE COMPANY OF NEW YORK — B — Good

Major Rating Factors: Good quality investment portfolio (6.5 on a scale of 0 to 10) despite mixed results such as: minimal exposure to mortgages and large holdings of BBB rated bonds but small junk bond holdings. Good liquidity (5.8) with sufficient resources to handle a spike in claims as well as a significant increase in policy surrenders. Good overall results on stability tests (5.8) good operational trends and excellent risk diversification.

Other Rating Factors: Fair profitability (3.5). Strong capitalization (8.0) based on excellent risk adjusted capital (severe loss scenario).

Principal Business: Individual life insurance (74%), group health insurance (19%), group life insurance (5%), individual annuities (2%), and individual health insurance (1%).

Principal Investments: NonCMO investment grade bonds (67%), mortgages in good standing (9%), CMOs and structured securities (9%), policy loans (5%), and misc. investments (6%).

Investments in Affiliates: None

Group Affiliation: Voya Financial Inc

Licensed in: All states except PR

Commenced Business: September 1917

Address: 1000 WOODBURY ROAD STE 208, WOODBURY, NY 11797

Phone: (770) 980-5100 **Domicile State:** NY **NAIC Code:** 61360

Data Date	Rating	RACR #1	RACR #2	Total Assets ($mil)	Capital ($mil)	Net Premium ($mil)	Net Income ($mil)
9-18	B	3.11	1.68	2,927.2	276.6	101.0	14.7
9-17	B	3.51	1.89	2,999.8	314.9	107.9	5.4
2017	B	3.08	1.67	3,016.7	272.7	146.1	-32.1
2016	B	3.55	1.91	2,978.0	313.3	152.0	5.6
2015	B	3.52	1.89	3,053.7	314.9	146.6	16.6
2014	B	3.33	1.79	3,201.6	298.8	139.9	-40.7
2013	B-	3.86	2.04	3,208.8	329.5	139.2	20.5

Adverse Trends in Operations

Decrease in premium volume from 2016 to 2017 (4%)
Decrease in capital during 2017 (13%)
Decrease in asset base during 2016 (2%)
Decrease in asset base during 2015 (5%)
Decrease in capital during 2014 (9%)

RESERVE NATIONAL INSURANCE COMPANY — B- — Good

Major Rating Factors: Good current capitalization (5.3 on a scale of 0 to 10) based on mixed results -- excessive policy leverage mitigated by excellent risk adjusted capital (severe loss scenario) reflecting improvement over results in 2017. Fair liquidity (4.9) as cash from operations and sale of marketable assets may not be adequate to cover a spike in claims. Fair overall results on stability tests (4.9) including negative cash flow from operations for 2017.

Other Rating Factors: Weak profitability (1.5) with operating losses during the first nine months of 2018. High quality investment portfolio (7.5).

Principal Business: Individual health insurance (83%), individual life insurance (9%), reinsurance (3%), group health insurance (3%), and group life insurance (2%).

Principal Investments: NonCMO investment grade bonds (86%), CMOs and structured securities (7%), and noninv. grade bonds (2%).

Investments in Affiliates: None

Group Affiliation: Kemper Corporation

Licensed in: All states except NY, PR

Commenced Business: September 1956

Address: 601 EAST BRITTON ROAD, OKLAHOMA CITY, OK 73114

Phone: (405) 848-7931 **Domicile State:** OK **NAIC Code:** 68462

Data Date	Rating	RACR #1	RACR #2	Total Assets ($mil)	Capital ($mil)	Net Premium ($mil)	Net Income ($mil)
9-18	B-	1.52	1.15	136.2	37.6	121.3	-1.6
9-17	B-	1.41	1.06	118.6	31.6	112.6	-6.6
2017	B-	1.03	0.79	121.5	24.8	152.5	-9.3
2016	B+	1.77	1.34	126.9	40.2	143.6	-2.0
2015	A	2.18	1.66	122.8	45.1	132.7	-0.5
2014	A	2.44	1.88	118.2	51.0	131.8	1.7
2013	A	2.27	1.76	111.2	52.4	143.6	4.9

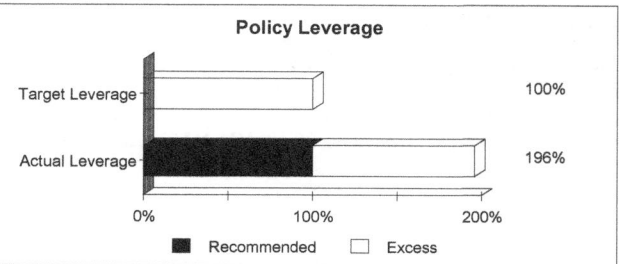

Policy Leverage

RGA REINSURANCE COMPANY — B- — Good

Major Rating Factors: Good overall capitalization (6.4 on a scale of 0 to 10) based on good risk adjusted capital (severe loss scenario). However, capital levels have fluctuated somewhat during past years. Good quality investment portfolio (5.2) despite large holdings of BBB rated bonds in addition to junk bond exposure equal to 75% of capital. Exposure to mortgages is significant, but the mortgage default rate has been low. Fair liquidity (4.9).

Other Rating Factors: Fair overall results on stability tests (4.5) including excessive premium growth. Excellent profitability (7.7).

Principal Business: Reinsurance (100%).

Principal Investments: NonCMO investment grade bonds (48%), mortgages in good standing (18%), CMOs and structured securities (15%), policy loans (6%), and misc. investments (12%).

Investments in Affiliates: 3%

Group Affiliation: Reinsurance Group of America Inc

Licensed in: All states, the District of Columbia and Puerto Rico

Commenced Business: October 1982

Address: 16600 Swingley Ridge Road, Chesterfield, MO 63017-1706

Phone: (636) 736-7000 **Domicile State:** MO **NAIC Code:** 93572

Data Date	Rating	RACR #1	RACR #2	Total Assets ($mil)	Capital ($mil)	Net Premium ($mil)	Net Income ($mil)
9-18	B-	1.75	0.92	37,286.1	1,771.9	6,718.9	289.5
9-17	B-	1.50	0.83	29,084.7	1,535.8	4,297.7	53.1
2017	B-	1.63	0.87	33,356.1	1,584.0	4,286.4	138.4
2016	B-	1.61	0.87	25,432.8	1,521.6	2,636.1	148.6
2015	B-	1.42	0.81	24,593.0	1,503.4	3,364.2	-23.6
2014	B	1.69	0.88	24,178.4	1,528.3	3,494.2	17.1
2013	B	1.70	0.90	23,259.8	1,550.1	2,305.6	115.8

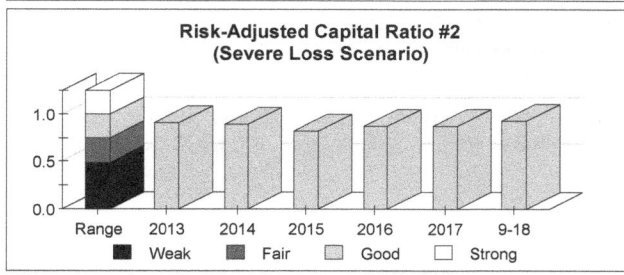

Risk-Adjusted Capital Ratio #2 (Severe Loss Scenario)

RIVERMONT LIFE INSURANCE COMPANY I — C — Fair

Major Rating Factors: Fair overall results on stability tests (3.7 on a scale of 0 to 10). Weak profitability (1.6) with operating losses during the first nine months of 2018. Strong overall capitalization (8.6) based on excellent risk adjusted capital (severe loss scenario). Nevertheless, capital levels have fluctuated during prior years.

Other Rating Factors: High quality investment portfolio (7.3). Excellent liquidity (7.0).

Principal Business: Reinsurance (100%).

Principal Investments: NonCMO investment grade bonds (78%) and CMOs and structured securities (19%).

Investments in Affiliates: None

Group Affiliation: Genworth Financial

Licensed in: SC

Commenced Business: October 2006

Address: 151 MEETING STREET SUITE 301, CHARLESTON, SC 29401

Phone: (843) 577-1026 **Domicile State:** SC **NAIC Code:** 13219

Data Date	Rating	RACR #1	RACR #2	Total Assets ($mil)	Capital ($mil)	Net Premium ($mil)	Net Income ($mil)
9-18	C	3.60	2.04	610.3	127.3	15.7	-0.5
9-17	C	3.76	2.15	588.1	128.2	16.9	-1.0
2017	C	3.46	1.97	594.3	122.6	22.3	-8.0
2016	C	3.72	2.14	569.4	128.7	24.1	-12.2
2015	C	3.90	2.22	544.0	129.8	28.5	-12.4
2014	C	4.93	2.75	533.2	145.0	26.9	-13.1
2013	C	4.64	2.54	502.6	153.8	29.1	-12.5

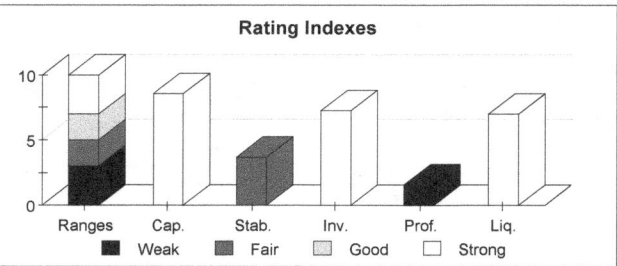

Rating Indexes

RIVERSOURCE LIFE INSURANCE COMPANY

C+   **Fair**

Major Rating Factors: Fair overall results on stability tests (4.7 on a scale of 0 to 10). Good quality investment portfolio (5.9) despite mixed results such as: large holdings of BBB rated bonds but junk bond exposure equal to 50% of capital. Good profitability (5.0) although investment income, in comparison to reserve requirements, is below regulatory standards.

Other Rating Factors: Strong capitalization (7.0) based on excellent risk adjusted capital (severe loss scenario). Excellent liquidity (7.8).

Principal Business: Individual annuities (73%), individual life insurance (20%), individual health insurance (6%), and group retirement contracts (1%).

Principal Investments: NonCMO investment grade bonds (42%), CMOs and structured securities (25%), mortgages in good standing (9%), noninv. grade bonds (5%), and misc. investments (6%).

Investments in Affiliates: 3%

Group Affiliation: Ameriprise Financial Inc

Licensed in: All states except NY, PR

Commenced Business: October 1957

Address: 227 AMERIPRISE FINANCIAL CNTR, MINNEAPOLIS, MN 55474

Phone: (612) 671-3131   **Domicile State:** MN   **NAIC Code:** 65005

Data Date	Rating	RACR #1	RACR #2	Total Assets ($mil)	Capital ($mil)	Net Premium ($mil)	Net Income ($mil)
9-18	C+	1.63	1.00	106,410	2,838.6	4,004.5	1,200.2
9-17	C	1.49	0.92	104,669	2,657.8	3,721.8	365.8
2017	C	1.40	0.86	107,010	2,390.0	5,082.8	222.0
2016	C	1.65	1.02	100,921	2,971.2	5,630.8	322.0
2015	C	2.05	1.27	100,564	3,650.1	6,222.2	632.7
2014	C	2.00	1.22	104,763	3,332.3	5,872.3	1,153.9
2013	C-	1.59	0.95	104,356	2,685.9	6,187.8	1,336.8

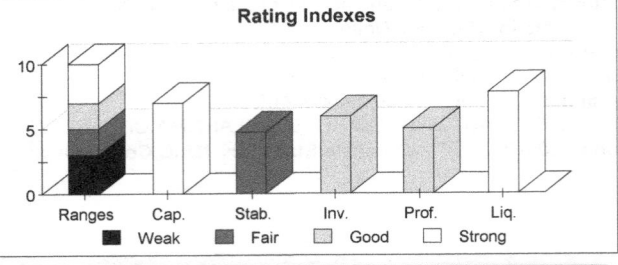

Rating Indexes

RIVERSOURCE LIFE INSURANCE COMPANY OF NEW YORK

C   **Fair**

Major Rating Factors: Fair overall results on stability tests (4.3 on a scale of 0 to 10). Good quality investment portfolio (6.0) despite mixed results such as: large holdings of BBB rated bonds but moderate junk bond exposure. Weak profitability (2.9) with investment income below regulatory standards in relation to interest assumptions of reserves.

Other Rating Factors: Strong capitalization (7.5) based on excellent risk adjusted capital (severe loss scenario). Excellent liquidity (7.6).

Principal Business: Individual annuities (75%), individual life insurance (18%), individual health insurance (4%), and group retirement contracts (3%).

Principal Investments: NonCMO investment grade bonds (54%), CMOs and structured securities (27%), mortgages in good standing (7%), noninv. grade bonds (3%), and policy loans (2%).

Investments in Affiliates: None

Group Affiliation: Ameriprise Financial Inc

Licensed in: NY

Commenced Business: October 1972

Address: 20 MADISON AVENUE EXTENSION, ALBANY, NY 12203-5326

Phone: (518) 869-8613   **Domicile State:** NY   **NAIC Code:** 80594

Data Date	Rating	RACR #1	RACR #2	Total Assets ($mil)	Capital ($mil)	Net Premium ($mil)	Net Income ($mil)
9-18	C	2.60	1.31	6,891.0	245.0	278.2	3.1
9-17	C	3.20	1.61	6,767.0	305.3	264.3	11.1
2017	C	2.82	1.42	6,911.3	269.1	372.1	1.7
2016	C	3.40	1.70	6,554.7	322.1	357.2	30.7
2015	C	3.50	1.76	6,497.2	325.5	412.4	48.9
2014	C	3.21	1.61	6,607.2	297.6	414.6	42.6
2013	C	2.67	1.34	6,315.7	250.3	428.1	90.4

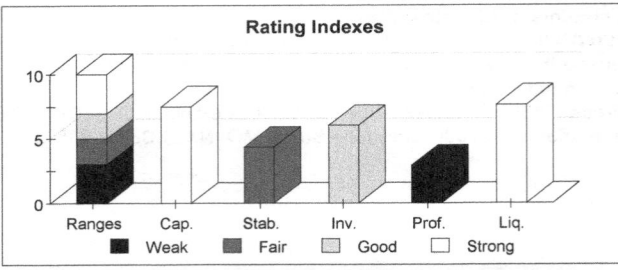

Rating Indexes

ROYAL STATE NATIONAL INSURANCE COMPANY LIMITED

C   **Fair**

Major Rating Factors: Fair profitability (4.0 on a scale of 0 to 10). Fair overall results on stability tests (4.2). Good quality investment portfolio (5.6) despite mixed results such as: no exposure to mortgages and large holdings of BBB rated bonds but no exposure to junk bonds.

Other Rating Factors: Strong capitalization (10.0) based on excellent risk adjusted capital (severe loss scenario). Excellent liquidity (7.1).

Principal Business: Group health insurance (54%), group life insurance (35%), individual life insurance (10%), and reinsurance (1%).

Principal Investments: NonCMO investment grade bonds (64%), common & preferred stock (17%), CMOs and structured securities (14%), cash (3%), and policy loans (1%).

Investments in Affiliates: None

Group Affiliation: Royal State Group

Licensed in: HI

Commenced Business: August 1961

Address: 819 SOUTH BERETANIA STREET, HONOLULU, HI 96813

Phone: (808) 539-1600   **Domicile State:** HI   **NAIC Code:** 68551

Data Date	Rating	RACR #1	RACR #2	Total Assets ($mil)	Capital ($mil)	Net Premium ($mil)	Net Income ($mil)
3-18	C	5.02	3.72	39.7	30.3	1.2	0.4
3-17	C	4.90	3.27	46.2	29.3	1.3	0.0
2017	C	5.14	3.70	46.8	29.8	5.1	0.2
2016	C	5.11	3.41	46.3	29.4	5.3	0.7
2015	C	4.91	3.29	45.3	28.6	7.0	-0.4
2014	B-	3.27	2.29	47.1	29.3	10.8	0.7
2013	B-	3.29	2.33	45.6	28.9	10.6	0.4

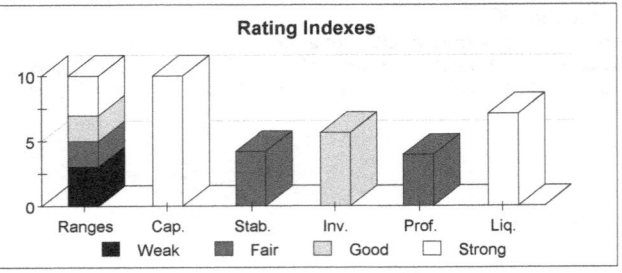

Rating Indexes

SAGICOR LIFE INSURANCE COMPANY   C-   Fair

Major Rating Factors: Fair quality investment portfolio (3.7 on a scale of 0 to 10). Fair liquidity (3.8) due, in part, to cash value policies that are subject to withdrawals with minimal or no penalty. Fair overall results on stability tests (3.1) including fair risk adjusted capital in prior years.

Other Rating Factors: Weak profitability (1.9) with operating losses during the first nine months of 2018. Good capitalization (5.1) based on good risk adjusted capital (moderate loss scenario).

Principal Business: Individual annuities (71%), individual life insurance (27%), and reinsurance (2%).

Principal Investments: NonCMO investment grade bonds (63%), CMOs and structured securities (23%), policy loans (3%), common & preferred stock (3%), and misc. investments (5%).

Investments in Affiliates: None
Group Affiliation: Sagicor Financial Corp
Licensed in: All states except AK, NY, PR
Commenced Business: April 1954
Address: 900 CONGRESS AVE SUITE 300, AUSTIN, TX 78701
Phone: (480) 425-5100 **Domicile State:** TX **NAIC Code:** 60445

Data Date	Rating	RACR #1	RACR #2	Total Assets ($mil)	Capital ($mil)	Net Premium ($mil)	Net Income ($mil)
9-18	C-	1.08	0.55	1,419.5	77.2	237.6	-5.9
9-17	C-	1.15	0.59	1,129.7	72.9	62.5	2.8
2017	C-	1.14	0.59	1,115.0	72.7	84.5	0.3
2016	C-	1.23	0.63	1,086.4	72.3	73.9	-27.7
2015	C-	1.49	0.75	1,193.8	82.1	80.8	6.3
2014	C-	1.33	0.69	1,214.9	74.2	74.2	0.2
2013	C-	1.43	0.74	1,176.2	75.8	87.4	1.1

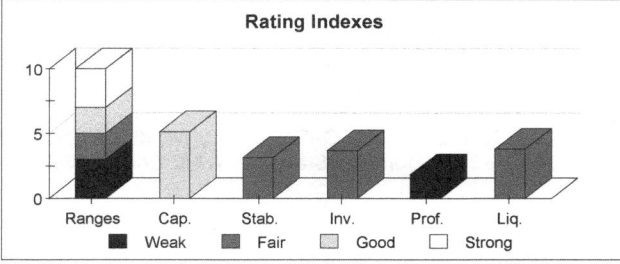

Rating Indexes

SAVINGS BANK LIFE INSURANCE COMPANY OF MASSACHUSE'   B+   Good

Major Rating Factors: Good quality investment portfolio (5.6 on a scale of 0 to 10) despite mixed results such as: large holdings of BBB rated bonds but junk bond exposure equal to 66% of capital. Good overall profitability (6.2). Excellent expense controls. Good liquidity (5.5) with sufficient resources to handle a spike in claims as well as a significant increase in policy surrenders.

Other Rating Factors: Good overall results on stability tests (6.4) despite negative cash flow from operations for 2017 good operational trends and excellent risk diversification. Strong capitalization (7.1) based on excellent risk adjusted capital (severe loss scenario).

Principal Business: Individual life insurance (99%) and individual annuities (1%).

Principal Investments: NonCMO investment grade bonds (71%), CMOs and structured securities (17%), noninv. grade bonds (4%), policy loans (3%), and common & preferred stock (2%).

Investments in Affiliates: 1%
Group Affiliation: Savings Bank Life Group
Licensed in: All states except NY, PR
Commenced Business: January 1992
Address: One Linscott Road, Woburn, MA 1801
Phone: (781) 938-3500 **Domicile State:** MA **NAIC Code:** 70435

Data Date	Rating	RACR #1	RACR #2	Total Assets ($mil)	Capital ($mil)	Net Premium ($mil)	Net Income ($mil)
9-18	B+	1.83	1.06	3,104.8	190.2	98.0	22.0
9-17	B+	1.57	0.98	3,015.1	202.3	106.3	20.9
2017	B+	1.96	1.14	3,032.4	202.5	140.5	46.8
2016	B+	1.84	1.15	3,016.4	225.6	158.6	26.6
2015	B+	1.70	1.11	2,919.1	224.0	215.7	11.7
2014	B+	1.77	1.21	2,795.6	256.8	198.7	12.9
2013	B+	2.90	1.60	2,534.4	213.6	169.1	17.9

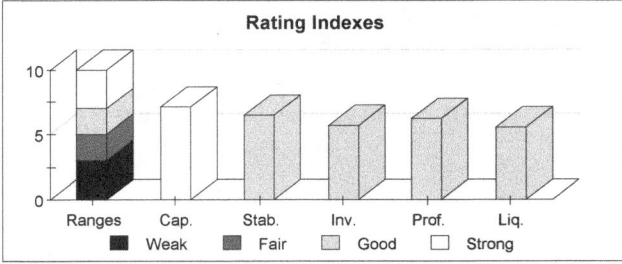

Rating Indexes

SBLI USA MUTUAL LIFE INSURANCE COMPANY INCORPORATE   B   Good

Major Rating Factors: Good current capitalization (6.8 on a scale of 0 to 10) based on good risk adjusted capital (severe loss scenario), although results have slipped from the excellent range over the last two years. Good quality investment portfolio (5.9) despite mixed results such as: minimal exposure to mortgages and large holdings of BBB rated bonds but minimal holdings in junk bonds. Good overall results on stability tests (5.1) despite excessive premium growth good operational trends and excellent risk diversification.

Other Rating Factors: Fair profitability (4.5) with investment income below regulatory standards in relation to interest assumptions of reserves. Fair liquidity (3.1).

Principal Business: Individual life insurance (52%), individual annuities (27%), group life insurance (16%), reinsurance (3%), and individual health insurance (2%).

Principal Investments: NonCMO investment grade bonds (73%), CMOs and structured securities (16%), policy loans (6%), common & preferred stock (1%), and cash (1%).

Investments in Affiliates: 1%
Group Affiliation: Reservoir Capital Group LLC
Licensed in: AK, AZ, AR, CO, DC, HI, IL, IA, MD, MI, MS, MO, MT, NH, NJ, NM, NY, NC, OH, OK, PA, SC, SD, TN, TX, UT, VT, WA, WV, PR
Commenced Business: January 2000
Address: 100 WEST 33RD STREET STE 1007, NEW YORK, NY 10001-2900
Phone: (212) 356-0300 **Domicile State:** NY **NAIC Code:** 60176

Data Date	Rating	RACR #1	RACR #2	Total Assets ($mil)	Capital ($mil)	Net Premium ($mil)	Net Income ($mil)
9-18	B	1.70	0.98	1,530.7	102.7	111.4	12.4
9-17	B	1.77	1.02	1,473.5	98.6	57.9	13.2
2017	B	1.70	0.98	1,474.0	95.4	81.2	16.8
2016	B	2.06	1.17	1,497.8	117.1	57.8	3.2
2015	B	2.06	1.15	1,518.8	121.5	59.4	15.7
2014	B-	1.69	0.94	1,530.9	102.2	62.3	-1.4
2013	B-	1.44	0.79	1,479.1	89.0	65.6	-2.2

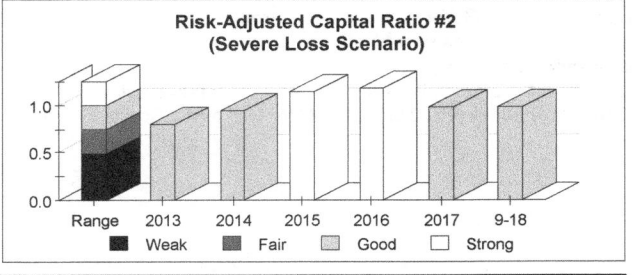

Risk-Adjusted Capital Ratio #2 (Severe Loss Scenario)

SCOR GLOBAL LIFE AMERICAS REINSURANCE COMPANY — B- — Good

Major Rating Factors: Good overall results on stability tests (5.0 on a scale of 0 to 10) despite fair financial strength of affiliated SCOR Reinsurance Group, excessive premium growth and fair risk adjusted capital in prior years. Other stability subfactors include good operational trends and excellent risk diversification. Good current capitalization (5.6) based on good risk adjusted capital (severe loss scenario) reflecting some improvement over results in 2013. Good liquidity (6.7).

Other Rating Factors: Fair profitability (3.0) with operating losses during the first nine months of 2018. High quality investment portfolio (7.1).

Principal Business: Reinsurance (100%).

Principal Investments: NonCMO investment grade bonds (64%), common & preferred stock (12%), CMOs and structured securities (12%), policy loans (2%), and cash (1%).

Investments in Affiliates: 12%

Group Affiliation: SCOR Reinsurance Group

Licensed in: All states except NY, PR

Commenced Business: April 1945

Address: 2711 CENTERVILLE ROAD STE 400, WILMINGTON, DE 19808

Phone: (704) 344-2700 **Domicile State:** DE **NAIC Code:** 64688

Data Date	Rating	RACR #1	RACR #2	Total Assets ($mil)	Capital ($mil)	Net Premium ($mil)	Net Income ($mil)
9-18	B-	1.12	0.82	1,057.7	231.1	139.1	-25.4
9-17	C+	1.01	0.74	1,063.0	188.4	95.7	3.4
2017	C+	1.14	0.84	1,112.0	208.0	130.5	8.9
2016	C	1.10	0.80	1,327.6	204.1	114.0	7.6
2015	C-	1.19	0.83	1,262.0	192.1	112.8	0.7
2014	C-	1.21	0.74	1,480.0	151.7	110.0	15.1
2013	C-	1.11	0.71	1,355.3	151.8	98.1	-40.6

SCOR Reinsurance Group
Composite Group Rating: C

Largest Group Members	Assets ($mil)	Rating
SCOR REINS CO	3542	C
SCOR GLOBAL LIFE AMERICAS REIN CO	1112	B-
SCOR GLOBAL LIFE USA RE CO	817	B-
GENERAL SECURITY NATIONAL INS CO	416	C-
SCOR GLOBAL LIFE REINS CO OF DE	375	C

SCOR GLOBAL LIFE REINSURANCE COMPANY OF DELAWARE — C — Fair

Major Rating Factors: Fair overall results on stability tests (4.3 on a scale of 0 to 10) including fair financial strength of affiliated SCOR Reinsurance Group and excessive premium growth. Good liquidity (6.5) with sufficient resources to handle a spike in claims as well as a significant increase in policy surrenders. Weak profitability (2.9) with investment income below regulatory standards in relation to interest assumptions of reserves.

Other Rating Factors: Strong capitalization (9.3) based on excellent risk adjusted capital (severe loss scenario). High quality investment portfolio (8.5).

Principal Business: Reinsurance (100%).

Principal Investments: NonCMO investment grade bonds (56%), CMOs and structured securities (33%), and policy loans (5%).

Investments in Affiliates: None

Group Affiliation: SCOR Reinsurance Group

Licensed in: All states except AL, PR

Commenced Business: May 1977

Address: 2711 CENTERVILLE ROAD STE 400, WILMINGTON, DE 19808

Phone: (704) 344-2700 **Domicile State:** DE **NAIC Code:** 87017

Data Date	Rating	RACR #1	RACR #2	Total Assets ($mil)	Capital ($mil)	Net Premium ($mil)	Net Income ($mil)
9-18	C	4.22	2.55	452.8	121.9	67.7	31.4
9-17	C	2.74	1.67	424.0	82.9	43.5	-15.9
2017	C	3.42	2.07	375.4	97.4	75.9	-1.5
2016	C	3.38	2.06	470.5	101.0	79.4	29.4
2015	C	2.71	1.68	368.3	78.1	65.7	16.2
2014	C	1.52	0.93	456.5	46.5	51.3	-4.5
2013	C-	1.70	1.04	470.0	51.3	37.9	-3.7

SCOR Reinsurance Group
Composite Group Rating: C

Largest Group Members	Assets ($mil)	Rating
SCOR REINS CO	3542	C
SCOR GLOBAL LIFE AMERICAS REIN CO	1112	B-
SCOR GLOBAL LIFE USA RE CO	817	B-
GENERAL SECURITY NATIONAL INS CO	416	C-
SCOR GLOBAL LIFE REINS CO OF DE	375	C

SCOR GLOBAL LIFE USA RE CO — B- — Good

Major Rating Factors: Good overall results on stability tests (5.0 on a scale of 0 to 10) despite fair financial strength of affiliated SCOR Reinsurance Group and excessive premium growth. Other stability subfactors include good operational trends and excellent risk diversification. Fair profitability (3.4). Excellent expense controls. Strong capitalization (8.8) based on excellent risk adjusted capital (severe loss scenario).

Other Rating Factors: High quality investment portfolio (7.4). Excellent liquidity (7.0).

Principal Business: Reinsurance (100%).

Principal Investments: NonCMO investment grade bonds (60%) and CMOs and structured securities (19%).

Investments in Affiliates: 14%

Group Affiliation: SCOR Reinsurance Group

Licensed in: All states except PR

Commenced Business: October 1982

Address: 2711 Centerville Road Ste 400, Wilmington, DE 19808

Phone: (913) 901-4600 **Domicile State:** DE **NAIC Code:** 97071

Data Date	Rating	RACR #1	RACR #2	Total Assets ($mil)	Capital ($mil)	Net Premium ($mil)	Net Income ($mil)
9-18	B-	3.72	2.21	836.9	251.1	187.8	0.2
9-17	B-	4.38	2.67	872.6	291.1	112.6	-5.3
2017	B-	4.13	2.46	817.3	277.1	133.8	-15.8
2016	C+	5.15	3.16	767.8	333.0	167.3	3.5
2015	C	6.10	3.84	736.8	360.3	160.8	18.4
2014	C	5.37	3.48	812.3	377.6	184.3	22.3
2013	C	8.20	5.04	949.3	422.6	908.2	61.6

SCOR Reinsurance Group
Composite Group Rating: C

Largest Group Members	Assets ($mil)	Rating
SCOR REINS CO	3542	C
SCOR GLOBAL LIFE AMERICAS REIN CO	1112	B-
SCOR GLOBAL LIFE USA RE CO	817	B-
GENERAL SECURITY NATIONAL INS CO	416	C-
SCOR GLOBAL LIFE REINS CO OF DE	375	C

SCOTTISH RE US INCORPORATED   E+   Very Weak

Major Rating Factors: Poor current capitalization (2.8 on a scale of 0 to 10) based on weak risk adjusted capital (moderate loss scenario), although results have slipped from the fair range during the last year. Low quality investment portfolio (0.8) containing large holdings of BBB rated bonds in addition to significant exposure to junk bonds. Weak profitability (2.9) with operating losses during the first nine months of 2018.

Other Rating Factors: Weak overall results on stability tests (0.4) including weak risk adjusted capital in prior years, negative cash flow from operations for 2017. Fair liquidity (3.2).

Principal Business: Reinsurance (100%).

Principal Investments: CMOs and structured securities (50%), nonCMO investment grade bonds (40%), noninv. grade bonds (3%), and cash (1%).

Investments in Affiliates: None

Group Affiliation: SRGL Acquisition LDC

Licensed in: All states except AK, PR

Commenced Business: September 1977

Address: 160 GREENTREE DRIVE SUITE 101, DOVER, DE 19904-7620

Phone: (704) 542-9192 **Domicile State:** DE **NAIC Code:** 87572

Data Date	Rating	RACR #1	RACR #2	Total Assets ($mil)	Capital ($mil)	Net Premium ($mil)	Net Income ($mil)
9-18	E+	0.73	0.37	1,556.8	37.6	102.1	-7.4
9-17	D+	0.83	0.43	1,673.5	53.1	88.0	3.0
2017	D+	0.82	0.41	1,654.5	50.1	108.7	45.2
2016	D+	0.91	0.48	1,501.8	56.7	118.3	13.1
2015	D+	1.08	0.57	1,570.3	80.9	13.8	-83.8
2014	C-	1.80	0.98	1,735.1	169.9	259.0	-1.3
2013	C-	1.73	0.95	1,808.2	171.7	251.2	-24.2

Junk Bonds as a % of Capital

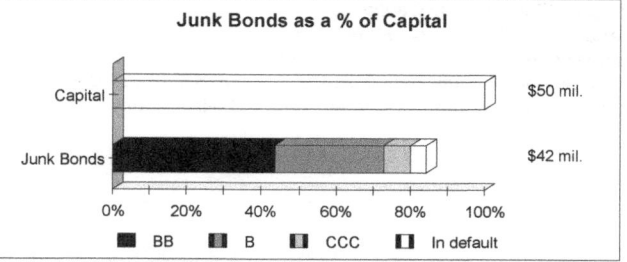

SECU LIFE INS CO   B   Good

Major Rating Factors: Good overall results on stability tests (5.7 on a scale of 0 to 10) despite excessive premium growth. Other stability subfactors include good operational trends and good risk diversification. Strong capitalization (10.0) based on excellent risk adjusted capital (severe loss scenario). Capital levels have been relatively consistent over the last five years. High quality investment portfolio (8.5).

Other Rating Factors: Excellent profitability (8.4) despite modest operating losses during 2013. Excellent liquidity (9.0).

Principal Business: Individual annuities (37%), individual life insurance (36%), and group life insurance (27%).

Principal Investments: NonCMO investment grade bonds (39%), mortgages in good standing (38%), and cash (23%).

Investments in Affiliates: None

Group Affiliation: State Employees Credit Union

Licensed in: NC

Commenced Business: January 2013

Address: 119 N Salisbury St Floor 10, Raleigh, NC 27603

Phone: (919) 839-5084 **Domicile State:** NC **NAIC Code:** 14924

Data Date	Rating	RACR #1	RACR #2	Total Assets ($mil)	Capital ($mil)	Net Premium ($mil)	Net Income ($mil)
9-18	B	4.72	4.25	49.2	28.4	7.3	0.9
9-17	C+	5.04	4.54	42.1	27.1	5.8	0.9
2017	B-	4.56	4.10	43.3	27.4	7.7	1.0
2016	C+	4.87	4.38	37.4	26.2	7.1	0.6
2015	C	5.37	4.83	31.6	25.5	6.3	0.9
2014	D+	5.89	5.30	26.3	24.6	2.1	0.3
2013	D	6.09	5.48	24.6	24.4	0.6	-0.7

Rating Indexes

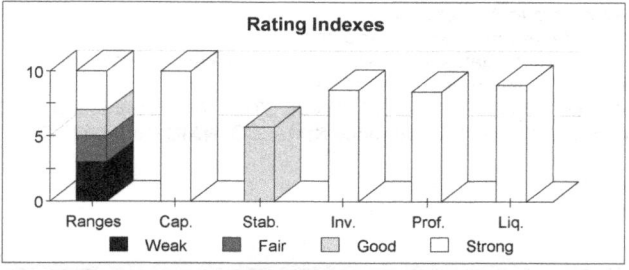

SECURIAN LIFE INSURANCE COMPANY   B   Good

Major Rating Factors: Good liquidity (6.8 on a scale of 0 to 10) with sufficient resources to handle a spike in claims as well as a significant increase in policy surrenders. Good overall results on stability tests (6.1) despite excessive premium growth. Strengths include good financial support from affiliation with Securian Financial Group, excellent operational trends and excellent risk diversification. Fair profitability (4.1).

Other Rating Factors: Strong capitalization (10.0) based on excellent risk adjusted capital (severe loss scenario). High quality investment portfolio (7.4).

Principal Business: Group life insurance (87%), group health insurance (6%), individual life insurance (3%), group retirement contracts (2%), and other lines (3%).

Principal Investments: NonCMO investment grade bonds (68%), CMOs and structured securities (19%), mortgages in good standing (6%), noninv. grade bonds (2%), and misc. investments (2%).

Investments in Affiliates: None

Group Affiliation: Securian Financial Group

Licensed in: All states, the District of Columbia and Puerto Rico

Commenced Business: December 1981

Address: 400 ROBERT STREET NORTH, ST. PAUL, MN 55101-2098

Phone: (651) 665-3500 **Domicile State:** MN **NAIC Code:** 93742

Data Date	Rating	RACR #1	RACR #2	Total Assets ($mil)	Capital ($mil)	Net Premium ($mil)	Net Income ($mil)
9-18	B	5.14	3.34	994.0	306.6	328.5	1.5
9-17	B	5.50	3.63	735.1	258.6	182.9	-5.7
2017	B	5.67	3.77	775.7	305.3	238.9	0.9
2016	A-	5.81	3.85	577.1	260.3	175.7	0.4
2015	A-	5.93	3.95	438.6	205.4	199.1	2.0
2014	A-	6.13	4.30	325.4	202.1	111.3	6.5
2013	B	6.47	4.56	207.8	131.5	83.2	-3.0

Securian Financial Group Composite Group Rating: B+ Largest Group Members	Assets ($mil)	Rating
MINNESOTA LIFE INS CO	46434	B+
SECURIAN LIFE INS CO	776	B
SECURIAN CASUALTY CO	328	B
AMERICAN MODERN LIFE INS CO	40	B
SOUTHERN PIONEER LIFE INS CO	16	A

SECURITY BENEFIT LIFE INSURANCE COMPANY — B — Good

Major Rating Factors: Good overall profitability (6.6 on a scale of 0 to 10). Fair quality investment portfolio (3.9) with large holdings of BBB rated bonds in addition to moderate junk bond exposure. Fair overall results on stability tests (4.9).

Other Rating Factors: Strong capitalization (7.3) based on excellent risk adjusted capital (severe loss scenario). Excellent liquidity (7.6).

Principal Business: Individual annuities (95%), group retirement contracts (4%), and individual life insurance (1%).

Principal Investments: CMOs and structured securities (55%), nonCMO investment grade bonds (9%), mortgages in good standing (5%), noninv. grade bonds (3%), and policy loans (2%).

Investments in Affiliates: 27%

Group Affiliation: NZC Captial LLC

Licensed in: All states except NY, PR

Commenced Business: February 1892

Address: One Security Benefit Place, Topeka, KS 66636-0001

Phone: (785) 431-3000 **Domicile State:** KS **NAIC Code:** 68675

Data Date	Rating	RACR #1	RACR #2	Total Assets ($mil)	Capital ($mil)	Net Premium ($mil)	Net Income ($mil)
9-18	B	2.60	1.19	33,665.2	2,051.6	1,491.6	235.9
9-17	B	2.11	0.96	32,367.7	1,904.0	2,280.0	160.2
2017	B	2.49	1.11	33,099.5	1,900.6	2,951.4	181.0
2016	B	2.18	1.00	29,812.9	1,561.7	3,665.5	-81.0
2015	B	1.93	0.90	27,787.4	1,286.4	2,270.7	75.4
2014	B	2.42	1.14	24,987.4	1,301.5	5,061.3	122.1
2013	B	2.31	1.12	20,702.3	1,044.8	6,191.9	163.6

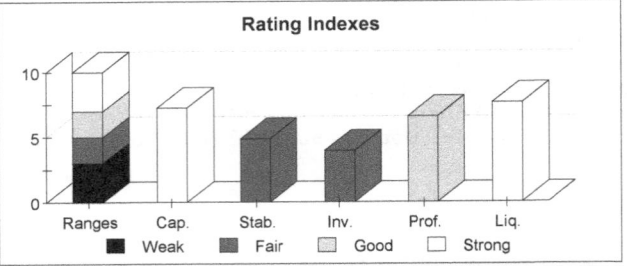

Rating Indexes

SECURITY LIFE OF DENVER INSURANCE COMPANY — B- — Good

Major Rating Factors: Good capitalization (5.6 on a scale of 0 to 10) based on good risk adjusted capital (moderate loss scenario). Good quality investment portfolio (5.6) despite large holdings of BBB rated bonds in addition to moderate junk bond exposure. Exposure to mortgages is significant, but the mortgage default rate has been low. Good overall profitability (5.4) despite operating losses during the first nine months of 2018.

Other Rating Factors: Good overall results on stability tests (5.0) good operational trends and excellent risk diversification. Fair liquidity (4.3).

Principal Business: Reinsurance (70%) and individual life insurance (30%).

Principal Investments: NonCMO investment grade bonds (58%), mortgages in good standing (10%), CMOs and structured securities (10%), policy loans (9%), and misc. investments (7%).

Investments in Affiliates: 3%

Group Affiliation: Voya Financial Inc

Licensed in: All states, the District of Columbia and Puerto Rico

Commenced Business: May 1950

Address: 8055 EAST TUFTS AVENUE STE 710, DENVER, CO 80237

Phone: (770) 980-5100 **Domicile State:** CO **NAIC Code:** 68713

Data Date	Rating	RACR #1	RACR #2	Total Assets ($mil)	Capital ($mil)	Net Premium ($mil)	Net Income ($mil)
9-18	B-	1.42	0.81	14,698.8	860.7	570.6	-28.8
9-17	C+	1.70	0.99	14,202.1	979.0	519.1	77.6
2017	C+	1.60	0.92	14,548.2	950.5	693.4	58.2
2016	C+	1.59	0.93	13,294.8	897.1	534.8	93.2
2015	C+	1.48	0.86	13,249.1	858.3	13.6	-244.5
2014	C+	1.91	1.11	14,228.3	1,128.8	-61.3	141.6
2013	C+	1.80	1.04	15,066.6	1,034.0	910.8	-0.1

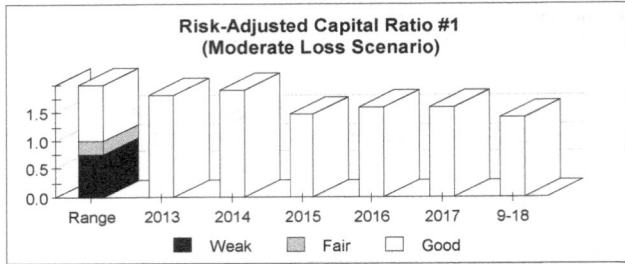

Risk-Adjusted Capital Ratio #1
(Moderate Loss Scenario)

SECURITY MUTUAL LIFE INSURANCE CO OF NEW YORK — C — Fair

Major Rating Factors: Good capitalization (6.2 on a scale of 0 to 10) based on good risk adjusted capital (severe loss scenario). Capital levels have been relatively consistent over the last five years. Good quality investment portfolio (6.2) despite mixed results such as: minimal exposure to mortgages and large holdings of BBB rated bonds but minimal holdings in junk bonds. Good overall profitability (5.4) although investment income, in comparison to reserve requirements, is below regulatory standards.

Other Rating Factors: Weak liquidity (0.7). Weak overall results on stability tests (2.9).

Principal Business: Individual life insurance (90%), group health insurance (4%), individual annuities (3%), and group life insurance (3%).

Principal Investments: NonCMO investment grade bonds (71%), policy loans (15%), mortgages in good standing (8%), CMOs and structured securities (3%), and noninv. grade bonds (1%).

Investments in Affiliates: None

Group Affiliation: None

Licensed in: All states except PR

Commenced Business: January 1887

Address: 100 COURT STREET, BINGHAMTON, NY 13901-3479

Phone: (607) 723-3551 **Domicile State:** NY **NAIC Code:** 68772

Data Date	Rating	RACR #1	RACR #2	Total Assets ($mil)	Capital ($mil)	Net Premium ($mil)	Net Income ($mil)
9-18	C	1.66	0.90	2,766.8	164.5	150.2	7.6
9-17	B-	1.66	0.89	2,737.7	158.1	159.4	2.3
2017	C	1.62	0.88	2,751.9	155.9	204.7	4.4
2016	B-	1.70	0.91	2,722.4	162.7	187.6	7.6
2015	B	1.55	0.84	2,667.8	136.5	174.6	6.9
2014	B	1.57	0.85	2,672.0	138.6	165.7	6.7
2013	B	1.52	0.83	2,676.4	133.6	170.7	8.4

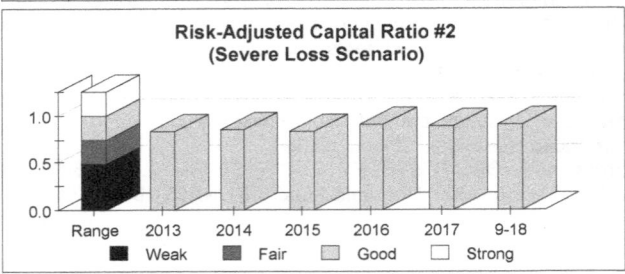

Risk-Adjusted Capital Ratio #2
(Severe Loss Scenario)

SECURITY NATIONAL LIFE INSURANCE COMPANY   D   Weak

Major Rating Factors: Weak overall results on stability tests (2.3 on a scale of 0 to 10) including weak risk adjusted capital in prior years. Fair quality investment portfolio (3.1) with large exposure to mortgages . Mortgage default rate has been low. Good capitalization for the current period (5.2) based on good risk adjusted capital (moderate loss scenario) reflecting some improvement over results in 2016.

Other Rating Factors: Good liquidity (5.9). Excellent profitability (7.3) despite modest operating losses during 2017.

Principal Business: Individual life insurance (86%), individual annuities (12%), and reinsurance (2%).

Principal Investments: Mortgages in good standing (36%), nonCMO investment grade bonds (30%), real estate (8%), common & preferred stock (4%), and misc. investments (7%).

Investments in Affiliates: 3%

Group Affiliation: Security National Life

Licensed in: AL, AK, AZ, AR, CA, CO, DC, DE, FL, GA, HI, ID, IL, IN, IA, KS, KY, LA, MD, MI, MN, MS, MO, MT, NE, NV, NM, ND, OK, OR, SC, SD, TN, TX, UT, VA, WI, WY

Commenced Business: July 1967

Address: 5300 SOUTH 360 WEST, SALT LAKE CITY, UT 84123

Phone: (801) 264-1060 **Domicile State:** UT **NAIC Code:** 69485

Data Date	Rating	RACR #1	RACR #2	Total Assets ($mil)	Capital ($mil)	Net Premium ($mil)	Net Income ($mil)
9-18	D	1.13	0.68	662.8	47.9	64.8	15.2
9-17	D-	0.50	0.33	580.3	34.2	61.4	-1.1
2017	D-	0.80	0.48	584.7	36.3	81.3	-3.0
2016	D-	0.53	0.35	567.1	36.8	74.5	2.6
2015	D-	0.85	0.51	544.1	32.8	67.0	3.5
2014	D-	0.62	0.38	507.8	34.4	61.5	5.1
2013	D	0.51	0.35	477.6	29.6	59.3	1.3

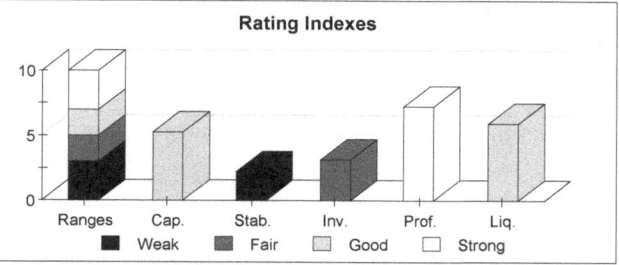

Rating Indexes

SENTINEL SECURITY LIFE INSURANCE COMPANY   C-   Fair

Major Rating Factors: Fair current capitalization (3.4 on a scale of 0 to 10) based on fair risk adjusted capital (moderate loss scenario), although results have slipped from the good range during the last year. Weak overall results on stability tests (2.9) including weak financial strength of affiliated Advantage Captial Partners LLC, excessive premium growth, weak risk adjusted capital in prior years and negative cash flow from operations for 2017. Low quality investment portfolio (1.7).

Other Rating Factors: Weak profitability (2.2) with investment income below regulatory standards in relation to interest assumptions of reserves. Excellent liquidity (7.6).

Principal Business: Individual annuities (78%), individual health insurance (18%), and individual life insurance (4%).

Principal Investments: CMOs and structured securities (45%), nonCMO investment grade bonds (24%), mortgages in good standing (8%), noninv. grade bonds (4%), and misc. investments (9%).

Investments in Affiliates: None

Group Affiliation: Advantage Captial Partners LLC

Licensed in: AZ, AR, CA, CO, DE, FL, GA, HI, ID, IL, IN, IA, KS, KY, LA, MD, MN, MS, MT, NE, NV, NM, NC, ND, OH, OK, OR, PA, RI, SD, TX, UT, WA, WY

Commenced Business: September 1948

Address: 1405 WEST 2200 SOUTH, SALT LAKE CITY, UT 84119

Phone: (801) 484-8514 **Domicile State:** UT **NAIC Code:** 68802

Data Date	Rating	RACR #1	RACR #2	Total Assets ($mil)	Capital ($mil)	Net Premium ($mil)	Net Income ($mil)
9-18	C-	0.81	0.37	1,103.6	41.7	37.5	2.4
9-17	C-	0.98	0.48	705.2	45.8	20.7	4.5
2017	C-	1.00	0.46	798.9	39.4	28.8	3.5
2016	C-	1.25	0.58	617.1	40.2	21.2	-2.5
2015	D	1.56	0.73	499.2	38.7	23.6	1.9
2014	D	1.10	0.50	479.5	25.7	31.6	-1.6
2013	D	1.13	0.54	403.7	15.2	17.1	-2.8

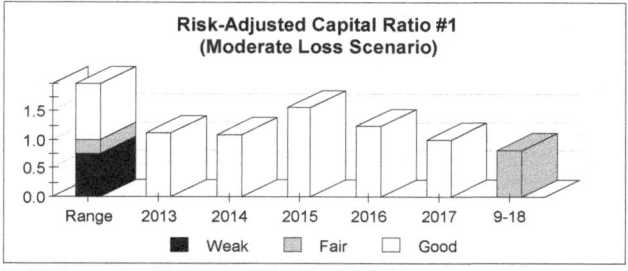

Risk-Adjusted Capital Ratio #1
(Moderate Loss Scenario)

SENTRY LIFE INSURANCE COMPANY *   A   Excellent

Major Rating Factors: Good overall profitability (6.4 on a scale of 0 to 10). Excellent overall results on stability tests (7.4). Strengths that enhance stability include excellent operational trends and excellent risk diversification. Strong capitalization (8.4) based on excellent risk adjusted capital (severe loss scenario). Furthermore, this high level of risk adjusted capital has been consistently maintained over the last five years.

Other Rating Factors: High quality investment portfolio (7.2). Excellent liquidity (8.2).

Principal Business: Group retirement contracts (94%), individual life insurance (4%), group health insurance (1%), individual annuities (1%), and group life insurance (1%).

Principal Investments: NonCMO investment grade bonds (90%), CMOs and structured securities (6%), and noninv. grade bonds (2%).

Investments in Affiliates: None

Group Affiliation: Sentry Ins Group

Licensed in: All states except NY, PR

Commenced Business: November 1958

Address: 1800 NORTH POINT DRIVE, STEVENS POINT, WI 54481

Phone: (715) 346-6000 **Domicile State:** WI **NAIC Code:** 68810

Data Date	Rating	RACR #1	RACR #2	Total Assets ($mil)	Capital ($mil)	Net Premium ($mil)	Net Income ($mil)
9-18	A	3.37	1.94	7,425.4	293.3	628.9	22.5
9-17	A	3.39	1.98	6,735.9	280.2	554.1	21.8
2017	A	3.24	1.89	6,958.1	272.9	751.9	28.0
2016	A	3.20	1.86	6,092.9	263.0	695.9	21.3
2015	A	3.50	2.07	5,560.2	268.8	660.9	13.6
2014	A	3.71	2.15	5,333.6	271.4	557.3	26.7
2013	A	3.77	2.16	4,909.7	272.5	502.1	26.2

Adverse Trends in Operations

Decrease in capital during 2016 (2%)
Increase in policy surrenders from 2013 to 2014 (33%)

SETTLERS LIFE INSURANCE COMPANY

B   **Good**

Major Rating Factors: Good overall results on stability tests (6.2 on a scale of 0 to 10). Stability strengths include excellent operational trends and good risk diversification. Good quality investment portfolio (6.1) despite mixed results such as: large holdings of BBB rated bonds but moderate junk bond exposure. Good overall profitability (5.7).

Other Rating Factors: Good liquidity (6.2). Strong capitalization (7.8) based on excellent risk adjusted capital (severe loss scenario).

Principal Business: Individual life insurance (91%) and group life insurance (9%).

Principal Investments: NonCMO investment grade bonds (82%), CMOs and structured securities (7%), noninv. grade bonds (4%), common & preferred stock (3%), and misc. investments (4%).

Investments in Affiliates: None

Group Affiliation: NGL Ins Group

Licensed in: All states except NY, PR

Commenced Business: September 1982

Address: 2 East Gilman Street, Madison, WI 53703-1494

Phone: (608) 257-5611 **Domicile State:** WI **NAIC Code:** 97241

Data Date	Rating	RACR #1	RACR #2	Total Assets ($mil)	Capital ($mil)	Net Premium ($mil)	Net Income ($mil)
9-18	B	2.80	1.53	423.1	46.2	40.5	2.7
9-17	B	2.71	1.47	413.7	43.9	40.2	1.0
2017	B	2.67	1.44	415.5	44.3	53.2	2.5
2016	B	2.67	1.44	401.8	42.1	51.8	2.8
2015	B	2.62	1.41	388.0	39.5	47.7	2.8
2014	B	3.40	1.83	394.2	52.6	44.8	7.1
2013	B	3.41	1.84	385.6	51.5	44.0	6.9

Adverse Trends in Operations

Increase in policy surrenders from 2014 to 2015 (44%)
Decrease in capital during 2015 (25%)
Decrease in asset base during 2015 (2%)

SHELTER LIFE INSURANCE COMPANY

B   **Good**

Major Rating Factors: Good liquidity (6.0 on a scale of 0 to 10) with sufficient resources to cover a large increase in policy surrenders. Good overall results on stability tests (5.5). Strengths include good financial support from affiliation with Shelter Ins Companies, excellent operational trends and excellent risk diversification. Fair profitability (3.3) with investment income below regulatory standards in relation to interest assumptions of reserves.

Other Rating Factors: Strong capitalization (9.2) based on excellent risk adjusted capital (severe loss scenario). High quality investment portfolio (7.6).

Principal Business: Individual life insurance (86%), group health insurance (8%), individual annuities (4%), and group life insurance (1%).

Principal Investments: NonCMO investment grade bonds (55%), CMOs and structured securities (37%), policy loans (2%), common & preferred stock (1%), and mortgages in good standing (1%).

Investments in Affiliates: 2%

Group Affiliation: Shelter Ins Companies

Licensed in: AR, CO, IL, IN, IA, KS, KY, LA, MS, MO, NE, NV, OH, OK, TN

Commenced Business: March 1959

Address: 1817 WEST BROADWAY, COLUMBIA, MO 65218-0001

Phone: (573) 445-8441 **Domicile State:** MO **NAIC Code:** 65757

Data Date	Rating	RACR #1	RACR #2	Total Assets ($mil)	Capital ($mil)	Net Premium ($mil)	Net Income ($mil)
9-18	B	3.89	2.45	1,268.8	225.5	101.1	14.8
9-17	B+	3.67	2.41	1,238.3	211.2	98.0	13.5
2017	B	3.70	2.35	1,236.6	206.5	130.8	11.6
2016	B+	3.42	2.24	1,198.9	196.0	126.7	16.2
2015	A-	3.34	2.19	1,157.4	184.1	119.9	7.5
2014	A-	3.45	2.23	1,118.2	178.0	115.3	-4.9
2013	A-	3.60	2.37	1,078.4	181.6	113.0	14.6

Shelter Ins Companies
Composite Group Rating: B
Largest Group Members

	Assets ($mil)	Rating
SHELTER MUTUAL INS CO	3381	B
SHELTER LIFE INS CO	1237	B
SHELTER REINS CO	473	B
SHELTER GENERAL INS CO	128	C
HAULERS INS CO	78	C+

SHELTERPOINT LIFE INSURANCE COMPANY *

A   **Excellent**

Major Rating Factors: Good overall results on stability tests (6.8 on a scale of 0 to 10) despite excessive premium growth. Strengths that enhance stability include excellent operational trends and good risk diversification. Strong capitalization (8.3) based on excellent risk adjusted capital (severe loss scenario). Furthermore, this high level of risk adjusted capital has been consistently maintained over the last five years. High quality investment portfolio (7.5).

Other Rating Factors: Excellent profitability (7.9). Excellent liquidity (7.0).

Principal Business: Group health insurance (98%), group life insurance (2%), and reinsurance (1%).

Principal Investments: NonCMO investment grade bonds (69%), CMOs and structured securities (16%), common & preferred stock (9%), cash (4%), and noninv. grade bonds (1%).

Investments in Affiliates: 9%

Group Affiliation: ShelterPoint Group Inc

Licensed in: CA, CO, CT, DC, DE, FL, IL, MD, MA, MI, MN, NJ, NY, NC, PA, RI, SC, TN

Commenced Business: November 1972

Address: 600 NORTHERN BLVD, GREAT NECK, NY 11530

Phone: (516) 829-8100 **Domicile State:** NY **NAIC Code:** 81434

Data Date	Rating	RACR #1	RACR #2	Total Assets ($mil)	Capital ($mil)	Net Premium ($mil)	Net Income ($mil)
9-18	A	2.19	1.85	151.3	66.7	149.2	5.9
9-17	A	2.51	2.11	110.1	62.2	75.7	3.8
2017	A	2.63	2.23	114.9	61.0	97.2	3.5
2016	A	2.47	2.09	106.5	58.8	91.8	5.5
2015	A	2.38	2.01	107.5	54.9	88.6	5.6
2014	A	2.40	2.03	104.4	54.9	86.7	10.0
2013	A	3.82	2.91	100.4	48.2	82.4	5.7

Rating Indexes

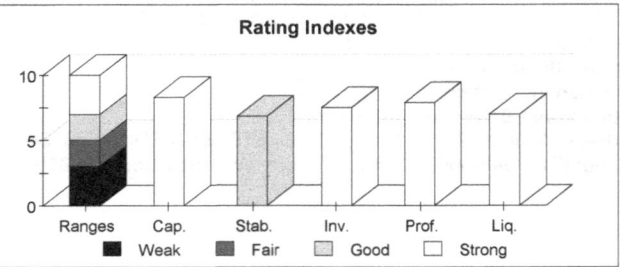

Ranges | Cap. | Stab. | Inv. | Prof. | Liq.
■ Weak   ▨ Fair   ▢ Good   □ Strong

SHENANDOAH LIFE INS CO — B- — Good

Major Rating Factors: Good quality investment portfolio (6.6 on a scale of 0 to 10) despite mixed results such as: minimal exposure to mortgages and large holdings of BBB rated bonds but minimal holdings in junk bonds. Good overall profitability (5.4) although investment income, in comparison to reserve requirements, is below regulatory standards. Fair liquidity (3.8).

Other Rating Factors: Fair overall results on stability tests (4.9) including negative cash flow from operations for 2017. Strong capitalization (7.7) based on excellent risk adjusted capital (severe loss scenario).

Principal Business: Individual life insurance (79%), individual health insurance (16%), reinsurance (4%), individual annuities (1%), and group life insurance (1%).

Principal Investments: NonCMO investment grade bonds (73%), CMOs and structured securities (17%), mortgages in good standing (5%), policy loans (3%), and common & preferred stock (1%).

Investments in Affiliates: 1%

Group Affiliation: Reservoir Capital Group LLC

Licensed in: AL, AK, AZ, AR, CO, DC, DE, FL, GA, HI, IL, IN, IA, KS, KY, LA, MD, MI, MN, MS, MO, NE, NH, NJ, NM, NC, ND, OH, OK, PA, SC, TN, TX, UT, VT, VA, WA, WV, WI, WY

Commenced Business: February 1916

Address: 4415 PHEASANT RIDGE RD STE 300, ROANOKE, VA 24014

Phone: (540) 985-4400 **Domicile State:** VA **NAIC Code:** 68845

Data Date	Rating	RACR #1	RACR #2	Total Assets ($mil)	Capital ($mil)	Net Premium ($mil)	Net Income ($mil)
9-18	B-	2.73	1.49	1,003.5	105.7	32.1	11.5
9-17	B-	2.39	1.28	1,055.1	94.8	30.5	24.9
2017	B-	2.52	1.37	1,036.4	94.6	40.4	27.4
2016	B-	2.09	1.10	1,077.4	83.7	59.8	14.1
2015	B-	2.11	1.11	1,131.8	87.9	44.8	21.0
2014	C	1.92	1.00	1,204.4	85.5	49.8	18.3
2013	C	1.74	0.93	1,278.8	81.1	54.7	12.6

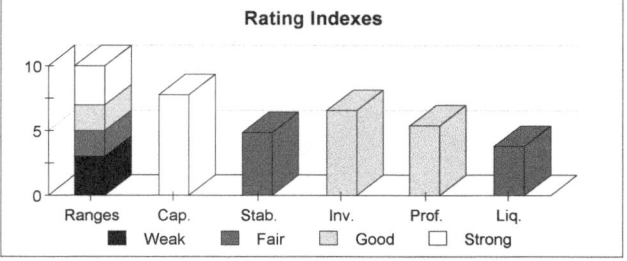

Rating Indexes

SOUTHERN FARM BUREAU LIFE INSURANCE COMPANY * — A — Excellent

Major Rating Factors: Good quality investment portfolio (6.0 on a scale of 0 to 10) despite significant exposure to mortgages . Mortgage default rate has been low. large holdings of BBB rated bonds in addition to small junk bond holdings. Good overall profitability (6.8). Good liquidity (6.3).

Other Rating Factors: Strong capitalization (9.1) based on excellent risk adjusted capital (severe loss scenario). Excellent overall results on stability tests (7.4) excellent operational trends and excellent risk diversification.

Principal Business: Individual life insurance (84%), individual annuities (12%), individual health insurance (3%), and group life insurance (1%).

Principal Investments: NonCMO investment grade bonds (54%), CMOs and structured securities (17%), mortgages in good standing (13%), common & preferred stock (5%), and misc. investments (11%).

Investments in Affiliates: None

Group Affiliation: Southern Farm Bureau Group

Licensed in: AL, AR, CO, FL, GA, KY, LA, MS, NC, SC, TN, TX, VA, PR

Commenced Business: December 1946

Address: 1401 Livingston Lane, Jackson, MS 39213

Phone: (601) 981-7422 **Domicile State:** MS **NAIC Code:** 68896

Data Date	Rating	RACR #1	RACR #2	Total Assets ($mil)	Capital ($mil)	Net Premium ($mil)	Net Income ($mil)
9-18	A	4.44	2.38	14,356.8	2,577.8	658.0	37.0
9-17	A	4.56	2.44	14,163.7	2,573.4	681.3	78.2
2017	A	4.47	2.40	14,191.7	2,558.7	882.3	115.6
2016	A	4.64	2.47	13,926.2	2,537.4	964.8	73.7
2015	A	4.55	2.45	13,307.9	2,456.8	904.7	77.0
2014	A	4.52	2.45	12,995.5	2,436.4	799.8	167.9
2013	A	4.42	2.42	12,679.3	2,327.2	785.7	149.8

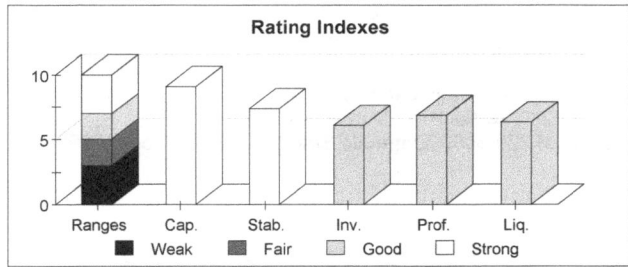

Rating Indexes

SOUTHERN FINANCIAL LIFE INSURANCE COMPANY — D+ — Weak

Major Rating Factors: Low quality investment portfolio (2.8 on a scale of 0 to 10) containing large holdings of BBB rated bonds in addition to moderate junk bond exposure. Weak overall results on stability tests (2.8). Good liquidity (6.7) with sufficient resources to handle a spike in claims.

Other Rating Factors: Strong capitalization (8.1) based on excellent risk adjusted capital (severe loss scenario). Excellent profitability (8.4).

Principal Business: Reinsurance (95%), credit life insurance (5%), and individual life insurance (1%).

Principal Investments: NonCMO investment grade bonds (48%), common & preferred stock (31%), noninv. grade bonds (11%), and cash (1%).

Investments in Affiliates: None

Group Affiliation: None

Licensed in: LA, TX

Commenced Business: June 1984

Address: 111 MATRIX LOOP, LAFAYETTE, LA 70507

Phone: (470) 639-8576 **Domicile State:** LA **NAIC Code:** 69418

Data Date	Rating	RACR #1	RACR #2	Total Assets ($mil)	Capital ($mil)	Net Premium ($mil)	Net Income ($mil)
9-18	D+	3.09	1.71	128.2	42.0	9.6	2.9
9-17	D+	3.04	1.66	119.5	35.4	13.5	3.0
2017	D+	2.98	1.64	123.6	37.1	17.4	4.1
2016	D+	2.88	1.55	109.9	31.6	15.4	2.3
2015	D+	2.67	1.46	106.2	29.0	17.8	2.0
2014	D+	2.63	1.45	104.7	27.8	12.8	1.9
2013	D+	2.43	1.33	102.4	24.7	9.9	3.6

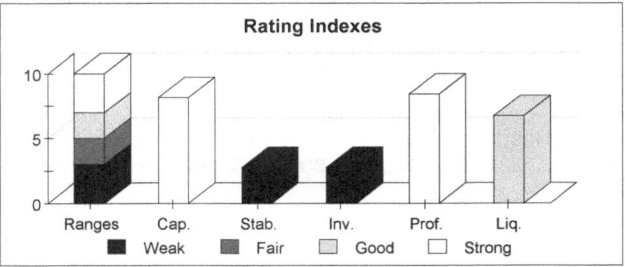

Rating Indexes

SOUTHERN LIFE & HEALTH INS CO   B   Good

Major Rating Factors: Good overall profitability (6.4 on a scale of 0 to 10). Good liquidity (6.9) with sufficient resources to handle a spike in claims. Fair overall results on stability tests (4.9) including negative cash flow from operations for 2017.
Other Rating Factors: Strong capitalization (8.0) based on excellent risk adjusted capital (severe loss scenario). High quality investment portfolio (7.2).
Principal Business: Reinsurance (100%).
Principal Investments: NonCMO investment grade bonds (63%), common & preferred stock (31%), and CMOs and structured securities (1%).
Investments in Affiliates: 25%
Group Affiliation: Geneve Holdings Inc
Licensed in: AL, DE, FL, LA, MS, TX, WI
Commenced Business: September 1890
Address: 1241 John Q Hammons Drive, Madison, WI 53717
Phone: (205) 414-3000 **Domicile State:** WI **NAIC Code:** 88323

Data Date	Rating	RACR #1	RACR #2	Total Assets ($mil)	Capital ($mil)	Net Premium ($mil)	Net Income ($mil)
9-18	B	1.74	1.65	71.2	32.0	-0.1	1.2
9-17	B-	1.63	1.54	75.2	31.2	0.2	1.6
2017	B	1.75	1.66	73.9	32.2	0.2	3.8
2016	C+	1.56	1.49	75.0	29.5	0.2	6.0
2015	U	1.86	1.73	85.5	33.4	0.0	7.9
2014	U	1.95	1.77	91.3	35.0	0.0	7.6
2013	U	1.96	1.78	95.0	34.9	0.1	8.1

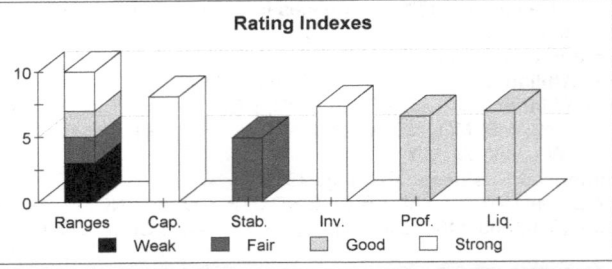

Rating Indexes

SOUTHLAND NATIONAL INSURANCE CORPORATION   D+   Weak

Major Rating Factors: Weak overall results on stability tests (1.8 on a scale of 0 to 10) including weak results on operational trends, negative cash flow from operations for 2017. Fair quality investment portfolio (3.8). Fair profitability (3.0) with operating losses during the first nine months of 2018.
Other Rating Factors: Good liquidity (6.9). Strong capitalization (7.1) based on excellent risk adjusted capital (severe loss scenario).
Principal Business: Reinsurance (46%), group health insurance (30%), individual life insurance (19%), group life insurance (4%), and individual health insurance (1%).
Principal Investments: NonCMO investment grade bonds (43%), CMOs and structured securities (28%), cash (10%), common & preferred stock (9%), and misc. investments (7%).
Investments in Affiliates: 13%
Group Affiliation: SNA Capital LLC
Licensed in: LA
Commenced Business: January 1969
Address: 2222 Sedwick Rd, Durham, NC 27713
Phone: (303) 220-8500 **Domicile State:** NC **NAIC Code:** 79057

Data Date	Rating	RACR #1	RACR #2	Total Assets ($mil)	Capital ($mil)	Net Premium ($mil)	Net Income ($mil)
9-18	D+	2.19	1.07	360.7	30.4	-38.3	-2.1
9-17	C-	N/A	N/A	414.0	29.0	5.6	-4.1
2017	C-	2.16	1.14	418.3	33.8	7.5	-5.4
2016	C-	1.50	0.96	385.4	36.6	94.4	-1.7
2015	C-	2.18	0.93	307.4	34.0	-152.4	16.4
2014	D	1.83	0.89	318.1	22.9	145.2	-7.2
2013	C	0.96	0.82	167.1	9.5	6.5	0.2

Adverse Trends in Operations

Increase in policy surrenders from 2016 to 2017 (438%)
Decrease in premium volume from 2016 to 2017 (92%)
Increase in policy surrenders from 2015 to 2016 (83%)
Decrease in premium volume from 2014 to 2015 (205%)
Change in asset mix during 2014 (5.3%)

STANDARD INSURANCE COMPANY *   B+   Good

Major Rating Factors: Good quality investment portfolio (5.1 on a scale of 0 to 10) despite substantial holdings of BBB bonds in addition to moderate junk bond exposure. Exposure to mortgages is large, but the mortgage default rate has been low. Good overall profitability (6.3). Good liquidity (6.8).
Other Rating Factors: Good overall results on stability tests (6.5) excellent operational trends and excellent risk diversification. Strong capitalization (7.3) based on excellent risk adjusted capital (severe loss scenario).
Principal Business: Group retirement contracts (42%), group health insurance (25%), group life insurance (16%), individual annuities (10%), and other lines (7%).
Principal Investments: NonCMO investment grade bonds (45%), mortgages in good standing (41%), CMOs and structured securities (6%), noninv. grade bonds (4%), and cash (1%).
Investments in Affiliates: None
Group Affiliation: Meiji Yasuda Life Ins Company
Licensed in: All states except NY
Commenced Business: April 1906
Address: 1100 SOUTHWEST SIXTH AVENUE, PORTLAND, OR 97204-1093
Phone: (503) 321-7000 **Domicile State:** OR **NAIC Code:** 69019

Data Date	Rating	RACR #1	RACR #2	Total Assets ($mil)	Capital ($mil)	Net Premium ($mil)	Net Income ($mil)
9-18	B+	2.31	1.19	24,530.4	1,258.7	3,002.2	157.0
9-17	B+	2.10	1.09	23,414.5	1,091.1	3,073.6	116.2
2017	B+	2.02	1.06	23,952.0	1,108.4	4,300.3	178.2
2016	B+	2.04	1.06	21,792.1	1,040.4	4,075.8	144.8
2015	B+	2.21	1.16	20,781.6	1,085.0	3,528.4	160.1
2014	B+	2.38	1.26	20,361.1	1,151.8	4,019.8	209.4
2013	B+	2.37	1.32	19,118.7	1,287.3	3,489.3	195.8

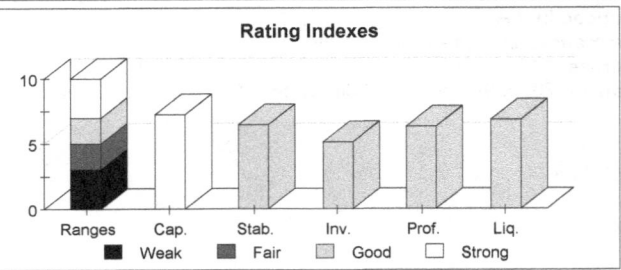

Rating Indexes

STANDARD LIFE & ACCIDENT INSURANCE COMPANY * A- Excellent

Major Rating Factors: Good overall results on stability tests (6.9 on a scale of 0 to 10) despite negative cash flow from operations for 2017. Strengths that enhance stability include excellent operational trends and excellent risk diversification. Good liquidity (6.9) with sufficient resources to handle a spike in claims as well as a significant increase in policy surrenders. Fair quality investment portfolio (4.9).

Other Rating Factors: Strong capitalization (10.0) based on excellent risk adjusted capital (severe loss scenario). Excellent profitability (7.9).

Principal Business: Reinsurance (40%), individual health insurance (35%), group health insurance (18%), and individual life insurance (7%).

Principal Investments: NonCMO investment grade bonds (75%), common & preferred stock (18%), noninv. grade bonds (3%), mortgages in good standing (3%), and misc. investments (2%).

Investments in Affiliates: None

Group Affiliation: American National Group Inc

Licensed in: All states except ME, NH, NJ, NY, PR

Commenced Business: June 1976

Address: ONE MOODY PLAZA, GALVESTON, TX 77550

Phone: (409) 763-4661 **Domicile State:** TX **NAIC Code:** 86355

Data Date	Rating	RACR #1	RACR #2	Total Assets ($mil)	Capital ($mil)	Net Premium ($mil)	Net Income ($mil)
9-18	A-	5.59	3.47	533.1	294.6	81.7	6.2
9-17	A-	6.18	3.79	516.7	287.7	73.0	8.2
2017	A-	5.78	3.59	521.6	289.5	98.3	10.7
2016	A-	6.21	3.82	518.8	287.1	95.1	13.6
2015	A-	5.93	3.68	514.5	278.1	105.2	8.6
2014	A-	5.09	3.17	530.2	259.1	120.7	20.6
2013	A-	5.22	3.20	527.6	252.2	108.7	18.0

Adverse Trends in Operations

Decrease in premium volume from 2015 to 2016 (10%)
Decrease in asset base during 2015 (3%)
Decrease in premium volume from 2014 to 2015 (13%)

STANDARD LIFE INSURANCE COMPANY OF NEW YORK * A- Excellent

Major Rating Factors: Excellent overall results on stability tests (7.2 on a scale of 0 to 10). Strengths that enhance stability include excellent operational trends and excellent risk diversification. Strong capitalization (10.0) based on excellent risk adjusted capital (severe loss scenario). Furthermore, this high level of risk adjusted capital has been consistently maintained over the last five years. High quality investment portfolio (7.4).

Other Rating Factors: Excellent profitability (7.9). Excellent liquidity (7.0).

Principal Business: Group health insurance (59%), group life insurance (36%), and individual health insurance (5%).

Principal Investments: Mortgages in good standing (49%), nonCMO investment grade bonds (48%), cash (2%), and noninv. grade bonds (1%).

Investments in Affiliates: None

Group Affiliation: Meiji Yasuda Life Ins Company

Licensed in: NY

Commenced Business: January 2001

Address: 360 HAMILTON AVENUE SUITE 210, WHITE PLAINS, NY 10601-1871

Phone: (914) 989-4400 **Domicile State:** NY **NAIC Code:** 89009

Data Date	Rating	RACR #1	RACR #2	Total Assets ($mil)	Capital ($mil)	Net Premium ($mil)	Net Income ($mil)
9-18	A-	4.75	3.12	296.6	96.9	76.3	0.1
9-17	A-	4.68	3.05	292.4	96.3	68.2	10.8
2017	A-	4.90	3.20	292.2	96.2	90.0	11.9
2016	A-	4.25	2.80	286.6	85.9	89.1	3.6
2015	A-	4.14	2.73	282.7	80.9	89.4	6.3
2014	A-	3.57	2.37	275.3	76.6	95.2	4.0
2013	A-	3.28	2.19	265.6	71.6	98.0	2.7

Adverse Trends in Operations

Increase in policy surrenders from 2016 to 2017 (375%)
Increase in policy surrenders from 2015 to 2016 (415%)
Decrease in premium volume from 2014 to 2015 (6%)
Decrease in premium volume from 2013 to 2014 (3%)

STANDARD SECURITY LIFE INSURANCE CO OF NEW YORK B Good

Major Rating Factors: Good overall results on stability tests (5.6 on a scale of 0 to 10) despite negative cash flow from operations for 2017. Other stability subfactors include good operational trends and excellent risk diversification. Good overall profitability (5.3). Good liquidity (6.9) with sufficient resources to handle a spike in claims.

Other Rating Factors: Strong capitalization (10.0) based on excellent risk adjusted capital (severe loss scenario). High quality investment portfolio (8.3).

Principal Business: Group health insurance (83%), individual health insurance (15%), and group life insurance (2%).

Principal Investments: NonCMO investment grade bonds (76%), common & preferred stock (16%), cash (2%), and CMOs and structured securities (1%).

Investments in Affiliates: 10%

Group Affiliation: Geneve Holdings Inc

Licensed in: All states, the District of Columbia and Puerto Rico

Commenced Business: December 1958

Address: 485 Madison Avenue 14th Floor, New York, NY 10022-5872

Phone: (212) 355-4141 **Domicile State:** NY **NAIC Code:** 69078

Data Date	Rating	RACR #1	RACR #2	Total Assets ($mil)	Capital ($mil)	Net Premium ($mil)	Net Income ($mil)
9-18	B	6.45	5.00	138.0	71.5	72.7	5.9
9-17	B	6.62	5.11	133.1	66.5	62.3	2.8
2017	B	6.77	5.23	131.5	65.6	80.3	3.6
2016	B+	6.84	5.28	154.9	70.6	84.7	-10.5
2015	A-	3.95	3.20	269.9	125.1	211.0	13.2
2014	B	3.55	2.81	252.4	116.5	207.3	12.1
2013	B	3.29	2.67	249.5	114.0	214.4	9.2

Adverse Trends in Operations

Decrease in asset base during 2017 (15%)
Decrease in premium volume from 2015 to 2016 (60%)
Decrease in asset base during 2016 (43%)
Decrease in capital during 2016 (44%)
Decrease in premium volume from 2013 to 2014 (3%)

STARMOUNT LIFE INSURANCE COMPANY   C+   Fair

Major Rating Factors: Fair overall results on stability tests (4.1 on a scale of 0 to 10) including negative cash flow from operations for 2017. Good overall capitalization (5.7) based on mixed results -- excessive policy leverage mitigated by good risk adjusted capital (severe loss scenario). Moreover, capital levels have been consistent over the last five years. Weak profitability (2.5) with operating losses during the first nine months of 2018.
Other Rating Factors: Weak liquidity (2.1). High quality investment portfolio (7.8).
Principal Business: Group health insurance (62%), reinsurance (21%), individual health insurance (13%), and individual life insurance (4%).
Principal Investments: NonCMO investment grade bonds (56%), cash (30%), real estate (9%), noninv. grade bonds (1%), and policy loans (1%).
Investments in Affiliates: None
Group Affiliation: Unum Group
Licensed in: All states except NY, PR
Commenced Business: August 1983
Address: 8485 Goodwood Blvd, Baton Rouge, LA 70806
Phone: (225) 926-2888 **Domicile State:** LA **NAIC Code:** 68985

Data Date	Rating	RACR #1	RACR #2	Total Assets ($mil)	Capital ($mil)	Net Premium ($mil)	Net Income ($mil)
9-18	C+	1.24	0.97	82.6	43.5	155.1	-7.6
9-17	B	1.11	0.86	76.4	34.8	133.0	-2.6
2017	B	1.18	0.92	79.9	37.4	179.7	-2.8
2016	B	1.20	0.94	76.2	32.3	144.3	-0.4
2015	B	N/A	N/A	65.9	28.3	121.0	4.0
2014	B	1.35	1.02	59.1	25.0	95.2	3.8
2013	B	1.46	1.08	51.1	22.3	79.7	4.2

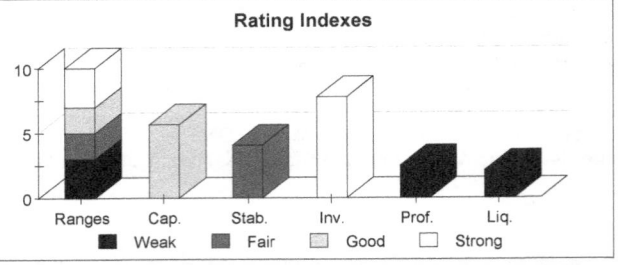

Rating Indexes

STATE FARM LIFE & ACCIDENT ASSURANCE COMPANY *   A+   Excellent

Major Rating Factors: Good overall profitability (5.4 on a scale of 0 to 10) although investment income, in comparison to reserve requirements, is below regulatory standards. Good liquidity (6.2) with sufficient resources to handle a spike in claims as well as a significant increase in policy surrenders. Excellent overall results on stability tests (7.9) excellent operational trends and excellent risk diversification.
Other Rating Factors: Strong capitalization (10.0) based on excellent risk adjusted capital (severe loss scenario). High quality investment portfolio (7.8).
Principal Business: Individual life insurance (91%) and individual annuities (9%).
Principal Investments: NonCMO investment grade bonds (69%), CMOs and structured securities (23%), policy loans (6%), and noninv. grade bonds (1%).
Investments in Affiliates: 1%
Group Affiliation: State Farm Group
Licensed in: CT, IL, NY, WI
Commenced Business: July 1961
Address: One State Farm Plaza, Bloomington, IL 61710
Phone: (309) 766-2311 **Domicile State:** IL **NAIC Code:** 69094

Data Date	Rating	RACR #1	RACR #2	Total Assets ($mil)	Capital ($mil)	Net Premium ($mil)	Net Income ($mil)
9-18	A+	5.53	3.13	3,003.4	524.9	181.3	20.8
9-17	A+	5.64	3.20	2,886.6	509.3	180.0	20.0
2017	A+	5.39	3.07	2,915.8	503.2	239.5	25.8
2016	A+	5.49	3.11	2,776.0	489.3	245.2	28.7
2015	A+	5.53	3.16	2,614.1	464.6	231.6	23.2
2014	A+	5.57	3.21	2,469.9	438.3	220.4	24.3
2013	A+	5.61	3.25	2,334.1	417.4	210.1	21.5

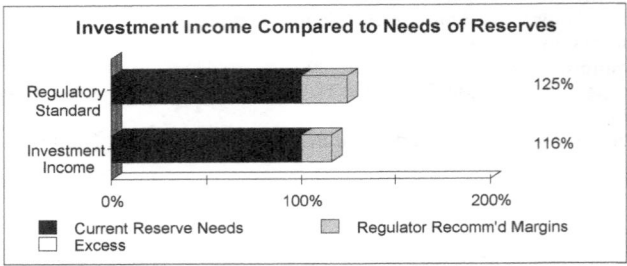

Investment Income Compared to Needs of Reserves

STATE FARM LIFE INSURANCE COMPANY *   A+   Excellent

Major Rating Factors: Good quality investment portfolio (6.5 on a scale of 0 to 10) despite significant exposure to mortgages . Mortgage default rate has been low. substantial holdings of BBB bonds in addition to minimal holdings in junk bonds. Good overall profitability (5.5) although investment income, in comparison to reserve requirements, is below regulatory standards. Good liquidity (6.0).
Other Rating Factors: Excellent overall results on stability tests (7.9) excellent operational trends and excellent risk diversification. Strong capitalization (9.3) based on excellent risk adjusted capital (severe loss scenario).
Principal Business: Individual life insurance (90%), individual annuities (8%), and group life insurance (1%).
Principal Investments: NonCMO investment grade bonds (53%), CMOs and structured securities (19%), mortgages in good standing (11%), policy loans (6%), and common & preferred stock (6%).
Investments in Affiliates: 3%
Group Affiliation: State Farm Group
Licensed in: All states except MA, NY, WI, PR
Commenced Business: April 1929
Address: One State Farm Plaza, Bloomington, IL 61710
Phone: (309) 766-2311 **Domicile State:** IL **NAIC Code:** 69108

Data Date	Rating	RACR #1	RACR #2	Total Assets ($mil)	Capital ($mil)	Net Premium ($mil)	Net Income ($mil)
9-18	A+	4.51	2.54	74,940.7	11,502.7	3,769.7	416.6
9-17	A+	4.53	2.55	72,335.9	10,855.5	3,764.8	304.5
2017	A+	4.47	2.52	73,080.0	10,904.7	5,018.7	466.4
2016	A+	4.46	2.51	70,061.3	10,177.3	5,418.7	533.1
2015	A+	4.46	2.53	66,498.2	9,559.9	5,224.3	644.2
2014	A+	4.32	2.47	63,530.5	9,001.1	5,002.1	497.5
2013	A+	4.30	2.46	60,442.0	8,444.7	4,750.7	433.6

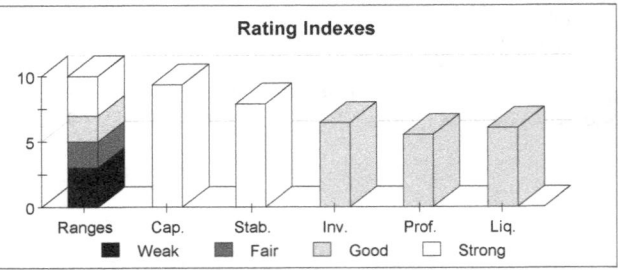

Rating Indexes

STATE LIFE INSURANCE COMPANY — B — Good

Major Rating Factors: Fair overall capitalization (3.0 on a scale of 0 to 10) based on mixed results -- excessive policy leverage mitigated by good risk adjusted capital (moderate loss scenario). Capital levels have been relatively consistent over the last five years. Fair quality investment portfolio (4.6) with large holdings of BBB rated bonds in addition to moderate junk bond exposure. Fair liquidity (3.9).

Other Rating Factors: Fair overall results on stability tests (4.2). Excellent profitability (7.6).

Principal Business: Individual life insurance (56%), individual annuities (38%), reinsurance (4%), and individual health insurance (2%).

Principal Investments: NonCMO investment grade bonds (62%), CMOs and structured securities (23%), mortgages in good standing (10%), noninv. grade bonds (2%), and misc. investments (2%).

Investments in Affiliates: None
Group Affiliation: American United Life Group
Licensed in: All states except NY, PR
Commenced Business: September 1894
Address: ONE AMERICAN SQUARE, INDIANAPOLIS, IN 46282-0001
Phone: (317) 285-2300 **Domicile State:** IN **NAIC Code:** 69116

Data Date	Rating	RACR #1	RACR #2	Total Assets ($mil)	Capital ($mil)	Net Premium ($mil)	Net Income ($mil)
9-18	B	1.65	0.83	8,378.9	461.0	499.8	25.1
9-17	B	2.01	1.04	7,619.4	472.4	599.8	13.0
2017	B	1.63	0.82	7,828.0	438.8	31.3	20.0
2016	B	2.06	1.07	6,754.1	459.8	788.4	16.9
2015	B	2.14	1.12	6,119.3	426.9	643.7	37.3
2014	B	1.97	1.02	5,522.2	354.2	599.3	23.5
2013	B	2.02	1.05	5,010.6	332.0	524.0	29.5

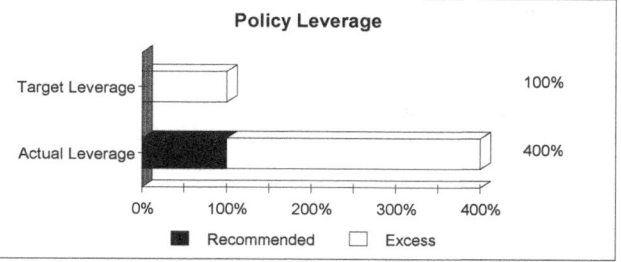

Policy Leverage

Target Leverage — 100%
Actual Leverage — 400%

0%   100%   200%   300%   400%

■ Recommended   □ Excess

STATE MUTUAL INSURANCE COMPANY — D+ — Weak

Major Rating Factors: Low quality investment portfolio (2.9 on a scale of 0 to 10) containing large holdings of BBB rated bonds in addition to junk bond exposure equal to 50% of capital. Weak profitability (2.0) with operating losses during the first nine months of 2018. Weak overall results on stability tests (2.5) including negative cash flow from operations for 2017 and weak results on operational trends.

Other Rating Factors: Fair overall capitalization (4.0) based on mixed results -- excessive policy leverage mitigated by good risk adjusted capital (moderate loss scenario). Good liquidity (6.4).

Principal Business: Individual health insurance (54%), individual life insurance (32%), and reinsurance (14%).

Principal Investments: NonCMO investment grade bonds (43%), CMOs and structured securities (16%), real estate (8%), common & preferred stock (7%), and misc. investments (23%).

Investments in Affiliates: 6%
Group Affiliation: None
Licensed in: All states except CA, CT, ME, NH, NJ, NY, PR
Commenced Business: October 1890
Address: 210 E Second Avenue Suite 301, Rome, GA 30161
Phone: (706) 291-1054 **Domicile State:** GA **NAIC Code:** 69132

Data Date	Rating	RACR #1	RACR #2	Total Assets ($mil)	Capital ($mil)	Net Premium ($mil)	Net Income ($mil)
9-18	D+	1.15	0.73	188.6	26.5	16.1	-3.9
9-17	C-	1.21	0.80	274.1	29.9	-30.9	-2.2
2017	C-	1.19	0.77	267.3	29.1	-33.1	-7.8
2016	C-	1.05	0.73	279.4	26.1	22.8	-9.0
2015	D+	2.31	1.27	286.7	33.7	18.7	1.0
2014	C	1.64	1.02	292.5	33.9	0.4	0.2
2013	C	1.73	1.04	296.8	30.0	21.5	0.8

Adverse Trends in Operations

Decrease in premium volume from 2016 to 2017 (245%)
Decrease in capital during 2016 (23%)
Decrease in asset base during 2014 (1%)
Change in premium mix from 2013 to 2014 (376.8%)
Decrease in premium volume from 2013 to 2014 (98%)

SUN LIFE & HEALTH INSURANCE COMPANY — D — Weak

Major Rating Factors: Weak overall results on stability tests (2.0 on a scale of 0 to 10) including potential financial drain due to affiliation with Sun Life Assurance Group and negative cash flow from operations for 2017, weak results on operational trends. Weak profitability (1.0) with investment income below regulatory standards in relation to interest assumptions of reserves. Good liquidity (6.3).

Other Rating Factors: Strong capitalization (8.6) based on excellent risk adjusted capital (severe loss scenario). High quality investment portfolio (7.2).

Principal Business: Reinsurance (71%), group health insurance (20%), and group life insurance (9%).

Principal Investments: NonCMO investment grade bonds (66%), CMOs and structured securities (22%), mortgages in good standing (7%), noninv. grade bonds (1%), and misc. investments (4%).

Investments in Affiliates: None
Group Affiliation: Sun Life Assurance Group
Licensed in: All states, the District of Columbia and Puerto Rico
Commenced Business: January 1975
Address: 201 Townsend Street Ste 900, Lansing, MI 48933
Phone: (781) 237-6030 **Domicile State:** MI **NAIC Code:** 80926

Data Date	Rating	RACR #1	RACR #2	Total Assets ($mil)	Capital ($mil)	Net Premium ($mil)	Net Income ($mil)
9-18	D	3.58	2.04	955.2	139.2	86.5	9.3
9-17	D	5.37	3.36	504.8	205.6	83.1	8.7
2017	D	2.95	1.74	943.2	129.9	644.6	-68.3
2016	D-	4.36	2.91	485.3	198.5	248.1	-44.8
2015	C	6.46	4.17	447.7	241.5	173.5	17.2
2014	C-	4.77	3.13	371.8	175.5	168.0	-1.4
2013	C-	5.38	3.67	353.7	182.0	166.8	-35.8

Sun Life Assurance Group
Composite Group Rating: D-
Largest Group Members

	Assets ($mil)	Rating
SUN LIFE ASR CO OF CANADA	19086	D-
INDEPENDENCE LIFE ANNUITY CO	3144	D
SUN LIFE HEALTH INS CO	943	D
PROFESSIONAL INS CO	110	D

SUN LIFE ASSURANCE COMPANY OF CANADA   D   Weak

Major Rating Factors: Poor capitalization (2.4 on a scale of 0 to 10) based on weak risk adjusted capital (moderate loss scenario). Low quality investment portfolio (2.1) containing significant exposure to mortgages . Mortgage default rate has been low. Weak profitability (2.3).

Other Rating Factors: Weak overall results on stability tests (1.7) including weak risk adjusted capital in prior years and excessive premium growth. Good liquidity (5.1).

Principal Business: Group health insurance (53%), individual life insurance (16%), group life insurance (16%), and reinsurance (15%).

Principal Investments: NonCMO investment grade bonds (54%), mortgages in good standing (18%), CMOs and structured securities (10%), real estate (6%), and misc. investments (10%).

Investments in Affiliates: 1%

Group Affiliation: Sun Life Assurance Group

Licensed in: All states except NY

Commenced Business: May 1871

Address: 150 King Street West, Toronto, ON 2481

Phone: (781) 237-6030 **Domicile State:** MI **NAIC Code:** 80802

Data Date	Rating	RACR #1	RACR #2	Total Assets ($mil)	Capital ($mil)	Net Premium ($mil)	Net Income ($mil)
9-18	D	0.67	0.40	18,767.4	1,192.5	2,646.3	414.9
9-17	D-	0.64	0.38	20,032.5	1,142.6	1,769.5	127.9
2017	D-	0.62	0.35	19,086.1	916.9	1,789.4	259.6
2016	E	0.53	0.32	19,562.8	1,019.0	3,803.2	-535.1
2015	D	1.27	0.74	18,222.4	1,925.8	2,207.2	86.4
2014	D	0.75	0.43	17,090.4	940.3	2,349.1	-64.3
2013	D	0.53	0.30	15,368.9	766.7	-919.7	234.8

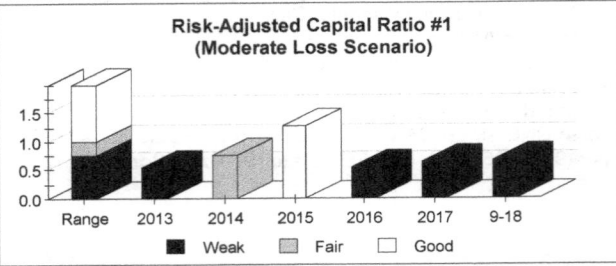

Risk-Adjusted Capital Ratio #1 (Moderate Loss Scenario)

SUNSET LIFE INSURANCE COMPANY OF AMERICA   B-   Good

Major Rating Factors: Good quality investment portfolio (6.2 on a scale of 0 to 10) despite significant exposure to mortgages . Mortgage default rate has been low. large holdings of BBB rated bonds in addition to minimal holdings in junk bonds. Good liquidity (5.2) with sufficient resources to cover a large increase in policy surrenders. Good overall results on stability tests (5.0) despite negative cash flow from operations for 2017 good operational trends and good risk diversification.

Other Rating Factors: Fair profitability (3.4). Strong capitalization (7.6) based on excellent risk adjusted capital (severe loss scenario).

Principal Business: Individual life insurance (78%) and individual annuities (22%).

Principal Investments: NonCMO investment grade bonds (73%), mortgages in good standing (17%), CMOs and structured securities (6%), policy loans (2%), and common & preferred stock (1%).

Investments in Affiliates: None

Group Affiliation: Kansas City Life Group

Licensed in: All states except AL, NH, NJ, NY, TN, VT, WI, PR

Commenced Business: May 1937

Address: 3520 Broadway, Kansas City, MO 64111-2565

Phone: (816) 753-7000 **Domicile State:** MO **NAIC Code:** 69272

Data Date	Rating	RACR #1	RACR #2	Total Assets ($mil)	Capital ($mil)	Net Premium ($mil)	Net Income ($mil)
9-18	B-	2.68	1.40	310.0	27.1	6.6	1.9
9-17	B	3.30	1.73	323.5	35.0	7.3	2.9
2017	B-	2.51	1.31	316.3	25.2	9.1	-3.7
2016	B	3.06	1.61	329.1	32.4	6.9	2.7
2015	B	2.66	1.38	338.7	29.4	8.3	2.8
2014	B-	2.75	1.41	354.1	32.0	16.0	4.4
2013	B-	2.61	1.34	355.7	31.2	15.3	4.8

Adverse Trends in Operations

Decrease in capital during 2017 (22%)
Decrease in asset base during 2017 (4%)
Decrease in premium volume from 2015 to 2016 (17%)
Decrease in capital during 2015 (8%)
Decrease in premium volume from 2014 to 2015 (48%)

SUPERIOR FUNERAL & LIFE INSURANCE COMPANY   C+   Fair

Major Rating Factors: Fair quality investment portfolio (4.1 on a scale of 0 to 10) with large holdings of BBB rated bonds in addition to junk bond exposure equal to 82% of capital. Fair overall results on stability tests (4.8). Good liquidity (5.8) with sufficient resources to cover a large increase in policy surrenders.

Other Rating Factors: Strong capitalization (7.6) based on excellent risk adjusted capital (severe loss scenario). Excellent profitability (7.8).

Principal Business: Individual life insurance (65%) and individual annuities (35%).

Principal Investments: NonCMO investment grade bonds (72%), noninv. grade bonds (11%), CMOs and structured securities (9%), common & preferred stock (5%), and cash (2%).

Investments in Affiliates: None

Group Affiliation: Superior Funeral and Life Insurance

Licensed in: AR, LA, MS, OK

Commenced Business: October 1960

Address: 119 CONVENTION BOULEVARD, HOT SPRINGS, AR 71901

Phone: (501) 624-2172 **Domicile State:** AR **NAIC Code:** 83836

Data Date	Rating	RACR #1	RACR #2	Total Assets ($mil)	Capital ($mil)	Net Premium ($mil)	Net Income ($mil)
9-18	C+	2.72	1.40	184.0	25.1	11.7	0.6
9-17	C+	2.65	1.36	179.8	24.4	11.4	0.7
2017	C+	2.67	1.36	181.7	24.5	15.2	0.6
2016	C+	2.53	1.32	176.7	23.2	15.4	0.8
2015	C+	2.40	1.41	171.5	22.0	15.1	0.7
2014	C+	2.47	1.50	169.4	22.7	15.0	0.8
2013	C+	2.52	1.58	168.1	25.2	16.1	0.6

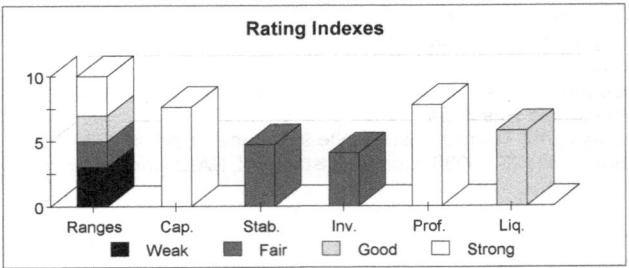

Rating Indexes

SWISS RE LIFE & HEALTH AMERICA INCORPORATED   C   Fair

Major Rating Factors: Fair overall results on stability tests (3.8 on a scale of 0 to 10). Good quality investment portfolio (6.6) despite mixed results such as: minimal exposure to mortgages and large holdings of BBB rated bonds but small junk bond holdings. Good liquidity (5.8) with sufficient resources to handle a spike in claims as well as a significant increase in policy surrenders.

Other Rating Factors: Weak profitability (1.7) with operating losses during the first nine months of 2018. Strong capitalization (7.2) based on excellent risk adjusted capital (severe loss scenario).

Principal Business: Reinsurance (100%).

Principal Investments: NonCMO investment grade bonds (68%), CMOs and structured securities (16%), mortgages in good standing (7%), noninv. grade bonds (3%), and common & preferred stock (1%).

Investments in Affiliates: 7%

Group Affiliation: Swiss Reinsurance Group

Licensed in: All states, the District of Columbia and Puerto Rico

Commenced Business: September 1967

Address: 237 EAST HIGH STREET, JEFFERSON CITY, MO 65101

Phone: (914) 828-8000   **Domicile State:** MO   **NAIC Code:** 82627

Data Date	Rating	RACR #1	RACR #2	Total Assets ($mil)	Capital ($mil)	Net Premium ($mil)	Net Income ($mil)
9-18	C	1.83	1.15	15,359.0	1,569.5	5,106.8	-1,570.0
9-17	C	1.74	1.09	14,355.3	1,457.4	1,827.3	189.9
2017	C	1.36	0.86	14,134.1	1,157.4	2,548.5	139.9
2016	C	1.57	0.99	14,226.8	1,380.9	2,289.7	-5.8
2015	C	1.83	1.08	12,264.0	1,318.3	2,983.5	85.8
2014	C	1.69	1.12	11,247.5	1,461.0	2,107.9	-924.1
2013	C	1.86	1.31	9,994.7	1,644.0	1,644.4	95.4

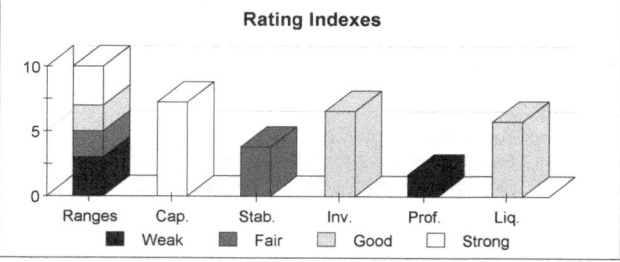

Rating Indexes

SYMETRA LIFE INSURANCE COMPANY   B   Good

Major Rating Factors: Good current capitalization (6.5 on a scale of 0 to 10) based on good risk adjusted capital (severe loss scenario), although results have slipped from the excellent range over the last two years. Good quality investment portfolio (5.2) despite large holdings of BBB rated bonds in addition to moderate junk bond exposure. Exposure to mortgages is significant, but the mortgage default rate has been low. Good overall profitability (5.6) although investment income, in comparison to reserve requirements, is below regulatory standards.

Other Rating Factors: Good liquidity (6.2). Good overall results on stability tests (6.3) good operational trends and excellent risk diversification.

Principal Business: Individual annuities (68%), group health insurance (19%), individual life insurance (11%), group life insurance (2%), and group retirement contracts (1%).

Principal Investments: NonCMO investment grade bonds (61%), mortgages in good standing (18%), CMOs and structured securities (11%), noninv. grade bonds (3%), and misc. investments (5%).

Investments in Affiliates: None

Group Affiliation: Sumitomo Life Ins Company

Licensed in: All states except NY

Commenced Business: April 1957

Address: 4125 WESTOWN PARKWAY SUITE 102, WEST DES MOINES, IA 50266

Phone: (425) 256-8000   **Domicile State:** IA   **NAIC Code:** 68608

Data Date	Rating	RACR #1	RACR #2	Total Assets ($mil)	Capital ($mil)	Net Premium ($mil)	Net Income ($mil)
9-18	B	1.76	0.94	37,769.4	2,158.0	-986.3	22.0
9-17	B+	2.05	1.10	36,133.8	2,198.7	3,251.4	61.8
2017	B	1.80	0.98	36,482.8	2,218.9	4,116.2	267.8
2016	B+	1.99	1.07	34,289.2	2,082.4	4,421.8	43.4
2015	B+	2.13	1.16	31,806.9	2,081.5	4,587.1	205.5
2014	B+	2.24	1.23	29,151.7	2,078.3	3,254.2	241.0
2013	B+	2.18	1.19	27,220.0	1,869.7	2,995.6	183.6

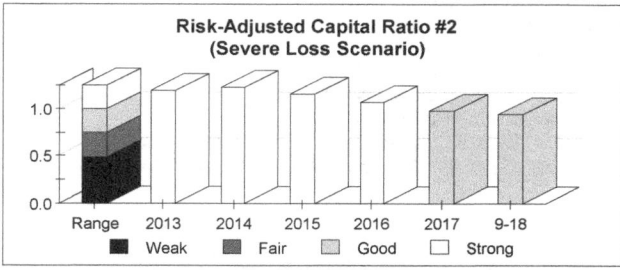

Risk-Adjusted Capital Ratio #2
(Severe Loss Scenario)

TEACHERS INSURANCE & ANNUITY ASSOCIATION OF AMERICA   A+   Excellent

Major Rating Factors: Good quality investment portfolio (6.5 on a scale of 0 to 10) despite substantial holdings of BBB bonds in addition to moderate junk bond exposure. Exposure to mortgages is significant, but the mortgage default rate has been low. Strong capitalization (8.9) based on excellent risk adjusted capital (severe loss scenario). Furthermore, this high level of risk adjusted capital has been consistently maintained over the last five years. Excellent profitability (8.1).

Other Rating Factors: Excellent liquidity (7.0). Excellent overall results on stability tests (7.9) excellent operational trends and excellent risk diversification.

Principal Business: Individual annuities (50%), group retirement contracts (49%), and individual life insurance (2%).

Principal Investments: NonCMO investment grade bonds (42%), CMOs and structured securities (24%), mortgages in good standing (11%), noninv. grade bonds (7%), and misc. investments (16%).

Investments in Affiliates: 11%

Group Affiliation: TIAA

Licensed in: All states, the District of Columbia and Puerto Rico

Commenced Business: May 1918

Address: 730 THIRD AVENUE, NEW YORK, NY 10017

Phone: (212) 490-9000   **Domicile State:** NY   **NAIC Code:** 69345

Data Date	Rating	RACR #1	RACR #2	Total Assets ($mil)	Capital ($mil)	Net Premium ($mil)	Net Income ($mil)
9-18	A+	3.83	2.24	302,803	37,328.4	10,981.0	1,267.8
9-17	A+	4.73	2.54	293,835	37,068.0	11,601.1	349.7
2017	A+	3.83	2.26	295,147	36,336.1	15,386.5	1,020.4
2016	A+	4.92	2.64	282,442	35,583.1	15,184.1	1,489.7
2015	A+	5.24	2.80	270,094	34,735.5	11,950.9	1,254.0
2014	A+	5.63	2.96	262,634	33,919.9	11,185.7	984.3
2013	A+	5.68	3.00	250,494	30,779.1	12,580.2	1,751.5

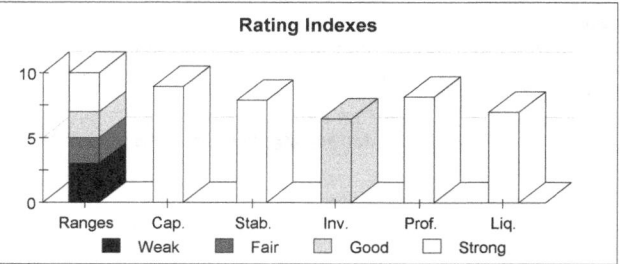

Rating Indexes

TENNESSEE FARMERS LIFE INSURANCE COMPANY * B+ Good

Major Rating Factors: Good overall results on stability tests (6.6 on a scale of 0 to 10). Stability strengths include excellent operational trends and excellent risk diversification. Good quality investment portfolio (5.7) despite mixed results such as: large holdings of BBB rated bonds but moderate junk bond exposure. Good liquidity (6.2).

Other Rating Factors: Fair profitability (4.2) with investment income below regulatory standards in relation to interest assumptions of reserves. Strong capitalization (8.0) based on excellent risk adjusted capital (severe loss scenario).

Principal Business: Individual life insurance (80%), individual annuities (18%), and reinsurance (2%).

Principal Investments: NonCMO investment grade bonds (80%), common & preferred stock (11%), noninv. grade bonds (7%), policy loans (1%), and real estate (1%).

Investments in Affiliates: 3%
Group Affiliation: Tennessee Farmers Ins Companies
Licensed in: TN
Commenced Business: September 1973
Address: 147 Bear Creek Pike, Columbia, TN 38401-2266
Phone: (931) 388-7872 **Domicile State:** TN **NAIC Code:** 82759

Data Date	Rating	RACR #1	RACR #2	Total Assets ($mil)	Capital ($mil)	Net Premium ($mil)	Net Income ($mil)
9-18	B+	2.58	1.66	2,318.6	465.9	129.6	32.6
9-17	B+	2.61	1.68	2,271.7	440.7	136.9	23.5
2017	B+	3.18	1.88	2,276.8	442.1	175.4	28.7
2016	B+	2.51	1.64	2,201.1	419.0	197.9	28.5
2015	A	2.25	1.48	2,090.6	375.6	184.5	25.2
2014	A	2.29	1.50	2,003.7	357.0	170.6	35.2
2013	A	2.24	1.46	1,913.6	328.1	185.5	34.5

Adverse Trends in Operations

Decrease in premium volume from 2016 to 2017 (11%)
Decrease in premium volume from 2013 to 2014 (8%)

TEXAS LIFE INSURANCE COMPANY B- Good

Major Rating Factors: Good overall capitalization (6.3 on a scale of 0 to 10) based on good risk adjusted capital (severe loss scenario). Nevertheless, capital levels have fluctuated during prior years. Good liquidity (5.9) with sufficient resources to handle a spike in claims as well as a significant increase in policy surrenders. Fair overall results on stability tests (4.7) including fair financial strength of affiliated Wilton Re Holdings Ltd.

Other Rating Factors: Fair quality investment portfolio (3.8). Fair profitability (3.0) with investment income below regulatory standards in relation to interest assumptions of reserves.

Principal Business: Individual life insurance (100%).

Principal Investments: NonCMO investment grade bonds (51%), CMOs and structured securities (36%), policy loans (4%), noninv. grade bonds (3%), and misc. investments (5%).

Investments in Affiliates: None
Group Affiliation: Wilton Re Holdings Ltd
Licensed in: All states except NY, PR
Commenced Business: April 1901
Address: P O BOX 830, WACO, TX 76703-0830
Phone: (254) 752-6521 **Domicile State:** TX **NAIC Code:** 69396

Data Date	Rating	RACR #1	RACR #2	Total Assets ($mil)	Capital ($mil)	Net Premium ($mil)	Net Income ($mil)
9-18	B-	1.69	0.91	1,204.2	86.2	192.6	29.5
9-17	B	2.01	1.11	1,158.0	98.1	185.7	29.4
2017	B	1.60	0.90	1,158.1	74.4	254.9	37.0
2016	B	1.70	0.95	1,104.9	79.7	238.5	30.8
2015	B	2.12	1.17	1,076.3	98.4	218.4	50.0
2014	B	1.68	0.92	1,016.6	68.9	208.1	25.6
2013	B	1.96	1.07	952.9	80.4	197.7	33.2

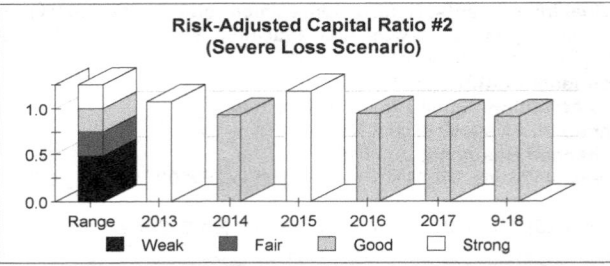

Risk-Adjusted Capital Ratio #2
(Severe Loss Scenario)

THRIVENT LIFE INSURANCE COMPANY B Good

Major Rating Factors: Good capitalization (6.4 on a scale of 0 to 10) based on good risk adjusted capital (severe loss scenario). Good overall results on stability tests (5.5). Stability strengths include excellent operational trends and excellent risk diversification. Fair quality investment portfolio (4.5) with large holdings of BBB rated bonds in addition to junk bond exposure equal to 88% of capital.

Other Rating Factors: Fair profitability (3.0) with investment income below regulatory standards in relation to interest assumptions of reserves. Fair liquidity (4.7).

Principal Business: Individual annuities (94%) and individual life insurance (6%).

Principal Investments: NonCMO investment grade bonds (64%), CMOs and structured securities (28%), noninv. grade bonds (7%), and policy loans (1%).

Investments in Affiliates: 1%
Group Affiliation: Thrivent Financial for Lutherans Grp
Licensed in: All states except GA, ME, MA, NH, NY, NC, RI, VT, WY, PR
Commenced Business: December 1982
Address: 625 4th Ave S MS-Reg Financial, Appleton, WI 54919-0001
Phone: (800) 847-4836 **Domicile State:** WI **NAIC Code:** 97721

Data Date	Rating	RACR #1	RACR #2	Total Assets ($mil)	Capital ($mil)	Net Premium ($mil)	Net Income ($mil)
9-18	B	1.88	0.93	3,939.4	167.2	102.4	11.0
9-17	B	1.89	0.93	3,809.6	161.2	102.2	2.8
2017	B	1.79	0.88	3,840.6	156.6	130.8	8.9
2016	B	1.87	0.92	3,615.3	156.4	154.0	6.7
2015	B	1.91	0.94	3,519.4	149.5	144.9	13.6
2014	B+	2.13	1.05	3,500.4	159.7	115.4	23.3
2013	B+	2.35	1.13	3,468.2	162.6	147.9	25.2

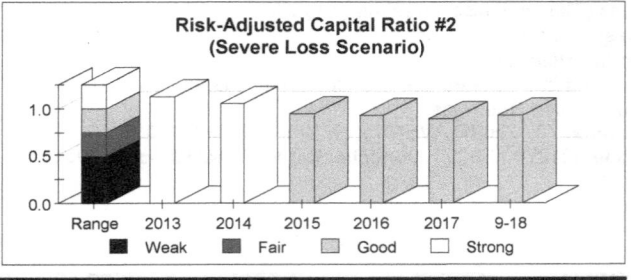

Risk-Adjusted Capital Ratio #2
(Severe Loss Scenario)

TIAA-CREF LIFE INSURANCE COMPANY
B   Good

Major Rating Factors: Good current capitalization (6.5 on a scale of 0 to 10) based on good risk adjusted capital (severe loss scenario), although results have slipped from the excellent range over the last two years. Good quality investment portfolio (5.1) despite mixed results such as: no exposure to mortgages and large holdings of BBB rated bonds but small junk bond holdings. Good overall results on stability tests (6.3) excellent operational trends and excellent risk diversification.

Other Rating Factors: Fair profitability (3.9). Fair liquidity (4.7).

Principal Business: Individual life insurance (46%), individual annuities (41%), group life insurance (12%), and individual health insurance (1%).

Principal Investments: NonCMO investment grade bonds (87%), CMOs and structured securities (12%), and noninv. grade bonds (1%).

Investments in Affiliates: None

Group Affiliation: TIAA

Licensed in: All states except PR

Commenced Business: December 1996

Address: 730 THIRD AVENUE, NEW YORK, NY 10017

Phone: (212) 490-9000 **Domicile State:** NY **NAIC Code:** 60142

Data Date	Rating	RACR #1	RACR #2	Total Assets ($mil)	Capital ($mil)	Net Premium ($mil)	Net Income ($mil)
9-18	B	1.80	0.94	13,320.7	418.8	509.6	1.8
9-17	B	2.02	1.06	13,026.7	413.2	543.6	8.0
2017	B	1.81	0.96	12,556.7	411.5	734.6	29.2
2016	B	2.08	1.10	11,882.5	409.7	692.3	2.6
2015	B	1.93	1.02	10,774.2	362.5	713.4	-39.8
2014	B	2.13	1.13	9,803.2	354.6	675.5	-17.5
2013	B	2.49	1.32	7,988.6	373.8	480.9	-29.3

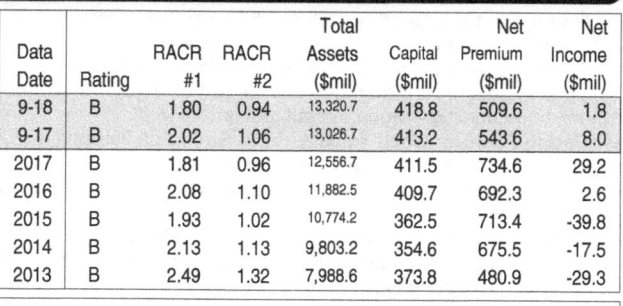

Risk-Adjusted Capital Ratio #2
(Severe Loss Scenario)

Weak   Fair   Good   Strong

TIME INSURANCE COMPANY
C+   Fair

Major Rating Factors: Fair profitability (3.0 on a scale of 0 to 10). Fair overall results on stability tests (3.0) including weak results on operational trends, negative cash flow from operations for 2017. Good quality investment portfolio (6.1) despite mixed results such as: no exposure to mortgages and substantial holdings of BBB bonds but minimal holdings in junk bonds.

Other Rating Factors: Weak liquidity (1.4). Strong capitalization (10.0) based on excellent risk adjusted capital (severe loss scenario).

Principal Business: Individual health insurance (60%), individual life insurance (20%), and group health insurance (20%).

Principal Investments: NonCMO investment grade bonds (43%), CMOs and structured securities (31%), real estate (17%), common & preferred stock (2%), and misc. investments (2%).

Investments in Affiliates: None

Group Affiliation: Assurant Inc

Licensed in: All states except NY, PR

Commenced Business: March 1910

Address: 501 WEST MICHIGAN STREET, MILWAUKEE, WI 53203

Phone: (414) 271-3011 **Domicile State:** WI **NAIC Code:** 69477

Data Date	Rating	RACR #1	RACR #2	Total Assets ($mil)	Capital ($mil)	Net Premium ($mil)	Net Income ($mil)
9-18	C+	5.19	3.24	62.3	36.7	0.4	2.7
9-17	C+	5.57	4.84	108.9	50.1	5.3	35.1
2017	C+	5.90	3.05	82.2	42.5	6.7	44.4
2016	C+	9.64	7.15	219.8	91.0	18.2	37.5
2015	C+	1.44	1.16	1,157.9	471.7	2,031.9	-389.3
2014	C+	1.46	1.15	991.0	389.7	1,755.5	-64.6
2013	B-	1.14	0.88	691.5	212.0	1,269.5	5.6

Adverse Trends in Operations

Decrease in capital during 2017 (53%)
Decrease in premium volume from 2016 to 2017 (63%)
Decrease in premium volume from 2015 to 2016 (99%)
Decrease in capital during 2016 (81%)
Increase in policy surrenders from 2015 to 2016 (738%)

TRANS OCEANIC LIFE INSURANCE COMPANY *
A-   Excellent

Major Rating Factors: Good overall results on stability tests (6.4 on a scale of 0 to 10). Strengths that enhance stability include good operational trends and good risk diversification. Fair quality investment portfolio (4.8). Strong capitalization (8.0) based on excellent risk adjusted capital (severe loss scenario).

Other Rating Factors: Excellent profitability (7.5). Excellent liquidity (8.0).

Principal Business: Individual health insurance (92%) and individual life insurance (7%).

Principal Investments: NonCMO investment grade bonds (53%), common & preferred stock (14%), CMOs and structured securities (12%), real estate (10%), and cash (8%).

Investments in Affiliates: None

Group Affiliation: Trans-Oceanic Group Inc

Licensed in: FL, PR

Commenced Business: December 1959

Address: # 121 ONEILL, SAN JUAN, PR 00918-2404

Phone: (787) 620-2680 **Domicile State:** PR **NAIC Code:** 69523

Data Date	Rating	RACR #1	RACR #2	Total Assets ($mil)	Capital ($mil)	Net Premium ($mil)	Net Income ($mil)
9-18	A-	2.61	1.65	75.3	34.9	22.1	1.6
9-17	A-	2.45	1.55	71.4	32.7	22.7	0.9
2017	A-	2.59	1.65	72.5	33.3	30.1	1.9
2016	A-	2.54	1.61	70.6	32.8	30.7	1.2
2015	A	3.12	1.95	67.4	35.2	30.4	4.7
2014	A	3.09	2.06	65.1	33.7	29.8	4.6
2013	B+	2.67	1.83	58.9	29.5	29.8	6.0

Adverse Trends in Operations

Decrease in premium volume from 2016 to 2017 (2%)
Change in asset mix during 2016 (4%)
Decrease in capital during 2016 (9%)
Increase in policy surrenders from 2015 to 2016 (8879%)

TRANS WORLD ASSURANCE COMPANY *   B+   Good

Major Rating Factors: Good overall results on stability tests (6.7 on a scale of 0 to 10). Stability strengths include excellent operational trends and good risk diversification. Good quality investment portfolio (6.0) despite mixed results such as: minimal exposure to mortgages and large holdings of BBB rated bonds but small junk bond holdings. Good overall profitability (6.8).

Other Rating Factors: Good liquidity (6.5). Strong capitalization (8.4) based on excellent risk adjusted capital (severe loss scenario).

Principal Business: Individual life insurance (73%), individual annuities (15%), and reinsurance (12%).

Principal Investments: NonCMO investment grade bonds (73%), common & preferred stock (9%), mortgages in good standing (8%), noninv. grade bonds (3%), and misc. investments (7%).

Investments in Affiliates: 17%

Group Affiliation: TWA Corp

Licensed in: All states except NH, NY, VT, PR

Commenced Business: December 1963

Address: 885 S El Camino Real, San Mateo, CA 94402

Phone: (850) 456-7401 **Domicile State:** CA **NAIC Code:** 69566

Data Date	Rating	RACR #1	RACR #2	Total Assets ($mil)	Capital ($mil)	Net Premium ($mil)	Net Income ($mil)
9-18	B+	2.49	1.90	344.9	86.3	9.0	1.4
9-17	B+	2.47	1.87	347.4	85.5	8.6	1.3
2017	B+	2.50	1.91	346.8	86.3	11.4	3.1
2016	B	2.52	1.93	354.4	87.0	10.7	4.8
2015	B	2.38	1.83	350.8	83.0	10.1	6.4
2014	B	2.20	1.73	350.1	81.4	11.0	4.6
2013	B	2.06	1.62	347.8	77.1	11.0	4.9

Adverse Trends in Operations

Decrease in asset base during 2017 (2%)
Increase in policy surrenders from 2016 to 2017 (44%)
Decrease in premium volume from 2014 to 2015 (8%)
Increase in policy surrenders from 2013 to 2014 (26%)

TRANSAMERICA ADVISORS LIFE INSURANCE COMPANY   B-   Good

Major Rating Factors: Good overall profitability (5.1 on a scale of 0 to 10). Good liquidity (6.7) with sufficient resources to handle a spike in claims as well as a significant increase in policy surrenders. Fair overall results on stability tests (3.6) including excessive premium growth.

Other Rating Factors: Strong capitalization (10.0) based on excellent risk adjusted capital (severe loss scenario). High quality investment portfolio (7.4).

Principal Business: Individual life insurance (88%), individual annuities (11%), and group retirement contracts (1%).

Principal Investments: NonCMO investment grade bonds (49%), policy loans (26%), CMOs and structured securities (9%), noninv. grade bonds (2%), and mortgages in good standing (1%).

Investments in Affiliates: None

Group Affiliation: AEGON USA Group

Licensed in: All states except NY, PR

Commenced Business: December 1986

Address: 425 West Capitol Ave Ste 1800, Little Rock, AR 72201

Phone: (800) 535-5549 **Domicile State:** AR **NAIC Code:** 79022

Data Date	Rating	RACR #1	RACR #2	Total Assets ($mil)	Capital ($mil)	Net Premium ($mil)	Net Income ($mil)
9-18	B-	8.54	4.40	7,770.6	570.4	5.5	50.2
9-17	B-	10.76	5.44	8,348.4	822.0	4.1	127.5
2017	B-	10.37	5.18	8,261.5	731.1	6.5	194.0
2016	B-	9.00	4.53	8,309.6	696.0	9.3	71.1
2015	B-	9.52	4.77	8,752.6	790.3	11.1	-24.1
2014	B-	10.27	5.14	9,692.5	912.1	9.3	201.5
2013	B-	8.73	4.45	10,135.2	733.4	18.0	196.6

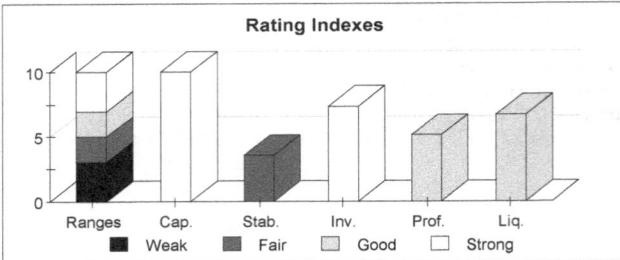

Rating Indexes

Ranges | Cap. | Stab. | Inv. | Prof. | Liq.

■ Weak   ■ Fair   ☐ Good   ☐ Strong

TRANSAMERICA FINANCIAL LIFE INSURANCE COMPANY   B   Good

Major Rating Factors: Good overall results on stability tests (5.1 on a scale of 0 to 10). Stability strengths include good operational trends and excellent risk diversification. Good quality investment portfolio (5.3) despite large holdings of BBB rated bonds in addition to moderate junk bond exposure. Exposure to mortgages is significant, but the mortgage default rate has been low. Good overall profitability (6.5).

Other Rating Factors: Strong capitalization (7.6) based on excellent risk adjusted capital (severe loss scenario). Excellent liquidity (9.3).

Principal Business: Group retirement contracts (82%), reinsurance (9%), individual annuities (5%), individual life insurance (3%), and other lines (2%).

Principal Investments: NonCMO investment grade bonds (50%), mortgages in good standing (15%), CMOs and structured securities (14%), noninv. grade bonds (5%), and policy loans (1%).

Investments in Affiliates: 4%

Group Affiliation: AEGON USA Group

Licensed in: All states except PR

Commenced Business: October 1947

Address: 440 Mamaroneck Avenue, Harrison, NY 10528

Phone: (914) 627-3630 **Domicile State:** NY **NAIC Code:** 70688

Data Date	Rating	RACR #1	RACR #2	Total Assets ($mil)	Capital ($mil)	Net Premium ($mil)	Net Income ($mil)
9-18	B	2.96	1.43	32,230.0	1,054.1	4,294.2	123.5
9-17	B	3.05	1.50	33,707.4	1,114.6	3,862.9	135.1
2017	B	2.97	1.45	34,192.5	1,050.4	5,150.0	158.7
2016	B	3.05	1.49	32,318.4	1,092.3	5,768.8	225.0
2015	B	3.15	1.54	31,535.3	1,167.4	5,807.6	259.9
2014	B	2.69	1.31	31,099.3	957.7	5,434.3	23.9
2013	B	2.71	1.32	29,402.4	934.6	5,239.6	226.1

Adverse Trends in Operations

Decrease in capital during 2017 (4%)
Decrease in premium volume from 2016 to 2017 (11%)
Decrease in capital during 2016 (6%)
Increase in policy surrenders from 2013 to 2014 (29%)

TRANSAMERICA LIFE INSURANCE COMPANY   B   Good

Major Rating Factors: Good quality investment portfolio (6.3 on a scale of 0 to 10) despite substantial holdings of BBB bonds in addition to moderate junk bond exposure. Exposure to mortgages is significant, but the mortgage default rate has been low. Fair current capitalization (4.0) based on mixed results -- excessive policy leverage mitigated by good risk adjusted capital (severe loss scenario), although results have slipped from the excellent range during the last year. Fair overall results on stability tests (4.2) including negative cash flow from operations for 2017.

Other Rating Factors: Excellent profitability (7.4) despite operating losses during the first nine months of 2018. Excellent liquidity (7.2).

Principal Business: Group retirement contracts (50%), individual life insurance (16%), individual annuities (14%), reinsurance (11%), and other lines (9%).

Principal Investments: NonCMO investment grade bonds (51%), mortgages in good standing (10%), CMOs and structured securities (10%), common & preferred stock (7%), and misc. investments (10%).

Investments in Affiliates: 9%

Group Affiliation: AEGON USA Group

Licensed in: All states except NY

Commenced Business: March 1962

Address: 4333 Edgewood Rd NE, Cedar Rapids, IA 52499

Phone: (319) 355-8511 **Domicile State:** IA **NAIC Code:** 86231

Data Date	Rating	RACR #1	RACR #2	Total Assets ($mil)	Capital ($mil)	Net Premium ($mil)	Net Income ($mil)
9-18	B	1.33	0.98	122,999	5,727.4	8,535.5	-59.4
9-17	B	1.40	0.97	129,680	5,065.4	-2,970.4	258.2
2017	B	1.47	1.07	125,308	5,411.7	-3,259.8	381.4
2016	B	1.44	0.99	131,790	5,234.8	13,943.3	471.1
2015	B	1.58	1.06	126,036	5,458.6	14,777.9	-250.9
2014	B-	2.09	1.34	124,486	5,835.3	15,782.9	233.6
2013	B-	1.63	1.02	115,276	4,717.9	15,446.5	57.5

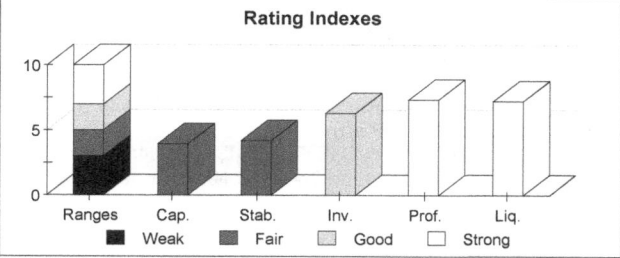

Rating Indexes

TRANSAMERICA PREMIER LIFE INSURANCE COMPANY   C+   Fair

Major Rating Factors: Fair profitability (3.6 on a scale of 0 to 10) with investment income below regulatory standards in relation to interest assumptions of reserves. Fair overall results on stability tests (3.3). Good current capitalization (6.3) based on good risk adjusted capital (severe loss scenario), although results have slipped from the excellent range over the last two years.

Other Rating Factors: Good quality investment portfolio (5.4). Good liquidity (6.4).

Principal Business: Reinsurance (38%), individual life insurance (32%), individual annuities (14%), group health insurance (10%), and other lines (7%).

Principal Investments: NonCMO investment grade bonds (61%), CMOs and structured securities (10%), mortgages in good standing (9%), noninv. grade bonds (5%), and misc. investments (9%).

Investments in Affiliates: 3%

Group Affiliation: AEGON USA Group

Licensed in: All states except NY

Commenced Business: May 1860

Address: 4333 Edgewood Rd NE, Cedar Rapids, IA 52499

Phone: (319) 355-8511 **Domicile State:** IA **NAIC Code:** 66281

Data Date	Rating	RACR #1	RACR #2	Total Assets ($mil)	Capital ($mil)	Net Premium ($mil)	Net Income ($mil)
9-18	C+	1.59	0.91	50,487.4	1,821.9	2,666.1	272.5
9-17	C+	2.03	1.05	41,444.3	1,494.5	-364.5	274.8
2017	C+	1.56	0.86	49,940.8	1,593.3	2,250.5	-308.0
2016	C+	1.98	1.07	41,515.6	1,677.7	3,298.0	338.9
2015	C+	1.41	0.81	41,649.4	1,508.0	3,094.9	213.8
2014	C+	1.53	0.88	42,248.2	1,774.7	6,292.5	350.7
2013	C+	1.58	0.78	31,879.6	971.2	1,586.3	166.9

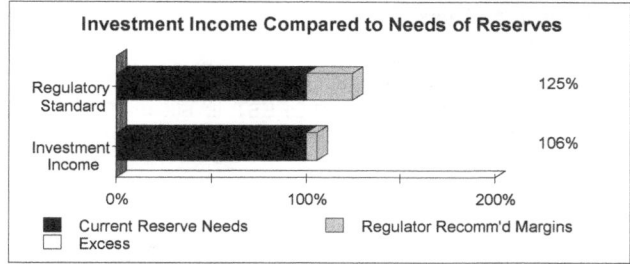

Investment Income Compared to Needs of Reserves

TRIPLE S VIDA INCORPORATED   B-   Good

Major Rating Factors: Good overall results on stability tests (5.2 on a scale of 0 to 10) despite fair risk adjusted capital in prior years. Other stability subfactors include excellent operational trends and good risk diversification. Good capitalization (5.2) based on good risk adjusted capital (moderate loss scenario). Good overall profitability (6.5).

Other Rating Factors: Fair quality investment portfolio (4.1). Fair liquidity (3.9).

Principal Business: Individual life insurance (55%), individual health insurance (32%), group life insurance (5%), group health insurance (4%), and other lines (4%).

Principal Investments: NonCMO investment grade bonds (79%), common & preferred stock (17%), policy loans (2%), and cash (2%).

Investments in Affiliates: 1%

Group Affiliation: Triple-S Management Corp

Licensed in: PR

Commenced Business: September 1964

Address: 1052 Munoz Rivera, San Juan, PR 927

Phone: (787) 758-4888 **Domicile State:** PR **NAIC Code:** 73814

Data Date	Rating	RACR #1	RACR #2	Total Assets ($mil)	Capital ($mil)	Net Premium ($mil)	Net Income ($mil)
9-18	B-	1.12	0.73	650.2	60.7	136.0	4.8
9-17	B-	1.14	0.75	637.5	59.6	129.0	3.9
2017	B-	1.27	0.83	637.9	67.1	169.6	10.9
2016	B-	1.16	0.75	601.8	62.0	170.9	9.5
2015	B-	N/A	N/A	572.2	59.1	161.0	5.3
2014	B-	1.19	0.81	550.3	64.8	158.3	12.3
2013	B-	1.00	0.69	512.7	61.1	147.3	6.0

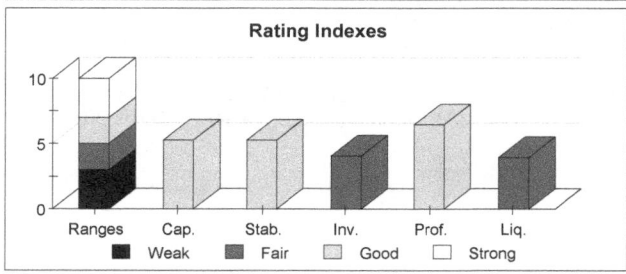

Rating Indexes

TRUSTMARK INSURANCE COMPANY *   B+   Good

Major Rating Factors: Good overall profitability (6.9 on a scale of 0 to 10). Good liquidity (6.9) with sufficient resources to handle a spike in claims as well as a significant increase in policy surrenders. Good overall results on stability tests (6.8). Stability strengths include excellent operational trends and excellent risk diversification.

Other Rating Factors: Fair quality investment portfolio (4.8). Strong capitalization (7.9) based on excellent risk adjusted capital (severe loss scenario).

Principal Business: Group life insurance (44%), group health insurance (26%), individual health insurance (20%), individual life insurance (9%), and reinsurance (1%).

Principal Investments: NonCMO investment grade bonds (39%), CMOs and structured securities (27%), common & preferred stock (10%), noninv. grade bonds (6%), and misc. investments (12%).

Investments in Affiliates: None

Group Affiliation: Trustmark Group Inc

Licensed in: All states, the District of Columbia and Puerto Rico

Commenced Business: January 1913

Address: 400 FIELD DRIVE, LAKE FOREST, IL 60045-2581

Phone: (847) 615-1500   **Domicile State:** IL   **NAIC Code:** 61425

Data Date	Rating	RACR #1	RACR #2	Total Assets ($mil)	Capital ($mil)	Net Premium ($mil)	Net Income ($mil)
9-18	B+	2.83	1.60	1,606.0	342.6	271.1	13.6
9-17	B+	2.83	1.60	1,532.5	317.5	253.3	19.8
2017	B+	3.12	1.77	1,548.0	323.8	343.3	22.6
2016	B+	3.12	1.77	1,460.2	294.8	322.0	21.0
2015	B+	3.15	1.77	1,406.8	286.7	293.6	16.3
2014	B+	3.02	1.75	1,393.5	287.7	312.2	18.9
2013	B+	3.24	1.89	1,369.8	297.8	294.0	30.0

Adverse Trends in Operations

Decrease in premium volume from 2014 to 2015 (6%)
Decrease in capital during 2014 (3%)

TRUSTMARK LIFE INSURANCE COMPANY *   B+   Good

Major Rating Factors: Good liquidity (6.9 on a scale of 0 to 10) with sufficient resources to handle a spike in claims. Good overall results on stability tests (6.5). Strengths include good financial support from affiliation with Trustmark Group Inc, good operational trends and excellent risk diversification. Fair quality investment portfolio (4.8).

Other Rating Factors: Strong capitalization (10.0) based on excellent risk adjusted capital (severe loss scenario). Excellent profitability (7.4).

Principal Business: Group health insurance (96%) and group life insurance (4%).

Principal Investments: NonCMO investment grade bonds (69%), noninv. grade bonds (11%), CMOs and structured securities (9%), and common & preferred stock (5%).

Investments in Affiliates: None

Group Affiliation: Trustmark Group Inc

Licensed in: All states except PR

Commenced Business: February 1925

Address: 400 FIELD DRIVE, LAKE FOREST, IL 60045-2581

Phone: (847) 615-1500   **Domicile State:** IL   **NAIC Code:** 62863

Data Date	Rating	RACR #1	RACR #2	Total Assets ($mil)	Capital ($mil)	Net Premium ($mil)	Net Income ($mil)
9-18	B+	7.43	4.50	330.1	179.6	94.3	14.4
9-17	B+	7.86	5.00	320.1	178.0	85.6	13.5
2017	B+	7.49	4.70	303.0	164.4	112.6	17.4
2016	B+	6.63	4.33	308.6	162.7	137.4	16.7
2015	B+	5.62	3.77	321.3	159.8	163.7	8.4
2014	B+	4.41	3.01	353.2	162.6	206.9	14.0
2013	B+	3.61	2.53	365.5	160.6	264.5	13.9

Trustmark Group Inc
Composite Group Rating: B+
Largest Group Members

	Assets ($mil)	Rating
TRUSTMARK INS CO	1548	B+
TRUSTMARK LIFE INS CO	303	B+
TRUSTMARK LIFE INS CO OF NEW YORK	9	B

UNICARE LIFE & HEALTH INSURANCE COMPANY   B-   Good

Major Rating Factors: Good overall capitalization (5.9 on a scale of 0 to 10) based on mixed results -- excessive policy leverage mitigated by excellent risk adjusted capital (severe loss scenario). Nevertheless, capital levels have fluctuated during prior years. Good overall profitability (6.2). Excellent expense controls. Good overall results on stability tests (5.2) good operational trends, excellent risk adjusted capital for prior years and good risk diversification.

Other Rating Factors: Fair quality investment portfolio (3.8). Fair liquidity (4.5).

Principal Business: Reinsurance (49%), group life insurance (35%), group health insurance (11%), and individual health insurance (5%).

Principal Investments: NonCMO investment grade bonds (86%) and noninv. grade bonds (13%).

Investments in Affiliates: None

Group Affiliation: Anthem Inc

Licensed in: All states, the District of Columbia and Puerto Rico

Commenced Business: December 1980

Address: 120 MONUMENT CIRCLE, INDIANAPOLIS, IN 46204

Phone: (877) 864-2273   **Domicile State:** IN   **NAIC Code:** 80314

Data Date	Rating	RACR #1	RACR #2	Total Assets ($mil)	Capital ($mil)	Net Premium ($mil)	Net Income ($mil)
9-18	B-	1.89	1.43	282.8	79.7	255.2	11.7
9-17	B-	1.82	1.37	305.5	70.8	234.5	15.6
2017	B-	2.12	1.60	283.9	70.1	312.7	8.8
2016	B-	2.81	2.12	306.0	88.1	275.2	28.3
2015	B-	3.06	2.27	373.8	108.4	291.9	21.5
2014	B-	1.77	1.32	413.3	63.8	329.6	25.0
2013	B	3.13	2.32	469.1	126.3	321.7	43.7

Policy Leverage

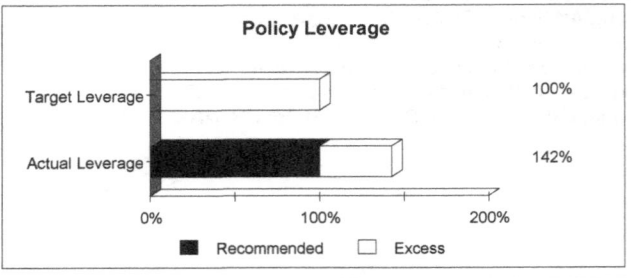

Target Leverage — 100%
Actual Leverage — 142%

0%   100%   200%

■ Recommended   □ Excess

UNIFIED LIFE INSURANCE COMPANY   B   Good

Major Rating Factors: Good overall profitability (6.8 on a scale of 0 to 10). Return on equity has been fair, averaging 8.6%. Good liquidity (5.1) with sufficient resources to handle a spike in claims as well as a significant increase in policy surrenders. Good overall results on stability tests (6.3) despite negative cash flow from operations for 2017 good operational trends and good risk diversification.

Other Rating Factors: Fair quality investment portfolio (4.6). Strong capitalization (7.5) based on excellent risk adjusted capital (severe loss scenario).

Principal Business: Group health insurance (69%), individual health insurance (14%), reinsurance (9%), and individual life insurance (8%).

Principal Investments: NonCMO investment grade bonds (63%), CMOs and structured securities (18%), policy loans (5%), noninv. grade bonds (5%), and misc. investments (3%).

Investments in Affiliates: None

Group Affiliation: William M Buchanan Group

Licensed in: All states except NY, PR

Commenced Business: May 2001

Address: CSC-Lawyers Inc Serv 211 E 7th, Dallas, TX 75201-3136

Phone: (877) 492-4678 **Domicile State:** TX **NAIC Code:** 11121

Data Date	Rating	RACR #1	RACR #2	Total Assets ($mil)	Capital ($mil)	Net Premium ($mil)	Net Income ($mil)
9-18	B	2.15	1.30	210.9	26.7	35.7	1.2
9-17	B	1.94	1.17	213.5	25.3	36.0	-0.6
2017	B	2.03	1.22	208.0	25.0	46.0	0.1
2016	B	1.78	1.09	219.0	25.9	60.4	1.2
2015	B	1.86	1.14	184.1	21.8	46.7	0.0
2014	B	2.55	1.55	183.5	24.9	33.7	2.7
2013	B	2.29	1.30	179.6	22.8	30.4	3.2

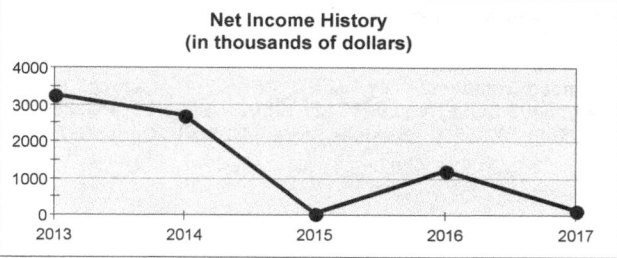

Net Income History
(in thousands of dollars)

UNIMERICA INSURANCE COMPANY   B   Good

Major Rating Factors: Good overall capitalization (5.8 on a scale of 0 to 10) based on mixed results -- excessive policy leverage mitigated by excellent risk adjusted capital (severe loss scenario). However, capital levels have fluctuated somewhat during past years. Good liquidity (5.9) with sufficient resources to handle a spike in claims. Fair overall results on stability tests (4.7) including fair financial strength of affiliated UnitedHealth Group Inc.

Other Rating Factors: High quality investment portfolio (8.5). Excellent profitability (8.7).

Principal Business: Reinsurance (59%), group health insurance (40%), and group life insurance (1%).

Principal Investments: NonCMO investment grade bonds (83%) and CMOs and structured securities (15%).

Investments in Affiliates: None

Group Affiliation: UnitedHealth Group Inc

Licensed in: All states except NY, PR

Commenced Business: December 1980

Address: 10701 WEST RESEARCH DRIVE, MILWAUKEE, WI 53226-0649

Phone: (952) 979-6128 **Domicile State:** WI **NAIC Code:** 91529

Data Date	Rating	RACR #1	RACR #2	Total Assets ($mil)	Capital ($mil)	Net Premium ($mil)	Net Income ($mil)
9-18	B	3.25	2.56	453.7	213.6	323.1	45.3
9-17	B	1.67	1.35	473.4	169.9	652.3	14.0
2017	B	1.73	1.39	502.5	186.1	874.3	31.4
2016	B	1.43	1.15	476.4	154.7	877.0	21.1
2015	B	1.99	1.59	435.9	167.7	669.4	65.7
2014	B	2.54	2.02	415.0	187.8	582.4	76.9
2013	B	2.82	2.24	410.1	181.1	489.2	43.3

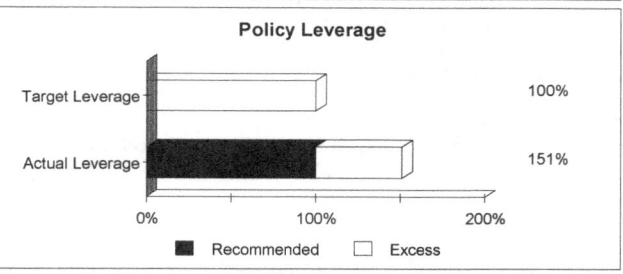

Policy Leverage

UNION FIDELITY LIFE INSURANCE COMPANY   E   Very Weak

Major Rating Factors: Low quality investment portfolio (2.8 on a scale of 0 to 10) containing large holdings of BBB rated bonds in addition to significant exposure to junk bonds. Weak profitability (1.4) with operating losses during the first nine months of 2018. Weak overall results on stability tests (0.1) including weak risk adjusted capital in prior years, negative cash flow from operations for 2017.

Other Rating Factors: Good capitalization (5.1) based on good risk adjusted capital (moderate loss scenario). Excellent liquidity (7.8).

Principal Business: Reinsurance (90%), group health insurance (5%), group life insurance (3%), individual life insurance (1%), and individual health insurance (1%).

Principal Investments: NonCMO investment grade bonds (78%), CMOs and structured securities (11%), mortgages in good standing (4%), and noninv. grade bonds (3%).

Investments in Affiliates: 1%

Group Affiliation: General Electric Corp Group

Licensed in: All states except NY, PR

Commenced Business: February 1926

Address: 7101 College Blvd Ste 1400, Overland Park, KS 66210

Phone: (913) 982-3700 **Domicile State:** KS **NAIC Code:** 62596

Data Date	Rating	RACR #1	RACR #2	Total Assets ($mil)	Capital ($mil)	Net Premium ($mil)	Net Income ($mil)
9-18	E	1.04	0.52	20,226.2	485.8	185.7	-49.9
9-17	C	1.58	0.79	19,526.8	748.4	192.4	-24.0
2017	E	1.14	0.57	20,435.4	536.6	263.9	-1,210.0
2016	D+	1.53	0.76	19,644.5	765.8	266.4	-65.0
2015	D+	0.89	0.46	19,365.0	428.3	276.3	-60.9
2014	D+	1.04	0.54	19,673.7	518.4	285.9	-280.8
2013	D+	1.07	0.55	19,510.6	569.3	305.7	6.3

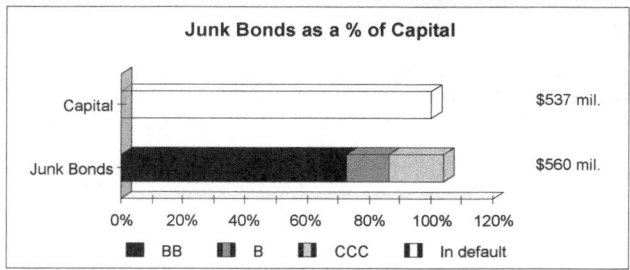

Junk Bonds as a % of Capital

UNION LABOR LIFE INSURANCE COMPANY
B   **Good**

Major Rating Factors: Good overall profitability (6.6 on a scale of 0 to 10). Good overall results on stability tests (6.3). Stability strengths include excellent operational trends and excellent risk diversification. Strong capitalization (7.6) based on excellent risk adjusted capital (severe loss scenario). Capital levels have been relatively consistent over the last five years.

Other Rating Factors: High quality investment portfolio (7.3). Excellent liquidity (7.6).

Principal Business: Group health insurance (55%), group life insurance (30%), reinsurance (9%), and group retirement contracts (5%).

Principal Investments: NonCMO investment grade bonds (54%), CMOs and structured securities (26%), common & preferred stock (6%), mortgages in good standing (3%), and noninv. grade bonds (1%).

Investments in Affiliates: 3%

Group Affiliation: ULLICO Inc

Licensed in: All states except PR

Commenced Business: May 1927

Address: 8403 COLESVILLE ROAD, SILVER SPRING, MD 20910

Phone: (202) 682-0900 **Domicile State:** MD **NAIC Code:** 69744

Data Date	Rating	RACR #1	RACR #2	Total Assets ($mil)	Capital ($mil)	Net Premium ($mil)	Net Income ($mil)
9-18	B	2.15	1.38	3,872.3	104.5	113.6	8.7
9-17	B	2.01	1.30	3,544.9	93.9	104.0	6.4
2017	B	2.03	1.31	3,614.2	94.2	138.1	9.3
2016	B-	2.04	1.32	3,354.7	89.2	124.2	10.2
2015	B-	1.52	1.07	3,238.8	79.6	138.3	3.5
2014	B-	1.42	1.00	3,337.5	76.4	142.1	1.4
2013	B-	1.66	1.20	2,813.7	87.7	139.5	-11.1

Adverse Trends in Operations

Decrease in premium volume from 2015 to 2016 (10%)
Decrease in premium volume from 2014 to 2015 (3%)
Decrease in asset base during 2015 (3%)
Decrease in capital during 2014 (13%)

UNION SECURITY INSURANCE COMPANY
B   **Good**

Major Rating Factors: Good quality investment portfolio (5.4 on a scale of 0 to 10) despite mixed results such as: large holdings of BBB rated bonds but moderate junk bond exposure. Good overall profitability (5.2). Fair overall results on stability tests (4.2) including negative cash flow from operations for 2017.

Other Rating Factors: Fair liquidity (4.5). Strong capitalization (7.8) based on excellent risk adjusted capital (severe loss scenario).

Principal Business: Group health insurance (67%), group life insurance (18%), individual health insurance (8%), individual life insurance (5%), and individual annuities (1%).

Principal Investments: NonCMO investment grade bonds (67%), mortgages in good standing (8%), CMOs and structured securities (8%), common & preferred stock (7%), and misc. investments (10%).

Investments in Affiliates: None

Group Affiliation: Assurant Inc

Licensed in: All states except NY, PR

Commenced Business: September 1910

Address: 2323 GRAND BOULEVARD, TOPEKA, KS 66614

Phone: (651) 361-4000 **Domicile State:** KS **NAIC Code:** 70408

Data Date	Rating	RACR #1	RACR #2	Total Assets ($mil)	Capital ($mil)	Net Premium ($mil)	Net Income ($mil)
9-18	B	2.91	1.52	2,758.2	134.3	2.9	70.3
9-17	B	2.61	1.37	2,690.2	129.1	3.3	81.9
2017	B	2.37	1.23	2,698.7	113.9	4.1	106.2
2016	B	3.14	1.62	2,690.3	158.5	-1,468.9	481.7
2015	B	1.91	1.26	4,711.8	428.4	1,028.4	71.5
2014	B	1.82	1.18	4,937.1	415.7	1,016.0	67.3
2013	B	1.88	1.21	5,085.8	434.7	986.2	85.4

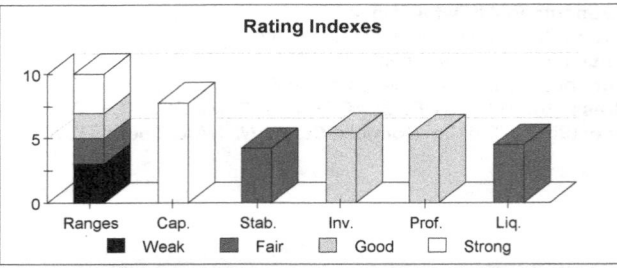

Rating Indexes

Ranges | Cap. | Stab. | Inv. | Prof. | Liq.

■ Weak ■ Fair ☐ Good ☐ Strong

UNION SECURITY LIFE INSURANCE COMPANY OF NEW YORK
C+   **Fair**

Major Rating Factors: Fair overall results on stability tests (3.0 on a scale of 0 to 10) including weak results on operational trends. Good overall profitability (6.2). Strong capitalization (10.0) based on excellent risk adjusted capital (severe loss scenario).

Other Rating Factors: High quality investment portfolio (8.1). Excellent liquidity (9.5).

Principal Business: Group health insurance (55%), individual health insurance (30%), group life insurance (9%), credit health insurance (2%), and other lines (4%).

Principal Investments: NonCMO investment grade bonds (71%), CMOs and structured securities (22%), noninv. grade bonds (2%), and cash (2%).

Investments in Affiliates: None

Group Affiliation: Assurant Inc

Licensed in: NY

Commenced Business: April 1974

Address: 212 HIGHBRIDGE STREET SUITE D, FAYETTEVILLE, NY 13066

Phone: (315) 637-4232 **Domicile State:** NY **NAIC Code:** 81477

Data Date	Rating	RACR #1	RACR #2	Total Assets ($mil)	Capital ($mil)	Net Premium ($mil)	Net Income ($mil)
9-18	C+	6.40	5.76	60.5	47.8	0.6	3.8
9-17	C+	6.51	5.86	74.4	52.8	0.7	4.7
2017	C+	7.06	6.36	66.7	52.7	1.0	6.3
2016	B-	8.30	7.47	81.0	67.4	-72.0	22.0
2015	B+	4.34	3.91	128.3	39.5	21.6	3.3
2014	B+	4.66	4.19	138.7	42.8	23.8	5.6
2013	B+	4.44	4.00	147.7	40.9	27.4	5.4

Adverse Trends in Operations

Change in asset mix during 2017 (11%)
Decrease in capital during 2017 (22%)
Change in asset mix during 2016 (10%)
Decrease in asset base during 2016 (37%)
Decrease in premium volume from 2015 to 2016 (433%)

UNITED AMERICAN INSURANCE COMPANY | B- | Good

Major Rating Factors: Fair current capitalization (4.9 on a scale of 0 to 10) based on fair risk adjusted capital (severe loss scenario), although results have slipped from the excellent range during the last year. Fair overall results on stability tests (4.4). Good quality investment portfolio (6.2).

Other Rating Factors: Good overall profitability (6.6). Good liquidity (5.6).

Principal Business: Individual health insurance (53%), group health insurance (35%), reinsurance (5%), individual annuities (4%), and individual life insurance (3%).

Principal Investments: NonCMO investment grade bonds (72%), common & preferred stock (8%), CMOs and structured securities (4%), noninv. grade bonds (3%), and policy loans (1%).

Investments in Affiliates: 10%

Group Affiliation: Torchmark Corp

Licensed in: All states except NY, PR

Commenced Business: August 1981

Address: 10306 REGENCY PARKWAY DR, OMAHA, NE 68114

Phone: (972) 529-5085 **Domicile State:** NE **NAIC Code:** 92916

Data Date	Rating	RACR #1	RACR #2	Total Assets ($mil)	Capital ($mil)	Net Premium ($mil)	Net Income ($mil)
9-18	B-	0.98	0.74	731.5	94.8	364.6	25.7
9-17	B-	1.65	1.23	1,006.6	206.2	359.5	65.8
2017	B-	1.56	1.17	766.7	162.0	481.4	88.1
2016	B-	1.07	0.78	1,563.3	157.7	706.0	37.1
2015	B-	1.24	0.90	1,559.7	192.7	815.3	80.1
2014	B-	1.01	0.74	1,694.9	178.4	870.9	29.5
2013	B	1.27	0.91	1,683.4	211.6	745.1	58.1

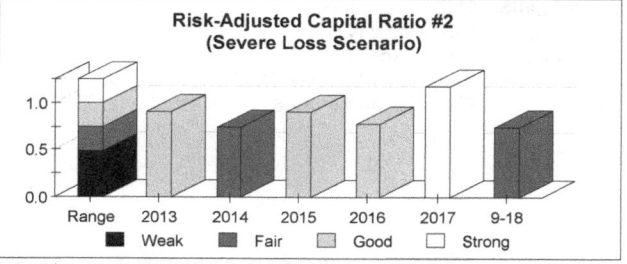

Risk-Adjusted Capital Ratio #2
(Severe Loss Scenario)

UNITED FARM FAMILY LIFE INSURANCE COMPANY * | A | Excellent

Major Rating Factors: Good quality investment portfolio (6.9 on a scale of 0 to 10) despite significant exposure to mortgages . Mortgage default rate has been low. large holdings of BBB rated bonds in addition to no exposure to junk bonds. Good overall profitability (5.9) although investment income, in comparison to reserve requirements, is below regulatory standards. Good liquidity (5.9).

Other Rating Factors: Strong capitalization (8.5) based on excellent risk adjusted capital (severe loss scenario). Excellent overall results on stability tests (7.4) excellent operational trends and excellent risk diversification.

Principal Business: Individual life insurance (77%), reinsurance (16%), and individual annuities (6%).

Principal Investments: NonCMO investment grade bonds (67%), mortgages in good standing (15%), CMOs and structured securities (9%), policy loans (4%), and common & preferred stock (3%).

Investments in Affiliates: 2%

Group Affiliation: Indiana Farm Bureau

Licensed in: AZ, CA, IL, IN, IA, MD, MA, NH, NJ, NC, ND, OH, PA

Commenced Business: May 1964

Address: 225 South East Street, Indianapolis, IN 46202

Phone: (317) 692-7200 **Domicile State:** IN **NAIC Code:** 69892

Data Date	Rating	RACR #1	RACR #2	Total Assets ($mil)	Capital ($mil)	Net Premium ($mil)	Net Income ($mil)
9-18	A	3.48	2.03	2,348.2	337.5	100.9	13.0
9-17	A	3.32	1.98	2,312.3	327.8	102.6	10.4
2017	A	3.43	2.01	2,321.9	326.3	136.5	18.2
2016	A	3.24	1.94	2,271.1	316.0	134.8	16.0
2015	A	3.21	1.92	2,203.5	301.5	136.5	16.6
2014	A	3.12	1.88	2,145.3	286.6	141.8	16.9
2013	A	3.07	1.84	2,087.0	275.2	144.3	12.8

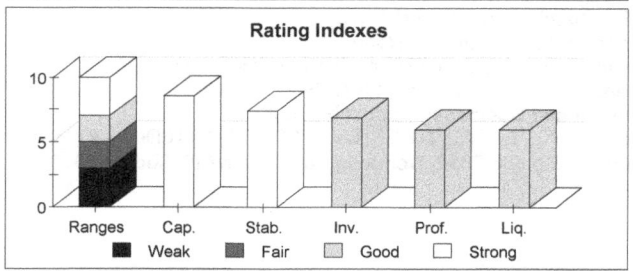

Rating Indexes

UNITED FIDELITY LIFE INSURANCE COMPANY | C | Fair

Major Rating Factors: Fair quality investment portfolio (3.1 on a scale of 0 to 10). Fair overall results on stability tests (4.0) including fair risk adjusted capital in prior years. Good current capitalization (5.4) based on good risk adjusted capital (severe loss scenario) reflecting some improvement over results in 2016.

Other Rating Factors: Good liquidity (6.8). Excellent profitability (7.5).

Principal Business: Individual life insurance (91%), individual annuities (5%), individual health insurance (2%), and reinsurance (2%).

Principal Investments: Common & preferred stock (82%), CMOs and structured securities (7%), nonCMO investment grade bonds (6%), policy loans (1%), and mortgages in good standing (1%).

Investments in Affiliates: 79%

Group Affiliation: Americo Life Inc

Licensed in: All states except CT, FL, HI, ME, MI, MN, NH, NJ, NY, VT, PR

Commenced Business: September 1977

Address: PO Box 139061, Dallas, TX 75313-9061

Phone: (816) 391-2000 **Domicile State:** TX **NAIC Code:** 87645

Data Date	Rating	RACR #1	RACR #2	Total Assets ($mil)	Capital ($mil)	Net Premium ($mil)	Net Income ($mil)
9-18	C	0.82	0.80	828.1	558.0	4.6	52.4
9-17	C	0.79	0.77	791.2	505.2	4.7	30.2
2017	C	0.77	0.75	802.9	520.0	6.3	29.6
2016	C	0.75	0.73	766.5	473.4	7.0	31.9
2015	C	0.75	0.73	755.3	450.6	7.5	52.5
2014	C	0.74	0.72	779.6	464.2	7.9	44.2
2013	C	0.74	0.72	778.2	450.2	8.6	44.2

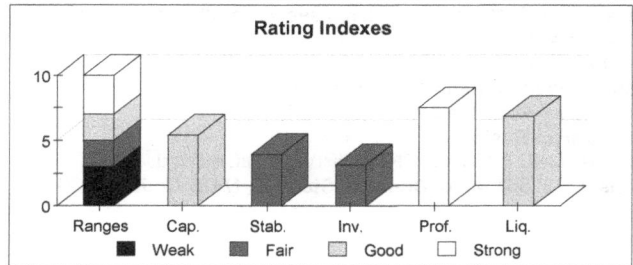

Rating Indexes

UNITED HEALTHCARE INSURANCE COMPANY
C   **Fair**

Major Rating Factors: Fair current capitalization (4.5 on a scale of 0 to 10) based on mixed results -- excessive policy leverage mitigated by good risk adjusted capital (severe loss scenario) reflecting some improvement over results in 2013. Fair overall results on stability tests (3.9) including fair risk adjusted capital in prior years. Good quality investment portfolio (6.4).

Other Rating Factors: Weak liquidity (1.9). Excellent profitability (9.0).

Principal Business: Group health insurance (85%), individual health insurance (10%), and reinsurance (5%).

Principal Investments: NonCMO investment grade bonds (53%), common & preferred stock (19%), CMOs and structured securities (15%), noninv. grade bonds (4%), and misc. investments (3%).

Investments in Affiliates: 15%

Group Affiliation: UnitedHealth Group Inc

Licensed in: All states except NY

Commenced Business: April 1972

Address: 185 ASYLUM STREET, HARTFORD, CT 06103-3408

Phone: (877) 832-7734 **Domicile State:** CT **NAIC Code:** 79413

Data Date	Rating	RACR #1	RACR #2	Total Assets ($mil)	Capital ($mil)	Net Premium ($mil)	Net Income ($mil)
9-18	C	0.96	0.80	19,448.9	6,211.7	40,911.5	1,718.1
9-17	C	0.85	0.72	20,075.9	5,039.7	38,027.9	1,692.6
2017	C	0.89	0.75	19,617.5	6,355.2	50,538.6	2,599.6
2016	C	0.79	0.67	17,922.6	5,250.4	44,379.2	1,924.6
2015	C	0.89	0.75	15,791.2	5,589.7	41,950.2	1,930.3
2014	C	0.82	0.69	15,113.4	5,595.8	43,936.4	2,658.1
2013	C	0.76	0.64	14,512.6	5,039.5	44,680.4	2,384.0

Policy Leverage

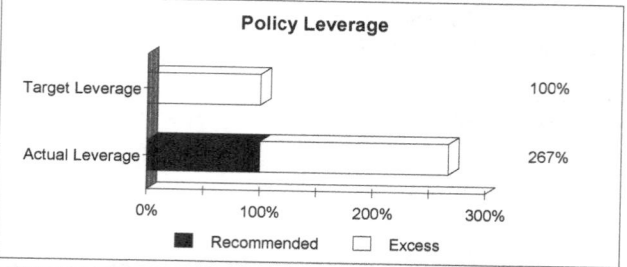

Target Leverage — 100%
Actual Leverage — 267%

0%   100%   200%   300%

■ Recommended   □ Excess

UNITED HERITAGE LIFE INSURANCE COMPANY
B   **Good**

Major Rating Factors: Good overall results on stability tests (5.7 on a scale of 0 to 10). Stability strengths include excellent operational trends and excellent risk diversification. Fair quality investment portfolio (4.0) with large holdings of BBB rated bonds in addition to junk bond exposure equal to 77% of capital. Fair liquidity (4.7).

Other Rating Factors: Strong capitalization (7.2) based on excellent risk adjusted capital (severe loss scenario). Excellent profitability (7.7).

Principal Business: Individual life insurance (68%), individual annuities (19%), group health insurance (6%), group life insurance (6%), and group retirement contracts (1%).

Principal Investments: NonCMO investment grade bonds (76%), noninv. grade bonds (9%), CMOs and structured securities (7%), common & preferred stock (3%), and misc. investments (5%).

Investments in Affiliates: None

Group Affiliation: United Heritage Mutual Holding Co

Licensed in: All states except NY, PR

Commenced Business: September 1935

Address: 707 E UNITED HERITAGE COURT, MERIDIAN, ID 83642-7785

Phone: (208) 466-7856 **Domicile State:** ID **NAIC Code:** 63983

Data Date	Rating	RACR #1	RACR #2	Total Assets ($mil)	Capital ($mil)	Net Premium ($mil)	Net Income ($mil)
9-18	B	2.38	1.15	597.7	65.9	59.3	3.7
9-17	B	2.63	1.30	570.9	63.3	56.4	3.9
2017	B	2.54	1.26	574.2	63.3	75.4	5.6
2016	B	2.65	1.32	559.1	62.0	70.5	4.2
2015	B	2.52	1.27	541.6	59.3	83.1	4.6
2014	B	2.69	1.38	522.6	58.0	63.0	6.3
2013	B-	2.71	1.40	520.1	55.4	68.1	5.9

Adverse Trends in Operations

Decrease in premium volume from 2015 to 2016 (15%)
Change in premium mix from 2014 to 2015 (4.5%)
Decrease in premium volume from 2013 to 2014 (8%)

UNITED INSURANCE COMPANY OF AMERICA
B-   **Good**

Major Rating Factors: Good quality investment portfolio (5.1 on a scale of 0 to 10) despite mixed results such as: large holdings of BBB rated bonds but junk bond exposure equal to 75% of capital. Good overall profitability (6.5). Good liquidity (5.0) with sufficient resources to handle a spike in claims as well as a significant increase in policy surrenders.

Other Rating Factors: Good overall results on stability tests (5.3) excellent operational trends, good risk adjusted capital for prior years and excellent risk diversification. Strong capitalization (7.2) based on excellent risk adjusted capital (severe loss scenario).

Principal Business: Reinsurance (53%), individual life insurance (45%), and individual health insurance (2%).

Principal Investments: NonCMO investment grade bonds (63%), noninv. grade bonds (10%), CMOs and structured securities (8%), policy loans (8%), and misc. investments (11%).

Investments in Affiliates: 3%

Group Affiliation: Kemper Corporation

Licensed in: All states except AK, NY, PR

Commenced Business: April 1928

Address: ONE EAST WACKER DRIVE, CHICAGO, IL 60601

Phone: (312) 661-4500 **Domicile State:** IL **NAIC Code:** 69930

Data Date	Rating	RACR #1	RACR #2	Total Assets ($mil)	Capital ($mil)	Net Premium ($mil)	Net Income ($mil)
9-18	B-	1.93	1.14	3,905.4	453.9	274.8	126.1
9-17	B-	1.76	1.04	3,823.5	430.4	275.9	57.0
2017	B-	1.82	1.04	3,833.6	421.8	362.5	84.8
2016	B-	1.68	0.99	3,776.0	407.4	359.9	32.0
2015	B-	1.59	0.93	3,675.8	405.4	364.2	64.8
2014	B-	1.67	1.00	3,644.8	439.4	362.7	122.5
2013	B-	1.53	0.95	3,591.7	436.1	375.0	79.0

Rating Indexes

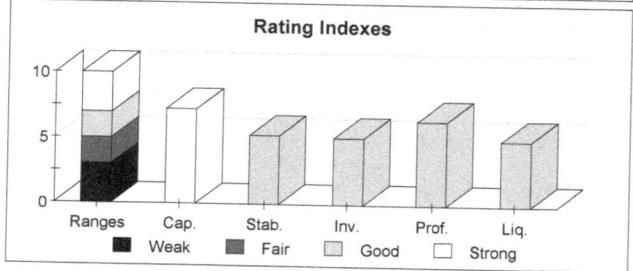

Ranges   Cap.   Stab.   Inv.   Prof.   Liq.

■ Weak   ■ Fair   □ Good   □ Strong

UNITED LIFE INSURANCE COMPANY
B **Good**

Major Rating Factors: Good quality investment portfolio (5.9 on a scale of 0 to 10) despite mixed results such as: large holdings of BBB rated bonds but moderate junk bond exposure. Good liquidity (5.5) with sufficient resources to cover a large increase in policy surrenders. Good overall results on stability tests (5.9) despite excessive premium growth and negative cash flow from operations for 2017 good operational trends and excellent risk diversification.

Other Rating Factors: Fair profitability (4.2) with investment income below regulatory standards in relation to interest assumptions of reserves. Strong capitalization (7.6) based on excellent risk adjusted capital (severe loss scenario).

Principal Business: Individual annuities (56%), individual life insurance (43%), and individual health insurance (1%).

Principal Investments: NonCMO investment grade bonds (70%), CMOs and structured securities (23%), noninv. grade bonds (3%), and common & preferred stock (2%).

Investments in Affiliates: None

Group Affiliation: United Fire & Casualty Group

Licensed in: AL, AZ, AR, CA, CO, DE, FL, ID, IL, IN, IA, KS, KY, LA, MD, MI, MN, MS, MO, MT, NE, NV, NJ, NM, NC, ND, OH, OK, PA, SD, TN, TX, UT, VA, WV, WI, WY

Commenced Business: October 1962

Address: 118 SECOND AVENUE SE, CEDAR RAPIDS, IA 52401-1212

Phone: (800) 553-7937 **Domicile State:** IA **NAIC Code:** 69973

Data Date	Rating	RACR #1	RACR #2	Total Assets ($mil)	Capital ($mil)	Net Premium ($mil)	Net Income ($mil)
9-18	B	2.66	1.38	1,549.3	143.4	122.9	20.2
9-17	B	2.92	1.56	1,502.8	145.0	85.9	4.2
2017	B	2.95	1.58	1,498.0	144.5	123.3	5.5
2016	B	2.78	1.48	1,524.6	139.8	135.5	-3.2
2015	B	2.76	1.47	1,535.9	138.9	143.0	-1.5
2014	B	2.83	1.50	1,635.4	155.7	198.8	3.5
2013	B	2.74	1.42	1,648.0	158.0	164.3	5.9

Adverse Trends in Operations

Decrease in asset base during 2017 (2%)
Change in premium mix from 2014 to 2015 (5.2%)
Decrease in asset base during 2015 (6%)
Decrease in capital during 2015 (11%)
Decrease in premium volume from 2014 to 2015 (28%)

UNITED OF OMAHA LIFE INSURANCE COMPANY
B **Good**

Major Rating Factors: Good quality investment portfolio (5.1 on a scale of 0 to 10) despite large holdings of BBB rated bonds in addition to moderate junk bond exposure. Exposure to mortgages is significant, but the mortgage default rate has been low. Good liquidity (6.0) with sufficient resources to cover a large increase in policy surrenders. Good overall results on stability tests (6.0) excellent operational trends and excellent risk diversification.

Other Rating Factors: Strong capitalization (7.2) based on excellent risk adjusted capital (severe loss scenario). Excellent profitability (7.2).

Principal Business: Individual life insurance (34%), individual health insurance (22%), group retirement contracts (17%), group health insurance (12%), and other lines (14%).

Principal Investments: NonCMO investment grade bonds (58%), CMOs and structured securities (21%), mortgages in good standing (12%), noninv. grade bonds (4%), and misc. investments (4%).

Investments in Affiliates: 2%

Group Affiliation: Mutual Of Omaha Group

Licensed in: All states except NY

Commenced Business: November 1926

Address: MUTUAL OF OMAHA PLAZA, OMAHA, NE 68175

Phone: (402) 342-7600 **Domicile State:** NE **NAIC Code:** 69868

Data Date	Rating	RACR #1	RACR #2	Total Assets ($mil)	Capital ($mil)	Net Premium ($mil)	Net Income ($mil)
9-18	B	1.98	1.13	23,546.4	1,600.8	3,165.1	43.2
9-17	B	1.85	1.05	22,326.3	1,460.5	2,913.5	55.3
2017	B	2.00	1.14	22,803.2	1,605.7	4,024.6	61.7
2016	B	1.89	1.06	20,698.2	1,429.5	3,692.0	9.0
2015	B	1.90	1.11	19,622.5	1,441.7	3,572.3	153.6
2014	B	1.95	1.15	18,786.7	1,422.7	2,712.4	164.4
2013	B	1.71	1.00	18,122.5	1,226.9	3,428.2	69.9

Adverse Trends in Operations

Change in premium mix from 2014 to 2015 (5.4%)
Change in premium mix from 2013 to 2014 (5.1%)
Increase in policy surrenders from 2013 to 2014 (30%)
Decrease in premium volume from 2013 to 2014 (21%)

UNITED STATES LIFE INSURANCE COMPANY IN NYC
B **Good**

Major Rating Factors: Good quality investment portfolio (5.1 on a scale of 0 to 10) despite large holdings of BBB rated bonds in addition to junk bond exposure equal to 66% of capital. Exposure to mortgages is significant, but the mortgage default rate has been low. Good overall profitability (6.4). Good liquidity (5.7).

Other Rating Factors: Fair overall results on stability tests (4.7). Strong capitalization (7.4) based on excellent risk adjusted capital (severe loss scenario).

Principal Business: Individual annuities (64%), individual life insurance (17%), group health insurance (9%), group life insurance (8%), and group retirement contracts (2%).

Principal Investments: NonCMO investment grade bonds (48%), CMOs and structured securities (27%), mortgages in good standing (12%), noninv. grade bonds (5%), and policy loans (1%).

Investments in Affiliates: 1%

Group Affiliation: American International Group

Licensed in: All states except PR

Commenced Business: March 1850

Address: 175 Water Street, New York, NY 10038

Phone: (713) 522-1111 **Domicile State:** NY **NAIC Code:** 70106

Data Date	Rating	RACR #1	RACR #2	Total Assets ($mil)	Capital ($mil)	Net Premium ($mil)	Net Income ($mil)
9-18	B	2.69	1.28	28,771.0	1,902.2	-4,021.0	353.3
9-17	B	2.47	1.21	28,940.0	1,939.9	945.3	210.0
2017	B	2.28	1.11	29,430.5	1,756.4	1,297.7	89.4
2016	B	2.26	1.12	28,609.9	1,837.0	1,742.9	93.2
2015	B	2.62	1.30	28,404.0	2,090.4	1,984.7	365.0
2014	B-	2.63	1.29	27,985.4	2,000.8	1,918.6	319.8
2013	B-	2.32	1.15	25,538.0	1,765.2	1,772.8	420.1

Rating Indexes

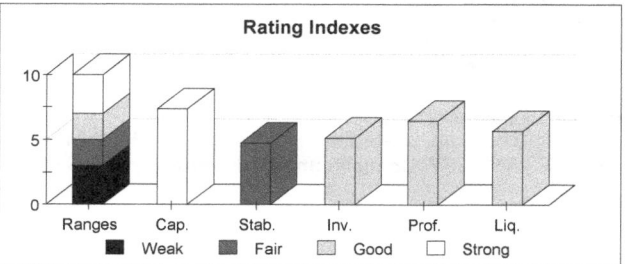

UNITED WORLD LIFE INSURANCE COMPANY *   B+   Good

Major Rating Factors: Good overall results on stability tests (6.5 on a scale of 0 to 10) despite negative cash flow from operations for 2017. Other stability subfactors include good operational trends and excellent risk diversification. Good overall profitability (5.3). Good liquidity (6.7) with sufficient resources to handle a spike in claims.

Other Rating Factors: Strong capitalization (8.3) based on excellent risk adjusted capital (severe loss scenario). High quality investment portfolio (7.6).

Principal Business: Individual health insurance (100%).

Principal Investments: NonCMO investment grade bonds (65%), CMOs and structured securities (27%), cash (5%), noninv. grade bonds (1%), and policy loans (1%).

Investments in Affiliates: None

Group Affiliation: Mutual Of Omaha Group

Licensed in: All states except CT, NY, PR

Commenced Business: April 1970

Address: MUTUAL OF OMAHA PLAZA, OMAHA, NE 68175

Phone: (402) 342-7600 **Domicile State:** NE **NAIC Code:** 72850

Data Date	Rating	RACR #1	RACR #2	Total Assets ($mil)	Capital ($mil)	Net Premium ($mil)	Net Income ($mil)
9-18	B+	4.36	1.84	119.5	46.4	0.8	2.2
9-17	B+	5.16	2.18	123.8	50.8	0.9	0.5
2017	B+	4.96	2.11	122.8	48.7	1.3	1.9
2016	B+	5.42	2.30	119.8	51.4	1.3	4.8
2015	B+	4.92	2.09	123.7	48.9	1.4	-0.5
2014	B+	4.62	1.95	119.4	49.4	1.5	1.6
2013	B+	4.19	1.76	114.9	48.6	1.6	1.2

Adverse Trends in Operations

Decrease in premium volume from 2016 to 2017 (6%)
Decrease in asset base during 2016 (3%)
Increase in policy surrenders from 2014 to 2015 (38%)
Decrease in premium volume from 2014 to 2015 (5%)
Decrease in premium volume from 2013 to 2014 (6%)

UNITEDHEALTHCARE LIFE INSURANCE COMPANY   C   Fair

Major Rating Factors: Good liquidity (6.6 on a scale of 0 to 10) with sufficient resources to handle a spike in claims. Weak profitability (1.9). Excellent expense controls. Weak overall results on stability tests (2.5) including weak results on operational trends, negative cash flow from operations for 2017.

Other Rating Factors: Strong capitalization (8.7) based on excellent risk adjusted capital (severe loss scenario). High quality investment portfolio (8.0).

Principal Business: Group health insurance (95%) and individual health insurance (5%).

Principal Investments: NonCMO investment grade bonds (59%) and CMOs and structured securities (41%).

Investments in Affiliates: None

Group Affiliation: UnitedHealth Group Inc

Licensed in: All states except MA, NY, PR

Commenced Business: December 1982

Address: 3100 AMS BOULEVARD, GREEN BAY, WI 54313

Phone: (800) 232-5432 **Domicile State:** WI **NAIC Code:** 97179

Data Date	Rating	RACR #1	RACR #2	Total Assets ($mil)	Capital ($mil)	Net Premium ($mil)	Net Income ($mil)
9-18	C	2.70	2.13	244.3	155.9	354.0	12.6
9-17	C	1.97	1.56	222.9	136.0	328.9	30.8
2017	C	2.68	2.12	224.2	142.9	435.6	32.1
2016	C	1.44	1.14	508.1	167.5	960.8	-9.0
2015	C	1.61	1.28	488.4	137.1	700.9	-143.0
2014	B	1.51	1.23	132.6	41.4	245.0	-15.4
2013	B	2.11	1.69	57.0	29.3	84.8	7.3

Adverse Trends in Operations

Decrease in capital during 2017 (15%)
Decrease in premium volume from 2016 to 2017 (55%)
Decrease in asset base during 2017 (56%)
Change in asset mix during 2016 (13%)
Change in asset mix during 2015 (6.4%)

UNIVERSAL GUARANTY LIFE INSURANCE COMPANY   C+   Fair

Major Rating Factors: Fair quality investment portfolio (3.0 on a scale of 0 to 10). Fair overall results on stability tests (4.8) including negative cash flow from operations for 2017, fair risk adjusted capital in prior years. Good overall profitability (5.6).

Other Rating Factors: Good liquidity (5.0). Strong capitalization (7.2) based on excellent risk adjusted capital (severe loss scenario).

Principal Business: Individual life insurance (96%), individual annuities (3%), and group life insurance (1%).

Principal Investments: NonCMO investment grade bonds (44%), common & preferred stock (16%), real estate (6%), mortgages in good standing (4%), and misc. investments (25%).

Investments in Affiliates: 5%

Group Affiliation: UTG Inc

Licensed in: AL, AZ, AR, CO, DE, GA, ID, IL, IN, IA, KS, KY, LA, MA, MN, MS, MO, MT, NE, NV, NM, NC, ND, OH, OK, OR, PA, RI, SC, SD, TN, TX, UT, VA, WA, WV, WI

Commenced Business: December 1966

Address: 65 East State Street Ste 2100, Columbus, OH 43215-4260

Phone: (877) 881-1777 **Domicile State:** OH **NAIC Code:** 70130

Data Date	Rating	RACR #1	RACR #2	Total Assets ($mil)	Capital ($mil)	Net Premium ($mil)	Net Income ($mil)
9-18	C+	1.96	1.14	363.9	70.0	4.1	5.9
9-17	C+	1.57	0.90	337.4	48.1	4.4	-0.9
2017	C+	1.82	1.03	343.3	54.7	5.6	5.4
2016	C+	1.52	0.86	337.7	45.2	6.4	4.6
2015	C+	1.39	0.79	334.8	39.8	6.8	0.3
2014	C+	1.44	0.89	343.2	41.1	7.3	12.2
2013	C	1.16	0.72	348.1	34.9	8.2	4.8

Rating Indexes

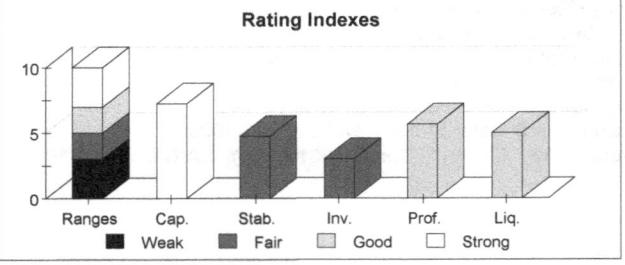

	Weak	Fair	Good	Strong

UNIVERSAL LIFE INSURANCE COMPANY *   B+   Good

Major Rating Factors: Good quality investment portfolio (6.6 on a scale of 0 to 10) despite mixed results such as: no exposure to mortgages and substantial holdings of BBB bonds but minimal holdings in junk bonds. Good overall results on stability tests (6.7). Stability strengths include excellent operational trends, good risk adjusted capital for prior years and excellent risk diversification. Strong capitalization (7.7) based on excellent risk adjusted capital (severe loss scenario).

Other Rating Factors: Excellent profitability (9.0). Excellent liquidity (9.2).

Principal Business: Individual annuities (94%), group life insurance (3%), group health insurance (2%), credit life insurance (1%), and individual life insurance (1%).

Principal Investments: NonCMO investment grade bonds (71%), CMOs and structured securities (19%), common & preferred stock (3%), cash (2%), and noninv. grade bonds (1%).

Investments in Affiliates: None
Group Affiliation: Universal Ins Co Group
Licensed in: PR
Commenced Business: September 1994
Address: Calle Bolivia #33 6to Piso, San Juan, PR 917
Phone: (787) 706-7337 **Domicile State:** PR **NAIC Code:** 60041

Data Date	Rating	RACR #1	RACR #2	Total Assets ($mil)	Capital ($mil)	Net Premium ($mil)	Net Income ($mil)
9-18	B+	2.73	1.44	1,569.7	111.6	86.5	21.9
9-17	B+	3.21	1.69	1,387.9	106.6	81.1	22.2
2017	B+	2.76	1.45	1,403.0	98.6	97.4	26.8
2016	B	2.32	1.22	1,137.4	68.5	103.8	22.4
2015	B	2.19	1.13	979.9	54.1	109.0	16.4
2014	B	2.03	1.07	814.2	42.8	132.2	16.0
2013	C+	1.34	0.77	773.5	29.4	140.7	3.6

Adverse Trends in Operations

Decrease in premium volume from 2016 to 2017 (6%)
Decrease in premium volume from 2015 to 2016 (5%)
Decrease in premium volume from 2014 to 2015 (18%)
Decrease in premium volume from 2013 to 2014 (6%)

UNUM INSURANCE COMPANY   C   Fair

Major Rating Factors: Fair overall results on stability tests (3.8 on a scale of 0 to 10). Good quality investment portfolio (5.7) despite mixed results such as: no exposure to mortgages and large holdings of BBB rated bonds but no exposure to junk bonds. Weak profitability (2.1) with investment income below regulatory standards in relation to interest assumptions of reserves.

Other Rating Factors: Strong capitalization (8.0) based on excellent risk adjusted capital (severe loss scenario). Excellent liquidity (10.0).

Principal Business: Individual life insurance (100%).

Principal Investments: NonCMO investment grade bonds (82%) and CMOs and structured securities (15%).

Investments in Affiliates: None
Group Affiliation: Unum Group
Licensed in: All states except NY, PR
Commenced Business: February 1966
Address: 2211 CONGRESS STREET, PORTLAND, ME 4122
Phone: (423) 294-1011 **Domicile State:** ME **NAIC Code:** 67601

Data Date	Rating	RACR #1	RACR #2	Total Assets ($mil)	Capital ($mil)	Net Premium ($mil)	Net Income ($mil)
9-18	C	7.05	4.55	63.9	47.0	3.3	1.2
9-17	C	6.93	4.65	59.7	46.0	0.0	1.4
2017	C	6.93	4.58	60.0	46.1	0.0	1.9
2016	C	6.79	4.45	59.5	45.0	0.0	1.8
2015	C	6.71	4.19	57.0	43.7	0.0	2.5
2014	C	6.46	3.96	56.2	41.6	0.0	2.3
2013	C	6.30	3.80	54.8	40.1	0.0	2.2

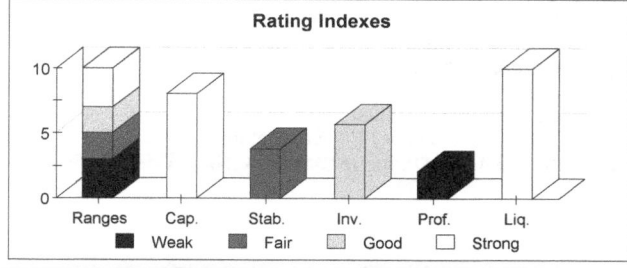

Rating Indexes

Legend: ■ Weak   ■ Fair   ▨ Good   ☐ Strong
(Categories: Ranges, Cap., Stab., Inv., Prof., Liq.)

UNUM LIFE INSURANCE COMPANY OF AMERICA   C+   Fair

Major Rating Factors: Fair quality investment portfolio (3.8 on a scale of 0 to 10) with large holdings of BBB rated bonds in addition to significant exposure to junk bonds. Fair overall results on stability tests (4.8). Strong capitalization (7.4) based on excellent risk adjusted capital (severe loss scenario). Capital levels have been relatively consistent over the last five years.

Other Rating Factors: Excellent profitability (8.0). Excellent liquidity (7.2).

Principal Business: Group health insurance (63%), group life insurance (29%), individual health insurance (6%), and reinsurance (2%).

Principal Investments: NonCMO investment grade bonds (73%), noninv. grade bonds (11%), CMOs and structured securities (7%), and mortgages in good standing (5%).

Investments in Affiliates: None
Group Affiliation: Unum Group
Licensed in: All states except NY
Commenced Business: September 1966
Address: 2211 CONGRESS STREET, PORTLAND, ME 4122
Phone: (207) 575-2211 **Domicile State:** ME **NAIC Code:** 62235

Data Date	Rating	RACR #1	RACR #2	Total Assets ($mil)	Capital ($mil)	Net Premium ($mil)	Net Income ($mil)
9-18	C+	2.34	1.24	21,839.2	1,762.4	2,709.5	384.6
9-17	C+	2.30	1.22	21,366.1	1,702.3	2,615.1	271.2
2017	C+	2.35	1.24	21,455.0	1,728.0	3,486.2	378.2
2016	C+	2.33	1.23	21,077.8	1,686.5	3,348.0	349.3
2015	C+	2.28	1.22	20,552.3	1,567.3	3,168.1	203.5
2014	C+	2.42	1.29	19,701.4	1,546.1	2,914.6	195.0
2013	C+	2.49	1.34	19,078.5	1,557.9	2,794.2	176.2

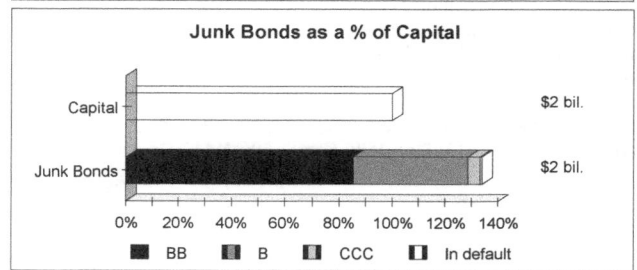

Junk Bonds as a % of Capital

Capital — $2 bil.
Junk Bonds — $2 bil.
(Scale: 0% 20% 40% 60% 80% 100% 120% 140%)
Legend: ■ BB   ▨ B   ☐ CCC   ☐ In default

US FINANCIAL LIFE INSURANCE COMPANY — B — Good

Major Rating Factors: Good liquidity (5.1 on a scale of 0 to 10) with sufficient resources to handle a spike in claims as well as a significant increase in policy surrenders. Good overall results on stability tests (5.8) despite negative cash flow from operations for 2017. Strengths include good financial support from affiliation with AXA Financial Inc, excellent operational trends and excellent risk diversification. Fair profitability (3.7) with investment income below regulatory standards in relation to interest assumptions of reserves.

Other Rating Factors: Strong capitalization (8.1) based on excellent risk adjusted capital (severe loss scenario). High quality investment portfolio (7.5).

Principal Business: Individual life insurance (100%).

Principal Investments: NonCMO investment grade bonds (94%), policy loans (5%), common & preferred stock (1%), and noninv. grade bonds (1%).

Investments in Affiliates: None

Group Affiliation: AXA Financial Inc

Licensed in: All states except NY, PR

Commenced Business: September 1974

Address: 4000 Smith Road Suite 300, Cincinnati, OH 45209

Phone: (201) 743-5073 **Domicile State:** OH **NAIC Code:** 84530

Data Date	Rating	RACR #1	RACR #2	Total Assets ($mil)	Capital ($mil)	Net Premium ($mil)	Net Income ($mil)
9-18	B	3.15	1.71	543.6	74.6	24.3	1.1
9-17	B	4.34	2.33	590.3	111.0	26.6	7.3
2017	B	3.09	1.67	541.4	73.4	36.0	9.0
2016	B	4.36	2.37	599.2	108.8	38.8	14.6
2015	B	3.53	1.90	597.3	93.7	35.1	14.9
2014	B	3.60	1.92	642.9	102.2	38.1	35.1
2013	B	2.08	1.10	638.1	62.5	43.3	8.0

AXA Financial Inc
Composite Group Rating: B+

Largest Group Members	Assets ($mil)	Rating
AXA EQUITABLE LIFE INS CO	194772	B+
MONY LIFE INS CO OF AMERICA	3735	B
US FINANCIAL LIFE INS CO	541	B
AXA EQUITABLE LIFE ANNUITY CO	486	C
AXA CORPORATE SOLUTIONS LIFE REINS	260	B

USAA LIFE INSURANCE COMPANY * — A — Excellent

Major Rating Factors: Good quality investment portfolio (6.7 on a scale of 0 to 10) despite mixed results such as: large holdings of BBB rated bonds but moderate junk bond exposure. Good liquidity (5.5) with sufficient resources to handle a spike in claims as well as a significant increase in policy surrenders. Excellent overall results on stability tests (7.4) excellent operational trends and excellent risk diversification.

Other Rating Factors: Strong capitalization (8.7) based on excellent risk adjusted capital (severe loss scenario). Excellent profitability (8.8).

Principal Business: Individual life insurance (47%), individual annuities (38%), and individual health insurance (15%).

Principal Investments: NonCMO investment grade bonds (73%), CMOs and structured securities (16%), noninv. grade bonds (5%), mortgages in good standing (4%), and misc. investments (2%).

Investments in Affiliates: 1%

Group Affiliation: USAA Group

Licensed in: All states except NY, PR

Commenced Business: August 1963

Address: 9800 Fredericksburg Rd, San Antonio, TX 78288

Phone: (210) 498-1411 **Domicile State:** TX **NAIC Code:** 69663

Data Date	Rating	RACR #1	RACR #2	Total Assets ($mil)	Capital ($mil)	Net Premium ($mil)	Net Income ($mil)
9-18	A	3.89	2.10	25,292.8	2,562.4	1,300.0	165.7
9-17	A	3.92	2.09	24,728.9	2,465.5	1,181.7	195.8
2017	A	3.83	2.06	24,666.8	2,466.7	1,530.2	245.3
2016	A	3.77	2.01	24,028.8	2,362.4	1,622.2	243.9
2015	A	3.87	2.11	22,777.1	2,256.2	1,423.7	218.7
2014	A	4.01	2.17	21,985.4	2,140.7	1,486.7	279.2
2013	A	3.83	2.05	21,114.0	1,973.4	1,786.6	244.5

Adverse Trends in Operations

Decrease in premium volume from 2016 to 2017 (6%)
Decrease in premium volume from 2014 to 2015 (4%)
Decrease in premium volume from 2013 to 2014 (17%)

USAA LIFE INSURANCE COMPANY OF NEW YORK * — B+ — Good

Major Rating Factors: Good overall results on stability tests (6.6 on a scale of 0 to 10). Stability strengths include excellent operational trends and excellent risk diversification. Good quality investment portfolio (5.9) despite mixed results such as: large holdings of BBB rated bonds but moderate junk bond exposure. Fair liquidity (4.9).

Other Rating Factors: Strong capitalization (7.6) based on excellent risk adjusted capital (severe loss scenario). Excellent profitability (8.4).

Principal Business: Individual life insurance (65%) and individual annuities (35%).

Principal Investments: NonCMO investment grade bonds (77%), CMOs and structured securities (15%), noninv. grade bonds (5%), common & preferred stock (1%), and policy loans (1%).

Investments in Affiliates: None

Group Affiliation: USAA Group

Licensed in: NY

Commenced Business: November 1997

Address: 529 Main Street, Highland Falls, NY 10928

Phone: (210) 498-1411 **Domicile State:** NY **NAIC Code:** 60228

Data Date	Rating	RACR #1	RACR #2	Total Assets ($mil)	Capital ($mil)	Net Premium ($mil)	Net Income ($mil)
9-18	B+	2.68	1.41	780.2	84.5	26.0	5.5
9-17	B+	2.58	1.34	764.3	79.3	28.5	2.2
2017	B+	2.50	1.31	757.9	78.5	36.8	2.5
2016	B+	2.50	1.30	734.6	77.2	41.2	5.7
2015	B+	2.51	1.32	699.4	72.5	35.1	3.6
2014	B+	2.50	1.31	665.4	68.0	36.9	5.7
2013	B+	2.41	1.25	641.1	62.9	39.3	3.8

Adverse Trends in Operations

Decrease in premium volume from 2016 to 2017 (11%)
Decrease in premium volume from 2014 to 2015 (5%)
Decrease in premium volume from 2013 to 2014 (6%)
Increase in policy surrenders from 2013 to 2014 (55%)

USABLE LIFE *   A-   Excellent

Major Rating Factors: Good liquidity (6.6 on a scale of 0 to 10) with sufficient resources to handle a spike in claims as well as a significant increase in policy surrenders. Strong capitalization (8.5) based on excellent risk adjusted capital (severe loss scenario). Furthermore, this high level of risk adjusted capital has been consistently maintained over the last five years. High quality investment portfolio (7.1).

Other Rating Factors: Excellent profitability (8.5). Excellent overall results on stability tests (7.3) excellent operational trends and excellent risk diversification.

Principal Business: Reinsurance (61%), group life insurance (19%), group health insurance (15%), individual health insurance (5%), and individual life insurance (1%).

Principal Investments: NonCMO investment grade bonds (74%), CMOs and structured securities (14%), common & preferred stock (5%), cash (3%), and misc. investments (3%).

Investments in Affiliates: None
Group Affiliation: Arkansas Bl Cross Bl Shield Group
Licensed in: All states except NY, PR
Commenced Business: December 1980
Address: 320 W Capitol Suite 700, Little Rock, AR 72201
Phone: (501) 375-7200 **Domicile State:** AR **NAIC Code:** 94358

Data Date	Rating	RACR #1	RACR #2	Total Assets ($mil)	Capital ($mil)	Net Premium ($mil)	Net Income ($mil)
9-18	A-	2.64	1.98	541.5	267.6	459.9	134.8
9-17	B+	2.62	1.95	510.9	263.9	436.0	19.9
2017	A-	2.80	2.10	535.3	278.1	586.1	37.8
2016	B+	2.41	1.80	498.2	241.6	587.8	24.3
2015	B+	2.07	1.52	467.9	215.3	580.2	27.3
2014	B+	1.83	1.34	446.0	194.3	591.7	24.6
2013	B+	1.60	1.17	408.3	166.3	570.0	11.5

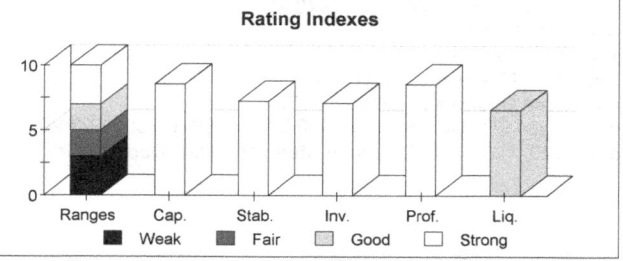

Rating Indexes

VANTIS LIFE INSURANCE COMPANY   C+   Fair

Major Rating Factors: Fair overall results on stability tests (4.2 on a scale of 0 to 10). Good quality investment portfolio (5.7) despite mixed results such as: minimal exposure to mortgages and large holdings of BBB rated bonds but minimal holdings in junk bonds. Good liquidity (6.5) with sufficient resources to cover a large increase in policy surrenders.

Other Rating Factors: Weak profitability (1.4) with operating losses during the first nine months of 2018. Strong capitalization (7.4) based on excellent risk adjusted capital (severe loss scenario).

Principal Business: Individual annuities (87%), individual life insurance (12%), and group life insurance (1%).

Principal Investments: NonCMO investment grade bonds (70%), CMOs and structured securities (16%), common & preferred stock (7%), policy loans (2%), and misc. investments (5%).

Investments in Affiliates: 6%
Group Affiliation: Penn Mutual Life Insurance Company
Licensed in: All states except NY, PR
Commenced Business: January 1964
Address: 200 Day Hill Road, Windsor, CT 6095
Phone: (860) 298-6001 **Domicile State:** CT **NAIC Code:** 68632

Data Date	Rating	RACR #1	RACR #2	Total Assets ($mil)	Capital ($mil)	Net Premium ($mil)	Net Income ($mil)
9-18	C+	1.89	1.29	482.0	68.6	66.8	-4.4
9-17	C+	2.93	1.75	368.1	47.6	134.8	-3.8
2017	C+	1.35	0.94	421.9	45.0	184.8	-1.8
2016	C	3.52	2.16	255.4	54.4	52.9	-15.0
2015	B-	5.07	3.02	251.6	87.3	-605.1	-0.5
2014	B-	1.89	1.04	874.4	69.6	33.3	3.0
2013	B-	1.89	1.04	896.3	71.7	34.4	1.8

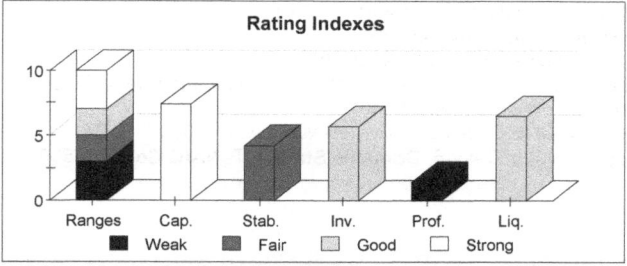

Rating Indexes

VARIABLE ANNUITY LIFE INSURANCE COMPANY   B   Good

Major Rating Factors: Good overall results on stability tests (5.8 on a scale of 0 to 10). Stability strengths include good operational trends and excellent risk diversification. Good overall profitability (6.7). Good liquidity (5.4) with sufficient resources to handle a spike in claims as well as a significant increase in policy surrenders.

Other Rating Factors: Fair quality investment portfolio (4.8). Strong capitalization (7.3) based on excellent risk adjusted capital (severe loss scenario).

Principal Business: Individual annuities (62%) and group retirement contracts (38%).

Principal Investments: NonCMO investment grade bonds (39%), CMOs and structured securities (37%), mortgages in good standing (13%), noninv. grade bonds (5%), and policy loans (1%).

Investments in Affiliates: 7%
Group Affiliation: American International Group
Licensed in: All states except PR
Commenced Business: May 1969
Address: 2929 Allen Parkway, Houston, TX 77019
Phone: (713) 522-1111 **Domicile State:** TX **NAIC Code:** 70238

Data Date	Rating	RACR #1	RACR #2	Total Assets ($mil)	Capital ($mil)	Net Premium ($mil)	Net Income ($mil)
9-18	B	2.51	1.18	83,441.4	2,914.9	3,546.6	446.1
9-17	B	2.41	1.14	80,671.2	2,747.5	3,123.5	455.6
2017	B	2.49	1.19	81,665.0	2,800.0	4,179.0	639.7
2016	B	2.20	1.05	76,674.8	2,387.8	4,608.2	757.7
2015	B	2.36	1.17	74,140.6	2,722.6	5,118.7	757.0
2014	B	3.03	1.45	77,095.2	3,618.1	4,830.3	1,024.6
2013	B	4.01	1.90	77,174.4	4,811.9	5,616.9	1,271.0

Adverse Trends in Operations

Decrease in premium volume from 2015 to 2016 (10%)
Decrease in capital during 2016 (12%)
Decrease in capital during 2015 (25%)
Decrease in premium volume from 2013 to 2014 (14%)
Decrease in capital during 2014 (25%)

VOYA INSURANCE & ANNUITY COMPANY

B-   **Good**

Major Rating Factors: Good overall capitalization (6.4 on a scale of 0 to 10) based on good risk adjusted capital (severe loss scenario). Nevertheless, capital levels have fluctuated during prior years. Good quality investment portfolio (5.2) despite large holdings of BBB rated bonds in addition to moderate junk bond exposure. Exposure to mortgages is significant, but the mortgage default rate has been low. Good liquidity (6.9).

Other Rating Factors: Fair profitability (3.5) with operating losses during the first nine months of 2018. Fair overall results on stability tests (3.7).

Principal Business: Individual annuities (77%), reinsurance (20%), group retirement contracts (2%), and individual life insurance (1%).

Principal Investments: NonCMO investment grade bonds (63%), mortgages in good standing (15%), CMOs and structured securities (11%), noninv. grade bonds (3%), and misc. investments (3%).

Investments in Affiliates: 1%

Group Affiliation: Voya Financial Inc

Licensed in: All states except NY, PR

Commenced Business: October 1973

Address: 909 LOCUST STREET, DES MOINES, IA 50309-3942

Phone: (610) 425-4310   **Domicile State:** IA   **NAIC Code:** 80942

Data Date	Rating	RACR #1	RACR #2	Total Assets ($mil)	Capital ($mil)	Net Premium ($mil)	Net Income ($mil)
9-18	B-	1.79	0.92	53,491.6	2,164.9	-14,615.3	-193.4
9-17	B-	1.71	0.84	59,991.4	1,856.9	1,375.1	507.0
2017	B-	1.70	0.84	58,725.1	1,835.2	1,806.7	513.7
2016	B-	1.79	0.89	60,761.9	1,906.2	2,098.1	232.4
2015	B-	1.95	0.97	63,981.2	2,074.8	2,654.4	553.3
2014	B	2.06	1.03	66,778.8	2,119.4	2,419.5	335.6
2013	B	1.86	0.93	69,266.0	1,941.6	6,164.9	-55.8

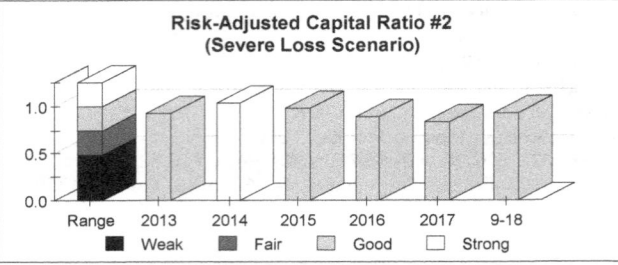

Risk-Adjusted Capital Ratio #2 (Severe Loss Scenario)

Range 2013 2014 2015 2016 2017 9-18
■ Weak ■ Fair □ Good □ Strong

VOYA RETIREMENT INSURANCE & ANNUITY COMPANY *

B+   **Good**

Major Rating Factors: Good overall profitability (5.2 on a scale of 0 to 10). Good overall results on stability tests (6.5). Stability strengths include excellent operational trends and excellent risk diversification. Fair quality investment portfolio (4.9) with large holdings of BBB rated bonds in addition to junk bond exposure equal to 65% of capital. Exposure to mortgages is significant, but the mortgage default rate has been low.

Other Rating Factors: Strong capitalization (7.0) based on excellent risk adjusted capital (severe loss scenario). Excellent liquidity (9.1).

Principal Business: Group retirement contracts (98%), individual life insurance (1%), and individual annuities (1%).

Principal Investments: NonCMO investment grade bonds (56%), mortgages in good standing (16%), CMOs and structured securities (15%), noninv. grade bonds (4%), and misc. investments (6%).

Investments in Affiliates: 2%

Group Affiliation: Voya Financial Inc

Licensed in: All states, the District of Columbia and Puerto Rico

Commenced Business: April 1976

Address: ONE ORANGE WAY, WINDSOR, CT 06095-4774

Phone: (860) 580-4646   **Domicile State:** CT   **NAIC Code:** 86509

Data Date	Rating	RACR #1	RACR #2	Total Assets ($mil)	Capital ($mil)	Net Premium ($mil)	Net Income ($mil)
9-18	B+	2.08	1.00	108,678	1,950.3	8,719.0	307.4
9-17	B+	2.09	1.02	104,964	1,829.0	9,652.0	161.5
2017	B+	2.05	1.00	104,543	1,792.7	12,592.5	194.9
2016	B+	2.39	1.17	93,159.7	1,959.3	12,396.2	266.2
2015	B+	2.62	1.29	87,214.1	2,030.2	12,041.8	317.5
2014	B	2.63	1.30	89,253.5	2,007.9	9,826.8	321.7
2013	B	2.65	1.30	85,670.1	2,010.8	9,439.7	175.2

Adverse Trends in Operations

Decrease in capital during 2017 (9%)
Decrease in capital during 2016 (3%)
Decrease in asset base during 2015 (2%)

WASHINGTON NATIONAL INSURANCE COMPANY

D+   **Weak**

Major Rating Factors: Weak overall results on stability tests (2.7 on a scale of 0 to 10) including potential financial drain due to affiliation with CNO Financial Group Inc. Fair quality investment portfolio (4.7) with large holdings of BBB rated bonds in addition to junk bond exposure equal to 54% of capital. Good capitalization (6.3) based on good risk adjusted capital (severe loss scenario).

Other Rating Factors: Good overall profitability (5.6). Good liquidity (6.5).

Principal Business: Individual health insurance (59%), group health insurance (29%), individual life insurance (7%), reinsurance (4%), and individual annuities (1%).

Principal Investments: NonCMO investment grade bonds (61%), CMOs and structured securities (21%), mortgages in good standing (5%), noninv. grade bonds (4%), and misc. investments (9%).

Investments in Affiliates: 1%

Group Affiliation: CNO Financial Group Inc

Licensed in: All states except NY

Commenced Business: September 1923

Address: 11825 NORTH PENNSYLVANIA STREE, CARMEL, IN 46032

Phone: (317) 817-6100   **Domicile State:** IN   **NAIC Code:** 70319

Data Date	Rating	RACR #1	RACR #2	Total Assets ($mil)	Capital ($mil)	Net Premium ($mil)	Net Income ($mil)
9-18	D+	1.62	0.91	5,465.1	361.4	527.1	48.2
9-17	D+	1.98	1.06	5,420.1	398.1	516.8	20.6
2017	D+	1.71	0.95	5,418.5	373.2	688.9	26.7
2016	D+	2.09	1.09	5,397.6	431.1	663.1	-53.0
2015	D+	1.70	0.93	4,807.8	333.1	649.7	60.9
2014	D+	1.67	0.90	4,775.3	327.0	610.0	50.8
2013	D+	2.20	1.15	5,286.1	431.9	540.7	59.6

CNO Financial Group Inc Composite Group Rating: D+ Largest Group Members	Assets ($mil)	Rating
BANKERS LIFE CAS CO	18274	D+
WASHINGTON NATIONAL INS CO	5418	D+
COLONIAL PENN LIFE INS CO	868	D+
BANKERS CONSECO LIFE INS CO	478	D

WEA INSURANCE CORPORATION　　　　　C　　Fair

Major Rating Factors: Fair quality investment portfolio (4.3 on a scale of 0 to 10). Fair overall results on stability tests (3.7) including negative cash flow from operations for 2017 and excessive premium growth. Good liquidity (6.2) with sufficient resources to handle a spike in claims.
Other Rating Factors: Weak profitability (2.3). Strong capitalization (7.4) based on excellent risk adjusted capital (severe loss scenario).
Principal Business: Group health insurance (100%).
Principal Investments: NonCMO investment grade bonds (48%), common & preferred stock (24%), CMOs and structured securities (22%), and cash (2%).
Investments in Affiliates: None
Group Affiliation: Wisconsin Education Assn Ins Trust
Licensed in: WI
Commenced Business: July 1985
Address: 45 NOB HILL ROAD, MADISON, WI 53713-0000
Phone: (608) 276-4000 **Domicile State:** WI **NAIC Code:** 72273

Data Date	Rating	RACR #1	RACR #2	Total Assets ($mil)	Capital ($mil)	Net Premium ($mil)	Net Income ($mil)
9-18	C	1.80	1.26	684.6	184.4	458.1	15.8
9-17	C	1.72	1.18	665.7	155.5	350.8	-3.7
2017	C	1.85	1.27	661.0	167.0	466.6	1.4
2016	C	1.57	1.09	644.9	140.9	496.6	1.1
2015	C	1.70	1.20	644.2	160.7	550.6	-34.2
2014	C	1.97	1.40	683.9	200.2	593.3	-28.0
2013	C	2.28	1.61	720.9	243.0	594.6	-15.1

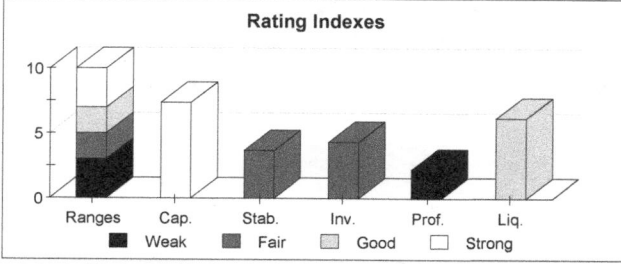

Rating Indexes

WEST COAST LIFE INSURANCE COMPANY　　　　B-　　Good

Major Rating Factors: Fair overall capitalization (4.0 on a scale of 0 to 10) based on mixed results -- excessive policy leverage mitigated by excellent risk adjusted capital (severe loss scenario). Nevertheless, capital levels have fluctuated during prior years. Fair quality investment portfolio (4.6) with large holdings of BBB rated bonds in addition to junk bond exposure equal to 77% of capital. Exposure to mortgages is significant, but the mortgage default rate has been low. Fair profitability (4.2) with operating losses during the first nine months of 2018.
Other Rating Factors: Fair overall results on stability tests (4.9). Good liquidity (5.6).
Principal Business: Individual life insurance (87%) and reinsurance (13%).
Principal Investments: NonCMO investment grade bonds (73%), mortgages in good standing (12%), noninv. grade bonds (6%), CMOs and structured securities (4%), and misc. investments (4%).
Investments in Affiliates: None
Group Affiliation: Dai-ichi Life Holdings Inc
Licensed in: All states except NY, PR
Commenced Business: February 1915
Address: 10306 REGENCY PARKWAY DRIVE, OMAHA, NE 68114
Phone: (205) 268-1000 **Domicile State:** NE **NAIC Code:** 70335

Data Date	Rating	RACR #1	RACR #2	Total Assets ($mil)	Capital ($mil)	Net Premium ($mil)	Net Income ($mil)
9-18	B-	2.13	1.03	5,319.9	351.3	-12.9	-10.4
9-17	B-	2.30	1.12	5,250.1	364.0	-9.2	-6.9
2017	B-	2.65	1.29	5,244.8	400.9	-21.1	70.5
2016	C+	2.97	1.45	5,158.4	448.4	-0.5	92.5
2015	C+	2.83	1.40	4,985.3	419.4	10.1	58.5
2014	C+	2.85	1.43	4,810.1	412.3	3.3	-89.2
2013	C+	3.24	1.62	4,516.1	450.0	24.6	12.5

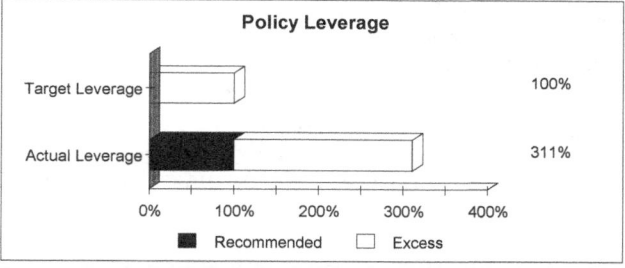

Policy Leverage

WESTERN & SOUTHERN LIFE INSURANCE COMPANY　　　B　　Good

Major Rating Factors: Good overall results on stability tests (5.7 on a scale of 0 to 10). Stability strengths include excellent operational trends and excellent risk diversification. Fair quality investment portfolio (3.4). Strong capitalization (8.1) based on excellent risk adjusted capital (severe loss scenario). Moreover, capital levels have been consistently high over the last five years.
Other Rating Factors: Excellent profitability (8.0). Excellent liquidity (7.1).
Principal Business: Individual life insurance (88%), individual health insurance (10%), group life insurance (1%), and reinsurance (1%).
Principal Investments: Common & preferred stock (39%), nonCMO investment grade bonds (31%), CMOs and structured securities (6%), noninv. grade bonds (3%), and misc. investments (21%).
Investments in Affiliates: 38%
Group Affiliation: Western & Southern Group
Licensed in: All states except AK, ME, MA, NY, PR
Commenced Business: April 1888
Address: 400 BROADWAY, CINCINNATI, OH 45202
Phone: (513) 357-4000 **Domicile State:** OH **NAIC Code:** 70483

Data Date	Rating	RACR #1	RACR #2	Total Assets ($mil)	Capital ($mil)	Net Premium ($mil)	Net Income ($mil)
9-18	B	2.09	1.75	10,735.7	5,319.9	173.5	178.3
9-17	B	1.97	1.64	10,626.1	5,103.2	181.8	49.9
2017	B	2.03	1.70	10,551.5	5,099.3	246.7	269.7
2016	B	1.92	1.63	10,107.7	4,815.5	253.7	53.6
2015	B	2.01	1.69	9,792.3	4,548.3	256.2	268.1
2014	B	1.87	1.56	9,918.3	4,294.2	263.2	519.5
2013	B	1.75	1.49	9,405.3	4,211.0	266.8	90.6

Adverse Trends in Operations

Decrease in premium volume from 2016 to 2017 (3%)
Decrease in asset base during 2015 (1%)
Decrease in premium volume from 2014 to 2015 (3%)
Decrease in premium volume from 2013 to 2014 (1%)

WESTERN UNITED LIFE ASSURANCE COMPANY | B- | Good

Major Rating Factors: Good capitalization (6.0 on a scale of 0 to 10) based on good risk adjusted capital (moderate loss scenario). Moreover, capital levels have been consistent over the last five years. Good overall results on stability tests (5.0). Stability strengths include good operational trends and excellent risk diversification. Fair quality investment portfolio (3.5).

Other Rating Factors: Fair liquidity (3.4). Excellent profitability (8.7).

Principal Business: Individual annuities (99%).

Principal Investments: NonCMO investment grade bonds (69%), CMOs and structured securities (21%), noninv. grade bonds (4%), common & preferred stock (1%), and misc. investments (2%).

Investments in Affiliates: None

Group Affiliation: Manhattan Life Group Inc

Licensed in: All states except CA, MN, NY, PR

Commenced Business: February 1975

Address: 929 West Sprague Ave, Spokane, WA 99201

Phone: (713) 529-0045 **Domicile State:** WA **NAIC Code:** 85189

Data Date	Rating	RACR #1	RACR #2	Total Assets ($mil)	Capital ($mil)	Net Premium ($mil)	Net Income ($mil)
9-18	B-	1.64	0.79	1,217.0	80.0	113.8	5.6
9-17	B-	1.67	0.80	1,194.8	76.7	106.7	6.3
2017	B-	1.70	0.82	1,201.0	78.0	138.5	7.8
2016	B-	1.66	0.80	1,157.8	74.7	148.5	8.4
2015	B-	1.68	0.81	1,096.3	70.5	191.6	12.5
2014	B-	1.61	0.79	990.7	61.8	239.8	11.5
2013	B-	2.59	2.33	14.8	7.4	0.6	0.2

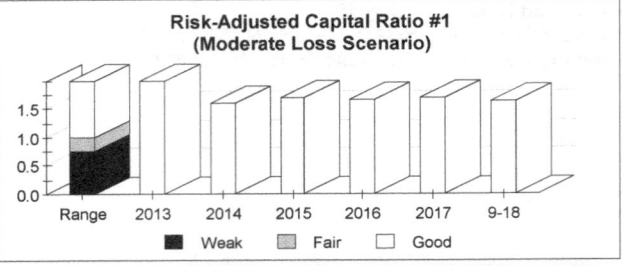

Risk-Adjusted Capital Ratio #1 (Moderate Loss Scenario)

WESTERN-SOUTHERN LIFE ASSURANCE COMPANY | B | Good

Major Rating Factors: Good quality investment portfolio (5.2 on a scale of 0 to 10) despite mixed results such as: large holdings of BBB rated bonds but junk bond exposure equal to 75% of capital. Good overall profitability (6.5). Excellent expense controls. Good liquidity (6.0) with sufficient resources to handle a spike in claims as well as a significant increase in policy surrenders.

Other Rating Factors: Fair overall results on stability tests (4.6). Strong capitalization (7.1) based on excellent risk adjusted capital (severe loss scenario).

Principal Business: Individual annuities (40%), group retirement contracts (28%), individual life insurance (21%), reinsurance (7%), and group life insurance (4%).

Principal Investments: NonCMO investment grade bonds (50%), CMOs and structured securities (29%), mortgages in good standing (8%), noninv. grade bonds (7%), and misc. investments (6%).

Investments in Affiliates: 3%

Group Affiliation: Western & Southern Group

Licensed in: All states except NY, PR

Commenced Business: March 1981

Address: 400 BROADWAY, CINCINNATI, OH 45202

Phone: (513) 357-4000 **Domicile State:** OH **NAIC Code:** 92622

Data Date	Rating	RACR #1	RACR #2	Total Assets ($mil)	Capital ($mil)	Net Premium ($mil)	Net Income ($mil)
9-18	B	1.99	1.09	12,464.1	1,010.8	493.1	36.9
9-17	B	2.45	1.31	12,383.1	1,179.0	494.0	61.3
2017	B	1.99	1.11	12,452.5	980.6	1,177.9	69.8
2016	B	2.34	1.24	12,350.1	1,092.8	612.1	55.2
2015	B	2.18	1.15	12,553.4	995.2	578.6	68.0
2014	B	2.20	1.15	13,147.0	1,051.3	801.5	179.6
2013	B	2.44	1.25	13,146.8	1,176.7	935.7	108.8

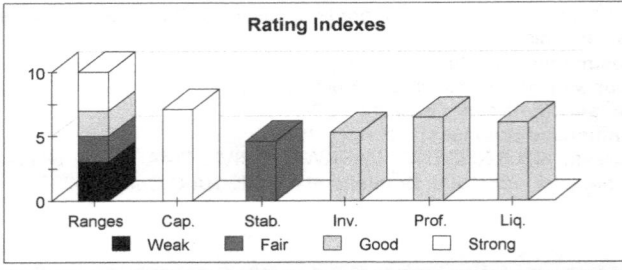

Rating Indexes

WILCAC LIFE INSURANCE COMPANY | C | Fair

Major Rating Factors: Fair overall capitalization (4.0 on a scale of 0 to 10) based on mixed results -- excessive policy leverage mitigated by excellent risk adjusted capital (severe loss scenario). Nevertheless, capital levels have fluctuated during prior years. Good quality investment portfolio (6.2) despite mixed results such as: large holdings of BBB rated bonds but moderate junk bond exposure. Good overall profitability (5.9).

Other Rating Factors: Weak overall results on stability tests (2.6) including fair financial strength of affiliated Wilton Re Holdings Ltd and weak results on operational trends, negative cash flow from operations for 2017. Excellent liquidity (9.3).

Principal Business: Individual life insurance (93%), group retirement contracts (4%), individual health insurance (2%), and individual annuities (1%).

Principal Investments: NonCMO investment grade bonds (70%), CMOs and structured securities (23%), common & preferred stock (3%), and noninv. grade bonds (2%).

Investments in Affiliates: None

Group Affiliation: Wilton Re Holdings Ltd

Licensed in: All states, the District of Columbia and Puerto Rico

Commenced Business: August 1911

Address: 1275A SANDUSKY ROAD, JACKSONVILLE, IL 62650

Phone: (203) 762-4400 **Domicile State:** IL **NAIC Code:** 62413

Data Date	Rating	RACR #1	RACR #2	Total Assets ($mil)	Capital ($mil)	Net Premium ($mil)	Net Income ($mil)
9-18	C	4.85	2.22	2,279.6	121.3	0.1	17.5
9-17	C	3.88	1.95	2,342.2	149.4	-1,561.9	6.3
2017	C	5.41	2.47	2,378.3	143.2	-1,561.9	10.3
2016	C	3.21	1.74	2,315.2	146.0	0.1	4.6
2015	C	3.19	1.71	2,479.9	139.4	0.3	25.2
2014	C	5.20	2.64	2,450.4	250.3	0.2	34.0
2013	C	7.87	3.84	2,937.9	597.3	0.5	47.7

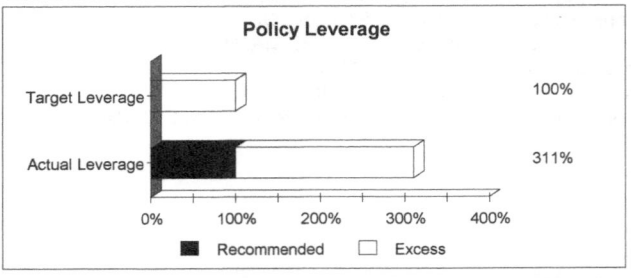

Policy Leverage

WILCO LIFE INSURANCE COMPANY　　　　　　C　　Fair

Major Rating Factors: Fair overall results on stability tests (4.2 on a scale of 0 to 10) including fair financial strength of affiliated Wilton Re Holdings Ltd and negative cash flow from operations for 2017, fair risk adjusted capital in prior years. Fair quality investment portfolio (3.8) with large holdings of BBB rated bonds in addition to junk bond exposure equal to 90% of capital. Fair liquidity (4.2).

Other Rating Factors: Good capitalization (5.8) based on good risk adjusted capital (moderate loss scenario). Good overall profitability (5.5).

Principal Business: Individual life insurance (86%), individual health insurance (13%), reinsurance (1%), and individual annuities (1%).

Principal Investments: NonCMO investment grade bonds (56%), CMOs and structured securities (26%), policy loans (5%), noninv. grade bonds (5%), and misc. investments (7%).

Investments in Affiliates: None

Group Affiliation: Wilton Re Holdings Ltd

Licensed in: All states except NY

Commenced Business: May 1962

Address: 12821 E NEW MARKET ST STE 250, CARMEL, IN 46032

Phone: (203) 762-4400　**Domicile State:** IN　**NAIC Code:** 65900

Data Date	Rating	RACR #1	RACR #2	Total Assets ($mil)	Capital ($mil)	Net Premium ($mil)	Net Income ($mil)
9-18	C	1.54	0.80	2,811.9	153.5	78.4	34.2
9-17	C	1.55	0.80	3,005.1	167.1	87.1	33.8
2017	C	1.19	0.61	2,902.2	113.8	108.7	2.2
2016	C	1.45	0.75	3,197.4	156.9	99.0	11.1
2015	C	1.78	0.93	3,485.6	200.6	128.4	56.2
2014	C-	1.76	0.93	3,732.0	225.3	155.6	62.6
2013	D	1.00	0.53	3,825.5	129.7	237.1	49.7

Wilton Re Holdings Ltd
Composite Group Rating: C
Largest Group Members

Largest Group Members	Assets ($mil)	Rating
WILTON REASSURANCE CO	15004	C
WILCO LIFE INS CO	2902	C
WILCAC LIFE INS CO	2378	C
TEXAS LIFE INS CO	1158	B-
WILTON REASSURANCE LIFE CO OF NY	896	C+

WILLIAM PENN LIFE INSURANCE COMPANY OF NEW YORK　　C　　Fair

Major Rating Factors: Fair quality investment portfolio (4.0 on a scale of 0 to 10) with large holdings of BBB rated bonds in addition to significant exposure to junk bonds. Exposure to mortgages is significant, but the mortgage default rate has been low. Fair overall results on stability tests (3.6). Good capitalization (6.5) based on good risk adjusted capital (severe loss scenario).

Other Rating Factors: Good liquidity (6.4). Weak profitability (1.7).

Principal Business: Individual life insurance (100%).

Principal Investments: NonCMO investment grade bonds (53%), mortgages in good standing (20%), noninv. grade bonds (12%), CMOs and structured securities (7%), and policy loans (3%).

Investments in Affiliates: None

Group Affiliation: Legal & General America Inc

Licensed in: AZ, CT, DC, FL, ID, IA, KS, KY, MD, MS, MT, NJ, NY, OK, OR, PA, RI, SC, SD, TX, VT

Commenced Business: February 1963

Address: 70 EAST SUNRISE HWY STE 500, VALLEY STREAM, NY 11581

Phone: (301) 279-4800　**Domicile State:** NY　**NAIC Code:** 66230

Data Date	Rating	RACR #1	RACR #2	Total Assets ($mil)	Capital ($mil)	Net Premium ($mil)	Net Income ($mil)
9-18	C	1.98	0.94	1,190.2	89.1	21.4	20.8
9-17	C-	2.95	1.37	1,185.0	143.3	26.9	47.1
2017	C-	2.53	1.20	1,186.2	117.3	24.0	41.7
2016	C-	3.11	1.47	1,169.6	144.3	-294.1	-213.4
2015	C-	2.80	1.32	1,158.7	133.2	24.8	-30.5
2014	C-	3.73	1.77	1,146.4	176.6	34.6	-15.1
2013	C-	4.50	2.19	1,134.1	195.9	47.2	-15.2

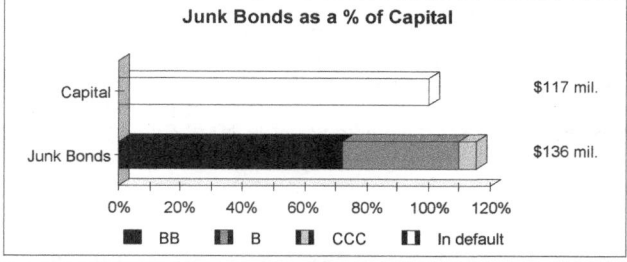

Junk Bonds as a % of Capital

Capital — $117 mil.
Junk Bonds — $136 mil.

0% 20% 40% 60% 80% 100% 120%

■ BB　▓ B　▥ CCC　□ In default

WILTON REASSURANCE COMPANY　　　　　　C　　Fair

Major Rating Factors: Fair overall results on stability tests (3.4 on a scale of 0 to 10) including weak risk adjusted capital in prior years. Good current capitalization (5.5) based on good risk adjusted capital (severe loss scenario) reflecting significant improvement over results in 2017. Good quality investment portfolio (5.6).

Other Rating Factors: Good overall profitability (5.9). Good liquidity (6.6).

Principal Business: Reinsurance (100%).

Principal Investments: NonCMO investment grade bonds (72%), CMOs and structured securities (12%), mortgages in good standing (8%), common & preferred stock (4%), and misc. investments (4%).

Investments in Affiliates: 3%

Group Affiliation: Wilton Re Holdings Ltd

Licensed in: All states except PR

Commenced Business: February 1901

Address: 5TH AVE TOWERS 100 S 5TH ST, MINNEAPOLIS, MN 55402

Phone: (203) 762-4400　**Domicile State:** MN　**NAIC Code:** 66133

Data Date	Rating	RACR #1	RACR #2	Total Assets ($mil)	Capital ($mil)	Net Premium ($mil)	Net Income ($mil)
9-18	C	1.26	0.81	19,124.8	1,184.8	3,857.3	106.9
9-17	C	0.67	0.44	15,018.2	733.7	151.1	-14.0
2017	C	0.68	0.46	15,004.1	655.7	190.1	21.4
2016	C+	0.83	0.72	2,866.6	674.2	183.8	21.4
2015	B-	1.03	0.90	3,039.3	866.4	183.0	184.1
2014	B-	1.00	0.89	3,095.5	842.6	606.0	450.6
2013	B	1.52	1.13	3,470.8	608.8	345.1	67.1

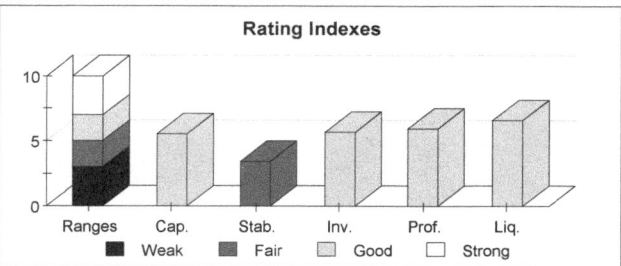

Rating Indexes

Ranges　Cap.　Stab.　Inv.　Prof.　Liq.

■ Weak　▓ Fair　▨ Good　□ Strong

WILTON REASSURANCE LIFE COMPANY OF NEW YORK   C+   Fair

Major Rating Factors: Fair overall results on stability tests (4.7 on a scale of 0 to 10) including fair financial strength of affiliated Wilton Re Holdings Ltd and negative cash flow from operations for 2017. Fair profitability (4.3). Excellent expense controls. Good quality investment portfolio (5.7).

Other Rating Factors: Good liquidity (5.2). Strong capitalization (7.5) based on excellent risk adjusted capital (severe loss scenario).

Principal Business: Individual life insurance (89%), individual annuities (9%), and reinsurance (2%).

Principal Investments: NonCMO investment grade bonds (53%), CMOs and structured securities (38%), policy loans (2%), noninv. grade bonds (2%), and misc. investments (3%).

Investments in Affiliates: None

Group Affiliation: Wilton Re Holdings Ltd

Licensed in: All states except PR

Commenced Business: November 1956

Address: 800 WESTCHESTER AVE STE 641 N, RYE BROOK, NY 10573

Phone: (203) 762-4400 **Domicile State:** NY **NAIC Code:** 60704

Data Date	Rating	RACR #1	RACR #2	Total Assets ($mil)	Capital ($mil)	Net Premium ($mil)	Net Income ($mil)
9-18	C+	2.63	1.32	879.3	98.2	9.6	6.8
9-17	B-	2.87	1.44	897.1	102.2	11.0	9.8
2017	B-	2.58	1.30	895.8	92.9	14.2	7.8
2016	B-	2.71	1.36	905.1	96.3	18.2	4.9
2015	B-	2.62	1.31	902.2	90.8	17.9	-12.1
2014	B-	3.02	1.52	910.8	106.6	17.3	-1.7
2013	C+	3.18	1.59	901.3	113.1	-32.5	13.7

Wilton Re Holdings Ltd Composite Group Rating: C Largest Group Members	Assets ($mil)	Rating
WILTON REASSURANCE CO	15004	C
WILCO LIFE INS CO	2902	C
WILCAC LIFE INS CO	2378	C
TEXAS LIFE INS CO	1158	B-
WILTON REASSURANCE LIFE CO OF NY	896	C+

ZURICH AMERICAN LIFE INSURANCE COMPANY   C   Fair

Major Rating Factors: Good current capitalization (6.1 on a scale of 0 to 10) based on good risk adjusted capital (severe loss scenario), although results have slipped from the excellent range over the last two years. Weak profitability (1.6) with operating losses during the first nine months of 2018. Weak overall results on stability tests (2.7) including weak results on operational trends.

Other Rating Factors: High quality investment portfolio (7.9). Excellent liquidity (9.5).

Principal Business: Group life insurance (85%), individual life insurance (9%), and individual annuities (6%).

Principal Investments: NonCMO investment grade bonds (53%), CMOs and structured securities (26%), policy loans (9%), common & preferred stock (3%), and noninv. grade bonds (1%).

Investments in Affiliates: 3%

Group Affiliation: Zurich Financial Services Group

Licensed in: All states except NY, PR

Commenced Business: September 1947

Address: 1400 AMERICAN LANE, SCHAUMBURG, IL 60196-1056

Phone: (877) 301-5376 **Domicile State:** IL **NAIC Code:** 90557

Data Date	Rating	RACR #1	RACR #2	Total Assets ($mil)	Capital ($mil)	Net Premium ($mil)	Net Income ($mil)
9-18	C	1.56	0.89	14,241.3	110.9	-122.2	-38.6
9-17	C	1.66	0.91	14,265.7	118.4	1,621.2	-21.9
2017	C	1.62	0.92	14,226.5	119.6	1,579.9	-33.4
2016	C	1.80	1.02	12,330.2	124.4	-31.0	-21.3
2015	C	1.87	1.05	12,270.8	125.6	17.1	-23.2
2014	C	2.02	1.18	12,689.3	146.9	0.0	3.9
2013	C	1.86	1.08	12,968.6	132.1	-295.0	-49.5

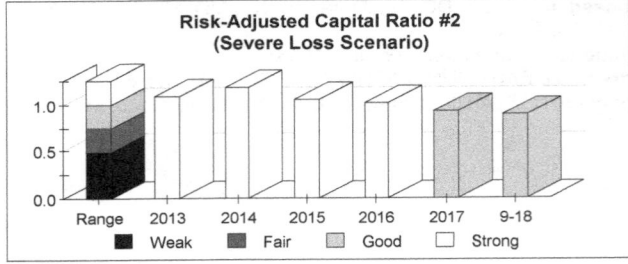

Risk-Adjusted Capital Ratio #2 (Severe Loss Scenario)

Range, 2013, 2014, 2015, 2016, 2017, 9-18

■ Weak ■ Fair ☐ Good ☐ Strong

Section III

Weiss Ratings
Recommended Companies

A compilation of those

U.S. Life and Annuity Insurers

receiving a Weiss Safety Rating
of A+, A, A- or B+.

Companies are listed in alphabetical order.

Section III Contents

This section provides a list of recommended carriers along with additional information you should have when shopping for insurance. It contains all insurers receiving a Weiss Safety Rating of A+, A, A-, or B+. If an insurer is not on this list, it should not be automatically assumed that the firm is weak. Indeed, there are many firms that have not achieved a B+ or better rating but are in relatively good condition with adequate resources to cover their risk during an average recession. Not being included in this list should not be construed as a recommendation to surrender policies.

Left Pages

1. **Safety Rating**

    Our rating is measured on a scale from A to F and considers a wide range of factors. Highly-rated companies are, in our opinion, less likely to experience financial difficulties than lower rated firms. See *About Weiss Safety Ratings* for more information.

2. **Insurance Company Name**

    The legally registered name, which can sometimes differ from the name that the company uses for advertising. An insurer's name can be very similar to the name of other companies which may not be on our Recommended List, so make sure you note the exact name before contacting your agent.

3. **Address**

    The address of the main office where you can contact the firm for additional financial data or for the location of local branches and/or registered agents.

4. **Telephone Number**

    The number to call for additional financial data or for the phone numbers of local branches and/or registered agents.

Right Pages

The right-side pages present the percentage of the company's business that is involved in each type of insurance. Specifically, the numbers shown are the amounts of premium (including certain annuity payments and other deposit funds not technically called premiums) for each line of business as a percent of total premiums. The amounts shown are net premiums and, therefore, include only policies for which the company carries risk.

1. **Domicile State**

    The state which has primary regulatory responsibility for the company. It may differ from the location of the company's corporate headquarters. You do not have to be living in the domicile state to purchase insurance from this firm, provided it is licensed to do business in your state.

2. **Individual Life**

    Life insurance policies offered to individual customers where a single contract covers a single person.

3. **Individual Health**

    Health insurance policies for individual customers that are acquired by a person on his/her own, not through an employer.

4. **Individual Annuities**   A retirement investment vehicle for individual customers which may be fixed and/or variable annuity contracts.

5. **Group Life**   Life insurance policies that can only be acquired through an employer, a public institution, or a union.

6. **Group Health**   Health insurance policies for groups such as the employees of a corporation, public institution or union.

7. **Group Annuities**   Annuity contracts for groups such as the employees of a corporation, public institution or union.

8. **Credit Life**   Life insurance policies designed to protect lenders against the eventual death of the borrower. Typically, if the borrower dies, the policy guarantees repayment of the loan balance.

9. **Credit Health**   Health insurance policies designed to protect lenders against the sickness of the borrower. Typically, if the borrower becomes ill, the policy guarantees repayment of the loan balance.

10. **Supplemental Contracts**   Policies in which the premium is paid from the benefits of another contract.

Weiss Safety Ratings are not deemed to be a recommendation concerning the purchase or sale of the securities of any insurance company that is publicly owned.

RATING	INSURANCE COMPANY NAME	ADDRESS	CITY	STATE	ZIP	PHONE
B+	ADVANCE INS CO OF KANSAS	1133 SW TOPEKA BLVD	TOPEKA	KS	66629	(800) 530-5989
B+	ALLIANZ LIFE INS CO OF NY	28 LIBERTY STREET 38TH FLOOR	NEW YORK	NY	10005	(800) 950-5872
A	AMALGAMATED LIFE INS CO	333 WESTCHESTER AVENUE	WHITE PLAINS	NY	10604	(914) 367-5000
A-	AMERICAN FAMILY LIFE ASR CO OF NY	22 CORPORATE WOODS BLVD STE 2	ALBANY	NY	12211	(800) 992-3522
A+	AMERICAN FAMILY LIFE INS CO	6000 AMERICAN PARKWAY	MADISON	WI	53783	(800) 692-6326
B+	AMERICAN FIDELITY ASR CO	9000 CAMERON PARKWAY	OKLAHOMA CITY	OK	73114	(800) 654-8489
A-	AMERICAN HEALTH & LIFE INS CO	3001 MEACHAM BLVD STE 100	FORT WORTH	TX	76137	(800) 316-5607
B+	AMERICAN UNITED LIFE INS CO	ONE AMERICAN SQUARE	INDIANAPOLIS	IN	46282	(317) 285-1877
B+	AMICA LIFE INS CO	100 AMICA WAY	LINCOLN	RI	02865	(800) 652-6422
A-	ANNUITY INVESTORS LIFE INS CO	301 EAST FOURTH STREET	CINCINNATI	OH	45202	(888) 497-8556
B+	ASSURITY LIFE INS CO	2000 Q STREET	LINCOLN	NE	68503	(800) 869-0355
B+	AXA EQUITABLE LIFE INS CO	1290 AVENUE OF THE AMERICAS	NEW YORK	NY	10104	(800) 777-6510
A	BERKLEY LIFE & HEALTH INS CO	11201 DOUGLAS AVE	URBANDALE	IA	50322	(800) 866-2308
B+	BEST LIFE & HEALTH INS CO	AUSTIN	AUSTIN	TX	78752	(800) 433-0088
B+	BLUEBONNET LIFE INS CO	3545 LAKELAND DR	FLOWOOD	MS	39232	(800) 222-8046
B+	BOSTON MUTUAL LIFE INS CO	120 ROYALL STREET	CANTON	MA	02021	(800) 669-2668
B+	CHESAPEAKE LIFE INS CO	1833 SOUTH MORGAN ROAD	OKLAHOMA CITY	OK	73128	(800) 733-1110
B+	CHRISTIAN FIDELITY LIFE INS CO	1999 BRYAN STREET SUITE 900	DALLAS	TX	75201	(866) 361-1634
A-	CIGNA LIFE INS CO OF NEW YORK	140 EAST 45TH STREET	NEW YORK	NY	10017	(215) 761-1000
B+	COMPANION LIFE INS CO	2501 FARAWAY DRIVE	COLUMBIA	SC	29219	(800) 753-0404
A-	COTTON STATES LIFE INS CO	13560 MORRIS ROAD SUITE 4000	ALPHARETTA	GA	30004	(866) 714-6902
A-	COUNTRY INVESTORS LIFE ASR CO	1701 N TOWANDA AVENUE	BLOOMINGTON	IL	61701	(866) 268-6879
A+	COUNTRY LIFE INS CO	1701 N TOWANDA AVENUE	BLOOMINGTON	IL	61701	(866) 268-6879
B+	DEARBORN NATIONAL LIFE INS CO	300 EAST RANDOLPH STREET	CHICAGO	IL	60601	(800) 348-4512
B+	DEARBORN NATIONAL LIFE INS CO OF NY	1250 PITTSFORD VICTOR ROAD	PITTSFORD	NY	14534	(888) 851-9156
B+	DELAWARE AMERICAN LIFE INS CO	1209 ORANGE STREET	WILMINGTON	DE	19801	(302) 594-2000
B+	EAGLE LIFE INS CO	6000 WESTOWN PARKWAY	WEST DES MOINES	IA	50266	(888) 221-1234
B+	EMPIRE FIDELITY INVESTMENTS L I C	640 FIFTH AVENUE 5TH FLOOR	NEW YORK	NY	10019	(800) 634-9361
B+	ENTERPRISE LIFE INS CO	300 BURNETT STREET SUITE 200	FORT WORTH	TX	76102	(817) 878-3300
A-	ERIE FAMILY LIFE INS CO	100 ERIE INSURANCE PLACE	ERIE	PA	16530	(800) 458-0811
B+	FAMILY HERITAGE LIFE INS CO OF AMER	6001 EAST ROYALTON RD STE 200	CLEVELAND	OH	44147	(440) 922-5200
B+	FARM BUREAU LIFE INS CO	5400 UNIVERSITY AVENUE	WEST DES MOINES	IA	50266	(800) 247-4170
A-	FARM BUREAU LIFE INS CO OF MICHIGAN	7373 WEST SAGINAW HIGHWAY	LANSING	MI	48917	(800) 292-2680
A-	FARM BUREAU LIFE INS CO OF MISSOURI	701 SOUTH COUNTRY CLUB DRIVE	JEFFERSON CITY	MO	65109	(800) 778-6452
A	FEDERATED LIFE INS CO	121 EAST PARK SQUARE	OWATONNA	MN	55060	(888) 333-4949
A-	FIDELITY INVESTMENTS LIFE INS CO	49 NORTH 400 WEST 6TH FLOOR	SALT LAKE CITY	UT	84101	(800) 634-9361
A-	FIRST RELIANCE STANDARD LIFE INS CO	590 MADISON AVENUE 29TH FLOOR	NEW YORK	NY	10022	(800) 353-3986
B+	FIRST SYMETRA NATL LIFE INS CO OF NY	420 LEXINGTON AVE SUITE 300	NEW YORK	NY	10170	(800) 796-3872
A	FRANDISCO LIFE INS CO	135 EAST TUGALO STREET	TOCCOA	GA	30577	(706) 886-7571
B+	FREEDOM LIFE INS CO OF AMERICA	300 BURNETT STREET SUITE 200	FORT WORTH	TX	76102	(817) 878-3300
A	GARDEN STATE LIFE INS CO	ONE MOODY PLAZA	GALVESTON	TX	77550	(800) 638-8565
B+	GERBER LIFE INS CO	1311 MAMARONECK AVENUE	WHITE PLAINS	NY	10605	(800) 704-2180
A	GUARDIAN LIFE INS CO OF AMERICA	7 HANOVER SQUARE	NEW YORK	NY	10004	(800) 441-6455
B+	HANNOVER LIFE REASSURANCE CO OF AMER	200 S ORANGE AVE STE 1900	ORLANDO	FL	32801	(800) 327-1910
A-	LIFE INS CO OF BOSTON & NEW YORK	4300 CAMP ROAD PO BOX 331	ATHOL SPRINGS	NY	14010	(800) 645-2317
A	LIFEWISE ASR CO	7001 220TH STREET SW	MOUNTLAKE TERRACE	WA	98043	(800) 258-0394
B+	LOCOMOTIVE ENGRS&COND MUT PROT ASSN	4000 TOWN CENTER SUITE 1250	SOUTHFIELD	MI	48075	(800) 514-0010
B+	M LIFE INS CO	THE CORP CO 7700 E ARAPAHOE RD	CENTENNIAL	CO	80112	(503) 414-7336
A-	MASSACHUSETTS MUTUAL LIFE INS CO	1295 STATE STREET	SPRINGFIELD	MA	1111	(800) 272-2216
B+	MIDLAND NATIONAL LIFE INS CO	4350 WESTOWN PARKWAY	WEST DES MOINES	IA	50266	(800) 923-3223
B+	MINNESOTA LIFE INS CO	400 ROBERT STREET NORTH	ST. PAUL	MN	55101	(651) 665-3500
A-	MUTUAL OF AMERICA LIFE INS CO	320 PARK AVENUE	NEW YORK	NY	10022	(800) 468-3785
B+	NATIONAL BENEFIT LIFE INS CO	ONE COURT SQUARE	LONG ISLAND CITY	NY	11120	(800) 222-2062
B+	NATIONAL FARMERS UNION LIFE INS CO	PO BOX 139061	DALLAS	TX	75313	(800) 366-6565
B+	NATIONAL FOUNDATION LIFE INS CO	300 BURNETT STREET SUITE 200	FORT WORTH	TX	76102	(800) 221-9039
B+	NATIONAL INCOME LIFE INS CO	301 PLAINFIELD RD STE 150	SYRACUSE	NY	13212	(315) 451-8180

DOM. STATE	IND. LIFE	IND. HEALTH	IND. ANNU.	GROUP LIFE	GROUP HEALTH	GROUP ANNU	CREDIT LIFE	CREDIT HEALTH	SUP. CONTR.	OTHER	INSURANCE COMPANY NAME
KS	13	0	0	58	29	0	0	0	0	0	ADVANCE INS CO OF KANSAS
NY	0	1	99	0	0	0	0	0	0	0	ALLIANZ LIFE INS CO OF NY
NY	3	3	0	68	26	0	0	0	0	0	AMALGAMATED LIFE INS CO
NY	4	94	0	0	2	0	0	0	0	0	AMERICAN FAMILY LIFE ASR CO OF NY
WI	94	1	3	1	0	0	0	0	0	0	AMERICAN FAMILY LIFE INS CO
OK	12	32	16	0	39	0	0	0	0	0	AMERICAN FIDELITY ASR CO
TX	13	0	0	7	2	0	38	40	0	0	AMERICAN HEALTH & LIFE INS CO
IN	6	0	4	3	3	85	0	0	0	0	AMERICAN UNITED LIFE INS CO
RI	80	0	13	6	0	0	0	0	0	0	AMICA LIFE INS CO
OH	0	0	91	0	0	9	0	0	0	0	ANNUITY INVESTORS LIFE INS CO
NE	54	32	6	4	4	0	0	0	0	0	ASSURITY LIFE INS CO
NY	17	0	61	0	0	22	0	0	0	0	AXA EQUITABLE LIFE INS CO
IA	0	0	0	0	100	0	0	0	0	0	BERKLEY LIFE & HEALTH INS CO
TX	0	35	0	2	63	0	0	0	0	0	BEST LIFE & HEALTH INS CO
MS	2	0	0	97	0	0	0	0	0	0	BLUEBONNET LIFE INS CO
MA	64	4	0	15	17	0	0	0	0	0	BOSTON MUTUAL LIFE INS CO
OK	2	98	0	0	0	0	0	0	0	0	CHESAPEAKE LIFE INS CO
TX	5	88	0	0	8	0	0	0	0	0	CHRISTIAN FIDELITY LIFE INS CO
NY	0	0	0	32	68	0	0	0	0	0	CIGNA LIFE INS CO OF NEW YORK
SC	0	1	0	11	88	0	0	0	0	0	COMPANION LIFE INS CO
GA	99	0	1	0	0	0	0	0	0	0	COTTON STATES LIFE INS CO
IL	0	0	0	0	0	0	0	0	0	0	COUNTRY INVESTORS LIFE ASR CO
IL	62	14	13	1	10	0	0	0	0	0	COUNTRY LIFE INS CO
IL	2	0	1	69	28	0	0	0	0	0	DEARBORN NATIONAL LIFE INS CO
NY	1	0	0	74	26	0	0	0	0	0	DEARBORN NATIONAL LIFE INS CO OF NY
DE	4	5	0	8	84	0	0	0	0	0	DELAWARE AMERICAN LIFE INS CO
IA	0	0	100	0	0	0	0	0	0	0	EAGLE LIFE INS CO
NY	0	0	100	0	0	0	0	0	0	0	EMPIRE FIDELITY INVESTMENTS L I C
TX	0	9	0	0	91	0	0	0	0	0	ENTERPRISE LIFE INS CO
PA	82	0	18	0	0	0	0	0	0	0	ERIE FAMILY LIFE INS CO
OH	10	86	0	0	4	0	0	0	0	0	FAMILY HERITAGE LIFE INS CO OF AMER
IA	51	0	47	0	0	1	0	0	0	0	FARM BUREAU LIFE INS CO
MI	48	0	50	0	0	2	0	0	0	0	FARM BUREAU LIFE INS CO OF MICHIGAN
MO	83	0	16	1	0	0	0	0	0	0	FARM BUREAU LIFE INS CO OF MISSOURI
MN	71	15	11	3	0	0	0	0	0	0	FEDERATED LIFE INS CO
UT	0	0	100	0	0	0	0	0	0	0	FIDELITY INVESTMENTS LIFE INS CO
NY	0	0	0	20	80	0	0	0	0	0	FIRST RELIANCE STANDARD LIFE INS CO
NY	0	0	93	1	5	0	0	0	0	0	FIRST SYMETRA NATL LIFE INS CO OF NY
GA	0	0	0	0	0	0	40	60	0	0	FRANDISCO LIFE INS CO
TX	15	26	0	0	60	0	0	0	0	0	FREEDOM LIFE INS CO OF AMERICA
TX	98	0	0	0	2	0	0	0	0	0	GARDEN STATE LIFE INS CO
NY	64	2	0	0	34	0	0	0	0	0	GERBER LIFE INS CO
NY	50	6	0	7	37	0	0	0	0	0	GUARDIAN LIFE INS CO OF AMERICA
FL	76	6	0	1	17	0	0	0	0	0	HANNOVER LIFE REASSURANCE CO OF AMER
NY	74	24	0	0	2	0	0	0	0	0	LIFE INS CO OF BOSTON & NEW YORK
WA	0	0	0	0	100	0	0	0	0	0	LIFEWISE ASR CO
MI	100	0	0	0	0	0	0	0	0	0	LOCOMOTIVE ENGRS&COND MUT PROT ASSN
CO	99	1	0	0	0	0	0	0	0	0	M LIFE INS CO
MA	35	4	13	-15	0	63	0	0	0	0	MASSACHUSETTS MUTUAL LIFE INS CO
IA	35	0	60	0	0	5	0	0	0	0	MIDLAND NATIONAL LIFE INS CO
MN	21	0	9	21	3	44	1	1	0	0	MINNESOTA LIFE INS CO
NY	0	0	23	0	0	77	0	0	0	0	MUTUAL OF AMERICA LIFE INS CO
NY	99	0	0	0	1	0	0	0	0	0	NATIONAL BENEFIT LIFE INS CO
TX	97	0	1	1	0	0	0	0	0	0	NATIONAL FARMERS UNION LIFE INS CO
TX	6	50	0	0	43	0	0	0	0	0	NATIONAL FOUNDATION LIFE INS CO
NY	92	8	0	0	0	0	0	0	0	0	NATIONAL INCOME LIFE INS CO

RATING	INSURANCE COMPANY NAME	ADDRESS	CITY	STATE	ZIP	PHONE
A	NATIONAL WESTERN LIFE INS CO	7700 E ARAPAHOE ROAD SUITE 220	CENTENNIAL	CO	80112	(800) 531-5442
B+	NEW YORK LIFE INS & ANNUITY CORP	200 CONTINENTAL DRIVE STE 306	NEWARK	DE	19713	(212) 576-7000
A-	NEW YORK LIFE INS CO	51 MADISON AVENUE	NEW YORK	NY	10010	(212) 576-7000
A-	NIPPON LIFE INS CO OF AMERICA	7115 VISTA DRIVE	WEST DES MOINES	IA	50266	(800) 374-1835
B+	NORTH AMERICAN INS CO	575 DONOFRIO DRIVE SUITE 100	MADISON	WI	53719	(800) 308-2318
B+	NORTHWESTERN MUTUAL LIFE INS CO	720 EAST WISCONSIN AVENUE	MILWAUKEE	WI	53202	(414) 271-1444
B+	OHIO NATIONAL LIFE ASR CORP	ONE FINANCIAL WAY	CINCINNATI	OH	45242	(800) 366-6654
B+	OXFORD LIFE INS CO	2721 NORTH CENTRAL AVENUE	PHOENIX	AZ	85004	(800) 308-2318
A-	PACIFIC GUARDIAN LIFE INS CO LTD	1440 KAPIOLANI BLVD STE 1600	HONOLULU	HI	96814	(800) 432-3306
B+	PACIFIC LIFE & ANNUITY CO	3800 N CENTRAL AVE STE 460	PHOENIX	AZ	85012	(800) 800-7646
A-	PACIFIC LIFE INS CO	6750 MERCY ROAD	OMAHA	NE	68106	(800) 800-7646
B+	PAN AMERICAN ASR CO	PAN-AMERICAN LIFE CENTER 601	NEW ORLEANS	LA	70130	(877) 939-4550
A	PARKER CENTENNIAL ASR CO	1800 NORTH POINT DRIVE	STEVENS POINT	WI	54481	(800) 373-6879
A-	PHYSICIANS LIFE INS CO	2600 DODGE STREET	OMAHA	NE	68131	(800) 228-9100
A+	PHYSICIANS MUTUAL INS CO	2600 DODGE STREET	OMAHA	NE	68131	(800) 228-9100
B+	PRINCIPAL LIFE INS CO	711 HIGH STREET	DES MOINES	IA	50392	(800) 986-3343
B+	SB MUTL LIFE INS CO OF MA	ONE LINSCOTT ROAD	WOBURN	MA	1801	(888) 438-7254
A	SENTRY LIFE INS CO	1800 NORTH POINT DRIVE	STEVENS POINT	WI	54481	(800) 373-6879
A	SHELTERPOINT LIFE INS CO	1225 FRANKLIN AVE STE 475	GARDEN CITY	NY	11530	(800) 365-4999
A	SOUTHERN FARM BUREAU LIFE INS CO	1401 LIVINGSTON LANE	JACKSON	MS	39213	(800) 457-9611
A-	SOUTHERN PIONEER LIFE INS CO	124 WEST CAPITOL AVE STE 1900	LITTLE ROCK	AR	72201	(866) 884-6167
B+	STANDARD INS CO	1100 SOUTHWEST SIXTH AVENUE	PORTLAND	OR	97204	(503) 321-7000
A-	STANDARD LIFE & ACCIDENT INS CO	ONE MOODY PLAZA	GALVESTON	TX	77550	(888) 290-1085
A-	STANDARD LIFE INS CO OF NY	360 HAMILTON AVENUE SUITE 210	WHITE PLAINS	NY	10601	(914) 989-4400
A+	STATE FARM LIFE & ACCIDENT ASR CO	ONE STATE FARM PLAZA	BLOOMINGTON	IL	61710	(855) 733-7333
A+	STATE FARM LIFE INS CO	ONE STATE FARM PLAZA	BLOOMINGTON	IL	61710	(855) 733-7333
B+	SWBC LIFE INS CO	9311 SAN PEDRO STE 600	SAN ANTONIO	TX	78216	(866) 252-1920
A-	SYMETRA NATIONAL LIFE INS CO	4125 WESTOWN PARKWAY SUITE 102	WEST DES MOINES	IA	50266	(800) 796-3872
A+	TEACHERS INS & ANNUITY ASN OF AM	730 THIRD AVENUE	NEW YORK	NY	10017	(800) 842-2252
B+	TENNESSEE FARMERS LIFE INS CO	147 BEAR CREEK PIKE	COLUMBIA	TN	38401	(931) 388-7872
A-	TRANS OCEANIC LIFE INS CO	#121 ONEILL	SAN JUAN	PR	00918	(787) 620-2680
B+	TRANS WORLD ASR CO	885 S EL CAMINO REAL	SAN MATEO	CA	94402	(866) 997-6349
B+	TRUSTMARK INS CO	400 FIELD DRIVE	LAKE FOREST	IL	60045	(800) 366-6663
B+	TRUSTMARK LIFE INS CO	400 FIELD DRIVE	LAKE FOREST	IL	60045	(800) 366-6663
A	UNITED FARM FAMILY LIFE INS CO	225 SOUTH EAST STREET	INDIANAPOLIS	IN	46202	(800) 723-3276
B+	UNITED WORLD LIFE INS CO	MUTUAL OF OMAHA PLAZA	OMAHA	NE	68175	(800) 228-7104
B+	UNIVERSAL LIFE INS CO	CALLE BOLIVIA #33 6TO PISO	SAN JUAN	PR	917	(787) 706-7337
A	USAA LIFE INS CO	9800 FREDERICKSBURG RD	SAN ANTONIO	TX	78288	(210) 498-8000
B+	USAA LIFE INS CO OF NEW YORK	529 MAIN STREET	HIGHLAND FALLS	NY	10928	(210) 498-8000
A-	USABLE LIFE	320 W CAPITOL SUITE 700	LITTLE ROCK	AR	72201	(800) 370-5856
B+	UTIC INS CO	450 RIVERCHASE PARKWAY EAST	BIRMINGHAM	AL	35244	(205) 220-2100
B+	VOYA RETIREMENT INS & ANNUITY CO	ONE ORANGE WAY	WINDSOR	CT	06095	(877) 886-5050

DOM. STATE	IND. LIFE	IND. HEALTH	IND. ANNU.	GROUP LIFE	GROUP HEALTH	GROUP ANNU	CREDIT LIFE	CREDIT HEALTH	SUP. CONTR.	OTHER	INSURANCE COMPANY NAME
CO	29	0	70	0	0	0	0	0	0	0	NATIONAL WESTERN LIFE INS CO
DE	12	0	87	1	0	1	0	0	0	0	NEW YORK LIFE INS & ANNUITY CORP
NY	51	2	2	15	1	29	0	0	0	0	NEW YORK LIFE INS CO
IA	0	0	0	1	99	0	0	0	0	0	NIPPON LIFE INS CO OF AMERICA
WI	0	100	0	0	0	0	0	0	0	0	NORTH AMERICAN INS CO
WI	76	11	12	0	0	1	0	0	0	0	NORTHWESTERN MUTUAL LIFE INS CO
OH	92	7	0	0	0	0	0	0	0	0	OHIO NATIONAL LIFE ASR CORP
AZ	15	12	73	0	0	0	0	0	0	0	OXFORD LIFE INS CO
HI	35	0	0	9	56	0	0	0	0	0	PACIFIC GUARDIAN LIFE INS CO LTD
AZ	5	0	95	0	0	0	0	0	0	0	PACIFIC LIFE & ANNUITY CO
NE	35	0	56	0	0	9	0	0	0	0	PACIFIC LIFE INS CO
LA	100	0	0	0	0	0	0	0	0	0	PAN AMERICAN ASR CO
WI	0	0	0	0	0	100	0	0	0	0	PARKER CENTENNIAL ASR CO
NE	62	0	16	21	0	0	0	0	0	0	PHYSICIANS LIFE INS CO
NE	0	90	0	0	10	0	0	0	0	0	PHYSICIANS MUTUAL INS CO
IA	11	4	31	5	15	33	0	0	0	0	PRINCIPAL LIFE INS CO
MA	97	0	3	0	0	0	0	0	0	0	SB MUTL LIFE INS CO OF MA
WI	3	0	1	1	0	95	0	0	0	0	SENTRY LIFE INS CO
NY	0	0	0	2	98	0	0	0	0	0	SHELTERPOINT LIFE INS CO
MS	85	1	13	1	0	0	0	0	0	0	SOUTHERN FARM BUREAU LIFE INS CO
AR	4	0	0	0	0	0	68	29	0	0	SOUTHERN PIONEER LIFE INS CO
OR	0	5	12	3	29	52	0	0	0	0	STANDARD INS CO
TX	13	66	0	0	21	0	0	0	0	0	STANDARD LIFE & ACCIDENT INS CO
NY	0	3	0	37	60	0	0	0	0	0	STANDARD LIFE INS CO OF NY
IL	91	0	9	0	0	0	0	0	0	0	STATE FARM LIFE & ACCIDENT ASR CO
IL	90	0	8	1	0	0	0	0	0	0	STATE FARM LIFE INS CO
TX	1	0	0	0	6	0	41	52	0	0	SWBC LIFE INS CO
IA	100	0	0	0	0	0	0	0	0	0	SYMETRA NATIONAL LIFE INS CO
NY	2	0	50	0	0	49	0	0	0	0	TEACHERS INS & ANNUITY ASN OF AM
TN	78	0	20	0	2	0	0	0	0	0	TENNESSEE FARMERS LIFE INS CO
PR	7	93	0	0	0	0	0	0	0	0	TRANS OCEANIC LIFE INS CO
CA	73	0	16	11	0	0	0	0	0	0	TRANS WORLD ASR CO
IL	8	15	1	47	29	0	0	0	0	0	TRUSTMARK INS CO
IL	0	0	0	4	96	0	0	0	0	0	TRUSTMARK LIFE INS CO
IN	92	0	8	0	0	0	0	0	0	0	UNITED FARM FAMILY LIFE INS CO
NE	100	0	0	0	0	0	0	0	0	0	UNITED WORLD LIFE INS CO
PR	1	0	85	7	5	0	3	0	0	0	UNIVERSAL LIFE INS CO
TX	39	21	40	0	0	0	0	0	0	0	USAA LIFE INS CO
NY	54	0	46	0	0	0	0	0	0	0	USAA LIFE INS CO OF NEW YORK
AR	1	18	0	21	60	0	0	0	0	0	USABLE LIFE
AL	0	78	0	0	22	0	0	0	0	0	UTIC INS CO
CT	0	0	1	0	0	99	0	0	0	0	VOYA RETIREMENT INS & ANNUITY CO

Section IV

Weiss Ratings Recommended Companies by State

A compilation of those

U.S. Life and Annuity Insurers

receiving a Weiss Safety Rating
of A+, A, A- or B+.

Companies are ranked by Safety Rating
in each state where they are licensed to do business.

Section IV Contents

This section provides a list of the recommended carriers licensed to do business in each state. It contains all insurers receiving a Weiss Safety Rating of A+, A, A-, or B+. If an insurer is not on this list, it should not be automatically assumed that the firm is weak. Indeed, there are many firms that have not achieved a B+ or better rating but are in relatively good condition with adequate resources to cover their risk during an average recession. Not being included in this list should not be construed as a recommendation to surrender policies.

Companies are ranked within each state by their Safety Rating. However, companies with the same rating should be viewed as having the same relative strength regardless of their ranking in this table. While the specific order in which they appear on the page is based upon differences in our underlying indexes, you can assume that companies with the same rating have differences that are only minor and relatively inconsequential.

1. Safety Rating	Our rating is measured on a scale from A to F and considers a wide range of factors. Highly-rated companies are, in our opinion, less likely to experience financial difficulties than lower rated firms. See *About Weiss Safety Ratings* for more information.
2. Insurance Company Name	The legally registered name, which can sometimes differ from the name that the company uses for advertising. An insurer's name can be very similar to the name of other companies which may not be on our Recommended List, so make sure you note the exact name before contacting your agent.
3. Domicile State	The state which has primary regulatory responsibility for the company. It may differ from the location of the company's corporate headquarters. You do not have to be living in the domicile state to purchase insurance from this firm, provided it is licensed to do business in your state.
4. Total Assets	All assets admitted by state insurance regulators in millions of dollars. This includes investments, current business assets, and separate accounts.

Weiss Safety Ratings are not deemed to be a recommendation concerning the purchase or sale of the securities of any insurance company that is publicly owned.

Alabama

INSURANCE COMPANY NAME	DOM. STATE	TOTAL ASSETS ($MIL)

Rating: A+

INSURANCE COMPANY NAME	DOM. STATE	TOTAL ASSETS ($MIL)
AMERICAN FAMILY LIFE INS CO	WI	5,269.9
COUNTRY LIFE INS CO	IL	9,673.9
PHYSICIANS MUTUAL INS CO	NE	2,367.4
STATE FARM LIFE INS CO	IL	74,940.7
TEACHERS INS & ANNUITY ASN OF AM	NY	302,803.1

Rating: A

INSURANCE COMPANY NAME	DOM. STATE	TOTAL ASSETS ($MIL)
AMALGAMATED LIFE INS CO	NY	140.3
BERKLEY LIFE & HEALTH INS CO	IA	325.8
FEDERATED LIFE INS CO	MN	1,969.7
GARDEN STATE LIFE INS CO	TX	135.5
GUARDIAN LIFE INS CO OF AMERICA	NY	57,852.7
NATIONAL WESTERN LIFE INS CO	CO	11,114.0
PARKER CENTENNIAL ASR CO	WI	96.0
SENTRY LIFE INS CO	WI	7,425.4
SOUTHERN FARM BUREAU LIFE INS CO	MS	14,356.8
USAA LIFE INS CO	TX	25,292.8

Rating: A-

INSURANCE COMPANY NAME	DOM. STATE	TOTAL ASSETS ($MIL)
AMERICAN HEALTH & LIFE INS CO	TX	1,018.0
ANNUITY INVESTORS LIFE INS CO	OH	3,232.6
CIGNA LIFE INS CO OF NEW YORK	NY	407.5
COTTON STATES LIFE INS CO	GA	339.7
COUNTRY INVESTORS LIFE ASR CO	IL	303.5
FIDELITY INVESTMENTS LIFE INS CO	UT	30,960.8
MASSACHUSETTS MUTUAL LIFE INS CO	MA	245,872.2
MUTUAL OF AMERICA LIFE INS CO	NY	21,758.9
NEW YORK LIFE INS CO	NY	178,706.9
NIPPON LIFE INS CO OF AMERICA	IA	219.2
PACIFIC LIFE INS CO	NE	133,288.3
PHYSICIANS LIFE INS CO	NE	1,664.1
SOUTHERN PIONEER LIFE INS CO	AR	14.6
STANDARD LIFE & ACCIDENT INS CO	TX	533.1
SYMETRA NATIONAL LIFE INS CO	IA	18.6
USABLE LIFE	AR	541.5

Rating: B+

INSURANCE COMPANY NAME	DOM. STATE	TOTAL ASSETS ($MIL)
AMERICAN FIDELITY ASR CO	OK	6,090.1
AMERICAN UNITED LIFE INS CO	IN	29,575.8
AMICA LIFE INS CO	RI	1,302.6
ASSURITY LIFE INS CO	NE	2,729.5
AXA EQUITABLE LIFE INS CO	NY	191,807.0
BEST LIFE & HEALTH INS CO	TX	22.7
BLUEBONNET LIFE INS CO	MS	64.3
BOSTON MUTUAL LIFE INS CO	MA	1,461.7
CHESAPEAKE LIFE INS CO	OK	195.4
CHRISTIAN FIDELITY LIFE INS CO	TX	64.2
COMPANION LIFE INS CO	SC	401.6
DEARBORN NATIONAL LIFE INS CO	IL	1,737.6
DELAWARE AMERICAN LIFE INS CO	DE	122.9
EAGLE LIFE INS CO	IA	1,070.1
FAMILY HERITAGE LIFE INS CO OF AMER	OH	1,444.8
FREEDOM LIFE INS CO OF AMERICA	TX	213.2
GERBER LIFE INS CO	NY	3,909.7
HANNOVER LIFE REASSURANCE CO OF AMER	FL	16,338.8

INSURANCE COMPANY NAME	DOM. STATE	TOTAL ASSETS ($MIL)
MIDLAND NATIONAL LIFE INS CO	IA	58,240.4
MINNESOTA LIFE INS CO	MN	49,271.3
NATIONAL BENEFIT LIFE INS CO	NY	564.7
NATIONAL FOUNDATION LIFE INS CO	TX	50.6
NEW YORK LIFE INS & ANNUITY CORP	DE	156,175.5
NORTH AMERICAN INS CO	WI	19.2
NORTHWESTERN MUTUAL LIFE INS CO	WI	273,304.0
OHIO NATIONAL LIFE ASR CORP	OH	4,098.9
OXFORD LIFE INS CO	AZ	2,192.1
PACIFIC LIFE & ANNUITY CO	AZ	7,409.8
PAN AMERICAN ASR CO	LA	26.7
PRINCIPAL LIFE INS CO	IA	197,908.3
SB MUTL LIFE INS CO OF MA	MA	3,104.8
STANDARD INS CO	OR	24,530.4
TRANS WORLD ASR CO	CA	344.9
TRUSTMARK INS CO	IL	1,606.0
TRUSTMARK LIFE INS CO	IL	330.1
UNITED WORLD LIFE INS CO	NE	119.5
UTIC INS CO	AL	102.4
VOYA RETIREMENT INS & ANNUITY CO	CT	108,678.3

Alaska

INSURANCE COMPANY NAME	DOM. STATE	TOTAL ASSETS ($MIL)
Rating: A+		
AMERICAN FAMILY LIFE INS CO	WI	5,269.9
COUNTRY LIFE INS CO	IL	9,673.9
PHYSICIANS MUTUAL INS CO	NE	2,367.4
STATE FARM LIFE INS CO	IL	74,940.7
TEACHERS INS & ANNUITY ASN OF AM	NY	302,803.1
Rating: A		
AMALGAMATED LIFE INS CO	NY	140.3
BERKLEY LIFE & HEALTH INS CO	IA	325.8
GARDEN STATE LIFE INS CO	TX	135.5
GUARDIAN LIFE INS CO OF AMERICA	NY	57,852.7
LIFEWISE ASR CO	WA	193.1
NATIONAL WESTERN LIFE INS CO	CO	11,114.0
PARKER CENTENNIAL ASR CO	WI	96.0
SENTRY LIFE INS CO	WI	7,425.4
USAA LIFE INS CO	TX	25,292.8
Rating: A-		
AMERICAN HEALTH & LIFE INS CO	TX	1,018.0
ANNUITY INVESTORS LIFE INS CO	OH	3,232.6
COUNTRY INVESTORS LIFE ASR CO	IL	303.5
FIDELITY INVESTMENTS LIFE INS CO	UT	30,960.8
MASSACHUSETTS MUTUAL LIFE INS CO	MA	245,872.2
MUTUAL OF AMERICA LIFE INS CO	NY	21,758.9
NEW YORK LIFE INS CO	NY	178,706.9
NIPPON LIFE INS CO OF AMERICA	IA	219.2
PACIFIC GUARDIAN LIFE INS CO LTD	HI	559.1
PACIFIC LIFE INS CO	NE	133,288.3
PHYSICIANS LIFE INS CO	NE	1,664.1
STANDARD LIFE & ACCIDENT INS CO	TX	533.1
USABLE LIFE	AR	541.5
Rating: B+		
AMERICAN FIDELITY ASR CO	OK	6,090.1
AMERICAN UNITED LIFE INS CO	IN	29,575.8
AMICA LIFE INS CO	RI	1,302.6
ASSURITY LIFE INS CO	NE	2,729.5
AXA EQUITABLE LIFE INS CO	NY	191,807.0
BEST LIFE & HEALTH INS CO	TX	22.7
BOSTON MUTUAL LIFE INS CO	MA	1,461.7
CHESAPEAKE LIFE INS CO	OK	195.4
COMPANION LIFE INS CO	SC	401.6
DEARBORN NATIONAL LIFE INS CO	IL	1,737.6
DELAWARE AMERICAN LIFE INS CO	DE	122.9
EAGLE LIFE INS CO	IA	1,070.1
FAMILY HERITAGE LIFE INS CO OF AMER	OH	1,444.8
GERBER LIFE INS CO	NY	3,909.7
HANNOVER LIFE REASSURANCE CO OF AMER	FL	16,338.8
MIDLAND NATIONAL LIFE INS CO	IA	58,240.4
MINNESOTA LIFE INS CO	MN	49,271.3
NATIONAL BENEFIT LIFE INS CO	NY	564.7
NATIONAL FARMERS UNION LIFE INS CO	TX	193.3
NATIONAL FOUNDATION LIFE INS CO	TX	50.6
NEW YORK LIFE INS & ANNUITY CORP	DE	156,175.5
NORTHWESTERN MUTUAL LIFE INS CO	WI	273,304.0

INSURANCE COMPANY NAME	DOM. STATE	TOTAL ASSETS ($MIL)
OHIO NATIONAL LIFE ASR CORP	OH	4,098.9
OXFORD LIFE INS CO	AZ	2,192.1
PACIFIC LIFE & ANNUITY CO	AZ	7,409.8
PRINCIPAL LIFE INS CO	IA	197,908.3
SB MUTL LIFE INS CO OF MA	MA	3,104.8
STANDARD INS CO	OR	24,530.4
TRANS WORLD ASR CO	CA	344.9
TRUSTMARK INS CO	IL	1,606.0
TRUSTMARK LIFE INS CO	IL	330.1
UNITED WORLD LIFE INS CO	NE	119.5
VOYA RETIREMENT INS & ANNUITY CO	CT	108,678.3

Arizona

INSURANCE COMPANY NAME	DOM. STATE	TOTAL ASSETS ($MIL)
Rating: A+		
AMERICAN FAMILY LIFE INS CO	WI	5,269.9
COUNTRY LIFE INS CO	IL	9,673.9
PHYSICIANS MUTUAL INS CO	NE	2,367.4
STATE FARM LIFE INS CO	IL	74,940.7
TEACHERS INS & ANNUITY ASN OF AM	NY	302,803.1
Rating: A		
AMALGAMATED LIFE INS CO	NY	140.3
BERKLEY LIFE & HEALTH INS CO	IA	325.8
FEDERATED LIFE INS CO	MN	1,969.7
GARDEN STATE LIFE INS CO	TX	135.5
GUARDIAN LIFE INS CO OF AMERICA	NY	57,852.7
NATIONAL WESTERN LIFE INS CO	CO	11,114.0
PARKER CENTENNIAL ASR CO	WI	96.0
SENTRY LIFE INS CO	WI	7,425.4
UNITED FARM FAMILY LIFE INS CO	IN	2,348.2
USAA LIFE INS CO	TX	25,292.8
Rating: A-		
AMERICAN HEALTH & LIFE INS CO	TX	1,018.0
ANNUITY INVESTORS LIFE INS CO	OH	3,232.6
COUNTRY INVESTORS LIFE ASR CO	IL	303.5
FIDELITY INVESTMENTS LIFE INS CO	UT	30,960.8
MASSACHUSETTS MUTUAL LIFE INS CO	MA	245,872.2
MUTUAL OF AMERICA LIFE INS CO	NY	21,758.9
NEW YORK LIFE INS CO	NY	178,706.9
NIPPON LIFE INS CO OF AMERICA	IA	219.2
PACIFIC GUARDIAN LIFE INS CO LTD	HI	559.1
PACIFIC LIFE INS CO	NE	133,288.3
PHYSICIANS LIFE INS CO	NE	1,664.1
STANDARD LIFE & ACCIDENT INS CO	TX	533.1
SYMETRA NATIONAL LIFE INS CO	IA	18.6
USABLE LIFE	AR	541.5
Rating: B+		
AMERICAN FIDELITY ASR CO	OK	6,090.1
AMERICAN UNITED LIFE INS CO	IN	29,575.8
AMICA LIFE INS CO	RI	1,302.6
ASSURITY LIFE INS CO	NE	2,729.5
AXA EQUITABLE LIFE INS CO	NY	191,807.0
BEST LIFE & HEALTH INS CO	TX	22.7
BOSTON MUTUAL LIFE INS CO	MA	1,461.7
CHESAPEAKE LIFE INS CO	OK	195.4
CHRISTIAN FIDELITY LIFE INS CO	TX	64.2
COMPANION LIFE INS CO	SC	401.6
DEARBORN NATIONAL LIFE INS CO	IL	1,737.6
DELAWARE AMERICAN LIFE INS CO	DE	122.9
EAGLE LIFE INS CO	IA	1,070.1
ENTERPRISE LIFE INS CO	TX	73.7
FAMILY HERITAGE LIFE INS CO OF AMER	OH	1,444.8
FARM BUREAU LIFE INS CO	IA	9,267.1
FREEDOM LIFE INS CO OF AMERICA	TX	213.2
GERBER LIFE INS CO	NY	3,909.7
HANNOVER LIFE REASSURANCE CO OF AMER	FL	16,338.8
M LIFE INS CO	CO	307.3

INSURANCE COMPANY NAME	DOM. STATE	TOTAL ASSETS ($MIL)
MIDLAND NATIONAL LIFE INS CO	IA	58,240.4
MINNESOTA LIFE INS CO	MN	49,271.3
NATIONAL BENEFIT LIFE INS CO	NY	564.7
NATIONAL FARMERS UNION LIFE INS CO	TX	193.3
NATIONAL FOUNDATION LIFE INS CO	TX	50.6
NEW YORK LIFE INS & ANNUITY CORP	DE	156,175.5
NORTHWESTERN MUTUAL LIFE INS CO	WI	273,304.0
OHIO NATIONAL LIFE ASR CORP	OH	4,098.9
OXFORD LIFE INS CO	AZ	2,192.1
PACIFIC LIFE & ANNUITY CO	AZ	7,409.8
PAN AMERICAN ASR CO	LA	26.7
PRINCIPAL LIFE INS CO	IA	197,908.3
SB MUTL LIFE INS CO OF MA	MA	3,104.8
STANDARD INS CO	OR	24,530.4
TRANS WORLD ASR CO	CA	344.9
TRUSTMARK INS CO	IL	1,606.0
TRUSTMARK LIFE INS CO	IL	330.1
UNITED WORLD LIFE INS CO	NE	119.5
VOYA RETIREMENT INS & ANNUITY CO	CT	108,678.3

Arkansas

INSURANCE COMPANY NAME	DOM. STATE	TOTAL ASSETS ($MIL)
Rating: A+		
AMERICAN FAMILY LIFE INS CO	WI	5,269.9
COUNTRY LIFE INS CO	IL	9,673.9
PHYSICIANS MUTUAL INS CO	NE	2,367.4
STATE FARM LIFE INS CO	IL	74,940.7
TEACHERS INS & ANNUITY ASN OF AM	NY	302,803.1
Rating: A		
AMALGAMATED LIFE INS CO	NY	140.3
BERKLEY LIFE & HEALTH INS CO	IA	325.8
FEDERATED LIFE INS CO	MN	1,969.7
GARDEN STATE LIFE INS CO	TX	135.5
GUARDIAN LIFE INS CO OF AMERICA	NY	57,852.7
NATIONAL WESTERN LIFE INS CO	CO	11,114.0
PARKER CENTENNIAL ASR CO	WI	96.0
SENTRY LIFE INS CO	WI	7,425.4
SOUTHERN FARM BUREAU LIFE INS CO	MS	14,356.8
USAA LIFE INS CO	TX	25,292.8
Rating: A-		
AMERICAN HEALTH & LIFE INS CO	TX	1,018.0
ANNUITY INVESTORS LIFE INS CO	OH	3,232.6
COUNTRY INVESTORS LIFE ASR CO	IL	303.5
FIDELITY INVESTMENTS LIFE INS CO	UT	30,960.8
MASSACHUSETTS MUTUAL LIFE INS CO	MA	245,872.2
MUTUAL OF AMERICA LIFE INS CO	NY	21,758.9
NEW YORK LIFE INS CO	NY	178,706.9
NIPPON LIFE INS CO OF AMERICA	IA	219.2
PACIFIC LIFE INS CO	NE	133,288.3
PHYSICIANS LIFE INS CO	NE	1,664.1
SOUTHERN PIONEER LIFE INS CO	AR	14.6
STANDARD LIFE & ACCIDENT INS CO	TX	533.1
SYMETRA NATIONAL LIFE INS CO	IA	18.6
USABLE LIFE	AR	541.5
Rating: B+		
AMERICAN FIDELITY ASR CO	OK	6,090.1
AMERICAN UNITED LIFE INS CO	IN	29,575.8
AMICA LIFE INS CO	RI	1,302.6
ASSURITY LIFE INS CO	NE	2,729.5
AXA EQUITABLE LIFE INS CO	NY	191,807.0
BEST LIFE & HEALTH INS CO	TX	22.7
BLUEBONNET LIFE INS CO	MS	64.3
BOSTON MUTUAL LIFE INS CO	MA	1,461.7
CHESAPEAKE LIFE INS CO	OK	195.4
CHRISTIAN FIDELITY LIFE INS CO	TX	64.2
COMPANION LIFE INS CO	SC	401.6
DEARBORN NATIONAL LIFE INS CO	IL	1,737.6
DELAWARE AMERICAN LIFE INS CO	DE	122.9
EAGLE LIFE INS CO	IA	1,070.1
ENTERPRISE LIFE INS CO	TX	73.7
FAMILY HERITAGE LIFE INS CO OF AMER	OH	1,444.8
FREEDOM LIFE INS CO OF AMERICA	TX	213.2
GERBER LIFE INS CO	NY	3,909.7
HANNOVER LIFE REASSURANCE CO OF AMER	FL	16,338.8
MIDLAND NATIONAL LIFE INS CO	IA	58,240.4

INSURANCE COMPANY NAME	DOM. STATE	TOTAL ASSETS ($MIL)
MINNESOTA LIFE INS CO	MN	49,271.3
NATIONAL BENEFIT LIFE INS CO	NY	564.7
NATIONAL FARMERS UNION LIFE INS CO	TX	193.3
NATIONAL FOUNDATION LIFE INS CO	TX	50.6
NEW YORK LIFE INS & ANNUITY CORP	DE	156,175.5
NORTHWESTERN MUTUAL LIFE INS CO	WI	273,304.0
OHIO NATIONAL LIFE ASR CORP	OH	4,098.9
OXFORD LIFE INS CO	AZ	2,192.1
PACIFIC LIFE & ANNUITY CO	AZ	7,409.8
PAN AMERICAN ASR CO	LA	26.7
PRINCIPAL LIFE INS CO	IA	197,908.3
SB MUTL LIFE INS CO OF MA	MA	3,104.8
STANDARD INS CO	OR	24,530.4
TRANS WORLD ASR CO	CA	344.9
TRUSTMARK INS CO	IL	1,606.0
TRUSTMARK LIFE INS CO	IL	330.1
UNITED WORLD LIFE INS CO	NE	119.5
VOYA RETIREMENT INS & ANNUITY CO	CT	108,678.3

California

INSURANCE COMPANY NAME	DOM. STATE	TOTAL ASSETS ($MIL)

Rating: A+

INSURANCE COMPANY NAME	DOM. STATE	TOTAL ASSETS ($MIL)
AMERICAN FAMILY LIFE INS CO	WI	5,269.9
PHYSICIANS MUTUAL INS CO	NE	2,367.4
STATE FARM LIFE INS CO	IL	74,940.7
TEACHERS INS & ANNUITY ASN OF AM	NY	302,803.1

Rating: A

INSURANCE COMPANY NAME	DOM. STATE	TOTAL ASSETS ($MIL)
AMALGAMATED LIFE INS CO	NY	140.3
BERKLEY LIFE & HEALTH INS CO	IA	325.8
FEDERATED LIFE INS CO	MN	1,969.7
GARDEN STATE LIFE INS CO	TX	135.5
GUARDIAN LIFE INS CO OF AMERICA	NY	57,852.7
LIFEWISE ASR CO	WA	193.1
NATIONAL WESTERN LIFE INS CO	CO	11,114.0
PARKER CENTENNIAL ASR CO	WI	96.0
SENTRY LIFE INS CO	WI	7,425.4
SHELTERPOINT LIFE INS CO	NY	151.3
UNITED FARM FAMILY LIFE INS CO	IN	2,348.2
USAA LIFE INS CO	TX	25,292.8

Rating: A-

INSURANCE COMPANY NAME	DOM. STATE	TOTAL ASSETS ($MIL)
AMERICAN HEALTH & LIFE INS CO	TX	1,018.0
ANNUITY INVESTORS LIFE INS CO	OH	3,232.6
FIDELITY INVESTMENTS LIFE INS CO	UT	30,960.8
MASSACHUSETTS MUTUAL LIFE INS CO	MA	245,872.2
MUTUAL OF AMERICA LIFE INS CO	NY	21,758.9
NEW YORK LIFE INS CO	NY	178,706.9
NIPPON LIFE INS CO OF AMERICA	IA	219.2
PACIFIC GUARDIAN LIFE INS CO LTD	HI	559.1
PACIFIC LIFE INS CO	NE	133,288.3
PHYSICIANS LIFE INS CO	NE	1,664.1
STANDARD LIFE & ACCIDENT INS CO	TX	533.1
SYMETRA NATIONAL LIFE INS CO	IA	18.6
USABLE LIFE	AR	541.5

Rating: B+

INSURANCE COMPANY NAME	DOM. STATE	TOTAL ASSETS ($MIL)
AMERICAN FIDELITY ASR CO	OK	6,090.1
AMERICAN UNITED LIFE INS CO	IN	29,575.8
AMICA LIFE INS CO	RI	1,302.6
ASSURITY LIFE INS CO	NE	2,729.5
AXA EQUITABLE LIFE INS CO	NY	191,807.0
BEST LIFE & HEALTH INS CO	TX	22.7
BOSTON MUTUAL LIFE INS CO	MA	1,461.7
CHESAPEAKE LIFE INS CO	OK	195.4
DEARBORN NATIONAL LIFE INS CO	IL	1,737.6
DELAWARE AMERICAN LIFE INS CO	DE	122.9
EAGLE LIFE INS CO	IA	1,070.1
FAMILY HERITAGE LIFE INS CO OF AMER	OH	1,444.8
GERBER LIFE INS CO	NY	3,909.7
HANNOVER LIFE REASSURANCE CO OF AMER	FL	16,338.8
MIDLAND NATIONAL LIFE INS CO	IA	58,240.4
MINNESOTA LIFE INS CO	MN	49,271.3
NATIONAL BENEFIT LIFE INS CO	NY	564.7
NATIONAL FARMERS UNION LIFE INS CO	TX	193.3
NATIONAL FOUNDATION LIFE INS CO	TX	50.6
NEW YORK LIFE INS & ANNUITY CORP	DE	156,175.5

INSURANCE COMPANY NAME	DOM. STATE	TOTAL ASSETS ($MIL)
NORTHWESTERN MUTUAL LIFE INS CO	WI	273,304.0
OHIO NATIONAL LIFE ASR CORP	OH	4,098.9
OXFORD LIFE INS CO	AZ	2,192.1
PACIFIC LIFE & ANNUITY CO	AZ	7,409.8
PAN AMERICAN ASR CO	LA	26.7
PRINCIPAL LIFE INS CO	IA	197,908.3
SB MUTL LIFE INS CO OF MA	MA	3,104.8
STANDARD INS CO	OR	24,530.4
TRANS WORLD ASR CO	CA	344.9
TRUSTMARK INS CO	IL	1,606.0
TRUSTMARK LIFE INS CO	IL	330.1
UNITED WORLD LIFE INS CO	NE	119.5
VOYA RETIREMENT INS & ANNUITY CO	CT	108,678.3

Colorado

INSURANCE COMPANY NAME	DOM. STATE	TOTAL ASSETS ($MIL)

Rating: A+

INSURANCE COMPANY NAME	DOM. STATE	TOTAL ASSETS ($MIL)
AMERICAN FAMILY LIFE INS CO	WI	5,269.9
COUNTRY LIFE INS CO	IL	9,673.9
PHYSICIANS MUTUAL INS CO	NE	2,367.4
STATE FARM LIFE INS CO	IL	74,940.7
TEACHERS INS & ANNUITY ASN OF AM	NY	302,803.1

Rating: A

INSURANCE COMPANY NAME	DOM. STATE	TOTAL ASSETS ($MIL)
AMALGAMATED LIFE INS CO	NY	140.3
BERKLEY LIFE & HEALTH INS CO	IA	325.8
FEDERATED LIFE INS CO	MN	1,969.7
GARDEN STATE LIFE INS CO	TX	135.5
GUARDIAN LIFE INS CO OF AMERICA	NY	57,852.7
NATIONAL WESTERN LIFE INS CO	CO	11,114.0
PARKER CENTENNIAL ASR CO	WI	96.0
SENTRY LIFE INS CO	WI	7,425.4
SHELTERPOINT LIFE INS CO	NY	151.3
SOUTHERN FARM BUREAU LIFE INS CO	MS	14,356.8
USAA LIFE INS CO	TX	25,292.8

Rating: A-

INSURANCE COMPANY NAME	DOM. STATE	TOTAL ASSETS ($MIL)
AMERICAN HEALTH & LIFE INS CO	TX	1,018.0
ANNUITY INVESTORS LIFE INS CO	OH	3,232.6
COUNTRY INVESTORS LIFE ASR CO	IL	303.5
FIDELITY INVESTMENTS LIFE INS CO	UT	30,960.8
MASSACHUSETTS MUTUAL LIFE INS CO	MA	245,872.2
MUTUAL OF AMERICA LIFE INS CO	NY	21,758.9
NEW YORK LIFE INS CO	NY	178,706.9
NIPPON LIFE INS CO OF AMERICA	IA	219.2
PACIFIC GUARDIAN LIFE INS CO LTD	HI	559.1
PACIFIC LIFE INS CO	NE	133,288.3
PHYSICIANS LIFE INS CO	NE	1,664.1
STANDARD LIFE & ACCIDENT INS CO	TX	533.1
SYMETRA NATIONAL LIFE INS CO	IA	18.6
USABLE LIFE	AR	541.5

Rating: B+

INSURANCE COMPANY NAME	DOM. STATE	TOTAL ASSETS ($MIL)
AMERICAN FIDELITY ASR CO	OK	6,090.1
AMERICAN UNITED LIFE INS CO	IN	29,575.8
AMICA LIFE INS CO	RI	1,302.6
ASSURITY LIFE INS CO	NE	2,729.5
AXA EQUITABLE LIFE INS CO	NY	191,807.0
BEST LIFE & HEALTH INS CO	TX	22.7
BOSTON MUTUAL LIFE INS CO	MA	1,461.7
CHESAPEAKE LIFE INS CO	OK	195.4
CHRISTIAN FIDELITY LIFE INS CO	TX	64.2
COMPANION LIFE INS CO	SC	401.6
DEARBORN NATIONAL LIFE INS CO	IL	1,737.6
DELAWARE AMERICAN LIFE INS CO	DE	122.9
EAGLE LIFE INS CO	IA	1,070.1
FAMILY HERITAGE LIFE INS CO OF AMER	OH	1,444.8
FARM BUREAU LIFE INS CO	IA	9,267.1
FREEDOM LIFE INS CO OF AMERICA	TX	213.2
GERBER LIFE INS CO	NY	3,909.7
HANNOVER LIFE REASSURANCE CO OF AMER	FL	16,338.8
M LIFE INS CO	CO	307.3

INSURANCE COMPANY NAME	DOM. STATE	TOTAL ASSETS ($MIL)
MIDLAND NATIONAL LIFE INS CO	IA	58,240.4
MINNESOTA LIFE INS CO	MN	49,271.3
NATIONAL BENEFIT LIFE INS CO	NY	564.7
NATIONAL FARMERS UNION LIFE INS CO	TX	193.3
NATIONAL FOUNDATION LIFE INS CO	TX	50.6
NEW YORK LIFE INS & ANNUITY CORP	DE	156,175.5
NORTH AMERICAN INS CO	WI	19.2
NORTHWESTERN MUTUAL LIFE INS CO	WI	273,304.0
OHIO NATIONAL LIFE ASR CORP	OH	4,098.9
OXFORD LIFE INS CO	AZ	2,192.1
PACIFIC LIFE & ANNUITY CO	AZ	7,409.8
PAN AMERICAN ASR CO	LA	26.7
PRINCIPAL LIFE INS CO	IA	197,908.3
SB MUTL LIFE INS CO OF MA	MA	3,104.8
STANDARD INS CO	OR	24,530.4
TRANS WORLD ASR CO	CA	344.9
TRUSTMARK INS CO	IL	1,606.0
TRUSTMARK LIFE INS CO	IL	330.1
UNITED WORLD LIFE INS CO	NE	119.5
VOYA RETIREMENT INS & ANNUITY CO	CT	108,678.3

Connecticut

INSURANCE COMPANY NAME	DOM. STATE	TOTAL ASSETS ($MIL)
Rating: A+		
AMERICAN FAMILY LIFE INS CO	WI	5,269.9
COUNTRY LIFE INS CO	IL	9,673.9
PHYSICIANS MUTUAL INS CO	NE	2,367.4
STATE FARM LIFE & ACCIDENT ASR CO	IL	3,003.4
STATE FARM LIFE INS CO	IL	74,940.7
TEACHERS INS & ANNUITY ASN OF AM	NY	302,803.1
Rating: A		
AMALGAMATED LIFE INS CO	NY	140.3
BERKLEY LIFE & HEALTH INS CO	IA	325.8
FEDERATED LIFE INS CO	MN	1,969.7
GARDEN STATE LIFE INS CO	TX	135.5
GUARDIAN LIFE INS CO OF AMERICA	NY	57,852.7
NATIONAL WESTERN LIFE INS CO	CO	11,114.0
PARKER CENTENNIAL ASR CO	WI	96.0
SENTRY LIFE INS CO	WI	7,425.4
SHELTERPOINT LIFE INS CO	NY	151.3
USAA LIFE INS CO	TX	25,292.8
Rating: A-		
AMERICAN FAMILY LIFE ASR CO OF NY	NY	1,000.3
AMERICAN HEALTH & LIFE INS CO	TX	1,018.0
ANNUITY INVESTORS LIFE INS CO	OH	3,232.6
COUNTRY INVESTORS LIFE ASR CO	IL	303.5
FIDELITY INVESTMENTS LIFE INS CO	UT	30,960.8
MASSACHUSETTS MUTUAL LIFE INS CO	MA	245,872.2
MUTUAL OF AMERICA LIFE INS CO	NY	21,758.9
NEW YORK LIFE INS CO	NY	178,706.9
NIPPON LIFE INS CO OF AMERICA	IA	219.2
PACIFIC LIFE INS CO	NE	133,288.3
PHYSICIANS LIFE INS CO	NE	1,664.1
STANDARD LIFE & ACCIDENT INS CO	TX	533.1
SYMETRA NATIONAL LIFE INS CO	IA	18.6
USABLE LIFE	AR	541.5
Rating: B+		
ALLIANZ LIFE INS CO OF NY	NY	3,461.1
AMERICAN FIDELITY ASR CO	OK	6,090.1
AMERICAN UNITED LIFE INS CO	IN	29,575.8
AMICA LIFE INS CO	RI	1,302.6
ASSURITY LIFE INS CO	NE	2,729.5
AXA EQUITABLE LIFE INS CO	NY	191,807.0
BOSTON MUTUAL LIFE INS CO	MA	1,461.7
CHESAPEAKE LIFE INS CO	OK	195.4
DEARBORN NATIONAL LIFE INS CO	IL	1,737.6
DELAWARE AMERICAN LIFE INS CO	DE	122.9
EAGLE LIFE INS CO	IA	1,070.1
FAMILY HERITAGE LIFE INS CO OF AMER	OH	1,444.8
GERBER LIFE INS CO	NY	3,909.7
HANNOVER LIFE REASSURANCE CO OF AMER	FL	16,338.8
MIDLAND NATIONAL LIFE INS CO	IA	58,240.4
MINNESOTA LIFE INS CO	MN	49,271.3
NATIONAL BENEFIT LIFE INS CO	NY	564.7
NEW YORK LIFE INS & ANNUITY CORP	DE	156,175.5
NORTHWESTERN MUTUAL LIFE INS CO	WI	273,304.0

INSURANCE COMPANY NAME	DOM. STATE	TOTAL ASSETS ($MIL)
OHIO NATIONAL LIFE ASR CORP	OH	4,098.9
OXFORD LIFE INS CO	AZ	2,192.1
PACIFIC LIFE & ANNUITY CO	AZ	7,409.8
PAN AMERICAN ASR CO	LA	26.7
PRINCIPAL LIFE INS CO	IA	197,908.3
SB MUTL LIFE INS CO OF MA	MA	3,104.8
STANDARD INS CO	OR	24,530.4
TRANS WORLD ASR CO	CA	344.9
TRUSTMARK INS CO	IL	1,606.0
TRUSTMARK LIFE INS CO	IL	330.1
VOYA RETIREMENT INS & ANNUITY CO	CT	108,678.3

Delaware

INSURANCE COMPANY NAME	DOM. STATE	TOTAL ASSETS ($MIL)
Rating: A+		
AMERICAN FAMILY LIFE INS CO	WI	5,269.9
COUNTRY LIFE INS CO	IL	9,673.9
PHYSICIANS MUTUAL INS CO	NE	2,367.4
STATE FARM LIFE INS CO	IL	74,940.7
TEACHERS INS & ANNUITY ASN OF AM	NY	302,803.1
Rating: A		
AMALGAMATED LIFE INS CO	NY	140.3
BERKLEY LIFE & HEALTH INS CO	IA	325.8
FEDERATED LIFE INS CO	MN	1,969.7
GARDEN STATE LIFE INS CO	TX	135.5
GUARDIAN LIFE INS CO OF AMERICA	NY	57,852.7
NATIONAL WESTERN LIFE INS CO	CO	11,114.0
PARKER CENTENNIAL ASR CO	WI	96.0
SENTRY LIFE INS CO	WI	7,425.4
SHELTERPOINT LIFE INS CO	NY	151.3
USAA LIFE INS CO	TX	25,292.8
Rating: A-		
AMERICAN HEALTH & LIFE INS CO	TX	1,018.0
ANNUITY INVESTORS LIFE INS CO	OH	3,232.6
COUNTRY INVESTORS LIFE ASR CO	IL	303.5
FIDELITY INVESTMENTS LIFE INS CO	UT	30,960.8
FIRST RELIANCE STANDARD LIFE INS CO	NY	208.0
MASSACHUSETTS MUTUAL LIFE INS CO	MA	245,872.2
MUTUAL OF AMERICA LIFE INS CO	NY	21,758.9
NEW YORK LIFE INS CO	NY	178,706.9
NIPPON LIFE INS CO OF AMERICA	IA	219.2
PACIFIC LIFE INS CO	NE	133,288.3
PHYSICIANS LIFE INS CO	NE	1,664.1
STANDARD LIFE & ACCIDENT INS CO	TX	533.1
SYMETRA NATIONAL LIFE INS CO	IA	18.6
USABLE LIFE	AR	541.5
Rating: B+		
AMERICAN FIDELITY ASR CO	OK	6,090.1
AMERICAN UNITED LIFE INS CO	IN	29,575.8
AMICA LIFE INS CO	RI	1,302.6
ASSURITY LIFE INS CO	NE	2,729.5
AXA EQUITABLE LIFE INS CO	NY	191,807.0
BOSTON MUTUAL LIFE INS CO	MA	1,461.7
CHESAPEAKE LIFE INS CO	OK	195.4
COMPANION LIFE INS CO	SC	401.6
DEARBORN NATIONAL LIFE INS CO	IL	1,737.6
DELAWARE AMERICAN LIFE INS CO	DE	122.9
EAGLE LIFE INS CO	IA	1,070.1
FAMILY HERITAGE LIFE INS CO OF AMER	OH	1,444.8
FREEDOM LIFE INS CO OF AMERICA	TX	213.2
GERBER LIFE INS CO	NY	3,909.7
HANNOVER LIFE REASSURANCE CO OF AMER	FL	16,338.8
M LIFE INS CO	CO	307.3
MIDLAND NATIONAL LIFE INS CO	IA	58,240.4
MINNESOTA LIFE INS CO	MN	49,271.3
NATIONAL BENEFIT LIFE INS CO	NY	564.7
NATIONAL FOUNDATION LIFE INS CO	TX	50.6

INSURANCE COMPANY NAME	DOM. STATE	TOTAL ASSETS ($MIL)
NEW YORK LIFE INS & ANNUITY CORP	DE	156,175.5
NORTHWESTERN MUTUAL LIFE INS CO	WI	273,304.0
OHIO NATIONAL LIFE ASR CORP	OH	4,098.9
OXFORD LIFE INS CO	AZ	2,192.1
PACIFIC LIFE & ANNUITY CO	AZ	7,409.8
PAN AMERICAN ASR CO	LA	26.7
PRINCIPAL LIFE INS CO	IA	197,908.3
SB MUTL LIFE INS CO OF MA	MA	3,104.8
STANDARD INS CO	OR	24,530.4
TRANS WORLD ASR CO	CA	344.9
TRUSTMARK INS CO	IL	1,606.0
TRUSTMARK LIFE INS CO	IL	330.1
UNITED WORLD LIFE INS CO	NE	119.5
VOYA RETIREMENT INS & ANNUITY CO	CT	108,678.3

District Of Columbia

INSURANCE COMPANY NAME	DOM. STATE	TOTAL ASSETS ($MIL)

Rating: A+

INSURANCE COMPANY NAME	DOM. STATE	TOTAL ASSETS ($MIL)
AMERICAN FAMILY LIFE INS CO	WI	5,269.9
PHYSICIANS MUTUAL INS CO	NE	2,367.4
STATE FARM LIFE INS CO	IL	74,940.7
TEACHERS INS & ANNUITY ASN OF AM	NY	302,803.1

Rating: A

INSURANCE COMPANY NAME	DOM. STATE	TOTAL ASSETS ($MIL)
AMALGAMATED LIFE INS CO	NY	140.3
BERKLEY LIFE & HEALTH INS CO	IA	325.8
GARDEN STATE LIFE INS CO	TX	135.5
GUARDIAN LIFE INS CO OF AMERICA	NY	57,852.7
NATIONAL WESTERN LIFE INS CO	CO	11,114.0
PARKER CENTENNIAL ASR CO	WI	96.0
SENTRY LIFE INS CO	WI	7,425.4
SHELTERPOINT LIFE INS CO	NY	151.3
USAA LIFE INS CO	TX	25,292.8

Rating: A-

INSURANCE COMPANY NAME	DOM. STATE	TOTAL ASSETS ($MIL)
AMERICAN HEALTH & LIFE INS CO	TX	1,018.0
ANNUITY INVESTORS LIFE INS CO	OH	3,232.6
CIGNA LIFE INS CO OF NEW YORK	NY	407.5
ERIE FAMILY LIFE INS CO	PA	2,512.1
FIDELITY INVESTMENTS LIFE INS CO	UT	30,960.8
FIRST RELIANCE STANDARD LIFE INS CO	NY	208.0
MASSACHUSETTS MUTUAL LIFE INS CO	MA	245,872.2
MUTUAL OF AMERICA LIFE INS CO	NY	21,758.9
NEW YORK LIFE INS CO	NY	178,706.9
NIPPON LIFE INS CO OF AMERICA	IA	219.2
PACIFIC LIFE INS CO	NE	133,288.3
PHYSICIANS LIFE INS CO	NE	1,664.1
STANDARD LIFE & ACCIDENT INS CO	TX	533.1
SYMETRA NATIONAL LIFE INS CO	IA	18.6
USABLE LIFE	AR	541.5

Rating: B+

INSURANCE COMPANY NAME	DOM. STATE	TOTAL ASSETS ($MIL)
ALLIANZ LIFE INS CO OF NY	NY	3,461.1
AMERICAN FIDELITY ASR CO	OK	6,090.1
AMERICAN UNITED LIFE INS CO	IN	29,575.8
AMICA LIFE INS CO	RI	1,302.6
ASSURITY LIFE INS CO	NE	2,729.5
AXA EQUITABLE LIFE INS CO	NY	191,807.0
BEST LIFE & HEALTH INS CO	TX	22.7
BOSTON MUTUAL LIFE INS CO	MA	1,461.7
CHESAPEAKE LIFE INS CO	OK	195.4
COMPANION LIFE INS CO	SC	401.6
DEARBORN NATIONAL LIFE INS CO	IL	1,737.6
DELAWARE AMERICAN LIFE INS CO	DE	122.9
EAGLE LIFE INS CO	IA	1,070.1
FAMILY HERITAGE LIFE INS CO OF AMER	OH	1,444.8
GERBER LIFE INS CO	NY	3,909.7
HANNOVER LIFE REASSURANCE CO OF AMER	FL	16,338.8
MIDLAND NATIONAL LIFE INS CO	IA	58,240.4
MINNESOTA LIFE INS CO	MN	49,271.3
NATIONAL BENEFIT LIFE INS CO	NY	564.7
NATIONAL FARMERS UNION LIFE INS CO	TX	193.3
NATIONAL FOUNDATION LIFE INS CO	TX	50.6

INSURANCE COMPANY NAME	DOM. STATE	TOTAL ASSETS ($MIL)
NEW YORK LIFE INS & ANNUITY CORP	DE	156,175.5
NORTH AMERICAN INS CO	WI	19.2
NORTHWESTERN MUTUAL LIFE INS CO	WI	273,304.0
OHIO NATIONAL LIFE ASR CORP	OH	4,098.9
OXFORD LIFE INS CO	AZ	2,192.1
PACIFIC LIFE & ANNUITY CO	AZ	7,409.8
PAN AMERICAN ASR CO	LA	26.7
PRINCIPAL LIFE INS CO	IA	197,908.3
SB MUTL LIFE INS CO OF MA	MA	3,104.8
STANDARD INS CO	OR	24,530.4
TRANS WORLD ASR CO	CA	344.9
TRUSTMARK INS CO	IL	1,606.0
TRUSTMARK LIFE INS CO	IL	330.1
UNITED WORLD LIFE INS CO	NE	119.5
VOYA RETIREMENT INS & ANNUITY CO	CT	108,678.3

Florida

INSURANCE COMPANY NAME	DOM. STATE	TOTAL ASSETS ($MIL)

Rating: A+

INSURANCE COMPANY NAME	DOM. STATE	TOTAL ASSETS ($MIL)
AMERICAN FAMILY LIFE INS CO	WI	5,269.9
COUNTRY LIFE INS CO	IL	9,673.9
PHYSICIANS MUTUAL INS CO	NE	2,367.4
STATE FARM LIFE INS CO	IL	74,940.7
TEACHERS INS & ANNUITY ASN OF AM	NY	302,803.1

Rating: A

INSURANCE COMPANY NAME	DOM. STATE	TOTAL ASSETS ($MIL)
AMALGAMATED LIFE INS CO	NY	140.3
BERKLEY LIFE & HEALTH INS CO	IA	325.8
FEDERATED LIFE INS CO	MN	1,969.7
GARDEN STATE LIFE INS CO	TX	135.5
GUARDIAN LIFE INS CO OF AMERICA	NY	57,852.7
NATIONAL WESTERN LIFE INS CO	CO	11,114.0
PARKER CENTENNIAL ASR CO	WI	96.0
SENTRY LIFE INS CO	WI	7,425.4
SHELTERPOINT LIFE INS CO	NY	151.3
SOUTHERN FARM BUREAU LIFE INS CO	MS	14,356.8
USAA LIFE INS CO	TX	25,292.8

Rating: A-

INSURANCE COMPANY NAME	DOM. STATE	TOTAL ASSETS ($MIL)
AMERICAN HEALTH & LIFE INS CO	TX	1,018.0
ANNUITY INVESTORS LIFE INS CO	OH	3,232.6
COTTON STATES LIFE INS CO	GA	339.7
COUNTRY INVESTORS LIFE ASR CO	IL	303.5
FIDELITY INVESTMENTS LIFE INS CO	UT	30,960.8
MASSACHUSETTS MUTUAL LIFE INS CO	MA	245,872.2
MUTUAL OF AMERICA LIFE INS CO	NY	21,758.9
NEW YORK LIFE INS CO	NY	178,706.9
NIPPON LIFE INS CO OF AMERICA	IA	219.2
PACIFIC LIFE INS CO	NE	133,288.3
PHYSICIANS LIFE INS CO	NE	1,664.1
STANDARD LIFE & ACCIDENT INS CO	TX	533.1
SYMETRA NATIONAL LIFE INS CO	IA	18.6
TRANS OCEANIC LIFE INS CO	PR	75.3
USABLE LIFE	AR	541.5

Rating: B+

INSURANCE COMPANY NAME	DOM. STATE	TOTAL ASSETS ($MIL)
AMERICAN FIDELITY ASR CO	OK	6,090.1
AMERICAN UNITED LIFE INS CO	IN	29,575.8
AMICA LIFE INS CO	RI	1,302.6
ASSURITY LIFE INS CO	NE	2,729.5
AXA EQUITABLE LIFE INS CO	NY	191,807.0
BEST LIFE & HEALTH INS CO	TX	22.7
BOSTON MUTUAL LIFE INS CO	MA	1,461.7
CHESAPEAKE LIFE INS CO	OK	195.4
CHRISTIAN FIDELITY LIFE INS CO	TX	64.2
COMPANION LIFE INS CO	SC	401.6
DEARBORN NATIONAL LIFE INS CO	IL	1,737.6
DELAWARE AMERICAN LIFE INS CO	DE	122.9
EAGLE LIFE INS CO	IA	1,070.1
FAMILY HERITAGE LIFE INS CO OF AMER	OH	1,444.8
FREEDOM LIFE INS CO OF AMERICA	TX	213.2
GERBER LIFE INS CO	NY	3,909.7
HANNOVER LIFE REASSURANCE CO OF AMER	FL	16,338.8
MIDLAND NATIONAL LIFE INS CO	IA	58,240.4

INSURANCE COMPANY NAME	DOM. STATE	TOTAL ASSETS ($MIL)
MINNESOTA LIFE INS CO	MN	49,271.3
NATIONAL BENEFIT LIFE INS CO	NY	564.7
NEW YORK LIFE INS & ANNUITY CORP	DE	156,175.5
NORTHWESTERN MUTUAL LIFE INS CO	WI	273,304.0
OHIO NATIONAL LIFE ASR CORP	OH	4,098.9
OXFORD LIFE INS CO	AZ	2,192.1
PACIFIC LIFE & ANNUITY CO	AZ	7,409.8
PAN AMERICAN ASR CO	LA	26.7
PRINCIPAL LIFE INS CO	IA	197,908.3
SB MUTL LIFE INS CO OF MA	MA	3,104.8
STANDARD INS CO	OR	24,530.4
TRANS WORLD ASR CO	CA	344.9
TRUSTMARK INS CO	IL	1,606.0
TRUSTMARK LIFE INS CO	IL	330.1
UNITED WORLD LIFE INS CO	NE	119.5
VOYA RETIREMENT INS & ANNUITY CO	CT	108,678.3

Georgia

INSURANCE COMPANY NAME	DOM. STATE	TOTAL ASSETS ($MIL)

Rating: A+

INSURANCE COMPANY NAME	DOM. STATE	TOTAL ASSETS ($MIL)
AMERICAN FAMILY LIFE INS CO	WI	5,269.9
COUNTRY LIFE INS CO	IL	9,673.9
PHYSICIANS MUTUAL INS CO	NE	2,367.4
STATE FARM LIFE INS CO	IL	74,940.7
TEACHERS INS & ANNUITY ASN OF AM	NY	302,803.1

Rating: A

INSURANCE COMPANY NAME	DOM. STATE	TOTAL ASSETS ($MIL)
AMALGAMATED LIFE INS CO	NY	140.3
BERKLEY LIFE & HEALTH INS CO	IA	325.8
FEDERATED LIFE INS CO	MN	1,969.7
FRANDISCO LIFE INS CO	GA	93.8
GARDEN STATE LIFE INS CO	TX	135.5
GUARDIAN LIFE INS CO OF AMERICA	NY	57,852.7
NATIONAL WESTERN LIFE INS CO	CO	11,114.0
PARKER CENTENNIAL ASR CO	WI	96.0
SENTRY LIFE INS CO	WI	7,425.4
SOUTHERN FARM BUREAU LIFE INS CO	MS	14,356.8
USAA LIFE INS CO	TX	25,292.8

Rating: A-

INSURANCE COMPANY NAME	DOM. STATE	TOTAL ASSETS ($MIL)
AMERICAN HEALTH & LIFE INS CO	TX	1,018.0
ANNUITY INVESTORS LIFE INS CO	OH	3,232.6
COTTON STATES LIFE INS CO	GA	339.7
COUNTRY INVESTORS LIFE ASR CO	IL	303.5
FIDELITY INVESTMENTS LIFE INS CO	UT	30,960.8
MASSACHUSETTS MUTUAL LIFE INS CO	MA	245,872.2
MUTUAL OF AMERICA LIFE INS CO	NY	21,758.9
NEW YORK LIFE INS CO	NY	178,706.9
NIPPON LIFE INS CO OF AMERICA	IA	219.2
PACIFIC LIFE INS CO	NE	133,288.3
PHYSICIANS LIFE INS CO	NE	1,664.1
SOUTHERN PIONEER LIFE INS CO	AR	14.6
STANDARD LIFE & ACCIDENT INS CO	TX	533.1
SYMETRA NATIONAL LIFE INS CO	IA	18.6
USABLE LIFE	AR	541.5

Rating: B+

INSURANCE COMPANY NAME	DOM. STATE	TOTAL ASSETS ($MIL)
AMERICAN FIDELITY ASR CO	OK	6,090.1
AMERICAN UNITED LIFE INS CO	IN	29,575.8
AMICA LIFE INS CO	RI	1,302.6
ASSURITY LIFE INS CO	NE	2,729.5
AXA EQUITABLE LIFE INS CO	NY	191,807.0
BEST LIFE & HEALTH INS CO	TX	22.7
BOSTON MUTUAL LIFE INS CO	MA	1,461.7
CHESAPEAKE LIFE INS CO	OK	195.4
CHRISTIAN FIDELITY LIFE INS CO	TX	64.2
COMPANION LIFE INS CO	SC	401.6
DEARBORN NATIONAL LIFE INS CO	IL	1,737.6
DELAWARE AMERICAN LIFE INS CO	DE	122.9
EAGLE LIFE INS CO	IA	1,070.1
FAMILY HERITAGE LIFE INS CO OF AMER	OH	1,444.8
FREEDOM LIFE INS CO OF AMERICA	TX	213.2
GERBER LIFE INS CO	NY	3,909.7
HANNOVER LIFE REASSURANCE CO OF AMER	FL	16,338.8
MIDLAND NATIONAL LIFE INS CO	IA	58,240.4

INSURANCE COMPANY NAME	DOM. STATE	TOTAL ASSETS ($MIL)
MINNESOTA LIFE INS CO	MN	49,271.3
NATIONAL BENEFIT LIFE INS CO	NY	564.7
NATIONAL FOUNDATION LIFE INS CO	TX	50.6
NEW YORK LIFE INS & ANNUITY CORP	DE	156,175.5
NORTHWESTERN MUTUAL LIFE INS CO	WI	273,304.0
OHIO NATIONAL LIFE ASR CORP	OH	4,098.9
OXFORD LIFE INS CO	AZ	2,192.1
PACIFIC LIFE & ANNUITY CO	AZ	7,409.8
PAN AMERICAN ASR CO	LA	26.7
PRINCIPAL LIFE INS CO	IA	197,908.3
SB MUTL LIFE INS CO OF MA	MA	3,104.8
STANDARD INS CO	OR	24,530.4
SWBC LIFE INS CO	TX	32.6
TRANS WORLD ASR CO	CA	344.9
TRUSTMARK INS CO	IL	1,606.0
TRUSTMARK LIFE INS CO	IL	330.1
UNITED WORLD LIFE INS CO	NE	119.5
VOYA RETIREMENT INS & ANNUITY CO	CT	108,678.3

Hawaii

INSURANCE COMPANY NAME	DOM. STATE	TOTAL ASSETS ($MIL)

Rating: A+

INSURANCE COMPANY NAME	DOM. STATE	TOTAL ASSETS ($MIL)
AMERICAN FAMILY LIFE INS CO	WI	5,269.9
PHYSICIANS MUTUAL INS CO	NE	2,367.4
STATE FARM LIFE INS CO	IL	74,940.7
TEACHERS INS & ANNUITY ASN OF AM	NY	302,803.1

Rating: A

INSURANCE COMPANY NAME	DOM. STATE	TOTAL ASSETS ($MIL)
AMALGAMATED LIFE INS CO	NY	140.3
BERKLEY LIFE & HEALTH INS CO	IA	325.8
GARDEN STATE LIFE INS CO	TX	135.5
GUARDIAN LIFE INS CO OF AMERICA	NY	57,852.7
NATIONAL WESTERN LIFE INS CO	CO	11,114.0
PARKER CENTENNIAL ASR CO	WI	96.0
SENTRY LIFE INS CO	WI	7,425.4
USAA LIFE INS CO	TX	25,292.8

Rating: A-

INSURANCE COMPANY NAME	DOM. STATE	TOTAL ASSETS ($MIL)
AMERICAN HEALTH & LIFE INS CO	TX	1,018.0
ANNUITY INVESTORS LIFE INS CO	OH	3,232.6
FIDELITY INVESTMENTS LIFE INS CO	UT	30,960.8
MASSACHUSETTS MUTUAL LIFE INS CO	MA	245,872.2
MUTUAL OF AMERICA LIFE INS CO	NY	21,758.9
NEW YORK LIFE INS CO	NY	178,706.9
NIPPON LIFE INS CO OF AMERICA	IA	219.2
PACIFIC GUARDIAN LIFE INS CO LTD	HI	559.1
PACIFIC LIFE INS CO	NE	133,288.3
PHYSICIANS LIFE INS CO	NE	1,664.1
STANDARD LIFE & ACCIDENT INS CO	TX	533.1
USABLE LIFE	AR	541.5

Rating: B+

INSURANCE COMPANY NAME	DOM. STATE	TOTAL ASSETS ($MIL)
AMERICAN FIDELITY ASR CO	OK	6,090.1
AMERICAN UNITED LIFE INS CO	IN	29,575.8
AMICA LIFE INS CO	RI	1,302.6
ASSURITY LIFE INS CO	NE	2,729.5
AXA EQUITABLE LIFE INS CO	NY	191,807.0
BEST LIFE & HEALTH INS CO	TX	22.7
BOSTON MUTUAL LIFE INS CO	MA	1,461.7
CHESAPEAKE LIFE INS CO	OK	195.4
DEARBORN NATIONAL LIFE INS CO	IL	1,737.6
DELAWARE AMERICAN LIFE INS CO	DE	122.9
EAGLE LIFE INS CO	IA	1,070.1
FAMILY HERITAGE LIFE INS CO OF AMER	OH	1,444.8
GERBER LIFE INS CO	NY	3,909.7
HANNOVER LIFE REASSURANCE CO OF AMER	FL	16,338.8
MIDLAND NATIONAL LIFE INS CO	IA	58,240.4
MINNESOTA LIFE INS CO	MN	49,271.3
NATIONAL BENEFIT LIFE INS CO	NY	564.7
NEW YORK LIFE INS & ANNUITY CORP	DE	156,175.5
NORTHWESTERN MUTUAL LIFE INS CO	WI	273,304.0
OHIO NATIONAL LIFE ASR CORP	OH	4,098.9
OXFORD LIFE INS CO	AZ	2,192.1
PACIFIC LIFE & ANNUITY CO	AZ	7,409.8
PAN AMERICAN ASR CO	LA	26.7
PRINCIPAL LIFE INS CO	IA	197,908.3
SB MUTL LIFE INS CO OF MA	MA	3,104.8

INSURANCE COMPANY NAME	DOM. STATE	TOTAL ASSETS ($MIL)
STANDARD INS CO	OR	24,530.4
TRANS WORLD ASR CO	CA	344.9
TRUSTMARK INS CO	IL	1,606.0
TRUSTMARK LIFE INS CO	IL	330.1
UNITED WORLD LIFE INS CO	NE	119.5
VOYA RETIREMENT INS & ANNUITY CO	CT	108,678.3

Idaho

INSURANCE COMPANY NAME	DOM. STATE	TOTAL ASSETS ($MIL)
Rating: A+		
AMERICAN FAMILY LIFE INS CO	WI	5,269.9
COUNTRY LIFE INS CO	IL	9,673.9
PHYSICIANS MUTUAL INS CO	NE	2,367.4
STATE FARM LIFE INS CO	IL	74,940.7
TEACHERS INS & ANNUITY ASN OF AM	NY	302,803.1
Rating: A		
AMALGAMATED LIFE INS CO	NY	140.3
BERKLEY LIFE & HEALTH INS CO	IA	325.8
FEDERATED LIFE INS CO	MN	1,969.7
GARDEN STATE LIFE INS CO	TX	135.5
GUARDIAN LIFE INS CO OF AMERICA	NY	57,852.7
LIFEWISE ASR CO	WA	193.1
NATIONAL WESTERN LIFE INS CO	CO	11,114.0
PARKER CENTENNIAL ASR CO	WI	96.0
SENTRY LIFE INS CO	WI	7,425.4
USAA LIFE INS CO	TX	25,292.8
Rating: A-		
AMERICAN HEALTH & LIFE INS CO	TX	1,018.0
ANNUITY INVESTORS LIFE INS CO	OH	3,232.6
COUNTRY INVESTORS LIFE ASR CO	IL	303.5
FIDELITY INVESTMENTS LIFE INS CO	UT	30,960.8
MASSACHUSETTS MUTUAL LIFE INS CO	MA	245,872.2
MUTUAL OF AMERICA LIFE INS CO	NY	21,758.9
NEW YORK LIFE INS CO	NY	178,706.9
NIPPON LIFE INS CO OF AMERICA	IA	219.2
PACIFIC GUARDIAN LIFE INS CO LTD	HI	559.1
PACIFIC LIFE INS CO	NE	133,288.3
PHYSICIANS LIFE INS CO	NE	1,664.1
STANDARD LIFE & ACCIDENT INS CO	TX	533.1
SYMETRA NATIONAL LIFE INS CO	IA	18.6
USABLE LIFE	AR	541.5
Rating: B+		
AMERICAN FIDELITY ASR CO	OK	6,090.1
AMERICAN UNITED LIFE INS CO	IN	29,575.8
AMICA LIFE INS CO	RI	1,302.6
ASSURITY LIFE INS CO	NE	2,729.5
AXA EQUITABLE LIFE INS CO	NY	191,807.0
BEST LIFE & HEALTH INS CO	TX	22.7
BOSTON MUTUAL LIFE INS CO	MA	1,461.7
CHESAPEAKE LIFE INS CO	OK	195.4
CHRISTIAN FIDELITY LIFE INS CO	TX	64.2
COMPANION LIFE INS CO	SC	401.6
DEARBORN NATIONAL LIFE INS CO	IL	1,737.6
DELAWARE AMERICAN LIFE INS CO	DE	122.9
FAMILY HERITAGE LIFE INS CO OF AMER	OH	1,444.8
FARM BUREAU LIFE INS CO	IA	9,267.1
GERBER LIFE INS CO	NY	3,909.7
HANNOVER LIFE REASSURANCE CO OF AMER	FL	16,338.8
MIDLAND NATIONAL LIFE INS CO	IA	58,240.4
MINNESOTA LIFE INS CO	MN	49,271.3
NATIONAL BENEFIT LIFE INS CO	NY	564.7
NATIONAL FARMERS UNION LIFE INS CO	TX	193.3

INSURANCE COMPANY NAME	DOM. STATE	TOTAL ASSETS ($MIL)
NATIONAL FOUNDATION LIFE INS CO	TX	50.6
NEW YORK LIFE INS & ANNUITY CORP	DE	156,175.5
NORTHWESTERN MUTUAL LIFE INS CO	WI	273,304.0
OHIO NATIONAL LIFE ASR CORP	OH	4,098.9
OXFORD LIFE INS CO	AZ	2,192.1
PACIFIC LIFE & ANNUITY CO	AZ	7,409.8
PAN AMERICAN ASR CO	LA	26.7
PRINCIPAL LIFE INS CO	IA	197,908.3
SB MUTL LIFE INS CO OF MA	MA	3,104.8
STANDARD INS CO	OR	24,530.4
TRANS WORLD ASR CO	CA	344.9
TRUSTMARK INS CO	IL	1,606.0
TRUSTMARK LIFE INS CO	IL	330.1
UNITED WORLD LIFE INS CO	NE	119.5
VOYA RETIREMENT INS & ANNUITY CO	CT	108,678.3

Illinois

INSURANCE COMPANY NAME	DOM. STATE	TOTAL ASSETS ($MIL)

Rating: A+

INSURANCE COMPANY NAME	DOM. STATE	TOTAL ASSETS ($MIL)
AMERICAN FAMILY LIFE INS CO	WI	5,269.9
COUNTRY LIFE INS CO	IL	9,673.9
PHYSICIANS MUTUAL INS CO	NE	2,367.4
STATE FARM LIFE & ACCIDENT ASR CO	IL	3,003.4
STATE FARM LIFE INS CO	IL	74,940.7
TEACHERS INS & ANNUITY ASN OF AM	NY	302,803.1

Rating: A

INSURANCE COMPANY NAME	DOM. STATE	TOTAL ASSETS ($MIL)
AMALGAMATED LIFE INS CO	NY	140.3
BERKLEY LIFE & HEALTH INS CO	IA	325.8
FEDERATED LIFE INS CO	MN	1,969.7
GARDEN STATE LIFE INS CO	TX	135.5
GUARDIAN LIFE INS CO OF AMERICA	NY	57,852.7
NATIONAL WESTERN LIFE INS CO	CO	11,114.0
PARKER CENTENNIAL ASR CO	WI	96.0
SENTRY LIFE INS CO	WI	7,425.4
SHELTERPOINT LIFE INS CO	NY	151.3
UNITED FARM FAMILY LIFE INS CO	IN	2,348.2
USAA LIFE INS CO	TX	25,292.8

Rating: A-

INSURANCE COMPANY NAME	DOM. STATE	TOTAL ASSETS ($MIL)
AMERICAN HEALTH & LIFE INS CO	TX	1,018.0
ANNUITY INVESTORS LIFE INS CO	OH	3,232.6
COUNTRY INVESTORS LIFE ASR CO	IL	303.5
ERIE FAMILY LIFE INS CO	PA	2,512.1
FIDELITY INVESTMENTS LIFE INS CO	UT	30,960.8
MASSACHUSETTS MUTUAL LIFE INS CO	MA	245,872.2
MUTUAL OF AMERICA LIFE INS CO	NY	21,758.9
NEW YORK LIFE INS CO	NY	178,706.9
NIPPON LIFE INS CO OF AMERICA	IA	219.2
PACIFIC LIFE INS CO	NE	133,288.3
PHYSICIANS LIFE INS CO	NE	1,664.1
STANDARD LIFE & ACCIDENT INS CO	TX	533.1
SYMETRA NATIONAL LIFE INS CO	IA	18.6
USABLE LIFE	AR	541.5

Rating: B+

INSURANCE COMPANY NAME	DOM. STATE	TOTAL ASSETS ($MIL)
ALLIANZ LIFE INS CO OF NY	NY	3,461.1
AMERICAN FIDELITY ASR CO	OK	6,090.1
AMERICAN UNITED LIFE INS CO	IN	29,575.8
AMICA LIFE INS CO	RI	1,302.6
ASSURITY LIFE INS CO	NE	2,729.5
AXA EQUITABLE LIFE INS CO	NY	191,807.0
BEST LIFE & HEALTH INS CO	TX	22.7
BOSTON MUTUAL LIFE INS CO	MA	1,461.7
CHESAPEAKE LIFE INS CO	OK	195.4
CHRISTIAN FIDELITY LIFE INS CO	TX	64.2
COMPANION LIFE INS CO	SC	401.6
DEARBORN NATIONAL LIFE INS CO	IL	1,737.6
DELAWARE AMERICAN LIFE INS CO	DE	122.9
EAGLE LIFE INS CO	IA	1,070.1
ENTERPRISE LIFE INS CO	TX	73.7
FAMILY HERITAGE LIFE INS CO OF AMER	OH	1,444.8
FREEDOM LIFE INS CO OF AMERICA	TX	213.2
GERBER LIFE INS CO	NY	3,909.7

INSURANCE COMPANY NAME	DOM. STATE	TOTAL ASSETS ($MIL)
HANNOVER LIFE REASSURANCE CO OF AMER	FL	16,338.8
MIDLAND NATIONAL LIFE INS CO	IA	58,240.4
MINNESOTA LIFE INS CO	MN	49,271.3
NATIONAL BENEFIT LIFE INS CO	NY	564.7
NATIONAL FARMERS UNION LIFE INS CO	TX	193.3
NEW YORK LIFE INS & ANNUITY CORP	DE	156,175.5
NORTH AMERICAN INS CO	WI	19.2
NORTHWESTERN MUTUAL LIFE INS CO	WI	273,304.0
OHIO NATIONAL LIFE ASR CORP	OH	4,098.9
OXFORD LIFE INS CO	AZ	2,192.1
PACIFIC LIFE & ANNUITY CO	AZ	7,409.8
PAN AMERICAN ASR CO	LA	26.7
PRINCIPAL LIFE INS CO	IA	197,908.3
SB MUTL LIFE INS CO OF MA	MA	3,104.8
STANDARD INS CO	OR	24,530.4
TRANS WORLD ASR CO	CA	344.9
TRUSTMARK INS CO	IL	1,606.0
TRUSTMARK LIFE INS CO	IL	330.1
UNITED WORLD LIFE INS CO	NE	119.5
VOYA RETIREMENT INS & ANNUITY CO	CT	108,678.3

Indiana

INSURANCE COMPANY NAME	DOM. STATE	TOTAL ASSETS ($MIL)
NATIONAL BENEFIT LIFE INS CO	NY	564.7
NATIONAL FARMERS UNION LIFE INS CO	TX	193.3
NATIONAL FOUNDATION LIFE INS CO	TX	50.6
NEW YORK LIFE INS & ANNUITY CORP	DE	156,175.5
NORTH AMERICAN INS CO	WI	19.2
NORTHWESTERN MUTUAL LIFE INS CO	WI	273,304.0
OHIO NATIONAL LIFE ASR CORP	OH	4,098.9
OXFORD LIFE INS CO	AZ	2,192.1
PACIFIC LIFE & ANNUITY CO	AZ	7,409.8
PAN AMERICAN ASR CO	LA	26.7
PRINCIPAL LIFE INS CO	IA	197,908.3
SB MUTL LIFE INS CO OF MA	MA	3,104.8
STANDARD INS CO	OR	24,530.4
TRANS WORLD ASR CO	CA	344.9
TRUSTMARK INS CO	IL	1,606.0
TRUSTMARK LIFE INS CO	IL	330.1
UNITED WORLD LIFE INS CO	NE	119.5
VOYA RETIREMENT INS & ANNUITY CO	CT	108,678.3

Rating: A+

INSURANCE COMPANY NAME	DOM. STATE	TOTAL ASSETS ($MIL)
AMERICAN FAMILY LIFE INS CO	WI	5,269.9
COUNTRY LIFE INS CO	IL	9,673.9
PHYSICIANS MUTUAL INS CO	NE	2,367.4
STATE FARM LIFE INS CO	IL	74,940.7
TEACHERS INS & ANNUITY ASN OF AM	NY	302,803.1

Rating: A

INSURANCE COMPANY NAME	DOM. STATE	TOTAL ASSETS ($MIL)
AMALGAMATED LIFE INS CO	NY	140.3
BERKLEY LIFE & HEALTH INS CO	IA	325.8
FEDERATED LIFE INS CO	MN	1,969.7
GARDEN STATE LIFE INS CO	TX	135.5
GUARDIAN LIFE INS CO OF AMERICA	NY	57,852.7
NATIONAL WESTERN LIFE INS CO	CO	11,114.0
PARKER CENTENNIAL ASR CO	WI	96.0
SENTRY LIFE INS CO	WI	7,425.4
UNITED FARM FAMILY LIFE INS CO	IN	2,348.2
USAA LIFE INS CO	TX	25,292.8

Rating: A-

INSURANCE COMPANY NAME	DOM. STATE	TOTAL ASSETS ($MIL)
AMERICAN HEALTH & LIFE INS CO	TX	1,018.0
ANNUITY INVESTORS LIFE INS CO	OH	3,232.6
COUNTRY INVESTORS LIFE ASR CO	IL	303.5
ERIE FAMILY LIFE INS CO	PA	2,512.1
FIDELITY INVESTMENTS LIFE INS CO	UT	30,960.8
MASSACHUSETTS MUTUAL LIFE INS CO	MA	245,872.2
MUTUAL OF AMERICA LIFE INS CO	NY	21,758.9
NEW YORK LIFE INS CO	NY	178,706.9
NIPPON LIFE INS CO OF AMERICA	IA	219.2
PACIFIC LIFE INS CO	NE	133,288.3
PHYSICIANS LIFE INS CO	NE	1,664.1
SOUTHERN PIONEER LIFE INS CO	AR	14.6
STANDARD LIFE & ACCIDENT INS CO	TX	533.1
SYMETRA NATIONAL LIFE INS CO	IA	18.6
USABLE LIFE	AR	541.5

Rating: B+

INSURANCE COMPANY NAME	DOM. STATE	TOTAL ASSETS ($MIL)
AMERICAN FIDELITY ASR CO	OK	6,090.1
AMERICAN UNITED LIFE INS CO	IN	29,575.8
AMICA LIFE INS CO	RI	1,302.6
ASSURITY LIFE INS CO	NE	2,729.5
AXA EQUITABLE LIFE INS CO	NY	191,807.0
BEST LIFE & HEALTH INS CO	TX	22.7
BOSTON MUTUAL LIFE INS CO	MA	1,461.7
CHESAPEAKE LIFE INS CO	OK	195.4
CHRISTIAN FIDELITY LIFE INS CO	TX	64.2
COMPANION LIFE INS CO	SC	401.6
DEARBORN NATIONAL LIFE INS CO	IL	1,737.6
DELAWARE AMERICAN LIFE INS CO	DE	122.9
EAGLE LIFE INS CO	IA	1,070.1
FAMILY HERITAGE LIFE INS CO OF AMER	OH	1,444.8
FREEDOM LIFE INS CO OF AMERICA	TX	213.2
GERBER LIFE INS CO	NY	3,909.7
HANNOVER LIFE REASSURANCE CO OF AMER	FL	16,338.8
MIDLAND NATIONAL LIFE INS CO	IA	58,240.4
MINNESOTA LIFE INS CO	MN	49,271.3

Iowa

INSURANCE COMPANY NAME	DOM. STATE	TOTAL ASSETS ($MIL)
Rating: A+		
AMERICAN FAMILY LIFE INS CO	WI	5,269.9
COUNTRY LIFE INS CO	IL	9,673.9
PHYSICIANS MUTUAL INS CO	NE	2,367.4
STATE FARM LIFE INS CO	IL	74,940.7
TEACHERS INS & ANNUITY ASN OF AM	NY	302,803.1
Rating: A		
AMALGAMATED LIFE INS CO	NY	140.3
BERKLEY LIFE & HEALTH INS CO	IA	325.8
FEDERATED LIFE INS CO	MN	1,969.7
GARDEN STATE LIFE INS CO	TX	135.5
GUARDIAN LIFE INS CO OF AMERICA	NY	57,852.7
NATIONAL WESTERN LIFE INS CO	CO	11,114.0
PARKER CENTENNIAL ASR CO	WI	96.0
SENTRY LIFE INS CO	WI	7,425.4
UNITED FARM FAMILY LIFE INS CO	IN	2,348.2
USAA LIFE INS CO	TX	25,292.8
Rating: A-		
AMERICAN HEALTH & LIFE INS CO	TX	1,018.0
ANNUITY INVESTORS LIFE INS CO	OH	3,232.6
COUNTRY INVESTORS LIFE ASR CO	IL	303.5
FIDELITY INVESTMENTS LIFE INS CO	UT	30,960.8
MASSACHUSETTS MUTUAL LIFE INS CO	MA	245,872.2
MUTUAL OF AMERICA LIFE INS CO	NY	21,758.9
NEW YORK LIFE INS CO	NY	178,706.9
NIPPON LIFE INS CO OF AMERICA	IA	219.2
PACIFIC GUARDIAN LIFE INS CO LTD	HI	559.1
PACIFIC LIFE INS CO	NE	133,288.3
PHYSICIANS LIFE INS CO	NE	1,664.1
STANDARD LIFE & ACCIDENT INS CO	TX	533.1
SYMETRA NATIONAL LIFE INS CO	IA	18.6
USABLE LIFE	AR	541.5
Rating: B+		
AMERICAN FIDELITY ASR CO	OK	6,090.1
AMERICAN UNITED LIFE INS CO	IN	29,575.8
AMICA LIFE INS CO	RI	1,302.6
ASSURITY LIFE INS CO	NE	2,729.5
AXA EQUITABLE LIFE INS CO	NY	191,807.0
BEST LIFE & HEALTH INS CO	TX	22.7
BOSTON MUTUAL LIFE INS CO	MA	1,461.7
CHESAPEAKE LIFE INS CO	OK	195.4
COMPANION LIFE INS CO	SC	401.6
DEARBORN NATIONAL LIFE INS CO	IL	1,737.6
DELAWARE AMERICAN LIFE INS CO	DE	122.9
EAGLE LIFE INS CO	IA	1,070.1
FAMILY HERITAGE LIFE INS CO OF AMER	OH	1,444.8
FARM BUREAU LIFE INS CO	IA	9,267.1
FREEDOM LIFE INS CO OF AMERICA	TX	213.2
GERBER LIFE INS CO	NY	3,909.7
HANNOVER LIFE REASSURANCE CO OF AMER	FL	16,338.8
MIDLAND NATIONAL LIFE INS CO	IA	58,240.4
MINNESOTA LIFE INS CO	MN	49,271.3
NATIONAL BENEFIT LIFE INS CO	NY	564.7

INSURANCE COMPANY NAME	DOM. STATE	TOTAL ASSETS ($MIL)
NATIONAL FARMERS UNION LIFE INS CO	TX	193.3
NATIONAL FOUNDATION LIFE INS CO	TX	50.6
NEW YORK LIFE INS & ANNUITY CORP	DE	156,175.5
NORTHWESTERN MUTUAL LIFE INS CO	WI	273,304.0
OHIO NATIONAL LIFE ASR CORP	OH	4,098.9
OXFORD LIFE INS CO	AZ	2,192.1
PACIFIC LIFE & ANNUITY CO	AZ	7,409.8
PRINCIPAL LIFE INS CO	IA	197,908.3
SB MUTL LIFE INS CO OF MA	MA	3,104.8
STANDARD INS CO	OR	24,530.4
TRANS WORLD ASR CO	CA	344.9
TRUSTMARK INS CO	IL	1,606.0
TRUSTMARK LIFE INS CO	IL	330.1
UNITED WORLD LIFE INS CO	NE	119.5
VOYA RETIREMENT INS & ANNUITY CO	CT	108,678.3

Kansas

INSURANCE COMPANY NAME	DOM. STATE	TOTAL ASSETS ($MIL)
Rating: A+		
AMERICAN FAMILY LIFE INS CO	WI	5,269.9
COUNTRY LIFE INS CO	IL	9,673.9
PHYSICIANS MUTUAL INS CO	NE	2,367.4
STATE FARM LIFE INS CO	IL	74,940.7
TEACHERS INS & ANNUITY ASN OF AM	NY	302,803.1
Rating: A		
AMALGAMATED LIFE INS CO	NY	140.3
BERKLEY LIFE & HEALTH INS CO	IA	325.8
FEDERATED LIFE INS CO	MN	1,969.7
GARDEN STATE LIFE INS CO	TX	135.5
GUARDIAN LIFE INS CO OF AMERICA	NY	57,852.7
NATIONAL WESTERN LIFE INS CO	CO	11,114.0
PARKER CENTENNIAL ASR CO	WI	96.0
SENTRY LIFE INS CO	WI	7,425.4
USAA LIFE INS CO	TX	25,292.8
Rating: A-		
AMERICAN HEALTH & LIFE INS CO	TX	1,018.0
ANNUITY INVESTORS LIFE INS CO	OH	3,232.6
COUNTRY INVESTORS LIFE ASR CO	IL	303.5
FIDELITY INVESTMENTS LIFE INS CO	UT	30,960.8
MASSACHUSETTS MUTUAL LIFE INS CO	MA	245,872.2
MUTUAL OF AMERICA LIFE INS CO	NY	21,758.9
NEW YORK LIFE INS CO	NY	178,706.9
NIPPON LIFE INS CO OF AMERICA	IA	219.2
PACIFIC LIFE INS CO	NE	133,288.3
PHYSICIANS LIFE INS CO	NE	1,664.1
SOUTHERN PIONEER LIFE INS CO	AR	14.6
STANDARD LIFE & ACCIDENT INS CO	TX	533.1
SYMETRA NATIONAL LIFE INS CO	IA	18.6
USABLE LIFE	AR	541.5
Rating: B+		
ADVANCE INS CO OF KANSAS	KS	61.6
AMERICAN FIDELITY ASR CO	OK	6,090.1
AMERICAN UNITED LIFE INS CO	IN	29,575.8
AMICA LIFE INS CO	RI	1,302.6
ASSURITY LIFE INS CO	NE	2,729.5
AXA EQUITABLE LIFE INS CO	NY	191,807.0
BEST LIFE & HEALTH INS CO	TX	22.7
BOSTON MUTUAL LIFE INS CO	MA	1,461.7
CHESAPEAKE LIFE INS CO	OK	195.4
CHRISTIAN FIDELITY LIFE INS CO	TX	64.2
COMPANION LIFE INS CO	SC	401.6
DEARBORN NATIONAL LIFE INS CO	IL	1,737.6
DELAWARE AMERICAN LIFE INS CO	DE	122.9
EAGLE LIFE INS CO	IA	1,070.1
ENTERPRISE LIFE INS CO	TX	73.7
FAMILY HERITAGE LIFE INS CO OF AMER	OH	1,444.8
FARM BUREAU LIFE INS CO	IA	9,267.1
FREEDOM LIFE INS CO OF AMERICA	TX	213.2
GERBER LIFE INS CO	NY	3,909.7
HANNOVER LIFE REASSURANCE CO OF AMER	FL	16,338.8
MIDLAND NATIONAL LIFE INS CO	IA	58,240.4

INSURANCE COMPANY NAME	DOM. STATE	TOTAL ASSETS ($MIL)
MINNESOTA LIFE INS CO	MN	49,271.3
NATIONAL BENEFIT LIFE INS CO	NY	564.7
NATIONAL FARMERS UNION LIFE INS CO	TX	193.3
NATIONAL FOUNDATION LIFE INS CO	TX	50.6
NEW YORK LIFE INS & ANNUITY CORP	DE	156,175.5
NORTH AMERICAN INS CO	WI	19.2
NORTHWESTERN MUTUAL LIFE INS CO	WI	273,304.0
OHIO NATIONAL LIFE ASR CORP	OH	4,098.9
OXFORD LIFE INS CO	AZ	2,192.1
PACIFIC LIFE & ANNUITY CO	AZ	7,409.8
PAN AMERICAN ASR CO	LA	26.7
PRINCIPAL LIFE INS CO	IA	197,908.3
SB MUTL LIFE INS CO OF MA	MA	3,104.8
STANDARD INS CO	OR	24,530.4
TRANS WORLD ASR CO	CA	344.9
TRUSTMARK INS CO	IL	1,606.0
TRUSTMARK LIFE INS CO	IL	330.1
UNITED WORLD LIFE INS CO	NE	119.5
VOYA RETIREMENT INS & ANNUITY CO	CT	108,678.3

Kentucky

INSURANCE COMPANY NAME	DOM. STATE	TOTAL ASSETS ($MIL)	INSURANCE COMPANY NAME	DOM. STATE	TOTAL ASSETS ($MIL)
Rating: A+			MINNESOTA LIFE INS CO	MN	49,271.3
			NATIONAL BENEFIT LIFE INS CO	NY	564.7
AMERICAN FAMILY LIFE INS CO	WI	5,269.9	NATIONAL FARMERS UNION LIFE INS CO	TX	193.3
COUNTRY LIFE INS CO	IL	9,673.9	NATIONAL FOUNDATION LIFE INS CO	TX	50.6
PHYSICIANS MUTUAL INS CO	NE	2,367.4	NEW YORK LIFE INS & ANNUITY CORP	DE	156,175.5
STATE FARM LIFE INS CO	IL	74,940.7	NORTHWESTERN MUTUAL LIFE INS CO	WI	273,304.0
TEACHERS INS & ANNUITY ASN OF AM	NY	302,803.1	OHIO NATIONAL LIFE ASR CORP	OH	4,098.9
			OXFORD LIFE INS CO	AZ	2,192.1
Rating: A			PACIFIC LIFE & ANNUITY CO	AZ	7,409.8
			PAN AMERICAN ASR CO	LA	26.7
AMALGAMATED LIFE INS CO	NY	140.3	PRINCIPAL LIFE INS CO	IA	197,908.3
BERKLEY LIFE & HEALTH INS CO	IA	325.8	SB MUTL LIFE INS CO OF MA	MA	3,104.8
FEDERATED LIFE INS CO	MN	1,969.7	STANDARD INS CO	OR	24,530.4
GARDEN STATE LIFE INS CO	TX	135.5	TRANS WORLD ASR CO	CA	344.9
GUARDIAN LIFE INS CO OF AMERICA	NY	57,852.7	TRUSTMARK INS CO	IL	1,606.0
NATIONAL WESTERN LIFE INS CO	CO	11,114.0	TRUSTMARK LIFE INS CO	IL	330.1
PARKER CENTENNIAL ASR CO	WI	96.0	UNITED WORLD LIFE INS CO	NE	119.5
SENTRY LIFE INS CO	WI	7,425.4	VOYA RETIREMENT INS & ANNUITY CO	CT	108,678.3
SOUTHERN FARM BUREAU LIFE INS CO	MS	14,356.8			
USAA LIFE INS CO	TX	25,292.8			

Rating: A-

INSURANCE COMPANY NAME	DOM. STATE	TOTAL ASSETS ($MIL)
AMERICAN HEALTH & LIFE INS CO	TX	1,018.0
ANNUITY INVESTORS LIFE INS CO	OH	3,232.6
COTTON STATES LIFE INS CO	GA	339.7
COUNTRY INVESTORS LIFE ASR CO	IL	303.5
ERIE FAMILY LIFE INS CO	PA	2,512.1
FIDELITY INVESTMENTS LIFE INS CO	UT	30,960.8
MASSACHUSETTS MUTUAL LIFE INS CO	MA	245,872.2
MUTUAL OF AMERICA LIFE INS CO	NY	21,758.9
NEW YORK LIFE INS CO	NY	178,706.9
NIPPON LIFE INS CO OF AMERICA	IA	219.2
PACIFIC LIFE INS CO	NE	133,288.3
PHYSICIANS LIFE INS CO	NE	1,664.1
SOUTHERN PIONEER LIFE INS CO	AR	14.6
STANDARD LIFE & ACCIDENT INS CO	TX	533.1
SYMETRA NATIONAL LIFE INS CO	IA	18.6
USABLE LIFE	AR	541.5

Rating: B+

INSURANCE COMPANY NAME	DOM. STATE	TOTAL ASSETS ($MIL)
AMERICAN FIDELITY ASR CO	OK	6,090.1
AMERICAN UNITED LIFE INS CO	IN	29,575.8
AMICA LIFE INS CO	RI	1,302.6
ASSURITY LIFE INS CO	NE	2,729.5
AXA EQUITABLE LIFE INS CO	NY	191,807.0
BEST LIFE & HEALTH INS CO	TX	22.7
BOSTON MUTUAL LIFE INS CO	MA	1,461.7
CHESAPEAKE LIFE INS CO	OK	195.4
CHRISTIAN FIDELITY LIFE INS CO	TX	64.2
COMPANION LIFE INS CO	SC	401.6
DEARBORN NATIONAL LIFE INS CO	IL	1,737.6
DELAWARE AMERICAN LIFE INS CO	DE	122.9
EAGLE LIFE INS CO	IA	1,070.1
FAMILY HERITAGE LIFE INS CO OF AMER	OH	1,444.8
FREEDOM LIFE INS CO OF AMERICA	TX	213.2
GERBER LIFE INS CO	NY	3,909.7
HANNOVER LIFE REASSURANCE CO OF AMER	FL	16,338.8
MIDLAND NATIONAL LIFE INS CO	IA	58,240.4

Louisiana

INSURANCE COMPANY NAME	DOM. STATE	TOTAL ASSETS ($MIL)

Rating: A+

INSURANCE COMPANY NAME	DOM. STATE	TOTAL ASSETS ($MIL)
AMERICAN FAMILY LIFE INS CO	WI	5,269.9
COUNTRY LIFE INS CO	IL	9,673.9
PHYSICIANS MUTUAL INS CO	NE	2,367.4
STATE FARM LIFE INS CO	IL	74,940.7
TEACHERS INS & ANNUITY ASN OF AM	NY	302,803.1

Rating: A

INSURANCE COMPANY NAME	DOM. STATE	TOTAL ASSETS ($MIL)
AMALGAMATED LIFE INS CO	NY	140.3
BERKLEY LIFE & HEALTH INS CO	IA	325.8
FEDERATED LIFE INS CO	MN	1,969.7
GARDEN STATE LIFE INS CO	TX	135.5
GUARDIAN LIFE INS CO OF AMERICA	NY	57,852.7
NATIONAL WESTERN LIFE INS CO	CO	11,114.0
PARKER CENTENNIAL ASR CO	WI	96.0
SENTRY LIFE INS CO	WI	7,425.4
SOUTHERN FARM BUREAU LIFE INS CO	MS	14,356.8
USAA LIFE INS CO	TX	25,292.8

Rating: A-

INSURANCE COMPANY NAME	DOM. STATE	TOTAL ASSETS ($MIL)
AMERICAN HEALTH & LIFE INS CO	TX	1,018.0
ANNUITY INVESTORS LIFE INS CO	OH	3,232.6
COTTON STATES LIFE INS CO	GA	339.7
COUNTRY INVESTORS LIFE ASR CO	IL	303.5
FIDELITY INVESTMENTS LIFE INS CO	UT	30,960.8
MASSACHUSETTS MUTUAL LIFE INS CO	MA	245,872.2
MUTUAL OF AMERICA LIFE INS CO	NY	21,758.9
NEW YORK LIFE INS CO	NY	178,706.9
NIPPON LIFE INS CO OF AMERICA	IA	219.2
PACIFIC GUARDIAN LIFE INS CO LTD	HI	559.1
PACIFIC LIFE INS CO	NE	133,288.3
PHYSICIANS LIFE INS CO	NE	1,664.1
SOUTHERN PIONEER LIFE INS CO	AR	14.6
STANDARD LIFE & ACCIDENT INS CO	TX	533.1
SYMETRA NATIONAL LIFE INS CO	IA	18.6
USABLE LIFE	AR	541.5

Rating: B+

INSURANCE COMPANY NAME	DOM. STATE	TOTAL ASSETS ($MIL)
AMERICAN FIDELITY ASR CO	OK	6,090.1
AMERICAN UNITED LIFE INS CO	IN	29,575.8
AMICA LIFE INS CO	RI	1,302.6
ASSURITY LIFE INS CO	NE	2,729.5
AXA EQUITABLE LIFE INS CO	NY	191,807.0
BEST LIFE & HEALTH INS CO	TX	22.7
BLUEBONNET LIFE INS CO	MS	64.3
BOSTON MUTUAL LIFE INS CO	MA	1,461.7
CHESAPEAKE LIFE INS CO	OK	195.4
CHRISTIAN FIDELITY LIFE INS CO	TX	64.2
COMPANION LIFE INS CO	SC	401.6
DEARBORN NATIONAL LIFE INS CO	IL	1,737.6
DELAWARE AMERICAN LIFE INS CO	DE	122.9
EAGLE LIFE INS CO	IA	1,070.1
ENTERPRISE LIFE INS CO	TX	73.7
FAMILY HERITAGE LIFE INS CO OF AMER	OH	1,444.8
FREEDOM LIFE INS CO OF AMERICA	TX	213.2
GERBER LIFE INS CO	NY	3,909.7

INSURANCE COMPANY NAME	DOM. STATE	TOTAL ASSETS ($MIL)
HANNOVER LIFE REASSURANCE CO OF AMER	FL	16,338.8
MIDLAND NATIONAL LIFE INS CO	IA	58,240.4
MINNESOTA LIFE INS CO	MN	49,271.3
NATIONAL BENEFIT LIFE INS CO	NY	564.7
NATIONAL FOUNDATION LIFE INS CO	TX	50.6
NEW YORK LIFE INS & ANNUITY CORP	DE	156,175.5
NORTH AMERICAN INS CO	WI	19.2
NORTHWESTERN MUTUAL LIFE INS CO	WI	273,304.0
OHIO NATIONAL LIFE ASR CORP	OH	4,098.9
OXFORD LIFE INS CO	AZ	2,192.1
PACIFIC LIFE & ANNUITY CO	AZ	7,409.8
PAN AMERICAN ASR CO	LA	26.7
PRINCIPAL LIFE INS CO	IA	197,908.3
SB MUTL LIFE INS CO OF MA	MA	3,104.8
STANDARD INS CO	OR	24,530.4
SWBC LIFE INS CO	TX	32.6
TRANS WORLD ASR CO	CA	344.9
TRUSTMARK INS CO	IL	1,606.0
TRUSTMARK LIFE INS CO	IL	330.1
UNITED WORLD LIFE INS CO	NE	119.5
VOYA RETIREMENT INS & ANNUITY CO	CT	108,678.3

Maine

INSURANCE COMPANY NAME	DOM. STATE	TOTAL ASSETS ($MIL)

Rating: A+

INSURANCE COMPANY NAME	DOM. STATE	TOTAL ASSETS ($MIL)
AMERICAN FAMILY LIFE INS CO	WI	5,269.9
COUNTRY LIFE INS CO	IL	9,673.9
PHYSICIANS MUTUAL INS CO	NE	2,367.4
STATE FARM LIFE INS CO	IL	74,940.7
TEACHERS INS & ANNUITY ASN OF AM	NY	302,803.1

Rating: A

INSURANCE COMPANY NAME	DOM. STATE	TOTAL ASSETS ($MIL)
AMALGAMATED LIFE INS CO	NY	140.3
BERKLEY LIFE & HEALTH INS CO	IA	325.8
FEDERATED LIFE INS CO	MN	1,969.7
GARDEN STATE LIFE INS CO	TX	135.5
GUARDIAN LIFE INS CO OF AMERICA	NY	57,852.7
NATIONAL WESTERN LIFE INS CO	CO	11,114.0
PARKER CENTENNIAL ASR CO	WI	96.0
SENTRY LIFE INS CO	WI	7,425.4
USAA LIFE INS CO	TX	25,292.8

Rating: A-

INSURANCE COMPANY NAME	DOM. STATE	TOTAL ASSETS ($MIL)
AMERICAN HEALTH & LIFE INS CO	TX	1,018.0
ANNUITY INVESTORS LIFE INS CO	OH	3,232.6
COUNTRY INVESTORS LIFE ASR CO	IL	303.5
FIDELITY INVESTMENTS LIFE INS CO	UT	30,960.8
MASSACHUSETTS MUTUAL LIFE INS CO	MA	245,872.2
MUTUAL OF AMERICA LIFE INS CO	NY	21,758.9
NEW YORK LIFE INS CO	NY	178,706.9
PACIFIC LIFE INS CO	NE	133,288.3
PHYSICIANS LIFE INS CO	NE	1,664.1
USABLE LIFE	AR	541.5

Rating: B+

INSURANCE COMPANY NAME	DOM. STATE	TOTAL ASSETS ($MIL)
AMERICAN FIDELITY ASR CO	OK	6,090.1
AMERICAN UNITED LIFE INS CO	IN	29,575.8
AMICA LIFE INS CO	RI	1,302.6
ASSURITY LIFE INS CO	NE	2,729.5
AXA EQUITABLE LIFE INS CO	NY	191,807.0
BOSTON MUTUAL LIFE INS CO	MA	1,461.7
CHESAPEAKE LIFE INS CO	OK	195.4
COMPANION LIFE INS CO	SC	401.6
DEARBORN NATIONAL LIFE INS CO	IL	1,737.6
DELAWARE AMERICAN LIFE INS CO	DE	122.9
EAGLE LIFE INS CO	IA	1,070.1
FAMILY HERITAGE LIFE INS CO OF AMER	OH	1,444.8
GERBER LIFE INS CO	NY	3,909.7
HANNOVER LIFE REASSURANCE CO OF AMER	FL	16,338.8
MIDLAND NATIONAL LIFE INS CO	IA	58,240.4
MINNESOTA LIFE INS CO	MN	49,271.3
NATIONAL BENEFIT LIFE INS CO	NY	564.7
NATIONAL FOUNDATION LIFE INS CO	TX	50.6
NEW YORK LIFE INS & ANNUITY CORP	DE	156,175.5
NORTHWESTERN MUTUAL LIFE INS CO	WI	273,304.0
OHIO NATIONAL LIFE ASR CORP	OH	4,098.9
OXFORD LIFE INS CO	AZ	2,192.1
PACIFIC LIFE & ANNUITY CO	AZ	7,409.8
PRINCIPAL LIFE INS CO	IA	197,908.3
SB MUTL LIFE INS CO OF MA	MA	3,104.8

INSURANCE COMPANY NAME	DOM. STATE	TOTAL ASSETS ($MIL)
STANDARD INS CO	OR	24,530.4
TRANS WORLD ASR CO	CA	344.9
TRUSTMARK INS CO	IL	1,606.0
TRUSTMARK LIFE INS CO	IL	330.1
UNITED WORLD LIFE INS CO	NE	119.5
VOYA RETIREMENT INS & ANNUITY CO	CT	108,678.3

Maryland

INSURANCE COMPANY NAME	DOM. STATE	TOTAL ASSETS ($MIL)
Rating: A+		
AMERICAN FAMILY LIFE INS CO	WI	5,269.9
COUNTRY LIFE INS CO	IL	9,673.9
PHYSICIANS MUTUAL INS CO	NE	2,367.4
STATE FARM LIFE INS CO	IL	74,940.7
TEACHERS INS & ANNUITY ASN OF AM	NY	302,803.1
Rating: A		
AMALGAMATED LIFE INS CO	NY	140.3
BERKLEY LIFE & HEALTH INS CO	IA	325.8
FEDERATED LIFE INS CO	MN	1,969.7
GARDEN STATE LIFE INS CO	TX	135.5
GUARDIAN LIFE INS CO OF AMERICA	NY	57,852.7
LIFEWISE ASR CO	WA	193.1
NATIONAL WESTERN LIFE INS CO	CO	11,114.0
PARKER CENTENNIAL ASR CO	WI	96.0
SENTRY LIFE INS CO	WI	7,425.4
SHELTERPOINT LIFE INS CO	NY	151.3
UNITED FARM FAMILY LIFE INS CO	IN	2,348.2
USAA LIFE INS CO	TX	25,292.8
Rating: A-		
AMERICAN HEALTH & LIFE INS CO	TX	1,018.0
ANNUITY INVESTORS LIFE INS CO	OH	3,232.6
COUNTRY INVESTORS LIFE ASR CO	IL	303.5
ERIE FAMILY LIFE INS CO	PA	2,512.1
FIDELITY INVESTMENTS LIFE INS CO	UT	30,960.8
MASSACHUSETTS MUTUAL LIFE INS CO	MA	245,872.2
MUTUAL OF AMERICA LIFE INS CO	NY	21,758.9
NEW YORK LIFE INS CO	NY	178,706.9
NIPPON LIFE INS CO OF AMERICA	IA	219.2
PACIFIC LIFE INS CO	NE	133,288.3
PHYSICIANS LIFE INS CO	NE	1,664.1
STANDARD LIFE & ACCIDENT INS CO	TX	533.1
SYMETRA NATIONAL LIFE INS CO	IA	18.6
USABLE LIFE	AR	541.5
Rating: B+		
AMERICAN FIDELITY ASR CO	OK	6,090.1
AMERICAN UNITED LIFE INS CO	IN	29,575.8
AMICA LIFE INS CO	RI	1,302.6
ASSURITY LIFE INS CO	NE	2,729.5
AXA EQUITABLE LIFE INS CO	NY	191,807.0
BEST LIFE & HEALTH INS CO	TX	22.7
BOSTON MUTUAL LIFE INS CO	MA	1,461.7
CHESAPEAKE LIFE INS CO	OK	195.4
COMPANION LIFE INS CO	SC	401.6
DEARBORN NATIONAL LIFE INS CO	IL	1,737.6
DELAWARE AMERICAN LIFE INS CO	DE	122.9
EAGLE LIFE INS CO	IA	1,070.1
FAMILY HERITAGE LIFE INS CO OF AMER	OH	1,444.8
FREEDOM LIFE INS CO OF AMERICA	TX	213.2
GERBER LIFE INS CO	NY	3,909.7
HANNOVER LIFE REASSURANCE CO OF AMER	FL	16,338.8
MIDLAND NATIONAL LIFE INS CO	IA	58,240.4
MINNESOTA LIFE INS CO	MN	49,271.3

INSURANCE COMPANY NAME	DOM. STATE	TOTAL ASSETS ($MIL)
NATIONAL BENEFIT LIFE INS CO	NY	564.7
NEW YORK LIFE INS & ANNUITY CORP	DE	156,175.5
NORTH AMERICAN INS CO	WI	19.2
NORTHWESTERN MUTUAL LIFE INS CO	WI	273,304.0
OHIO NATIONAL LIFE ASR CORP	OH	4,098.9
OXFORD LIFE INS CO	AZ	2,192.1
PACIFIC LIFE & ANNUITY CO	AZ	7,409.8
PAN AMERICAN ASR CO	LA	26.7
PRINCIPAL LIFE INS CO	IA	197,908.3
SB MUTL LIFE INS CO OF MA	MA	3,104.8
STANDARD INS CO	OR	24,530.4
TRANS WORLD ASR CO	CA	344.9
TRUSTMARK INS CO	IL	1,606.0
TRUSTMARK LIFE INS CO	IL	330.1
UNITED WORLD LIFE INS CO	NE	119.5
VOYA RETIREMENT INS & ANNUITY CO	CT	108,678.3

Massachusetts

INSURANCE COMPANY NAME	DOM. STATE	TOTAL ASSETS ($MIL)

Rating: A+

INSURANCE COMPANY NAME	DOM. STATE	TOTAL ASSETS ($MIL)
AMERICAN FAMILY LIFE INS CO	WI	5,269.9
COUNTRY LIFE INS CO	IL	9,673.9
PHYSICIANS MUTUAL INS CO	NE	2,367.4
TEACHERS INS & ANNUITY ASN OF AM	NY	302,803.1

Rating: A

INSURANCE COMPANY NAME	DOM. STATE	TOTAL ASSETS ($MIL)
AMALGAMATED LIFE INS CO	NY	140.3
BERKLEY LIFE & HEALTH INS CO	IA	325.8
FEDERATED LIFE INS CO	MN	1,969.7
GARDEN STATE LIFE INS CO	TX	135.5
GUARDIAN LIFE INS CO OF AMERICA	NY	57,852.7
NATIONAL WESTERN LIFE INS CO	CO	11,114.0
PARKER CENTENNIAL ASR CO	WI	96.0
SENTRY LIFE INS CO	WI	7,425.4
SHELTERPOINT LIFE INS CO	NY	151.3
UNITED FARM FAMILY LIFE INS CO	IN	2,348.2
USAA LIFE INS CO	TX	25,292.8

Rating: A-

INSURANCE COMPANY NAME	DOM. STATE	TOTAL ASSETS ($MIL)
AMERICAN FAMILY LIFE ASR CO OF NY	NY	1,000.3
AMERICAN HEALTH & LIFE INS CO	TX	1,018.0
ANNUITY INVESTORS LIFE INS CO	OH	3,232.6
COUNTRY INVESTORS LIFE ASR CO	IL	303.5
FIDELITY INVESTMENTS LIFE INS CO	UT	30,960.8
MASSACHUSETTS MUTUAL LIFE INS CO	MA	245,872.2
MUTUAL OF AMERICA LIFE INS CO	NY	21,758.9
NEW YORK LIFE INS CO	NY	178,706.9
NIPPON LIFE INS CO OF AMERICA	IA	219.2
PACIFIC LIFE INS CO	NE	133,288.3
PHYSICIANS LIFE INS CO	NE	1,664.1
STANDARD LIFE & ACCIDENT INS CO	TX	533.1
USABLE LIFE	AR	541.5

Rating: B+

INSURANCE COMPANY NAME	DOM. STATE	TOTAL ASSETS ($MIL)
AMERICAN FIDELITY ASR CO	OK	6,090.1
AMERICAN UNITED LIFE INS CO	IN	29,575.8
AMICA LIFE INS CO	RI	1,302.6
ASSURITY LIFE INS CO	NE	2,729.5
AXA EQUITABLE LIFE INS CO	NY	191,807.0
BOSTON MUTUAL LIFE INS CO	MA	1,461.7
CHESAPEAKE LIFE INS CO	OK	195.4
COMPANION LIFE INS CO	SC	401.6
DEARBORN NATIONAL LIFE INS CO	IL	1,737.6
DELAWARE AMERICAN LIFE INS CO	DE	122.9
EAGLE LIFE INS CO	IA	1,070.1
FAMILY HERITAGE LIFE INS CO OF AMER	OH	1,444.8
GERBER LIFE INS CO	NY	3,909.7
HANNOVER LIFE REASSURANCE CO OF AMER	FL	16,338.8
MIDLAND NATIONAL LIFE INS CO	IA	58,240.4
MINNESOTA LIFE INS CO	MN	49,271.3
NATIONAL BENEFIT LIFE INS CO	NY	564.7
NEW YORK LIFE INS & ANNUITY CORP	DE	156,175.5
NORTHWESTERN MUTUAL LIFE INS CO	WI	273,304.0
OHIO NATIONAL LIFE ASR CORP	OH	4,098.9
OXFORD LIFE INS CO	AZ	2,192.1

INSURANCE COMPANY NAME	DOM. STATE	TOTAL ASSETS ($MIL)
PACIFIC LIFE & ANNUITY CO	AZ	7,409.8
PRINCIPAL LIFE INS CO	IA	197,908.3
SB MUTL LIFE INS CO OF MA	MA	3,104.8
STANDARD INS CO	OR	24,530.4
TRANS WORLD ASR CO	CA	344.9
TRUSTMARK INS CO	IL	1,606.0
TRUSTMARK LIFE INS CO	IL	330.1
UNITED WORLD LIFE INS CO	NE	119.5
VOYA RETIREMENT INS & ANNUITY CO	CT	108,678.3

Michigan

INSURANCE COMPANY NAME	DOM. STATE	TOTAL ASSETS ($MIL)

Rating: A+

INSURANCE COMPANY NAME	DOM. STATE	TOTAL ASSETS ($MIL)
AMERICAN FAMILY LIFE INS CO	WI	5,269.9
COUNTRY LIFE INS CO	IL	9,673.9
PHYSICIANS MUTUAL INS CO	NE	2,367.4
STATE FARM LIFE INS CO	IL	74,940.7
TEACHERS INS & ANNUITY ASN OF AM	NY	302,803.1

Rating: A

INSURANCE COMPANY NAME	DOM. STATE	TOTAL ASSETS ($MIL)
AMALGAMATED LIFE INS CO	NY	140.3
BERKLEY LIFE & HEALTH INS CO	IA	325.8
FEDERATED LIFE INS CO	MN	1,969.7
GARDEN STATE LIFE INS CO	TX	135.5
GUARDIAN LIFE INS CO OF AMERICA	NY	57,852.7
NATIONAL WESTERN LIFE INS CO	CO	11,114.0
PARKER CENTENNIAL ASR CO	WI	96.0
SENTRY LIFE INS CO	WI	7,425.4
SHELTERPOINT LIFE INS CO	NY	151.3
USAA LIFE INS CO	TX	25,292.8

Rating: A-

INSURANCE COMPANY NAME	DOM. STATE	TOTAL ASSETS ($MIL)
AMERICAN HEALTH & LIFE INS CO	TX	1,018.0
ANNUITY INVESTORS LIFE INS CO	OH	3,232.6
COUNTRY INVESTORS LIFE ASR CO	IL	303.5
FARM BUREAU LIFE INS CO OF MICHIGAN	MI	2,502.3
FIDELITY INVESTMENTS LIFE INS CO	UT	30,960.8
MASSACHUSETTS MUTUAL LIFE INS CO	MA	245,872.2
MUTUAL OF AMERICA LIFE INS CO	NY	21,758.9
NEW YORK LIFE INS CO	NY	178,706.9
NIPPON LIFE INS CO OF AMERICA	IA	219.2
PACIFIC LIFE INS CO	NE	133,288.3
PHYSICIANS LIFE INS CO	NE	1,664.1
STANDARD LIFE & ACCIDENT INS CO	TX	533.1
SYMETRA NATIONAL LIFE INS CO	IA	18.6
USABLE LIFE	AR	541.5

Rating: B+

INSURANCE COMPANY NAME	DOM. STATE	TOTAL ASSETS ($MIL)
AMERICAN FIDELITY ASR CO	OK	6,090.1
AMERICAN UNITED LIFE INS CO	IN	29,575.8
AMICA LIFE INS CO	RI	1,302.6
ASSURITY LIFE INS CO	NE	2,729.5
AXA EQUITABLE LIFE INS CO	NY	191,807.0
BEST LIFE & HEALTH INS CO	TX	22.7
BOSTON MUTUAL LIFE INS CO	MA	1,461.7
CHESAPEAKE LIFE INS CO	OK	195.4
COMPANION LIFE INS CO	SC	401.6
DEARBORN NATIONAL LIFE INS CO	IL	1,737.6
DELAWARE AMERICAN LIFE INS CO	DE	122.9
EAGLE LIFE INS CO	IA	1,070.1
FAMILY HERITAGE LIFE INS CO OF AMER	OH	1,444.8
FREEDOM LIFE INS CO OF AMERICA	TX	213.2
GERBER LIFE INS CO	NY	3,909.7
HANNOVER LIFE REASSURANCE CO OF AMER	FL	16,338.8
LOCOMOTIVE ENGRS&COND MUT PROT ASSN	MI	73.6
M LIFE INS CO	CO	307.3
MIDLAND NATIONAL LIFE INS CO	IA	58,240.4
MINNESOTA LIFE INS CO	MN	49,271.3

INSURANCE COMPANY NAME	DOM. STATE	TOTAL ASSETS ($MIL)
NATIONAL BENEFIT LIFE INS CO	NY	564.7
NATIONAL FARMERS UNION LIFE INS CO	TX	193.3
NEW YORK LIFE INS & ANNUITY CORP	DE	156,175.5
NORTH AMERICAN INS CO	WI	19.2
NORTHWESTERN MUTUAL LIFE INS CO	WI	273,304.0
OHIO NATIONAL LIFE ASR CORP	OH	4,098.9
OXFORD LIFE INS CO	AZ	2,192.1
PACIFIC LIFE & ANNUITY CO	AZ	7,409.8
PAN AMERICAN ASR CO	LA	26.7
PRINCIPAL LIFE INS CO	IA	197,908.3
SB MUTL LIFE INS CO OF MA	MA	3,104.8
STANDARD INS CO	OR	24,530.4
SWBC LIFE INS CO	TX	32.6
TRANS WORLD ASR CO	CA	344.9
TRUSTMARK INS CO	IL	1,606.0
TRUSTMARK LIFE INS CO	IL	330.1
UNITED WORLD LIFE INS CO	NE	119.5
VOYA RETIREMENT INS & ANNUITY CO	CT	108,678.3

Minnesota

INSURANCE COMPANY NAME	DOM. STATE	TOTAL ASSETS ($MIL)

Rating: A+

INSURANCE COMPANY NAME	DOM. STATE	TOTAL ASSETS ($MIL)
AMERICAN FAMILY LIFE INS CO	WI	5,269.9
COUNTRY LIFE INS CO	IL	9,673.9
PHYSICIANS MUTUAL INS CO	NE	2,367.4
STATE FARM LIFE INS CO	IL	74,940.7
TEACHERS INS & ANNUITY ASN OF AM	NY	302,803.1

Rating: A

INSURANCE COMPANY NAME	DOM. STATE	TOTAL ASSETS ($MIL)
AMALGAMATED LIFE INS CO	NY	140.3
BERKLEY LIFE & HEALTH INS CO	IA	325.8
FEDERATED LIFE INS CO	MN	1,969.7
GARDEN STATE LIFE INS CO	TX	135.5
GUARDIAN LIFE INS CO OF AMERICA	NY	57,852.7
NATIONAL WESTERN LIFE INS CO	CO	11,114.0
PARKER CENTENNIAL ASR CO	WI	96.0
SENTRY LIFE INS CO	WI	7,425.4
SHELTERPOINT LIFE INS CO	NY	151.3
USAA LIFE INS CO	TX	25,292.8

Rating: A-

INSURANCE COMPANY NAME	DOM. STATE	TOTAL ASSETS ($MIL)
AMERICAN HEALTH & LIFE INS CO	TX	1,018.0
ANNUITY INVESTORS LIFE INS CO	OH	3,232.6
COUNTRY INVESTORS LIFE ASR CO	IL	303.5
ERIE FAMILY LIFE INS CO	PA	2,512.1
FIDELITY INVESTMENTS LIFE INS CO	UT	30,960.8
MASSACHUSETTS MUTUAL LIFE INS CO	MA	245,872.2
MUTUAL OF AMERICA LIFE INS CO	NY	21,758.9
NEW YORK LIFE INS CO	NY	178,706.9
NIPPON LIFE INS CO OF AMERICA	IA	219.2
PACIFIC LIFE INS CO	NE	133,288.3
PHYSICIANS LIFE INS CO	NE	1,664.1
STANDARD LIFE & ACCIDENT INS CO	TX	533.1
SYMETRA NATIONAL LIFE INS CO	IA	18.6
USABLE LIFE	AR	541.5

Rating: B+

INSURANCE COMPANY NAME	DOM. STATE	TOTAL ASSETS ($MIL)
ALLIANZ LIFE INS CO OF NY	NY	3,461.1
AMERICAN FIDELITY ASR CO	OK	6,090.1
AMERICAN UNITED LIFE INS CO	IN	29,575.8
AMICA LIFE INS CO	RI	1,302.6
ASSURITY LIFE INS CO	NE	2,729.5
AXA EQUITABLE LIFE INS CO	NY	191,807.0
BOSTON MUTUAL LIFE INS CO	MA	1,461.7
CHESAPEAKE LIFE INS CO	OK	195.4
COMPANION LIFE INS CO	SC	401.6
DEARBORN NATIONAL LIFE INS CO	IL	1,737.6
DELAWARE AMERICAN LIFE INS CO	DE	122.9
EAGLE LIFE INS CO	IA	1,070.1
FAMILY HERITAGE LIFE INS CO OF AMER	OH	1,444.8
FARM BUREAU LIFE INS CO	IA	9,267.1
FREEDOM LIFE INS CO OF AMERICA	TX	213.2
GERBER LIFE INS CO	NY	3,909.7
HANNOVER LIFE REASSURANCE CO OF AMER	FL	16,338.8
MIDLAND NATIONAL LIFE INS CO	IA	58,240.4
MINNESOTA LIFE INS CO	MN	49,271.3
NATIONAL BENEFIT LIFE INS CO	NY	564.7

INSURANCE COMPANY NAME	DOM. STATE	TOTAL ASSETS ($MIL)
NATIONAL FARMERS UNION LIFE INS CO	TX	193.3
NEW YORK LIFE INS & ANNUITY CORP	DE	156,175.5
NORTH AMERICAN INS CO	WI	19.2
NORTHWESTERN MUTUAL LIFE INS CO	WI	273,304.0
OHIO NATIONAL LIFE ASR CORP	OH	4,098.9
OXFORD LIFE INS CO	AZ	2,192.1
PACIFIC LIFE & ANNUITY CO	AZ	7,409.8
PAN AMERICAN ASR CO	LA	26.7
PRINCIPAL LIFE INS CO	IA	197,908.3
SB MUTL LIFE INS CO OF MA	MA	3,104.8
STANDARD INS CO	OR	24,530.4
TRANS WORLD ASR CO	CA	344.9
TRUSTMARK INS CO	IL	1,606.0
TRUSTMARK LIFE INS CO	IL	330.1
UNITED WORLD LIFE INS CO	NE	119.5
VOYA RETIREMENT INS & ANNUITY CO	CT	108,678.3

Mississippi

INSURANCE COMPANY NAME	DOM. STATE	TOTAL ASSETS ($MIL)

Rating: A+

INSURANCE COMPANY NAME	DOM. STATE	TOTAL ASSETS ($MIL)
AMERICAN FAMILY LIFE INS CO	WI	5,269.9
COUNTRY LIFE INS CO	IL	9,673.9
PHYSICIANS MUTUAL INS CO	NE	2,367.4
STATE FARM LIFE INS CO	IL	74,940.7
TEACHERS INS & ANNUITY ASN OF AM	NY	302,803.1

Rating: A

INSURANCE COMPANY NAME	DOM. STATE	TOTAL ASSETS ($MIL)
AMALGAMATED LIFE INS CO	NY	140.3
BERKLEY LIFE & HEALTH INS CO	IA	325.8
FEDERATED LIFE INS CO	MN	1,969.7
GARDEN STATE LIFE INS CO	TX	135.5
GUARDIAN LIFE INS CO OF AMERICA	NY	57,852.7
NATIONAL WESTERN LIFE INS CO	CO	11,114.0
PARKER CENTENNIAL ASR CO	WI	96.0
SENTRY LIFE INS CO	WI	7,425.4
SOUTHERN FARM BUREAU LIFE INS CO	MS	14,356.8
USAA LIFE INS CO	TX	25,292.8

Rating: A-

INSURANCE COMPANY NAME	DOM. STATE	TOTAL ASSETS ($MIL)
AMERICAN HEALTH & LIFE INS CO	TX	1,018.0
ANNUITY INVESTORS LIFE INS CO	OH	3,232.6
COTTON STATES LIFE INS CO	GA	339.7
COUNTRY INVESTORS LIFE ASR CO	IL	303.5
FIDELITY INVESTMENTS LIFE INS CO	UT	30,960.8
MASSACHUSETTS MUTUAL LIFE INS CO	MA	245,872.2
MUTUAL OF AMERICA LIFE INS CO	NY	21,758.9
NEW YORK LIFE INS CO	NY	178,706.9
NIPPON LIFE INS CO OF AMERICA	IA	219.2
PACIFIC LIFE INS CO	NE	133,288.3
PHYSICIANS LIFE INS CO	NE	1,664.1
SOUTHERN PIONEER LIFE INS CO	AR	14.6
STANDARD LIFE & ACCIDENT INS CO	TX	533.1
SYMETRA NATIONAL LIFE INS CO	IA	18.6
USABLE LIFE	AR	541.5

Rating: B+

INSURANCE COMPANY NAME	DOM. STATE	TOTAL ASSETS ($MIL)
AMERICAN FIDELITY ASR CO	OK	6,090.1
AMERICAN UNITED LIFE INS CO	IN	29,575.8
AMICA LIFE INS CO	RI	1,302.6
ASSURITY LIFE INS CO	NE	2,729.5
AXA EQUITABLE LIFE INS CO	NY	191,807.0
BEST LIFE & HEALTH INS CO	TX	22.7
BLUEBONNET LIFE INS CO	MS	64.3
BOSTON MUTUAL LIFE INS CO	MA	1,461.7
CHESAPEAKE LIFE INS CO	OK	195.4
CHRISTIAN FIDELITY LIFE INS CO	TX	64.2
COMPANION LIFE INS CO	SC	401.6
DEARBORN NATIONAL LIFE INS CO	IL	1,737.6
DELAWARE AMERICAN LIFE INS CO	DE	122.9
EAGLE LIFE INS CO	IA	1,070.1
ENTERPRISE LIFE INS CO	TX	73.7
FAMILY HERITAGE LIFE INS CO OF AMER	OH	1,444.8
FREEDOM LIFE INS CO OF AMERICA	TX	213.2
GERBER LIFE INS CO	NY	3,909.7
HANNOVER LIFE REASSURANCE CO OF AMER	FL	16,338.8

INSURANCE COMPANY NAME	DOM. STATE	TOTAL ASSETS ($MIL)
MIDLAND NATIONAL LIFE INS CO	IA	58,240.4
MINNESOTA LIFE INS CO	MN	49,271.3
NATIONAL BENEFIT LIFE INS CO	NY	564.7
NATIONAL FARMERS UNION LIFE INS CO	TX	193.3
NATIONAL FOUNDATION LIFE INS CO	TX	50.6
NEW YORK LIFE INS & ANNUITY CORP	DE	156,175.5
NORTHWESTERN MUTUAL LIFE INS CO	WI	273,304.0
OHIO NATIONAL LIFE ASR CORP	OH	4,098.9
OXFORD LIFE INS CO	AZ	2,192.1
PACIFIC LIFE & ANNUITY CO	AZ	7,409.8
PAN AMERICAN ASR CO	LA	26.7
PRINCIPAL LIFE INS CO	IA	197,908.3
SB MUTL LIFE INS CO OF MA	MA	3,104.8
STANDARD INS CO	OR	24,530.4
TRANS WORLD ASR CO	CA	344.9
TRUSTMARK INS CO	IL	1,606.0
TRUSTMARK LIFE INS CO	IL	330.1
UNITED WORLD LIFE INS CO	NE	119.5
VOYA RETIREMENT INS & ANNUITY CO	CT	108,678.3

Missouri

INSURANCE COMPANY NAME	DOM. STATE	TOTAL ASSETS ($MIL)

Rating: A+

INSURANCE COMPANY NAME	DOM. STATE	TOTAL ASSETS ($MIL)
AMERICAN FAMILY LIFE INS CO	WI	5,269.9
COUNTRY LIFE INS CO	IL	9,673.9
PHYSICIANS MUTUAL INS CO	NE	2,367.4
STATE FARM LIFE INS CO	IL	74,940.7
TEACHERS INS & ANNUITY ASN OF AM	NY	302,803.1

Rating: A

INSURANCE COMPANY NAME	DOM. STATE	TOTAL ASSETS ($MIL)
AMALGAMATED LIFE INS CO	NY	140.3
BERKLEY LIFE & HEALTH INS CO	IA	325.8
FEDERATED LIFE INS CO	MN	1,969.7
GARDEN STATE LIFE INS CO	TX	135.5
GUARDIAN LIFE INS CO OF AMERICA	NY	57,852.7
NATIONAL WESTERN LIFE INS CO	CO	11,114.0
PARKER CENTENNIAL ASR CO	WI	96.0
SENTRY LIFE INS CO	WI	7,425.4
USAA LIFE INS CO	TX	25,292.8

Rating: A-

INSURANCE COMPANY NAME	DOM. STATE	TOTAL ASSETS ($MIL)
AMERICAN HEALTH & LIFE INS CO	TX	1,018.0
ANNUITY INVESTORS LIFE INS CO	OH	3,232.6
CIGNA LIFE INS CO OF NEW YORK	NY	407.5
COUNTRY INVESTORS LIFE ASR CO	IL	303.5
FARM BUREAU LIFE INS CO OF MISSOURI	MO	604.4
FIDELITY INVESTMENTS LIFE INS CO	UT	30,960.8
MASSACHUSETTS MUTUAL LIFE INS CO	MA	245,872.2
MUTUAL OF AMERICA LIFE INS CO	NY	21,758.9
NEW YORK LIFE INS CO	NY	178,706.9
NIPPON LIFE INS CO OF AMERICA	IA	219.2
PACIFIC GUARDIAN LIFE INS CO LTD	HI	559.1
PACIFIC LIFE INS CO	NE	133,288.3
PHYSICIANS LIFE INS CO	NE	1,664.1
SOUTHERN PIONEER LIFE INS CO	AR	14.6
STANDARD LIFE & ACCIDENT INS CO	TX	533.1
SYMETRA NATIONAL LIFE INS CO	IA	18.6
USABLE LIFE	AR	541.5

Rating: B+

INSURANCE COMPANY NAME	DOM. STATE	TOTAL ASSETS ($MIL)
ALLIANZ LIFE INS CO OF NY	NY	3,461.1
AMERICAN FIDELITY ASR CO	OK	6,090.1
AMERICAN UNITED LIFE INS CO	IN	29,575.8
AMICA LIFE INS CO	RI	1,302.6
ASSURITY LIFE INS CO	NE	2,729.5
AXA EQUITABLE LIFE INS CO	NY	191,807.0
BEST LIFE & HEALTH INS CO	TX	22.7
BOSTON MUTUAL LIFE INS CO	MA	1,461.7
CHESAPEAKE LIFE INS CO	OK	195.4
CHRISTIAN FIDELITY LIFE INS CO	TX	64.2
COMPANION LIFE INS CO	SC	401.6
DEARBORN NATIONAL LIFE INS CO	IL	1,737.6
DELAWARE AMERICAN LIFE INS CO	DE	122.9
EAGLE LIFE INS CO	IA	1,070.1
FAMILY HERITAGE LIFE INS CO OF AMER	OH	1,444.8
FREEDOM LIFE INS CO OF AMERICA	TX	213.2
GERBER LIFE INS CO	NY	3,909.7
HANNOVER LIFE REASSURANCE CO OF AMER	FL	16,338.8

INSURANCE COMPANY NAME	DOM. STATE	TOTAL ASSETS ($MIL)
MIDLAND NATIONAL LIFE INS CO	IA	58,240.4
MINNESOTA LIFE INS CO	MN	49,271.3
NATIONAL BENEFIT LIFE INS CO	NY	564.7
NATIONAL FARMERS UNION LIFE INS CO	TX	193.3
NATIONAL FOUNDATION LIFE INS CO	TX	50.6
NEW YORK LIFE INS & ANNUITY CORP	DE	156,175.5
NORTH AMERICAN INS CO	WI	19.2
NORTHWESTERN MUTUAL LIFE INS CO	WI	273,304.0
OHIO NATIONAL LIFE ASR CORP	OH	4,098.9
OXFORD LIFE INS CO	AZ	2,192.1
PACIFIC LIFE & ANNUITY CO	AZ	7,409.8
PAN AMERICAN ASR CO	LA	26.7
PRINCIPAL LIFE INS CO	IA	197,908.3
SB MUTL LIFE INS CO OF MA	MA	3,104.8
STANDARD INS CO	OR	24,530.4
TRANS WORLD ASR CO	CA	344.9
TRUSTMARK INS CO	IL	1,606.0
TRUSTMARK LIFE INS CO	IL	330.1
UNITED WORLD LIFE INS CO	NE	119.5
VOYA RETIREMENT INS & ANNUITY CO	CT	108,678.3

Montana

INSURANCE COMPANY NAME	DOM. STATE	TOTAL ASSETS ($MIL)
Rating: A+		
AMERICAN FAMILY LIFE INS CO	WI	5,269.9
COUNTRY LIFE INS CO	IL	9,673.9
PHYSICIANS MUTUAL INS CO	NE	2,367.4
STATE FARM LIFE INS CO	IL	74,940.7
TEACHERS INS & ANNUITY ASN OF AM	NY	302,803.1
Rating: A		
AMALGAMATED LIFE INS CO	NY	140.3
BERKLEY LIFE & HEALTH INS CO	IA	325.8
FEDERATED LIFE INS CO	MN	1,969.7
GARDEN STATE LIFE INS CO	TX	135.5
GUARDIAN LIFE INS CO OF AMERICA	NY	57,852.7
NATIONAL WESTERN LIFE INS CO	CO	11,114.0
PARKER CENTENNIAL ASR CO	WI	96.0
SENTRY LIFE INS CO	WI	7,425.4
USAA LIFE INS CO	TX	25,292.8
Rating: A-		
AMERICAN HEALTH & LIFE INS CO	TX	1,018.0
ANNUITY INVESTORS LIFE INS CO	OH	3,232.6
COUNTRY INVESTORS LIFE ASR CO	IL	303.5
FIDELITY INVESTMENTS LIFE INS CO	UT	30,960.8
MASSACHUSETTS MUTUAL LIFE INS CO	MA	245,872.2
MUTUAL OF AMERICA LIFE INS CO	NY	21,758.9
NEW YORK LIFE INS CO	NY	178,706.9
NIPPON LIFE INS CO OF AMERICA	IA	219.2
PACIFIC GUARDIAN LIFE INS CO LTD	HI	559.1
PACIFIC LIFE INS CO	NE	133,288.3
PHYSICIANS LIFE INS CO	NE	1,664.1
STANDARD LIFE & ACCIDENT INS CO	TX	533.1
SYMETRA NATIONAL LIFE INS CO	IA	18.6
USABLE LIFE	AR	541.5
Rating: B+		
AMERICAN FIDELITY ASR CO	OK	6,090.1
AMERICAN UNITED LIFE INS CO	IN	29,575.8
AMICA LIFE INS CO	RI	1,302.6
ASSURITY LIFE INS CO	NE	2,729.5
AXA EQUITABLE LIFE INS CO	NY	191,807.0
BEST LIFE & HEALTH INS CO	TX	22.7
BOSTON MUTUAL LIFE INS CO	MA	1,461.7
CHESAPEAKE LIFE INS CO	OK	195.4
CHRISTIAN FIDELITY LIFE INS CO	TX	64.2
COMPANION LIFE INS CO	SC	401.6
DEARBORN NATIONAL LIFE INS CO	IL	1,737.6
DELAWARE AMERICAN LIFE INS CO	DE	122.9
EAGLE LIFE INS CO	IA	1,070.1
FAMILY HERITAGE LIFE INS CO OF AMER	OH	1,444.8
FARM BUREAU LIFE INS CO	IA	9,267.1
GERBER LIFE INS CO	NY	3,909.7
HANNOVER LIFE REASSURANCE CO OF AMER	FL	16,338.8
MIDLAND NATIONAL LIFE INS CO	IA	58,240.4
MINNESOTA LIFE INS CO	MN	49,271.3
NATIONAL BENEFIT LIFE INS CO	NY	564.7
NATIONAL FARMERS UNION LIFE INS CO	TX	193.3

INSURANCE COMPANY NAME	DOM. STATE	TOTAL ASSETS ($MIL)
NATIONAL FOUNDATION LIFE INS CO	TX	50.6
NEW YORK LIFE INS & ANNUITY CORP	DE	156,175.5
NORTHWESTERN MUTUAL LIFE INS CO	WI	273,304.0
OHIO NATIONAL LIFE ASR CORP	OH	4,098.9
OXFORD LIFE INS CO	AZ	2,192.1
PACIFIC LIFE & ANNUITY CO	AZ	7,409.8
PAN AMERICAN ASR CO	LA	26.7
PRINCIPAL LIFE INS CO	IA	197,908.3
SB MUTL LIFE INS CO OF MA	MA	3,104.8
STANDARD INS CO	OR	24,530.4
TRANS WORLD ASR CO	CA	344.9
TRUSTMARK INS CO	IL	1,606.0
TRUSTMARK LIFE INS CO	IL	330.1
UNITED WORLD LIFE INS CO	NE	119.5
VOYA RETIREMENT INS & ANNUITY CO	CT	108,678.3

Nebraska

INSURANCE COMPANY NAME	DOM. STATE	TOTAL ASSETS ($MIL)

Rating: A+

INSURANCE COMPANY NAME	DOM. STATE	TOTAL ASSETS ($MIL)
AMERICAN FAMILY LIFE INS CO	WI	5,269.9
COUNTRY LIFE INS CO	IL	9,673.9
PHYSICIANS MUTUAL INS CO	NE	2,367.4
STATE FARM LIFE INS CO	IL	74,940.7
TEACHERS INS & ANNUITY ASN OF AM	NY	302,803.1

Rating: A

INSURANCE COMPANY NAME	DOM. STATE	TOTAL ASSETS ($MIL)
AMALGAMATED LIFE INS CO	NY	140.3
BERKLEY LIFE & HEALTH INS CO	IA	325.8
FEDERATED LIFE INS CO	MN	1,969.7
GARDEN STATE LIFE INS CO	TX	135.5
GUARDIAN LIFE INS CO OF AMERICA	NY	57,852.7
NATIONAL WESTERN LIFE INS CO	CO	11,114.0
PARKER CENTENNIAL ASR CO	WI	96.0
SENTRY LIFE INS CO	WI	7,425.4
USAA LIFE INS CO	TX	25,292.8

Rating: A-

INSURANCE COMPANY NAME	DOM. STATE	TOTAL ASSETS ($MIL)
AMERICAN HEALTH & LIFE INS CO	TX	1,018.0
ANNUITY INVESTORS LIFE INS CO	OH	3,232.6
COUNTRY INVESTORS LIFE ASR CO	IL	303.5
FIDELITY INVESTMENTS LIFE INS CO	UT	30,960.8
MASSACHUSETTS MUTUAL LIFE INS CO	MA	245,872.2
MUTUAL OF AMERICA LIFE INS CO	NY	21,758.9
NEW YORK LIFE INS CO	NY	178,706.9
NIPPON LIFE INS CO OF AMERICA	IA	219.2
PACIFIC GUARDIAN LIFE INS CO LTD	HI	559.1
PACIFIC LIFE INS CO	NE	133,288.3
PHYSICIANS LIFE INS CO	NE	1,664.1
STANDARD LIFE & ACCIDENT INS CO	TX	533.1
SYMETRA NATIONAL LIFE INS CO	IA	18.6
USABLE LIFE	AR	541.5

Rating: B+

INSURANCE COMPANY NAME	DOM. STATE	TOTAL ASSETS ($MIL)
AMERICAN FIDELITY ASR CO	OK	6,090.1
AMERICAN UNITED LIFE INS CO	IN	29,575.8
AMICA LIFE INS CO	RI	1,302.6
ASSURITY LIFE INS CO	NE	2,729.5
AXA EQUITABLE LIFE INS CO	NY	191,807.0
BEST LIFE & HEALTH INS CO	TX	22.7
BOSTON MUTUAL LIFE INS CO	MA	1,461.7
CHESAPEAKE LIFE INS CO	OK	195.4
CHRISTIAN FIDELITY LIFE INS CO	TX	64.2
COMPANION LIFE INS CO	SC	401.6
DEARBORN NATIONAL LIFE INS CO	IL	1,737.6
DELAWARE AMERICAN LIFE INS CO	DE	122.9
EAGLE LIFE INS CO	IA	1,070.1
ENTERPRISE LIFE INS CO	TX	73.7
FAMILY HERITAGE LIFE INS CO OF AMER	OH	1,444.8
FARM BUREAU LIFE INS CO	IA	9,267.1
FREEDOM LIFE INS CO OF AMERICA	TX	213.2
GERBER LIFE INS CO	NY	3,909.7
HANNOVER LIFE REASSURANCE CO OF AMER	FL	16,338.8
LOCOMOTIVE ENGRS&COND MUT PROT ASSN	MI	73.6
M LIFE INS CO	CO	307.3

INSURANCE COMPANY NAME	DOM. STATE	TOTAL ASSETS ($MIL)
MIDLAND NATIONAL LIFE INS CO	IA	58,240.4
MINNESOTA LIFE INS CO	MN	49,271.3
NATIONAL BENEFIT LIFE INS CO	NY	564.7
NATIONAL FARMERS UNION LIFE INS CO	TX	193.3
NATIONAL FOUNDATION LIFE INS CO	TX	50.6
NEW YORK LIFE INS & ANNUITY CORP	DE	156,175.5
NORTHWESTERN MUTUAL LIFE INS CO	WI	273,304.0
OHIO NATIONAL LIFE ASR CORP	OH	4,098.9
OXFORD LIFE INS CO	AZ	2,192.1
PACIFIC LIFE & ANNUITY CO	AZ	7,409.8
PAN AMERICAN ASR CO	LA	26.7
PRINCIPAL LIFE INS CO	IA	197,908.3
SB MUTL LIFE INS CO OF MA	MA	3,104.8
STANDARD INS CO	OR	24,530.4
TRANS WORLD ASR CO	CA	344.9
TRUSTMARK INS CO	IL	1,606.0
TRUSTMARK LIFE INS CO	IL	330.1
UNITED WORLD LIFE INS CO	NE	119.5
VOYA RETIREMENT INS & ANNUITY CO	CT	108,678.3

Nevada

INSURANCE COMPANY NAME	DOM. STATE	TOTAL ASSETS ($MIL)

Rating: A+

INSURANCE COMPANY NAME	DOM. STATE	TOTAL ASSETS ($MIL)
AMERICAN FAMILY LIFE INS CO	WI	5,269.9
COUNTRY LIFE INS CO	IL	9,673.9
PHYSICIANS MUTUAL INS CO	NE	2,367.4
STATE FARM LIFE INS CO	IL	74,940.7
TEACHERS INS & ANNUITY ASN OF AM	NY	302,803.1

Rating: A

INSURANCE COMPANY NAME	DOM. STATE	TOTAL ASSETS ($MIL)
AMALGAMATED LIFE INS CO	NY	140.3
BERKLEY LIFE & HEALTH INS CO	IA	325.8
FEDERATED LIFE INS CO	MN	1,969.7
GARDEN STATE LIFE INS CO	TX	135.5
GUARDIAN LIFE INS CO OF AMERICA	NY	57,852.7
NATIONAL WESTERN LIFE INS CO	CO	11,114.0
PARKER CENTENNIAL ASR CO	WI	96.0
SENTRY LIFE INS CO	WI	7,425.4
USAA LIFE INS CO	TX	25,292.8

Rating: A-

INSURANCE COMPANY NAME	DOM. STATE	TOTAL ASSETS ($MIL)
AMERICAN HEALTH & LIFE INS CO	TX	1,018.0
ANNUITY INVESTORS LIFE INS CO	OH	3,232.6
COUNTRY INVESTORS LIFE ASR CO	IL	303.5
FIDELITY INVESTMENTS LIFE INS CO	UT	30,960.8
MASSACHUSETTS MUTUAL LIFE INS CO	MA	245,872.2
MUTUAL OF AMERICA LIFE INS CO	NY	21,758.9
NEW YORK LIFE INS CO	NY	178,706.9
NIPPON LIFE INS CO OF AMERICA	IA	219.2
PACIFIC GUARDIAN LIFE INS CO LTD	HI	559.1
PACIFIC LIFE INS CO	NE	133,288.3
PHYSICIANS LIFE INS CO	NE	1,664.1
STANDARD LIFE & ACCIDENT INS CO	TX	533.1
SYMETRA NATIONAL LIFE INS CO	IA	18.6
USABLE LIFE	AR	541.5

Rating: B+

INSURANCE COMPANY NAME	DOM. STATE	TOTAL ASSETS ($MIL)
AMERICAN FIDELITY ASR CO	OK	6,090.1
AMERICAN UNITED LIFE INS CO	IN	29,575.8
AMICA LIFE INS CO	RI	1,302.6
ASSURITY LIFE INS CO	NE	2,729.5
AXA EQUITABLE LIFE INS CO	NY	191,807.0
BEST LIFE & HEALTH INS CO	TX	22.7
BOSTON MUTUAL LIFE INS CO	MA	1,461.7
CHESAPEAKE LIFE INS CO	OK	195.4
CHRISTIAN FIDELITY LIFE INS CO	TX	64.2
COMPANION LIFE INS CO	SC	401.6
DEARBORN NATIONAL LIFE INS CO	IL	1,737.6
DELAWARE AMERICAN LIFE INS CO	DE	122.9
EAGLE LIFE INS CO	IA	1,070.1
FAMILY HERITAGE LIFE INS CO OF AMER	OH	1,444.8
FARM BUREAU LIFE INS CO	IA	9,267.1
FREEDOM LIFE INS CO OF AMERICA	TX	213.2
GERBER LIFE INS CO	NY	3,909.7
HANNOVER LIFE REASSURANCE CO OF AMER	FL	16,338.8
MIDLAND NATIONAL LIFE INS CO	IA	58,240.4
MINNESOTA LIFE INS CO	MN	49,271.3
NATIONAL BENEFIT LIFE INS CO	NY	564.7
NATIONAL FARMERS UNION LIFE INS CO	TX	193.3
NATIONAL FOUNDATION LIFE INS CO	TX	50.6
NEW YORK LIFE INS & ANNUITY CORP	DE	156,175.5
NORTHWESTERN MUTUAL LIFE INS CO	WI	273,304.0
OHIO NATIONAL LIFE ASR CORP	OH	4,098.9
OXFORD LIFE INS CO	AZ	2,192.1
PACIFIC LIFE & ANNUITY CO	AZ	7,409.8
PAN AMERICAN ASR CO	LA	26.7
PRINCIPAL LIFE INS CO	IA	197,908.3
SB MUTL LIFE INS CO OF MA	MA	3,104.8
STANDARD INS CO	OR	24,530.4
TRANS WORLD ASR CO	CA	344.9
TRUSTMARK INS CO	IL	1,606.0
TRUSTMARK LIFE INS CO	IL	330.1
UNITED WORLD LIFE INS CO	NE	119.5
VOYA RETIREMENT INS & ANNUITY CO	CT	108,678.3

New Hampshire

INSURANCE COMPANY NAME	DOM. STATE	TOTAL ASSETS ($MIL)
Rating: A+		
AMERICAN FAMILY LIFE INS CO	WI	5,269.9
PHYSICIANS MUTUAL INS CO	NE	2,367.4
STATE FARM LIFE INS CO	IL	74,940.7
TEACHERS INS & ANNUITY ASN OF AM	NY	302,803.1
Rating: A		
AMALGAMATED LIFE INS CO	NY	140.3
BERKLEY LIFE & HEALTH INS CO	IA	325.8
FEDERATED LIFE INS CO	MN	1,969.7
GARDEN STATE LIFE INS CO	TX	135.5
GUARDIAN LIFE INS CO OF AMERICA	NY	57,852.7
NATIONAL WESTERN LIFE INS CO	CO	11,114.0
PARKER CENTENNIAL ASR CO	WI	96.0
SENTRY LIFE INS CO	WI	7,425.4
UNITED FARM FAMILY LIFE INS CO	IN	2,348.2
USAA LIFE INS CO	TX	25,292.8
Rating: A-		
AMERICAN HEALTH & LIFE INS CO	TX	1,018.0
ANNUITY INVESTORS LIFE INS CO	OH	3,232.6
FIDELITY INVESTMENTS LIFE INS CO	UT	30,960.8
MASSACHUSETTS MUTUAL LIFE INS CO	MA	245,872.2
MUTUAL OF AMERICA LIFE INS CO	NY	21,758.9
NEW YORK LIFE INS CO	NY	178,706.9
PACIFIC LIFE INS CO	NE	133,288.3
PHYSICIANS LIFE INS CO	NE	1,664.1
USABLE LIFE	AR	541.5
Rating: B+		
AMERICAN FIDELITY ASR CO	OK	6,090.1
AMERICAN UNITED LIFE INS CO	IN	29,575.8
AMICA LIFE INS CO	RI	1,302.6
ASSURITY LIFE INS CO	NE	2,729.5
AXA EQUITABLE LIFE INS CO	NY	191,807.0
BOSTON MUTUAL LIFE INS CO	MA	1,461.7
CHESAPEAKE LIFE INS CO	OK	195.4
COMPANION LIFE INS CO	SC	401.6
DEARBORN NATIONAL LIFE INS CO	IL	1,737.6
DELAWARE AMERICAN LIFE INS CO	DE	122.9
EAGLE LIFE INS CO	IA	1,070.1
FAMILY HERITAGE LIFE INS CO OF AMER	OH	1,444.8
GERBER LIFE INS CO	NY	3,909.7
HANNOVER LIFE REASSURANCE CO OF AMER	FL	16,338.8
MIDLAND NATIONAL LIFE INS CO	IA	58,240.4
MINNESOTA LIFE INS CO	MN	49,271.3
NATIONAL BENEFIT LIFE INS CO	NY	564.7
NEW YORK LIFE INS & ANNUITY CORP	DE	156,175.5
NORTHWESTERN MUTUAL LIFE INS CO	WI	273,304.0
OHIO NATIONAL LIFE ASR CORP	OH	4,098.9
OXFORD LIFE INS CO	AZ	2,192.1
PACIFIC LIFE & ANNUITY CO	AZ	7,409.8
PRINCIPAL LIFE INS CO	IA	197,908.3
SB MUTL LIFE INS CO OF MA	MA	3,104.8
STANDARD INS CO	OR	24,530.4
TRUSTMARK INS CO	IL	1,606.0

INSURANCE COMPANY NAME	DOM. STATE	TOTAL ASSETS ($MIL)
TRUSTMARK LIFE INS CO	IL	330.1
UNITED WORLD LIFE INS CO	NE	119.5
VOYA RETIREMENT INS & ANNUITY CO	CT	108,678.3

New Jersey

INSURANCE COMPANY NAME	DOM. STATE	TOTAL ASSETS ($MIL)	INSURANCE COMPANY NAME	DOM. STATE	TOTAL ASSETS ($MIL)
			SB MUTL LIFE INS CO OF MA	MA	3,104.8
			STANDARD INS CO	OR	24,530.4
			TRANS WORLD ASR CO	CA	344.9
			TRUSTMARK INS CO	IL	1,606.0
			TRUSTMARK LIFE INS CO	IL	330.1
			UNITED WORLD LIFE INS CO	NE	119.5
			VOYA RETIREMENT INS & ANNUITY CO	CT	108,678.3

Rating: A+

INSURANCE COMPANY NAME	DOM. STATE	TOTAL ASSETS ($MIL)
AMERICAN FAMILY LIFE INS CO	WI	5,269.9
PHYSICIANS MUTUAL INS CO	NE	2,367.4
STATE FARM LIFE INS CO	IL	74,940.7
TEACHERS INS & ANNUITY ASN OF AM	NY	302,803.1

Rating: A

INSURANCE COMPANY NAME	DOM. STATE	TOTAL ASSETS ($MIL)
AMALGAMATED LIFE INS CO	NY	140.3
BERKLEY LIFE & HEALTH INS CO	IA	325.8
FEDERATED LIFE INS CO	MN	1,969.7
GARDEN STATE LIFE INS CO	TX	135.5
GUARDIAN LIFE INS CO OF AMERICA	NY	57,852.7
NATIONAL WESTERN LIFE INS CO	CO	11,114.0
PARKER CENTENNIAL ASR CO	WI	96.0
SENTRY LIFE INS CO	WI	7,425.4
SHELTERPOINT LIFE INS CO	NY	151.3
UNITED FARM FAMILY LIFE INS CO	IN	2,348.2
USAA LIFE INS CO	TX	25,292.8

Rating: A-

INSURANCE COMPANY NAME	DOM. STATE	TOTAL ASSETS ($MIL)
AMERICAN FAMILY LIFE ASR CO OF NY	NY	1,000.3
AMERICAN HEALTH & LIFE INS CO	TX	1,018.0
ANNUITY INVESTORS LIFE INS CO	OH	3,232.6
FIDELITY INVESTMENTS LIFE INS CO	UT	30,960.8
MASSACHUSETTS MUTUAL LIFE INS CO	MA	245,872.2
MUTUAL OF AMERICA LIFE INS CO	NY	21,758.9
NEW YORK LIFE INS CO	NY	178,706.9
NIPPON LIFE INS CO OF AMERICA	IA	219.2
PACIFIC LIFE INS CO	NE	133,288.3
PHYSICIANS LIFE INS CO	NE	1,664.1
USABLE LIFE	AR	541.5

Rating: B+

INSURANCE COMPANY NAME	DOM. STATE	TOTAL ASSETS ($MIL)
AMERICAN FIDELITY ASR CO	OK	6,090.1
AMERICAN UNITED LIFE INS CO	IN	29,575.8
AMICA LIFE INS CO	RI	1,302.6
ASSURITY LIFE INS CO	NE	2,729.5
AXA EQUITABLE LIFE INS CO	NY	191,807.0
BOSTON MUTUAL LIFE INS CO	MA	1,461.7
DEARBORN NATIONAL LIFE INS CO	IL	1,737.6
DELAWARE AMERICAN LIFE INS CO	DE	122.9
EAGLE LIFE INS CO	IA	1,070.1
FAMILY HERITAGE LIFE INS CO OF AMER	OH	1,444.8
GERBER LIFE INS CO	NY	3,909.7
HANNOVER LIFE REASSURANCE CO OF AMER	FL	16,338.8
M LIFE INS CO	CO	307.3
MIDLAND NATIONAL LIFE INS CO	IA	58,240.4
MINNESOTA LIFE INS CO	MN	49,271.3
NATIONAL BENEFIT LIFE INS CO	NY	564.7
NEW YORK LIFE INS & ANNUITY CORP	DE	156,175.5
NORTHWESTERN MUTUAL LIFE INS CO	WI	273,304.0
OHIO NATIONAL LIFE ASR CORP	OH	4,098.9
OXFORD LIFE INS CO	AZ	2,192.1
PACIFIC LIFE & ANNUITY CO	AZ	7,409.8
PAN AMERICAN ASR CO	LA	26.7
PRINCIPAL LIFE INS CO	IA	197,908.3

New Mexico

INSURANCE COMPANY NAME	DOM. STATE	TOTAL ASSETS ($MIL)

Rating: A+

INSURANCE COMPANY NAME	DOM. STATE	TOTAL ASSETS ($MIL)
AMERICAN FAMILY LIFE INS CO	WI	5,269.9
COUNTRY LIFE INS CO	IL	9,673.9
PHYSICIANS MUTUAL INS CO	NE	2,367.4
STATE FARM LIFE INS CO	IL	74,940.7
TEACHERS INS & ANNUITY ASN OF AM	NY	302,803.1

Rating: A

INSURANCE COMPANY NAME	DOM. STATE	TOTAL ASSETS ($MIL)
AMALGAMATED LIFE INS CO	NY	140.3
BERKLEY LIFE & HEALTH INS CO	IA	325.8
FEDERATED LIFE INS CO	MN	1,969.7
GARDEN STATE LIFE INS CO	TX	135.5
GUARDIAN LIFE INS CO OF AMERICA	NY	57,852.7
NATIONAL WESTERN LIFE INS CO	CO	11,114.0
PARKER CENTENNIAL ASR CO	WI	96.0
SENTRY LIFE INS CO	WI	7,425.4
USAA LIFE INS CO	TX	25,292.8

Rating: A-

INSURANCE COMPANY NAME	DOM. STATE	TOTAL ASSETS ($MIL)
AMERICAN HEALTH & LIFE INS CO	TX	1,018.0
ANNUITY INVESTORS LIFE INS CO	OH	3,232.6
COUNTRY INVESTORS LIFE ASR CO	IL	303.5
FIDELITY INVESTMENTS LIFE INS CO	UT	30,960.8
MASSACHUSETTS MUTUAL LIFE INS CO	MA	245,872.2
MUTUAL OF AMERICA LIFE INS CO	NY	21,758.9
NEW YORK LIFE INS CO	NY	178,706.9
NIPPON LIFE INS CO OF AMERICA	IA	219.2
PACIFIC GUARDIAN LIFE INS CO LTD	HI	559.1
PACIFIC LIFE INS CO	NE	133,288.3
PHYSICIANS LIFE INS CO	NE	1,664.1
SOUTHERN PIONEER LIFE INS CO	AR	14.6
STANDARD LIFE & ACCIDENT INS CO	TX	533.1
SYMETRA NATIONAL LIFE INS CO	IA	18.6
USABLE LIFE	AR	541.5

Rating: B+

INSURANCE COMPANY NAME	DOM. STATE	TOTAL ASSETS ($MIL)
AMERICAN FIDELITY ASR CO	OK	6,090.1
AMERICAN UNITED LIFE INS CO	IN	29,575.8
AMICA LIFE INS CO	RI	1,302.6
ASSURITY LIFE INS CO	NE	2,729.5
AXA EQUITABLE LIFE INS CO	NY	191,807.0
BEST LIFE & HEALTH INS CO	TX	22.7
BOSTON MUTUAL LIFE INS CO	MA	1,461.7
CHESAPEAKE LIFE INS CO	OK	195.4
CHRISTIAN FIDELITY LIFE INS CO	TX	64.2
COMPANION LIFE INS CO	SC	401.6
DEARBORN NATIONAL LIFE INS CO	IL	1,737.6
DELAWARE AMERICAN LIFE INS CO	DE	122.9
EAGLE LIFE INS CO	IA	1,070.1
ENTERPRISE LIFE INS CO	TX	73.7
FAMILY HERITAGE LIFE INS CO OF AMER	OH	1,444.8
FARM BUREAU LIFE INS CO	IA	9,267.1
FREEDOM LIFE INS CO OF AMERICA	TX	213.2
GERBER LIFE INS CO	NY	3,909.7
HANNOVER LIFE REASSURANCE CO OF AMER	FL	16,338.8
LOCOMOTIVE ENGRS&COND MUT PROT ASSN	MI	73.6

INSURANCE COMPANY NAME	DOM. STATE	TOTAL ASSETS ($MIL)
MIDLAND NATIONAL LIFE INS CO	IA	58,240.4
MINNESOTA LIFE INS CO	MN	49,271.3
NATIONAL BENEFIT LIFE INS CO	NY	564.7
NATIONAL FARMERS UNION LIFE INS CO	TX	193.3
NATIONAL FOUNDATION LIFE INS CO	TX	50.6
NEW YORK LIFE INS & ANNUITY CORP	DE	156,175.5
NORTH AMERICAN INS CO	WI	19.2
NORTHWESTERN MUTUAL LIFE INS CO	WI	273,304.0
OHIO NATIONAL LIFE ASR CORP	OH	4,098.9
OXFORD LIFE INS CO	AZ	2,192.1
PACIFIC LIFE & ANNUITY CO	AZ	7,409.8
PAN AMERICAN ASR CO	LA	26.7
PRINCIPAL LIFE INS CO	IA	197,908.3
SB MUTL LIFE INS CO OF MA	MA	3,104.8
STANDARD INS CO	OR	24,530.4
TRANS WORLD ASR CO	CA	344.9
TRUSTMARK INS CO	IL	1,606.0
TRUSTMARK LIFE INS CO	IL	330.1
UNITED WORLD LIFE INS CO	NE	119.5
VOYA RETIREMENT INS & ANNUITY CO	CT	108,678.3

New York

INSURANCE COMPANY NAME	DOM. STATE	TOTAL ASSETS ($MIL)
Rating: A+		
PHYSICIANS MUTUAL INS CO	NE	2,367.4
STATE FARM LIFE & ACCIDENT ASR CO	IL	3,003.4
TEACHERS INS & ANNUITY ASN OF AM	NY	302,803.1
Rating: A		
AMALGAMATED LIFE INS CO	NY	140.3
BERKLEY LIFE & HEALTH INS CO	IA	325.8
FEDERATED LIFE INS CO	MN	1,969.7
GARDEN STATE LIFE INS CO	TX	135.5
GUARDIAN LIFE INS CO OF AMERICA	NY	57,852.7
SHELTERPOINT LIFE INS CO	NY	151.3
Rating: A-		
AMERICAN FAMILY LIFE ASR CO OF NY	NY	1,000.3
CIGNA LIFE INS CO OF NEW YORK	NY	407.5
FIRST RELIANCE STANDARD LIFE INS CO	NY	208.0
LIFE INS CO OF BOSTON & NEW YORK	NY	157.5
MASSACHUSETTS MUTUAL LIFE INS CO	MA	245,872.2
MUTUAL OF AMERICA LIFE INS CO	NY	21,758.9
NEW YORK LIFE INS CO	NY	178,706.9
NIPPON LIFE INS CO OF AMERICA	IA	219.2
STANDARD LIFE INS CO OF NY	NY	296.6
Rating: B+		
ALLIANZ LIFE INS CO OF NY	NY	3,461.1
AMERICAN UNITED LIFE INS CO	IN	29,575.8
AMICA LIFE INS CO	RI	1,302.6
AXA EQUITABLE LIFE INS CO	NY	191,807.0
BOSTON MUTUAL LIFE INS CO	MA	1,461.7
DEARBORN NATIONAL LIFE INS CO OF NY	NY	23.6
DELAWARE AMERICAN LIFE INS CO	DE	122.9
EMPIRE FIDELITY INVESTMENTS L I C	NY	3,035.0
FIRST SYMETRA NATL LIFE INS CO OF NY	NY	2,070.2
GERBER LIFE INS CO	NY	3,909.7
HANNOVER LIFE REASSURANCE CO OF AMER	FL	16,338.8
NATIONAL BENEFIT LIFE INS CO	NY	564.7
NATIONAL INCOME LIFE INS CO	NY	261.9
NEW YORK LIFE INS & ANNUITY CORP	DE	156,175.5
NORTHWESTERN MUTUAL LIFE INS CO	WI	273,304.0
PACIFIC LIFE & ANNUITY CO	AZ	7,409.8
PRINCIPAL LIFE INS CO	IA	197,908.3
TRUSTMARK INS CO	IL	1,606.0
TRUSTMARK LIFE INS CO	IL	330.1
USAA LIFE INS CO OF NEW YORK	NY	780.2
VOYA RETIREMENT INS & ANNUITY CO	CT	108,678.3

North Carolina

INSURANCE COMPANY NAME	DOM. STATE	TOTAL ASSETS ($MIL)

Rating: A+

INSURANCE COMPANY NAME	DOM. STATE	TOTAL ASSETS ($MIL)
AMERICAN FAMILY LIFE INS CO	WI	5,269.9
COUNTRY LIFE INS CO	IL	9,673.9
PHYSICIANS MUTUAL INS CO	NE	2,367.4
STATE FARM LIFE INS CO	IL	74,940.7
TEACHERS INS & ANNUITY ASN OF AM	NY	302,803.1

Rating: A

INSURANCE COMPANY NAME	DOM. STATE	TOTAL ASSETS ($MIL)
AMALGAMATED LIFE INS CO	NY	140.3
BERKLEY LIFE & HEALTH INS CO	IA	325.8
FEDERATED LIFE INS CO	MN	1,969.7
GARDEN STATE LIFE INS CO	TX	135.5
GUARDIAN LIFE INS CO OF AMERICA	NY	57,852.7
NATIONAL WESTERN LIFE INS CO	CO	11,114.0
PARKER CENTENNIAL ASR CO	WI	96.0
SENTRY LIFE INS CO	WI	7,425.4
SHELTERPOINT LIFE INS CO	NY	151.3
SOUTHERN FARM BUREAU LIFE INS CO	MS	14,356.8
UNITED FARM FAMILY LIFE INS CO	IN	2,348.2
USAA LIFE INS CO	TX	25,292.8

Rating: A-

INSURANCE COMPANY NAME	DOM. STATE	TOTAL ASSETS ($MIL)
AMERICAN HEALTH & LIFE INS CO	TX	1,018.0
ANNUITY INVESTORS LIFE INS CO	OH	3,232.6
COTTON STATES LIFE INS CO	GA	339.7
COUNTRY INVESTORS LIFE ASR CO	IL	303.5
ERIE FAMILY LIFE INS CO	PA	2,512.1
FIDELITY INVESTMENTS LIFE INS CO	UT	30,960.8
MASSACHUSETTS MUTUAL LIFE INS CO	MA	245,872.2
MUTUAL OF AMERICA LIFE INS CO	NY	21,758.9
NEW YORK LIFE INS CO	NY	178,706.9
NIPPON LIFE INS CO OF AMERICA	IA	219.2
PACIFIC LIFE INS CO	NE	133,288.3
PHYSICIANS LIFE INS CO	NE	1,664.1
STANDARD LIFE & ACCIDENT INS CO	TX	533.1
SYMETRA NATIONAL LIFE INS CO	IA	18.6
USABLE LIFE	AR	541.5

Rating: B+

INSURANCE COMPANY NAME	DOM. STATE	TOTAL ASSETS ($MIL)
AMERICAN FIDELITY ASR CO	OK	6,090.1
AMERICAN UNITED LIFE INS CO	IN	29,575.8
AMICA LIFE INS CO	RI	1,302.6
ASSURITY LIFE INS CO	NE	2,729.5
AXA EQUITABLE LIFE INS CO	NY	191,807.0
BEST LIFE & HEALTH INS CO	TX	22.7
BOSTON MUTUAL LIFE INS CO	MA	1,461.7
CHESAPEAKE LIFE INS CO	OK	195.4
COMPANION LIFE INS CO	SC	401.6
DEARBORN NATIONAL LIFE INS CO	IL	1,737.6
DELAWARE AMERICAN LIFE INS CO	DE	122.9
EAGLE LIFE INS CO	IA	1,070.1
FAMILY HERITAGE LIFE INS CO OF AMER	OH	1,444.8
FREEDOM LIFE INS CO OF AMERICA	TX	213.2
GERBER LIFE INS CO	NY	3,909.7
HANNOVER LIFE REASSURANCE CO OF AMER	FL	16,338.8
MIDLAND NATIONAL LIFE INS CO	IA	58,240.4

INSURANCE COMPANY NAME	DOM. STATE	TOTAL ASSETS ($MIL)
MINNESOTA LIFE INS CO	MN	49,271.3
NATIONAL BENEFIT LIFE INS CO	NY	564.7
NATIONAL FOUNDATION LIFE INS CO	TX	50.6
NEW YORK LIFE INS & ANNUITY CORP	DE	156,175.5
NORTHWESTERN MUTUAL LIFE INS CO	WI	273,304.0
OHIO NATIONAL LIFE ASR CORP	OH	4,098.9
OXFORD LIFE INS CO	AZ	2,192.1
PACIFIC LIFE & ANNUITY CO	AZ	7,409.8
PAN AMERICAN ASR CO	LA	26.7
PRINCIPAL LIFE INS CO	IA	197,908.3
SB MUTL LIFE INS CO OF MA	MA	3,104.8
STANDARD INS CO	OR	24,530.4
TRANS WORLD ASR CO	CA	344.9
TRUSTMARK INS CO	IL	1,606.0
TRUSTMARK LIFE INS CO	IL	330.1
UNITED WORLD LIFE INS CO	NE	119.5
VOYA RETIREMENT INS & ANNUITY CO	CT	108,678.3

North Dakota

INSURANCE COMPANY NAME	DOM. STATE	TOTAL ASSETS ($MIL)
Rating: A+		
AMERICAN FAMILY LIFE INS CO	WI	5,269.9
COUNTRY LIFE INS CO	IL	9,673.9
PHYSICIANS MUTUAL INS CO	NE	2,367.4
STATE FARM LIFE INS CO	IL	74,940.7
TEACHERS INS & ANNUITY ASN OF AM	NY	302,803.1
Rating: A		
AMALGAMATED LIFE INS CO	NY	140.3
BERKLEY LIFE & HEALTH INS CO	IA	325.8
FEDERATED LIFE INS CO	MN	1,969.7
GARDEN STATE LIFE INS CO	TX	135.5
GUARDIAN LIFE INS CO OF AMERICA	NY	57,852.7
NATIONAL WESTERN LIFE INS CO	CO	11,114.0
PARKER CENTENNIAL ASR CO	WI	96.0
SENTRY LIFE INS CO	WI	7,425.4
UNITED FARM FAMILY LIFE INS CO	IN	2,348.2
USAA LIFE INS CO	TX	25,292.8
Rating: A-		
AMERICAN FAMILY LIFE ASR CO OF NY	NY	1,000.3
AMERICAN HEALTH & LIFE INS CO	TX	1,018.0
ANNUITY INVESTORS LIFE INS CO	OH	3,232.6
COUNTRY INVESTORS LIFE ASR CO	IL	303.5
FIDELITY INVESTMENTS LIFE INS CO	UT	30,960.8
MASSACHUSETTS MUTUAL LIFE INS CO	MA	245,872.2
MUTUAL OF AMERICA LIFE INS CO	NY	21,758.9
NEW YORK LIFE INS CO	NY	178,706.9
NIPPON LIFE INS CO OF AMERICA	IA	219.2
PACIFIC LIFE INS CO	NE	133,288.3
PHYSICIANS LIFE INS CO	NE	1,664.1
STANDARD LIFE & ACCIDENT INS CO	TX	533.1
SYMETRA NATIONAL LIFE INS CO	IA	18.6
USABLE LIFE	AR	541.5
Rating: B+		
ALLIANZ LIFE INS CO OF NY	NY	3,461.1
AMERICAN FIDELITY ASR CO	OK	6,090.1
AMERICAN UNITED LIFE INS CO	IN	29,575.8
AMICA LIFE INS CO	RI	1,302.6
ASSURITY LIFE INS CO	NE	2,729.5
AXA EQUITABLE LIFE INS CO	NY	191,807.0
BEST LIFE & HEALTH INS CO	TX	22.7
BOSTON MUTUAL LIFE INS CO	MA	1,461.7
CHESAPEAKE LIFE INS CO	OK	195.4
CHRISTIAN FIDELITY LIFE INS CO	TX	64.2
COMPANION LIFE INS CO	SC	401.6
DEARBORN NATIONAL LIFE INS CO	IL	1,737.6
DELAWARE AMERICAN LIFE INS CO	DE	122.9
EAGLE LIFE INS CO	IA	1,070.1
FAMILY HERITAGE LIFE INS CO OF AMER	OH	1,444.8
FARM BUREAU LIFE INS CO	IA	9,267.1
GERBER LIFE INS CO	NY	3,909.7
HANNOVER LIFE REASSURANCE CO OF AMER	FL	16,338.8
MIDLAND NATIONAL LIFE INS CO	IA	58,240.4
MINNESOTA LIFE INS CO	MN	49,271.3

INSURANCE COMPANY NAME	DOM. STATE	TOTAL ASSETS ($MIL)
NATIONAL BENEFIT LIFE INS CO	NY	564.7
NATIONAL FARMERS UNION LIFE INS CO	TX	193.3
NATIONAL FOUNDATION LIFE INS CO	TX	50.6
NEW YORK LIFE INS & ANNUITY CORP	DE	156,175.5
NORTH AMERICAN INS CO	WI	19.2
NORTHWESTERN MUTUAL LIFE INS CO	WI	273,304.0
OHIO NATIONAL LIFE ASR CORP	OH	4,098.9
OXFORD LIFE INS CO	AZ	2,192.1
PACIFIC LIFE & ANNUITY CO	AZ	7,409.8
PAN AMERICAN ASR CO	LA	26.7
PRINCIPAL LIFE INS CO	IA	197,908.3
SB MUTL LIFE INS CO OF MA	MA	3,104.8
STANDARD INS CO	OR	24,530.4
TRANS WORLD ASR CO	CA	344.9
TRUSTMARK INS CO	IL	1,606.0
TRUSTMARK LIFE INS CO	IL	330.1
UNITED WORLD LIFE INS CO	NE	119.5
VOYA RETIREMENT INS & ANNUITY CO	CT	108,678.3

Ohio

INSURANCE COMPANY NAME	DOM. STATE	TOTAL ASSETS ($MIL)
### Rating: A+		
AMERICAN FAMILY LIFE INS CO	WI	5,269.9
COUNTRY LIFE INS CO	IL	9,673.9
PHYSICIANS MUTUAL INS CO	NE	2,367.4
STATE FARM LIFE INS CO	IL	74,940.7
TEACHERS INS & ANNUITY ASN OF AM	NY	302,803.1
### Rating: A		
AMALGAMATED LIFE INS CO	NY	140.3
BERKLEY LIFE & HEALTH INS CO	IA	325.8
FEDERATED LIFE INS CO	MN	1,969.7
GARDEN STATE LIFE INS CO	TX	135.5
GUARDIAN LIFE INS CO OF AMERICA	NY	57,852.7
NATIONAL WESTERN LIFE INS CO	CO	11,114.0
PARKER CENTENNIAL ASR CO	WI	96.0
SENTRY LIFE INS CO	WI	7,425.4
UNITED FARM FAMILY LIFE INS CO	IN	2,348.2
USAA LIFE INS CO	TX	25,292.8
### Rating: A-		
AMERICAN HEALTH & LIFE INS CO	TX	1,018.0
ANNUITY INVESTORS LIFE INS CO	OH	3,232.6
COUNTRY INVESTORS LIFE ASR CO	IL	303.5
ERIE FAMILY LIFE INS CO	PA	2,512.1
FIDELITY INVESTMENTS LIFE INS CO	UT	30,960.8
MASSACHUSETTS MUTUAL LIFE INS CO	MA	245,872.2
MUTUAL OF AMERICA LIFE INS CO	NY	21,758.9
NEW YORK LIFE INS CO	NY	178,706.9
NIPPON LIFE INS CO OF AMERICA	IA	219.2
PACIFIC LIFE INS CO	NE	133,288.3
PHYSICIANS LIFE INS CO	NE	1,664.1
STANDARD LIFE & ACCIDENT INS CO	TX	533.1
SYMETRA NATIONAL LIFE INS CO	IA	18.6
USABLE LIFE	AR	541.5
### Rating: B+		
AMERICAN FIDELITY ASR CO	OK	6,090.1
AMERICAN UNITED LIFE INS CO	IN	29,575.8
AMICA LIFE INS CO	RI	1,302.6
ASSURITY LIFE INS CO	NE	2,729.5
AXA EQUITABLE LIFE INS CO	NY	191,807.0
BEST LIFE & HEALTH INS CO	TX	22.7
BOSTON MUTUAL LIFE INS CO	MA	1,461.7
CHESAPEAKE LIFE INS CO	OK	195.4
CHRISTIAN FIDELITY LIFE INS CO	TX	64.2
COMPANION LIFE INS CO	SC	401.6
DEARBORN NATIONAL LIFE INS CO	IL	1,737.6
DELAWARE AMERICAN LIFE INS CO	DE	122.9
EAGLE LIFE INS CO	IA	1,070.1
FAMILY HERITAGE LIFE INS CO OF AMER	OH	1,444.8
FREEDOM LIFE INS CO OF AMERICA	TX	213.2
GERBER LIFE INS CO	NY	3,909.7
HANNOVER LIFE REASSURANCE CO OF AMER	FL	16,338.8
M LIFE INS CO	CO	307.3
MIDLAND NATIONAL LIFE INS CO	IA	58,240.4
MINNESOTA LIFE INS CO	MN	49,271.3

INSURANCE COMPANY NAME	DOM. STATE	TOTAL ASSETS ($MIL)
NATIONAL BENEFIT LIFE INS CO	NY	564.7
NATIONAL FARMERS UNION LIFE INS CO	TX	193.3
NATIONAL FOUNDATION LIFE INS CO	TX	50.6
NEW YORK LIFE INS & ANNUITY CORP	DE	156,175.5
NORTH AMERICAN INS CO	WI	19.2
NORTHWESTERN MUTUAL LIFE INS CO	WI	273,304.0
OHIO NATIONAL LIFE ASR CORP	OH	4,098.9
OXFORD LIFE INS CO	AZ	2,192.1
PACIFIC LIFE & ANNUITY CO	AZ	7,409.8
PAN AMERICAN ASR CO	LA	26.7
PRINCIPAL LIFE INS CO	IA	197,908.3
SB MUTL LIFE INS CO OF MA	MA	3,104.8
STANDARD INS CO	OR	24,530.4
TRANS WORLD ASR CO	CA	344.9
TRUSTMARK INS CO	IL	1,606.0
TRUSTMARK LIFE INS CO	IL	330.1
UNITED WORLD LIFE INS CO	NE	119.5
VOYA RETIREMENT INS & ANNUITY CO	CT	108,678.3

Oklahoma

INSURANCE COMPANY NAME	DOM. STATE	TOTAL ASSETS ($MIL)
Rating: A+		
AMERICAN FAMILY LIFE INS CO	WI	5,269.9
COUNTRY LIFE INS CO	IL	9,673.9
PHYSICIANS MUTUAL INS CO	NE	2,367.4
STATE FARM LIFE INS CO	IL	74,940.7
TEACHERS INS & ANNUITY ASN OF AM	NY	302,803.1
Rating: A		
AMALGAMATED LIFE INS CO	NY	140.3
BERKLEY LIFE & HEALTH INS CO	IA	325.8
FEDERATED LIFE INS CO	MN	1,969.7
GARDEN STATE LIFE INS CO	TX	135.5
GUARDIAN LIFE INS CO OF AMERICA	NY	57,852.7
NATIONAL WESTERN LIFE INS CO	CO	11,114.0
PARKER CENTENNIAL ASR CO	WI	96.0
SENTRY LIFE INS CO	WI	7,425.4
USAA LIFE INS CO	TX	25,292.8
Rating: A-		
AMERICAN HEALTH & LIFE INS CO	TX	1,018.0
ANNUITY INVESTORS LIFE INS CO	OH	3,232.6
COUNTRY INVESTORS LIFE ASR CO	IL	303.5
FIDELITY INVESTMENTS LIFE INS CO	UT	30,960.8
MASSACHUSETTS MUTUAL LIFE INS CO	MA	245,872.2
MUTUAL OF AMERICA LIFE INS CO	NY	21,758.9
NEW YORK LIFE INS CO	NY	178,706.9
NIPPON LIFE INS CO OF AMERICA	IA	219.2
PACIFIC GUARDIAN LIFE INS CO LTD	HI	559.1
PACIFIC LIFE INS CO	NE	133,288.3
PHYSICIANS LIFE INS CO	NE	1,664.1
SOUTHERN PIONEER LIFE INS CO	AR	14.6
STANDARD LIFE & ACCIDENT INS CO	TX	533.1
SYMETRA NATIONAL LIFE INS CO	IA	18.6
USABLE LIFE	AR	541.5
Rating: B+		
AMERICAN FIDELITY ASR CO	OK	6,090.1
AMERICAN UNITED LIFE INS CO	IN	29,575.8
AMICA LIFE INS CO	RI	1,302.6
ASSURITY LIFE INS CO	NE	2,729.5
AXA EQUITABLE LIFE INS CO	NY	191,807.0
BEST LIFE & HEALTH INS CO	TX	22.7
BOSTON MUTUAL LIFE INS CO	MA	1,461.7
CHESAPEAKE LIFE INS CO	OK	195.4
CHRISTIAN FIDELITY LIFE INS CO	TX	64.2
COMPANION LIFE INS CO	SC	401.6
DEARBORN NATIONAL LIFE INS CO	IL	1,737.6
DELAWARE AMERICAN LIFE INS CO	DE	122.9
EAGLE LIFE INS CO	IA	1,070.1
ENTERPRISE LIFE INS CO	TX	73.7
FAMILY HERITAGE LIFE INS CO OF AMER	OH	1,444.8
FARM BUREAU LIFE INS CO	IA	9,267.1
FREEDOM LIFE INS CO OF AMERICA	TX	213.2
GERBER LIFE INS CO	NY	3,909.7
HANNOVER LIFE REASSURANCE CO OF AMER	FL	16,338.8
MIDLAND NATIONAL LIFE INS CO	IA	58,240.4

INSURANCE COMPANY NAME	DOM. STATE	TOTAL ASSETS ($MIL)
MINNESOTA LIFE INS CO	MN	49,271.3
NATIONAL BENEFIT LIFE INS CO	NY	564.7
NATIONAL FARMERS UNION LIFE INS CO	TX	193.3
NATIONAL FOUNDATION LIFE INS CO	TX	50.6
NEW YORK LIFE INS & ANNUITY CORP	DE	156,175.5
NORTH AMERICAN INS CO	WI	19.2
NORTHWESTERN MUTUAL LIFE INS CO	WI	273,304.0
OHIO NATIONAL LIFE ASR CORP	OH	4,098.9
OXFORD LIFE INS CO	AZ	2,192.1
PACIFIC LIFE & ANNUITY CO	AZ	7,409.8
PAN AMERICAN ASR CO	LA	26.7
PRINCIPAL LIFE INS CO	IA	197,908.3
SB MUTL LIFE INS CO OF MA	MA	3,104.8
STANDARD INS CO	OR	24,530.4
SWBC LIFE INS CO	TX	32.6
TRANS WORLD ASR CO	CA	344.9
TRUSTMARK INS CO	IL	1,606.0
TRUSTMARK LIFE INS CO	IL	330.1
UNITED WORLD LIFE INS CO	NE	119.5
VOYA RETIREMENT INS & ANNUITY CO	CT	108,678.3

Oregon

INSURANCE COMPANY NAME	DOM. STATE	TOTAL ASSETS ($MIL)

Rating: A+

INSURANCE COMPANY NAME	DOM. STATE	TOTAL ASSETS ($MIL)
AMERICAN FAMILY LIFE INS CO	WI	5,269.9
COUNTRY LIFE INS CO	IL	9,673.9
PHYSICIANS MUTUAL INS CO	NE	2,367.4
STATE FARM LIFE INS CO	IL	74,940.7
TEACHERS INS & ANNUITY ASN OF AM	NY	302,803.1

Rating: A

INSURANCE COMPANY NAME	DOM. STATE	TOTAL ASSETS ($MIL)
AMALGAMATED LIFE INS CO	NY	140.3
BERKLEY LIFE & HEALTH INS CO	IA	325.8
FEDERATED LIFE INS CO	MN	1,969.7
GARDEN STATE LIFE INS CO	TX	135.5
GUARDIAN LIFE INS CO OF AMERICA	NY	57,852.7
LIFEWISE ASR CO	WA	193.1
NATIONAL WESTERN LIFE INS CO	CO	11,114.0
PARKER CENTENNIAL ASR CO	WI	96.0
SENTRY LIFE INS CO	WI	7,425.4
USAA LIFE INS CO	TX	25,292.8

Rating: A-

INSURANCE COMPANY NAME	DOM. STATE	TOTAL ASSETS ($MIL)
AMERICAN HEALTH & LIFE INS CO	TX	1,018.0
ANNUITY INVESTORS LIFE INS CO	OH	3,232.6
COUNTRY INVESTORS LIFE ASR CO	IL	303.5
FIDELITY INVESTMENTS LIFE INS CO	UT	30,960.8
MASSACHUSETTS MUTUAL LIFE INS CO	MA	245,872.2
MUTUAL OF AMERICA LIFE INS CO	NY	21,758.9
NEW YORK LIFE INS CO	NY	178,706.9
NIPPON LIFE INS CO OF AMERICA	IA	219.2
PACIFIC GUARDIAN LIFE INS CO LTD	HI	559.1
PACIFIC LIFE INS CO	NE	133,288.3
PHYSICIANS LIFE INS CO	NE	1,664.1
STANDARD LIFE & ACCIDENT INS CO	TX	533.1
SYMETRA NATIONAL LIFE INS CO	IA	18.6
USABLE LIFE	AR	541.5

Rating: B+

INSURANCE COMPANY NAME	DOM. STATE	TOTAL ASSETS ($MIL)
AMERICAN FIDELITY ASR CO	OK	6,090.1
AMERICAN UNITED LIFE INS CO	IN	29,575.8
AMICA LIFE INS CO	RI	1,302.6
ASSURITY LIFE INS CO	NE	2,729.5
AXA EQUITABLE LIFE INS CO	NY	191,807.0
BEST LIFE & HEALTH INS CO	TX	22.7
BOSTON MUTUAL LIFE INS CO	MA	1,461.7
CHESAPEAKE LIFE INS CO	OK	195.4
CHRISTIAN FIDELITY LIFE INS CO	TX	64.2
COMPANION LIFE INS CO	SC	401.6
DEARBORN NATIONAL LIFE INS CO	IL	1,737.6
DELAWARE AMERICAN LIFE INS CO	DE	122.9
EAGLE LIFE INS CO	IA	1,070.1
ENTERPRISE LIFE INS CO	TX	73.7
FAMILY HERITAGE LIFE INS CO OF AMER	OH	1,444.8
FARM BUREAU LIFE INS CO	IA	9,267.1
FREEDOM LIFE INS CO OF AMERICA	TX	213.2
GERBER LIFE INS CO	NY	3,909.7
HANNOVER LIFE REASSURANCE CO OF AMER	FL	16,338.8
MIDLAND NATIONAL LIFE INS CO	IA	58,240.4

INSURANCE COMPANY NAME	DOM. STATE	TOTAL ASSETS ($MIL)
MINNESOTA LIFE INS CO	MN	49,271.3
NATIONAL BENEFIT LIFE INS CO	NY	564.7
NATIONAL FARMERS UNION LIFE INS CO	TX	193.3
NATIONAL FOUNDATION LIFE INS CO	TX	50.6
NEW YORK LIFE INS & ANNUITY CORP	DE	156,175.5
NORTH AMERICAN INS CO	WI	19.2
NORTHWESTERN MUTUAL LIFE INS CO	WI	273,304.0
OHIO NATIONAL LIFE ASR CORP	OH	4,098.9
OXFORD LIFE INS CO	AZ	2,192.1
PACIFIC LIFE & ANNUITY CO	AZ	7,409.8
PAN AMERICAN ASR CO	LA	26.7
PRINCIPAL LIFE INS CO	IA	197,908.3
SB MUTL LIFE INS CO OF MA	MA	3,104.8
STANDARD INS CO	OR	24,530.4
TRANS WORLD ASR CO	CA	344.9
TRUSTMARK INS CO	IL	1,606.0
TRUSTMARK LIFE INS CO	IL	330.1
UNITED WORLD LIFE INS CO	NE	119.5
VOYA RETIREMENT INS & ANNUITY CO	CT	108,678.3

Pennsylvania

INSURANCE COMPANY NAME	DOM. STATE	TOTAL ASSETS ($MIL)

Rating: A+

INSURANCE COMPANY NAME	DOM. STATE	TOTAL ASSETS ($MIL)
AMERICAN FAMILY LIFE INS CO	WI	5,269.9
COUNTRY LIFE INS CO	IL	9,673.9
PHYSICIANS MUTUAL INS CO	NE	2,367.4
STATE FARM LIFE INS CO	IL	74,940.7
TEACHERS INS & ANNUITY ASN OF AM	NY	302,803.1

Rating: A

INSURANCE COMPANY NAME	DOM. STATE	TOTAL ASSETS ($MIL)
AMALGAMATED LIFE INS CO	NY	140.3
BERKLEY LIFE & HEALTH INS CO	IA	325.8
FEDERATED LIFE INS CO	MN	1,969.7
GARDEN STATE LIFE INS CO	TX	135.5
GUARDIAN LIFE INS CO OF AMERICA	NY	57,852.7
NATIONAL WESTERN LIFE INS CO	CO	11,114.0
PARKER CENTENNIAL ASR CO	WI	96.0
SENTRY LIFE INS CO	WI	7,425.4
SHELTERPOINT LIFE INS CO	NY	151.3
UNITED FARM FAMILY LIFE INS CO	IN	2,348.2
USAA LIFE INS CO	TX	25,292.8

Rating: A-

INSURANCE COMPANY NAME	DOM. STATE	TOTAL ASSETS ($MIL)
AMERICAN HEALTH & LIFE INS CO	TX	1,018.0
ANNUITY INVESTORS LIFE INS CO	OH	3,232.6
CIGNA LIFE INS CO OF NEW YORK	NY	407.5
COUNTRY INVESTORS LIFE ASR CO	IL	303.5
ERIE FAMILY LIFE INS CO	PA	2,512.1
FIDELITY INVESTMENTS LIFE INS CO	UT	30,960.8
MASSACHUSETTS MUTUAL LIFE INS CO	MA	245,872.2
MUTUAL OF AMERICA LIFE INS CO	NY	21,758.9
NEW YORK LIFE INS CO	NY	178,706.9
NIPPON LIFE INS CO OF AMERICA	IA	219.2
PACIFIC LIFE INS CO	NE	133,288.3
PHYSICIANS LIFE INS CO	NE	1,664.1
STANDARD LIFE & ACCIDENT INS CO	TX	533.1
SYMETRA NATIONAL LIFE INS CO	IA	18.6
USABLE LIFE	AR	541.5

Rating: B+

INSURANCE COMPANY NAME	DOM. STATE	TOTAL ASSETS ($MIL)
AMERICAN FIDELITY ASR CO	OK	6,090.1
AMERICAN UNITED LIFE INS CO	IN	29,575.8
AMICA LIFE INS CO	RI	1,302.6
ASSURITY LIFE INS CO	NE	2,729.5
AXA EQUITABLE LIFE INS CO	NY	191,807.0
BEST LIFE & HEALTH INS CO	TX	22.7
BOSTON MUTUAL LIFE INS CO	MA	1,461.7
CHESAPEAKE LIFE INS CO	OK	195.4
COMPANION LIFE INS CO	SC	401.6
DEARBORN NATIONAL LIFE INS CO	IL	1,737.6
DELAWARE AMERICAN LIFE INS CO	DE	122.9
EAGLE LIFE INS CO	IA	1,070.1
FAMILY HERITAGE LIFE INS CO OF AMER	OH	1,444.8
FREEDOM LIFE INS CO OF AMERICA	TX	213.2
GERBER LIFE INS CO	NY	3,909.7
HANNOVER LIFE REASSURANCE CO OF AMER	FL	16,338.8
MIDLAND NATIONAL LIFE INS CO	IA	58,240.4
MINNESOTA LIFE INS CO	MN	49,271.3

INSURANCE COMPANY NAME	DOM. STATE	TOTAL ASSETS ($MIL)
NATIONAL BENEFIT LIFE INS CO	NY	564.7
NATIONAL FARMERS UNION LIFE INS CO	TX	193.3
NATIONAL FOUNDATION LIFE INS CO	TX	50.6
NEW YORK LIFE INS & ANNUITY CORP	DE	156,175.5
NORTH AMERICAN INS CO	WI	19.2
NORTHWESTERN MUTUAL LIFE INS CO	WI	273,304.0
OHIO NATIONAL LIFE ASR CORP	OH	4,098.9
OXFORD LIFE INS CO	AZ	2,192.1
PACIFIC LIFE & ANNUITY CO	AZ	7,409.8
PAN AMERICAN ASR CO	LA	26.7
PRINCIPAL LIFE INS CO	IA	197,908.3
SB MUTL LIFE INS CO OF MA	MA	3,104.8
STANDARD INS CO	OR	24,530.4
TRANS WORLD ASR CO	CA	344.9
TRUSTMARK INS CO	IL	1,606.0
TRUSTMARK LIFE INS CO	IL	330.1
UNITED WORLD LIFE INS CO	NE	119.5
VOYA RETIREMENT INS & ANNUITY CO	CT	108,678.3

Puerto Rico

INSURANCE COMPANY NAME	DOM. STATE	TOTAL ASSETS ($MIL)
### Rating: A+		
TEACHERS INS & ANNUITY ASN OF AM	NY	302,803.1
### Rating: A		
NATIONAL WESTERN LIFE INS CO	CO	11,114.0
SOUTHERN FARM BUREAU LIFE INS CO	MS	14,356.8
### Rating: A-		
MASSACHUSETTS MUTUAL LIFE INS CO	MA	245,872.2
NEW YORK LIFE INS CO	NY	178,706.9
TRANS OCEANIC LIFE INS CO	PR	75.3
### Rating: B+		
AMERICAN FIDELITY ASR CO	OK	6,090.1
AXA EQUITABLE LIFE INS CO	NY	191,807.0
BOSTON MUTUAL LIFE INS CO	MA	1,461.7
DEARBORN NATIONAL LIFE INS CO	IL	1,737.6
FAMILY HERITAGE LIFE INS CO OF AMER	OH	1,444.8
GERBER LIFE INS CO	NY	3,909.7
HANNOVER LIFE REASSURANCE CO OF AMER	FL	16,338.8
MIDLAND NATIONAL LIFE INS CO	IA	58,240.4
MINNESOTA LIFE INS CO	MN	49,271.3
OHIO NATIONAL LIFE ASR CORP	OH	4,098.9
PAN AMERICAN ASR CO	LA	26.7
PRINCIPAL LIFE INS CO	IA	197,908.3
STANDARD INS CO	OR	24,530.4
TRUSTMARK INS CO	IL	1,606.0
UNIVERSAL LIFE INS CO	PR	1,569.7
VOYA RETIREMENT INS & ANNUITY CO	CT	108,678.3

Rhode Island

INSURANCE COMPANY NAME	DOM. STATE	TOTAL ASSETS ($MIL)

Rating: A+

INSURANCE COMPANY NAME	DOM. STATE	TOTAL ASSETS ($MIL)
AMERICAN FAMILY LIFE INS CO	WI	5,269.9
COUNTRY LIFE INS CO	IL	9,673.9
PHYSICIANS MUTUAL INS CO	NE	2,367.4
STATE FARM LIFE INS CO	IL	74,940.7
TEACHERS INS & ANNUITY ASN OF AM	NY	302,803.1

Rating: A

INSURANCE COMPANY NAME	DOM. STATE	TOTAL ASSETS ($MIL)
AMALGAMATED LIFE INS CO	NY	140.3
BERKLEY LIFE & HEALTH INS CO	IA	325.8
FEDERATED LIFE INS CO	MN	1,969.7
GARDEN STATE LIFE INS CO	TX	135.5
GUARDIAN LIFE INS CO OF AMERICA	NY	57,852.7
NATIONAL WESTERN LIFE INS CO	CO	11,114.0
PARKER CENTENNIAL ASR CO	WI	96.0
SENTRY LIFE INS CO	WI	7,425.4
SHELTERPOINT LIFE INS CO	NY	151.3
USAA LIFE INS CO	TX	25,292.8

Rating: A-

INSURANCE COMPANY NAME	DOM. STATE	TOTAL ASSETS ($MIL)
AMERICAN HEALTH & LIFE INS CO	TX	1,018.0
ANNUITY INVESTORS LIFE INS CO	OH	3,232.6
COUNTRY INVESTORS LIFE ASR CO	IL	303.5
FIDELITY INVESTMENTS LIFE INS CO	UT	30,960.8
MASSACHUSETTS MUTUAL LIFE INS CO	MA	245,872.2
MUTUAL OF AMERICA LIFE INS CO	NY	21,758.9
NEW YORK LIFE INS CO	NY	178,706.9
NIPPON LIFE INS CO OF AMERICA	IA	219.2
PACIFIC LIFE INS CO	NE	133,288.3
PHYSICIANS LIFE INS CO	NE	1,664.1
STANDARD LIFE & ACCIDENT INS CO	TX	533.1
USABLE LIFE	AR	541.5

Rating: B+

INSURANCE COMPANY NAME	DOM. STATE	TOTAL ASSETS ($MIL)
AMERICAN FIDELITY ASR CO	OK	6,090.1
AMERICAN UNITED LIFE INS CO	IN	29,575.8
AMICA LIFE INS CO	RI	1,302.6
ASSURITY LIFE INS CO	NE	2,729.5
AXA EQUITABLE LIFE INS CO	NY	191,807.0
BOSTON MUTUAL LIFE INS CO	MA	1,461.7
CHESAPEAKE LIFE INS CO	OK	195.4
COMPANION LIFE INS CO	SC	401.6
DEARBORN NATIONAL LIFE INS CO	IL	1,737.6
DELAWARE AMERICAN LIFE INS CO	DE	122.9
EAGLE LIFE INS CO	IA	1,070.1
FAMILY HERITAGE LIFE INS CO OF AMER	OH	1,444.8
GERBER LIFE INS CO	NY	3,909.7
HANNOVER LIFE REASSURANCE CO OF AMER	FL	16,338.8
MIDLAND NATIONAL LIFE INS CO	IA	58,240.4
MINNESOTA LIFE INS CO	MN	49,271.3
NATIONAL BENEFIT LIFE INS CO	NY	564.7
NEW YORK LIFE INS & ANNUITY CORP	DE	156,175.5
NORTHWESTERN MUTUAL LIFE INS CO	WI	273,304.0
OHIO NATIONAL LIFE ASR CORP	OH	4,098.9
OXFORD LIFE INS CO	AZ	2,192.1
PACIFIC LIFE & ANNUITY CO	AZ	7,409.8

INSURANCE COMPANY NAME	DOM. STATE	TOTAL ASSETS ($MIL)
PRINCIPAL LIFE INS CO	IA	197,908.3
SB MUTL LIFE INS CO OF MA	MA	3,104.8
STANDARD INS CO	OR	24,530.4
TRANS WORLD ASR CO	CA	344.9
TRUSTMARK INS CO	IL	1,606.0
TRUSTMARK LIFE INS CO	IL	330.1
UNITED WORLD LIFE INS CO	NE	119.5
VOYA RETIREMENT INS & ANNUITY CO	CT	108,678.3

South Carolina

INSURANCE COMPANY NAME	DOM. STATE	TOTAL ASSETS ($MIL)
Rating: A+		
AMERICAN FAMILY LIFE INS CO	WI	5,269.9
COUNTRY LIFE INS CO	IL	9,673.9
PHYSICIANS MUTUAL INS CO	NE	2,367.4
STATE FARM LIFE INS CO	IL	74,940.7
TEACHERS INS & ANNUITY ASN OF AM	NY	302,803.1
Rating: A		
AMALGAMATED LIFE INS CO	NY	140.3
BERKLEY LIFE & HEALTH INS CO	IA	325.8
FEDERATED LIFE INS CO	MN	1,969.7
GARDEN STATE LIFE INS CO	TX	135.5
GUARDIAN LIFE INS CO OF AMERICA	NY	57,852.7
NATIONAL WESTERN LIFE INS CO	CO	11,114.0
PARKER CENTENNIAL ASR CO	WI	96.0
SENTRY LIFE INS CO	WI	7,425.4
SHELTERPOINT LIFE INS CO	NY	151.3
SOUTHERN FARM BUREAU LIFE INS CO	MS	14,356.8
USAA LIFE INS CO	TX	25,292.8
Rating: A-		
AMERICAN HEALTH & LIFE INS CO	TX	1,018.0
ANNUITY INVESTORS LIFE INS CO	OH	3,232.6
COTTON STATES LIFE INS CO	GA	339.7
COUNTRY INVESTORS LIFE ASR CO	IL	303.5
FIDELITY INVESTMENTS LIFE INS CO	UT	30,960.8
MASSACHUSETTS MUTUAL LIFE INS CO	MA	245,872.2
MUTUAL OF AMERICA LIFE INS CO	NY	21,758.9
NEW YORK LIFE INS CO	NY	178,706.9
NIPPON LIFE INS CO OF AMERICA	IA	219.2
PACIFIC LIFE INS CO	NE	133,288.3
PHYSICIANS LIFE INS CO	NE	1,664.1
SOUTHERN PIONEER LIFE INS CO	AR	14.6
STANDARD LIFE & ACCIDENT INS CO	TX	533.1
SYMETRA NATIONAL LIFE INS CO	IA	18.6
USABLE LIFE	AR	541.5
Rating: B+		
AMERICAN FIDELITY ASR CO	OK	6,090.1
AMERICAN UNITED LIFE INS CO	IN	29,575.8
AMICA LIFE INS CO	RI	1,302.6
ASSURITY LIFE INS CO	NE	2,729.5
AXA EQUITABLE LIFE INS CO	NY	191,807.0
BEST LIFE & HEALTH INS CO	TX	22.7
BOSTON MUTUAL LIFE INS CO	MA	1,461.7
CHESAPEAKE LIFE INS CO	OK	195.4
CHRISTIAN FIDELITY LIFE INS CO	TX	64.2
COMPANION LIFE INS CO	SC	401.6
DEARBORN NATIONAL LIFE INS CO	IL	1,737.6
DELAWARE AMERICAN LIFE INS CO	DE	122.9
EAGLE LIFE INS CO	IA	1,070.1
FAMILY HERITAGE LIFE INS CO OF AMER	OH	1,444.8
FREEDOM LIFE INS CO OF AMERICA	TX	213.2
GERBER LIFE INS CO	NY	3,909.7
HANNOVER LIFE REASSURANCE CO OF AMER	FL	16,338.8
MIDLAND NATIONAL LIFE INS CO	IA	58,240.4

INSURANCE COMPANY NAME	DOM. STATE	TOTAL ASSETS ($MIL)
MINNESOTA LIFE INS CO	MN	49,271.3
NATIONAL BENEFIT LIFE INS CO	NY	564.7
NATIONAL FOUNDATION LIFE INS CO	TX	50.6
NEW YORK LIFE INS & ANNUITY CORP	DE	156,175.5
NORTH AMERICAN INS CO	WI	19.2
NORTHWESTERN MUTUAL LIFE INS CO	WI	273,304.0
OHIO NATIONAL LIFE ASR CORP	OH	4,098.9
OXFORD LIFE INS CO	AZ	2,192.1
PACIFIC LIFE & ANNUITY CO	AZ	7,409.8
PAN AMERICAN ASR CO	LA	26.7
PRINCIPAL LIFE INS CO	IA	197,908.3
SB MUTL LIFE INS CO OF MA	MA	3,104.8
STANDARD INS CO	OR	24,530.4
TRANS WORLD ASR CO	CA	344.9
TRUSTMARK INS CO	IL	1,606.0
TRUSTMARK LIFE INS CO	IL	330.1
UNITED WORLD LIFE INS CO	NE	119.5
VOYA RETIREMENT INS & ANNUITY CO	CT	108,678.3

South Dakota

INSURANCE COMPANY NAME	DOM. STATE	TOTAL ASSETS ($MIL)

Rating: A+

INSURANCE COMPANY NAME	DOM. STATE	TOTAL ASSETS ($MIL)
AMERICAN FAMILY LIFE INS CO	WI	5,269.9
COUNTRY LIFE INS CO	IL	9,673.9
PHYSICIANS MUTUAL INS CO	NE	2,367.4
STATE FARM LIFE INS CO	IL	74,940.7
TEACHERS INS & ANNUITY ASN OF AM	NY	302,803.1

Rating: A

INSURANCE COMPANY NAME	DOM. STATE	TOTAL ASSETS ($MIL)
AMALGAMATED LIFE INS CO	NY	140.3
BERKLEY LIFE & HEALTH INS CO	IA	325.8
FEDERATED LIFE INS CO	MN	1,969.7
GARDEN STATE LIFE INS CO	TX	135.5
GUARDIAN LIFE INS CO OF AMERICA	NY	57,852.7
NATIONAL WESTERN LIFE INS CO	CO	11,114.0
PARKER CENTENNIAL ASR CO	WI	96.0
SENTRY LIFE INS CO	WI	7,425.4
USAA LIFE INS CO	TX	25,292.8

Rating: A-

INSURANCE COMPANY NAME	DOM. STATE	TOTAL ASSETS ($MIL)
AMERICAN HEALTH & LIFE INS CO	TX	1,018.0
ANNUITY INVESTORS LIFE INS CO	OH	3,232.6
COUNTRY INVESTORS LIFE ASR CO	IL	303.5
FIDELITY INVESTMENTS LIFE INS CO	UT	30,960.8
MASSACHUSETTS MUTUAL LIFE INS CO	MA	245,872.2
MUTUAL OF AMERICA LIFE INS CO	NY	21,758.9
NEW YORK LIFE INS CO	NY	178,706.9
NIPPON LIFE INS CO OF AMERICA	IA	219.2
PACIFIC GUARDIAN LIFE INS CO LTD	HI	559.1
PACIFIC LIFE INS CO	NE	133,288.3
PHYSICIANS LIFE INS CO	NE	1,664.1
STANDARD LIFE & ACCIDENT INS CO	TX	533.1
SYMETRA NATIONAL LIFE INS CO	IA	18.6
USABLE LIFE	AR	541.5

Rating: B+

INSURANCE COMPANY NAME	DOM. STATE	TOTAL ASSETS ($MIL)
AMERICAN FIDELITY ASR CO	OK	6,090.1
AMERICAN UNITED LIFE INS CO	IN	29,575.8
AMICA LIFE INS CO	RI	1,302.6
ASSURITY LIFE INS CO	NE	2,729.5
AXA EQUITABLE LIFE INS CO	NY	191,807.0
BEST LIFE & HEALTH INS CO	TX	22.7
BOSTON MUTUAL LIFE INS CO	MA	1,461.7
CHESAPEAKE LIFE INS CO	OK	195.4
CHRISTIAN FIDELITY LIFE INS CO	TX	64.2
COMPANION LIFE INS CO	SC	401.6
DEARBORN NATIONAL LIFE INS CO	IL	1,737.6
DELAWARE AMERICAN LIFE INS CO	DE	122.9
EAGLE LIFE INS CO	IA	1,070.1
FAMILY HERITAGE LIFE INS CO OF AMER	OH	1,444.8
FARM BUREAU LIFE INS CO	IA	9,267.1
FREEDOM LIFE INS CO OF AMERICA	TX	213.2
GERBER LIFE INS CO	NY	3,909.7
HANNOVER LIFE REASSURANCE CO OF AMER	FL	16,338.8
MIDLAND NATIONAL LIFE INS CO	IA	58,240.4
MINNESOTA LIFE INS CO	MN	49,271.3
NATIONAL BENEFIT LIFE INS CO	NY	564.7

INSURANCE COMPANY NAME	DOM. STATE	TOTAL ASSETS ($MIL)
NATIONAL FARMERS UNION LIFE INS CO	TX	193.3
NATIONAL FOUNDATION LIFE INS CO	TX	50.6
NEW YORK LIFE INS & ANNUITY CORP	DE	156,175.5
NORTHWESTERN MUTUAL LIFE INS CO	WI	273,304.0
OHIO NATIONAL LIFE ASR CORP	OH	4,098.9
OXFORD LIFE INS CO	AZ	2,192.1
PACIFIC LIFE & ANNUITY CO	AZ	7,409.8
PRINCIPAL LIFE INS CO	IA	197,908.3
SB MUTL LIFE INS CO OF MA	MA	3,104.8
STANDARD INS CO	OR	24,530.4
TRANS WORLD ASR CO	CA	344.9
TRUSTMARK INS CO	IL	1,606.0
TRUSTMARK LIFE INS CO	IL	330.1
UNITED WORLD LIFE INS CO	NE	119.5
VOYA RETIREMENT INS & ANNUITY CO	CT	108,678.3

Tennessee

INSURANCE COMPANY NAME	DOM. STATE	TOTAL ASSETS ($MIL)
Rating: A+		
AMERICAN FAMILY LIFE INS CO	WI	5,269.9
COUNTRY LIFE INS CO	IL	9,673.9
PHYSICIANS MUTUAL INS CO	NE	2,367.4
STATE FARM LIFE INS CO	IL	74,940.7
TEACHERS INS & ANNUITY ASN OF AM	NY	302,803.1
Rating: A		
AMALGAMATED LIFE INS CO	NY	140.3
BERKLEY LIFE & HEALTH INS CO	IA	325.8
FEDERATED LIFE INS CO	MN	1,969.7
GARDEN STATE LIFE INS CO	TX	135.5
GUARDIAN LIFE INS CO OF AMERICA	NY	57,852.7
NATIONAL WESTERN LIFE INS CO	CO	11,114.0
PARKER CENTENNIAL ASR CO	WI	96.0
SENTRY LIFE INS CO	WI	7,425.4
SHELTERPOINT LIFE INS CO	NY	151.3
SOUTHERN FARM BUREAU LIFE INS CO	MS	14,356.8
USAA LIFE INS CO	TX	25,292.8
Rating: A-		
AMERICAN HEALTH & LIFE INS CO	TX	1,018.0
ANNUITY INVESTORS LIFE INS CO	OH	3,232.6
CIGNA LIFE INS CO OF NEW YORK	NY	407.5
COTTON STATES LIFE INS CO	GA	339.7
COUNTRY INVESTORS LIFE ASR CO	IL	303.5
ERIE FAMILY LIFE INS CO	PA	2,512.1
FIDELITY INVESTMENTS LIFE INS CO	UT	30,960.8
MASSACHUSETTS MUTUAL LIFE INS CO	MA	245,872.2
MUTUAL OF AMERICA LIFE INS CO	NY	21,758.9
NEW YORK LIFE INS CO	NY	178,706.9
NIPPON LIFE INS CO OF AMERICA	IA	219.2
PACIFIC LIFE INS CO	NE	133,288.3
PHYSICIANS LIFE INS CO	NE	1,664.1
SOUTHERN PIONEER LIFE INS CO	AR	14.6
STANDARD LIFE & ACCIDENT INS CO	TX	533.1
SYMETRA NATIONAL LIFE INS CO	IA	18.6
USABLE LIFE	AR	541.5
Rating: B+		
AMERICAN FIDELITY ASR CO	OK	6,090.1
AMERICAN UNITED LIFE INS CO	IN	29,575.8
AMICA LIFE INS CO	RI	1,302.6
ASSURITY LIFE INS CO	NE	2,729.5
AXA EQUITABLE LIFE INS CO	NY	191,807.0
BEST LIFE & HEALTH INS CO	TX	22.7
BLUEBONNET LIFE INS CO	MS	64.3
BOSTON MUTUAL LIFE INS CO	MA	1,461.7
CHESAPEAKE LIFE INS CO	OK	195.4
CHRISTIAN FIDELITY LIFE INS CO	TX	64.2
COMPANION LIFE INS CO	SC	401.6
DEARBORN NATIONAL LIFE INS CO	IL	1,737.6
DELAWARE AMERICAN LIFE INS CO	DE	122.9
EAGLE LIFE INS CO	IA	1,070.1
FAMILY HERITAGE LIFE INS CO OF AMER	OH	1,444.8
FREEDOM LIFE INS CO OF AMERICA	TX	213.2

INSURANCE COMPANY NAME	DOM. STATE	TOTAL ASSETS ($MIL)
GERBER LIFE INS CO	NY	3,909.7
HANNOVER LIFE REASSURANCE CO OF AMER	FL	16,338.8
MIDLAND NATIONAL LIFE INS CO	IA	58,240.4
MINNESOTA LIFE INS CO	MN	49,271.3
NATIONAL BENEFIT LIFE INS CO	NY	564.7
NATIONAL FOUNDATION LIFE INS CO	TX	50.6
NEW YORK LIFE INS & ANNUITY CORP	DE	156,175.5
NORTHWESTERN MUTUAL LIFE INS CO	WI	273,304.0
OHIO NATIONAL LIFE ASR CORP	OH	4,098.9
OXFORD LIFE INS CO	AZ	2,192.1
PACIFIC LIFE & ANNUITY CO	AZ	7,409.8
PAN AMERICAN ASR CO	LA	26.7
PRINCIPAL LIFE INS CO	IA	197,908.3
SB MUTL LIFE INS CO OF MA	MA	3,104.8
STANDARD INS CO	OR	24,530.4
SWBC LIFE INS CO	TX	32.6
TENNESSEE FARMERS LIFE INS CO	TN	2,318.6
TRANS WORLD ASR CO	CA	344.9
TRUSTMARK INS CO	IL	1,606.0
TRUSTMARK LIFE INS CO	IL	330.1
UNITED WORLD LIFE INS CO	NE	119.5
UTIC INS CO	AL	102.4
VOYA RETIREMENT INS & ANNUITY CO	CT	108,678.3

Texas

INSURANCE COMPANY NAME	DOM. STATE	TOTAL ASSETS ($MIL)

Rating: A+

INSURANCE COMPANY NAME	DOM. STATE	TOTAL ASSETS ($MIL)
AMERICAN FAMILY LIFE INS CO	WI	5,269.9
COUNTRY LIFE INS CO	IL	9,673.9
PHYSICIANS MUTUAL INS CO	NE	2,367.4
STATE FARM LIFE INS CO	IL	74,940.7
TEACHERS INS & ANNUITY ASN OF AM	NY	302,803.1

Rating: A

INSURANCE COMPANY NAME	DOM. STATE	TOTAL ASSETS ($MIL)
AMALGAMATED LIFE INS CO	NY	140.3
BERKLEY LIFE & HEALTH INS CO	IA	325.8
FEDERATED LIFE INS CO	MN	1,969.7
GARDEN STATE LIFE INS CO	TX	135.5
GUARDIAN LIFE INS CO OF AMERICA	NY	57,852.7
NATIONAL WESTERN LIFE INS CO	CO	11,114.0
PARKER CENTENNIAL ASR CO	WI	96.0
SENTRY LIFE INS CO	WI	7,425.4
SOUTHERN FARM BUREAU LIFE INS CO	MS	14,356.8
USAA LIFE INS CO	TX	25,292.8

Rating: A-

INSURANCE COMPANY NAME	DOM. STATE	TOTAL ASSETS ($MIL)
AMERICAN HEALTH & LIFE INS CO	TX	1,018.0
ANNUITY INVESTORS LIFE INS CO	OH	3,232.6
COUNTRY INVESTORS LIFE ASR CO	IL	303.5
FIDELITY INVESTMENTS LIFE INS CO	UT	30,960.8
MASSACHUSETTS MUTUAL LIFE INS CO	MA	245,872.2
MUTUAL OF AMERICA LIFE INS CO	NY	21,758.9
NEW YORK LIFE INS CO	NY	178,706.9
NIPPON LIFE INS CO OF AMERICA	IA	219.2
PACIFIC GUARDIAN LIFE INS CO LTD	HI	559.1
PACIFIC LIFE INS CO	NE	133,288.3
PHYSICIANS LIFE INS CO	NE	1,664.1
SOUTHERN PIONEER LIFE INS CO	AR	14.6
STANDARD LIFE & ACCIDENT INS CO	TX	533.1
SYMETRA NATIONAL LIFE INS CO	IA	18.6
USABLE LIFE	AR	541.5

Rating: B+

INSURANCE COMPANY NAME	DOM. STATE	TOTAL ASSETS ($MIL)
AMERICAN FIDELITY ASR CO	OK	6,090.1
AMERICAN UNITED LIFE INS CO	IN	29,575.8
AMICA LIFE INS CO	RI	1,302.6
ASSURITY LIFE INS CO	NE	2,729.5
AXA EQUITABLE LIFE INS CO	NY	191,807.0
BEST LIFE & HEALTH INS CO	TX	22.7
BOSTON MUTUAL LIFE INS CO	MA	1,461.7
CHESAPEAKE LIFE INS CO	OK	195.4
CHRISTIAN FIDELITY LIFE INS CO	TX	64.2
COMPANION LIFE INS CO	SC	401.6
DEARBORN NATIONAL LIFE INS CO	IL	1,737.6
DELAWARE AMERICAN LIFE INS CO	DE	122.9
EAGLE LIFE INS CO	IA	1,070.1
ENTERPRISE LIFE INS CO	TX	73.7
FAMILY HERITAGE LIFE INS CO OF AMER	OH	1,444.8
FREEDOM LIFE INS CO OF AMERICA	TX	213.2
GERBER LIFE INS CO	NY	3,909.7
HANNOVER LIFE REASSURANCE CO OF AMER	FL	16,338.8
LOCOMOTIVE ENGRS&COND MUT PROT ASSN	MI	73.6

INSURANCE COMPANY NAME	DOM. STATE	TOTAL ASSETS ($MIL)
MIDLAND NATIONAL LIFE INS CO	IA	58,240.4
MINNESOTA LIFE INS CO	MN	49,271.3
NATIONAL BENEFIT LIFE INS CO	NY	564.7
NATIONAL FARMERS UNION LIFE INS CO	TX	193.3
NATIONAL FOUNDATION LIFE INS CO	TX	50.6
NEW YORK LIFE INS & ANNUITY CORP	DE	156,175.5
NORTH AMERICAN INS CO	WI	19.2
NORTHWESTERN MUTUAL LIFE INS CO	WI	273,304.0
OHIO NATIONAL LIFE ASR CORP	OH	4,098.9
OXFORD LIFE INS CO	AZ	2,192.1
PACIFIC LIFE & ANNUITY CO	AZ	7,409.8
PAN AMERICAN ASR CO	LA	26.7
PRINCIPAL LIFE INS CO	IA	197,908.3
SB MUTL LIFE INS CO OF MA	MA	3,104.8
STANDARD INS CO	OR	24,530.4
SWBC LIFE INS CO	TX	32.6
TRANS WORLD ASR CO	CA	344.9
TRUSTMARK INS CO	IL	1,606.0
TRUSTMARK LIFE INS CO	IL	330.1
UNITED WORLD LIFE INS CO	NE	119.5
VOYA RETIREMENT INS & ANNUITY CO	CT	108,678.3

Utah

INSURANCE COMPANY NAME	DOM. STATE	TOTAL ASSETS ($MIL)
Rating: A+		
AMERICAN FAMILY LIFE INS CO	WI	5,269.9
COUNTRY LIFE INS CO	IL	9,673.9
PHYSICIANS MUTUAL INS CO	NE	2,367.4
STATE FARM LIFE INS CO	IL	74,940.7
TEACHERS INS & ANNUITY ASN OF AM	NY	302,803.1
Rating: A		
AMALGAMATED LIFE INS CO	NY	140.3
BERKLEY LIFE & HEALTH INS CO	IA	325.8
FEDERATED LIFE INS CO	MN	1,969.7
GARDEN STATE LIFE INS CO	TX	135.5
GUARDIAN LIFE INS CO OF AMERICA	NY	57,852.7
NATIONAL WESTERN LIFE INS CO	CO	11,114.0
PARKER CENTENNIAL ASR CO	WI	96.0
SENTRY LIFE INS CO	WI	7,425.4
USAA LIFE INS CO	TX	25,292.8
Rating: A-		
AMERICAN HEALTH & LIFE INS CO	TX	1,018.0
ANNUITY INVESTORS LIFE INS CO	OH	3,232.6
FIDELITY INVESTMENTS LIFE INS CO	UT	30,960.8
MASSACHUSETTS MUTUAL LIFE INS CO	MA	245,872.2
MUTUAL OF AMERICA LIFE INS CO	NY	21,758.9
NEW YORK LIFE INS CO	NY	178,706.9
NIPPON LIFE INS CO OF AMERICA	IA	219.2
PACIFIC GUARDIAN LIFE INS CO LTD	HI	559.1
PACIFIC LIFE INS CO	NE	133,288.3
PHYSICIANS LIFE INS CO	NE	1,664.1
STANDARD LIFE & ACCIDENT INS CO	TX	533.1
SYMETRA NATIONAL LIFE INS CO	IA	18.6
USABLE LIFE	AR	541.5
Rating: B+		
AMERICAN FIDELITY ASR CO	OK	6,090.1
AMERICAN UNITED LIFE INS CO	IN	29,575.8
AMICA LIFE INS CO	RI	1,302.6
ASSURITY LIFE INS CO	NE	2,729.5
AXA EQUITABLE LIFE INS CO	NY	191,807.0
BEST LIFE & HEALTH INS CO	TX	22.7
BOSTON MUTUAL LIFE INS CO	MA	1,461.7
CHESAPEAKE LIFE INS CO	OK	195.4
CHRISTIAN FIDELITY LIFE INS CO	TX	64.2
COMPANION LIFE INS CO	SC	401.6
DEARBORN NATIONAL LIFE INS CO	IL	1,737.6
DELAWARE AMERICAN LIFE INS CO	DE	122.9
EAGLE LIFE INS CO	IA	1,070.1
FAMILY HERITAGE LIFE INS CO OF AMER	OH	1,444.8
FARM BUREAU LIFE INS CO	IA	9,267.1
FREEDOM LIFE INS CO OF AMERICA	TX	213.2
GERBER LIFE INS CO	NY	3,909.7
HANNOVER LIFE REASSURANCE CO OF AMER	FL	16,338.8
MIDLAND NATIONAL LIFE INS CO	IA	58,240.4
MINNESOTA LIFE INS CO	MN	49,271.3
NATIONAL BENEFIT LIFE INS CO	NY	564.7
NATIONAL FARMERS UNION LIFE INS CO	TX	193.3

INSURANCE COMPANY NAME	DOM. STATE	TOTAL ASSETS ($MIL)
NATIONAL FOUNDATION LIFE INS CO	TX	50.6
NEW YORK LIFE INS & ANNUITY CORP	DE	156,175.5
NORTHWESTERN MUTUAL LIFE INS CO	WI	273,304.0
OHIO NATIONAL LIFE ASR CORP	OH	4,098.9
OXFORD LIFE INS CO	AZ	2,192.1
PACIFIC LIFE & ANNUITY CO	AZ	7,409.8
PAN AMERICAN ASR CO	LA	26.7
PRINCIPAL LIFE INS CO	IA	197,908.3
SB MUTL LIFE INS CO OF MA	MA	3,104.8
STANDARD INS CO	OR	24,530.4
SWBC LIFE INS CO	TX	32.6
TRANS WORLD ASR CO	CA	344.9
TRUSTMARK INS CO	IL	1,606.0
TRUSTMARK LIFE INS CO	IL	330.1
UNITED WORLD LIFE INS CO	NE	119.5
VOYA RETIREMENT INS & ANNUITY CO	CT	108,678.3

Vermont

INSURANCE COMPANY NAME	DOM. STATE	TOTAL ASSETS ($MIL)	INSURANCE COMPANY NAME	DOM. STATE	TOTAL ASSETS ($MIL)
			UNITED WORLD LIFE INS CO	NE	119.5
			VOYA RETIREMENT INS & ANNUITY CO	CT	108,678.3

Rating: A+

INSURANCE COMPANY NAME	DOM. STATE	TOTAL ASSETS ($MIL)
AMERICAN FAMILY LIFE INS CO	WI	5,269.9
PHYSICIANS MUTUAL INS CO	NE	2,367.4
STATE FARM LIFE INS CO	IL	74,940.7
TEACHERS INS & ANNUITY ASN OF AM	NY	302,803.1

Rating: A

INSURANCE COMPANY NAME	DOM. STATE	TOTAL ASSETS ($MIL)
AMALGAMATED LIFE INS CO	NY	140.3
BERKLEY LIFE & HEALTH INS CO	IA	325.8
FEDERATED LIFE INS CO	MN	1,969.7
GARDEN STATE LIFE INS CO	TX	135.5
GUARDIAN LIFE INS CO OF AMERICA	NY	57,852.7
NATIONAL WESTERN LIFE INS CO	CO	11,114.0
PARKER CENTENNIAL ASR CO	WI	96.0
SENTRY LIFE INS CO	WI	7,425.4
USAA LIFE INS CO	TX	25,292.8

Rating: A-

INSURANCE COMPANY NAME	DOM. STATE	TOTAL ASSETS ($MIL)
AMERICAN FAMILY LIFE ASR CO OF NY	NY	1,000.3
AMERICAN HEALTH & LIFE INS CO	TX	1,018.0
FIDELITY INVESTMENTS LIFE INS CO	UT	30,960.8
MASSACHUSETTS MUTUAL LIFE INS CO	MA	245,872.2
MUTUAL OF AMERICA LIFE INS CO	NY	21,758.9
NEW YORK LIFE INS CO	NY	178,706.9
NIPPON LIFE INS CO OF AMERICA	IA	219.2
PACIFIC LIFE INS CO	NE	133,288.3
PHYSICIANS LIFE INS CO	NE	1,664.1
STANDARD LIFE & ACCIDENT INS CO	TX	533.1
USABLE LIFE	AR	541.5

Rating: B+

INSURANCE COMPANY NAME	DOM. STATE	TOTAL ASSETS ($MIL)
AMERICAN FIDELITY ASR CO	OK	6,090.1
AMERICAN UNITED LIFE INS CO	IN	29,575.8
AMICA LIFE INS CO	RI	1,302.6
ASSURITY LIFE INS CO	NE	2,729.5
AXA EQUITABLE LIFE INS CO	NY	191,807.0
BOSTON MUTUAL LIFE INS CO	MA	1,461.7
COMPANION LIFE INS CO	SC	401.6
DEARBORN NATIONAL LIFE INS CO	IL	1,737.6
DELAWARE AMERICAN LIFE INS CO	DE	122.9
EAGLE LIFE INS CO	IA	1,070.1
FAMILY HERITAGE LIFE INS CO OF AMER	OH	1,444.8
GERBER LIFE INS CO	NY	3,909.7
HANNOVER LIFE REASSURANCE CO OF AMER	FL	16,338.8
MIDLAND NATIONAL LIFE INS CO	IA	58,240.4
MINNESOTA LIFE INS CO	MN	49,271.3
NATIONAL BENEFIT LIFE INS CO	NY	564.7
NEW YORK LIFE INS & ANNUITY CORP	DE	156,175.5
NORTHWESTERN MUTUAL LIFE INS CO	WI	273,304.0
OHIO NATIONAL LIFE ASR CORP	OH	4,098.9
PACIFIC LIFE & ANNUITY CO	AZ	7,409.8
PRINCIPAL LIFE INS CO	IA	197,908.3
SB MUTL LIFE INS CO OF MA	MA	3,104.8
STANDARD INS CO	OR	24,530.4
TRUSTMARK INS CO	IL	1,606.0
TRUSTMARK LIFE INS CO	IL	330.1

Virginia

INSURANCE COMPANY NAME	DOM. STATE	TOTAL ASSETS ($MIL)

Rating: A+

INSURANCE COMPANY NAME	DOM. STATE	TOTAL ASSETS ($MIL)
AMERICAN FAMILY LIFE INS CO	WI	5,269.9
COUNTRY LIFE INS CO	IL	9,673.9
PHYSICIANS MUTUAL INS CO	NE	2,367.4
STATE FARM LIFE INS CO	IL	74,940.7
TEACHERS INS & ANNUITY ASN OF AM	NY	302,803.1

Rating: A

INSURANCE COMPANY NAME	DOM. STATE	TOTAL ASSETS ($MIL)
AMALGAMATED LIFE INS CO	NY	140.3
BERKLEY LIFE & HEALTH INS CO	IA	325.8
FEDERATED LIFE INS CO	MN	1,969.7
GARDEN STATE LIFE INS CO	TX	135.5
GUARDIAN LIFE INS CO OF AMERICA	NY	57,852.7
NATIONAL WESTERN LIFE INS CO	CO	11,114.0
PARKER CENTENNIAL ASR CO	WI	96.0
SENTRY LIFE INS CO	WI	7,425.4
SOUTHERN FARM BUREAU LIFE INS CO	MS	14,356.8
USAA LIFE INS CO	TX	25,292.8

Rating: A-

INSURANCE COMPANY NAME	DOM. STATE	TOTAL ASSETS ($MIL)
AMERICAN HEALTH & LIFE INS CO	TX	1,018.0
ANNUITY INVESTORS LIFE INS CO	OH	3,232.6
COTTON STATES LIFE INS CO	GA	339.7
COUNTRY INVESTORS LIFE ASR CO	IL	303.5
ERIE FAMILY LIFE INS CO	PA	2,512.1
FIDELITY INVESTMENTS LIFE INS CO	UT	30,960.8
MASSACHUSETTS MUTUAL LIFE INS CO	MA	245,872.2
MUTUAL OF AMERICA LIFE INS CO	NY	21,758.9
NEW YORK LIFE INS CO	NY	178,706.9
NIPPON LIFE INS CO OF AMERICA	IA	219.2
PACIFIC LIFE INS CO	NE	133,288.3
PHYSICIANS LIFE INS CO	NE	1,664.1
STANDARD LIFE & ACCIDENT INS CO	TX	533.1
SYMETRA NATIONAL LIFE INS CO	IA	18.6
USABLE LIFE	AR	541.5

Rating: B+

INSURANCE COMPANY NAME	DOM. STATE	TOTAL ASSETS ($MIL)
AMERICAN FIDELITY ASR CO	OK	6,090.1
AMERICAN UNITED LIFE INS CO	IN	29,575.8
AMICA LIFE INS CO	RI	1,302.6
ASSURITY LIFE INS CO	NE	2,729.5
AXA EQUITABLE LIFE INS CO	NY	191,807.0
BEST LIFE & HEALTH INS CO	TX	22.7
BOSTON MUTUAL LIFE INS CO	MA	1,461.7
CHESAPEAKE LIFE INS CO	OK	195.4
CHRISTIAN FIDELITY LIFE INS CO	TX	64.2
COMPANION LIFE INS CO	SC	401.6
DEARBORN NATIONAL LIFE INS CO	IL	1,737.6
DELAWARE AMERICAN LIFE INS CO	DE	122.9
EAGLE LIFE INS CO	IA	1,070.1
FAMILY HERITAGE LIFE INS CO OF AMER	OH	1,444.8
FREEDOM LIFE INS CO OF AMERICA	TX	213.2
GERBER LIFE INS CO	NY	3,909.7
HANNOVER LIFE REASSURANCE CO OF AMER	FL	16,338.8
MIDLAND NATIONAL LIFE INS CO	IA	58,240.4
MINNESOTA LIFE INS CO	MN	49,271.3

INSURANCE COMPANY NAME	DOM. STATE	TOTAL ASSETS ($MIL)
NATIONAL BENEFIT LIFE INS CO	NY	564.7
NATIONAL FARMERS UNION LIFE INS CO	TX	193.3
NATIONAL FOUNDATION LIFE INS CO	TX	50.6
NEW YORK LIFE INS & ANNUITY CORP	DE	156,175.5
NORTHWESTERN MUTUAL LIFE INS CO	WI	273,304.0
OHIO NATIONAL LIFE ASR CORP	OH	4,098.9
OXFORD LIFE INS CO	AZ	2,192.1
PACIFIC LIFE & ANNUITY CO	AZ	7,409.8
PAN AMERICAN ASR CO	LA	26.7
PRINCIPAL LIFE INS CO	IA	197,908.3
SB MUTL LIFE INS CO OF MA	MA	3,104.8
STANDARD INS CO	OR	24,530.4
SWBC LIFE INS CO	TX	32.6
TRANS WORLD ASR CO	CA	344.9
TRUSTMARK INS CO	IL	1,606.0
TRUSTMARK LIFE INS CO	IL	330.1
UNITED WORLD LIFE INS CO	NE	119.5
VOYA RETIREMENT INS & ANNUITY CO	CT	108,678.3

Washington

INSURANCE COMPANY NAME	DOM. STATE	TOTAL ASSETS ($MIL)
Rating: A+		
AMERICAN FAMILY LIFE INS CO	WI	5,269.9
COUNTRY LIFE INS CO	IL	9,673.9
PHYSICIANS MUTUAL INS CO	NE	2,367.4
STATE FARM LIFE INS CO	IL	74,940.7
TEACHERS INS & ANNUITY ASN OF AM	NY	302,803.1
Rating: A		
AMALGAMATED LIFE INS CO	NY	140.3
BERKLEY LIFE & HEALTH INS CO	IA	325.8
FEDERATED LIFE INS CO	MN	1,969.7
GARDEN STATE LIFE INS CO	TX	135.5
GUARDIAN LIFE INS CO OF AMERICA	NY	57,852.7
LIFEWISE ASR CO	WA	193.1
NATIONAL WESTERN LIFE INS CO	CO	11,114.0
PARKER CENTENNIAL ASR CO	WI	96.0
SENTRY LIFE INS CO	WI	7,425.4
USAA LIFE INS CO	TX	25,292.8
Rating: A-		
AMERICAN HEALTH & LIFE INS CO	TX	1,018.0
ANNUITY INVESTORS LIFE INS CO	OH	3,232.6
COUNTRY INVESTORS LIFE ASR CO	IL	303.5
FIDELITY INVESTMENTS LIFE INS CO	UT	30,960.8
MASSACHUSETTS MUTUAL LIFE INS CO	MA	245,872.2
MUTUAL OF AMERICA LIFE INS CO	NY	21,758.9
NEW YORK LIFE INS CO	NY	178,706.9
NIPPON LIFE INS CO OF AMERICA	IA	219.2
PACIFIC GUARDIAN LIFE INS CO LTD	HI	559.1
PACIFIC LIFE INS CO	NE	133,288.3
PHYSICIANS LIFE INS CO	NE	1,664.1
STANDARD LIFE & ACCIDENT INS CO	TX	533.1
SYMETRA NATIONAL LIFE INS CO	IA	18.6
USABLE LIFE	AR	541.5
Rating: B+		
AMERICAN FIDELITY ASR CO	OK	6,090.1
AMERICAN UNITED LIFE INS CO	IN	29,575.8
AMICA LIFE INS CO	RI	1,302.6
ASSURITY LIFE INS CO	NE	2,729.5
AXA EQUITABLE LIFE INS CO	NY	191,807.0
BEST LIFE & HEALTH INS CO	TX	22.7
BOSTON MUTUAL LIFE INS CO	MA	1,461.7
CHESAPEAKE LIFE INS CO	OK	195.4
CHRISTIAN FIDELITY LIFE INS CO	TX	64.2
COMPANION LIFE INS CO	SC	401.6
DEARBORN NATIONAL LIFE INS CO	IL	1,737.6
DELAWARE AMERICAN LIFE INS CO	DE	122.9
EAGLE LIFE INS CO	IA	1,070.1
FAMILY HERITAGE LIFE INS CO OF AMER	OH	1,444.8
FARM BUREAU LIFE INS CO	IA	9,267.1
FREEDOM LIFE INS CO OF AMERICA	TX	213.2
GERBER LIFE INS CO	NY	3,909.7
HANNOVER LIFE REASSURANCE CO OF AMER	FL	16,338.8
MIDLAND NATIONAL LIFE INS CO	IA	58,240.4
MINNESOTA LIFE INS CO	MN	49,271.3

INSURANCE COMPANY NAME	DOM. STATE	TOTAL ASSETS ($MIL)
NATIONAL BENEFIT LIFE INS CO	NY	564.7
NATIONAL FARMERS UNION LIFE INS CO	TX	193.3
NATIONAL FOUNDATION LIFE INS CO	TX	50.6
NEW YORK LIFE INS & ANNUITY CORP	DE	156,175.5
NORTHWESTERN MUTUAL LIFE INS CO	WI	273,304.0
OHIO NATIONAL LIFE ASR CORP	OH	4,098.9
OXFORD LIFE INS CO	AZ	2,192.1
PACIFIC LIFE & ANNUITY CO	AZ	7,409.8
PAN AMERICAN ASR CO	LA	26.7
PRINCIPAL LIFE INS CO	IA	197,908.3
SB MUTL LIFE INS CO OF MA	MA	3,104.8
STANDARD INS CO	OR	24,530.4
TRANS WORLD ASR CO	CA	344.9
TRUSTMARK INS CO	IL	1,606.0
TRUSTMARK LIFE INS CO	IL	330.1
UNITED WORLD LIFE INS CO	NE	119.5
VOYA RETIREMENT INS & ANNUITY CO	CT	108,678.3

West Virginia

INSURANCE COMPANY NAME	DOM. STATE	TOTAL ASSETS ($MIL)
Rating: A+		
AMERICAN FAMILY LIFE INS CO	WI	5,269.9
COUNTRY LIFE INS CO	IL	9,673.9
PHYSICIANS MUTUAL INS CO	NE	2,367.4
STATE FARM LIFE INS CO	IL	74,940.7
TEACHERS INS & ANNUITY ASN OF AM	NY	302,803.1
Rating: A		
AMALGAMATED LIFE INS CO	NY	140.3
BERKLEY LIFE & HEALTH INS CO	IA	325.8
FEDERATED LIFE INS CO	MN	1,969.7
GARDEN STATE LIFE INS CO	TX	135.5
GUARDIAN LIFE INS CO OF AMERICA	NY	57,852.7
NATIONAL WESTERN LIFE INS CO	CO	11,114.0
PARKER CENTENNIAL ASR CO	WI	96.0
SENTRY LIFE INS CO	WI	7,425.4
USAA LIFE INS CO	TX	25,292.8
Rating: A-		
AMERICAN HEALTH & LIFE INS CO	TX	1,018.0
ANNUITY INVESTORS LIFE INS CO	OH	3,232.6
COUNTRY INVESTORS LIFE ASR CO	IL	303.5
ERIE FAMILY LIFE INS CO	PA	2,512.1
FIDELITY INVESTMENTS LIFE INS CO	UT	30,960.8
MASSACHUSETTS MUTUAL LIFE INS CO	MA	245,872.2
MUTUAL OF AMERICA LIFE INS CO	NY	21,758.9
NEW YORK LIFE INS CO	NY	178,706.9
NIPPON LIFE INS CO OF AMERICA	IA	219.2
PACIFIC LIFE INS CO	NE	133,288.3
PHYSICIANS LIFE INS CO	NE	1,664.1
STANDARD LIFE & ACCIDENT INS CO	TX	533.1
SYMETRA NATIONAL LIFE INS CO	IA	18.6
USABLE LIFE	AR	541.5
Rating: B+		
AMERICAN FIDELITY ASR CO	OK	6,090.1
AMERICAN UNITED LIFE INS CO	IN	29,575.8
AMICA LIFE INS CO	RI	1,302.6
ASSURITY LIFE INS CO	NE	2,729.5
AXA EQUITABLE LIFE INS CO	NY	191,807.0
BOSTON MUTUAL LIFE INS CO	MA	1,461.7
CHESAPEAKE LIFE INS CO	OK	195.4
CHRISTIAN FIDELITY LIFE INS CO	TX	64.2
COMPANION LIFE INS CO	SC	401.6
DEARBORN NATIONAL LIFE INS CO	IL	1,737.6
DELAWARE AMERICAN LIFE INS CO	DE	122.9
EAGLE LIFE INS CO	IA	1,070.1
FAMILY HERITAGE LIFE INS CO OF AMER	OH	1,444.8
FREEDOM LIFE INS CO OF AMERICA	TX	213.2
GERBER LIFE INS CO	NY	3,909.7
HANNOVER LIFE REASSURANCE CO OF AMER	FL	16,338.8
MIDLAND NATIONAL LIFE INS CO	IA	58,240.4
MINNESOTA LIFE INS CO	MN	49,271.3
NATIONAL BENEFIT LIFE INS CO	NY	564.7
NEW YORK LIFE INS & ANNUITY CORP	DE	156,175.5
NORTHWESTERN MUTUAL LIFE INS CO	WI	273,304.0

INSURANCE COMPANY NAME	DOM. STATE	TOTAL ASSETS ($MIL)
OHIO NATIONAL LIFE ASR CORP	OH	4,098.9
OXFORD LIFE INS CO	AZ	2,192.1
PACIFIC LIFE & ANNUITY CO	AZ	7,409.8
PAN AMERICAN ASR CO	LA	26.7
PRINCIPAL LIFE INS CO	IA	197,908.3
SB MUTL LIFE INS CO OF MA	MA	3,104.8
STANDARD INS CO	OR	24,530.4
TRANS WORLD ASR CO	CA	344.9
TRUSTMARK INS CO	IL	1,606.0
TRUSTMARK LIFE INS CO	IL	330.1
UNITED WORLD LIFE INS CO	NE	119.5
VOYA RETIREMENT INS & ANNUITY CO	CT	108,678.3

Wisconsin

INSURANCE COMPANY NAME	DOM. STATE	TOTAL ASSETS ($MIL)

Rating: A+

INSURANCE COMPANY NAME	DOM. STATE	TOTAL ASSETS ($MIL)
AMERICAN FAMILY LIFE INS CO	WI	5,269.9
COUNTRY LIFE INS CO	IL	9,673.9
PHYSICIANS MUTUAL INS CO	NE	2,367.4
STATE FARM LIFE & ACCIDENT ASR CO	IL	3,003.4
TEACHERS INS & ANNUITY ASN OF AM	NY	302,803.1

Rating: A

INSURANCE COMPANY NAME	DOM. STATE	TOTAL ASSETS ($MIL)
AMALGAMATED LIFE INS CO	NY	140.3
BERKLEY LIFE & HEALTH INS CO	IA	325.8
FEDERATED LIFE INS CO	MN	1,969.7
GARDEN STATE LIFE INS CO	TX	135.5
GUARDIAN LIFE INS CO OF AMERICA	NY	57,852.7
NATIONAL WESTERN LIFE INS CO	CO	11,114.0
PARKER CENTENNIAL ASR CO	WI	96.0
SENTRY LIFE INS CO	WI	7,425.4
USAA LIFE INS CO	TX	25,292.8

Rating: A-

INSURANCE COMPANY NAME	DOM. STATE	TOTAL ASSETS ($MIL)
AMERICAN HEALTH & LIFE INS CO	TX	1,018.0
ANNUITY INVESTORS LIFE INS CO	OH	3,232.6
COUNTRY INVESTORS LIFE ASR CO	IL	303.5
ERIE FAMILY LIFE INS CO	PA	2,512.1
FIDELITY INVESTMENTS LIFE INS CO	UT	30,960.8
MASSACHUSETTS MUTUAL LIFE INS CO	MA	245,872.2
MUTUAL OF AMERICA LIFE INS CO	NY	21,758.9
NEW YORK LIFE INS CO	NY	178,706.9
NIPPON LIFE INS CO OF AMERICA	IA	219.2
PACIFIC LIFE INS CO	NE	133,288.3
PHYSICIANS LIFE INS CO	NE	1,664.1
STANDARD LIFE & ACCIDENT INS CO	TX	533.1
SYMETRA NATIONAL LIFE INS CO	IA	18.6
USABLE LIFE	AR	541.5

Rating: B+

INSURANCE COMPANY NAME	DOM. STATE	TOTAL ASSETS ($MIL)
AMERICAN FIDELITY ASR CO	OK	6,090.1
AMERICAN UNITED LIFE INS CO	IN	29,575.8
AMICA LIFE INS CO	RI	1,302.6
ASSURITY LIFE INS CO	NE	2,729.5
AXA EQUITABLE LIFE INS CO	NY	191,807.0
BOSTON MUTUAL LIFE INS CO	MA	1,461.7
CHESAPEAKE LIFE INS CO	OK	195.4
COMPANION LIFE INS CO	SC	401.6
DEARBORN NATIONAL LIFE INS CO	IL	1,737.6
DELAWARE AMERICAN LIFE INS CO	DE	122.9
EAGLE LIFE INS CO	IA	1,070.1
ENTERPRISE LIFE INS CO	TX	73.7
FAMILY HERITAGE LIFE INS CO OF AMER	OH	1,444.8
FARM BUREAU LIFE INS CO	IA	9,267.1
GERBER LIFE INS CO	NY	3,909.7
HANNOVER LIFE REASSURANCE CO OF AMER	FL	16,338.8
MIDLAND NATIONAL LIFE INS CO	IA	58,240.4
MINNESOTA LIFE INS CO	MN	49,271.3
NATIONAL BENEFIT LIFE INS CO	NY	564.7
NATIONAL FARMERS UNION LIFE INS CO	TX	193.3
NEW YORK LIFE INS & ANNUITY CORP	DE	156,175.5

INSURANCE COMPANY NAME	DOM. STATE	TOTAL ASSETS ($MIL)
NORTH AMERICAN INS CO	WI	19.2
NORTHWESTERN MUTUAL LIFE INS CO	WI	273,304.0
OHIO NATIONAL LIFE ASR CORP	OH	4,098.9
OXFORD LIFE INS CO	AZ	2,192.1
PACIFIC LIFE & ANNUITY CO	AZ	7,409.8
PAN AMERICAN ASR CO	LA	26.7
PRINCIPAL LIFE INS CO	IA	197,908.3
SB MUTL LIFE INS CO OF MA	MA	3,104.8
STANDARD INS CO	OR	24,530.4
TRANS WORLD ASR CO	CA	344.9
TRUSTMARK INS CO	IL	1,606.0
TRUSTMARK LIFE INS CO	IL	330.1
UNITED WORLD LIFE INS CO	NE	119.5
VOYA RETIREMENT INS & ANNUITY CO	CT	108,678.3

Wyoming

INSURANCE COMPANY NAME	DOM. STATE	TOTAL ASSETS ($MIL)

Rating: A+

INSURANCE COMPANY NAME	DOM. STATE	TOTAL ASSETS ($MIL)
AMERICAN FAMILY LIFE INS CO	WI	5,269.9
COUNTRY LIFE INS CO	IL	9,673.9
PHYSICIANS MUTUAL INS CO	NE	2,367.4
STATE FARM LIFE INS CO	IL	74,940.7
TEACHERS INS & ANNUITY ASN OF AM	NY	302,803.1

Rating: A

INSURANCE COMPANY NAME	DOM. STATE	TOTAL ASSETS ($MIL)
AMALGAMATED LIFE INS CO	NY	140.3
BERKLEY LIFE & HEALTH INS CO	IA	325.8
FEDERATED LIFE INS CO	MN	1,969.7
GARDEN STATE LIFE INS CO	TX	135.5
GUARDIAN LIFE INS CO OF AMERICA	NY	57,852.7
NATIONAL WESTERN LIFE INS CO	CO	11,114.0
PARKER CENTENNIAL ASR CO	WI	96.0
SENTRY LIFE INS CO	WI	7,425.4
USAA LIFE INS CO	TX	25,292.8

Rating: A-

INSURANCE COMPANY NAME	DOM. STATE	TOTAL ASSETS ($MIL)
AMERICAN HEALTH & LIFE INS CO	TX	1,018.0
ANNUITY INVESTORS LIFE INS CO	OH	3,232.6
COUNTRY INVESTORS LIFE ASR CO	IL	303.5
FIDELITY INVESTMENTS LIFE INS CO	UT	30,960.8
MASSACHUSETTS MUTUAL LIFE INS CO	MA	245,872.2
MUTUAL OF AMERICA LIFE INS CO	NY	21,758.9
NEW YORK LIFE INS CO	NY	178,706.9
PACIFIC GUARDIAN LIFE INS CO LTD	HI	559.1
PACIFIC LIFE INS CO	NE	133,288.3
PHYSICIANS LIFE INS CO	NE	1,664.1
STANDARD LIFE & ACCIDENT INS CO	TX	533.1
USABLE LIFE	AR	541.5

Rating: B+

INSURANCE COMPANY NAME	DOM. STATE	TOTAL ASSETS ($MIL)
AMERICAN FIDELITY ASR CO	OK	6,090.1
AMERICAN UNITED LIFE INS CO	IN	29,575.8
AMICA LIFE INS CO	RI	1,302.6
ASSURITY LIFE INS CO	NE	2,729.5
AXA EQUITABLE LIFE INS CO	NY	191,807.0
BEST LIFE & HEALTH INS CO	TX	22.7
BOSTON MUTUAL LIFE INS CO	MA	1,461.7
CHESAPEAKE LIFE INS CO	OK	195.4
CHRISTIAN FIDELITY LIFE INS CO	TX	64.2
COMPANION LIFE INS CO	SC	401.6
DEARBORN NATIONAL LIFE INS CO	IL	1,737.6
DELAWARE AMERICAN LIFE INS CO	DE	122.9
EAGLE LIFE INS CO	IA	1,070.1
FAMILY HERITAGE LIFE INS CO OF AMER	OH	1,444.8
FARM BUREAU LIFE INS CO	IA	9,267.1
FREEDOM LIFE INS CO OF AMERICA	TX	213.2
GERBER LIFE INS CO	NY	3,909.7
HANNOVER LIFE REASSURANCE CO OF AMER	FL	16,338.8
MIDLAND NATIONAL LIFE INS CO	IA	58,240.4
MINNESOTA LIFE INS CO	MN	49,271.3
NATIONAL BENEFIT LIFE INS CO	NY	564.7
NATIONAL FARMERS UNION LIFE INS CO	TX	193.3
NATIONAL FOUNDATION LIFE INS CO	TX	50.6

INSURANCE COMPANY NAME	DOM. STATE	TOTAL ASSETS ($MIL)
NEW YORK LIFE INS & ANNUITY CORP	DE	156,175.5
NORTHWESTERN MUTUAL LIFE INS CO	WI	273,304.0
OHIO NATIONAL LIFE ASR CORP	OH	4,098.9
OXFORD LIFE INS CO	AZ	2,192.1
PACIFIC LIFE & ANNUITY CO	AZ	7,409.8
PRINCIPAL LIFE INS CO	IA	197,908.3
SB MUTL LIFE INS CO OF MA	MA	3,104.8
STANDARD INS CO	OR	24,530.4
TRANS WORLD ASR CO	CA	344.9
TRUSTMARK INS CO	IL	1,606.0
TRUSTMARK LIFE INS CO	IL	330.1
UNITED WORLD LIFE INS CO	NE	119.5
VOYA RETIREMENT INS & ANNUITY CO	CT	108,678.3

Section V

All Companies
Listed by Rating

A list of all rated and unrated

U.S. Life and Annuity Insurers

Companies are ranked by Weiss Safety Rating
and then listed alphabetically within each rating category.

Section V Contents

This section sorts all companies by their Weiss Safety Rating and then lists them alphabetically within each rating category. The purpose of this section is to provide in one place all of those companies receiving a given rating. Companies with the same rating should be viewed as having the same relative risk regardless of their order in this table.

1. Safety Rating   Our rating is measured on a scale from A to F and considers a wide range of factors. Highly rated companies are, in our opinion, less likely to experience financial difficulties than lower rated firms. See *About Weiss Safety Ratings* for more information.

2. Insurance Company Name   The legally registered name, which can sometimes differ from the name that the company uses for advertising. An insurer's name can be very similar to that of another, so verify the company's exact name and state of domicile to make sure you are looking at the correct company.

3. Domicile State   The state which has primary regulatory responsibility for the company. It may differ from the location of the company's corporate headquarters. You do not have to be living in the domicile state to purchase insurance from this firm, provided it is licensed to do business in your state.

4. Total Assets   All assets admitted by state insurance regulators in millions of dollars. This includes investments, current business assets and separate accounts.

INSURANCE COMPANY NAME	DOM. STATE	TOTAL ASSETS ($MIL)
Rating: A+		
AMERICAN FAMILY LIFE INS CO	WI	5,269.9
COUNTRY LIFE INS CO	IL	9,673.9
PHYSICIANS MUTUAL INS CO	NE	2,367.4
STATE FARM LIFE & ACCIDENT ASR CO	IL	3,003.4
STATE FARM LIFE INS CO	IL	74,940.7
TEACHERS INS & ANNUITY ASN OF AM	NY	302,803.1
Rating: A		
AMALGAMATED LIFE INS CO	NY	140.3
BERKLEY LIFE & HEALTH INS CO	IA	325.8
FEDERATED LIFE INS CO	MN	1,969.7
FRANDISCO LIFE INS CO	GA	93.8
GARDEN STATE LIFE INS CO	TX	135.5
GUARDIAN LIFE INS CO OF AMERICA	NY	57,852.7
LIFEWISE ASR CO	WA	193.1
NATIONAL WESTERN LIFE INS CO	CO	11,114.0
PARKER CENTENNIAL ASR CO	WI	96.0
SENTRY LIFE INS CO	WI	7,425.4
SHELTERPOINT LIFE INS CO	NY	151.3
SOUTHERN FARM BUREAU LIFE INS CO	MS	14,356.8
UNITED FARM FAMILY LIFE INS CO	IN	2,348.2
USAA LIFE INS CO	TX	25,292.8
Rating: A-		
AMERICAN FAMILY LIFE ASR CO OF NY	NY	1,000.3
AMERICAN HEALTH & LIFE INS CO	TX	1,018.0
ANNUITY INVESTORS LIFE INS CO	OH	3,232.6
CIGNA LIFE INS CO OF NEW YORK	NY	407.5
COTTON STATES LIFE INS CO	GA	339.7
COUNTRY INVESTORS LIFE ASR CO	IL	303.5
ERIE FAMILY LIFE INS CO	PA	2,512.1
FARM BUREAU LIFE INS CO OF MICHIGAN	MI	2,502.3
FARM BUREAU LIFE INS CO OF MISSOURI	MO	604.4
FIDELITY INVESTMENTS LIFE INS CO	UT	30,960.8
FIRST RELIANCE STANDARD LIFE INS CO	NY	208.0
LIFE INS CO OF BOSTON & NEW YORK	NY	157.5
MASSACHUSETTS MUTUAL LIFE INS CO	MA	245,872.2
MUTUAL OF AMERICA LIFE INS CO	NY	21,758.9
NEW YORK LIFE INS CO	NY	178,706.9
NIPPON LIFE INS CO OF AMERICA	IA	219.2
PACIFIC GUARDIAN LIFE INS CO LTD	HI	559.1
PACIFIC LIFE INS CO	NE	133,288.3
PHYSICIANS LIFE INS CO	NE	1,664.1
SOUTHERN PIONEER LIFE INS CO	AR	14.6
STANDARD LIFE & ACCIDENT INS CO	TX	533.1
STANDARD LIFE INS CO OF NY	NY	296.6
SYMETRA NATIONAL LIFE INS CO	IA	18.6
TRANS OCEANIC LIFE INS CO	PR	75.3
USABLE LIFE	AR	541.5
Rating: B+		
ADVANCE INS CO OF KANSAS	KS	61.6
ALLIANZ LIFE INS CO OF NY	NY	3,461.1

INSURANCE COMPANY NAME	DOM. STATE	TOTAL ASSETS ($MIL)
AMERICAN FIDELITY ASR CO	OK	6,090.1
AMERICAN UNITED LIFE INS CO	IN	29,575.8
AMICA LIFE INS CO	RI	1,302.6
ASSURITY LIFE INS CO	NE	2,729.5
AXA EQUITABLE LIFE INS CO	NY	191,807.0
BEST LIFE & HEALTH INS CO	TX	22.7
BLUEBONNET LIFE INS CO	MS	64.3
BOSTON MUTUAL LIFE INS CO	MA	1,461.7
CHESAPEAKE LIFE INS CO	OK	195.4
CHRISTIAN FIDELITY LIFE INS CO	TX	64.2
COMPANION LIFE INS CO	SC	401.6
DEARBORN NATIONAL LIFE INS CO	IL	1,737.6
DEARBORN NATIONAL LIFE INS CO OF NY	NY	23.6
DELAWARE AMERICAN LIFE INS CO	DE	122.9
EAGLE LIFE INS CO	IA	1,070.1
EMPIRE FIDELITY INVESTMENTS L I C	NY	3,035.0
ENTERPRISE LIFE INS CO	TX	73.7
FAMILY HERITAGE LIFE INS CO OF AMER	OH	1,444.8
FARM BUREAU LIFE INS CO	IA	9,267.1
FIRST SYMETRA NATL LIFE INS CO OF NY	NY	2,070.2
FREEDOM LIFE INS CO OF AMERICA	TX	213.2
GERBER LIFE INS CO	NY	3,909.7
HANNOVER LIFE REASSURANCE CO OF AMER	FL	16,338.8
LOCOMOTIVE ENGRS&COND MUT PROT ASSN	MI	73.6
M LIFE INS CO	CO	307.3
MIDLAND NATIONAL LIFE INS CO	IA	58,240.4
MINNESOTA LIFE INS CO	MN	49,271.3
NATIONAL BENEFIT LIFE INS CO	NY	564.7
NATIONAL FARMERS UNION LIFE INS CO	TX	193.3
NATIONAL FOUNDATION LIFE INS CO	TX	50.6
NATIONAL INCOME LIFE INS CO	NY	261.9
NEW YORK LIFE INS & ANNUITY CORP	DE	156,175.5
NORTH AMERICAN INS CO	WI	19.2
NORTHWESTERN MUTUAL LIFE INS CO	WI	273,304.0
OHIO NATIONAL LIFE ASR CORP	OH	4,098.9
OXFORD LIFE INS CO	AZ	2,192.1
PACIFIC LIFE & ANNUITY CO	AZ	7,409.8
PAN AMERICAN ASR CO	LA	26.7
PRINCIPAL LIFE INS CO	IA	197,908.3
SB MUTL LIFE INS CO OF MA	MA	3,104.8
STANDARD INS CO	OR	24,530.4
SWBC LIFE INS CO	TX	32.6
TENNESSEE FARMERS LIFE INS CO	TN	2,318.6
TRANS WORLD ASR CO	CA	344.9
TRUSTMARK INS CO	IL	1,606.0
TRUSTMARK LIFE INS CO	IL	330.1
UNITED WORLD LIFE INS CO	NE	119.5
UNIVERSAL LIFE INS CO	PR	1,569.7
USAA LIFE INS CO OF NEW YORK	NY	780.2
UTIC INS CO	AL	102.4
VOYA RETIREMENT INS & ANNUITY CO	CT	108,678.3
Rating: B		
4 EVER LIFE INS CO	IL	190.1

INSURANCE COMPANY NAME	DOM. STATE	TOTAL ASSETS ($MIL)	INSURANCE COMPANY NAME	DOM. STATE	TOTAL ASSETS ($MIL)
Rating: B (Continued)			GREAT-WEST LIFE & ANNUITY INS OF NY	NY	2,258.1
AAA LIFE INS CO	MI	677.0	GREATER GEORGIA LIFE INS CO	GA	61.0
AAA LIFE INS CO OF NY	NY	7.7	GREENFIELDS LIFE INS CO	CO	16.1
AETNA LIFE INS CO	CT	21,702.3	GUARANTEE TRUST LIFE INS CO	IL	637.7
ALLSTATE LIFE INS CO	IL	30,993.3	GUARANTY INCOME LIFE INS CO	LA	812.7
AMERICAN EQUITY INVESTMENT LIFE NY	NY	201.4	GUARDIAN INS & ANNUITY CO INC	DE	15,824.8
AMERICAN FARM LIFE INS CO	TX	4.5	HARLEYSVILLE LIFE INS CO	OH	401.8
AMERICAN FEDERATED LIFE INS CO	MS	31.6	HCC LIFE INS CO	IN	1,086.9
AMERICAN FIDELITY LIFE INS CO	FL	402.5	HM LIFE INS CO	PA	721.2
AMERICAN GENERAL LIFE INS CO	TX	179,039.2	HM LIFE INS CO OF NEW YORK	NY	67.2
AMERICAN HERITAGE LIFE INS CO	FL	2,026.5	HOMESTEADERS LIFE CO	IA	3,035.3
AMERICAN MODERN LIFE INS CO	OH	38.3	HORACE MANN LIFE INS CO	IL	9,548.2
AMERICAN NATIONAL INS CO	TX	20,831.3	HUMANA INS CO OF KENTUCKY	KY	209.8
AMERICAN PUBLIC LIFE INS CO	OK	99.1	ILLINOIS MUTUAL LIFE INS CO	IL	1,447.8
AMERICAN SERVICE LIFE INS CO	AR	1.3	INTRAMERICA LIFE INS CO	NY	34.8
AMERITAS LIFE INS CORP	NE	21,881.9	INVESTORS LIFE INS CO NORTH AMERICA	TX	597.6
ANTHEM LIFE & DISABILITY INS CO	NY	24.6	JACKSON NATIONAL LIFE INS CO	MI	237,904.4
ANTHEM LIFE INS CO	IN	720.0	JACKSON NATIONAL LIFE INS CO OF NY	NY	13,730.6
ASSURITY LIFE INS CO OF NY	NY	8.3	JOHN HANCOCK LIFE & HEALTH INS CO	MA	13,974.9
AURORA NATIONAL LIFE ASR CO	CA	3,097.8	JOHN HANCOCK LIFE INS CO (USA)	MI	240,600.9
AUTO-OWNERS LIFE INS CO	MI	3,995.6	JOHN HANCOCK LIFE INS CO OF NY	NY	17,266.2
AXA CORPORATE SOLUTIONS LIFE REINS	DE	258.4	KANSAS CITY LIFE INS CO	MO	3,401.6
AXA EQUITABLE LIFE & ANNUITY CO	CO	474.4	LAFAYETTE LIFE INS CO	OH	5,572.4
BALTIMORE LIFE INS CO	MD	1,286.6	LEADERS LIFE INS CO	OK	6.2
BENEFICIAL LIFE INS CO	UT	2,157.1	LIBERTY NATIONAL LIFE INS CO	NE	7,484.1
BERKSHIRE LIFE INS CO OF AMERICA	MA	3,893.2	LIFE INS CO OF ALABAMA	AL	124.2
BLUE CROSS BLUE SHIELD OF KANSAS INC	KS	1,791.6	LIFE INS CO OF NORTH AMERICA	PA	8,743.9
BLUE SHIELD OF CALIFORNIA L&H INS CO	CA	303.9	LIFE INS CO OF THE SOUTHWEST	TX	19,754.5
BRIGHTHOUSE LIFE INSURANCE CO	DE	172,096.6	LINCOLN LIFE & ANNUITY CO OF NY	NY	15,062.1
CARIBBEAN AMERICAN LIFE ASR CO	PR	39.7	LINCOLN NATIONAL LIFE INS CO	IN	249,329.3
CENTRAL STATES H & L CO OF OMAHA	NE	389.7	LONGEVITY INS CO	TX	7.8
CHURCH LIFE INS CORP	NY	303.4	MADISON NATIONAL LIFE INS CO INC	WI	339.1
CIGNA HEALTH & LIFE INS CO	CT	10,572.2	MANHATTAN LIFE INS CO	NY	623.8
CM LIFE INS CO	CT	8,471.3	MEDAMERICA INS CO OF FL	FL	44.5
COLUMBIAN MUTUAL LIFE INS CO	NY	1,454.3	MERIT LIFE INS CO	IN	386.6
COMPANION LIFE INS CO OF CA	CA	24.4	MIDWESTERN UNITED LIFE INS CO	IN	234.5
CONSUMERS LIFE INS CO	OH	44.4	MML BAY STATE LIFE INS CO	CT	5,026.5
CONTINENTAL AMERICAN INS CO	SC	804.5	MONITOR LIFE INS CO OF NEW YORK	NY	21.0
DESERET MUTUAL INS CO	UT	42.8	MONY LIFE INS CO OF AMERICA	AZ	3,981.0
EMC NATIONAL LIFE CO	IA	963.0	MOTORISTS LIFE INS CO	OH	491.5
FARM FAMILY LIFE INS CO	NY	2,259.2	MUTUAL OF OMAHA INS CO	NE	7,924.2
FIDELITY SECURITY LIFE INS CO	MO	931.6	MUTUAL SAVINGS LIFE INS CO	AL	480.7
FIDELITY SECURITY LIFE INS CO OF NY	NY	44.4	MUTUAL TRUST LIFE INS CO	IL	2,038.5
FIRST ALLMERICA FINANCIAL LIFE INS	MA	3,333.8	NATIONAL FARM LIFE INS CO	TX	417.6
FIRST ASR LIFE OF AMERICA	LA	41.6	NATIONAL SECURITY INS CO	AL	57.0
FIRST PENN-PACIFIC LIFE INS CO	IN	1,418.1	NATIONAL SECURITY LIFE & ANNUITY CO	NY	491.9
FIRST SECURITY BENEFIT LIFE & ANN	NY	599.1	NATIONAL TEACHERS ASSOCIATES L I C	TX	572.9
FORETHOUGHT LIFE INS CO	IN	30,391.4	NEW ENGLAND LIFE INS CO	MA	9,964.8
GLOBE LIFE INSURANCE CO OF NY	NY	248.9	NIAGARA LIFE & HEALTH INS CO	NY	18.2
GOLDEN RULE INS CO	IN	534.7	NORTH AMERICAN CO FOR LIFE & H INS	IA	27,148.1
GOVERNMENT PERSONNEL MUTUAL L I C	TX	821.2	NORTHWESTERN LONG TERM CARE INS CO	WI	204.5
GPM HEALTH & LIFE INS CO	WA	143.3	NTA LIFE INS CO OF NEW YORK	NY	7.8
GREAT SOUTHERN LIFE INS CO	TX	212.0	NYLIFE INS CO OF ARIZONA	AZ	175.9
			OHIO NATIONAL LIFE INS CO	OH	32,065.5

INSURANCE COMPANY NAME	DOM. STATE	TOTAL ASSETS ($MIL)
Rating: B (Continued)		
OLD UNITED LIFE INS CO	AZ	89.4
OPTUM INS OF OH INC	OH	264.1
PACIFICARE LIFE & HEALTH INS CO	IN	186.3
PAN AMERICAN LIFE INS CO OF PR	PR	9.6
PAN-AMERICAN LIFE INS CO	LA	1,215.8
PARK AVENUE LIFE INS CO	DE	234.6
PEKIN LIFE INS CO	IL	1,496.7
PENN MUTUAL LIFE INS CO	PA	21,664.0
PHILADELPHIA AMERICAN LIFE INS CO	TX	297.6
PIONEER MUTUAL LIFE INS CO	ND	509.5
POPULAR LIFE RE	PR	69.3
PRENEED REINS CO OF AMERICA	AZ	43.0
PRIMERICA LIFE INS CO	TN	1,617.7
PRINCIPAL NATIONAL LIFE INS CO	IA	368.2
PROTECTIVE LIFE INS CO	TN	59,054.5
PROVIDENT AMER LIFE & HEALTH INS CO	OH	9.0
PRUDENTIAL INS CO OF AMERICA	NJ	269,548.9
RELIASTAR LIFE INS CO OF NEW YORK	NY	2,927.2
S USA LIFE INS CO INC	AZ	25.6
SBLI USA MUT LIFE INS CO INC	NY	1,530.7
SECU LIFE INS CO	NC	49.2
SECURIAN LIFE INS CO	MN	994.0
SECURITY BENEFIT LIFE INS CO	KS	33,665.2
SENTRY LIFE INS CO OF NEW YORK	NY	118.6
SETTLERS LIFE INS CO	WI	423.1
SHELTER LIFE INS CO	MO	1,268.8
SHELTERPOINT INS CO	FL	9.0
SOUTHERN LIFE & HEALTH INS CO	WI	71.2
SOUTHERN NATL LIFE INS CO INC	LA	16.9
STANDARD SECURITY LIFE INS CO OF NY	NY	138.0
STATE LIFE INS CO	IN	8,378.9
STATE LIFE INS FUND	WI	111.9
SYMETRA LIFE INS CO	IA	37,769.4
TEXAS DIRECTORS LIFE INS CO	TX	5.5
THE UNION LABOR LIFE INS CO	MD	3,872.3
THRIVENT LIFE INS CO	WI	3,939.4
TIAA-CREF LIFE INS CO	NY	13,320.7
TPM LIFE INS CO	PA	18.9
TRANSAMERICA FINANCIAL LIFE INS CO	NY	32,230.0
TRANSAMERICA LIFE INS CO	IA	122,998.5
TRUSTMARK LIFE INS CO OF NEW YORK	NY	10.0
UNIFIED LIFE INS CO	TX	210.9
UNIMERICA INS CO	WI	453.7
UNIMERICA LIFE INS CO OF NY	NY	41.0
UNION NATIONAL LIFE INS CO	LA	21.0
UNION SECURITY INS CO	KS	2,758.2
UNITED HERITAGE LIFE INS CO	ID	597.7
UNITED HOME LIFE INS CO	IN	96.4
UNITED LIFE INS CO	IA	1,549.3
UNITED NATIONAL LIFE INS CO OF AM	IL	32.5
UNITED OF OMAHA LIFE INS CO	NE	23,546.4
UNITED STATES LIFE INS CO IN NYC	NY	28,771.0

INSURANCE COMPANY NAME	DOM. STATE	TOTAL ASSETS ($MIL)
US FINANCIAL LIFE INS CO	OH	543.6
VANTISLIFE INS CO OF NEW YORK	NY	168.4
VARIABLE ANNUITY LIFE INS CO	TX	83,441.4
WESTERN & SOUTHERN LIFE INS CO	OH	10,735.7
WESTERN-SOUTHERN LIFE ASR CO	OH	12,464.1
Rating: B-		
ACE LIFE INS CO	CT	45.9
ALFA LIFE INS CORP	AL	1,479.5
ALLSTATE LIFE INS CO OF NEW YORK	NY	6,223.9
AMERICAN EQUITY INVEST LIFE INS CO	IA	54,487.2
AMERICAN INCOME LIFE INS CO	IN	4,094.0
AMERICAN MATURITY LIFE INS CO	CT	63.1
AMERICAN MEMORIAL LIFE INS CO	SD	3,314.8
AMERICAN NATIONAL LIFE INS CO OF TX	TX	127.2
AMERICAN REPUBLIC INS CO	IA	1,016.1
AMERICO FINANCIAL LIFE & ANNUITY INS	TX	4,642.1
AMERITAS LIFE INS CORP OF NY	NY	1,316.4
ATLANTIC COAST LIFE INS CO	SC	542.2
AUTOMOBILE CLUB OF SOUTHERN CA INS	CA	1,285.6
BANNER LIFE INS CO	MD	4,020.8
BEST MERIDIAN INS CO	FL	348.6
BROOKE LIFE INS CO	MI	4,657.8
CENTRE LIFE INS CO	MA	1,703.5
CIGNA NATIONAL HEALTH INS CO	OH	14.6
CIGNA WORLDWIDE INS CO	DE	63.0
CINCINNATI LIFE INS CO	OH	4,517.0
CMFG LIFE INS CO	IA	18,854.8
COMBINED INS CO OF AMERICA	IL	1,561.1
COMM TRAVELERS LIFE INS CO	NY	27.1
COMMONWEALTH ANNUITY & LIFE INS CO	MA	19,628.2
COMPANION LIFE INS CO	NY	1,170.0
CONNECTICUT GENERAL LIFE INS CO	CT	19,355.3
CSI LIFE INS CO	NE	24.6
DELAWARE LIFE INS CO OF NEW YORK	NY	2,382.2
EQUITRUST LIFE INS CO	IL	18,410.4
FARMERS NEW WORLD LIFE INS CO	WA	5,159.1
FIDELITY & GUARANTY LIFE INS CO NY	NY	539.9
FIRST COMMAND LIFE INS CO	TX	41.3
FUNERAL DIRECTORS LIFE INS CO	TX	1,386.8
GREAT AMERICAN LIFE INS CO	OH	35,805.2
GREAT-WEST LIFE & ANNUITY INS CO	CO	57,765.4
GUGGENHEIM LIFE & ANNUITY CO	DE	13,884.9
HEARTLAND NATIONAL LIFE INS CO	IN	13.0
IDEALIFE INS CO	CT	21.5
INTEGRITY LIFE INS CO	OH	9,713.5
JAMESTOWN LIFE INS CO	VA	127.3
JEFFERSON NATIONAL LIFE INS CO OF NY	NY	110.2
JOHN ALDEN LIFE INS CO	WI	208.0
KENTUCKY FUNERAL DIRECTORS LIFE INS	KY	22.8
LIBERTY LIFE ASR CO OF BOSTON	NH	4,034.0
LIFEMAP ASR CO	OR	100.7
LIFESHIELD NATIONAL INS CO	OK	86.1
LINCOLN HERITAGE LIFE INS CO	IL	1,018.0

INSURANCE COMPANY NAME	DOM. STATE	TOTAL ASSETS ($MIL)
Rating: B- (Continued)		
LONDON LIFE INS CO	MI	21.1
LOYAL AMERICAN LIFE INS CO	OH	334.0
MANHATTAN NATIONAL LIFE INS CO	OH	152.0
MEDICO CORP LIFE INS CO	NE	70.6
MEDICO INS CO	NE	84.6
METROPOLITAN LIFE INS CO	NY	389,582.7
METROPOLITAN TOWER LIFE INS CO	NE	5,013.0
MONY LIFE INS CO	NY	7,114.0
NATIONAL GUARDIAN LIFE INS CO	WI	4,065.8
NATIONAL INTEGRITY LIFE INS CO	NY	4,583.7
NATIONAL LIFE INS CO	VT	9,786.2
NATIONWIDE LIFE INS CO	OH	146,933.0
OHIO STATE LIFE INS CO	TX	13.2
OLD AMERICAN INS CO	MO	266.3
OLD REPUBLIC LIFE INS CO	IL	113.7
OMAHA INS CO	NE	89.4
OZARK NATIONAL LIFE INS CO	MO	836.8
PERFORMANCE LIFE OF AMERICA	LA	31.9
PROFESSIONAL LIFE & CAS CO	IL	180.9
PROVIDENT LIFE & CAS INS CO	TN	746.1
PRUCO LIFE INS CO OF NEW JERSEY	NJ	16,367.8
PRUDENTIAL ANNUITIES LIFE ASR CORP	AZ	53,916.6
PRUDENTIAL RETIREMENT INS & ANNUITY	CT	75,563.2
RELIABLE LIFE INS CO	MO	21.2
RELIASTAR LIFE INS CO	MN	20,768.8
RESERVE NATIONAL INS CO	OK	136.2
RGA REINSURANCE CO	MO	37,286.1
SCOR GLOBAL LIFE AMERICAS REIN CO	DE	1,057.7
SCOR GLOBAL LIFE USA RE CO	DE	836.9
SECURITY LIFE OF DENVER INS CO	CO	14,698.8
SHENANDOAH LIFE INS CO	VA	1,003.5
STERLING INVESTORS LIFE INS CO	IN	70.0
STERLING LIFE INS CO	IL	39.9
SUNSET LIFE INS CO OF AMERICA	MO	310.0
TALCOTT RESOLUTION LIFE	CT	36,933.6
TEXAS LIFE INS CO	TX	1,204.2
TRANSAMERICA ADVISORS LIFE INS CO	AR	7,770.6
TRIPLE S VIDA INC	PR	650.2
UNICARE LIFE & HEALTH INS CO	IN	282.8
UNITED AMERICAN INS CO	NE	731.5
UNITED INS CO OF AMERICA	IL	3,905.4
VERSANT LIFE INS CO	MS	6.5
VOYA INS & ANNUITY CO	IA	53,491.6
WEST COAST LIFE INS CO	NE	5,319.9
WESTERN UNITED LIFE ASR CO	WA	1,217.0
WINDSOR LIFE INS CO	TX	3.2
ZURICH AMERICAN LIFE INS CO OF NY	NY	78.2
Rating: C+		
ALLSTATE ASR CO	IL	699.2
AMERICAN BANKERS LIFE ASR CO OF FL	FL	334.1
AMERICAN CONTINENTAL INS CO	TN	268.1

INSURANCE COMPANY NAME	DOM. STATE	TOTAL ASSETS ($MIL)
AMERICAN RETIREMENT LIFE INS CO	OH	120.7
AUTO CLUB LIFE INS CO	MI	814.0
BANKERS FIDELITY ASR CO	GA	11.2
BERKSHIRE HATHAWAY LIFE INS CO OF NE	NE	18,380.3
BRIGHTHOUSE LIFE INS CO OF NY	NY	8,005.3
CITIZENS FIDELITY INS CO	AR	70.3
COLONIAL LIFE & ACCIDENT INS CO	SC	3,368.4
COLUMBUS LIFE INS CO	OH	4,144.8
COMBINED LIFE INS CO OF NEW YORK	NY	464.1
CONTINENTAL GENERAL INS CO	OH	1,407.1
CONTINENTAL LIFE INS CO OF BRENTWOOD	TN	376.4
ELCO MUTUAL LIFE & ANNUITY	IL	821.4
EQUITABLE LIFE & CASUALTY INS CO	UT	371.9
FIDELITY & GUARANTY LIFE INS CO	IA	24,281.8
FIDELITY LIFE ASSN A LEGAL RESERVE	IL	404.2
FIRST BERKSHIRE HATHAWAY LIFE INS CO	NY	215.8
FIRST HEALTH LIFE & HEALTH INS CO	TX	420.1
FIRST UNUM LIFE INS CO	NY	3,656.0
FORESTERS LIFE INS & ANNUITY CO	NY	2,619.6
GENWORTH LIFE INS CO	DE	39,956.4
GERMANIA LIFE INS CO	TX	94.3
GLOBE LIFE & ACCIDENT INS CO	NE	4,652.8
GREAT CENTRAL LIFE INS CO	LA	24.9
GREAT WEST LIFE ASR CO	MI	73.3
GULF GUARANTY LIFE INS CO	MS	18.6
HERITAGE LIFE INS CO	AZ	3,923.4
HUMANA INS CO OF PUERTO RICO INC	PR	77.8
IA AMERICAN LIFE INS CO	TX	140.8
INVESTORS HERITAGE LIFE INS CO	KY	466.9
LINCOLN BENEFIT LIFE CO	NE	10,952.9
LONDON LIFE REINSURANCE CO	PA	200.0
MID-WEST NATIONAL LIFE INS CO OF TN	TX	62.6
MOLINA HEALTHCARE OF TEXAS INS CO	TX	9.0
NEW ERA LIFE INS CO OF THE MIDWEST	TX	138.4
OPTIMUM RE INS CO	TX	191.2
PATRIOT LIFE INS CO	MI	21.9
PAUL REVERE LIFE INS CO	MA	3,479.2
PENN INS & ANNUITY CO	DE	6,128.0
PROTEC INS CO	IL	5.1
PROTECTIVE LIFE & ANNUITY INS CO	AL	5,029.6
PROVIDENT LIFE & ACCIDENT INS CO	TN	8,041.3
PRUCO LIFE INS CO	AZ	123,473.2
RELIANCE STANDARD LIFE INS CO	IL	13,947.8
RIVERSOURCE LIFE INS CO	MN	106,410.1
RX LIFE INSURANCE CO	AZ	9.3
STARMOUNT LIFE INS CO	LA	82.6
SUPERIOR FUNERAL & LIFE INS CO	AR	184.0
TALCOTT RESOLUTION LIFE INS CO	CT	90,215.7
TIME INS CO	WI	62.3
TRANSAMERICA PREMIER LIFE INS CO	IA	50,487.4
UNION SECURITY LIFE INS CO OF NY	NY	60.5
UNIVERSAL GUARANTY LIFE INS CO	OH	363.9
UNUM LIFE INS CO OF AMERICA	ME	21,839.2
USIC LIFE INS CO	PR	10.8

INSURANCE COMPANY NAME	DOM. STATE	TOTAL ASSETS ($MIL)
Rating: C+ (Continued)		
VANTIS LIFE INS CO	CT	482.0
WILTON REASSURANCE LIFE CO OF NY	NY	879.3
Rating: C		
ACCORDIA LIFE & ANNUITY CO	IA	9,246.6
AETNA HEALTH & LIFE INS CO	CT	175.2
ALL SAVERS INS CO	IN	703.8
ALLIANZ LIFE INS CO OF NORTH AMERICA	MN	147,319.7
AMALGAMATED LIFE & HEALTH INS CO	IL	5.0
AMERICAN BENEFIT LIFE INS CO	OK	158.3
AMERICAN FARMERS & RANCHERS LIFE INS	OK	30.2
AMERICAN LIFE & ACC INS CO OF KY	KY	252.6
AMERICAN LIFE INS CO	DE	10,706.5
AMERICAN PROGRESSIVE L&H I C OF NY	NY	259.4
AMERICAN REPUBLIC CORP INS CO	IA	21.7
AMERICAN SAVINGS LIFE INS CO	AZ	62.0
AMERICAN-AMICABLE LIFE INS CO OF TX	TX	303.0
ATHENE ANNUITY & LIFE ASR CO	DE	20,718.3
ATHENE ANNUITY & LIFE ASR CO OF NY	NY	3,174.7
ATHENE ANNUITY & LIFE CO	IA	57,378.9
ATHENE LIFE INS CO OF NEW YORK	NY	970.0
BANKERS FIDELITY LIFE INS CO	GA	146.1
BANKERS LIFE OF LOUISIANA	LA	18.3
CANADA LIFE ASSURANCE CO-US BRANCH	MI	4,624.3
CAPITOL LIFE INS CO	TX	299.9
CENTURION LIFE INS CO	IA	1,047.7
CHESTERFIELD REINS CO	MO	330.3
CITIZENS NATIONAL LIFE INS CO	TX	11.9
CITIZENS SECURITY LIFE INS CO	KY	29.5
COLORADO BANKERS LIFE INS CO	NC	2,618.4
COLUMBIAN LIFE INS CO	IL	342.1
DELAWARE LIFE INS CO	DE	37,022.2
DIRECT GENERAL LIFE INS CO	SC	32.4
EPIC LIFE INSURANCE CO	WI	33.2
FAMILY BENEFIT LIFE INS CO	MO	159.1
FAMILY LIFE INS CO	TX	146.4
FAMILY SECURITY LIFE INS CO INC	MS	6.8
FIRST NATIONAL LIFE INS CO	NE	6.9
FIVE STAR LIFE INS CO	NE	294.2
FLORIDA COMBINED LIFE INS CO INC	FL	70.5
GENERAL FIDELITY LIFE INS CO	SC	22.1
GENERAL RE LIFE CORP	CT	4,272.2
GENWORTH LIFE INS CO OF NEW YORK	NY	7,736.8
GRANGE LIFE INS CO	OH	390.8
HALLMARK LIFE INS CO	AZ	4.8
HARTFORD LIFE & ACCIDENT INS CO	CT	12,962.6
HAWKEYE LIFE INS GROUP INC	IA	12.5
HEALTH NET LIFE INS CO	CA	748.8
INDUSTRIAL ALLIANCE INS & FIN SERV	TX	272.5
JEFFERSON NATIONAL LIFE INS CO	TX	6,534.9
LANDMARK LIFE INS CO	TX	46.2
LANGHORNE REINSURANCE AZ LTD	AZ	8.6

INSURANCE COMPANY NAME	DOM. STATE	TOTAL ASSETS ($MIL)
LEWER LIFE INS CO	MO	32.9
LIFE OF AMERICA INS CO	TX	12.0
LIFE OF THE SOUTH INS CO	GA	106.6
LIFECARE ASSURANCE CO	AZ	2,516.7
LUMICO LIFE INSURANCE CO	MO	58.4
MAGNOLIA GUARANTY LIFE INS CO	MS	10.7
MANHATTANLIFE ASSR CO OF AM	AR	675.1
MAPFRE LIFE INS CO	DE	40.7
MEDAMERICA INS CO	PA	973.5
MEDAMERICA INS CO OF NEW YORK	NY	808.5
MEDICO LIFE & HEALTH INS CO	IA	15.6
MEMBERS LIFE INS CO	IA	151.4
MEMORIAL LIFE INS CO	LA	3.6
MUNICH AMERICAN REASSURANCE CO	GA	8,459.3
NATIONAL FAMILY CARE LIFE INS CO	TX	16.0
NATIONAL HEALTH INS CO	TX	54.5
NATIONWIDE LIFE & ANNUITY INS CO	OH	24,689.8
NEW ERA LIFE INS CO	TX	543.6
NORTH AMERICAN NATIONAL RE INS CO	AZ	36.6
OCCIDENTAL LIFE INS CO OF NC	TX	258.8
OLD SPARTAN LIFE INS CO INC	SC	24.6
OLD SURETY LIFE INS CO	OK	29.5
PARTNERRE LIFE RE CO OF AM	AR	63.8
PAVONIA LIFE INS CO OF MICHIGAN	MI	1,149.3
PAVONIA LIFE INS CO OF NEW YORK	NY	29.0
PHYSICIANS BENEFITS TRUST LIFE INS	IL	6.2
PIONEER AMERICAN INS CO	TX	68.4
PIONEER SECURITY LIFE INS CO	TX	76.3
PLATEAU INS CO	TN	27.4
PRESIDENTIAL LIFE INS CO	TX	4.3
PROVIDENT AMERICAN INS CO	TX	18.8
REINSURANCE CO OF MO INC	MO	1,952.2
RIVERMONT LIFE INS CO I	SC	610.3
RIVERSOURCE LIFE INS CO OF NY	NY	6,891.0
ROYAL STATE NATIONAL INS CO LTD	HI	39.7
SCOR GLOBAL LIFE REINS CO OF DE	DE	452.8
SECURITY MUTUAL LIFE INS CO OF NY	NY	2,766.8
SOUTHERN FINANCIAL LIFE INS CO	KY	9.8
SURENCY LIFE & HEALTH INS CO	KS	12.7
SWISS RE LIFE & HEALTH AMER INC	MO	15,359.0
UNITED FIDELITY LIFE INS CO	TX	828.1
UNITED HEALTHCARE INS CO	CT	19,448.9
UNITEDHEALTHCARE LIFE INS CO	WI	244.3
UNUM INS CO	ME	63.9
WEA INS CORP	WI	684.6
WILCAC LIFE INS CO	IL	2,279.6
WILCO LIFE INS CO	IN	2,811.9
WILLIAM PENN LIFE INS CO OF NEW YORK	NY	1,190.2
WILTON REASSURANCE CO	MN	19,124.8
ZURICH AMERICAN LIFE INS CO	IL	14,241.3
Rating: C-		
AMERICAN CENTURY LIFE INS CO TX	TX	7.4
AMERICAN HOME LIFE INS CO	KS	263.0

INSURANCE COMPANY NAME	DOM. STATE	TOTAL ASSETS ($MIL)

Rating: C- (Continued)

INSURANCE COMPANY NAME	DOM. STATE	TOTAL ASSETS ($MIL)
AMERICAN INTEGRITY LIFE INS CO	AR	1.4
BANKERS LIFE INS CO	FL	385.7
COLONIAL LIFE INS CO OF TX	TX	20.1
CONTINENTAL LIFE INS CO	PA	27.7
COOPERATIVA DE SEGUROS DE VIDA DE PR	PR	511.4
FEDERAL LIFE INS CO	IL	241.1
FRINGE BENEFIT LIFE INS CO	TX	27.2
GENWORTH LIFE & ANNUITY INS CO	VA	22,016.7
GREAT WESTERN INS CO	UT	1,402.4
KENTUCKY HOME LIFE INS CO	KY	5.2
LIFE ASSURANCE CO INC	OK	4.1
MAPFRE LIFE INS CO OF PR	PR	58.5
MOUNTAIN LIFE INS CO	TN	6.0
MULTINATIONAL LIFE INS CO	PR	118.1
PURITAN LIFE INS CO	TX	23.6
RABENHORST LIFE INS CO	LA	30.7
SAGICOR LIFE INS CO	TX	1,419.5
SECURITY PLAN LIFE INS CO	LA	307.0
SENTINEL SECURITY LIFE INS CO	UT	1,103.6
SHERIDAN LIFE INS CO	OK	2.2
SURETY LIFE & CASUALTY INS CO	ND	12.6
TEXAS SERVICE LIFE INS CO	TX	88.9
TOWN & COUNTRY LIFE INS CO	UT	7.8
TRANS CITY LIFE INS CO	AZ	19.4
UNITY FINANCIAL LIFE INS CO	OH	295.8
USA INS CO	MS	3.9
WICHITA NATIONAL LIFE INS CO	OK	15.7

Rating: D+

INSURANCE COMPANY NAME	DOM. STATE	TOTAL ASSETS ($MIL)
AMERICAN CENTURY LIFE INS CO	OK	84.3
AMERICAN LIFE & ANNUITY CO	AR	53.4
ATLANTA LIFE INS CO	GA	22.7
BANKERS LIFE & CAS CO	IL	15,550.0
BANKERS LIFE INS CO OF AMERICA	TX	6.1
CENTRAL SECURITY LIFE INS CO	TX	87.2
COLONIAL PENN LIFE INS CO	PA	871.8
COLONIAL SECURITY LIFE INS CO	TX	2.7
LIBERTY BANKERS LIFE INS CO	OK	1,974.6
MARQUETTE INDEMNITY & LIFE INS CO	AZ	5.6
PRUDENTIAL LEGACY INS CO OF NJ	NJ	59,813.8
PURITAN LIFE INS CO OF AMERICA	TX	130.4
SENIOR LIFE INS CO	GA	63.6
SOUTHERN FINANCIAL LIFE INS CO	LA	128.2
SOUTHERN SECURITY LIFE INS CO INC	MS	1.6
SOUTHLAND NATIONAL INS CORP	NC	360.7
STATE MUTUAL INS CO	GA	188.6
T J M LIFE INS CO	TX	17.2
USA LIFE ONE INS CO OF INDIANA	IN	33.8
WASHINGTON NATIONAL INS CO	IN	5,465.1
WESTERN AMERICAN LIFE INS CO	TX	26.7

Rating: D

INSURANCE COMPANY NAME	DOM. STATE	TOTAL ASSETS ($MIL)
ABILITY INS CO	NE	1,320.8

INSURANCE COMPANY NAME	DOM. STATE	TOTAL ASSETS ($MIL)
ALABAMA LIFE REINS CO INC	AL	24.3
AMERICAN FINANCIAL SECURITY L I C	MO	14.3
AMERICAN LABOR LIFE INS CO	AZ	10.4
ARKANSAS BANKERS LIFE INS CO	AR	2.6
BANKERS CONSECO LIFE INS CO	NY	494.3
BENEVOLENT LIFE INS CO INC	LA	2.1
CICA LIFE INS CO OF AMERICA	CO	169.5
CINCINNATI EQUITABLE LIFE INS CO	OH	154.8
CONSTITUTION LIFE INS CO	TX	393.5
COOPERATIVE LIFE INS CO	AR	6.9
DAKOTA CAPITAL LIFE INS CO	ND	7.2
EMPLOYERS REASSURANCE CORP	KS	13,630.6
FAMILY LIBERTY LIFE INS CO	TX	34.9
FIRST GUARANTY INS CO	LA	54.2
FOUNDATION LIFE INS CO OF AR	AR	5.5
HAWTHORN LIFE INS CO	TX	10.1
HAYMARKET INS CO	NE	1,016.4
INDEPENDENCE LIFE & ANNUITY CO	DE	3,172.7
INDIVIDUAL ASR CO LIFE HEALTH & ACC	OK	26.6
JEFF DAVIS MORTUARY BENEFIT ASSOC	LA	7.9
JEFFERSON LIFE INS CO	TX	2.2
LIFE INS CO OF LOUISIANA	LA	10.4
LIFESECURE INS CO	MI	404.4
MAJESTIC LIFE INS CO	LA	12.8
MEDICAL BENEFITS MUTUAL LIFE INS CO	OH	14.9
MELANCON LIFE INS CO	LA	10.8
MEMORIAL INS CO OF AMERICA	AR	1.1
MULHEARN PROTECTIVE INS CO	LA	12.4
NASSAU LIFE & ANNUITY CO	CT	31.0
PELLERIN LIFE INS CO	LA	11.8
PHL VARIABLE INS CO	CT	6,103.7
PROFESSIONAL INS CO	TX	109.9
PYRAMID LIFE INS CO	KS	72.6
ROYALTY CAPITAL LIFE INS CO	MO	3.6
SECURICO LIFE INS CO	TX	2.3
SECURITY NATIONAL LIFE INS CO	UT	662.8
STANDARD LIFE & CAS INS CO	UT	31.1
SUN LIFE & HEALTH INS CO	MI	955.2
SUN LIFE ASR CO OF CANADA	MI	18,767.4
SURETY LIFE INS CO	NE	18.8
TEXAS REPUB LIFE INS CO	TX	7.2
TRIPLE-S BLUE II	PR	14.8
UNITED FUNERAL BENEFIT LIFE INS CO	OK	48.0
UNITED FUNERAL DIR BENEFIT LIC	TX	118.5
UNIVERSAL FIDELITY LIFE INS CO	OK	15.5
US ALLIANCE LIFE & SECURITY CO	KS	28.0

Rating: D-

INSURANCE COMPANY NAME	DOM. STATE	TOTAL ASSETS ($MIL)
CAPITOL SECURITY LIFE INS CO	TX	4.3
FINANCIAL AMERICAN LIFE INS CO	KS	3.5
FIRST CONTINENTAL LIFE & ACC INS CO	TX	3.0
JACKSON GRIFFIN INS CO	AR	12.8
K-TENN INSURANCE CO	TN	2.2
MCS LIFE INS CO	PR	92.7

INSURANCE COMPANY NAME	DOM. STATE	TOTAL ASSETS ($MIL)	INSURANCE COMPANY NAME	DOM. STATE	TOTAL ASSETS ($MIL)
Rating: D- (Continued)			CANYON STATE LIFE INS CO	AZ	--
			CAREAMERICA LIFE INS CO	CA	--
NASSAU LIFE INSURANCE CO	NY	12,246.6	CASS COUNTY LIFE INSURANCE CO	TX	--
REGAL LIFE OF AMERICA INS CO	TX	7.4	CATERPILLAR LIFE INS CO	MO	--
SOUTHWEST SERVICE LIFE INS CO	TX	11.8	CIGNA ARBOR LIFE INS CO	CT	--
TRINITY LIFE INS CO	OK	230.9	CLEAR SPRING LIFE INS CO	TX	--
UNITED ASR LIFE INS CO	TX	2.3	COMMENCEMENT BAY RISK MGMT INS	WA	--
Rating: E+			COMMONWEALTH DEALERS LIFE INS CO	VA	--
			CONSECO LIFE INS CO OF TX	TX	--
DELTA LIFE INS CO	GA	65.0	CORVESTA LIFE INS CO	AZ	--
DIRECTORS LIFE ASR CO	OK	36.4	DESTINY HEALTH INS CO	IL	--
ELAN INSURANCE USVI INC	VI	2.6	DL REINSURANCE CO	DE	--
FIDELITY STANDARD LIFE INS CO	AR	3.4	EDUCATORS LIFE INS CO OF AMERICA	IL	--
KILPATRICK LIFE INS CO	LA	193.2	EQUITABLE NATIONAL LIFE INS CO	CT	--
LILY LIFE INS CO	TX	2.0	EVERENCE INS CO	IN	--
NETCARE LIFE & HEALTH INS CO	GU	29.0	EVERGREEN LIFE INS CO	TX	--
RELIABLE LIFE INS CO	LA	7.7	FAMILY SERVICE LIFE INS CO	TX	--
SCOTTISH RE US INC	DE	1,556.8	FINANCIAL ASSURANCE LIFE INS CO	TX	--
UNITED SECURITY ASR CO OF PA	PA	26.4	FIRST DIMENSION LIFE INS CO INC	OK	--
Rating: E			FIRST LANDMARK LIFE INS CO	NE	--
			FORETHOUGHT NATIONAL LIFE INS CO	TX	--
AMERICAN HOME LIFE INS CO	AR	22.6	GENWORTH INSURANCE CO	NC	--
CROWN GLOBAL INS CO OF AMERICA	DE	661.2	GMHP HEALTH INS LMTD	GU	--
INVESTORS PREFERRED LIFE INS CO	SD	478.0	GREAT WESTERN LIFE INS CO	MT	--
LOMBARD INTL LIFE ASR CO	PA	7,065.7	GRIFFIN LEGGETT BURIAL INS CO	AR	--
SMITH BURIAL & LIFE INS CO	AR	4.7	GULF STATES LIFE INS CO INC	LA	--
UNION FIDELITY LIFE INS CO	KS	20,226.2	IBC LIFE INS CO	TX	--
WILLIAMS PROGRESSIVE LIFE & ACC I C	LA	11.1	INDEPENDENCE INS INC	DE	--
Rating: E-			INTERNATIONAL AMERICAN LIFE INS CO	TX	--
			JRD LIFE INS CO	AZ	--
AMERICAN LIFE & SECURITY CORP	NE	21.1	LANDCAR LIFE INS CO	UT	--
NORTH CAROLINA MUTUAL LIFE INS CO	NC	26.7	LASSO HEALTHCARE INSURANCE CO	TX	--
RHODES LIFE INS CO OF LA INC	LA	3.8	LEGACY LIFE INS CO OF MO	MO	--
SENIOR HEALTH INS CO OF PENNSYLVANIA	PA	2,688.5	LIFE ASR CO OF AMERICA	IL	--
Rating: F			LOMBARD INTL LIFE ASR CO OF NY	NY	--
			MELLON LIFE INS CO	DE	--
AMERICAN COMMUNITY MUT INS CO	MI	--	METLIFE INSURANCE LTD	GU	--
CONCERT HEALTH PLAN INS CO	IL	--	MILILANI LIFE INS CO	HI	--
FIDELITY MUTUAL LIFE INS CO	PA	--	MUNICH RE US LIFE CORP	GA	--
FREMONT LIFE INS CO	CA	--	NATIONAL PROSPERITY L&H INS CO	TX	--
GERTRUDE GEDDES WILLIS LIFE INS CO	LA	--	OMAHA HEALTH INS CO	NE	--
GREAT REPUBLIC LIFE INS CO	WA	--	PACIFIC CENTURY LIFE INS CORP	AZ	--
HIGGINBOTHAM BURIAL INS CO	AR	--	PAN AMERICAN ASR CO INTL INC	FL	--
JORDAN FUNERAL & INS CO INC	AL	--	PINE BELT LIFE INS CO	MS	--
LONE STAR LIFE INS CO	TX	--	PIONEER MILITARY INS CO	NV	--
MONARCH LIFE INS CO	MA	669.5	PREFERRED SECURITY LIFE INS CO	TX	--
Rating: U			PRINCIPAL LIFE INS CO IOWA	IA	--
			REGAL REINSURANCE COMPANY	MA	--
ACADEME INC	WA	--	RELIABLE SERVICE INS CO	LA	--
AGC LIFE INS CO	MO	--	RELIANCE STANDARD LIFE INS CO OF TX	TX	--
ALL SAVERS LIFE INS CO OF CA	CA	--	RESOURCE LIFE INS CO	IL	--
ALLIED FINANCIAL INS CO	TX	--	SENTINEL AMERICAN LIFE INS CO	TX	--
AMERICAN CREDITORS LIFE INS CO	DE	--	SERVICE LIFE & CAS INS CO	TX	--
ATHENE LIFE INS CO	DE	--	SOUTHERN FIDELITY LIFE INS CO	AR	--
BLUE SPIRIT INS CO	VT	--			
CALPERS LONG-TERM CARE PROGRAM		--			

INSURANCE COMPANY NAME	DOM. STATE	TOTAL ASSETS ($MIL)	INSURANCE COMPANY NAME	DOM. STATE	TOTAL ASSETS ($MIL)
Rating: U (Continued)					
SOUTHWEST CREDIT LIFE INC	NM	--			
SQUIRE REASSURANCE CO LLC	MI	--			
STATE FARM HEALTH INS CO	IL	--			
STRUCTURED ANNUITY RE CO	IA	--			
TALCOTT RESOLUTION INTL LIFE	CT	--			
TIER ONE INSURANCE CO	OK	--			
TRANS-WESTERN LIFE INS CO	TX	--			
UBS LIFE INS CO USA	CA	--			
UNITED BENEFIT LIFE INS CO	OH	--			
UNIVANTAGE INS CO	UT	--			

Section VI

Rating Upgrades
and Downgrades

A list of all

U.S. Life and Annuity Insurers

receiving a rating upgrade or downgrade
during the current quarter.

Section VI Contents

This section identifies those companies receiving a rating change since the previous edition of this publication, whether it be a rating upgrade, rating downgrade, newly-rated company or the withdrawal of a rating. A rating may be withdrawn due to a merger, dissolution, liquidation or lack of information. A rating upgrade or downgrade may entail a change from one letter grade to another, or it may mean the addition or deletion of a plus or minus sign within the same letter grade previously assigned to the company. Each rating upgrade and downgrade is accompanied by a brief explanation of why the rating was changed. Ratings are normally updated once each quarter of the year. In some instances, however, a company's rating may be downgraded outside of the normal updates due to overriding circumstances. The tables for new and withdrawn ratings will contain some or all of the following information:

1. **Insurance Company Name**

The legally registered name, which can sometimes differ from the name that the company uses for advertising. An insurer's name can be very similar to that of another, so verify the company's exact name and state of domicile to make sure you are looking at the correct company.

2. **Domicile State**

The state which has primary regulatory responsibility for the company. It may differ from the location of the company's corporate headquarters. You do not have to be living in the domicile state to purchase insurance from this firm, provided it is licensed to do business in your state.

3. **Total Assets**

All assets admitted by state insurance regulators in millions of dollars. This includes investments, current business assets, and separate accounts.

4. **New Safety Rating**

The rating assigned to the company as of the date of this Guide's publication. Our rating is measured on a scale from A to F and considers a wide range of factors. Highly rated companies are, in our opinion, less likely to experience financial difficulties than lower-rated firms. See *About Weiss Safety Ratings* for more information.

5. **Previous Safety Rating**

The rating assigned to the company prior to its most recent change.

6. **Date of Change**

The date that the rating upgrade or downgrade officially occurred. Normally, all rating changes are put into effect on a single day each quarter of the year. In some instances, however, a rating may have been changed outside of this normal update.

New Ratings

INSURANCE COMPANY NAME	DOM. STATE	TOTAL ASSETS ($MIL)	NEW RATING	PREVIOUS RATING	DATE OF CHANGE

No new ratings are being released in this edition.

Withdrawn Ratings

INSURANCE COMPANY NAME	DOM. STATE	TOTAL ASSETS ($MIL)	NEW RATING	PREVIOUS RATING	DATE OF CHANGE
KANAWHA INS CO	SC	2,234.9	U	B	01/15/19

Rating Upgrades

ALABAMA LIFE REINS CO INC was upgraded to D from E+ in January 2019 based on an improved capitalization index, a higher five-year profitability index and a markedly improved stability index.

AXA EQUITABLE LIFE & ANNUITY CO was upgraded to B from C in January 2019 based on a greatly improved capitalization index and a greatly improved investment safety index.

CHESAPEAKE LIFE INS CO was upgraded to B+ from B in January 2019 based on a higher capitalization index and a higher five-year profitability index.

CIGNA WORLDWIDE INS CO was upgraded to B- from C in January 2019 based on a greatly improved capitalization index, a greatly improved investment safety index, a higher five-year profitability index and a higher stability index.

CONTINENTAL LIFE INS CO was upgraded to C- from D+ in January 2019 based on a higher capitalization index, a markedly improved five-year profitability index and a higher stability index.

DIRECTORS LIFE ASR CO was upgraded to E+ from E in January 2019 based on an improved capitalization index, a higher five-year profitability index and a markedly improved stability index.

ENTERPRISE LIFE INS CO was upgraded to B+ from B in January 2019 based on a higher capitalization index and a markedly improved stability index. enhanced financial strength of affiliates in Credit Suisse Group.

GENERAL FIDELITY LIFE INS CO was upgraded to C from C- in January 2019 based on a higher stability index. enhanced financial strength of affiliates in Bank of America Corp Group.

GUARANTY INCOME LIFE INS CO was upgraded to B from B- in January 2019 based on a higher investment safety index and a higher stability index.

JACKSON GRIFFIN INS CO was upgraded to D- from E in January 2019 based on a markedly improved capitalization index, a markedly improved investment safety index and a greatly improved stability index.

MEDAMERICA INS CO OF FL was upgraded to B from B- in January 2019 based on a higher capitalization index and a higher five-year profitability index. composite rating for affiliated Lifetime Healthcare Inc Group rose to B from B-.

MID-WEST NATIONAL LIFE INS CO OF TN was upgraded to C+ from C in January 2019 based on a higher five-year profitability index and an improved stability index. composite rating for affiliated Blackstone Investor Group rose to B from B-, notably the recent upgrade of affiliated company CHESAPEAKE LIFE INS CO to B+ from B.

MOLINA HEALTHCARE OF TEXAS INS CO was upgraded to C+ from C in January 2019 based on capitalization index. enhanced financial strength of affiliates in Molina Healthcare Inc Group.

NASSAU LIFE & ANNUITY CO was upgraded to D from D- in January 2019 based on capitalization index, a markedly improved five-year profitability index and a higher stability index.

NIPPON LIFE INS CO OF AMERICA was upgraded to A- from B in January 2019 based on a markedly improved five-year profitability index.

NORTH AMERICAN INS CO was upgraded to B+ from B in January 2019 based on a higher capitalization index, a markedly improved five-year profitability index and an improved stability index.

RELIASTAR LIFE INS CO was upgraded to B- from C+ in January 2019 based on an improved capitalization index, an improved investment safety index and an improved five-year profitability index. enhanced financial strength of affiliates in Voya Financial Inc Group.

SECURITY LIFE OF DENVER INS CO was upgraded to B- from C+ in January 2019 based on a higher five-year profitability index. enhanced financial strength of affiliates in Voya Financial Inc Group, notably the recent upgrade of affiliated company RELIASTAR LIFE INS CO to B- from C+.

SUN LIFE ASR CO OF CANADA was upgraded to D from D- in January 2019 based on a higher capitalization index, a higher investment safety index, a higher five-year profitability index and a markedly improved stability index.

US ALLIANCE LIFE & SECURITY CO was upgraded to D from D- in January 2019 based on a higher capitalization index and an improved five-year profitability index.

WESTERN AMERICAN LIFE INS CO was upgraded to D+ from D in January 2019 based on an improved capitalization index, an improved investment safety index and a higher stability index. enhanced financial strength of affiliates in Maximum Corporation Group.

Rating Downgrades

AMERICAN LIFE & SECURITY CORP was downgraded to E- from E+ in January 2019 due to a substantially lower capitalization index, a substantially lower investment safety index and a significant decline in its five-year profitability index.

AMERICAN MATURITY LIFE INS CO was downgraded to B- from B in January 2019 due to a significant decline in its stability index.

CINCINNATI EQUITABLE LIFE INS CO was downgraded to D from C- in January 2019 due to capitalization index and a significant decline in its five-year profitability index.

FIRST RELIANCE STANDARD LIFE INS CO was downgraded to A- from A in January 2019 due to a lower five-year profitability index. In addition, the composite rating for affiliated Tokio Marine Holdings Inc Group fell to C+ from B-.

GENERAL RE LIFE CORP was downgraded to C from C+ in January 2019 due to a substantially lower capitalization index and a declining investment safety index.

HUMANA INS CO OF PUERTO RICO INC was downgraded to C+ from B in January 2019 due to a significant decline in its stability index. In addition, the composite rating for affiliated Humana Inc Group fell to B from B+.

RX LIFE INSURANCE CO was downgraded to C+ from B in January 2019 due to a substantially lower stability index. In addition, the composite rating for affiliated Calton Holdings LLC Group fell to C+ from B.

SOUTHERN PIONEER LIFE INS CO was downgraded to A- from A in January 2019 due to a significant decline in its stability index.

SOUTHLAND NATIONAL INS CORP was downgraded to D+ from C- in January 2019 due to a declining capitalization index, a significant decline in its investment safety index, a declining five-year profitability index and a declining stability index. In addition, the financial strength of affiliates in SNA Capital LLC is declining Group.

Appendix

State Guaranty Associations

The states have established insurance guaranty associations to help pay claims to policyholders of failed insurance companies. However, there are several cautions which you must be aware of with respect to this coverage:

1. Most of the guaranty associations do not set aside funds in advance. Rather, states assess contributions from other insurance companies after an insolvency occurs.

2. There can be an unacceptably long delay before claims are paid.

3. Each state is governed by its own legislation, providing a wide range of coverage and conditions that may apply. According to the National Organization of Life and Health Guaranty Associations (NOLHGA), the issues are extremely complex with unique variables for each individual state.

4. The table on the following page is designed to help you sort out these issues. However, it is not intended to handle all of them. If your carrier has failed and you need a complete answer, we recommend you contact your State Insurance Official or NOLHGA at 703-481-5206.

State guaranty associations are set up to cover policyholders residing in their own state. This essentially means that each individual state is responsible for policyholders residing in that state, no matter where the insolvent insurer is domiciled.

Non-resident coverage is provided only under certain circumstances listed in the state's statutes. The general conditions are typically as follows:

a) The insurer of the policyholder must be domiciled and licensed in the state in which the non-resident is seeking coverage;

b) When the contracts were sold, the insurers that issued the policies were not licensed in the state in which the policyholder resides;

c) The non-resident policyholder is not eligible for coverage from his or her state of residence;

d) The state where the policyholder resides must have a guaranty association similar to that of the state in which he or she is seeking non-resident coverage.

Warning: Be sure to contact the specific state guaranty association for information in that state's laws. Conditions and limitations are subject to individual state statutes and can change.

Following is a brief explanation of each of the columns in the table.

1. **Maximum Aggregate Benefits for All Lines of Insurance**   The maximum amount payable by the State Guaranty Fund to cover all types of insurance including life insurance, health insurance, disability and annuities.

2. **Maximum Death Benefit with Respect to Any One Life**   The maximum amount payable by the State Guaranty Fund for a death claim on a single life. If the policy benefits are higher than the Guaranty Fund's coverage limits, policyholders may typically be able to file a claim with the court-appointed Liquidator of the insolvent insurance company to try to recover the difference. But success is uncertain.

3. **Liability for Cash or Withdrawal Value of Life Insurance Policy**   The maximum cash value or withdrawal value the Guaranty Fund will assume responsibility for related to an individual life insurance policy.

4. **Maximum Liability for Present Value of an Annuity Contract**   The maximum cash value or withdrawal value the Guaranty Fund will assume responsibility for related to an individual annuity contract. The coverage may be higher if the annuity is in the payout phase.

Coverage of State Guaranty Funds

State	Max. Aggregate Benefits for All Lines of Insurance	Max. Death Benefit with Respect to Any One Life	Max. Liability for Cash or Withdrawal Value of Life Insurance Policy	Max. Liability for Present Value of an Annuity Contract	State Guaranty Association Phone Numbers	State Guaranty Web Address
Alabama	$300,000	$300,000	$100,000	$250,000	(205) 879-2202	www.allifega.org
Alaska	$300,000	$300,000	$100,000	$100,000	(907) 243-2311	www.aklifega.org
Arizona	$300,000	$300,000	$100,000	$250,000	(602) 364-3863	www.id.state.az.us
Arkansas	$300,000	$300,000	$300,000	$300,000	(501) 375-9151	www.arlifega.org
California	80% not to exceed $300,000	80% not to exceed $300,000	80% not to exceed $100,000	80% not to exceed $250,000	(323) 782-0182	www.califega.org
Colorado	$300,000	$300,000	$100,000	$250,000	(303) 292-5022	www.colifega.org
Connecticut	$500,000	$500,000	$500,000	$500,000	(860) 647-1054	www.ctlifega.org
Delaware	$300,000	$300,000	$100,000	$250,000	(302) 456-3656	www.delifega.org
Dist. of Col.	$300,000	$300,000	$100,000	$300,000	(202) 434-8771	www.dclifega.org
Florida	$300,000	$300,000	$100,000	$250,000	(904) 398-3644	www.flahiga.org
Georgia	$300,000	$300,000	$100,000	$250,000	(770) 621-9835	www.gaiga.org
Hawaii	$300,000	$300,000	$100,000	$100,000	(808) 528-5400	www.hilifega.org
Idaho	$300,000	$300,000	$100,000	$250,000	(208) 378-9510	www.idlifega.org
Illinois	$300,000	$300,000	$100,000	$250,000	(773) 714-8050	www.ilhiga.org
Indiana	$300,000	$300,000	$100,000	$100,000	(317) 692-0574	www.inlifega.org
Iowa	$300,000	$300,000	$100,000	$250,000	(515) 248-5712	www.ialifega.org
Kansas	$300,000	$300,000	$100,000	$250,000	(785) 271-1199	www.kslifega.org
Kentucky	$300,000	$300,000	$100,000	$250,000	(502) 895-5915	www.klhiga.org
Louisiana	$500,000	$300,000	$100,000	$250,000	(225) 381-0656	www.lalifega.org
Maine	$300,000	$300,000	$100,000	$250,000	(207) 633-1090	www.melifega.org
Maryland	$300,000	$300,000	$100,000	$250,000	(410) 248-0407	www.mdlifega.org
Massachusetts	$300,000	$300,000	$100,000	$250,000	(413) 744-8483	www.malifega.org
Michigan	$300,000	$300,000	$100,000	$250,000	(517) 339-1755	www.milifega.org
Minnesota	$500,000	$500,000	$130,000	$250,000	(651) 407-3149	www.mnlifega.org
Mississippi	$300,000	$300,000	$100,000	$100,000	(601) 981-0755	www.mslifega.org
Missouri	$300,000	$300,000	$100,000	$100,000	(573) 634-8455	www.mo-iga.org
Montana	$300,000	$300,000	$100,000	$250,000	(262) 965-5761	www.mtlifega.org
Nebraska	$300,000	$300,000	$100,000	$250,000	(402) 474-6900	www.nelifega.org
Nevada	$300,000	$300,000	$100,000	$250,000	(775) 329-8387	www.nvlifega.org
New Hampshire	$300,000	$300,000	$100,000	$100,000	(603) 472-3734	www.nhlifega.org
New Jersey	$500,000	$500,000	$100,000	$100,000	(732) 345-5200	www.njlifega.org
New Mexico	$300,000	$300,000	$100,000	$250,000	(505) 820-7355	www.nmlifega.org
New York	$500,000	$500,000	$500,000	$500,000	(212) 202-4243	www.nylifega.org
North Carolina	$300,000	$300,000	$300,000	$300,000	(919) 833-6838	www.nclifega.org
North Dakota	$300,000	$300,000	$100,000	$250,000	(701) 235-4108	www.ndlifega.org
Ohio	$300,000	$300,000	$100,000	$250,000	(614) 442-6601	www.olhiga.org
Oklahoma	$300,000	$300,000	$100,000	$300,000	(405) 272-9221	www.oklifega.org
Oregon	$300,000	$300,000	$100,000	$250,000	(855) 378-9510	www.orlifega.org
Pennsylvania	$300,000	$300,000	$100,000	$100,000	(610) 975-0572	www.palifega.org
Puerto Rico	$300,000	$300,000	$100,000	$100,000	(787) 765-2095	www.ocs.gobierno.pr
Rhode Island	$300,000	$300,000	$100,000	$250,000	(401) 273-2921	www.rilifega.org
South Carolina	$300,000	$300,000	$300,000	$300,000	(803) 783-4947	www.sclifega.org
South Dakota	$300,000	$300,000	$100,000	$250,000	(605) 336-0177	www.sdlifega.org
Tennessee	$300,000	$300,000	$100,000	$250,000	(615) 242-8758	www.tnlifega.org
Texas	$300,000	$300,000	$100,000	$250,000	(512) 476-5101	www.txlifega.org
Utah	$500,000	$500,000	$200,000	$200,000	(801) 302-9955	www.utlifega.org
Vermont	$300,000	$300,000	$100,000	$250,000	(802) 249-0284	www.vtlifega.org
Virginia	$350,000	$300,000	$100,000	$250,000	(804) 282-2240	www.valifega.org
Washington	$500,000	$500,000	$500,000	$500,000	(360) 426-6744	www.walifega.org
West Virginia	$300,000	$300,000	$100,000	$250,000	(304) 733-6904	www.wvlifega.org
Wisconsin	$300,000	$300,000	$300,000	$300,000	(608) 242-9473	www.wilifega.org
Wyoming	$500,000	$300,000	$100,000	$250,000	(303) 292-5022	www.wylifega.org

State Insurance Commissioners'
Website and Departmental Phone Numbers

State	Official's Title	Website Address	Phone Number
Alabama	Commissioner	www.aldoi.org	(334) 269-3550
Alaska	Director	https://www.commerce.alaska.gov/web/ins/	(800) 467-8725
Arizona	Director	https://insurance.az.gov/	(602) 364-2499
Arkansas	Commissioner	www.insurance.arkansas.gov	(800) 282-9134
California	Commissioner	www.insurance.ca.gov	(800) 927-4357
Colorado	Commissioner	https://www.colorado.gov/dora/division-insurance	(800) 886-7675
Connecticut	Commissioner	http://www.ct.gov/cid/site/default.asp	(800) 203-3447
Delaware	Commissioner	http://delawareinsurance.gov/	(800) 282-8611
Dist. of Columbia	Commissioner	http://disb.dc.gov/	(202) 727-8000
Florida	Commissioner	www.floir.com/	(850) 413-3140
Georgia	Commissioner	www.oci.ga.gov/	(800) 656-2298
Hawaii	Commissioner	http://cca.hawaii.gov/ins/	(808) 586-2790
Idaho	Director	www.doi.idaho.gov	(800) 721-3272
Illinois	Director	www.insurance.illinois.gov/	(866) 445-5364
Indiana	Commissioner	www.in.gov/idoi/	(317) 232-2385
Iowa	Commissioner	www.iid.state.ia.us	(877) 955-1212
Kansas	Commissioner	www.ksinsurance.org	(800) 432-2484
Kentucky	Commissioner	http://insurance.ky.gov/	(800) 595-6053
Louisiana	Commissioner	www.ldi.la.gov/	(800) 259-5300
Maine	Superintendent	www.maine.gov/pfr/insurance/	(800) 300-5000
Maryland	Commissioner	http://insurance.maryland.gov/Pages/default.aspx	(800) 492-6116
Massachusetts	Commissioner	www.mass.gov/ocabr/government/oca-agencies/doi-lp/	(877) 563-4467
Michigan	Director	http://www.michigan.gov/difs	(877) 999-6442
Minnesota	Commissioner	http://mn.gov/commerce/	(651) 539-1500
Mississippi	Commissioner	http://www.mid.ms.gov/	(601) 359-3569
Missouri	Director	www.insurance.mo.gov	(800) 726-7390
Montana	Commissioner	http://csimt.gov/	(800) 332-6148
Nebraska	Director	www.doi.nebraska.gov/	(402) 471-2201
Nevada	Commissioner	www.doi.nv.gov/	(888) 872-3234
New Hampshire	Commissioner	www.nh.gov/insurance/	(800) 852-3416
New Jersey	Commissioner	www.state.nj.us/dobi/	(800) 446-7467
New Mexico	Superintendent	www.osi.state.nm.us/	(855) 427-5674
New York	Superintendent	www.dfs.ny.gov/	(800) 342-3736
North Carolina	Commissioner	www.ncdoi.com	(800) 546-5664
North Dakota	Commissioner	www.nd.gov/ndins	(800) 247-0560
Ohio	Lieutenant Governor	www.insurance.ohio.gov/	(800) 686-1526
Oklahoma	Commissioner	www.ok.gov/oid/	(800) 522-0071
Oregon	Insurance Commissioner	www.oregon.gov/dcbs/insurance/Pages/index.aspx	(888) 877-4894
Pennsylvania	Commissioner	www.insurance.pa.gov/	(877) 881-6388
Puerto Rico	Commissioner	www.ocs.gobierno.pr	(787) 304-8686
Rhode Island	Superintendent	www.dbr.state.ri.us/divisions/insurance/	(401) 462-9500
South Carolina	Director	www.doi.sc.gov	(803) 737-6160
South Dakota	Director	http://dlr.sd.gov/insurance/default.aspx	(605) 773-3563
Tennessee	Commissioner	www.tn.gov/insurance/	(615) 741-2241
Texas	Commissioner	www.tdi.texas.gov/	(800) 252-3439
Utah	Commissioner	www.insurance.utah.gov	(800) 439-3805
Vermont	Commissioner	www.dfr.vermont.gov/	(802) 828-3301
Virgin Islands	Lieutenant Governor	http://ltg.gov.vi/division-of-banking-and-insurance.html	(340) 774-7166
Virginia	Commissioner	www.scc.virginia.gov/boi/	(804) 371-9741
Washington	Commissioner	www.insurance.wa.gov	(800) 562-6900
West Virginia	Commissioner	www.wvinsurance.gov	(888) 879-9842
Wisconsin	Commissioner	oci.wi.gov	(800) 236-8517
Wyoming	Commissioner	http://doi.wyo.gov/	(800) 438-5768

Risk-Adjusted Capital for Life and Annuity Insurers in Weiss Rating Model

Among the most important indicators used in the analysis of an individual company are our two risk-adjusted capital ratios, which are useful tools in determining exposure to investment, liquidity and insurance risk in relation to the capital the company has to cover those risks.

The first risk-adjusted capital ratio evaluates the company's ability to withstand a moderate loss scenario. The second ratio evaluates the company's ability to withstand a severe loss scenario.

In order to calculate these risk-adjusted capital ratios, we follow these steps:

1. Capital Resources
First, we add up all of the company's resources which could be used to cover losses. These include capital, surplus, the Asset Valuation Reserve (AVR), and a portion of the provision for future policyholders' dividends, where appropriate. Additional credit may also be given for the use of conservative reserving assumptions and other "hidden capital" when applicable.

2. Target Capital
Next, we determine the company's target capital. This answers the question: Based upon the company's level of risk in both its insurance business and its investment portfolio, how much capital would it need to cover potential losses during a moderate loss scenario? In other words, we determine how much capital we believe this company *should* have.

3. Risk-Adjusted Capital Ratio #1
We compare the results of step 1 with those of step 2. Specifically, we divide the "capital resources" by the "target capital" and express it in terms of a ratio. This ratio is called RACR #1. (See next page for more detail on methodology.)

If a company has a Risk-Adjusted Capital Ratio of 1.0 or more, it means the company has all of the capital we believe it requires to withstand potential losses which could be inflicted by a moderate loss scenario. If the company has less than 1.0, it does not currently have all of the basic capital resources we think it needs. During times of financial distress, companies often have access to additional capital through contributions from a parent company, current profits or reductions in policyholder dividends. Therefore, an allowance is made in our rating system for firms with somewhat less than 1.0 Risk-Adjusted Capital Ratios.

4. Risk-Adjusted Capital Ratio #2
We repeat steps 2 and 3, but now assuming a severe loss scenario. This ratio is called RACR #2.

5. Capitalization Index
We convert RACR #1 and #2 into an index. It is measured on a scale of zero to ten, with ten being the best and seven or better considered strong. A company whose capital, surplus and AVR equal its target capital will have a Risk-Adjusted Capital Ratio of 1.0 and a Risk-Adjusted Capital Index of 7.0.

How We Determine Target Capital

The basic procedure for determining target capital is to ask these questions:

1.   What is the breakdown of the company's investment portfolio and types of business?

2.   For each category, what are the potential losses which could be incurred in the loss scenario?

3.   In order to cover those potential losses, how much in capital resources does the company need? It stands to reason that more capital is needed as a cushion for losses on high-risk investments, such as junk bonds, than would be necessary for low-risk investments, such as AAA-rated utility bonds.

Unfortunately, the same questions we have raised about Wall Street rating systems with respect to how they rate insurance companies can be asked about the way they rate bonds. However, we do not rate bonds ourselves. Therefore, we must rely upon the bond ratings of other rating agencies. This is another reason why we have stricter capital requirements for the insurance companies. It accounts for the fact that they may need some extra protection in case an AAA-rated bond may not be quite as good as it appears to be.

Finally, target capital is adjusted for the company's spread of risk in the diversification of its investment portfolio, the size and number of the policies it writes and the diversification of its business.

Table 1 on the next page shows target capital percentages used in Weiss Risk-Adjusted Capital Ratios #1 and #2 (RACR #1 and RACR #2).

The percentages shown in the table answer the question: How much should the firm hold in capital resources for every $100 it has committed to each category? Several of the items in Table 1 are expressed as ranges. The actual percentages used in the calculation of target capital for an individual company may vary due to the levels of risks in the operations, investments or policy obligations of that specific company.

Table 1. Target Capital Percentages

Asset Risk		Weiss Ratings	
		RACR#1 (%)	RACR#2 (%)
Bonds			
	Government guaranteed bonds	0	0
	Class 1	.5-.75	1-1.5
	Class 2	2	5
	Class 3	5	15
	Class 4	10	30
	Class 5	20	60
	Class 6	20	60
Mortgages			
	In good standing	0.5	1
	90 days overdue	1.7-20	3.8-25
	In process of foreclosure	25-33	33-50
Real Estate			
	Class 1	20	50
	Class 2	10	33
Preferred Stock			
	Class 1	3	5
	Class 2	4	6
	Class 3	7	9
	Class 4	12	15
	Class 5	22	29
	Class 6	30	39
	Class 7	3-30	5-39
Common Stock			
	Unaffiliated	25	33
	Affiliated	25-100	33-100
Short-term investment		0.5	1
Premium notes		2	5
Collateral loans		2	5
Separate account equity		25	33
Other invested assets		5	10
Insurance Risk			
Individual life reserves*		.06-.15	.08-.21
Group life reserves*		.05-.12	.06-.16
Individual Health Premiums			
	Class 1	12-20	15-25
	Class 2	9.6	12
	Class 3	6.4	8
	Class 4	12-28	15-35
	Class 5	12-20	15-25
Group Health Premiums			
	Class 1	5.6-12	7-15
	Class 2	20	25
	Class 3	9.6	12
	Class 4	6.4	8
	Class 5	12-20	15-25
Managed care credit		5-40	6-50
Premiums subject to rate guarantees		100-209	120-250
Individual claim reserves		4	5
Group claim reserves		4	5
Reinsurance		0-2	0-5
Interest Rate Risk			
Policy loans		0-2	0-5
Life reserves		1-2	1-3
Individual annuity reserves		1-3	1-5
Group annuity reserves		1-2	1-3
Guaranteed interest contract reserves		1-2	1-3

All numbers are shown for illustrative purposes. Figures actually used in the formula vary annually based on industry experience.
*Based on net amount at risk.

Investment Class

Descriptions

Government guaranteed bonds		Guaranteed bonds issued by U.S. and other governments which receive the top rating of state insurance commissioners.
Bonds	Class 1	Investment grade bonds rated AAA, AA or A by Moody's or Standard & Poor's or deemed AAA - A equivalent by state insurance commissioners.
	Class 2	Investment grade bonds with some speculative elements, rated BBB or equivalent.
	Class 3	Noninvestment grade bonds, rated BB or equivalent.
	Class 4	Noninvestment grade bonds, rated B or equivalent.
	Class 5	Noninvestment grade bonds, rated CCC, CC or C or equivalent.
	Class 6	Noninvestment grade bonds, in or near default.
Mortgages		Mortgages in good standing
		Mortgages 90 days past due
		Mortgages in process of foreclosure
Real Estate	Class 1	Properties acquired in satisfaction of debt.
	Class 2	Company occupied and other investment properties.
Preferred stock	Class 1	Highest quality unaffiliated preferred stock.
	Class 2	High quality unaffiliated preferred stock.
	Class 3	Medium quality unaffiliated preferred stock.
	Class 4	Low quality unaffiliated preferred stock.
	Class 5	Lowest quality unaffiliated preferred stock.
	Class 6	Unaffiliated preferred stock, in or near default.
	Class 7	Affiliated preferred stock.
Common stock		Unaffiliated common stock.
		Affiliated common stock.
Short-term investments		All investments whose maturities at the time of acquisition were one year or less.
Premium Notes		Loans for payment of premiums.
Collateral loans		Loans made to a company or individual where the underlying security is in the form of bonds, stocks, or other marketable securities.
Separate account assets		Investments held in an account segregated from the general assets of the company, generally used to provide variable annuity benefits.
Other invested assets		Any invested assets that do not fit under the main categories above.
Individual life reserves		Funds set aside for payment of life insurance benefits under an individual contract rather than a company or group, underwriting based on individual profile.
Group life reserves		Funds set aside for payment of life insurance benefits under a contract with at least 10 people whereby all members have a common interest and are joined for a reason other than to obtain insurance.
Individual health premiums	Class 1	Usual and customary hospital and medical premiums which include traditional medical reimbursement plans that are subject to annual rate increases based on the company's claims experience.
	Class 2	Medicare supplement, dental, and other limited benefits anticipating rate increases.
	Class 3	Hospital indemnity plans, accidental death and dismemberment policies, and other limited benefits not anticipating rate increases.
	Class 4	Noncancelable disability income.
	Class 5	Guaranteed renewable disability income.

Group health premiums	Class 1	Usual and customary hospital and medical premiums which include traditional medical reimbursement plans that are subject to annual rate increases based on the company's claims experience.
	Class 2	Stop loss and minimum premium where a known claims liability is minimal or nonexistent.
	Class 3	Medicare supplement, dental, and other limited benefits anticipating rate increases.
	Class 4	Hospital indemnity plans, accidental death and dismemberment policies, and other limited benefits not anticipating rate increases.
	Class 5	Disability Income.

Managed care credit	Premiums for HMO and PPO business which carry less risk than traditional indemnity business. Included in this credit are provider compensation arrangements such as salary, capitation and fixed payment per service.
Premiums subject to rate guarantees	Health insurance premiums from policies where the rate paid by the policyholder is guaranteed for a period of time, such as one year, 15 months, 27 months or 37 months.
Individual claim reserves	Accident and health reserves for claims on individual policies.
Group claim reserves	Accident and health reserves for claims on group policies.
Reinsurance	Amounts recoverable on paid and unpaid losses for all reinsurance ceded; unearned premiums on accident and health reinsurance ceded; and funds held with unauthorized reinsurers.
Policy loans	Loans against the cash value of a life insurance policy.
Life reserves	Reserves for life insurance claims net of reinsurance and policy loans.
Individual annuity reserves	Reserves held in order to pay off maturing individual annuities or those surrendered before maturity.
Group annuity reserves	Reserves held in order to pay off maturing group annuities or those surrendered before maturity.
GIC reserves	Reserves held to pay off maturing guaranteed interest contracts.

Table 2. Bond Default Rates - potential losses as a percent of bond portfolio

Bond Rating	(1) Moody's 15 Yr Rate (%)	(2) Moody's 12 Yr Rate (%)	(3) Worst Year (%)	(4) 3 Cum. Recession Years (%)	(5) Weiss 15 Year Rate (%)	(6) Assumed Loss Rate (%)	(7) Losses as % of Holdings (%)	(8) RACR #2 Rate (%)
Aaa	0.73	0.55	0.08	0.24	0.79	50	0.95	1.00
Aa	1.39	1.04	0.13	0.39	1.43	50	1.09	1.00
A	4.05	2.96	0.35	1.05	4.02	55	2.02	1.00
Baa	7.27	5.29	0.67	2.02	7.31	60	5.15	5.00
Ba	23.93	19.57	2.04	6.11	25.68	65	23.71	15.00
B	43.37	39.30	4.99	14.96	54.26	70	43.57	30.00

Comments On Target Capital Percentages

The factors that are chiefly responsible for the conservative results of our Risk-Adjusted Capital Ratios are the investment risks of bond Classes 2 - 6, mortgages, real estate and affiliate common stock as well as the interest rate risk for annuities and GICs. Comments on the basis of these figures are found below. Additional comments address factors that vary, based on particular performance or risk characteristics of the individual company.

Bonds   Target capital percentages for bonds are derived from a model that factors in historical cumulative bond default rates from the last 45 years and the additional loss potential during a prolonged economic decline. **Table 2** shows how this was done for each bond rating classification. A 15-year cumulative default rate is used (column 1), due to the 15-year average maturity at issue of bonds held by life insurance companies. These are historical default rates for 1970-2015 for each bond class, taken from *Moody's Annual Default Study*.

To factor in the additional loss potential of a severe three-year-long economic decline, we reduced the base to Moody's 12-year rate (column 2), determined the worst single year experience (column 3), extended that experience over three years (column 4), and added the historical 12-year rate to the 3-year projection to derive Weiss Ratings 15-year default rate (column 5).

The next step was to determine the losses that could be expected from these defaults. This would be equivalent to the capital a company should have to cover those losses. Loss rates were assigned for each bond class (column 6), based on the fact that higher-rated issues generally carry less debt and the fact that the debt is also better secured, leading to higher recovery rates upon default. Column 7 shows losses as a percent of holdings for each bond class. Column 8 shows the target capital percentages that are used in RACR #2 (Table 1, RACR #2 column, Bonds - classes 1 to 6).

Regulations limiting junk bond holdings of insurers to a set percent of assets are a tacit acknowledgement that the reserve requirements used by State Insurance Commissioners are inadequate. If the figure adequately represented full loss potential, there would be no need to limit holdings through legislation since an adequate loss reserve would provide sufficient capital to absorb potential losses.

Mortgages

Mortgage default rates for the Risk-Adjusted Capital Ratios are derived from historical studies of mortgage and real estate losses in selected depressed markets. The rate for RACR #2 (Table 1, RACR #2 column, Mortgages – 90 days overdue) will vary between 3.8 and 25%, based on the performance of the company's mortgage portfolio in terms of mortgage loans 90 days or more past due, in process of foreclosure and foreclosed during the previous year.

Real Estate

The 33% rate (Table 1, RACR #2 column, Real Estate – Class 2) used for potential real estate losses in Weiss ratios is based on historical losses in depressed markets.

Affiliate Common Stock

The target capital rate on affiliate common stock for RACR #2 can vary between 33% and 100% (Table 1, RACR #2 column, Common stock - Affiliate) depending on the financial strength of the affiliate and the prospects for obtaining capital from the affiliate should the need arise.

Insurance Risk

Calculations of target capital for insurance risk vary according to categories. For individual and group life insurance, target capital is a percentage of net amount at risk (total amount of insurance in force less reserves). Individual and group health insurance risk is calculated as a percentage of premium. Categories vary from "usual and customary hospital and medical premiums" where risk is relatively low, because losses from one year are recouped by annual rate increases to "noncancellable disability income" where the risk of loss is greater because disability benefits are paid in future years without the possibility of recovery.

Reinsurance

This factor varies with the quality of the reinsuring companies and the type of reinsurance being used (e.g. co-insurance, modified co-insurance, yearly renewable term, etc.).

Interest Rate Risk On Annuities

The 1 - 5% rate on individual annuities as a percentage of reserves (Table 1, RACR #2 column 3, Individual annuity reserves) and the 1 - 3% rate for group annuities as a percentage of reserves (Table 1, RACR #2 column 3, Group annuity reserves and GICs) are derived from studies of potential losses that can occur when assets and liabilities are not properly matched.

Companies are especially prone to losses in this area for one of two reasons: (1) They promise high interest rates on their annuities and have not locked in corresponding yields on their investments. If interest rates fall, the company will have difficulties earning the promised rate. (2) They lock in high returns on their investments but allow policy surrenders without market value adjustments. If market values decline and surrenders increase, liquidity problems can result in substantial losses.

The target capital figure used for each company is based on the surrender characteristics of its policies, the interest rate used in calculating reserves and the actuarial analysis found in New York Regulation 126 filing or similar studies where applicable.

RECENT INDUSTRY FAILURES
2018

Institution	Headquarters	Industry	Date of Failure	At Date of Failure	
				Total Assets ($Mil)	Safety Rating
Healthcare Providers Ins. Exch	Pennsylvania	P&C	01/12/18	32.6	E- (Very Weak)
Access Ins. Co	Texas	P&C	03/18/18	214.1	C (Fair)
Touchstone Health HMO Inc	New York	Health	04/09/18	12.5	E+ (Very Weak)
Reliamax Surety Co	South Dakota	P&C	06/27/18	63.0	C (Fair)
Paramount Ins. Co	Maryland	P&C	09/13/18	13.2	D- (Weak)
Real Legacy Asr Co Inc	Puerto Rico	P&C	09/28/18	230.4	D+ (Weak)

2017

Institution	Headquarters	Industry	Date of Failure	At Date of Failure	
				Total Assets ($Mil)	Safety Rating
IFA Ins Co	New Jersey	P&C	03/07/17	8.4	E (Very Weak)
Public Service Ins. Co	New York	P&C	03/16/17	278.5	E (Very Weak)
Zoom Health Plan Inc	Oregon	Health	04/26/17	6.0	U (Unrated)
Galen Ins Co	Missouri	P&C	05/31/17	10.0	E- (Very Weak)
Fiduciary Ins. Co of America	New York	P&C	07/25/17	13.9	E- (Very Weak)
Evergreen Health Inc	Maryland	Health	07/27/17	37.2	E- (Very Weak)
Minuteman Health Inc	Massachusetts	Health	08/02/17	111.7	E- (Very Weak)
Sawgrass Mutual Ins. Co	Florida	P&C	08/22/17	32.3	D+ (Weak)
Guarantee Ins. Co	Florida	P&C	08/28/17	400.4	E+ (Very Weak)
Oceanus Ins. Co A RRG	South Carolina	P&C	09/04/17	52.9	D- (Weak)

2016

Institution	Headquarters	Industry	Date of Failure	At Date of Failure Total Assets ($Mil)	At Date of Failure Safety Rating
Consumers Choice Health Ins. Co	S Carolina	Health	01/06/16	92.4	D- (Weak)
Moda Health Plan Inc	Oregon	Health	01/28/16	445.5	D+ (Weak)
Family Health Hawaii MBS	Hawaii	Health	04/07/16	5.5	D (Weak)
Health Republic Ins. of NY Corp	New York	Health	04/22/16	525.3	D+ (Weak)
Coordinated Health Mut Inc	Ohio	Health	05/26/16	94.9	E (Very Weak)
HealthyCT Inc.	Connecticut	Health	07/01/16	112.3	D+ (Weak)
Oregons Health Co-op	Oregon	Health	07/11/16	46.6	D (Weak)
Land of Lincoln Mut Hlth Ins. Co	Illinois	Health	07/14/16	107.8	D+ (Weak)
Excalibur Reins Corp	Pennsylvania	P&C	07/18/16	9.0	U (Unrated)
Castlepoint Florida Ins	Florida	P&C	07/28/16	100.0	D (Weak)
Castlepoint Insurance Co	New York	P&C	07/28/16	178.4	E (Very Weak)
Castlepoint National Ins. Co	California	P&C	07/28/16	355.2	C- (Fair)
Hermitage Insurance Co	New York	P&C	07/28/16	167.6	E+ (Very Weak)
Massachusetts Homeland Ins Co	Massachusetts	P&C	07/28/16	8.9	C (Fair)
North East Insurance Co	Maine	P&C	07/28/16	35.9	D (Weak)
York Insurance Co of Maine	Maine	P&C	07/28/16	47.0	C (Fair)
Careconcepts Ins Inc A RRG	Montana	P&C	08/08/16	3.8	E (Very Weak)
Freelancers Consumer Operated	New Jersey	Health	09/12/16	135.3	D+ (Weak)
Doctors & Surgeons Natl RRG Ic	Kentucky	P&C	10/07/16	9.1	E+ (Very Weak)
American Medical & Life Ins. Co	New York	Life	12/28/16	4.4	U (Unrated)

2015

Institution	Headquarters	Industry	Date of Failure	Total Assets ($Mil)	Safety Rating
				At Date of Failure	
Millers Classified Ins Co	Illinois	P&C	01/20/15	2.7	E (Very Weak)
Eveready Ins Co	New York	P&C	01/29/15	10.6	E- (Very Weak)
Jordan Funeral and Ins Co, Inc	Alabama	L&H	02/17/15	1.1	U (Unrated)
Drivers Insurance Co	New York	P&C	03/12/15	3.0	E- (Very Weak)
Lumbermens UW Alliance	Missouri	P&C	05/19/15	354.3	E- (Very Weak)
Pinelands Ins Co RRG, Inc	D. C.	P&C	08/25/15	4.9	E (Very Weak)
Louisiana Health Cooperative, Inc	Louisiana	Health	09/01/15	59.5	E (Very Weak)
Affirmative Ins Co	Illinois	P&C	09/16/15	181.2	E (Very Weak)
Affirmative Casualty Ins Co	Louisiana	P&C	10/05/15	32.6	D+ (Weak)
Affirmative Direct Ins Co	New York	P&C	10/05/15	5.3	U (Unrated)
Nevada Health Co-op	Nevada	Health	10/14/15	47.9	E- (Very Weak)
Winhealth Partners	Wyoming	Health	10/21/15	34.0	D (Weak)
Health Republic Ins Co	Oregon	Health	10/21/15	8.8	E (Very Weak)
Affirmative Ins Co of Michigan	Texas	P&C	10/29/15	9.3	U (Unrated)
Kentucky Health Cooperative Inc	Kentucky	Health	10/29/15	189.5	D+ (Weak)
Meritus Mutual Health Partners	Arizona	Health	10/30/15	45.8	D (Weak)
Meritus Health Partners	Arizona	Health	10/30/15	43.0	D+ (Weak)
Regis Ins Co	Pennsylvania	P&C	10/30/15	.6	E- (Very Weak)
Arches Mutual Ins Co	Utah	Health	11/02/15	77.2	D (Weak)
Lincoln General Ins Co	Pennsylvania	P&C	11/05/15	65.6	E- (Very Weak)
Advantage Health Solutions Inc	Indiana	Health	11/06/15	64.2	E (Very Weak)
Colorado Hlth Ins Cooperative Inc	Colorado	Health	11/10/15	108.7	D+ (Weak)
Consumers Mutual Ins of MI	Michigan	Health	11/13/15	60.4	E- (Very Weak)

2014

Institution	Headquarters	Industry	Date of Failure	At Date of Failure Total Assets ($Mil)	Safety Rating
Union Mutual Ins Co	Oklahoma	P&C	01/24/14	5.1	E+ (Very Weak)
Commonwealth Ins Co	Pennsylvania	P&C	03/20/14	1.1	E (Very Weak)
LEMIC Ins Co	Louisiana	P&C	03/31/14	51.6	D (Weak)
Interstate Bankers Casualty Co	Illinois	P&C	04/16/14	16.2	D+ (Weak)
Freestone Ins Co	Delaware	P&C	04/28/14	421.2	D- (Weak)
Alameda Alliance For Health	California	Health	05/05/14	176.3	D (Weak)
Sunshine State Ins Co	Florida	P&C	06/03/14	22.9	E+ (Very Weak)
Physicians United Plan Inc	Florida	Health	06/09/14	110.7	E (Very Weak)
Red Rock Ins Co	Oklahoma	P&C	08/01/14	28.5	E+ (Very Weak)
DLE Life Ins Co	Louisiana	L&H	10/02/14	39.3	D- (Weak)
Mothe Life Ins Co	Louisiana	L&H	10/02/14	15.2	E- (Very Weak)
First Keystone RRG Inc	S. Carolina	P&C	10/21/14	13.6	E+ (Very Weak)
SeeChange Health Ins Co	California	Health	11/19/14	23.4	D (Weak)
PROAIR Risk Retention Grp Inc	Nevada	P&C	11/12/14	0.5	U (Unrated)
Florida Healthcare Plus, Inc	Florida	Health	12/10/14	11.1	U (Unrated)
CoOportunity Health, Inc	Iowa	Health	12/23/14	195.7	U (Unrated)

2013

Institution	Headquarters	Industry	Date of Failure	Total Assets ($Mil)	Safety Rating
Partnership Health Plan Inc	Wisconsin	Health	01/18/13	27.1	D (Weak)
Driver's Insurance Co	Oklahoma	P&C	02/21/13	33.1	D+ (Weak)
Lewis & Clark LTC RRG	Nevada	P&C	02/28/13	16.4	E (Very Weak)
Pride National Ins Co	Oklahoma	P&C	03/08/13	17.1	E+ (Very Weak)
Santa Fe Auto	Texas	P&C	03/08/13	22.9	E (Very Weak)
Ullico Casualty Co	Delaware	P&C	03/11/13	327.7	D (Weak)
Builders Ins Co Inc	Nevada	P&C	03/15/13	15.0	U (Unrated)
Nevada Contractors Ins Co Inc	Nevada	P&C	03/15/13	49.0	U (Unrated)
Universal Health Care Ins Co Inc	Florida	Health	03/22/13	106.1	C (Fair)
Universal Health Care Inc	Florida	Health	03/25/13	109.0	D (Weak)
Universal HMO of Texas	Texas	Health	04/18/13	15.3	C- (Fair)
Universal Health Care of NV Inc	Nevada	Health	06/03/13	1.9	D+ (Weak)
Liberty First RRG Ins Co	Utah	P&C	08/06/13	2.5	E (Very Weak)
United Contractors Ins Co Inc, RRG	Delaware	P&C	08/22/13	17.0	E (Very Weak)
Advance Physicians Ins RRG, Inc	Arizona	P&C	08/29/13	1.9	D (Weak)
Georgia Mutual Ins Co	Georgia	P&C	09/10/13	3.3	D (Weak)
Ocean Risk Retention Group	D. C.	P&C	09/6/13	7.9	E (Very Weak)
Gertrude Geddes Willis LIC	Louisiana	L&H	10/24/13	4.9	U (Unrated)
San Antonio Indemnity Co	Texas	P&C	10/31/13	2.8	E+ (Very Weak)
Higginbotham Burial Ins Co	Arkansas	L&H	11/04/13	1.3	U (Unrated)
Indemnity Ins Corp RRG	Delaware	P&C	11/07/13	83.2	D- (Weak)
Concert Health Plan Ins Co	Illinois	L&H	12/10/13	1.8	D- (Weak)
ICM Insurance Co	New York	P&C	12/23/13	5.0	E+ (Very Weak)

Glossary

This glossary contains the most important terms used in this publication.

Admitted Assets
The total of all investments and business interests that are acceptable under statutory accounting rules.

Asset/Liability Matching
The designation of particular investments (assets) to particular policy obligations (liabilities) so that investments mature at the appropriate times and with appropriate yields to meet policy obligations as they come due.

Asset Valuation Reserve (AVR)
A liability established under statutory accounting rules whose purpose is to protect the company's surplus from the effects of defaults and market value fluctuation on stocks, bonds, mortgages and real estate. This replaces the Mandatory Securities Valuation Reserve (MSVR) and is more comprehensive in that it includes a mortgage loss reserve, whereas the MSVR did not.

Average Recession
A recession involving a decline in real GDP which is approximately equivalent to the average of the postwar recessions of 1957-58, 1960, 1970, 1974-75, 1980, 1981-82,1990-1991, 2001, and 2007-2009. It is assumed, however, that in today's market, the financial losses suffered from a recession of that magnitude would be greater than those experienced in previous decades. (See also "Severe Recession.")

Capital
Strictly speaking, capital refers to funds raised through the sale of common and preferred stock. Mutual companies have capital in the form of retained earnings. In a more general sense, the term capital is commonly used to refer to a company's equity or net worth, that is, the difference between assets and liabilities (i.e., capital and surplus as shown on the balance sheet).

Capital Resources
The sum of various resources which serve as a capital cushion to losses, including capital, surplus and Asset Valuation Reserve (AVR).

Capitalization Index
An index, expressed on a scale of zero to ten, with seven or higher considered excellent, that measures the adequacy of the company's capital resources to deal with a variety of business and economic scenarios. It combines Risk-Adjusted Capital Ratios #1 and #2 as well as a leverage test that examines pricing risk.

Cash and Demand Deposits
Includes cash on hand and on deposit. A negative figure indicates that the company has more checks outstanding than current funds to cover those checks. This is not an unusual situation for an insurance company.

Collateralized Mortgage Obligation (CMO)	Mortgage-backed bond that splits the payments from mortgage pools into different classes, called tranches. The investor may purchase a bond or tranche that passes through to him or her the principal and interest payments made by the mortgage holders in that specific maturity class (usually two, five, 10 or 20 years). The risk associated with a CMO is in the variation of the payment speed on the mortgage pool which, if different than originally assumed, can cause the total return to vary greatly.
Common and Preferred Stocks	See "Stocks".
Deposit Funds	Accumulated contributions of a group out of which immediate annuities are purchased as the individual members of the group retire.
Direct Premiums Written	Total gross premiums derived from policies issued directly by the company. This figure excludes the impact of reinsurance.
Safety Rating	Weiss Safety Ratings grade insurers on a scale from A (Excellent) to F (Failed). Ratings are based on five major factors: investment safety, policy leverage, capitalization, profitability and stability of operations.
Five-Year Profitability Index	See "Profitability Index."
Government Securities	Securities issued and/or guaranteed by U.S. and foreign governments which are rated as highest quality (Class 1) by state insurance commissioners. Included in this category are bonds issued by governmental agencies and guaranteed with the full faith and credit of the government. Regardless of the issuing entity, they are viewed as being relatively safer than the other investment categories. See "Investment Grade Bonds" to determine which items are excluded from this category.
Health Claims Reserve	Funds set aside from premiums for the eventual payment of health benefits after the end of the statement year.
Insurance Risk	The risk that the level of claims and related expenses will exceed current premiums plus reserves allocated for their payment.
Interest Rate Risk	The risk that, due to changes in interest rates, investment income will not meet the needs of policy commitments. This risk can be reduced by effective asset/liability matching.
Invested Assets	The total size of the firm's investment portfolio.
Investment Grade Bonds	This covers all investment grade bonds other than those listed in "Government Securities" (above). Specifically, this includes: (1) nonguaranteed obligations of governments; (2) obligations of governments rated as Class 2 by state insurance commissioners; (3) state and municipal bonds; plus (4) investment grade corporate bonds.

Investment Safety Index	Measured on a scale of zero to ten, with ten being the best and seven or better considered strong. Each investment area is rated as to quality and vulnerability during an unfavorable economic environment (updated using quarterly data when available).
Investments in Affiliates	Includes bonds, preferred stocks and common stocks, as well as other vehicles which many insurance companies use to invest in, and establish a corporate link with, affiliated companies
Life and Annuity Claims Reserve	Funds set aside from premiums for the eventual payment of life and annuity claims.
Liquidity Index	An index, expressed on a scale from zero to ten, with seven or higher considered excellent, which measures the company's ability to raise the necessary cash to meet policyholder obligations. This index includes a stress test which considers the consequences of a spike in claims or a run on policy surrenders. Sometimes a company may appear to have the necessary resources, but may be unable to sell its investments at the prices at which they are valued in the company's financial statements.
Mandatory Security Valuation Reserve (MSVR)	Reserve for investment losses and asset value fluctuation mandated by the state insurance commissioners for companies registered as life and health insurers. As of December 31, 1992, this was replaced by the Asset Valuation Reserve.
Moderate Loss Scenario	An economic decline from current levels approximately equivalent to that of the average postwar recession.
Mortgages in Good Standing	Mortgages which are current in their payments (excludes mortgage-backed securities).
Net Premiums Written	The total dollar volume of premiums retained by the company. This figure is equal to direct premiums written, plus reinsurance assumed less reinsurance ceded.
Noninvestment Grade Bonds	Low-rated issues, commonly known as "junk bonds," which carry a high risk as defined by the state insurance commissioners. These include bond Classes 3 - 6.
Nonperforming Mortgages	Mortgages which are (a) 90 days or more past due or (b) in process of foreclosure.
Other Investments	Items not included in any of the other categories such as premium notes, collateral loans, short-term investments and other miscellaneous items.
Other Structured Securities	Nonresidential mortgage related and other securitized loan-backed or asset-backed securities. This category also includes CMOs with noninvestment grade ratings.

Policy Leverage

A measure of insurance risk based on the relationship of net premiums to capital resources.

Policy Loans

Loans to policyholders under insurance contracts.

Profitability Index

Measured on a scale of zero to ten, with ten being the best and seven or better considered strong. A composite of five factors: (1) gain or loss on operations; (2) consistency of operating results; (3) impact of operating results on surplus; (4) adequacy of investment income as compared to the needs of policy reserves; and (5) expenses in relation to industry averages. Thus, the overall index is an indicator of the health of a company's current and past operations.

Purchase Money Mortgages

Mortgages written by an insurance company to facilitate the sale of property owned by the company.

Real Estate

Direct real estate investments including property (a) occupied by the company; (b) acquired through foreclosure and (c) purchased as an investment.

Reinsurance Assumed

Insurance risk acquired by taking on partial or full responsibility for claims on policies written by other companies. (See "Reinsurance Ceded.")

Reinsurance Ceded

Insurance risk sold to another company.

Risk-Adjusted Capital

The capital resources that would be needed in a worsening economic environment (same as "Target Capital").

Risk-Adjusted Capital Ratio #1

The capital resources which a company currently has, in relation to the resources that would be needed to deal with a moderate loss scenario. This scenario is based on historical experience during an average recession and adjusted to reflect current conditions and vulnerabilities (updated using quarterly data when available).

Risk-Adjusted Capital Ratio #2

The capital resources which a company currently has, in relation to the resources that would be needed to deal with a severe loss scenario. This scenario is based on historical experience of the postwar period and adjusted to reflect current conditions and the potential impact of a severe recession (updated using quarterly data when available).

Separate Accounts

Funds segregated from the general account and valued at market. Used to fund indexed products, such as variable life and variable annuity products.

Severe Loss Scenario

An economic decline from current levels in which the loss experience of the single worst year of the postwar period is extended for a period of three years. (See also "Moderate Loss Scenario".)

Severe Recession

A prolonged economic slowdown in which the single worst year of the postwar period is extended for a period of three years. (See also "Average Recession".)

Stability Index	Measured on a scale of zero to ten. This integrates a wide variety of factors that reflects the company's financial stability and diversification of risk.
State of Domicile	Although most insurance companies are licensed to do business in many states, they have only one state of domicile. This is the state which has primary regulatory responsibility for the company. Use the state of domicile to make absolutely sure that you have the correct company. Bear in mind, however, that this need not be the state where the company's main offices are located.
State Guaranty Funds	Funds that are designed to raise cash from existing insurance carriers to cover policy claims of bankrupt insurance companies.
Stocks	Common and preferred equities, including ownership in affiliates.
Surplus	The difference between assets and liabilities, including paid-in contributed surplus, plus the statutory equivalent of "retained earnings" in non-insurance business corporations.
Target Capital	See "Risk-Adjusted Capital."
Total Assets	Total admitted assets, including investments and other business assets. See "Admitted Assets."